World War 1
The First Culture War

Best wishes

Robert Owles

By the same author

*Counterattack: Montgomery
and the Battle of the Bulge*

*Everything you wanted to know
about the EU but were afraid to ask*

Montgomery and the First War on Terror

Moralitis, A Cultural Virus
with Dr Niall McCrae.

Paperback: 978-1-8380658-0-5

Audiobook: 978-1-7393152-4-5

Ebook: 978-1-7393152-5-2

Copyright © Robert Oulds

Published in 2023 by The Bruges Group

Bruges Group Publications Office
246 Linen Hall, 162-168 Regent Street, London W1B 5TB
www.brugesgroup.com

Scan me for Bruges Group

Twitter 🐦 @brugesgroup, LinkedIn 🔗 @brugesgroup,
GETTR 🔵 @brugesgroup, Telegram ✈ t.me/brugesgroup, Facebook 🔵 @brugesgroup,
Instagram 📷 @brugesgroup, YouTube ▶ @brugesgroup

How culture determined victory
and defeat in World War II

World War II
The First Culture War

This book explores the history, politics, economics, and thinking behind the
military strategies of Hitler, the Axis, and the Allies

Robert Oulds

www.brugesgroup.com

ABOUT THE AUTHOR

ROBERT OULDS M.A., FRSA, is the author of *Montgomery and the First War on Terror*. The book details a little-known period of Monty's career. Bernard Law Montgomery, later Field Marshal Viscount Montgomery of Alamein, faced guerrilla forces in Ireland in the early 1920s and Palestine on the eve of the Second World War. That book explores the lessons of Monty's victories in those conflicts and how they should be applied today in the modern war on terror.

Robert is the author of *Counterattack: Montgomery and the Battle of the Bulge* and *Everything you wanted to know about the EU but were afraid to ask*. Amongst other works he is also the co-author of *Moralitis, A Cultural Virus*. He is the longstanding Director of the Bruges Group, the respected think tank which since 1989 has been at the forefront of the debate about the UK's relationship with the EU and the wider world. The President of the Bruges Group was the former Prime Minister, the late Baroness Margaret Thatcher. Robert regularly appears on television and radio debating topical issues.

He was the Standard Bearer and Treasurer for his local branch of the Royal British Legion (RBL) which is an organisation established to help the welfare of ex-Servicemen. It also campaigns on issues relating to the armed forces. The RBL are the custodians of the nation's Remembrance services; they organise and run the annual Poppy Appeal which raises funds in aid of our soldiers, sailors, airmen, and women, as well as their dependents.

Robert is proud of his grandfather's service in World War Two that took Leslie Frank Oulds from Egypt, across North Africa, to Sicily and Italy, and onto Arnhem. He survived those many engagements.

To my son Robin,
So you will know,
It is not the state,
That makes a nation great,
It is when the government is made to let go,
That power and prosperity will flow.

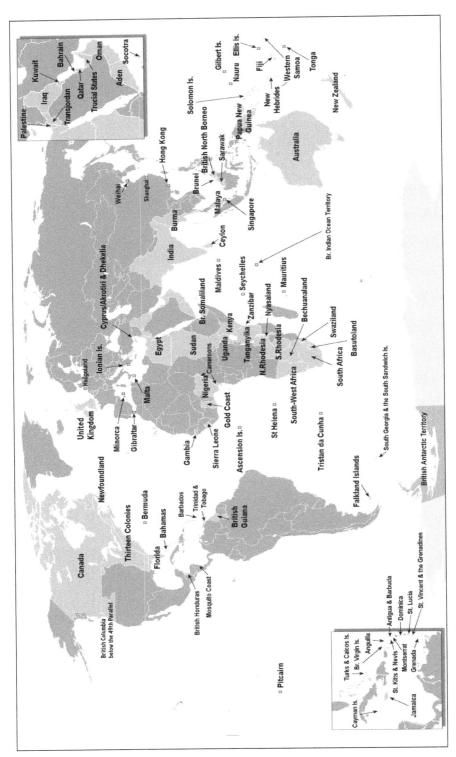

The totality of the British Empire

Synopsis

The global conflict of WWII, the bloodiest yet in human history, was as much a clash of cultures as it was a clash of arms. Different world visions collided as fiercely as the great armies which encountered each other on the battlefields of Europe, Asia, and Africa. The struggle of ideas was as vicious as the battle on, and below the waves as was the fight in the skies above. Indeed, the culture war and national differences drove the conflict and influenced where, when, why, and even how, the war was fought.

Churchill, Stalin, and Roosevelt – as well as their opponents; Hitler, Mussolini, and Hirohito – shaped events. However, these intractable enemies were governed by the hand which history gave them, the political directed the personal, as they wrangled for control of the future.

Despite the initial successes of Nazi Germany and Japan, Hitler and his Axis were eventually outgunned and outthought.

How much can we consider that German and Japanese capitulation was inevitable? And what drove so few men to command so many – and devastate so much? Economic and cultural factors, as well as military power, determined victory for some and subjected others to defeat and utter ruin.

In many regards, Second World War throws up more questions than answers, but *World War II: The First Culture War* addresses certain controversial and unpalatable issues.

The war fighting skills and the ability to manufacture the weapons that were so effectively wielded by the Allies were begotten by the notions of individual freedom, limited government, and property rights. Those concepts emerged in one place only, mediaeval England. The culture that produced Anglo-Saxon exceptionalism, and colonialism, gave Britain and her Allies the advantage over the Nazis.

Initiative, imagination, industriousness, innovation, ingenuity, and inventiveness; encouraged by the powerful inducement that is a lust for private profit – though now unpopular in some circles – proved to be the basis for the superior social, economic, political, and military system which confronted the Axis.

For some time, Great Britain and its Empire stood alone against the might and menace of the Axis powers. Churchill, embodying a culture of defiance, believed that the English-speaking peoples would ultimately triumph. He was right.

World War II: The First Culture War asserts why he was right and how this great victory was fought.

Contents

"Blood, blood, blood and blood again."

"Strategy is the art of distributing and applying military means, such as armed forces and supplies, to fulfil the ends of policy. Tactics means the dispositions for, and control of, military forces and techniques in actual fighting. Put more shortly: strategy is the art of the conduct of war, tactics the art of fighting."
— **Field Marshal Viscount Montgomery of Alamein,** *A History of Warfare*, **Collins. London, 1968**

The nazi party

On 23rd August 1939, nearly the eve of war, the drum beat to humanity's greatest and most vicious conflict grew steadily louder and faster. That evening an astonishing agreement between Nazi Germany and communist Russia, known as the Molotov-Ribbentrop Pact was announced. This paved the way to war. The 'peace' agreement between the two natural foes was named after the Foreign Ministers of those expanding empires. Eventually they would run into each other and much of Europe would be laid waste. That same evening on the terrace of the Führer's private residence at the Berghof, in the Bavarian Alps near the town of Berchtesgaden, horrific skies had people entranced. A Hungarian associate of Hitler, a female guest at this one of his many parties, saw the mountains at sunset bathed in red light as if caught in a deluge of the gory liquid. She turned to him and exclaimed "My Führer this augers nothing good. It means blood, blood, blood and blood again. Destruction and terrible suffering. Blood and blood again." A shocked Hitler snapped back "If it has to be, then let it be now." The die was cast, the admonition was true. Less than ten days later Germany invaded Poland.

Hitler's guest's ramblings rightly foretold the atmospheric phenomena as auguring in man's inhumanity to man which plunged to new depths. The omens did point to war. The blood did flow, in proportions never seen before in human history. Millions were consumed in the following six years in a great conflagration. The great dictator, from his mountaintop retreat, saw it all as inevitable, even part of his divinely inspired mission. The drenching of the mountains in the evenings reddened sunlight signalled what was to come. What followed is known, yet the causes of this monumental murder and how and why it played out as it did have been little understood, that is until now.

The origins of the war go back further than the decisions taken in 1939 that careered the world to yet another apocalyptic conflict. What became a world war was a long time coming, and Hitler knew it, he desired it, and willed its creation. He unwittingly enabled the destruction of his country and deliberately pillaged numerous other nations along the way. Yet he was merely an actor on a stage. It was a combination of factors both large and small that brought this conflict to life. Cultural and historic forces delivered the deaths of millions and set in course the rise of the American and Soviet empires, and the destruction of both the Third Reich, and Imperial Japan. This is the big history of World War Two.

'Victory or annihilation'

In 1938 Hitler predicted that, unlike the First World War, the next conflict will not end with an armistice like that of 11th November 1918 but with either 'victory or annihilation'. So it came to pass. The biggest conflict in human history deserves its bigger picture to be properly understood. This history does not just look at what happened, it gets to the heart of explaining why events unfolded as they did. History is a web of competing interests.

This book explores the important military strategies that governed the fate of nations and it explains the political and even psychological aspects that set-in motion the thinking behind the fighting. We will explore the military strategies adopted by each belligerent nation in humanity's most bloody conflict. To complete our analysis of how and why the Nazis lost the war, we must put events in their wider context. The fate of the Second World War depended upon key strategic decisions based upon the hand that history and mother nature had dealt the belligerents.

Despite the strength of Hitler's Will, he could not escape his fate. His delusional state of invincibility was merely a symptom of post-traumatic stress disorder brought on through his experiences in the First World War. Nor could the Third Reich avoid the same inherent weaknesses that had bedevilled the earlier Reich which was defeated in 1918. For a time, however, it looked as if the Nazis would be victorious, and their leader's willpower would overturn the world. Hitler thought of himself as a strategic genius and declared himself as such when he posed by the Eiffel Tower after routing the French, thought to be Europe's preeminent land power, in just a matter of weeks. Hitler was certainly a gifted amateur, but he made strategic mistakes which cost Germany the war. He could not make the best of the bad hand that geography and geology had given the Axis powers; the Nazis and their central European conspirators were doomed. Hitler was also a gambler, the stakes were high for soldiers and civilians alike, as they were ultimately for him. The aggressor's actions in the Second World War were always haphazard, even long pre-planned attacks were little more than throws of the dice. In Hitler's speech on Blitzkrieg in 1935 he stated, "I would not make lengthy preparations but will hurl myself on the enemy… " There was little choice; the die was cast. German ambitions had not changed from generations before.

Gamblers need luck; at first the leader of Nazi Germany was blessed with good fortune most notably in the enemies that he cultivated both at home and abroad. These enfeebled foes were the weak and ill Neville Chamberlain, the isolationist United States of America, unreproductive France, and the beleaguered behemoth that was Soviet Russia. The USSR had had its heart ripped out through Joseph Stalin's purges and persecution which caused the deaths of millions of Soviet citizens. Hitler was also blessed by the world body charged with keeping the peace, the League of Nations. On the day that the Second World War began, the League of Nations was discussing the standardisation of level crossings; such is the effectiveness of supranational organisations and the Olympians who toy at being at the 'commanding' heights of such bodies, they just preach from their ivory towers.

The other 'bigger' conflict
The Second World War was not just a war conducted against German imperial ambitions. There were two separate, but interlinked, conflicts on opposite sides of the globe. When we think of the Second World War, our mind's eye produces dark images. We see Swastikas, destruction of cities from bombs and bombardment from the king of the battlefield, artillery, we see victims of kidnap and murder on an industrial scale.

Those hateful horrors and the slaughter known as the 'Holocaust', a word derived from the Greek *holokauston* meaning meaning a burnt sacrifice offered to a god, were committed with a bureaucratic coldness, even an efficiency rare for *fonctionnaires*. In this, one of history's great crimes; Freemasons, homosexuals, political opponents, Roma, Sinti, as well as Jews, and many others were worked to death in slave and extermination camps, others were killed with a variety of methods such as the bullet, carbon monoxide, or Zyklon B, a gas developed in Germany from a cyanide-based pesticide. Many more on all sides perished by other unimaginable horrors that have since been largely forgotten after nearly six years of destructive war. Those images are from the European theatre of operations. Much of a whole continent was consumed by those terrors, which spilt out beyond its borders to the Middle East and North Africa where European nations battled for pride, resources, and to outflank their opponents.

Few realise that World War Two began earlier than 1939. It started with Japan's 1937 attack on China and continued until September 1945, when the Empire of the Sun signed the formal instrument of surrender to the Allies. Cordial and normalised relations between the United States and Japan officially came with the Treaty of San Francisco in 1952. Peace between Japan and the Soviet Union was achieved through the Soviet–Japanese Joint Declaration of 1956. Some isolated pockets of limited Japanese resistance lasted as late as 1974 when Hirō Onoda finally surrendered his weapon to his commander in the Philippines.

Not only did the Pacific war last longer, but it also covered a wider area when one considers the breadth of fighting over both land and sea. With Tokyo at the centre, the fighting engulfed islands off the coast of Alaska in the north, to Mongolia in the northwest, and India to the west of Japan. War even reached Australia in the south and went beyond that continent to the middle of the Pacific as far as Hawai'i and touched mainland USA. Japan's rapid conquest and America's dogged fight back from island to island meant that death came to the South Seas paradise. Our imagination perceives the beauties of this part of the world, deserted desert islands and in China, perhaps the oldest continuous civilisation on Earth. Yet for a period in the last century, they turned from places of wonder which some of us can only dream of, veritable idylls, to places of terror where no quarter was given and countless lives eradicated, treasurers plundered, land pillaged, and an ancient people raped.

Both conflicts showed people at their worst, but conversely the braveness and stoicism shown by many combatants and civilians presented humanity at its best. The greatest generation of Allied heroes are role models to lionise and perhaps even idolise to this day. Some combatants received a favourable judgement from history, others damned for posterity. The court of public opinion and the judgement of historians can be a fickle mistress. Whilst Hitler remains the great ogre, modern public discourse assigns him ideological partners that bare no similarity whatsoever to his creed. Churchill the saviour of a great democracy at its darkest hour is now condemned as a racist. Stalin, a man whose story is a mirror image of Hitler and a tyrant in similar proportions, is now lauded by some in Russia and even in the free world. Stalin has been rehabilitated, almost.

These two conflicts in Europe, Asia, Africa, as well as Australasia, cannot be divorced from each other. The lessons learned in one of those struggles informed the fighting in the other. Military planning changed and led to a dark evolution of war being introduced in other theatres. For instance, the concept of aerial bombing was taken from Europe and brought to the Japanese. These different, but connected wars, also drained resources which altered the calculus of military planning and functioned as a catalyst for America's formal entry into the Second World War.

Historical materialism

In the Second World War there were many strategies raging against each other. This book looks at the strategies used in World War Two; and explains how strategy, the art of the conduct of war during that great conflagration, determined its outcome and the future of the modern world. However, history set those strategies in stone long before the first bullet was fired in anger.

This book does not look at events and other factors in isolation, important as they may be, but considers them as part of the wider picture, as part of the big history. In this study we look at but go beyond analysing the tactics that gave the Allies victory. We get to the heart of what happened in World War Two and look at the events holistically as part of history's unfolding master plan and how it combined with the serendipity of happenstance. Whilst it is true that economic factors were largely responsible for the Allies' success, particularly the industrial foundations of the belligerents, this itself was determined by the resources the earth provided; and yet it is still not the whole picture. This work marries the macro with the minutia of understanding the human element at work as part of why World War II happened as it did. The strategic thinking of the war's main military thinkers and leaders, which in part is determined by their personalities, will also be explained as the pages are turned. However, above all else, war is downstream of culture, from which all else flowed.

This war thankfully remains the largest in human history, at least so far, although the next may be much worse. We must therefore learn from history, both the blunders as well as the deft moves of generals and their political masters, to uncover and illuminate the fighting but also consider the sublime to the bizarre. Little can be weirder than the true story of the Nazi suicide pilots to the impact of partisans and the air war which devastated so many cities around the globe. This book will show how the events relate to each other and it will look at how the development of weapons and tactics were largely shaped by the demands of national military strategy, ideology, and culture. Tactics can be altered; new and improved weapons could be and were developed; it was the strategy that was the key to victory or defeat in World War Two. And national strategy was predestined by tradition. Indeed, the strategies and the following events themselves were manifestations of the demands and opportunities placed on each belligerent by the weight of history and the hand that fate had given them.

Genesis of Evil

"You see, it's been [Germany's] misfortune to have the wrong religion. Why didn't we have the religion of the Japanese, who regard sacrifice for the Fatherland as the highest good? The Mohammedan religion [Islam] too would have been more compatible to us than Christianity. Why did it have to be Christianity with its meekness and flabbiness?" — **Adolf Hitler**

Drang nach Osten

Hitler wanted war; he was the ultimate warmonger. He divided the globe into two camps, intent on the other's destruction. We know who won World War Two, this book explains why one side lost and the other was victorious. We begin with the historical forces driving this gargantuan clash of ideas, peoples, and nations.

Hitler wanted to reform both Germany and the Germans. His was a revolutionary doctrine, seen by some as a progressive movement that would transform society and eliminate the enemies of his German-led European Utopia. Brutality and extermination would be the nursemaid of this new order, but behind their revolution in society was an age-old scheme that was merely adopted and adapted by the Nazis. Hitler and his gang, like other German elites before them, put into place an off-the-shelf plan for European domination.

The plot behind the Second World War was merely a rebadging of German grand strategy. The only distinct real difference was that the Nazis sought to take the riches for themselves along with the glory, or infamy if defeated. They used German ambition to spread a twisted ideology and perverted pseudo-science known as Nazism. For a time, it even looked as though they may succeed. However, like the others who went before them, history would see them defeated. Behind the war was Germany's doctrine of *Drang nach Osten,* meaning drive to the East. It had caused countless other conflicts in generations gone before.

Germany was on a collision course with Russia, the Teutons coveted their territory. The Nazis were no different. They took the concept of *Lebensraum,* 'living space'; the belief that Germany did not have enough land was not new and dated back to the nineteenth century. They desired to seize territory in the east, someone else's home, and provide it to Germans to work as a free people.

The existing lesser residents would serve as a slave or serf class who were to prepare the soil for the emigrating east farmers and their families.

The Nazis had a romanticised view of history; at the time it was common to look back to the past for inspiration. Generations before other nations had romanticised Charlemagne, the Arthurian Romances, or the Roman Empire – all to gain a cultural legitimacy for emerging national identities. Germany was no different. The cultural leadership of the Germans was an important prize for the statelets that were eventually forged into the German Empire. The manipulation of the past was a means to unite these differing peoples, the mercantilist north with the conservative south. German nationalists aimed to unite the Protestant and the Roman Catholic in this new nation. Germany was a nation made in war for war. The Nazis found inspiration for their warrior class in German mythology, and from real history, both of which were used to justify and even guide their territorial ambitions in the east.

During the migration era, the Germanic tribe known as the Goths had briefly settled on the Pontic Steppe close to the Black Sea. The German Knights of the Teutonic Order had conquered much of the east in their crusade against paganism and the Russian Orthodox inhabitants of Slavic lands. Incidentally, they were useful propaganda tools for Stalin's regime, which used the spirit of Alexander Nevsky whose victory in 1242 over the German and Swedish forces of the Livonian Order was immortalised by Sergei Eisenstein. This patriotic film was named after the main protagonist. It was released in 1938.

The Nazi desire for ethnic Germans to be the overlords of a first to be subdued, then expelled population in the east was not as outlandish as it was terrible. European colonists had done the same in another part of the world, 'twas ever thus. What is more, the ruling class of nations such as Estonia and Latvia on the Baltic Sea were predominantly ethnic Germans. They had ruled there for 700 years until their overthrow in the tumultuous events at the end of the First World War in 1918. They did not go easily: *Freikorps* units fought both against Bolshevik uprisings in ethnic German controlled regions and against the mutually anti-Bolshevik and anti-Russian forces of Baltic citizen soldiers. These militants had carved out the independent new-born Baltic states of Estonia and Latvia from the ashes of the Russian Empire. This was a triumph of liberal nationalism and an underclass throwing off the vestiges of feudalism. In this struggle the Estonians received significant amounts of British aid as well as the support of the Royal Navy. With the defeat of both the Bolshevik and the German forces in the Baltic states, the *Freikorps* retreated to Germany. Some, however, took with them a sacred Estonian symbol which they painted on their helmets to identify themselves when fighting against other Germans. In these operations *Freikorps* paramilitaries crushed the communist revolution which broke out in Germany after Kaiser Wilhelm II's abdication and his defeat in the Great War. The symbol they used was the Swastika.

Not all German influence and settlement in Russian lands was the result of aggression. Many Germans peacefully settled by the Volga River in the 18th Century, and some still reside in the former Union of Soviet Socialist Republics (USSR), most notably in Kazakhstan. Further German settlement in the Ukraine was encouraged by Catherine the Great to lessen the influence of Turkic peoples who were living there. A semi-autonomous Volga German oblast, or region, was created for them in Russia, lasting from 1924 until its abolition in 1941. Whereas many ethnic Germans retreated to the Fatherland as the fortunes of war turned against their cousins in the Wehrmacht, the Volga Germans were deported from their ancestral homeland in Russia, most of which did not return even after their persecution was brought to an end. Since then, others have settled as far afield as the United States.

Nazi dreams

In Nazi Germany, Hitler was seen as the saviour that was seeking to restore the *status quo ante*. Yet Hitler's ideas were quixotic and justified by unscientific racial theory. Indeed, at the heart of all Nazi thinking was the concept of race. Despite the deposed German Kaiser, the man responsible for the First World War, being loathed by Hitler who in turn disliked Germany's new leader; they did share some similar views. Both had imperial ambitions, both saw their respective conflicts as a fight between Teutons and Slavs, and both were opposed to Anglo-Saxon free markets and Jewish finance. Hitler had in one sense inherited his throne and taken on board some of the Kaiser's aims and ideals. However, these would be magnified to previously unimaginable levels of depravity beyond anything the German Emperor desired. Hitler's loathing of the former Kaiser was because, like many soldiers in the First World War, he partly blamed him for what was until 1945 Germany's greatest defeat. Hitler took the Kaiser's ambitions to a whole new level and would inflict an even greater defeat on his adopted nation.

The quest for *Lebensraum* proved to be counter-productive for many of the disparate German communities who had to leave their homes in other countries when the war turned against Germany. Thus, Hitler's quest for *Lebensraum* had been a disaster for his co-linguists. The German drive east was not just a territorial claim underpinned by racial politics; above that was an ideological competition. Hitler's propaganda chief, Joseph Goebbels, saw the war as a great battle between two versions of socialism. In the week prior to the beginning of Operation Barbarossa, he wrote on 16th June 1941 that the Nazis would replace the powers of the USSR but there would be no restoration for the previous order of priests, Tsars, and capitalists. The Nazi conquest of these eastern lands would usher in a new order in which the Germans would replace 'Jewish Bolshevism' with '*der echte Sozialismus*', real socialism.

The Nazis' version of collectivism contrasted itself with the divisive Bolshevik version that sought to exacerbate and capitalize on conflict between the worker and the owner class. The Nazis practised an exclusionary form of socialism. It had a strong racial element, but aimed to bring the different classes together, so long as they were of an acceptable ethnicity, part of the *volk*, the manufactured Aryan nation. George Watson, wrote in his book, *The Lost Literature of Socialism*, 'It is now clear beyond all reasonable doubt that Hitler and his associates believed they were socialists, and that others, including democratic socialists, thought so too.' Indeed, Nazism was a synthesis of two powerful dogmas, Marxism and racialism.

Hitler had spoken of a racially 'pure' greater Germania that would fulfil Germany's 'historic' and 'rightful' destiny. However, the reality was Germany's empire was multi-ethnic. Ethnicity would determine one's virtue and value in the Nazi system. In colonised pastoral Eastern Europe, German speakers would make a living from both the land and the conquered inhabitants. A degree of equality between Germans was intended; this overlord class of people would be expected to dress and eat the same food as everyone else. Yet, some were more equal than others; it was agrarian socialism for the few. Hitler intended his Germanic people to be the masters above a slave class. Those groups which the Nazis reviled would play the Morlocks in the Nazi's concept of Europe, serving the fair-haired Eloi. Some, however, had been earmarked for eradication. This was not a new idea nor unique to the Nazis. German communist theorists, Karl Marx, and Friedrich Engels had advocated that races that were not ready for socialism should be exterminated. In 1849, this idea was even put into print and expressed in Marx's newspaper *Neue Rheinische Zeitung*. In the following century both the USSR and Germany would liquidate those who the powers deemed to be unable or unwilling to conform to their vision of socialism.

The Jews would be chief amongst the victims of Nazi genocide. Yet, Hitler did not consider them to be lesser human beings. As detailed in *Mein Kampf*, he did not think that Jews were an inferior race. He wrote that the Jews and the Aryans were the two pre-eminently creative peoples on the planet and that there would be a struggle between them for world domination. The National

Socialists also believed that the Jews were unfairly privileged and exploited the disadvantaged German. Racism is often directed against those that are perceived to be economically successful. This has been shown throughout history from the persecution of Armenians and the Greek Orthodox in Turkey to Idi Amin's expulsion of the Ugandan Asians and was demonstrated by the destruction of the Greenwood District in Tulsa, USA, formerly known as "Negro Wall Street". This phenomenon is now exhibited by the modern epidemic of assaults carried out against people of Oriental heritage by African Americans. When prejudice is combined with a belief in the redistribution of wealth, the state, or even individuals, will sanction the obliteration of 'privileged' races; just as others have eliminated those perceived to be privileged classes.

Many socialists believed that human nature is malleable, Man, they thought, can be remade by the state. The belief that the world and all that is under the sun should be changed by government decree was popular towards the end of the nineteenth century and into the first half of the next hundred years. It was not long before high-minded thinkers put their great intellects to how best improve human stock. Marie Stopes and George Bernard Shaw, to name just two, promoted the idea of eugenics and advocated abolishing poverty by eradicating the poor; curing their penury by anti-natalist policies. The sterilisation of the mentally or morally deficient was not far behind. This would be taken up with delight by the National Socialists. From the twentieth century onwards race became politicised. Purveyors of identity politics blamed one ethnic group for disadvantaging another. Furthermore, identitarians did not, and do not, see all ethnic groups as being able or willing to adapt to whatever utopian future their book prescribed. Those outsider groups will enjoy a bleaker fate than that available to the insiders. It was not a great leap for such ideologues to believe that the morally suspect, undeservedly privileged, the culturally disadvantaged, and, or, intellectually challenged should not only be denied the rewards that modernity offered but should also have no place in that brave new world. Herein lay the roots of the Nazi genocide that was to come.

The Nazis received a degree of resistance from the Roman Catholic Church, which objected to their eugenics policy. Yet, many individual Roman Catholics were surprisingly receptive to the Nazis. The National Socialist movement had begun in earnest in Bavaria, traditionally a staunchly conservative and Roman Catholic statelet within Germany. However, the Nazis had expected to receive most of their support from the industrial and urban working class. The especially socialist Nazis, namely Joseph Goebbels and Gregor Strasser, hoped that the National Socialist German Workers Party would place a strong emphasis on socialism. Their propaganda was aimed at the working man, as was the campaign organisation that Strasser put in place. To their surprise, rural middle-class conservative Christians, especially women, but also men, became amongst Nazism's strongest adherents. The Frankfurt School of Communist theorists speculated at the time, and after the Second World War, that this devotion to Nazism was an expression of suppressed sexuality, and was the consequent of guilt, caused through the acceptance of Roman Catholic teaching in matters associated with the bedroom. Indeed, the Nazis did in time get most of their support from rural, and perhaps, repressed areas of Germany.

Militarism and homosexuality did at times make strange bedfellows. The Nazi hero, statesman, soldier, and King of Prussia, the renowned military strategist, Frederick the Great was almost certainly homosexual. Kaiser Wilhelm II, the last Emperor of Germany and chief provocateur of the Great War, though whilst he was heterosexual had a circle of homosexual bohemian friends in his youth. Berlin, during the decadent German Weimar Republic was the homosexual capital of Europe. This culture did not end; it just found new ways to express itself. The Nazi paramilitary wing, the SA, was a notorious hotbed of homosexuality. It can be argued that the Nazi artistic glorification of masculinity was part of a wider homosexual tradition that remains strong in Germany. Alternatively, it may be that the reverse was true with gay men borrowing and culturally appropriating the fashions from extremist movements dominated by masculine men. Whatever the case may be, the art and fashion of Nazi Germany did not end with the collapse of the Third Reich, cultural echoes can still be seen in the performances and record sleeves of German bands such as Kraftwerk. If aspects of discredited Nazi inspired cultural expressions survived to this day, it is only logical that previous cultural expressions, though contrary to official Nazi doctrine, may have had a role to play in developing the extreme behaviours displayed by the Nazis.

The Frankfurt School of Communist theorists, however, came to such a conclusion because they wanted to discredit both Nazism and traditional sexual and cultural norms. They thought conventional social mores were an impediment to their version of a socialist revolution. It was the Frankfurt School's belief that a culture war needed to be waged to tear down those customs and beliefs which they saw as preserving the capitalist order. The more likely hypothesis accounting for the rise of Hitler may be that with his moderating influence over the Nazis' social-economic program, the Nazi Party offered stability and a defence of private property in the face of a perceived communist threat from both home and abroad. Some of the blame for Germany's descent into extremism therefore rests with communist forces who sought revolution. Perhaps the Frankfurt School was engaging in an academic act of psychological projection driven by collective communist guilt. Hitler wanted his war more than he wanted reform at home. Further he did not want to completely smash the old Germany, merely co-opt it, and mould the country to serve his purposes.

It was a great irony of history that the Germans were largely responsible for the triumph of Bolshevism in Russia. The First World War had rocked the very foundations of the Russian order. Indeed, Russian communists were the political pawns in this deadly power game. Wilhelmine Germany used Lenin and the Bolsheviks to destabilise Tsarist Russia, sending him from his exile in Switzerland to the Russian capital, Petrograd, to ferment revolution. They further buttressed the Bolshevik revolution by reaching a peace agreement with Russia's new communist masters. Yet this agreement saw the Bolsheviks ceding large tracts of Russia to the Germans, who had won the Great War in the East. This was not the last time that Germany had sought to work alongside socialists in Russia. Both the Weimar Republic and Nazi Germany shared military technology with the USSR. The Nazis later entered a marriage made in hell with Stalin, dividing Poland between themselves, and accepted Soviet dominion over the Baltic states. Germany also relied upon materials supplied by Communist Russia to prosecute its war against Britain and France. When circumstances changed the British Prime Minister Winston Churchill, an ardent anti-communist, allied with Stalin to defeat their mutual foe, Hitler. History was repeating itself. Both Tsarist and Communist Russia had been a great rival to the British Empire but was a useful ally against the German Empire.

Dreams and nightmares

In the nineteenth century the Kingdom of Prussia, by possessing an effective military, had grown to become the dominant political force of the German speaking world. The competition for cultural leadership could be left to the Kingdom of Bavaria, and Vienna – the capital of the Austrian Empire. The Prussians gradually turned their military hegemony into an empire of their own. Trade agreements were amongst the weapons which they deployed to further bind Prussia's satellite states under Berlin's yoke.

The Zollverein Customs Union was one such tool. From 1834 that organisation was used to not only increase the market for German manufactures as well as reduce the cost of trade; but also forge an empire. This trade agreement would help consolidate Prussian control over its neighbours in central Europe and expand German power vis à vis France. This great power to Germany's west had earlier under Napoleon Bonaparte sought to use similar economic trade agreements to keep its subordinate states under its control. France would now be hoist with their own petard when Germany adopted this concept as their own and breathed fresh life into it during the First World War.

On 4th September 1914, less than seven weeks into World War One, German Chancellor Bethmann-Hollweg set out his empire's war aims. The fourth goal was to use trade treaties to create a European economic association. Once Germany had won the Great War, they would use this customs union to make France an economic vassal of the Kaiser's Reich. This central European bloc would include, France, Belgium, Netherlands, Denmark, Austria-Hungary, along with its south-eastern European empire, Poland, Switzerland and conceivably Italy, Sweden, and Norway. Furthermore, and not without reason, the borders of the Low Countries would be adjusted to create linguistic homogeneity within those states. The Grand Duchy of Luxembourg would be incorporated into Germany as a state in the larger federation. A German remaking of the map of western Europe would have inevitably increased the Reich's influence. On 9th September 1914, the Imperial Chancellor Theobald von Bethmann-Hollweg wrote:

"Russia must be pushed back as far as possible from Germany's Eastern frontier and her domination over non-Russian vassal people broken... We must create a Central European Economic Association through common customs treaties to include France, Belgium, Holland, Denmark, Austria-Hungary and perhaps Italy, Sweden and Norway. This association will not have any common constitutional supreme authority and all members will be formally equal but in practice under German leadership and must stabilise Germany's dominance over central Europe".

As the war progressed, not entirely in Germany's favour, the Germans sought a way out of their predicament that would allow them to win the peace. A separate accord was offered to Belgium; whose government was at the time in exile in the northern French coastal city of Le Havre. The deal was the withdrawal of German forces; the price that the Belgians would be expected to pay for peace, and for their country back, and in return the Belgians had to agree to a Belgian-German customs union. This bilateral arrangement would however be one sided, as Germany, the larger economy, would be dominant. The Allies, however, would not accept piecemeal agreements with individual countries.

By 1917, with stalemate on the Western Front, and trouble for the Triple Entente in Eastern Europe, a compromise peace with the German-led Quadruple Alliance may have been possible. However, the Wilhelmine Reich aimed to hold onto the German speaking region of Belgium and keep Alsace-Lorraine which had been awarded to Germany by France following the Franco-Prussian War of

1870-71 and France wanted this region returned. Notwithstanding that, Germany would have also been unyielding in their insistence on taking a leading role in a customs union, with Austria-Hungary as their junior partner. This would have solidified German domination over the middle of Europe making that area subordinate to the German economy. Trade policy is merely the continuation of war by other means.

From middle earth to middle Europe

As in a dark Tolkien fantasy, Germany would spread its grip over *Mitteleuropa* playing the role of Mordor, the English Shire was also in the Kaiser's sights. The plan was to isolate Britain. A third overriding goal was to carve up the Russian Empire and create a series of ethnocentric statelets that would exist under a *Pax Germanica*. Cultural hegemony would follow their economic and military supremacy as the suzerain of central Europe. Subordinate states would find themselves financially exploited. Germany would then be able to resume its colonisation of its puppet states, who would be subject to Germanisation. Through commercial agreements, business in these vassal nations which stretched from the Baltic to the Crimea would be dependent upon Germany. Whilst the native inhabitants would be reduced to serfdom, the underclass would be told that their subjugation would bring stability and was for their own economic benefit. German political plans would perpetuate the Reich's dominance. These plans were in part realised with the 1918 separate peace between the Central Powers and the Bolsheviks. The Treaty of Brest-Litovsk, recognised German speakers as the masters of the Ukraine, Belarus, and the Baltic states. Those nations which were not directly under the German yoke, and merely bound to their cause, would also be subject to the German Empire's influence. The Ottoman Turkish Empire would be made reliant on Germany. The close links between Turkey, the sultanate's successor state, and Germany existed into the late twentieth century.

The United Kingdom would also not be immune. This continental system had the aim of isolating Britain from markets in Europe. Through damaging the British Empire's opportunity to trade, the UK's economic might would be diminished, and its political and military influence would in theory follow suit and likewise be degraded. This plan alarmed the British government. The name of this concept was *Mitteleuropa* and was a prominent idea in Germany during the nineteenth and twentieth centuries. It was also the name of a book, published in 1915, by Friedrich Naumann, who helped inspire Nazi geopolitics. These plans, however, met a roadblock. Nationalist uprisings in eastern Europe, which rejected German authority, the armistice of November 1918, and the Treaty of Versailles, forced these schemes to be put on hold. Germany no longer had the opportunity, nor the capability, to implement them, at least not yet. German dark intentions were kept alive by the *Mitteleuropäischen Wirtschaftstag* think tank which lobbied for the expansion of German economic influence over central Europe. War would be their means to an end.

A game of two halves

The First World War was a disaster for Germany. There was dissension at home. The German military was on its knees and wanted to surrender on the best possible terms but did not want the army associated with the armistice. Erich Ludendorff, First Quartermaster-General of the German General Staff, and a later associate of Hitler during the 1924 failed Beerhall Putsch, advised that an armistice should be made as early as August 1918. Similarly, Field Marshal Paul von Hindenburg, later President of Germany, wanted democratic politicians to come to terms with the Allies so that the military would not be associated with defeat. This gave rise to the widely held belief that the fight could have still been won and that the military was betrayed. Indeed, no member of the German military attended the Armistice signing. This was signed in a railway carriage of Ferdinand Foch's train parked in the Forest of Compiègne. It was a humiliating capitulation.

Gefreiter Adolf Hitler twice awarded the Iron Cross, First and Second Class, had fought on the Western Front during the Great War. He had never reconciled himself to Germany's defeat. He was a devotee of the myth that the German army was victorious but had been stabbed in the back, *Dolchstoßlegende*, by the so-called November criminals. In his mind, a fantastical combination of Jews, Marxists, and liberal politicians took the blame for the Armistice agreement of 1918.

The Great War, as World War One was known, was thought to have ended with the ceasefire on 11th November. Not all on the Allied side were pleased with peace. The renowned French General, Charles Mangin, thought the armistice was a grave political mistake. His response to the peace proposal was, "No no no, we must go right into the heart of Germany. The Germans will not admit they were beaten, which is a fatal error and France will pay for it." Mangin, the hero of many First World War battles, was known for his concept of all-out war, *la guerre à outrance*. His statue in Paris was destroyed on the orders of Hitler. Mangin was an advocate of recruiting black colonial soldiers into the French army. During his time as commander of the 10th Army, which occupied the German Rhineland, he is alleged to have insisted that German authorities under his control provide local women in brothels to offer their services to his West African soldiers. Charles Mangin also intrigued to dismember Germany, seeking to create a pro-French Rhineland buffer state between France and the remainder of Germany. He saw the continuing threat but had helped to stoke a future conflict.

For the time being at least, the war was officially brought to a formal end with the signing of the Treaty of Versailles on 28th June 1919. The reality was as described by Marshal Ferdinand Jean Marie Foch, Supreme Allied Commander on the Western Front at the end of the First World War, "This is not a peace. It is an armistice for twenty years". History showed his words to be prophetic. War resumed with Germany invading Poland twenty years and 65 days later. The origins of the Second World War were based on the sense of injustice regarding the terms of the Versailles Treaty, especially those clauses which took away German territory. The desire for *Lebensraum* and the wars which Hitler wanted to start were given all the political cover that they needed in the seemingly rational desire in Germany for irredentism, the reclaiming of land that they considered to be unfairly occupied by neighbouring states. Hitler was far from alone in wanting to redeem these regions.

The bottom line is usually financial and recent German history and its treatment by its neighbours was a festering sore that Hitler intended to avenge. A key term of the Treaty of Versailles was the payment of reparations by Germany. The sums were excessive, and the German Government defaulted on the payments. As a result, in January 1923, the French and Belgium governments sent in soldiers to occupy the Ruhr, the industrial heart of Germany, they came in a manner akin to debt collectors seeking recompense for the defaulted funds by expropriating wealth. They did not depart until 1925. The Germans were not alone in feeling aggrieved by this. The British Labour Party considered the occupation unjustified and referred to France as the principal threat to peace in Europe. The French aggression of the 1920s was worsened in the minds of the Germans because many of the soldiers used in the 1918 to 1930 Allied occupation of Germany's Rhineland were from France's African colonies, most notably Senegal. Rumours of their sexual crimes against German women spread in what was known as the 'Black horror on the Rhine.'

The German Army wanted to avenge their country's humiliation. Hitler just had the means and the maliciousness to see through these plans, the motive was already there. The embers of resentment had been smouldering for years, and it was just a matter of time before they became the great conflagration which was

World War Two. When Hitler's expansionist plans were underway, the game plan was near identical to that of Germany in the First World War. It was as if a nation had succumbed to repetition compulsion.

The similarities were striking, and the conduct of many nations eerily similar to their actions more than 20 years earlier. The Schlieffen Plan of attacking France first before dealing with Russia found an echo in 1940 where the threat to Germany's western flank, from France, was eliminated before the conquest of the East was to begin. The Germans looted Poland in World War One and had the same intentions in the Second World War. Hitler favoured the gradual incorporation of Austria into the Third Reich, a policy goal known as *Anschluss*. During the First World War the Germans considered annexing Austria and taking it into the Kaiser's empire. In the First World War Germany deported Slavs to the west for forced labour. The same would happen in the Second World War. Indeed, the German army triumphant in the east in World War One, started cataloguing the different races in the newly conquered lands of Eastern Europe. Italy was a Central Power, aligned with Germany and Austria-Hungary, until it switched its allegiance in 1915. It came back to the authoritarian fold in the Second World War, when it joined with the Germans in 1940. They were not the only country to switch sides. Finland had been part of Russia but threw off their control in 1918. Towards the end of the First World War the newly independent Finland supported Germany, and had a German Prince as King, but later threw out the German influence. Prior to the First World War the Germans integrated their railway network with their armed forces to allow for the easy deployment of troops. Before the 1939 re-match the Nazis built autobahns which allowed for the Germans to quickly and easily move their armed forces across the country. The Bulgarians were associated with the Germans in both world wars. The list of similarities is expansive.

However there was one crucial, though similar difference. The Italians were a liability to the Allies in World War I. When Italy was confronted by Austrians and Germans, British troops had to be dispatched to Italy to reverse an Allied collapse in the Italian theatre. In World War II the Italians were a liability to the Germans, with Wehrmacht troops sent to prevent a complete collapse of Italian forces. These German soldiers were desperately needed elsewhere. Italy later switched to the Allied side. The politics were not too dissimilar either.

To strengthen support on the German home front for the Great War, German militarists founded the Fatherland Party. Their main goal ultimately failed as the civilian population turned against Germany's war leaders, as did the Kaiser's High Seas Fleet. However, many of its members later found a fitting home in

Adolf Hitler's National Socialist German Workers' Party, the *Nationalsozialistische Deutsche Arbeiterpartei*. The seeds were sown between 1914 and 1918 for an even larger conflict two decades later and took inspiration from long running disputes, chief amongst them the problem of Poland and its borders. This dilemma was not created by Hitler to justify his aggressive reworking of the world, he merely inherited this predicament.

The Polish question

After World War One, some German speakers had been severed from the Fatherland, their homes incorporated into a Polish state. It was a festering sore. Conflict and border disputes between Polish and German nationalists were not a new phenomenon. The spark that lit the Second World War was just the latest incarnation of a problem that had remained unresolved. Indeed, war between Germany and Poland could have come much earlier. Throughout 1920 and 1921 another crisis had begun to brew on the continent of Europe. This was the growing international dispute between the German government and Polish nationalists in Upper Silesia. Ironically, at this time British forces were being considered for peace keeping duties in that region, where they could have been acting in conjunction with Germany against French-backed ethnic Poles. Polish nationalists sought Upper Silesia's incorporation into the newly established Republic of Poland. War was a very real fear. As a result of this latest crisis in mainland Europe the British Army took the step of warning the government of British Prime Minister David Lloyd George that there was a risk that British policy was drawing the UK into a commitment which it most definitely did not have the resources to meet. This dispute was a conflict too far; adequate amounts of resources were not available if the peace keeping mission dragged Britain into yet another continental war. The problem was especially acute as the UK was engaged fighting an insurgency in Ireland.

The Chief of the Imperial General Staff, Field Marshal Sir Henry Wilson, from County Longford in Ireland who would later be assassinated by the IRA in 1922, and General Nevil Macready, the General Officer Commanding-in-Chief of British forces on the Emerald Isle, were becoming deeply concerned about the lack of troops on that island. The diary entries of Field Marshal Sir Henry Wilson show growing alarm. On 18th May 1921 he wrote:

'At 1.30 Curzon (the Foreign Secretary) rang me. He gave me a long sermon about the state of affairs in Silesia, ending by saying that the Prime Minister and he had decided that five battalions should go to Silesia. I at once attacked.

I said that, directly England was safe, every available man should go to Ireland, that even four battalions now on the Rhine ought also to go to Ireland. I said that the troops and the measures taken up to now had been quite inadequate, that I was terrified at the state of that country, and that, in my opinion, unless we crushed out the murder gang this summer, we should lose Ireland and the Empire. I spoke in the strongest manner and I frightened Curzon, who said he must refer it all to the Prime Minister.'

Britain for the time being stayed out of Silesia but the Polish question was not resolved. Certainly, Hitler was reliving the past, re-enacting it, and hoping for a different outcome. When the Nazis unleashed the opening phase of their plan for *Drang nach Osten* in 1939 they considered that they were merely reclaiming their own. Indeed, large parts of what we now consider to be Poland had not just been a part of the German empire but were also an intrinsic part of the Fatherland. However, Germany lost parts of Silesia, Pomerania, and Prussia to Poland; through force or arms Prussia was the founding German state creating a unified nation. Notwithstanding that, after World War One Germany was disembowelled and many regions on its periphery were awarded to France, Lithuania, and the newly independent Poland. That was despite the fact that there were significant German populations residing in "the monstrous bastard son of the Versailles Treaty" as Soviet Foreign Minister Molotov described Poland.

The situation was similar with the German annexation of the previously Czechoslovak controlled Sudetenland, which was once part of the German speaking Austrian Empire, itself brought into Hitler's Third Reich. The main difference to the conquest of Poland was that the swallowing of the then German speaking Sudetenland was reluctantly endorsed by the international community. Six months later, a blind eye was turned to the German occupation of Bohemia and Moravia, now known as Czechia, however, it did have the effect of sounding the alarm about Hitler's intentions; appeasement as a policy had reached the end of the road. There would be no more toleration of the Nazis desire to reunite these disparate German populations by bringing them into the Third Reich, as one people, one empire, one leader, *"Ein Volk, Ein Reich, Ein Führer"*. Hitler was hoping to correct the pain experienced in his past by bloody war. Repetition Compulsion was not the only psychological disorder that drove the Second World War.

High Hitler

Hitler was a mass of contradictions, a paradoxical fellow. He loved his people yet condemned many to death when he thought that they had failed him and, in his opinion, proved themselves to be the weaker race when compared to the Slav and Turkic peoples. Those ethnicities made up the Russian forces bearing down upon the Führerbunker in 1945. He was an environmentalist, yet he released industrial warfare, even industrial extermination, on the world. A vegetarian and animal lover, he cared deeply for his German Shepherd dog named Blondi, yet still killed his pet on 29th April 1945 by testing his cyanide capsules on his beloved animal before ingesting the poison himself. Blondi was not alone. Most of Hitler's romantic interests ranging from his niece to his wife either killed themselves or attempted suicide. For years he would not marry Eva Braun, his mistress of sorts, as he considered himself wedded to the German people. The women and children of the Fatherland did especially adore him, although from afar.

The adoration was, however, greatest from those to whom he was closest. Just as he had an obsessive nature, his associates were addicted to him. This is not an uncommon occurrence for those who suffer from bipolar disorder, what some will know as manic depression and those who suffer from narcissistic personality disorder. Hitler was either in a state of hypomania or depression, with bouts of enormous energy followed by extreme melancholy, then followed by passion and positivity. His devoted inner circle at times swung from being in awe of him to fearing that he may take his own life. Yet, he was no fool. He could easily outmanoeuvre those who were critical of his plans, such as the critics who came from the conservative Prussian military aristocracy. Hitler was a consummate politician, but ultimately proved too smart for his own good. The yes men that he appointed could not properly serve Germany's war as well as the talent that Hitler had removed, sometimes permanently and with extreme prejudice.

Germany had ultimately been schooled by the Allies in 1918. A crushing blow to a man that had become fiercely patriotic, the same despondency was felt by the nation that had been told they were winning. Indeed, whilst losing their colonies in Africa, the Pacific, and China they had won on the Eastern Front against Russia but were later forced to relinquish their newly won empire.

Extreme reactions are a familiar occurrence in societies that have suffered cataclysmic disasters, especially those at the hands of outside powers. The defeated often develop messianic movements. When the Plains Indians suffered defeats and deportation to often unsatisfactory reservations in what became the United States they developed numerous cults, such as the Ghost Dance movement. This promised to restore the adherents to their rightful place after apocalyptic cataclysms would befall the earth before ushering in a new and purer future. The most famous messianic cult is the one that grew after the Roman corruption, desecration, and eventual destruction of the Temple in Jerusalem. Christianity's revelations promised a new order after the devastation of the old. Although Christianity follows the teachings of Jesus and mostly espouses a desire to eschew war one of his recorded apostles was a Zealot, a far from peaceable sect. Biblical scholar Reza Aslan has suggested that Jesus of Nazareth was himself a zealot; this is a far from widely accepted belief and is improbable. What is certain is that Millenarian movements grow at times of rapid social change and upheaval. Germany had suffered defeat and humiliation after World War One, and Hitler promised a one-thousand Year Reich. It would restore the Aryan peoples to their rightful place, but first there had to be the cleansing fire.

The man now known as Hitler's chief propagandist, Joseph Goebbels, wrote a book titled *Michael* which was published in 1929. It promoted the need for a moral saviour and soldier to save society. Hitler was to be that man. Many Germans, including those influenced by the proto-Nazi Thule society, looked to a superman to save them. Why could Hitler not be that man? He had charisma, again a symptom of bipolar disorder and narcissistic personality disorder, which is often caused by parental neglect and childhood trauma, savaging a victim's self-esteem (Adolf as a child was not unaccustomed to beatings from his father, Alois). Hitler was an orator of great renown. Indeed, Hitler saw himself as a saviour, even a messianic figure like the German mythological hero romanticised by Wagner. Indeed, some saw Hitler as the veritable incarnation of the Wagnerian *beau idéal* Siegfried. This opera romanticised the legendary hero Sigurd who fought against invaders from the east but died after being betrayed. Hitler at the twilight of the Third Reich believed that his own army had been near treasonous. Hitler also believed that Germany had been double-crossed at the end of World War One. His was a paranoid mind, certainly not trusting of his military advisors and sometimes with good reason.

Dealing with defeat and the insecurities that this produces can lead to a reaction that is both equal and opposite. The German exceptionalism that followed was an extreme coping mechanism as well as an opportunity to start again on new and more solid foundations. Hitler had been figuratively born again after being blinded in a British mustard gas attack. Upon hearing of Germany's surrender whilst recuperating in hospital he lost his sight again in a bout of shock. Temporary hysterical blindness in rare cases can be a symptom of severe mental trauma and has been recorded amongst women in Cambodia who had seen terrors at the hands of Pol Pot's year-zero communists, the Khmer

Rouge. His vision was restored by a doctor that encouraged him to believe in himself. Hitler had been a brave soldier that had experienced the extreme horrors of war and was suffering from post-traumatic stress disorder, a variation of this affliction can lead sufferers to believe in their own invincibility. Hitler thought he could do no wrong. In his mind he was the Nietzschean superman, his time had come. Yet, this produced unsound military planning and does not constitute a winning strategy.

His many mental illnesses were exacerbated by drug use. He was hopelessly addicted to methamphetamine, what readers may call crystal meth. A prescription for raising hell if ever there was one. Hitler's unstable nature hardly helped the war effort, as a narcissist he was often more concerned with what people thought of him, surprising for the man who is now the most reviled person in history. His decision making was poor. He meddled in the minutiae of the war over the heads of his commanders and was often affected by his desire to divide his sub-ordinates and make them compete to be in his favour; he was the consummate politician. Hitler's tendency to forge irrational military strategies did have one advantage for the Germans. Information gathered through decryptions made by Ultra, Britain's wartime signals intelligence, found plotting his next move difficult as they could not take into account Hitler's irrationality, that is however a very small crumb of comfort, and it did not save the Nazis from their fate.

Hitler, whose rule was not universally popular with his own people, could not escape his destiny, however time after time he survived assassination attempts. Each added to his state or delirium and reinforced his belief in his own triumphant future even when logic and a dispassionate observation of the evidence dictated otherwise. The most notable occurrence of this phenomena was Hitler's survival of the July 1944 bomb plot conducted by Claus von Stauffenberg. This led to the Führer reinforcing his belief that victory was achievable, the fighting continued.

War is downstream of culture. The second great war was an expression of peoples' values, customs, heritage, and traditions. The society that had repeatedly spawned war again in the twentieth century dictated how it was fought and where. The rematch that was World War Two would have to be played out to the very end. The influence of racialist secret societies played a role in keeping Germany at war even when a rational logical mind could see that defeat was inevitable. The Nazi's had taken the beliefs of the Thule and Vril societies and expanded upon esoteric pseudo-science to construct a narrative that would give Germany's leadership the confidence to believe that they could win the war. The belief in a sacred energy that pure Aryans could harness and use, but only if the Germanic people were purged of pollution from other races, was used to justify the holocaust and keep Germany at war to carry out this ethnic reset. As German society had failed to win the previous war, Hitler, in what is known as a 'cope', expanded upon existing German notions of ethnic superiority.

Social Darwinism

The mistaken belief that the Aryans, a class to which the Germans did not belong, were the supreme race fueled Hitler's faith in victory. The principle of survival of the fittest was, however, not a phrase that Darwin used. The facts of human biology could not be undone by wishful thinking. Science does not support the idea of races having immutable psychological characteristics, it does not even endorse the concept of race. However, that was not the thinking at the time and the Nazis were intent on breeding the next generation of stormtroopers whilst recklessly allowing their active servicemen to wither and die.

Germans were to be a population that would be culturally, intellectually, and physically improved through successful breeding and the application of the latest science, and, for the time almost socially acceptable, eugenics. The improvement of the human race was a very long-term project that demanded looking far into the future. Building a new army required the long-term investment by both men and women in stable loving families. Germany did not have time for this nor the inclination. To create their super soldiers the Nazis attempted to bypass biology. As part of the *Lebensborn* programme the Germans stole children from their families in the hope that they could encourage these younglings to grow into ruthless hardened soldiers. It was not too dissimilar in concept from the Islamic tradition as practised by the Ottomans and Mamelukes of taking Christian children into slavery and indoctrinating them into becoming Muslim jihadists. This approach was recently revived by ISIS with Yazidi children being the object of their conversion programme. Yet, in Germany these child would-be world conquerors were deprived of their mother's love and affection too early and as a result, the *Lebensborn* association produced psychologically weak, damaged, and fearful individuals. Wilfully blind Nazi ideologues just ignored these negative results. Hitler's social policies and his approach to the role of women was to have an important effect later in the war, it led to a delayed call to action for Total War and prevented the mobilisation of the home front until it was too late. The consequences were that the flower of German womanhood, which the Nazis were trying to protect, would be defiled beyond their worst nightmares. The threat this time would come from the east.

Eurasia

Hitler endorsed many strange beliefs. Nevertheless, he was far from being alone in seemingly bizarre theories about what Germany's future role in the world should be. Strategic political thinkers at the time, such as Karl Ernst Haushofer and Rudolf Hess, believed that the different regions of the world should be divided into blocks. A school of thought was founded in Germany and created a unique brand of international relations named *Geopolitik*. This gave further justification and impetus to a German geopolitical strategy that desired to take the leadership of Europe and advance the cause of *Lebensraum*. Some even went as far as to pontificate on the Centre of World Power theory, the thesis of which concludes that whoever controlled the region of the earth north of the Black Sea would rule the world. These ideas may sound strange, until one considers the Orwellian way that some aspects of international relations are developing now. Nor did they seem outlandish at the time. Germany had briefly dominated this region after it had been ceded to them by Lenin's Bolshevik authorities in Moscow. They had accepted peace at any price and had made it clear that they would not walk away from negotiations with the Germans, forcing them to accept any deal they were offered. Ukraine was now in the German sphere of influence. Hitler wanted it back for the Germans, taking it into his sphere of influence and settling Ukraine with his own people who would make it the breadbasket for his empire. There existed towards the end of World War One an alliance between Ukraine and the Berlin dominated Central Powers. It was a thwarted historical destiny but one that German planners were determined to fulfil. To achieve these aims, Germany would need to defeat the USSR. German *autobahns* led to Russia via Poland and the Ukraine.

In the build-up to the war, some western countries favoured German control over Ukraine and sought to appease Hitler by satisfying his territorial ambitions by offering him control over a greater Ukraine; this was naturally alarming to Joseph Stalin. This was not the only act of appeasement designed to mitigate and moderate Hitler's ambitions. However, the deciding factor was Russophobia, which for many is not an irrational fear. Turning a blind eye or even endorsing some of the German Führer's aims and ambitions in Europe was a useful tool that existed for the purpose of containing both communism and Russia. This approach to international relations, and the very recent history, observed by Hitler, was a manifesto and justification for unfettered boldness. Hitler thought he could get away with his plans to expand his Reich. For far too long he did get away with it as did his international partners.

Axis appeasement

The renowned British economist John Maynard Keynes described the terms of the Treaty of Versailles as a "Carthaginian Peace", which means to impose brutal terms on an opponent as the Roman Republic did to the great city of Carthage in antiquity. Conversely, Marshal Ferdinand Foch thought the concord was too lenient and perceived that it would not stop Germany from rising again. However, short of pastoralising Germany, there was little more that could have been demanded of the defeated power. Eventually, a middle way was followed; the terms were not cancelled but merely ceased to be enforced, but by then the damage had already been done.

Hitler's ambitions started early, in 1934 he tried to force a union with his native Austria. This move was checked by Benito Mussolini, the Fascist dictator of Italy who moved troops to the Brenner Pass, which forms part of the border between Italy and Austria. *Il Duce*, the boss of Italy, was no fan of his counterpart in Germany, indeed he was terrified of him. For Adolf Hitler, Benito Mussolini was probably the closest person he could consider to be a friend. Italy was the first nation to be appeased. The British and French failed to stop the 1935 invasion of Abyssinia, now known as Ethiopia. In this act of aggression, the Italians used poison gas, overthrowing the Emperor Haile Selassie I, the *Ras* Täfäri Mäkonnän. It ended the political freedom of the hitherto last independent nation in Africa, bar the *de facto* American protectorate of Liberia. This emboldened the Italians as well as Hitler, and led to the Mediterranean Crisis, discredited the League of Nations, and even influenced the Arab Uprising against British rule in the Palestine Mandate.

The failure in 1936 to stop Hitler reoccupying the Rhineland with his troops, (prior to this it was meant to be devoid of German soldiers), gave encouragement to the Führer. Hitler was also encouraged by the official French and British policy of the same year favouring non-intervention in the Spanish Civil War. This inaction undermined the standing of the British and French governments and by the war's end, France found herself nearly surrounded by an axis of like-minded states. The Spanish Civil War which began in 1936 ran until 1939. The faint echoes of this conflict still reverberate in Spain to this day. At the time its implications were enormous for the whole of Europe and beyond. Intervention went beyond the now romanticised volunteers that made up the international brigades who fought for the Popular Front, a potpourri of socialist forces each with their own idea as to how to reach the promised land. Whilst, the UK and France stayed out, Germany, Italy, and Russia did not. The Germans and Italians aided the Nationalist side, which General Franco emerged to lead. The Soviets aided the Republicans and came into conflict with their future Axis friends and later opponents. The communist's defeat in the Spanish Civil War proved to be a boon to the Soviets. They realised the inadequacy of their tanks and aircraft which they redesigned; the new models faired more than favourably during the Second World War. Stalin had used the Spanish Civil War in the same way as he used the coming conflict between the Axis and the Allies. It kept the Italians and Germans occupied whilst he built-up Soviet military strength.

Incidentally Hitler, Mussolini, and Stalin were not the only statesmen of World War Two that made use of the fighting in Spain. Josip Tito, who would later lead Yugoslavia, gained experience there and he learnt the art of guerrilla warfare.

The most famous act of appeasement remains the awarding of the rich industrial part of Czechoslovakia, the Sudetenland, which had a German speaking majority, to Germany. France had a treaty to defend the territorial integrity of that country, a state that has since peacefully divided itself in two, forming Czechia and Slovakia. Czechoslovakia was one of many states born out of the fall of the Austro-Hungarian Empire. History has shown that its territorial integrity did not survive, and its borders were indeed ill-thought through. The historical memory, and source of many latter-day memes, is the 1938 Munich Conference. This meeting involved the side-lining of the Czechoslovakian President, Edvard Beneš, and the resultant Munich Agreement gave Hitler the land he wanted but not the war he craved. The British Prime Minister Neville Chamberlain gets much of the blame for this. Whilst it is true that the UK persuaded the French not to honour their agreement, many other European nations consented to handing the Sudetenland to Nazi Germany. High amongst the reasons for this taking place was not the desire to appease Hitler; rather it was to contain the Soviet leader, Joseph Stalin. Many countries in eastern Europe feared Russia more than Germany, indeed many still do and this informs policy making as to which camp a nation aligns with to this day, particularly Poland.

Stalin had proposed supplying one-million soldiers to the fight against Germany, so long as Britain and France also joined the battle against Hitler. Poland rejected this proposal and in time the Soviets entered their unholy marriage with Nazi Germany; a union that would be consummated in Poland. Neville Chamberlain, the poster boy for appeasement, was largely persuaded by the Poles to follow this policy. Poland was under a dictatorship of its own and its recent historical memory, one of partition between the German and Russian Empires, showed them that German domination was less severe. Germany during World War One was less anti-Semitic towards Poland's Jews than their eastern European neighbours. Tsarist Russian rule was notorious for its pogroms.

Poland had seized from the Soviets swathes of territory in the 1919 to 1921 Polish-Soviet War. Poland had also invaded Ukraine in an unsuccessful attempt to expand its borders to the south-east. Following the endeavour for Polish *lebensraum* there was a fear that the territory they captured may be reclaimed. There was also the ever-present danger that the Bolsheviks would seek to export their revolution to Poland and use that country as a staging post to 'liberate' other nations and workers and support communist movements that were fighting for their 'freedom', by revolting, in other European states, including Germany. Ultimately the fear of a Russian threat to Polish sovereignty over its territory was very real, but only after the USSR had been attacked by the Germans using Poland as the bridge. That could have been prevented but the Poles were appeasing the Germans.

The Polish desire to placate Nazi Germany was much more than a necessity; it was a treaty commitment. Indeed, these two authoritarian states had been politically associated from the mid-1930s. On 26th January 1934 the German–Polish Non-Aggression Pact was signed, a trade agreement was entered into, and borders were settled, at least for the time being. To all intents and purposes, it was an alliance in all but name. There was also a cultural dimension that was as important as potential further disputes over territory. Poland's military rulers held views that were similar to those that would come to the fore in Nazi Germany, namely that Bolshevism and Judaism were somehow synonymous. In Poland it was said amongst the leadership "With the Germans we may lose our freedom, but with the Russians we shall lose our soul." The Soviet Union was a state where private property was restricted to an elite few. It was a nominally atheist state and where there was religion the citizens were predominately Eastern Orthodox, albeit with a significant Muslim population in parts. Devoutly Roman Catholic Poland was a world away.

It has been theorised that there is a schism in Europe between France and Germany. Whilst there has been a great power rivalry between those two nations the real schism is between the Roman Catholic populations and those who follow different Patriarchs in the Orthodox Churches of eastern and south-eastern Europe. This was formalised as long ago as 1054 AD when the Pope, the Bishop of Rome, excommunicated the Patriarch of Constantinople who retaliated with his own excommunication of his Roman counterpart. The seeds of the split were sown many years before and despite several half-hearted attempts at reconciliation the division, and its political implications, still exist to this day. Such is the divide that it has been the *casus belli* for numerous conflicts into the modern era; a real schism. The deeply Roman Catholic Poles had more in common with the Germans, many of which were followers of the Roman-led branch of Catholicism, indeed Hitler was a coreligionist. Brought up as a devout Roman Catholic, Hitler had been described by Rudolf Hess as 'a good Roman Catholic'. Richard Dawkins, however, noted that he was hardly a good anything. He was, however, a child of his time.

Hitler's economic vision

Adolf Hitler was not just a deluded romantic lusting after conquests to restore a nation's honour and fantasised of becoming a world leader by expropriating most of Europe. He understood the need to obtain and control natural resources. Germany had come late to the party of overseascolonisation. It was then playing catch-up with established economic powers. Most notably Britain and France, who could call upon resources in both men and materiel from their colonies to prosecute the war against what became a hopelessly strained German economy. Whist German industrialisation had been rapid before the outbreak of war in 1914 it had been retarded by a lack of political unity and from a dissipation of energy reserves. Germany's main resource was coal; this was the key fossil fuel of the 19th century. However, German coal fields were dispersed across the country. They could only make full use of these hydrocarbons once the railway network had been fully established, but this came too late for them to profit from the scramble for Africa. Germany's limited maritime strength, resulting from a lack of political unity and limited coastline, prevented them from dominating the land abutting the South Atlantic and the Indian and Pacific Oceans.

This failure both drove Germany's belligerency and ultimately hampered its effectiveness at waging a protracted modern war. To be a great power Germany had to look to its neighbours. For Germany energy security could only come via impinging upon someone else's energy sovereignty. Geology had not blessed Germany with significant reserves of oil, the premier hydrocarbon fuel of the 20th century. Whilst synthetic oil could be produced from coal and gas, this was not sufficient to power Hitler's ambitions. It could not meet his needs. Nor could Germany's mythic forests, or northern plain. Germany's great cities could not provide adequate grounds for the agriculture needed to feed its growing population. In 1918 the German people grew hungry, the Royal Navy had effectively blockaded Germany, and the resources needed to feed, clothe, and fuel not just the army at war but also the people on the home front, had run out.

The thinking in 1930s Germany was quite different. Germany's late entry into the great power overseasexpansion game, its defeat in the First World War, and the need to deliver resources to a growing economy led to Germany enviously gazing over its borders. They coveted areas that could produce the food and fuel the Third Reich needed. This was to be found in lands that were at the time part of the Soviet Union. Russia was the Great Economic Space that Germany needed to exploit. Russia had the natural resources to power the Nazis' drive for European leadership. Under the control of Moscow was coal and oil reserves that were waiting to be stolen, as was the agricultural production of the Ukraine; the Nazis aimed to seize them all. Hitler knew that to keep Germany ahead, they had to take the Ukraine for its food and the Caucasus region for its oil. The rebuilding of German power and prestige in the 1930s followed numerous disasters. Notably their defeat in the First World War, the French and Belgium occupation of the Ruhr in 1923, and the hyper-inflation which followed. The growing unemployment from 1927 onwards and the Great Depression following first the Wall Street Crash of 1929, and then the banking crisis soon after, shook Germany to the core and created a sense that Germany was on a knife edge. The risk of further economic shocks could not be tolerated. However, the foundations of the first German economic miracle of the mid 1930s was built on foundations that were much weaker than those used in the autobahn network. It was built on debt and excessive state borrowing. Germany had structural problems.

There comes a point when debt to GDP ratio becomes unsustainable and by the late 1930s this point had been reached. It is not uncommon for politicians and people alike to blame a murky world of Jewish financiers for their woes and Hitler was no exception. He thought their influence was driving the world to war, or at least that was his delusional self-justification for his actions that he owned. Hitler thought that Jewish international financiers were crippling Germany. In 1939 in the Reichstag, he threatened to annihilate the whole Jewish race in Europe, he tried and very nearly succeeded. Notwithstanding that, laws of economics are like the laws of physics, the German economy was a bubble that was due to burst. Its growth after the crash had not reached an escape velocity, like the V-2 rocket it was due to come crashing down on Germany's neighbours and then the Reich itself. Hitler despised capitalism, but German rearmament and expansionism was kept afloat by Swiss bankers. His preferred economic solution to Germany's impending crisis was plunder. The Swiss were not alone in their culpability. The Bank of England sold Nazi gold plundered from Czechoslovakia in June 1939.

The Nazi need for resources was not just restricted to oil and good arable land. The German's needed the resources of other nations, in particular their gold and financial reserves, to first payoff the debts incurred rebuilding its infrastructure and armed forces. Germany then had to cover the costs of previous invasions which were originally needed to gain resources to fund the German National Debt owed to financial institutions. They borrowed from these to buy the popularity of the German public and stimulate economic growth. It was a vicious debt cycle, with the emphasis on the word vicious. War finances war, further wars were used to finance both previous and future conflicts. It was unsustainable economics. It was not just people abroad that paid the price. The first victims of the Nazi government's reckless misuse of their exchequer were Germany's Jews. In 1938, to stave off the impending bankruptcy of the German state they were persecuted and fined for being Jewish. When Germany was further in debt, Hitler blamed the Jews again. The maliciousness knew no bounds.

Despite their barbarous crimes, the Nazis were not entirely barbarians. They wanted Germany to be the centre of, unlike the German Weimar Republic of the 1920s, a non-decadent high culture which possessed Europe's cultural treasurers. This putative Germanic Renaissance was, however, to be built on the looting of national treasures that belonged to others. This was hardly original; indeed, it was completely derivative. Hitler's own people were also ruthlessly exploited to serve his ends. An Austrian by birth he twice sought to annex his home country and absorb it into his German Reich and succeeded in 1938. Hitler wanted Austria's large deposits of iron ore and steel making industry, as well as its gold reserves, to develop his war machine. There was a powerful economic rationale behind his thinking, which for the time being justified Hitler's romantic vision of one people under his control. War was his answer to Germany's problems.

Blitzkrieg par excellence

Hitler was open minded to ideas that promised quick military solutions to Germany's crises. These plans came to be referred to by Germany's enemies as lightning war, *blitzkrieg*. Whilst not a coherent single military doctrine, it was a successful strategy. *Blitzkrieg*, as far as it existed, relied on the discombobulation of the enemy that would be put into a state of shock and awe. Through the speed of the advance as much as the pace of the initial and often unexpected breakthrough, the attack's ensuing disruption made the defender panic, and created military and political chaos. In that sense *blitzkrieg* was as much a political strategy as it was military; after all they are just different modes of achieving the goals of statecraft. *Blitzkrieg* is also psychological.

Hitler was willing to risk the lives of his men in order to add to his glory and that of his empire, the Reich. The Nazi war machine aimed to spread confusion and terror. This mental tactic was very fitting for the Führer who believed his will would be the deciding factor, the centre of gravity. The chosen mode of warfare was however far from original. The Wehrmacht's use of speed and mobility; move fast, hit hard, move fast again was a romantic vision, a propaganda success reminiscent of warrior knights charging into battle. The English tactic of the *Chevauchée*, with horse parties led by the Black Prince, raiding deep into the territory of the French King, reducing his lands productivity, was a medieval exemplar of fast paced economic warfare. Though by 1940 war was different, Hitler's army took ideas from the past and sought to disrupt the enemy behind their lines. Manoeuvre warfare was not new to the Germans either; it was known in German as *Bewegungskrieg*. This concept was already part of German army doctrine. Since the nineteenth century its strategists sought to defeat an enemy not by destroying strength and assets in a battle of attrition, but commanders would achieve victory through capturing strategic points in the battlespace. They aimed to deliver a bold move that could change the course of the war in the theatre of conflict. It did not always succeed, and such principles were not always followed.

In 1914, in the early stages of World War One, after the initial move to capture Paris had been checked, the front became a stalemate that resulted in trench warfare. The dugout itself was not a new concept and was used extensively by both sides in the later part of what is known as the American Civil War. In 1864 and 1865 they were a key feature of the Union's attempt to capture the city of Petersburg in Virginia and the Confederate capital Richmond. Comparably, trenches formed a key part of the South's attempt to defend their cities. Technology in World War One led to the scenario where firepower from artillery, machine guns, and even relatively fast to fire and reload rifles necessitated that those soldiers seek shelter. Their security was aided by the defensive implement of barbed wire, first invented in the United States in the late 1860s and refined by 1874. This obstacle made attack harder thus aiding the protection of soldiers entrenched and encamped in bunkers behind the wire. Improvements in communications, namely the telephone allowed for the defender to easily keep commanders abreast of developments and request reinforcements. Similarly, fixed positions could call on artillery to rain down defensive fire. Conversely, as these devices were not readily portable, the attacker could not refine their offense in real time. Furthermore, artillery firepower was not easily manoeuvrable and therefore an offensive could only proceed so far and would have difficulty breaking permanent lines primed with personnel who could keep fighting. The invention of tinned food and refined logistics meant soldiers at the front could be supplied all year round.

No longer would armies have to retreat to winter quarters. The monotony of spam accompanied the tedium of trench warfare.

Trench warfare worked for the French as it reduced casualties and stopped Germany from achieving any significant breakout from which they could go on to seize Paris. In World War One it was a successful system for the Allies. Trenches on the western front completely negated the German plan for a swift victory. It dashed German hopes for victory in the west, one that was intended to allow the Teuton to focus all their resources against Slavic Russia. Helmuth von Moltke the Younger, the German general and Chief of the Great General Staff, most probably knew that his side had lost the war as soon as they failed to capture the French capital. Germany could not afford to fight a war of attrition, and certainly not on multiple fronts. They were bogged down trying to overcome the trench and the defensive system supporting it.

Manoeuvre warfare partially returned in 1918 when the Germans attempted to break the Allies in the Spring offensive. This included using highly trained and well-equipped Stormtroopers probing for weaknesses in the Allied lines from which they hoped to break through and cause disruption to headquarters and strong points. These shock troops offered a vision of what the Nazi 'superman' could achieve. The Michael Offensive, as it was also known, succeeded in driving the British back but failed to win the war. There was still time for the Nietzschean concept of the superman to triumph. The French had also developed a similar, though less sophisticated approach to breaking the confines of trench warfare. Yet it was not needed; Germany was exhausted towards the close of World War One. Mobility truly returned to the Western Front with the Battle of Amiens at the start of the Hundred Days Offensive where the Allies sought to push the Germans back to the Fatherland. The Allies had learnt to coordinate aerial attacks working in unison with a plethora of tanks, the Germans only managed to produce twenty panzers in the Great War. Nevertheless, Allied casualties at this time of great success exceeded the losses from trench warfare. Clearly the Nazis' military innovations derived from others. *Blitzkrieg* was far from original.

The aim of achieving local superiority at a given point, from where operations would be developed had a long history. The Theban tactic, developed by Epaminondas and used against the Spartans at the Battle of Leuctra in 371 BC was an early iteration. It applied in the skies as well as on the ground. In World War One, the Luftwaffe attempted to make up for its' dearth of aircraft through the so-called Flying Circus, concentrating their aircraft on different points on the front line. This was first led by Baron von Richthofen, after his death Hermann Göring took charge of these airmen. The prominent Nazi was a celebrated war hero whose military career started in the infantry before he became a fighter pilot. He would later cover his reputation in infamy in the second stage of the German wars.

With the development of mechanised vehicles and their gradual proliferation into the armed forces of most developed nations, the war of manoeuvre would be institutionalised. Military theorists and commanders were free to plan how best to use their newfound mobility; the sky was the limit. The modern development of what is known as blitzkrieg, with the use of tanks and ground attack aircraft combined with infantry and artillery is often wrongly accredited to the Germans. Moreover, it began not in Germany but in Britain. Blitzkrieg-esque tactics were used at the Battle of Cambrai in late 1917. However, a German counterattack nullified and negated the British successes.

The word blitzkrieg was itself coined in Britain. The British Army were the first to learn the lessons from World War One and develop concepts that could affect a swift breakthrough. As early as 1928 Army exercises on Salisbury Plain used mechanised armoured units to practice how to make breakthroughs against infantry. British military theorists Basil Liddel-Hart and Major-General John Fuller were the initial advocates of tactics that centred on bypassing enemy strong points, with isolated units being destroyed at leisure. Their maxim was 'destroy the enemy's brain and not his body'. These ideas were a great influence on men in the German Army such as General Heinz Guderian, whose 1937 book *Achtung – Panzer!* was devoured by Adolf Hitler. Guderian had the notion that the tank's engine was as much the weapon as the gun which the tank mounted. Another famed German general, Erwin Rommel was also thinking along similar lines and expressed his ideas in his book *Infantry Attacks* first published in 1937. Both Guderian and Rommel would be instrumental in the Fall of France. Incidentally, Fuller later became an admirer of Adolf Hitler.

The future of the British Army's approach to warfare rested with Bernard Law Montgomery. He was a key planner behind the success of the Hundred Days Offensive in World War One. Lieutenant Colonel, later Field Marshal Montgomery, known as Monty to his men and the public, was an early advocate of the use of air power in conjunction with ground forces. And proposed integrating the different branches of the armed services, combining them in operations. Throughout the 1920s and the 1930s, Montgomery was a prolific author of articles on the successful execution of his profession – war. The future of much of the Allied war effort would to be in his hands. His works included, "Letter of Advice to a Newly Appointed Adjutant in the TA" (The editors changed his original title, "Training in the Territorial Army") *Army Quarterly*, published in the Autumn of 1924. In the mid-1920s, Montgomery published a five-part series entitled "The Growth of Modern Infantry Tactics" in the journal of the Royal Warwickshire Regiment, *The Antelope*. He followed this up in 1926 with an article titled "Some Problems of Mechanization" also published in *The Antelope*.

Most importantly Montgomery was later commissioned by the War Office in 1929 to write the British Army's *Infantry Training Manual*. Published in 1930, he alone developed the credo that would be adopted by the British Army. Montgomery and his doctrine of war, whilst using armour in concentrated attacks, was not the same as that preached by men like Fuller and Liddell-Hart. The differences were however nuanced. Liddell-Hart wanted armoured units to flow through following *ad hoc* attacks, rather than through a precisely planned piercing of the front line. Montgomery thought that the attack should be subordinate to the commander's overall objectives and conducted according to his plan. Montgomery's doctrine rested on his belief that victory was not determined just by mere materiel considerations relating to which side had the greater quantity of high-quality tanks for instance. Rather, it was Monty's considered view that the commander was the deciding factor.

Montgomery, displaying 3D thinking, also dealt with how best to manoeuvre in time and space. He also made the case that armoured divisions should be used for concentrated powerful blows to smash the enemy at a given point, and not spread out thinly along a broad front which would dissipate strength. Any failure to focus power would make an army vulnerable to attack. Monty devised a strategy to dictate the course of events. Yet, throughout the course of the war he could, and did, appreciate the advantage that multiple attacks in different sectors could give the Allies. Supporting offensives would make the enemy unbalanced, distracted, and confused. So much so that it would pull resources away from the area where the main blow would fall. Monty's doctrine would use massed artillery, tanks, and aeroplanes to break apart the enemy and destroy their power.

In his 1938 work *The Major Tactics of the Encounter Battle*, published in *The Army Quarterly*, Montgomery discussed the importance of ground. And laid down his theories on the new operational instructions that were needed in mechanized warfare and how these orders should be passed on by divisional commanders. These ideas were reiterated in "The Problem of the Encounter Battle as Affected by Modern British War Establishment" published in the *Royal Engineers Journal*, September 1938. Monty's theories were described by the Editor, Kenneth Stuart, as "the most thoughtful and valuable tactical discussion that has appeared in any British service journal for some considerable time."

Monty not only defined British strategy and tactics he also took an all-encompassing attitude to warfare from communication to motivating the home front and those under his command. Montgomery evangelised his ideas in print and taught other future leaders of the British Army. In 1926 Lieutenant Colonel Montgomery became an Instructor at the British Army Staff College based in Camberley. He was promoted to Colonel in the 1930s and he even taught as the Chief Instructor at the Indian Army Staff College based at Quetta, now in modern day Pakistan. Throughout the interwar period he also actively trained soldiers. Amongst many other drills, in 1938 Monty impressively organised a combined operations amphibious landing exercise. It would not be long before the history of Europe would depend upon such an operation carried out in the heat of battle.

The British and the Germans were not alone in formally adopting line-breaking ideas. Others would similarly develop doctrines that rested upon the use of firepower made mobile by the tank, self-propelled artillery, and trucks to transport soldiers in swift decisive moves supported by airpower and even using planes to take men into battle. In the inter-war period, the Soviet Red Army was amongst the first to develop and unify these theories which even included the use of airborne forces with paratroopers. The Russian concept was known as Deep Battle. This involved multiple coordinated attacks under the direction of the commander following a strategic objective. Offensives would be focused on many fronts, driving deep into the enemy lines, with other units following through, smashing the invaders logistics, dividing the opposing forces, and destroying both their will and ability to mount a defence. On the face of it there were similarities to the German method of war, indeed both nations' armed forces had collaborated in the 1920s in developing their respective strategies. The distinctive difference was that the Red Army would not be demanding a quick victory. Their concept would enable the enemy to first be surrounded, firmly isolated, and then effectively imprisoned in a self-guarding prison camp from where they would be gradually, but decisively, annihilated. Deep Battle did not seek a *coup de main*; Russia did not rely on the hope of one decisive victory but instead took a pioneering and holistic approach that included both defence of strategic points and offence. In the 1920s the Red Army and NKVD, the Soviet secret police, even invented the mixed martial art of Sambo to unite the nation and add to their citizens hand-to-hand combat skills. It took the best techniques from arts such as judo, jujutsu, and numerous styles of wrestling, to create a complete form of unarmed fighting.

Before Soviet communism fell into stagnation and just became about the management of a declining and failed system, the revolutionaries who took over Russia in the name of socialism were both energetic and inventive. Despite policies which caused enormous human hardship, mass deaths and misery for millions, they believed themselves to be modern and progressive, on the right side of history and bringing into being a rational and even scientific system. As such these highly driven men were open to innovation. They were also negatively incentivised to modernise their military and the thinking behind how the Soviet Union should defend itself. Military planners believed that the biggest external threat to their rule came from the industrially advanced capitalist countries. An attack was not without precedence, for several years following the First World War, multi-national forces were sent to crush the Moscow based Bolshevik government which was surrounded by those who wished to extinguish the Red revolution.

Deep Battle was much more than just a set of tactics and field regulations. It was a national strategy, a deep strategy. Planners in the Soviet Union knew that mobile warfare was the answer; the sheer expanse of Russia meant that mobility would always be possible. They also rightly concluded that the coming conflict would be a war of attrition. To that end the USSR set out to industrialise and modernise the state, especially, its armed forces to fight for its very survival in a war where manoeuvre was paramount. Preparation was everything, at least that was the plan.

The way in which Germany made war upon its neighbours was therefore nothing novel, nor out of the ordinary. The Nazi 'blitzkrieg' was actually a less well-defined approach to war than those developed by its rivals. Blitzkrieg was a vague notion and like everything in the Nazi state confused and *ad hoc*. It was a poorly managed and often uncoordinated approach to war. Indeed, Nazi Germany, unlike Fascist Italy, which was corporatist and structured, was, within ideological limits, pluralistic, and only brought together in the person of the Führer himself. Pluralism was partly driven by Hitler's paranoia, the politician in him wanted to prevent other people from becoming too powerful. There were rivalries between organisations, even intelligence divisions rarely cooperated. In fact, they were set against each other and had to seek Hitler's favour. There were seven different code breaking bodies with resources split between them, they were competing and not coordinating. German efficiency was merely a myth.

Always the Sun

"The war has developed not necessarily to Japan's advantage."
— **Tennō (天皇), Heavenly Sovereign (Emperor), Hirohito**

Islands in chains

Japan's position as a group of islands sitting on the Pacific rim's ring of fire gave it rich soils blessed with many nutrients. The land is surrounded by seas which also offered a bounty that could support a large population without the need for technical innovation. The abundance of minerals, a temperate climate, and the surrounding waters gave it a plenitude that fed a growing number of inhabitants. This in turn produced a glut of workers. Reliance on an oversupply of labour automatically made workers cheap, often they were compelled to toil for free. This held back Japan's technological development. There was no need and little return on investment in new technology. Japan's almost feudal rural society with its strict class system known as *shinōkōshō,* itself imported from China and derived from Confucianism, also prevented modernisation and meritocracy.

Other social conventions had fateful consequences. The employment of the Japanese concept of *Bushido* and the *Senjinkun* military code were a hangover from a society that had only recently emerged from feudalism, which was itself a consequence of Japan's physical and intellectual isolation. This was abruptly ended by the USA in July 1853 when their gunboats arrived in Edo Bay, now renamed Tokyo. Links between the United States and Japan quickly grew and almost developed into chains. There followed a period of Westernisation and in some cases imitation, adoption, and then replication of old-world science and technology, which were repackaged into mass produced tailored versions to suit Japanese requirements. The ability to do this has been a remarkable quality peculiar to the Japanese. It is shown in the use of Kanji characters adopted from China's writing system to the Chinese inspiration for the Samurai sword, the Katana. And is reflected in Karate which derives from Gung Fu and T'ai chi ch'üan. However, the flowing circular movements of those Chinese meditative arts became direct lines and abrupt angles aiming to deliver forceful and overwhelming strikes in a Japanese martial discipline. Japan has also taken metaphysical and material enrichment from abroad. From the spread of Buddhism in the past, to the present-day Japanese interest in cars and whisky being notable examples of such flattery. During the Second World War the idea for the use of aircraft carriers on 7th December 1941 had *gaikoku hito*, foreign, inspiration. The conservative society in Japan historically had little inherent creativity. The wheel, which originated far to the west, was not a significant part of their economy. Wheeled vehicles were unsuited to the terrain and were restricted during the Shogunate. Their use was too liberating for the lower classes who would be freed from manual haulage duties. Whilst Japan's economy was far from advanced, its society was, however, ruthlessly efficient and existed to fulfil the military caste's ego driven aims.

The land of the rising sun, the very fitting *sobriquet* for Japan, sitting on the edge of Asia with nothing but a great expanse of ocean lying to the east, is beautifully illustrated in the country's flag. And equally so in its naval ensign derived from the flag of its Shōgun rulers. The diffusionist school of thought regarding cultural and technological developments, helps explain Japan's distinct development that put it on its calamitous course of action. Isolation is not just a matter of lacking links with other nations, it is also a state of mind. Its isolation kept it free from migrating populations, a policy it follows to this day. It was also free from the conquering armies of the world's preeminent superpower, the Mongol hordes. This held back the economic and societal revolutions that we now call progress and solidified Japan's staid culture.

The seas surrounding the Japanese islands are like those that encompass the British Isles, a fortress built by nature for herself. A divine wind, *Kamikaze*, secured both island chains from the designs of less happy lands, the first divine wind saved Japan from conquest by the Mongol ruler Kublai Khan in 1274, destroying his poorly constructed keelless fleet. The second, Kamikaze, came in 1588 which saved Elizabethan England from the forces of the Roman Catholic King Phillip II of Spain, the Spanish Armada was also wrecked by powerful winds. Britain, especially England, is, similar to Japan both densely populated islands but that is where the similarities end. Japan's development followed a different course.

Resource poor, apart from coal, the English and later British nation looked overseas for opportunity. Japan, at first looked inward. Anglo-Celtic liberal traditions, inherited from Norse and western Germanic notions of devolved power to tribal and county institutions drove innovation. When this political culture became empowered by the individualistic protestant and capitalist ethos the United Kingdom burst onto the world stage in the first era of globalisation. England established a presence across the seas shortly after the age of discovery began. The Japanese Tsunami on the world came much later and was a desperate gamble for land and resources. Their short and brutal period of conquest, was, like the British Empire, partly conducted in a fit of absence of mind. Germany had a grand plan, Japan did not. Indeed, Japan was a victim of its own success. When the industrial revolution took hold of Japan its economic and population growth was so rapid that it could only be maintained by acquiring more resources from abroad. Japan was caught in a circular logic trap of its own making. It needed more riches; it was thought that conquest was necessary to gain those materials. Additional amounts were then required to power and produce their weapons of war, which begot the need for yet more land and the minerals and fuels that lay within the earth. The economic justification for war and nationalist sentiments quickly spun out of control.

Japan, like Germany, started its expansionist and imperial endeavours much later than western European nations. Japan had been a relatively isolationist state and was less wedded to the concept of subjugating its neighbours in east Asia. The Yamato people, as the main ethnic group of Japan are known, even came late to colonising and unifying their own home islands. The ethnic, cultural, and linguistic unification of Japan was only achieved after the suppression of the Ainu people of Hokkaidō in the north and the Ryukyuans of the Ryukyu Islands of which the largest isle is Okinawa to the South. Japan's home islands are an archipelago that stretches down into the East China Sea towards Taiwan. The Ryukyu's integration into Japan came in the nineteenth century. The political integration of Japan was delayed by its combination of mountainous terrain followed by islands that had emerged out of the Pacific Ocean. Both of those were in themselves a consequence of Japan's sitting on where the competing North American, Pacific, Eurasian, and Philippine tectonic plates clash. Indeed, the nation owes its existence to this natural phenomenon. To this day ¾ of Japan is either mountainous or forested land that is not easily conducive to enabling economic growth, that is until man learned to conqueror and control nature with the onset of industrialisation.

Identity politics
Beyond the mythology of the past with its pseudo-historical figures and legendary rulers, the political unification of Japan in anything that corresponds to history was not complete until the early 1590s. This was achieved when Toyotomi Hideyoshi, a samurai of humble origins rose to become a prominent *Daimyō*, a great noble. He fought and won control over Japan's home islands, which he then governed with the approval of the Emperor. Despite being of peasant stock

Hideyoshi enforced strict rules that differentiated the classes and deprived the lower orders of rights; Japan's stultified culture continued. He also desired to conquer China and Korea. To such an end, Japan's early militarists concocted a feudal Ponzi scheme. They envisaged this would spread their power across Asia in a manner akin to a domino effect. After initial conquests, Hideyoshi presumed that subjected peoples of first Korea, and then parts of China, could be pressed into the service of their new master and made to seize more territories from which other recruits would be drawn and so forth. Japan's violent ruling class were overly accustomed to receiving the service of their base underlings to comprehend the futility of these plans. The endeavour of capturing Korea and China spectacularly failed. Yet, Japan would try again centuries later. There were compelling spiritual beliefs that would have a powerful physical manifestation and contributed to the growing culture of conflict.

The Emperor is the highest authority of the Shinto religion, a direct descendant of the sun-goddess Amaterasu. Indeed, from the establishment of the first shogunate in 1192 until the Meiji restoration in 1867, temporal affairs were not his domain but instead belonged to effectively independent lords who were subordinated to various military dictators. The Emperor is called *Tennō* (天皇), which means "heavenly sovereign", also *Mikado* (帝), he dealt with heavenly affairs, religious rites, and formally recognised those who possessed power, granting them official government titles. Only from the Meiji Constitution of 1889 did the *de facto* and *de jure* overlordship of Japan became formalised in the divine person of the emperor. Religion played an important role. Shintōism and the belief in the emperor were founding myths useful for political purposes to unite what was a divided and fractious land. It had a powerful effect. The result was extreme nationalism, which is a common occurrence amongst newly invented politeias such as Germany, Italy, and the Republic of Turkey, and Japan for instance. The not-too-distant history of Japan however had provided little justification and evidence for this excessive form of exceptionalism. Indeed, it was a psychological correction to compensate for Japan's insecurity and inferiority in face of the powers and civilisations which surrounded the home islands.

Japanese political unity was stabilised under the Tokugawa Shogunate which had learned from the failures of interventions in foreign lands. During this period, rule over earthly matters was carried out by one military leader, this dynastic ruler held the title of Shōgun. Japanese isolation was far from complete and foreign naval powers began to impinge on Japan's otherness. Japan also began to influence its near abroad. Its seaborne trade with its neighbours was developed under the stewardship of an English sailor. William Adams, a Protestant who arrived in Japan in 1600 diffused to the Japanese the skills to build the latest sea going vessels and built trade links with its Pacific neighbours. In time he became a key advisor to Shōgun Tokugawa Ieyasu. This Japanese noble seized power in Japan in 1600 and was appointed as Japan's ruler by the nominal and religious leader, the Emperor, in 1603. In the same year Elizabeth I of England was succeeded by James VI of Scotland, henceforth known as James I.

The religious rivalries of the European continent were exported to Japan by the Jesuits and Roman Catholic Portuguese and Spanish traders. They tried unsuccessfully to limit the growing but still benign influence that Adams exercised over Ieyasu. In response the Protestant Adams persuaded the Shōgun to expel Roman Catholic influences from the country. This preserved Japan's independence and avoided it being dragged down by Spanish influence and its inquisition. To this day Spain's former colonies are, apart from those which now constitute a part of the USA, politically troubled and economically unstable.

Japan was largely freed from the cultural and religious invasion of western ideas. Because they did not close their eyes and kneel to pray as the Portuguese and Spanish missionaries desired, they were able to keep a watchful eye against any further Iberian incursion. The Portuguese were the prevailing colonists of this age and were to the world what the Phoenicians were to the ancient Mediterranean. Through the endeavours of the Order of the Knights of Our Lord Jesus Christ, reorganised from the Knights Templar, the Portuguese created trade links that sparked the development of civilisation. This was largely in response to the 15th century conquests of the Islamic Ottoman Empire which cut the overland trade routes between the occident and the orient, prompting, and necessitating the age of discovery. Here Portugal and Spain, and later others, sought direct access to the markets of the far-east by sea via the Cape of Good Hope. They explored and, in some cases, conquered nearly as far as the Japanese home islands, where their naval empires were halted. Spain was the superpower of that age, yet it could not overcome Adams; he had affected a turning point against the growing influence of these two alien empires.

Whilst Japan was far from barbarous, it still lagged behind Europe's imperial powers, particularly in weaponology. Its famed composite swords, a technology perfected in the 16th century using the forging together of steel with different amounts of carbon in the blade, had been practised by Anglo-Saxon bladesmiths in the 6th century. These devotees of Wayland the Smith used chemical etchants to show the shimmering lines of the many layers created by forging together the folds and twists of the metals that make up the blade. Each fold had differing properties to the next, alternating between hardness and flexibility. Despite the delayed development Japan had a distinct and resplendent culture that was economically prosperous as well as socially rich. While feudal Japan was not on the path to industrialisation, it did have enormous potential. This only occurred in the 1870s when the tumults caused through its contact with another Pacific imperial power, the USA, had settled.

When Japan was forcibly made to enter the modern world by an American trade mission of 1853. Conducted with overwhelming force, the shock led to the collapse of the Shogunate system of control where the ruling dynasty had held sway over Japan's islands for more than 250 years. It was replaced with the Meiji Restoration, restoring the emperors to their position of secular as well as religious authority; a state of affairs not seen in Japan for millennia. Japan, having seen the British defeat China, when the Chinese had had the temerity to reject Britain's demands, had no choice but to comply with American overtures. Nearly nine decades later, Japan's economy was yet to reach a stage of preparedness to compete in the age of total war. Even into the industrial age, most residential buildings, even in the capital city of Tokyo, were made of wood. This would prove to be a major structural failing that illuminated Japan's lack of development. In antiquity, it was assumed that Germanic tribesmen were less advanced than their Roman enemies because the Germans lived in wooden dwellings, the Romans however, would reside in houses built of stone. Indeed, the Roman established colony of Cologne was made of much more robust materials than those used by the Germans living on the other bank of the Rhine River. Medieval building materials would not stand in the way of the wolf of modern warfare. However, Japan's unique identity and culture, with great human potential alongside a large labour force, meant that it was not in awe of what is known as the 'West' but was keen to enter the world and take its place amongst the greater states of the globe. It was a nation in a hurry.

Trouble with the neighbours

Japan has now been replaced as the predominant power in the eastern Pacific by China, a country that was also expanding its control over its citizenry at home. And under the guise of infrastructure improvements, using debt slavery to secure control over resources and assets abroad. China is finally fulfilling the potential it showed in the early 15th century when Heng Tze's great fleet could have taken dominion of the world. However, in the late nineteenth century China once a great power, and will be so again, was a failed state. Its inability to modernise had left it at the mercy of European powers, even the United States.

Both Britain, Italy, and Germany had secured Chinese colonies, with the UK controlling Shanghai amongst other places and Germany holding the colonial concession of Tsingtao. China's territorial integrity was being gnawed away from abroad by western European states and from within by warlordism. The rot had set in much earlier, most notably in the Opium Wars. The failure to modernise its fleet meant that the Chinese navy was destroyed by the British acting on behalf of Jardine Matheson & Co, who wanted the right to traffic opium to the Chinese. Unlike Japan, which had largely rejected Christian influence, that religion had a long history in China; missionaries and European involvement expanded this exponentially.

In the mid-nineteenth century, under the guise of Christianity, Hong Xiuquan, who claimed to be the brother of Jesus Christ, inspired people to fight one of the most destructive wars in Chinese history. Estimates of the casualties from the Taiping Rebellion, as it became known, range from 20 million to 80 million dead. It is amongst the first examples of total war. This quasi-Prester John's rebellion was eventually crushed with the aid of British and French troops. The revolt's real inspiration was the much-needed root and branch reformation of Chinese government and society, although overpopulation, famine, defeat at the hands of European powers and economic hardship were the underlying causes. This along with China being gripped by numerous other rebellions made the Chinese state unviable. Hong Xiuquan's messianic movement was a symptom of a wider decline and part of the common desire to find saviours amongst improbable people.

China was now fully at the mercy of all and sundry, especially its ravenous neighbour Japan. However, China would not just give way, it still had pretensions to exert control over its neighbours, China's own near-abroad, it had become a broken land ripe for the Japanese to exploit. Japan's ambitions in China were the underlying cause of its cataclysmic conflict with the United States, which had not only forged an empire from the Atlantic to the Pacific, sea to shining sea, but also across the Pacific seizing territory in its steady advance. The USA had taken islands from the Polynesians and the Spanish. The Philippines, which abuts onto the South China Sea, was the prized American imperial possession which it had seized from Spain in 1898. The USA kept these islands to prevent other European powers, such as Germany, from moving in. They were also an essential staging post for American trade with China. The USA was always willing to fight for the Philippines and held this nation by crushing pro-independence Islamic insurrections.

Apart from that, and the positive cultural transfusion from China to Japan, the enmity between those two nations had a long history, and this was the ultimate cause of the war in the east. Whereas China was in relative decline, Japan, free from revolutions inspired by foreign ideologies, made some very real progress. A weakened China was waiting to be exploited by Japan, yet the immediate cause of conflict was a third country. Japan's Imperial expansion over established nations originally began with Korea in the late 16th century and resumed on the Korean peninsula three centuries later. The Korean peninsula with the Yellow Sea to the West and by the Sea of Japan to the East, was a security issue for the Japanese. The two nations are separated by the Korean Straight to the south of the peninsula. The proximity of that land was a cause for concern for Japan. The Japanese were concerned that a foreign power controlling Korea could threaten Japan itself. Korea was to Japan what Cuba is to the United States. In 1894 Japan and China went to war primarily over the status of Korea, the Japanese sought greater influence over their immediate neighbour. Aping European colonists, Japan also desired to obtain an economic advantage from the conflict. The now mercantilist Japanese adopted the war aim of forcing the Chinese to open its ports to their trade.

The 1894-95 Sino-Japanese war was concluded in Japan's favour. A broken China suing for peace had to cease involvement in Korea and later were forced to cede the Chinese island of Taiwan to Japan in perpetuity. China also lost part of Manchuria and land to the Northwest of Korea, including the city of Mukden. Japan however was humiliated by Germany, France, and Russia which in 1895 threatened war unless the Japanese gave back the ports it had seized, including the soon to be infamous Port Arthur. The Japanese were indignant. Japan's resentment against these colonial powers was born as was a burning sense of injustice. Vengeance was desired.

Korea became a Japanese Protectorate in 1905. In that year Japan had announced itself to the world as a force to be reckoned with. Tsarist Russia, initially an empire centred on the Grand Duchy of Moscow, flitted between eastward and westward expansion. At the turn of the last century Russia was seeking to expand its dominion to include the Chinese province of Manchuria and the Korean Peninsula. Despite Japanese complaints, Russia continued with its *de facto* annexation of Manchuria, a region that Japan considered to be part of its sphere of influence. Russia's endeavours around the Pacific rim demanded that they secure a port that did not freeze over in winter. To this end Russia took a port on the Yellow Sea from the Chinese, Port Arthur, which was usable all year-round. Russian policy is still determined by the need to secure accessible ports. Policy makers in other countries that do not allow for this geostrategic aim are wholly ignorant as it remains an overriding aim of the Russian state to this day, hence the 2014 reoccupation of the Crimean Peninsula, largely to secure the harbour, and warm water port, of Sevastopol, home to a major Russian naval base and their Black Sea Fleet.

Riding the tiger

In 1904, Japan declared war on the Russian bear. The *casus belli* was largely Russian intransigence on the status of Manchuria, and the exceptional Japanese interest in what was and still is a major Chinese province. The Tsar responded by sending his Baltic Fleet on an epic voyage across the globe to fight the Japanese. Russia was decisively defeated on land and sea. This victory was the cause of a great deal of national pride in Japan. A tiger had been awakened. The world was shocked,as the natural order as seen by European countries had been overturned. Being checked in the east, forced Russia to again look west where in less than a decade it again ran into the Ottoman Empire as well as Austria-Hungary, and Germany. In Japan the security rational for military intervention soon gave way to the concept of spheres of influence which was soon superseded by imperialism. Japan formally incorporated Korea into its nascent empire in 1910. Japan's exploitation of both its neighbour's resources and peoples were underway, as was the colonisation of Korea, by 1945 there were 850,000 Japanese living on the Korean Peninsula.

Japan was opportunistic and, in alliance with Britain, France, and Russia, declared war on Germany during World War One. This made China and Japan quasi-allies. China declared war on Germany in 1917, joining the Allied side in the First World War. Japan joined the fight towards the start, declaring war in 1914. This was a sound strategy. Germany's Chinese colony was seized by a combined British and Japanese force. After the war the Paris Peace Conference of 1919 awarded all of Germany's former oriental possessions north of the equator to Japan, including the territories in China. Yet, this still did not give the Japanese equality with their European and American partners. China, which had also declared war on Germany expected the colonies to be returned. The Chinese lobbied for their land to be given back to them, and in 1922, under American mediation Japan was forced to cede their conquests. The United States had stymied Japan's Imperial ambitions, this would not be forgotten, nor forgiven.

To make matters worse salt was poured into an open wound. Under the guise of preventing an expensive naval arms race, which could spiral out of control,

Japan's power was kept in check by American chicanery as was Britain's might. Formerly, the waves were ruled by Britannia which had for over a century been unchallenged at sea. *Pax Britannica* had reigned from 1812, when it had been at war with the United States, until 1914 when ships from the Kaiser's High Seas Fleet unsuccessfully fought the Royal Navy for control of the ocean. Its dominance continued throughout the war. Britain was able to continue its blockade of Germany. Ultimately, when the High Seas Fleet was ordered out in 1918 to fight the British, the Germans revolted; the Kaiser was broken. It was always highly unlikely that the Germans could wrest naval supremacy from the British. Since 1889 the UK followed the 'Two-power standard', maintaining a fleet more than twice the size of the two nearest naval powers.

A *prima facie* case can be made that the Great War had expanded Britain's position in the world. Imperial rivals had been eliminated and their overseas territories parcelled out and given to the European Allies of Britain and France. Indeed, the British Empire appeared to be triumphant. Yet, Britain, while not quite bankrupt, had lost much treasure as well as blood. Equally important was that the constitutional and economic liberalism that had enabled Britain to expand its economy and grow into a world power had died a strange death. However, another great threat had emerged. Two 'allies' had burst onto the scene that would threaten the Empire and ultimately humiliate it and act as a catalyst towards its disembodiment. One was the United States, the other Japan. The weakness of the British Empire could be sensed by those two predators. The biggest blow was delivered by pressure to end its naval advantage and thus abandon its domination of the seas. The 1922 Washington Naval Treaty allotted a 5/5/3 ratio for the navies of Great Britain, the United States, and Japan. It meant parity between the UK and the USA, but Japan could only possess an Imperial Navy that was three-fifths the size of for instance Britain's Royal Navy.

This agreement was meant to secure peace, as well as save money. However, the ending of *Pax Britannica*, often a force for world stability, left the market open to new more aggressive entrants. What is more, the Japanese were far from appeased, more militaristically minded people were outraged by the agreement, and felt they had been betrayed by their own politicians. Its terms meant that a protracted war with either Britain or the United States would end in defeat, and certainly so if those two forces were combined against the Japanese empire. The reality was that the treaty restricted the potential of Britain and especially the United States. Japan still lacked industrial capacity and could have been easily swept aside in any naval arms race with America. That is if the Americans were willing to engage in a cold war stand off against imperial Japan.

Allies and enemies

Much of Japan's development served the purpose of rejecting the links between the United States and the Empire of Japan. The Japanese had reason to believe that the United States of America was a land in crisis. It had been the land of the gangster during the prohibition era and organised crime remained a problem in parts of the US. The depression continued throughout the 1930s with mass unemployment and military expenditure was small as was the size of America's armed forces. This was mistakenly read as a weakness, when in fact a proper gap-analysis should have seen that America had enormous potential. Nature had blessed the United States with natural resources from iron ore to fossil fuels. America could turn these minerals into steel behemoths and then use the hydrocarbons to drive them forward into battle. Its common law legal system, inherited from England, gave the USA a stable environment that enabled its economic potential to be fulfilled.

The Common Law is an international open-source system that can adapt and learn from occurrences on other countries; important in a quickly developing world where new commercial opportunities are continually evolving. Common Law is seen as the basis for the commercial success of the states that use it. Rather than providing a broad and at times ambiguous set of principles, as in continental law, common law offers clear guidelines and protects property rights. The Anglo-Saxon system sets specific stipulations of what cannot be done; this provides businesses with surety as to the legal environment in which they are operating. This means that a business can make commercial decisions safe in the knowledge that they will not breach the law or suffer arbitrary loss of wealth at the whims of a politicised judgement.

America had re-adopted isolationism after the First World War just as Japan was looking to end its relative introversion. The Americans did know what independence looked like. Some American colonists had sought independence to preserve slavery. Their King, George III, had wanted England's prohibition of slavery extended throughout his empire. Furthermore, rebels feared that the judgment in the 1772 Somerset v Stewart case in the United Kingdom had the potential of outlawing chattel slavery in the Thirteen Colonies that were soon to revolt. Indeed, slaves in Massachusetts had filed legal cases against exploitation using that ruling. The economy, and society, of some colonies was originally built on the plantation. Another reason for rejecting British rule was that treaties with Red Indian tribes prevented the colonies from expanding westwards. This stopped individuals, namely George Washington, from claiming large swathes of native land. The Crown authorities refused to disavow their treaty obligations with the

'Savages', indeed when mainland Britain maintained its alliance with them in repeated conflicts with the colonists the British were labelled as 'race traitors'. From its inception the USA had in its national DNA, imperial expansion and a belligerency. The Japanese had miscalculated the *'merican* character. However, there was plenty of reason to believe that isolationism would continue.

One of the prominent reasons behind the desire of some in the Thirteen Colonies for independence was to be isolated, and insulated, from the Old World's troubles. George Washington set out the isolationist creed in his Farewell Address. This was originally known as *The Address of Gen. Washington to the People of America on His Declining the Presidency of the United States*. The reading of this became an annual tradition in both Houses of Congress. However, the House of Representatives ceased this practice in 1984, (an auspicious year). Generations before World War Two, Japan's leadership found that America was not isolated, indeed it had been the bane of Japan's militaristic ambitions. They were now gambling that America would remain true to one of its original values, isolationism; but the presumption that Americans were from Venus was a grave mistake. Their history showed otherwise; the United States had strong predatory instincts; the national emblem of the United States is the Bald Eagle, a free and powerful hunter. Perhaps the grizzly bear is an even more apt symbol. That mighty animal is slow to rise from its slumber but once roused this beast is indomitable. America, like Japan, had just not yet had the opportunity to show what it could do. Yet, the United States was starting from a very different position and had many innate advantages over Japan.

America's economic system, and the very foundation of the USA, were built upon a rejection of obsolete overlordship; it was far superior to Japan's feudal traditions. America's victory in World War Two was partly won through its inheritance from England, its ideological mother country. English colonists to America took with them their Anglo-Saxon legacy. This gave the young United States the principles which flowed from Magna Carta. The great charter, signed by King John of England in 1215 was a document built upon the native, pre-Norman conquest, English limitations on the King. Its repeated reaffirmation set-in train a political tradition that rejected the arbitrary rule of the state. Importantly, government could not tax without the consent of its people. The eventual liberation from feudalism and the restrictive practices of the guild system ensured that monopolies over land and trade were in time broken. This allowed private property, competition, social mobility, and innovation to flourish. By the time of Tudor England, free trade had become ingrained. When the Elizabethan religious settlement enshrined a version of Protestantism as the national religion,

England found itself isolated from Roman Catholic Europe and had no choice but to go global. A mercantilist power was born. Along with those who left England for the New World seeking freedom and opportunity, England, and then Great Britain, was able to export Anglo-Saxon liberties, the antithesis of feudalism, to the Americas. Those principles were taken across the Atlantic and made the bedrock of American political economy. Richard Hakluyt's vision of a protestant North America, and the principles which were reinforced by that theology, had been realised. It acted as a counterweight to absolutist nations. English settlement in North America was a success. A society that was built upon freedom and personal responsibility will perform more effectively than one built on the use of the whip. Those with practical experience will make superior decisions to those that are compelled to follow the edicts of distant bureaucrats in ivory towers, or distant capitals, or dizzyingly remote hierarchies. As well as the psychological endowment from England there were intrinsic physical advantages bestowed upon the USA which Japan could not compete with.

Until European settlers arrived, the physical isolation of the North American continent from the rest of the world kept its people from benefiting from the diffusion of technology, notably metallurgy and farming. Its short longitude at reasonable climes, when compared to Eurasia, limited the opportunity for pre-John Cabot North America to develop these technologies. It would thus easily fall prey to European immigrants, who would eventually outnumber the indigenous population who were consigned to unproductive reservations. Isolation, and the lack of animal husbandry in North America prevented native Americans from building-up resistance to diseases common in the Old World. Raising livestock was a major source of disease transmission to humans, yet the Red Indians had missed these and had no immunity to many diseases, they especially suffered when the variola virus eventually came. The accidentally spread Smallpox epidemic decimated American aboriginals. This made colonisation and conquest much easier. This was not all one-sided, New World natives may have sent syphilis back to Europe in return.

The United States was able to grow so quickly because nature had conspired to grant it land without a people. It was able to import from across the globe a growing mass of young productive workers intent on creating wealth. As population density was so low, immigration could easily be accommodated without the downside risk of overpopulation and the social, environmental, and economic consequences that would follow in smaller states. Japan did not have that blessing. What is more, America's settlers were free to be creative and their talents would be out to good use in a legal, social, and political environment that valued innovation. Japan did not have those advantages and conversely, as the Japanese hailed from an overcrowded set of islands, they looked at exporting, not importing, people. They follow a similar approach to this day and have decreasing demand at home, including falling asset prices, but rely on exporting manufactures abroad to keep afloat. Without that the Japanese home islands would metaphorically sink.

Japan with its thousands of years of civilisation looked down upon the barbarian, even degenerate United States. The Japanese leadership derogatorily regarded America as a society without class. Yet, American individualism and inventiveness, inherited from Britain, were attributes the Japanese in their history were lacking. Japan had none of the advantages, or even the pre-requisites for superpower success in the 20th century, yet it was still trying to compete with not only the United States but also the other leviathan the Soviet Union and all at a time when it was tied up fighting the not insignificant Chinese, which like Russia could afford to lose mass and manpower without being defeated. The slumbering American grizzly was gradually stirring into action, this was not due to events in Germany but was as a direct consequence of concerns about the actions of Japan against the USA's Chinese ally.

The deep state

The Kwantung Army, the forces of Japan occupying the northern parts of China, had their own imperial agenda. They were largely responsible for reigniting Sino-Japanese tensions, even going as far as staging false-flag attacks as a pretext for seizing more Chinese territory. This they did in the Mukden Incident of 1931. The remaining part of Manchuria was then invaded and quickly renamed Manchukuo, and turned into a puppet-state with Puyi, the last Emperor of China, as its nominal Head of State. Manchuria was rich in the resources that Japan lacked, such as iron ore and coal. Most importantly, this occupied province was three times the size of Spain.

Japan began to industrialise and colonise Manchuria. This land soon became vital for the Japanese war machine, of particular importance was the production of synthetic oil. Manchuria's other uses for the Japanese military was that its biological weapons programme was tested on its subjects in Manchukuo. Despite criticisms from the impotent League of Nations, which the Japanese duly left in 1933, Japanese aggression against China had been effectively appeased. Criticisms of Japanese expansion by other states who remained colonial powers were dismissed as hypocrisy by the Japanese. Emperor Hirohito did in time become concerned about Japanese expansion into China and the growth of extremists in the military and their influence over both domestic and foreign policy, but he could not stop the drift to war. It was certainly true that the Japanese military-industrial complex had a great deal of influence over Japanese policy. Japan's generals became increasingly brazen, in China they were operating out of the control of the High Command, like feudal lords on the rampage.

The eight-year war

The Republic of China was again attacked by Japan on 7th July 1937 in clashes that are known as the Marco Polo Bridge Incident. Thus began the Second Sino-Japanese War. It was a full-scale invasion of China and resulted in the deaths of tens of millions of Chinese civilians and millions of soldiers. Japan would sweep across China's seaboard and attempted to conquer the interior of its great neighbour. Other nations were appalled. Consequently, China was supported by both the United States and the Soviet Union. Extraordinarily the Chinese and Russians had earlier gone to war over Mongolia in 1929, but the USSR was now allied with China.

Such was the nature of the conflict that some consider 1937, not 1939, as the year in which World War II began. Indeed, it very nearly did become a global conflict. The Japanese did not stop at just attacking the Chinese. There was limited fighting directed against Russia; and both British and American interests in China were also threatened by Japan. In December 1937, to safeguard American economic interests, ships from the United States Asiatic Fleet whilst escorting oil tankers along the Yangtze and its tributaries found themselves under attack from Japan. US American vessels on the third longest river in the world were bombed by the Japanese, resulting in some US casualties and the sinking of a gunboat. American public opinion was outraged, however, the Japanese paid compensation to America and war was averted. The US War department could shelve for the time being Plan Orange, the name given to the planning for an eventual fight with Japan. That scheme may have run concurrently with War Plan Red, the US plan for war against Britain. Within four years the Japanese again deliberately sank US vessels.

Jihadi Japan

The Japanese did not accept the materialistic conception of history. They also had alternative other worldly tools in their arsenal. Many believed that spirit could overcome matter. In tune with the Hegel influenced Nazi Germany, the Japanese held an idealist conception of history thinking that their future was in the hands of a non-material power, understood in German as the "geist". This was a spiritual mind. Shintoism, at the time the state religion of Japan, advocated that as the gods had chosen the divine Emperor to rule over Japan so fate had it that the Yamato people were destined to achieve greatness and dominate others. Japan, naturally, sought to use their empire for her own ends; this was justified by the concept of *Hakkō ichiu*. This was taken from a purported prophecy made by Japan's legendary first Emperor, Jinmu Tennō, himself reputed to be a descendant of divine beings. It was believed that morally it gave the Empire of Japan the right to "unify the eight corners of the world."

The desire in sections of Japan for conquest was not just to fulfil its 'rightful' place amongst the great nations dominating the region, many of which had little legal justification to be there themselves. A creed was also at work. The Japanese fight for its own *Lebensraum* in China was considered a holy war, or *Seisen*. Whilst the Japanese Empire was far from altruistic, they professed a quasi-moral justification behind their conquests. The Japanese believed that their imperialism would impose order and the philosophy of *Musubi* over less developed, and generally disordered societies in the orient. The coming Japanese caliphate was known as the Greater East Asia Co-Prosperity Sphere, this innocuous sounding endeavour was just a cover for the exploitation and oppression of foreign lands and alien people. Despite its benevolent name, the call to support a new order in the east under Japanese leadership was merely useful propaganda for imperialism. It was little more than a euphemism and political cover for Japan's empire. The Japanese were told that their forces were bringing liberty to their Asian brothers and sisters, even those that they were murdering in China. The external struggle against non-Asiatic powers in the Pacific, Japan's perceived sphere of influence, and the reordering of less successful nations under Japanese leadership had at its heart an internal target. They were railing against social change at home, they objected to what is called 'westernisation'.

The latter-day jihadi strikes at the so-called west, all too often their real and usually main targets are fellow Muslims, the aim being to prevent or reverse the liberalisation of their society. Rapid modernisation of an economy causes social change that sits at odds with traditional values, it can also lead to economic hardship for some. Turning to the ideology and certainties of the past is a way to deal with the injustices and inequalities of the present. Pre-war Japan was no different. Militant forces were working to reform society, taking it back to an idealised *status quo ante*. Just as the Thule Society helped pave the way for

Nazism in Germany, Japanese secret societies lobbied for war and against liberal-left thought. These groups sought a more militaristic Japan. The National Foundation Society, League of Blood, the Black Dragons and the Cherry Blossom Society (*Sakurakai*) were amongst the propagators for militarism and war. These ultra-nationalist groups and secret societies manipulated events to create a conflict with China over Manchuria.

US influence had helped Japan expand, it forced it to embrace the economics of modernity. However, the influence of America and its culture angered traditionalists. Meiji Restoration Japan was built upon Shintoism, the native belief system of Japan, and devotion to their religious leader, the Emperor. In the so-called State Shinto period religion and its rituals were used to create loyalty, unity, and to direct that common purpose according to the wishes of its leaders. It was a tactic in Japan's nation-building after the fall of the Shōgun era. Japan's religion would be used to serve a very dark agenda. Japan's traditional codes and ethics would be perverted in order to serve intolerant and aggressive masters. The anger was, as always, directed against the United States of America; whose cultural traditions and influence were anathema to traditionalists, but was very seductive to others, particularly Japan's young citizens. Japan's own people were the real threat to the extremists.

Japan's destiny lay in China, or so they thought, but not just China. They desired to expand and settle to wherever was feasible, indeed, they believed that they had a natural right to migrate to territories from China to Australia. Andrew Roberts' has speculated that the Japanese were even reconnoitring Australia as an area perhaps suitable for colonisation as early as the 1920s, this would perhaps come after a possible putative attack many years before World War Two was thought to have begun.

Russia and Japan

The Russian Empire expanded eastwards until it abutted Japan. The history of bad blood between these two powers continued after the First World War and its aftermath. Japanese intervention in Manchuria increased when Japan joined the international coalition against the Bolsheviks. In this the Japanese fought alongside American servicemen to safeguard the Czechoslovak legion which had originally been sent to Russia to fight against Austria-Hungary but were re-employed to try and snuff-out communism. Japan's aims in Siberia and the Russian far east were to protect itself from Bolshevism, safeguard its frontier to the north and recapture lands taken by Russian imperialism under the Tsars. By the late 1930s border clashes had broken out between the Soviet Union and Japan over the ill-defined and disputed border between Russian controlled Mongolia and Japanese controlled Manchuria.

Japanese breaches of the line of control, led to a series of engagements from 1932 until the Red Army managed to decisively defeat the Japanese Kwantung Army in 1939. Superior Soviet armour was a factor, as was the talents of the Russian commander Georgy Zhukov. The Japanese were only experienced in fighting the technologically inferior Chinese and had not developed tanks suitable for modern mechanised warfare. This led to peace breaking out between Russia and Japan, both parties duly signed the Soviet–Japanese Neutrality Pact on 13th April 1941. Yet, Stalin kept 40 Divisions close to Japan protecting the Soviet frontier from Japanese forces in Manchuria.

Appeasement

Japan had been checked in its efforts to wrench territory from Russia. Yet, its war in China continued. So far, the Second Sino-Japanese War had only alienated the United States, but America's patience was being tested especially as Japan's foreign policy became sucked into the black hole that was China. In a bid to stop supplies reaching Chinese forces, the Japanese looked towards physically isolating China. In late June 1940 the British Prime Minister Winston Churchill acceded to Japanese pressure and closed the Burma Road through which Chiang Kai-shek's Republic of China Army were being supplied. This stymied Japan's enemies and emboldened the aggressor. On 29th June 1940, the military took power in Japan and officially announced the formation of the Greater East Asia Co-Prosperity Sphere.

The Kuomintang Government of China did not give up their fight. The Chinese Army was supplied through Vietnam, the Japanese responded by occupying that country as well. Technically Vichy France allowed the Japanese to be stationed in French Indochina. The reality was that they had little alternative. The Japanese occupation of Vichy French territory in southeast Asia was not seriously challenged apart from by the USA; the American response was to introduce sanctions against the Empire of Japan. President Franklin Delano Roosevelt wanted to bend Japan to his will and provoked a war, he froze Japan's assets and imposed an oil embargo on that country. The Japanese felt they were left with two choices; either face decline caused by US sanctions or go to war with the sleeping giant and bring the Americans to the negotiating table. The

Japanese attempted the latter option, but America would not compromise. Two very major miscalculations.

Japan and the Jews

As the war clouds spread across Asia, just as the atmosphere in Europe darkened and forewarned war, Japan looked admiringly towards Germany. Nazi expansionism and its successes were seen as setting a fine example. The Japanese sphere of influence was far enough removed from Europe to not be directly threatened by the Germans. Furthermore, Hitler did not regard the Japanese, nor the Chinese, as being inferior to the Germanic people.

The Nazis proved to be a bad role model. They did share common enemies; the Japanese had been at war with Russia and clashed with the Soviet Union. Hitler despised the United States of America and Japanese interests ran contrary to American foreign policy. Whilst German and Japanese expansionism had much in common, the two most eminent axis powers did not seek the same friends. Japan, eager to learn from the Nazis, studied Hitler's beliefs. One of the most prominent was anti-Semitism, this was a fundamental creed of the German leadership, this intrigued the Japanese.

Whereas the Nazis belief in the power of the international Jewish conspiracy led them to try and eliminate the entire Jewish race, the Japanese took a different strategy. They accepted as legitimate German theories about Jews as set out in Hitler's *Mein Kampf* and other popular fictions of the time. Yet, this enticed the Japanese to adopt a wildly differing approach. Believing this propaganda, they sought to bring the Jews onto their side and to encourage Jewish immigration into Japan to take advantage of their industrious nature and global links and to please the USA. This was known as the *Fugu* Plan. Whereas Germany saw Jews as the rivals of the Aryan race, and the Soviet Union libelled them as 'rootless cosmopolitans', the Japanese perceived an opportunity. They thought to co-opt them and hoped that their supposed international power would be at the disposal of the Japanese in a future conflict for global domination against Germany. To this day there is a small Jewish community in Japan that has lived there for centuries without the persecutions exhibited on them by other peoples. Jews were also given a safe home for those fleeing the holocaust. Japan took in Jewish refugees from Nazi Germany who had escaped via Russia. The Nazis later tried to stop this policy.

This was not the only obscure alliance in the Pacific theatre. Initially Nazi Germany supported the Chinese and was in alliance with the anti-communist

Kuomintang government in China led by Chiang Kai-shek, who was simultaneously fighting against a multitude of communist insurgents as well as the Japanese. Remarkable, given that Chiang Kai-shek was educated in Japan and trained by the Bolsheviks in Russia. The Chinese alliance with Nazi Germany, which included the provision of military aid, continued until the signing on 27th September 1940 of the Tripartite Pact between Germany-Italy-Japan. The Axis was born and soon a host of other central European states associated themselves with that alliance. This further encouraged war.

The opposing tectonic plates of the Japanese and American empires were on a collision course. American expansion westward, to the far east, laid the foundations for conflict with the emerging power of Japan. War was coming to the Pacific and much of Asia. Japan called the conflict The Greater East Asia War. Defeat for the Japanese when it clashed with the Red Army and the peace treaty with Russia, would make the Japanese leaders look out over the Pacific, here they would run into the western European countries who had imperial possessions on the Pacific's many islands. Imperial Japan's fate would be sealed.

Lightning Strikes

"Politics is war without bloodshed while war is politics with bloodshed." — **Mao Zedong**

Preparing to fail

Germany would not tolerate being disarmed for long, indeed it had no intention of honouring the terms of the treaty obligations demanded at Versailles. Hitler and the Nazis, who initially took power in Germany in 1933, had cemented their rule by 1934. History views the interregnum between the German Reichs from the period following the abdication of the Kaiser to Hitler taking power as an era when Germany was democratic, decadent, and pacifistic. The Weimar Republic, as the German state during this era had been unofficially called, was certainly presented as a time of degeneracy and weakness. However, when Hitler was just an obscure fringe figure, plans had already been developed to avenge the injustice, as many Germans saw it, of the Versailles *diktat*. Germany did not intend to be humbled for long.

In the shadows Germany prepared for war throughout the 1930s. This did not just include rearmament but also involved learning the art of how best to conduct a contemporary conflict. To this end they studied the tactics being developed by both Britain and Russia. Germany was especially eager to learn about those nations' use of tanks and integrate them into their military strategy. However, there was a fatal flaw – a lack of materiel. German greed far outstripped its willingness to delay consumption today for a better tomorrow. Germany was always behind the curve. For instance, planes were scarce, due to the terms of the Treaty of Versailles which forbade Germany from having an air force, so for a time they had to use gliders to train pilots.

Germany's rearmament plans preceded the Nazis by a decade and had been in place as early as 1924. The guns were to have a purpose. The military plans to redraw Germany's boundaries had been prepared long before and predated the emergence of the Third Reich. Hitler just dusted them off and put them into action. Upon Hitler seizing ownership of Germany's destiny, he became the willing instrument of the German deep state. He was merely the man who had the audacity to challenge the post-World War One political settlement. However, some senior career soldiers realised that German ambitions outstripped its capabilities. The Hitler effect was such that he would drive rearmament forward and use his political skill to nullify and outmanoeuvre the naysayers in the German General Staff who were sceptical or outright opposed to the magnitude of Hitler's ambitions. However, they would be united in a common cause of conquest.

The process of creating a unity of purpose between National Socialist ideologues and the German Army began with the 1934 Night of the Long Knives. Here the leadership of the Nazi affiliated *Sturmabteilung* (SA) militia group also known as the brown shirts were eliminated. This group, led by Ernst Röhm, had ambitions to fulfil the socialist transformation of German society with the SA becoming a popular army that would replace both the much smaller Reichswehr, as the German military was then known, and its old-school officer class. These ideas were similar to the military concepts of leading Bolsheviks, and the People's Commissar of Military and Naval Affairs of the Soviet Union, Leon Trotsky. He proposed a mass militia as opposed to the concept of a more professional, properly organised, and armed Red Army whose chief proponent was Trotsky's great rival, Joseph Stalin. Both the regimes of Hitler and Stalin originally had comparable military visions, and both demanded absolute obedience.

From the summer of 1934 onwards until the collapse of Nazi rule in 1945 the German military, as well as the nation's civil servants, had to swear loyalty to Adolf Hitler. For them it was a serious matter; an oath was binding and intertwined with loyalty and honour. Hitler announced his plans for conquest to his senior Generals in 1937, at that point Germany was far from ready for war, but Hitler was a man with a plan. Before beginning the conquest of the east, he had to unite the German people; those in Austria and the Czech Sudetenland were to be absorbed into his Reich. The generals that opposed his destructive plans, namely Werner von Blomberg and Werner von Fritsch, were manoeuvred out of office by the use of threats to expose personal scandals. Hitler had trouble directing armies, but no one could surpass his political manoeuvrings. Internal opposition was limited.

The Nazis, who wanted to be loved, prioritised consumer goods above armaments. They were always seeking to legitimise their rule, and themselves. This desire to please, even at the expense of the war, was perhaps a sign that deep down they knew that they were not as righteous and progressive as they pretended. If they did wholeheartedly believe in their cause and that there was a strong moral case for the war, they would have put everything into the war effort. And logically therefore the German population would, could, and should have been prepared to not only give up their creature comforts but also be willing to endure any hardship in pursuit of the greater good.

The Nazis were focused on the short term, and unless Hitler was aroused by some fit of rage or pique, or acting out of desperation, the Führer found it hard to plan and give direct and clear orders. The development of a logical and strategically sound plan of action beyond reacting to events troubled the Führer. Hitler, a man of contradictions, could successfully execute short term political schemes to manoeuvre himself into a position of power and make the system depend upon him, that was after all the Führer principle of one leader but, he did not have the solutions to German problems. Adolf Hitler could also dream about grand boulevards lined with even grander buildings to enthral the public. Hitler could dream of his utopia and use those who had to seek his patronage to indulge whatever his whims may have been at the time. He was a man of extremes – there was no middle way.

What preparation there was for war was too little and too late. Germany had become powerful under Hitler, but it was a false economy that was simply not equipped to deal with the maelstrom that the Nazis were to unleash. The magnitude of his ambitions was only matched by the size of the inevitable defeat. The German rearmament program let alone the coming conflict, and Hitler's audacious aims and fanciful ambitions were merely written on cheques that the war economy could not cash. The staggering German economic miracle that accompanied Hitler taking power was a mirage. This was paid for by borrowing, debt financing. Funding these programs would not come through selling off the family silver, it would be achieved through stealing someone else's along with their gold reserves. German rearmament had not succeeded in preparing Germany for the war that came too early for Hitler. The Führer knew that he must first build a nation dedicated to war and then subdue, or neutralise, enemies in the west. However, the war machine was simply not ready when conflict began. Hitler's Will however, wanted to quickly defeat his opponents. He thought France would be defeated in six weeks. And he even felt that in order to defeat the Soviet giant, "We have only to kick in the door and the whole rotten structure will come crashing down." To achieve those ends Hitler was keen to adopt ambitious strategies that promised fantastic outcomes, but he lacked the fundamentals.

Hitler saw war as an economic necessity, a Darwinian struggle for survival between races on an epic scale. The Führer wanted his war but not yet. 1944 was the preferred date, by then the Kriegsmarine would have been rebuilt and better prepared to deliver Hitler the hegemony he wanted. Helping him eliminate any rivals to German mastery of Europe and beyond. Hitler's super battleships would have been in service by this year. Like the Kaiser before him, Hitler was obsessed with size and Hitler, like the Kaiser, wanted to rule the waves with his capital ships. However, the Battleship of the Line was not only an outmoded concept but constructing them was also a drain on resources. It was a similar picture to the last conflict. The German leadership in 1914 did not want a major war but thought that if a war was coming it was better to have it sooner rather than later. Many fell into Thucydides' Trap. In 1939, Hitler did not want a war with Europe's other great powers, instead he favoured the mid-1940s as his preferred start date. Yet he could not avoid war without drastically changing course.

By 1939 German borrowing was out of control. It was politically inconceivable to have a financial crisis like that which had struck the German Weimar Republic. War was the way out of Germany's inherent fiscal weakness caused through building the house of Germany on debt. Hitler had mortgaged his country but had no intention of rewarding the international ('Jewish,' as he saw it) financial system with debilitating repayments and austerity measures at home. He had no intention of lowering the standard of living in Germany. To continue to provide for German citizens, plunder became the economic system of choice. Yet it was the economics of chasing the dragon. One conquest facilitated the need for another to feed the addiction to other peoples' resources. Hitler would bear no responsibility for this and his economic illiteracy. Instead, he believed that the 'international jew' was driving the world to war and not at a time that Hitler had appointed. Hitler had the issue the wrong way around, it was his paranoid anti-Semitism that was the deciding factor. Hitler was driven by events as much as he was creating them, but he was spurred on by an almost supernatural belief in conspiracies. He thought others were dictating the actions for which he was liable. Nevertheless, war as early as 1940 was still a possibility. Hitler had written of this to Hermann Göring in 1936 and emphasised the need to be ready for war in four years. After numerous provocations, Britain and France would eventually oblige Hitler.

The worm had turned
Following the loss of the Sudetenland to Germany the Czechs and Slovaks were at the mercy of their neighbours. In October 1938 Poland took back from Czechoslovakia the border region called Zaolzie. This was originally seized by Czechoslovakia when Poland itself was weakened after their invasion of Belarus and Ukraine during the Soviet-Polish War of 1919-1921. Poland prior to the

outbreak of World War Two was an illiberal state, that was no bastion of democracy, nor did it respect internationally agreed boundaries.

No one was truly blameless in the run up to the start of the Second World War. Each had their own territorial ambitions and the desire to right perceived wrongs. However, the Nazis took the conflicts that regularly occur over disputed boundaries and between rival nationalities to epic proportions. Hitler did not believe that Britain and France would stand up to Germany; they would, he thought, merely meekly protest his making a new acquisition. He was the gambler who judged future odds, on past performance. The variables, however, had changed; patience had run out and, Hitler failed to recognise this. Appeasement ended with the German invasion of Poland. After the German occupation of Bohemia and Moravia in March 1939, the core of the country that is now known as Czechia, Chamberlain made it clear to Hitler that further German territorial adventures would not be tolerated.

When the British Prime Minister gave a guarantee to Poland on 31st March 1939 Hitler said of Chamberlain "They are little worms. I saw them at Munich. I'll cook them a stew they'll choke on." The Führer did not expect Chamberlain to honour his commitment to defend Poland and was unnerved when Chamberlain threatened war. The giant conflagration of which Chamberlain had warned was to be unleashed on 1st September 1939. Hitler's war was to happen, but not at the appointed time and not according to his vague and undefined plan but through blunder worthy of European leaders a generation before.

Poland was the bastard of the Versailles Treaty, created from embers of the rival German and Russian empires. Imperia that would soon be reborn from the ashes of Poland. Hitler's attention turned to Poland in 1939, he made irredentist demands for the restitution of German lands and reuniting those *volk* that had been separated from the Reich when Poland was recreated following the Great War. As the omens of war grew, the Polish response was more appeasement. Poland was reluctant to complete a full mobilisation; it still hoped for peace and did not want to provoke the Germans. This craven policy was supported by Britain and France. These democratic imperial powers and the retrograde Polish government were reluctant to face the reality that war was coming, and religion played a part.

It has been speculated that Hitler was an occultist. In truth he disapproved of Heinrich Himmler's, the Nazi terror chief, obsession with esoteric religions and the occult. The head of the SS's beliefs were merely acceptable so long as he remained loyal to Hitler and ran an efficient police state. Whilst Hitler's only stipulation for belief in Nazi Germany was deism, Christianity remained predominant. Many Poles at the time saw atheistic state socialist Soviet Russia as the greatest threat. Poland along with other eastern European nations was to get a horrible lesson in wickedness under the Nazis and history would demonstrate that Soviet Communism was the lesser evil. Poland's leadership was especially alarmed when in response to Hitler's designs on Czechoslovakia's Sudetenland, Stalin promised to provide one-million men from the Red Army to meet and counter this threat so long as other nations committed to the fight. Poland did not want Soviet guarantees and military support as they feared the Nazis less than they feared the Soviets. Poland convinced Chamberlain to appease Germany, and even in late August 1939 when the augers predicted that there would be much blood, the Poles demobilised much of their army so as not to provoke their German neighbour. Chamberlin decided to turn down the prospect of a military alliance between the Soviet Union and France, to counter, contain and defeat Germany, at the request of the Poles, he also ignored calls in the UK to have an alliance with Russia.

The Polish effectively siding with German interests against the better judgement of many other European nations, especially the Soviet Union, which was to suffer a greater loss of human life than any other country in the war, changed the dynamic. The USSR was to make what appeared to be an extraordinary alliance, but in fact it was congruent with the Weimar Republic's earlier cooperation with Moscow. The European theatre of operations was not Stalin's only concern. Hitler's Axis partners, the Japanese, were competing with Russia over control of the far east. Stalin needed to make peace with the Nazis. He wanted to buy time and prepare for the seemingly inevitable clash between Teuton and Slav, Bolshevik and National Socialist, but also to preserve forces in the orient to fight the Japanese for control over Mongolia. Stalin also hoped that the Soviet's partnership with the Nazis, who were greatly admired by the belligerent Japanese militarists, would help end the war he was fighting in the east.

The most important factor that led to the Soviets re-entering their partnership with the Germans was Stalin's realisation that he could not rely on western European countries, let alone trust them. Recognising a change in foreign policy was needed, the Soviet leader removed as Foreign Minister Litvinov, a man who was well disposed to the so-called west and was a supporter of the League of Nations and replaced him with Vyacheslav Molotov. The new Russian Minister of Foreign Affairs concluded a trade treaty with Italy and then agreed with Germany, the infamous Molotov-Ribbentrop Pact. von Ribbentrop being the Foreign Minister of Nazi Germany. This treaty between the USSR and Germany divided up eastern Europe, especially Poland. Partitioning it almost as it had been before the First World War. Resource rich Russia had to supply the Germans with raw materials and the energy to fuel its war machine. In exchange the Nazis would supply technology to the USSR. Hitler was now free to strike at Poland and then turn west, just as Germany had planned in 1914, before moving its guns east in an attempt to conquer Russia. It could be said that Hitler had learnt nothing and forgotten nothing.

Stopping the wolf

Established military doctrine usually dictates that attackers need a three to one advantage. The Nazis had nothing like that superiority. Germany had only 66 divisions at the time of the invasion of Poland, ranged against them were 55 French and 30 Polish divisions. Poland had a further nine in reserve. Two British divisions were also available on the continent. The fight back against German expansionism would begin in Poland. Preparations started well. Prior to the invasion the Poles mobilised their armed forces. Germany was facing a war on two fronts against not only numerically greater forces but also, in some cases, the Allies had superior materiel as well as more men. French tanks were on paper more than a match for their German adversaries and even the Polish 7TP light tank was more effective than its German counterparts. It had a powerful and reliable diesel engine and was equipped with a Bofors wz. 37mm anti-tank gun that could penetrate the armour of its German rivals, including the excellent but small in number Panzer IV, of which a little over 200 hundred were involved in the invasion. This Polish tank was, however, too lightly armoured, and vulnerable to attack from the air. Yet, they were still deemed good enough to be incorporated into the German Army once the conquest of Poland was complete.

The invasion of Poland

Before the invasion, scheduled for 1st September 1939, Hitler conducted a strategic deception campaign. This included a series of false flag attacks on German border positions. The most notable was a feigned assault carried out by SS troops in Polish uniforms against a German border post and radio installation. The corpses of murdered concentration camp prisoners were dressed in Polish uniforms and placed at the scene of the 'attack'. It was hoped that would give the invasion international legitimacy and motivate the German soldiers for the coming offensive. Above all it was an attempt to isolate Poland from its allies. Hitler had reason to believe that it would be successful. Under pressure from the UK and France, as well as from the fear of provoking Germany, Poland had already taken the decision to demobilise its troops. Only for the Polish government to have to remobilise them again as tensions increased further over the status of the city of Danzig. This contradictory approach caused chaos and meant that only half the Polish army was ready to confront the German onslaught.

The Germans had asked for negotiations to return the Baltic port of Danzig, now Gdansk, to Germany. It had also asked to hold a plebiscite on the future of the Polish corridor, including the right to vote being awarded to no longer resident ethnically cleansed Germans. Granting them the opportunity to decide whether the stretch of land that connected Poland to the sea but separated East Prussia from the rest of the Fatherland, should be returned to Germany or not. As late as 28th August 1939, Britain and France hoped that a settlement could be found. Poland remained intransigent and instead relied on the promises that its western European allies would defend their sovereignty and territorial integrity if the Germans used force rather than negotiations to resolve the dispute. Hitler thought Chamberlain was bluffing, but on the 3rd September 1939 Britain and France declared war on Germany.

The UK promised Poland that it would bomb German cities in response to any German bombing of Polish cities. However, this help was not forthcoming and during the invasion Polish civilians were attacked without any UK response. Similarly, France had already made many pledges to Poland in the Franco-Polish alliance of 1921 and the Kasprzycki-Gamelin Convention of May 1939, they even promised to invade Germany within 15 days of any war breaking out. Indeed, the French army did make a half-hearted attempt to invade the Saarland region, a coal rich area bordering France. This area had been placed under French administration following the First World War. Under the terms of the Treaty of Versailles and as part of the punitive reparations that were enforced against Germany, the French were allowed to exploit it as they saw fit. The population of the Saare, as it is called in French, voted overwhelmingly to reunite with the rest of Germany in 1935. This French 'invasion' amounted to nothing of significance, and by mid-October they withdrew with just a little persuasion from the German army. It was a missed opportunity. German resources and factories fundamental to war in both the Ruhr and the Saar were within easy striking distance of the French. France did not come to the rescue of Poland.

The Polish soldier was very able, so much so, that a highly motivated and experienced quarter of a million Polish troops served alongside the British Army after fleeing to the UK they impressed their hosts with their skill and dedication. After they had made their way to western Europe these committed Polish soldiers were used by the British as shock troops and led many assaults. Furthermore, 400,000 Polish soldiers, in the so-called Home Army, never truly left the field. They stayed behind to fight against the German occupiers until the Soviets drove them out. The fable of the gallant but foolishly reckless Polish Lancer charging at the steel-clad German tanks was a product of Nazi myth making. It followed a skirmish where Polish cavalry had beaten back German infantry only to be driven back by machine gun fire. Some Panzers arrived at the scene after the battle had ended, but before German and Italian war correspondents arrived. The reporters erroneously concluded that men and horses were used against the hard horsepower of a modern panzer. An unflattering and false legend was born. It is worth noting that Germany not only relied upon the horse as a beast of burden to move its armaments but also deployed cavalry units on the Eastern Front until 1944, a practice replicated by the Russians.

The Red Army sealed the Pole's fate. On 17th September 1939, sixteen days after Germany invaded, the Soviets invaded from the East. The Soviet Union had the twin aim of improving the defence of Stalin's 'socialism in a single country' state, he was not yet ready to export communism to the rest of the world through force. He also sought to reunite the fractured Tsarist empire. By 6th October Poland was partitioned yet again between Germany and Russia. Indeed, it seemed that the natural state of Poland was for it to be divided and apportioned between these two rival empires.

The great man theory
It has been hypothesised that the course of history depends upon the decisions and actions of heroic men. Indeed, as Malvolio said in Shakespeare's Twelfth Night "Some are born great, some achieve greatness, and some have greatness thrust upon them." Yet, in reality, few can live up to the epitaph that history has turned on their bold and brave decisions. One such figure is the Father of Finland, Carl Mannerheim. During the tumults arising from World War One, he played a key part in preventing the Bolshevisation of Finland and helped achieve freedom for his homeland from Russia. He was to keep it independent and accordingly influenced the course of World War Two. Despite flirtations with two German empires, Finland was a reluctant satellite of the Third Reich, and Mannerheim was not afraid to pivot by 180 degrees to protect his lands territorial integrity.

Finland's history had flittered between favouring Russia at one time and more Germanic interests the next. The Grand Duchy of Finland was seized by Russia from Sweden during the Finnish War of the early nineteenth century and became an autonomous region within the Russian Empire. It achieved its independence in 1917 and then with support from the Kaiser's Reich the Whites defeated the Red side in its forthcoming civil war, seeing off a Bolshevik challenge. Finland firmly left the Russian axis, associating itself with Russia's great rival, Germany. It became the short-lived Kingdom of Finland with a German monarchy. This new state's borders were perilously close to the city that would be known as Leningrad. This great city, the Venice of the North, which was once the capital of Russia was previously known as Petrograd and St Petersburg, the name it has now resumed in the post-Communist era. It was so close to Finland that a station in this city is called Finland Station. This port city, built on a swamp and famed for its canals, was founded by the expansionist Russian Tsar Peter the Great as his window on the west. In the Great Northern War, the visionary Tsar, incidentally, took from Sweden the lands of Estonia, Livonia, and Courland, which approximate to modern day Estonia and Latvia. St Petersburg which became Petrograd was and renamed as Leningrad in 1924 was also a centre of industry; this prestigious city's position would be safeguarded by the contemporary ruler of Russia, the Red Tsar Joseph Stalin.

As well as taking land back from Poland that had been occupied by Warsaw a generation before, the terms of the Molotov-Ribbentrop Pact permitted the USSR with the connivance of the Germans, to reclaim for Moscow the Baltic states of Estonia, Latvia, and Lithuania. In the autumn of 1939, these three countries, through the terms of so-called mutual assistance treaties had to accept the presence of Red Army bases on their territory. These three small nations were then taken into the USSR in the summer of 1940. Initially just Estonia and Latvia were to be in the Soviet sphere, with Lithuania coming under German influence. However, following the conquest of Poland, the Polish occupation of parts of Lithuania was ended. The Lithuanian capital city of Vilnius was freed from Polish control and restored to Lithuania, the most southern and western of the three so-called Baltic states. The Soviet occupation had some limited support from trade unionists, and those that either thought communism was the future or accepted the perceived wisdom that these statelets did not have a viable future as independent countries. Indeed, with the might of the Soviet Union threatening to bear down upon them they had little choice but to allow the Red Army to enter. From then on there followed five decades of suzerainty to their Soviet masters. Logic dictated that Finland should follow suit; the Finns however would stand firm. The Soviets were alarmed by the growing friendliness between Finland and Nazi Germany. When German generals inspected Finland's defences in 1939 the Soviets feared that there may be a German invasion of Russia via Finland.

Border disputes and revisions are not unknown, especially in this region and they generally occur between the breakaway parts of dead or dying empires. To this day, Estonia has not agreed on its post-independence border with Russia. In 2017, there was even a campaign in Norway to give Finland the peak of Halti Mountain, on its northern border in Lapland, as a present to mark Finland's 100th birthday. However, under the Norwegian constitution this was not possible.

Initially, Stalin wanted to revise the border between Finland and the USSR to allow for the better defence of the crucial Russian city of Leningrad. At first, he tried persuasion. In exchange for moving the Finnish border away from Leningrad the Finns would be given land in less critical areas. The Finns under the leadership of Mannerheim would not be so obliging and boldly refused. When diplomacy failed Stalin turned to war. The Soviet High Command thought that the Finnish people were stricken by class conflict and thus would welcome the Red Army as liberators and the 450,000 soldiers earmarked for the attack would face little opposition.

The Red Army staged a false-flag incident, they shelled their own positions, and blamed the Finns for an attack and, just four days later, on 26th November 1939 the Soviet Union invaded Finland in overwhelming numbers. The Winter War as it is known was now underway. Initially this was a disaster for the communists; the Russian steamroller suffered appalling casualties. The usual Stalinist *modus operandi* followed, failed commanders were executed, and more able men came to the fore through a process of bullet in the head osmosis. The Soviets were also immensely practical, willing to innovate, learn from their own mistakes and failings. The Red Army was reorganised and the attacks on Finland renewed with added urgency and effectiveness.

Finland was not completely alone in its struggle against the behemoth bearing down on them. International volunteers arrived to support the Finns, but their numbers amounted to as few as 12,000 brave but forlorn cadres. The British and French governments considered sending a force to fight the Nazi aligned Soviet Union but could agree on little and achieved even less. Germany played no part in the Winter War of 1939 – 1940 and remained neutral. The war ended with the Soviets grinding down Finnish opposition, yet it appeared to be a Pyrrhic victory for the USSR. The Finns had defeated Russia in many a major battle and despite losing the war showed that the price of capturing Finland would be too high. Stalin was forced to accept Finnish sovereignty, though not its full territorial integrity, and came to the negotiating table. Following the Second

World War and for the duration of the cold war the USSR continued to recognise Finnish independence, however, Finland had economic agreements with its larger neighbour and was in the economic orbit of Russia.

Finland ultimately had to cede more territory to the USSR than that which was originally demanded by Stalin. The price for both sides was high, Finland had lost over ten per cent of its territory which comprised some of its most economically productive regions; consequently, Russia's economic capacity had been increased. Despite the Russian losses, the war was a net industrial gain. Furthermore, the Soviet Union could replace the men it lost, and its borders were secured, or so they thought. The global audience following this war drew different lessons. After the Red Army's abysmal showing in the Winter War, Hitler thought he could conquer Russia; one would only have to kick the door in and the whole rotten edifice, as he saw it, would collapse. The Allies also concluded that the USSR was inherently weak. Within a little more than a year and a quarter Finland and the Soviet Union would resume the hostilities and unfinished business would be continued. This time, however, Finland would be the aggressor and Germany would not be neutral.

Mannerheim had wanted an alliance with Britain and France but despite the French declarations of support and even in the face of German neutrality Finland drifted back into the German orbit, a position they had held at the end of the First World War. Mannerheim, who feared that it was just a matter of time before Russia attacked again, had to accept German help essentially to reclaim the territory that he had been forced to hand over to the Soviet Union. After the Winter War, however, the Red Army was reorganised and improved which made it a more effective organisation and better able to deal with the coming Nazi onslaught. The Russians drew enough of the correct lessons from the debacle just in time to save them against the Germans. But first Hitler had his own northern adventure to contend with.

The Bore War

Between October 1939 and April 1940, the absence of German military action is now best known by the American phrase, the Phoney War; but in Britain at the time this period of inaction was humorously described as the 'Bore War.' Alternatively, Winston Churchill called it the 'Twilight War'. The Germans referred to it as the '*Sitzkrieg*' which translates into English as the 'sitting war'. In France this inactivity is known as the *drôle de guerre.*; the funny war. When this bizarre time ended the joke however was soon to be on France.

During the 'Phoney War' the British dropped propaganda leaflets in Germany; called "truth raids". Perhaps peace would break out, perhaps the great conflagration which Chamberlain spoke of could be avoided, perhaps France and the UK would stand firm against the Germans. No, no, no. The standoff had to come to an end, and it duly did. This period of quiet was just the lull before the storm.

So far, the Fall of Poland, the following localised Winter War between the USSR and Finland, and least of all the submission of the so-called Baltic States, did not create anything like a world war. And these events certainly did not resemble the blundering into war that engulfed Europe a quarter of a century earlier. It was rather an anti-climax. This was about to end and the impetus for change came from Britain and France who planned to occupy neutral Norway. It was the catalyst for the Nazis to fulfil their Nordic fantasies.

Scandinavia

Germany invaded Denmark on 9th April 1940. The Danish surrendered after two hours with minimal casualties on both sides. This small state had once been a significant power dominating Scandinavia and ruling an empire that stretched across the Baltic ruling parts of what is now Estonia. Indeed, the Estonian capital, Tallinn, translates into English as 'City of the Danes'. Danish imperial ambitions across the Baltic Sea had been a part of a crusade against Estonian pagan tribes. The origin of the Danish flag and their national emblem, comes from their conquest of this city. Legend has it that the Dannebrog, as the flag is known, fell from the sky giving the crusaders the courage they needed to win the battle for the settlement. Later Denmark also held territories in the Americas and even in Asia. Their overseas possessions now consist of the Faroe Islands, in the North Atlantic and Greenland, both of which enjoy home rule. Greenland left the European Economic Community, the forerunner to the EU, in 1985. Denmark even once dominated a small part of what is now northern Germany, namely Schleswig and Holstein, Danish control over those provinces had led to a border dispute that was resolved in Germany's favour as late as 1920. The importance of Denmark to the Nazis was partly cultural, it had a small German speaking population and the Nazis had hoped that the Danes would join their Reich. After its conquest by Germany Denmark signed the Anti-Comintern Pact and, thus, preserved some degree of autonomy. Nevertheless, the Danish authorities had to ban communists as part of the agreement. There were other very practical considerations behind the invasion; that went beyond the Nazis idea of cultural hegemony; Denmark was the route to Norway.

Hitler rightly feared that Britain and France would invade Norway to cut-off Germany's supply of iron ore that came from Sweden via Norwegian ports such as Narvik, a port that despite its northern latitude was ice-free and thus accessible all year round. Hitler's fear was well-founded. Churchill, as First Lord of the Admiralty, did indeed plan to stop Swedish exports to Germany. This was intended to provoke Hitler, giving the British and French the opportunity to occupy neutral Norway. This was part of a greater strategy intended to blockade Germany, starving the Third Reich into submission by depriving the Nazis of the resources that were needed for war. However, Operation Wilfred, as it was known, was delayed due to indecision amongst the French, whose government was split and found itself unable to commit to a coherent plan as to how the war should be prosecuted. By the time the mission was underway, it was too late. Hitler acted before Norwegian ports could be blocked and cut-off from their German trade.

The German invasion of Norway began on 9th April 1940. As Germany had long coveted control over Norway's ports it was a well-planned operation. The invasion was swift. Allied forces, consisting of men from France, Britain, and Poland were committed to the defence of Norway. However, despite resistance continuing into June, by the end of April it was clear that Germany had been victorious. Sweden, a country that remained officially neutral, continued to supply Germany with the important ore and even allowed German soldiers to pass through its territory to enter Finland. In the closing stages of the war, however, it did allow the Allies to use Swedish airbases.

Later, in Norway, Vidkun Quisling was installed as the puppet leader of a Nazi Norway. His name became synonymous with collaboration. Quisling supplied Norwegian conscripts to aid the Nazi war effort, including ski soldiers, that fought alongside Finnish forces. They also delivered workers for German factories. As the war was clearly not going in the Allies favour, the conduct of the war raised serious questions, especially in Britain. On 10th May 1940, Neville Chamberlain resigned as the British Prime Minister and was succeeded by Winston Churchill. By then the German invasion of the Low Countries and France was already underway. Despite German success against Poland, and their seeing-off of the uninspiring French invasion which came in the autumn of 1939; Germany was still not ready for the war that the Fatherland had brought to the world. In spite of their lack of readiness they managed to defeat the French along with Norwegian, Polish, and British forces, in Norway. What they lacked in materiel they made up for in guile and boldness, unleashing what became known as lightning war.

New variant

The original plan to win in the west was eerily reminiscent of the attack used against France in 1914, namely drive through Belgium before attempting to wheel back around and encircle Paris, and the French Army, from the north and east. The Schlieffen Plan as it was called aimed to first defeat France, before taking on the Russian steamroller, as the Tsarist armed forces were known. In 1940, with Soviet Russia politically neutralised, Germany was now free to concentrate all its might against France and its allies. The plan, however, required a fundamental rethink.

The former King and ex-Emperor of India, Edward VIII, known as the Duke of Windsor and Prince Edward, was instrumental in this change of approach and thus aided the German invasion of France. The disgraced Duke informed the German Ambassador that the initial German plan to invade France via Belgium along the lines of the Schlieffen Plan had been discovered when a plane crashed which was carrying documents detailing the attack, thus confirming that the blueprints outlining the operation had not been destroyed. As such the Germans were forced to develop a new scheme.

The Duke also allowed it to be known that he believed that heavy bombing of civilians would make Britain ready for peace. This would have encouraged Hitler to believe that the Blitz would bring Britain to the negotiating table. This too directly influenced Hitler's military strategy and made him feel much more certain of victory. Prince Edward had previously met with Hitler. The former King's pro-Nazi sympathies may have led Hitler and the Nazi hierarchy to believe that there were a host of people in the British establishment who were willing to have an accommodation with the Germans. It was not the first time that the former monarch had given succour to the Axis. Earlier, the Duke of Windsor also gave away the secret that the Americans had cracked Italian codes. Eventually, the Duke was ordered out of continental Europe by British Prime Minister, Winston Churchill, who threatened Edward with a court martial if he did not comply; the former monarch monarch was a Major General in the British Army. In July 1940, Prince Edward was effectively exiled to the new world, safe from conducting any further intrigue. Churchill appointed him Governor of the Bahamas; a post he took up in August of that year. It was not a position of prestige.

A new plan had been developed by German general Erich von Manstein. His proposal consisted of three German fronts against the Low Countries and France. Whilst Army Group B, subdued the Dutch, Army Group C, immediately facing France across the German border, had the role of engaging the Maginot Line and supporting the southern shoulder of Army Group A. It was Army Group A, that was intended to be the decisive surprise for the Allies. This would cross into France through Luxembourg and Belgium, entering those countries via a region called the Ardennes. This heavily wooded and mountainous terrain was thought to be impassable to the movements of massed mechanised forces. It was a direction of attack which the French were simply not expecting, it was inconceivable to them that this would be the area through which the main thrust would pass. From there, instead of heading for Paris, they would race to the channel, thus separating the British forces from their French partners. Despite severe traffic jams, it was this bold *blitzkrieg* that gave the Nazis victory in 1940.

Hitler had independently of von Manstein proposed the idea of a breakthrough at Sedan in the Ardennes region of France. von Manstein however, saw the whole battle hinging upon victory around this small city. Upon hearing of these plans Hitler immediately ordered his general staff to adopt the proposals which they had buried. Amongst the reasons why this reckless gamble was accepted was that Germany was facing defeat. The chances of success were slight, therefore a strategy, any stratagem, that offered an outside chance of a quick decisive victory was needed. The dusting off of the Schlieffen Plan that was originally drawn up from as long ago as 1905 and 1906, nearly a decade before the war in which they would be employed, was no longer sufficient. Not only had these plans been uncovered by the Allies but it was becoming clear that encircling and directly engaging the might of the French Army meant creating what is known in German as a *Kesselschlacht*, which translates as cauldron battle. This would have resulted in high casualties for the attacker and lead to an inconclusive end to the fighting, indeed there was doubt that the Germans would have won such a battle. Even in the best-case scenario, it would have cost time which the Germans could not afford to lose. Therefore, conventional military logic, which included defence of the flanks, and properly organised logistics supplying reinforcements, were abandoned along with all caution. It was a surprising approach to war, but what was especially remarkable was the poor political and military leadership of the Allied nations which, at the start of the war, fell like dominoes.

Whilst Hitler did not intend to be underprepared for war, the fact is that the rearmament of the Fatherland had been woeful. The Wehrmacht and Kriegsmarine were five years from being ready. Nevertheless, delay would still not have given the Nazis victory. By the time German plans were complete Allied rearmament in response to the arms race, would still have been a match for Germany. A short war was needed. The boldness of lightning attacks was not incompatible with the need for quick and decisive victories delivered through a Hail Mary pass achieving a strategic victory. Indeed, whether Hitler was cognisant of it or not, such an approach was made a necessity by the weakness of the German war economy. To all intents and purposes blitzkrieg was war on a wing and a prayer. It would in time unravel but not before it became more dangerous. The theory behind it had been sharpened and honed through the conquest of Poland and the defeat of, the not inconsiderable in size, Norwegian and the Anglo-French forces protecting the Scandinavian nation. Blitzkrieg would then find its most perfect application against the French.

Hitler drives west

The Battle of France, or Fall of France, as Hitler's conquest of the French nation is also known, was accomplished in just six weeks from when the hammer first fell on 10th May 1940. In the firing line against Germany's main rival in western Europe were the so-called Benelux countries of Luxembourg, Belgium, and the Netherlands. These states were ostensibly collateral damage in the latest iteration of European great power rivalry. The Netherlands, however, would make a good incorporation into the Reich. The Dutch language is, like German, a West Germanic language, and has a similar route to the word Deutsch, the name for the German tongue. The Dutch are pejoratively known as "Swamp Germans". Also there were Nazi sympathisers in the Netherlands, the most prominent collaborator being Anton Mussert, the founder of the National Socialist Movement in the Netherlands. Indeed, up to 25,000 Dutchmen volunteered for the *Waffen-SS*, the military wing of the Nazi Party's Protection Squad (the SS) and served their German masters, often with the utmost ruthlessness, in Yugoslavia and Russia. The vision of Mussert was that although the Netherlands would not be an independent sovereign state it would become a stronger branch when attached to the German-led European tree trunk. Hitler was only too happy to oblige but on his own terms. Instead of adopting Mussert's idea of a Nordic Federation, Hitler merely gave him the title of *Leider* of the Dutch. This gave Mussert little real power.

Germany did not always feel the need to occupy its neighbours. Switzerland and Sweden are cases in point; on paper they were prime candidates for occupation but so long as they were obliging to German interests, Hitler's gaze would look elsewhere. Even Hungary was only occupied as late as 1944 and that was to ensure its continued obedience. The Netherlands, which took a neutral stance in 1940 may well have avoided German ambitions for a time. The Germans respected Dutch neutrality in the First World War, Wilhelm II, the German

Kaiser, made the Netherlands his home after his abdication and the collapse of the German Empire. In the Second World War the Dutch would not be left to their own devices. They would be attacked and the impetus for the German invasion was a practical consideration. The plan to attack France via Belgium included passing through part of Dutch territory, this is known as the Maastricht Corridor. It meant the Germans would thus be violating the neutrality of the Netherlands. Nazi logic concluded that the whole country must be subdued. In for a penny, in for a pound.

Ah, the French!

France was hardly a *putain* ripe for the German thrust, it was a country with a celebrated martial tradition whose soldiers, a century and half before had been the scourge of Europe. In defence of their own national revolution and in a quest for dominion over Europe the French in the Napoleonic Wars caused a death toll estimated to be between 3¼ million and 6½ million people.

France's automotive industry, particularly the Peugeot plant which had mastered mass production, was superior to the German car industry. In a long war the French had the potential to outproduce their Germanic neighbour. France, despite being a predominantly Roman Catholic country, had advanced industrial development spearheaded by protestant families of which the Peugeots were amongst the most notable. It has long been noted that there is a link between Protestantism and capitalism. The same phenomenon existed in Anglo-Saxon Britain and America and can be observed today in South Korea and China where in these modern times Christians are at the forefront of their respective capitalist class and subsequent economic development. Conversely, the mindset of the German Nazi hierarchy was pagan in the original meaning of the word. Pagan was a pejorative term meaning 'country dweller'. It denoted those who were backward and less sophisticated than their town and city dwelling contemporaries. The Nazi's origins were from the German Workers Party (DAP) founded by Anton Drexler. Hitler joined and turned it into the National Socialist German Workers Party, NSDAP, the Nazi Party. Hitler built upon the party's environmental and rural issues and put them at its core. The Nazis railed against capitalism and the materialistic world order. This was hardly a recipe for economic success, nor did they appreciate the development of the most efficient production techniques. Germany lacked many of the tools needed for victory.

France was not doomed to defeat, far from it. The French military possessed more guns than their German enemies. Germany had 7,378 artillery pieces and

France 10,700. The disparity did not stop there; the Germans could muster 2,439 tanks while the French had 3,254, most of which were bigger, better armed, and armoured than German panzers. The French also possessed 300,000 trucks. Germany had far fewer and could field just 120,000. Not only was France strong, but Germany also had inherent weaknesses. Only 16 of their 135 divisions were mechanised – that is, equipped with motorised transport. The rest depended on the horse and cart for transport, soldiers had to rely on their feet. France alone had 117 divisions, surely more than enough to keep the German's out. Yet, despite this France succumbed to Germany in less than six weeks, so what went wrong? The defeat was homegrown. The French had abandoned their attacking doctrine which was the hallmark of French military theory in the earlier part of World War One, *Attaque à outrance*, attack to excess. Instead, in land warfare they relied on outmoded tactics, a general defensive disposition, and an over reliance on fixed defences. The most famous of these was that which straddled the Franco-German border between Belgium and Switzerland, called the Maginot Line.

The Maginot Line performed well when attacked. It was no white elephant. The Italians were also stopped by French defences in the Alps in the south of France. The French, however, omitted to build this rampart on their vulnerable northern flank. This is where the problem arose, the French defensive wall was not completed along the border with Belgium. The Allied plan in the event of war with Germany was to hold the Hun at the Maginot Line and send British and French forces into Belgium. This well-made plan was sent into disarray when Belgium unilaterally declared neutrality, which should not have come as a surprise. The land which we now call Belgium was traditionally a buffer between the Romance phonic French and peoples who eschewed Latin influences and institutions favouring their Germanic linguistic inheritance and the religion of Luther and Calvin. The modern state of Belgium, traditionally a Roman Catholic land, was intended to be a neutral country. Indeed, a protocol signed by Britain and Europe's then great powers on 20th January 1831 enshrined this neutrality. The Belgium declaration of non-alignment and the repudiation of its military pact with France was a major problem. Despite German guarantees that it would honour Belgian neutrality the attack which came through Belgium was not entirely unexpected. Belgium had been amongst the most aggressive, perhaps even the cruellest, of the industrialised colonial countries up until the Second World War. Belgium had murdered its way up the Congo, but in the latter part of the 1930s switched its military posture to a defensive footing and began strengthening its own forts and building a national redoubt. Hitler and his core commanders had no intention of honouring the Kingdom's neutrality, they had other ideas. A sickle cut spearheaded by Army Group A went through Belgium and headed to the channel ports on the Atlantic coast. Belgian forts were either captured through daring raids using airborne troops or, like the Maginot Line itself, simply bypassed.

Fixed defensive positions, though bypassed by the Germans in 1940, still had their worth. The Germans had built fortified lines on their own border with France and revived this to guard the western boundaries of Germany when threatened later in the war. The Wehrmacht, under Luftwaffe *Generalfeldmarschall* Albert Kesselring, built throughout Italy a series of lines with fixed gun emplacements and other defences. Even Erwin Rommel, one of Germany's most famed tank commanders and Field Marshals, oversaw the building of fixed emplacements on his section of the Atlantic Wall. These proved to be inadequate, not because the concept was at fault but rather there were not enough resources to adequately construct and guard the coast from Spain to North Cape in Norway. These strategies were pursued because when the Nazis came to test the Maginot Line German assessments of French forts drew favourable conclusions and even earned a degree of respect from their assailants.

France's failure in 1940, a situation from which they were only saved four years later, with the help of the British Empire, Canada, the United States, and some dissident Frenchmen, was caused through a defeat of their will. Or in other words a collective collapse in the aggressive martial spirit for which France was once well known, from the spirit under Charles Martel who saved Europe from Arab invasion, to Charlemagne and the Napoleonic commanders. Yet, this lack of spirit was itself a symptom of a greater malaise that had befallen France both during and after the First World War. To a degree, the defensive posture was the logical conclusion of a crisis from a generation before. France lacked manpower.

Dereliction of duty
The experience at the 1916 Battle of Verdun hung heavy over France. The French drew the wrong lessons from their pyrrhic victory in this titanic struggle for what was an inconsequential, but prestigious, piece of French soil. The German trap that motivated their attack on Verdun was to kill Frenchmen, it worked, but not enough to give Kaiser Wilhelm and his son, the Crown Prince, victory in the first Great War. Unbeknownst to them, it helped give the Third Reich a stunning victory twenty-four years later. The Second World War was driven by the First, the French more than any other European power applied the lessons

from 1916 to the fighting in 1940. However, the French drew two very wrong, or at least outmoded, conclusions from the Battle of Verdun.

The first dubious deduction was that a chain of interconnected and mutually supporting forts, with well-orchestrated forces behind them, was how wars would be fought in the future. The French in World War One rightly observed that the defenders have the advantage, but incorrectly applied this to the Second. Gallic military planners and theorists presumed that any German attack would be broken by emplaced machine gun posts and forts, hence the idea for the Maginot Line. This super trench would break-up and then destroy a German army foolish enough to engage it. This belief was not so outlandish, even to this day conventional military doctrine dictates that for an attacker to be successful would need a three to one advantage in manpower over a defender. This mantra is still repeated despite the experience of the 1991 Gulf War which showed that other factors take precedence, just as they did in 1940. Before the Fall of France, the French had failed to appreciate how mechanised units incorporating tanks and troop carriers, supported by airpower and even paratroopers, could deliver spear like thrusts that bypass, if not breach, most static defences. Only the most robust positions stand firm against such assaults.

The second erroneous inference was that the hero of France, Marshal Pétain, the man who saved France in 1916 halting the German attack on Verdun, would save French honour in 1940. Marshal Philippe Pétain's inspirational leadership and superb organisation prevented a collapse in this sector. A generation later, there was no robust defence. His recall to lead the French state ushered in conquest followed by collaboration. The Germans passed through; France was out manoeuvred, outfought, and outthought. The problem was that France did not have the numbers. The First World War cast a long shadow, and not just for Germany. France was still reeling from the mauling they had suffered in the Great War. The French Army was psychologically exhausted, and as the 1917 mutinies show, they had lost much of their appetite to keep fighting.

Only the support of the British Empire and later the addition of American forces taking up the slack, alongside pressure from France's political leadership, had kept France in the fight until the armistice of 1918. Indeed, Georges Clemenceau, French Prime Minister, who was known for his successful and robust leadership of France at the close of World War One wrote that *War is too serious a matter to entrust to military men.'* In 1940 France had little resolve left and could not fully count on Britain and least of all the United States which after the First Word War was reluctant to become engaged in another European conflict.

Britain's contribution to the defence of France was lacklustre. The UK, like the USA, did not lust after yet another damaging continental entanglement.

In 1918 the butcher's bill after four years of war was too great for France, it caused long-term consequences. The death toll was the first part of a crisis in the French population. The situation worsened. In the final year of the Great War, from April 1918 France was hit by the Spanish Flu. This virus, a subtype of the H1N1 influenza A virus, left 240,000 people in France dead. It was particularly dangerous for what would otherwise have been fit and healthy young men, especially soldiers. This pandemic lasted until 1920 and took 40 million lives globally. France had structural problems and could not afford the losses. This, compounded with France's low birth rate in the 1920s, led to predictions that the French military would have a dire shortage of men and be incapable of competing with the size of Germany's army. This would rank high among the reasons for France's adoption of a defensive strategy, which itself resulted in the ill-fated decision to produce and rely on the Maginot Line. France had already been bled white during the First World War, suffering more than a million combat deaths, these crises affecting the population meant that French commanders lost their *va-va-voom* in military affairs. This came just as their young men and women were failing in affairs of the heart and not producing enough children.

When Germany attacked again in the Second World War, the next French generation was depleted of manpower and was too small in number to mount a proper resistance to the *Deutsches Heer* and *Waffen-SS* Divisions that bore down on France. Conversely, Germany's population had grown even after the First World War, whilst France was short of conscripts. Demographics are destiny. The people with the highest birth rate will win.

According to the National Bureau of Economic Research, a declining population is the cause of an economic downturn not the result of one. The phenomenon of a falling birth rate saps the spunk and virility out of a nation. A country with too few young people in relation to the elderly is one that will be cautious and generally risk averse. This was a psychological crisis that was compounded by the physical crises of the famine of reproduction, the pestilence of disease, and the fatalities caused through war at the hands of beastly Germans. The demographic decline of France reversed after World War II following the country's liberation. Post-war optimism and national independence inspired the surviving young people to thrive, rebuild, and repopulate France. Correspondingly the French economy also grew after the war.

The audacity of luck

Blitzkrieg, in practice, relied as much on the under preparedness of the opponent as much as it did on the initiative of the attacker. At a local level it secured a seemingly obscure part of the battlespace that would prove to be the decisive piece of ground through where the breakthrough and the breakout would be achieved. This is otherwise known as luck, but fortune in war is home grown. The side that is the most motivated and predatory are more likely to have lady luck on its side. This was the centre of gravity upon which blitzkrieg depended and enabled it to inflict a psychological shock upon defenders. Fortune favours the brave.

The German invasion of the Low Countries and France was a remarkable and risky gamble which even made many German generals nervous. Indeed, after navigating their way through the, thought to be impassable, Ardennes Forest, the next task was to cross the Meuse River. The French were on one bank, the Germans on the other. This time critical offensive could have foundered. It was enterprising German soldiers that managed to secure a bridgehead ensuring Army Group A had a foothold across this body of water. This was the decisive move in the Battle of Sedan which lasted from 12th to 15th May 1940. Here the Germans secured the victory that led to the collapse of French resistance, it allowed Allied forces in Belgium to be outflanked and left the path to the English Channel as good as open. The dash to the sea then began.

Blitzkrieg is only remembered when it is successful. When it failed, and the specific gamble did not pay off, it is described as a blunder, or as a reckless advance. In May 1940, the German attack had all the luck, they could have been stopped; but for the time being Allied commanders and the soldiers on the ground were unwilling to make the sacrifices that would offer the opportunity for them to become lucky.

Caution to excess

France had been, along with the United Kingdom, a pioneer of tank development during World War One. French factories produced machines that more closely resembled what in the modern era is viewed as a tank than those produced by even the British, or the cumbersome contraptions sent into battle by the Germans at that time. When it came to World War II the French, however, still thought that tanks were best used to support infantry and so, therefore, they did not concentrate their armour in fast moving thrusts that could penetrate enemy lines. French tanks, superior in numbers as well as in manoeuvrability, defence, and firepower, were spaced out too broadly to have a decisive impact on the battlefield. Again, the French military establishment were thinking in World War One terms where tanks could not operate without infantry support. The French were figuratively, almost literally, preparing to fight the last war. This was a problem observed and critiqued by a certain forward-thinking general who was to inherit the future after the war. In the book *Towards A Professional Army*, Charles De Gaulle put forward the counter view that tanks should be used in a more dynamic and focused fashion.

The heart of the matter was that there was little desire for a fight back. Pilots in the French air force in the Battle of France fought just one sortie a day. Those in the German Luftwaffe went on as many as four and sometimes up to six combat missions per day. Clearly de Gaulle had foreseen the catastrophic lackadaisical attitude to war, one that would cost France her national freedom and honour. Soon France, to all intents and purposes, found itself alone.

On 21st May 1940, a British counterattack known as the Battle of Arras, aimed south at the exposed flank of the German army's Hail Mary pass led by Erwin Rommel as his tanks advanced through the Somme Valley, heading towards the English Channel. The Allied move failed to breakthrough and the British were forced to retreat. The British Expeditionary Force fell back on Dunkirk, a channel port that was already in danger. The British contribution to preserving the honour of France was not great. Commanded by General Lord Gort, the British Expeditionary Force (BEF) as UK forces in France were known, was as few as approximately 350,000 soldiers. Despite the fact that this was the largest contingent of any Allied state outside France, this constituted just 10 per cent of the defending force. They were soon to begin the attempt to depart for home. Indeed, some could see the looming disaster before the Battle of France began. General Montgomery had his forces practice night manoeuvres should they need to withdraw under cover of darkness. On 15th May his Iron Division fought-off German attacks but as the other fronts collapsed that month, Monty's troops were ordered to withdraw to cover the retreat to Dunkirk; in this scenario their training found its purpose. Later in the month of May, and into early June, Montgomery commanded the BEF's II Corps and successfully withdrew from the continent. Monty was praised for his professional handling of the crisis that was not actually of his making.

Neither was the failure the fault of the BEF. The fiasco was caused elsewhere. Both the French and Belgian armies collapsed and retreated; the British Army were too few to make up for their host's lacklustre defence. It mattered not that British units all had the advantage that they could travel to, and back, from the front using vehicles. The British Army was fully mechanised. However, 85% of

German soldiers could not rely on powered vehicles to transport them and had to march. Had there been more British men, it would have been a quite different result. By the time the Second BEF was dispatched to France, the momentum was already with the invader, its deployment was again too little, and too late to turn the tide. The niggardly number of men committed to the fighting may seem like an omission, yet it was part of the United Kingdom's approach to war and security.

Britain had traditionally relied upon a smaller yet better equipped and well supplied professional army that could cooperate with allied nations, without the need to rely on plunder. This was because seizing supplies from the local populace was a practice that could rapidly turn friends into foes. Britain relied upon, and won her wars, using the combined strength of co-opted allies that would serve Britain's imperial ambitions. The men of the British Army would be delivered when and where they chose by the invictus Royal Navy. What resources were available were therefore given to the navy for that purpose, and to ensure the dominance of its merchant fleet. Rivals would either be conquered through divide and rule or suffocated by blockade into irrelevance and then submission. The control of global trade was the aim. However, Continental European states with often open and undefined borders, shared between less happier lands, relied upon massed armies of conscript soldiers that looted in order to keep on the move. That was true for the men of the Wehrmacht in 1940, ⅔ of which were not fully trained. For Great Britain, an island nation, security was guaranteed by both its mighty navy and its enormous merchant fleet; or so the British thought.

Soon the Germans could see the English White Cliffs of Dover from the occupied French shore. The final abandonment came when France asked the US President, Franklin Delano Roosevelt, to mediate a peace between France and Germany but he refused citing that he could not get involved in European affairs. Soon after France capitulated. The armistice was signed on 22ⁿᵈ June 1940 in the Forest of Compiègne and in the same railway carriage where the French and her allies had humiliated Germany in 1918 by forcing the Teutons to agree to a humiliating peace. This was poetic justice for the heartbreak which Hitler felt when Germany surrendered in the First World War. There then followed a period where France was drawn in to ever-closer alignment to Nazi Germany.

Volte-face

On 16ᵗʰ June 1940, just hours before the French government had formally decided to capitulate, Churchill offered the French an indissoluble union with the United Kingdom hoping this would keep them in the fight. France, however, chose Germany. Winston Churchill still harboured hopes that the French would at some point make another about-face. What happened, however, was that Germany took Northern France and its Atlantic seaboard under its occupation, as well as the once German region of Alsace and Lorraine; most of that territory, for the time being, officially remained a part of France but again became a *de facto* part of the Reich. Southern and Central France including Corsica and Algeria, and the French empire, would be administered by a new near puppet government based in the spa town of Vichy. From there the collaborationist regime took its unofficial name. It was officially called *État Français*, or in English, French State. Incidentally, the German state after World War One and before Hitler came to power, was known as the Weimar Republic. In 1919 after an attempted Communist coup in Berlin, the German government had fled to the city of Weimar.

Despite Churchill's hopes that the Vichy regime would at some point rejoin the Allied effort in the meantime at least, France had fallen. She was rocked and rolled over but had been spared the devastation that befell it at the hands of the Germans a generation before. France also avoided the violence that was meted out to countries in Eastern Europe, and even the Dutch, who were merely in the way of Hitler's wild right-hook. Rotterdam in the Netherlands, one of their principal cities, was devasted by German bombs. France surrendered before Paris would be bombed. The French had made peace with Germany.

There was also another factor at work. The 'peace' with Germany served a useful political purpose. Elements in France had Fascist tendencies. Many French supported a statist system, which was nationalistic, intolerant of both dissent and against Anglo-Saxon capitalism, and sought to manage life in an 'ethical' state. The aim was to impose morality from above and eliminate class conflict through corporatist governance. Those doctrines were intrinsic to fascism and not alien to the French. Even today, the *Grandes écoles* produce the educated elite that run the state in the best interests of the population whether they appreciate it or not. Just as Fascism had a counterpart amongst the Falangists of Spain, a similar ideology found an echo in France with the Vichy authorities.

The 1940 armistice with Germany, was an opportunity for them to enforce the precepts of fascism. French Fascism, like its Spanish and Italian counterparts, has its own unique cultural influences, tendencies, and traditions. The French manifestation of this system had its intellectual base in the medieval guild system and ideology of the Roman Catholic Church. France adapted easily to the corporatism of fascism. Furthermore, German muscle helped the Vichy Regime fulfil France's latent anti-Semitism. The Germans were also used by the Vichy government to take revenge on the Popular Front who they blamed for weakening France in the interwar years. Thus, such German 'help' with suppressing, and even eliminating socialists created a further rationale to justify collaboration. Conversely, when the Soviets and the Nazis were in alliance, the communists, on the orders of the Soviet leadership, did not initially oppose German dominion over France. Under instruction from their Russian leadership, who wanted peace with Germany as per the terms of the Molotov–Ribbentrop Pact, French communists were told not to oppose the Vichy Regime. They only took up arms against the German occupation of France when the Nazis invaded the Soviet Union. Other socialists found common cause with the corporatism of the Gallic version of fascism. Some Syndicalists, who followed a political ideology based around trade unionism, accepted, and lauded the idea that they be included into the state apparatus, they perceived it as integrating the proletariat into the national organism. However, the price of being at the top table was the workers' independent voice and would be champion became a mouthpiece for state control. It was a similar situation in Italy.

Voltafaccia

With both France and Britain effectively defeated on the continent of Europe, Italy played its hand. Italy's role in the war proved to be decisive, but not in the way that was intended. On 10th June 1940 Italy, under its Prime Minister, Benito Mussolini, declared war on the United Kingdom and France. This was the latest act in an ever-evolving national strategy. Italy had been the wildcard of Mediterranean politics, it practised many geopolitical turns. In this modern era Italy has been firmly aligned with Europe's central powers, but frustration at the stagnation caused by Europe's single currency and a lack of support for their national plight caused through the Covid-19 epidemic may initiate another 180-degree switch.

Italy was an aggressive military power before Mussolini took over the state in 1922. In the late nineteenth century, Italy colonised the area that became known as Italian Somaliland. In 1895 they also attempted to conquer Abyssinia, modern day Ethiopia. The Abyssinians however, aided by France and Russia, defeated the Italian invasion. Later Italy picked over the decaying Ottoman Empire, seizing modern day Libya from the Turks in 1911. Their imperial ambitions were not just centred on Africa. The Italians occupied the now Greek Dodecanese islands following the Italo-Turkish War of 1911 to 1912. This gave Italy a direct involvement in the Greek world.

In the First World War Italy, before it entered the fighting, was one of the Central Powers along with Germany and Austria-Hungary. They were a part of the Triple Alliance. After receiving promises of territory from Britain and France they entered the war on the British, French, and Russian side in 1915. Their reward included primarily German speaking territory from Austria-Hungary and the South Tyrol where the Ladin and Italian languages are also spoken. Italy was also promised some territory from the Ottoman Empire. The war did not go well for the Italians. After Austria received German assistance in the Alps the Italian front collapsed, it was in this fighting that Erwin Rommel showed great promise as a commander. When the Italian's crumpled, they had to be bolstered by troops from Britain. However, the addition of a new theatre of war opening against the Axis powers further drained German resources; this contributed to the Kaiser's defeat. The war against Germany and German speakers had many supporters in Italy.

Mussolini, a socialist, created the non-racialist and initially non-anti-Semitic, Fascist credo of a corporatist state as a way of eliminating class conflict. He was however, unlike other socialists and communists, firmly supportive of Italian involvement in the First World War against Germany. He denounced what he saw as the reactionary and imperialistic policies of the German and Austro-Hungarian Empires. He was also supportive of Britain and France. This continued when he came to power, he made Italy a guarantor of peace and signatory to the Lacarno Treaties which settled boundaries and borders in central and western Europe.

Mussolini was also the inheritor of Italian irredentism; a movement that wanted to annex lands in the north which many nationalists thought should be part of Italy. Ettore Tolomei, an Italian nationalist and fascist, tried to Italianise the German-speaking region of South Tyrol which had been annexed by Italy from Austria after the First World War. He made Italian the only official language in 1923 and invented approximately 8,000 Italian geographical place names to replace those used in German speaking settlements. Tolomei requested to be buried facing north, so that he could see the last German-speaking South Tyrolean leave. Tolomei was not successful and was later imprisoned by the Nazis. To this day the predominately German speaking South Tyrol region remains the most prosperous area of Italy.

Mussolini's grand plan extended beyond just addressing border issues with his immediate neighbours. He wanted a new Roman Empire, with dominion over Southern Europe, and control over much of North Africa and the Balkans; he even saw states such as Hungary and Austria as being in his orbit. He was more than willing to oppose German unification with Austria, known as *Anschluss*.

In 1934, furious at Hitler's meddling in Austrian affairs, Mussolini even sent troops to the Brenner Pass and threatened Germany with war if the German leader continued to undermine Austrian sovereignty. Hitler backed down, for the time being.

In 1935 Mussolini's pro-British and French disposition was renewed when he agreed to the Stresa Front. This pact united Italy, France and Britain against German expansion and came in response to German rearmament. It also further guaranteed the independence of Austria from Germany. To contain Germany, Mussolini did not just form alliances with Britain and France but also allied with the Soviet Union. In 1933 Italy agreed with the USSR, the Italo-Soviet Pact, officially titled the Pact of Friendship, Neutrality, and Nonaggression between Italy and the Soviet Union. Incidentally, Benito Mussolini's Italy was the first state in Western Europe to recognise the Soviet Union, establishing full diplomatic relations in 1924.

Hitler, however, admired Mussolini, particularly his takeover of Italy, and the Italian dictator was possibly the closest thing to a friend that existed in Adolf Hitler's life. The fate of Benito Mussolini would be an influence over the actions of Hitler in his final days. However, Mussolini was genuinely scared of both Hitler and German ambitions. He thought that the Nazi concept of the master race was nonsense and viewed Hitler as quite mad. However, Mussolini's approach to Germany was about to change.

As a result of the crisis in Abyssinia and British domination of the Mediterranean Sea, Mussolini began to reappraise his alliances. This included wanting closer relations with Japan. Italy, Germany, and Japan were quickly becoming international pariahs and were pushed closer to each other by an international order that was disgusted by Italian and Japanese imperialism. They were essentially cast out for doing in the late 1930s, what holier than thou states had done in some cases just decades before; that is conduct aggressive wars of conquest. In May 1939, Italy and Germany agreed to the so-called Pact of Steel, officially known as the Pact of Friendship and Alliance between Germany and Italy. Japan did not enter into the Axis at this point because it wanted to maintain relations with the United Kingdom and desired to oppose the Soviet Union, with which Italy was still in alliance. There was also another dynamic at work. As German power grew and as Hitler's area of control increased Mussolini felt that in order to keep Italy safe, he had to both hold Germany close to Italy and counterbalance the German empire by creating his own imperium in the Balkans. The overriding aim was still to preserve Italian independence from German influence and ensure that Germany would not become a suzerain over Italy. It failed.

The Italian intervention in the war was initially unsuccessful and resolutely resisted by the outnumbered French, who yielded only a limited amount of ground. The duplicity of the attack did have one important impact, it especially angered the American President, Franklin Delano Roosevelt. This nudged him further in the direction of getting involved in the war in Europe against the Axis. Whilst Italy was to arguably have a decisive and detrimental impact on the fate of the Third Reich, at the time, Hitler's alliance with Mussolini posed a threat to British forces in the Mediterranean Sea and after many defeats the UK and her empire would soon be fighting alone.

Spinning a victory out of the jaws of defeat

Vice-Admiral Bertram Ramsay, Commander-in-Chief Dover, based beneath Dover Castle, a great medieval construct of King Henry II, had responsibility for the English Channel. Accordingly, Ramsay was charged with organising the evacuation from Dunkirk of the British Expeditionary Force, the BEF. This castle from where the Vice-Admiral worked is known as the 'Key to England'; what Bertram Ramsay achieved saved England and by extension the UK from an ignominious political surrender that may have followed if the troops were not brought back safely and unilaterally.

The importance of getting British troops home went beyond the need to have a well-trained and adequately manned military. It was a matter of confidence, so much so that a lack of self-belief may have led to compromise and ultimately collaboration. The Fall of France left large sections of the French Army prisoners of war. Indeed, nearly two million had surrendered. In 1942 Pierre Laval, as the Chief of the Government of Vichy France, the French Prime Minister, struck a bargain with the German Reich. Germany short of industrial manpower, and with Laval hopeful for a Nazi victory against Russia, sought to get as many prisoners home as possible. His deal was that for every three workers supplied to Germany, one prisoner would be freed and returned home.

Laval thought that he could do business with Hitler. He certainly had, and for a time it was popular with the French public. The German Führer however was the consummate politician and knew that once a concession had been made to him, he could and would come back with further demands. The direction of travel had been set and became irresistible; Laval was hooked. In time Hitler had him eating out of his hand. Laval became dependent, he was subservient to the Germans and ran little more than a rump state puppet regime. Pierre Laval was repaid by a French firing squad, in 1945. Yet he died still believing that he was acting in the best interests of France, but "You cannot reason with a tiger when your head is in its mouth". Laval himself proved this to be true.

Laval had negotiated the 1935 French Russian alliance, known as the Franco-Soviet Treaty of Mutual Assistance which aimed to envelop Germany. It was, however, a useless treaty as it required Italy and the United Kingdom to approve any military action. Despite that, Pierre Laval had found himself on a remarkable political journey. Originally anti-German he became anti-British after the Hoare-Laval Pact of December 1935 unravelled. This treaty consented to Italian occupation of parts of Abyssinia in exchange for Italy pledging to continue to oppose Germany. Both he, and his British counterpart, the Foreign Secretary Samuel Hoare, lost their jobs over their scandalous acquiescence to Italian imperialism. Laval was forced to resign after this was leaked by the British and for that he never forgave his former allies, who, with the fortunes of war swinging against Britain, soon turned their back on crumbling France.

Bertram Ramsay, later Sir Bertram, was ordered to only save 45,000 men of the BEF from Dunkirk. This would have left hundreds of thousands of British servicemen in the hands of the Nazis. The Vice-Admiral and his Royal Navy, with the support of the privately held Little Ships assisting Operation Dynamo, however, saved 338,000 Servicemen. The evacuation of Dunkirk saved 193,000 British and 145,000 French troops marooned on the French coast. This miracle created a massive wave of confidence in Britain. The defeat of the BEF was spun as victory. Prime Minister Winston Churchill's position was emboldened. He won his battle to keep Britain in the war, facing down the architects and continued advocates of appeasement led by the Secretary of State for Foreign Affairs, Lord Halifax, and his Foreign Office. Halifax was destined to not only lose the argument but also lose his job. Churchill was hopeful that Halifax would help entice the United States of America into the war, and so later that year the crestfallen peer was sent to Washington D.C. to become the British Ambassador.

The situation could have been hugely different. The ever-decreasing perimeter around the British and French forces at Dunkirk was vulnerable from German armour that was bearing down on them. These tanks, however, advanced at such a pace that they outstripped their supplies and much of their infantry support. A compelling case could be made that they needed to wait. Logistics are all important as any student of the renowned Prussian military theorist, Carl von Clausewitz, will know. Hitler, on the advice of one of his generals, Gerd von Rundstedt, violated the principle of Mission Command, which allowed commanders on the ground to use their individual initiative, and make decisions for themselves. They ordered these fast-moving mechanised divisions to halt.

When they resumed their advance after being forced to pause their attack the Allied forces had the opportunity to mount their evacuation. Hitler had shown the first instance of his fateful meddling in affairs he knew not.

In terms of the war, the delay had cost Hitler the opportunity to capture over 300,00 troops at Dunkirk, a move that would have almost certainly strengthened the hand of those in the UK that wanted an armistice. Without the success of Operation Dynamo, enabled by Hitler as much as by British seafaring bravado, Britain may well have become a mere tributary state supplying men, money, and materials to serve the ambitions of a continental empire. It would have exchanged the risks of sovereignty for the certainties of suzerainty. Could the United Kingdom have followed the French example? France had fallen, but could Britain stand firm?

So Near Yet So Far

What would have happened if the Germans had invaded Britain?

"Supreme excellence consists of breaking the enemy's resistance without fighting."— **Sun Tzu**

The prawn cocktail offensive

Hitler's first assault on the British Isles was a charm offensive. The German leader sought to nullify the threat from the nation that had been thwarting European unions for the last four centuries. This was Britain's role from the time of Elizabeth I, when England aided the resistance against Habsburg dominion over the Spanish Netherlands, to Britain halting the ambitions of Louis XIV to rule western Europe. This policy continued to the time of the First World War and in its diplomacy after that Great War. Britain had proactively kept Europe divided, but, simultaneously free from authoritarian rule.

Unlike France, Germany's enduring enemy, Britain and its empire was much admired, if not properly understood, by Hitler. The Indian sub-continent, then a great land of three hundred million people, was on paper ruled by just twenty thousand British troops and civil servants. Hitler failed to appreciate the realities of the British Raj which co-opted and cooperated with native elites and to some extent incorporated them into the system. Rather than basing British rule on conquest and the force of arms, the empire in India was based on consent. In his desire to learn from, and emulate, the British Empire, Hitler drew the wrong lesson. His view was that his Germanic warriors could rule over and exploit the labour of a Helot class of Slavs to the east but this was just a fantasy, one that was reinforced by Hollywood. The 1935 film *The Lives of a Bengal Lancer*, starring Gary Cooper, was amongst the Führer's favourite films and became compulsory viewing for the SS. Hitler interpreted this movie as a romanticisation of the British, and by extension the white race's superiority over less advanced, as he saw it, and racially inferior peoples.

One of Hitler's overriding aims was an alliance between the German Reich and the English aristocracy. These nobles were arguably of Germanic descent through their Anglo-Saxon, Danish, and Norse in origin Norman lineages. Despite his

Bavarian military unit fighting against the British in World War I, or perhaps because of it, he was keen to avoid another war with the United Kingdom. Indeed, Hitler believed, or at least claimed, probably falsely that the sparing of his life by an English Tommy, Henry Tandey, in the closing stages of the war was in some way prophetic. Hitler opined that Britain could have its overseas empire; Germany would have Europe. To achieve that end Hitler sent his prime sycophant, the social climber Joachim von Ribbentrop, known disparagingly by some in Britain's establishment circles as von Ribbensnob. Hitler had reason to believe that this charmless man would be successful. He had earlier negotiated with Britain when on a previous errand for the Führer.

The Anglo-German Naval Agreement (AGNA) of 18th June 1935 was perceived by Hitler to be a great diplomatic triumph for von Ribbentrop. The truth of the matter was that Britain merely caved into German demands. The following summer Hitler appointed him Ambassador to the Court of St. James to negotiate a comprehensive Anglo-German alliance. Ultimately, the man that was to become Hitler's chief diplomat and Foreign Minister was simply offensive. He committed several *faux pas*, most notably giving the Nazi salute to the King. The abject failure of von Ribbentrop's mission did not quell Hitler's reverence for the 'sceptred isle', nor was he alone in his sycophancy. Hitler's arch henchman Heinrich Himmler also held Britain's supposed ruling elite in high regard. Himmler sought to model the SS leadership on his fantasy of the British aristocracy. At the SS' version of Britain's officer training centre Sandhurst, and its American equivalent West Point, Himmler tried to create a similar ruling class. At the Bad Tölz SS elite training school, the Nazi Party's military wing, alongside learning war fighting skills and receiving political indoctrination, also learnt how to horse ride and even play cricket. Fox hunting was however banned in Germany as Hitler was an animal lover. The Führer also saw the ban on hunting with hounds as an attack on Germany's own aristocracy which he despised.

Once war had broken out between the two putative allies Hitler still hoped that he could persuade Britain to leave the fight, Hitler was quoted as saying: "we are seeking contact with Britain on the basis of partitioning the world". Germany would have continental Europe; Britain would have the open sea. Any peace deal, however, with a single European state just 18 nautical miles from England's shoreline may in time have meant Britain would become a satellite of Nazi Germany. The pressure to conform to this European hegemon may have proved overwhelming. Yet, the UK was not alone. The conflict was not just between Britain and Germany. It was between a United Kingdom resourced by its empire and a Germany using money and materiel plundered from its newly won conquest, but not entirely. The German war effort in its fight against Britain relied upon debts racked up on the international financial market and via the Swiss banking system. Of prime importance were the supplies Germany received from the resource rich Soviet Union, these came as part of their alliance under the Ribbentrop-Molotov Pact.

The delivery of oil was particularly important to the German effort. Having this at their disposal greatly enhanced the military capabilities of the Nazi Regime. The fuel which powered the Luftwaffe attacks on Britain came from the USSR. Germany was reliant on fossil fuels under Russian control. Modern Germany was also dependent upon gas supplies from the Russian Federation which is somewhat cleaner than coal energy and until recently came via the Nord Stream gas pipeline. It passes through the Baltic Sea, connecting Vyborg in Russia with Greifswald in Germany, and was operated by Nord Stream AG and Russian state gas company Gazprom. The pipeline, and its expansion with the addition of the now considered politically unacceptable Nord Stream 2, has been disparagingly described by its political and environmental opponents in Poland, Estonia, and the United States, amongst others, as the Molotov-Ribbentrop Pipeline. Its destruction was an Anglo-American endeavour worthy of John le Carré. It is not a coincidence that a former German Chancellor, Gerhard Schröder, worked for the Russian gas giant Gazprom. Diplomacy and international relations are Germany's modern methods to achieve political power based on an economy that was once powered by cheap Russian gas. However, the relationship has again soured and disputes over the supply of resources are again threatening to derail peace and prosperity. *Plus ça change, plus c'est la même chose.*

If Russia and Germany had remained at peace, and if potential border disputes and zones of influence between the two powers had remained settled, then Hitler's dominion over a devastated Europe may have been cemented. And Hitler's ruthless ambition to co-opt Britain's global influence to serve his dastardly ends would have been emboldened. His war machine, then solely facing the United Kingdom and her empire, would have been further energised. Thus, markedly increasing Germany's potential to cow Britain. Yet, as Germany coveted the land to the east and sought to expand its influence over the Russian zone, the partnership between the two anti-democratic realms did not last long. European division allowed Britain to continue ruling its own house.

After the Fall of France and the accompanying evacuation of the continent by Britain and her allies, the entire seaboard from Spain to North Cape in Norway was occupied by Germany. Other nations on the Northern Atlantic coast of Europe were neutral, such as Ireland, which had ceased to be a dominion of the

UK in 1937. The Kingdom of Iceland, having been impartial, was occupied by Britain after the fall of Denmark to prevent pro-Nazi sympathisers and German citizens on the island from taking it into the Reich's orbit. The significant states on the continent of Europe, were, almost entirely at that time in one capacity or another acting against Britain. The dire situation could have further deteriorated.

Churchill was hoping to avoid a scenario where the French fleet would fall into German hands. He saw the potential for a defeated France to pose a very real danger to Britain. The French still possessed the fourth largest navy in the world. If this force joined with the German navy, Britannia would be imperilled. After France entered into an Armistice with both Germany and Italy, the French navy became a target for the British Prime Minister who launched Operation Catapult.

On 3rd July 1940 the bulk of the most powerful squadron of the French fleet, the *Marine Nationale*, was based at Mers-el-Kébir in Algeria, this country in North Africa was then considered an integral part and *département* of France. British forces made their presence known and gave the French the option to either join with the Royal Navy, scuttle their ships, or face destruction. They chose the latter and were preparing to resist. Britain intercepted an instruction to the French fleet to form up in battle order and the French fleet was consequently destroyed by the Royal Navy. French ships and a submarine of *La Royale*, as their national navy was also known, were captured when at rest in the English ports of Plymouth and Portsmouth and a French ship in British-held Alexandria in Egypt was voluntarily put out of action. Operations continued, and on 8th July at Oran, also in Algeria, other French ships and submarines were bombarded by British vessels. Operations were even conducted against the French in Senegal, West Africa, where as part of the Battle of Dakar, the Vichy French battleship *Richelieu*, amongst other craft, were attacked by a Royal Navy squadron. After her extensive damage was repaired, she defected to the Free French side.

In response French aircraft attacked Gibraltar and severed diplomatic relations with the United Kingdom, driving the French into a closer entanglement with Germany. France formally abolished the Third Republic and created Vichy France awarding Marshal Phillipe Pétain dictatorial powers. Although it never formally joined the German-led Axis, the Vichy government was collaborating with the Nazis. It was, however, a public relations success for Churchill. Operation Catapult showed to the world, particularly the United States, that Britain was intent on fighting on. The American President, Franklin Delano Roosevelt, concluded that Churchill and the UK would not surrender the Royal Navy to the Nazis. It was thought that handing this mighty force over to Germany would have been Hitler's main demand in a peace agreement. Americans could, therefore, invest in Britain's defence, especially her fleet, without the fear that they would inadvertently be helping Germany.

Any surrender of the Royal Navy would have been a mirror image of the German High Seas Fleet being gifted to Britain after the First World War. Notably, the German ships that sailed into captivity were scuttled by their crew on 21st June 1919. However, most were raised and salvaged. Some of their steel was later sold back to the Germans who used it to partly build a new fleet, the very one that threatened Britain in the Second World War.

Deal or no deal?

Britain had withdrawn from the continent but had no intention of agreeing to a deal with the German masters of the European mainland. To all intents and purposes, the British state was alone in Western Europe and was due to receive the full attention of Hitler's armed forces. This time the Luftwaffe would be used not to conquer but to bring the UK to the negotiating table and agree a deal with the Third Reich. With the Battle of France over and the Fall of France confirmed, the Battle of Britain was about to begin. The early phases saw the Germans attacking shipping and coastal cities. The Channel War was an attempt to clear the English Channel of shipping, it was the prelude to the aerial conflict we know as the Battle of Britain. Air Chief Marshal Hugh Dowding, the Air Officer Commanding RAF Fighter Command, did not defend the shipping, he wanted to save Britain's air power for the main conflict, the battle for air superiority over the skies of England.

The Battle of Britain began on 10th July 1940 and lasted until the end of October that same year. The Royal Air Force, and its bases, came under direct attack. This was the first demonstration in history of a battle being primarily fought in the air. The quest for air supremacy is now the first object of any aggressive action being the prerequisite for success in any conventional military conflict in the modern era. The events of 1940 marked a turning point in military thinking. Previously, command of the sea was regarded as all important by the British, indeed it was the very basis of not just her empire but also the nascent Japanese, American and, with their U-boats and commerce raiders, German imperia. Events and thinking were rapidly evolving.

The belief that the bomber will always get through was prevalent amongst all sides be they members of the Axis or the Allies. Airpower was being used to end the enemy's economic ability to wage war, destroying their infrastructure and capacity to produce arms. Bombing went even further than this material aim, it attempted to fight a psychological battle against an opponent's population. The German bombing campaign known as the Blitz was the intentional attacking of Britain's population, economic centres, and infrastructure, with London meted out for special attention. The Battle of London, as it became known, began on 7th September, it lasted 57 consecutive nights. It began after the Luftwaffe mistakenly hit civilian areas in London, and in response Britain attacked Berlin and provoked Hitler into hitting back with vigour against British civilians, especially those in Britain's capital. This period certainly allowed the RAF to recover, refit and repair planes, pilots and bases, after the desperate fighting for air superiority when they lost 466 planes in just two weeks from August 24th. The tide was now certainly turning against the Luftwaffe.

Traditionally the deliberate targeting of civilians was regarded as counter-productive and instead of knocking the fight out of a country it is thought that it strengthened resolve. However, this was not entirely the reality. As a result of German bombing of the industrial heart of Britain's capital city, the East End of London, the conflict was profoundly unpopular with locals who were the terrorised victims of the war. Communists were particularly opposed to this conflict; many saw it as the latest 'bosses' war.

Hitler, throughout the so-called Battle of Britain, and the fighting in North Africa that followed, was aiming to force the UK to the negotiating table and create a peace agreement on German terms. Hitler's militant strategy towards Britain was the extension of policy by other means. He sought to coax Britain into renouncing its conflict with the latest pretender to the title of European hegemon and induce Britain into agreeing to negotiations in 1940 and thus secure peace on his western flank, allowing him to look east. The strategy was four-pronged. Firstly, the Führer threatened invasion. The second phase involved attack from the air. This bombing aimed to not only degrade Britain's defences but sought to break the public's will to fight who would then force the government to agree to a settlement. Thirdly, to supplement the aerial conflict, and reduce the British Empire's capacity to wage war on the Reich, the Führer unleashed unrestricted submarine warfare and a raid on Britain's global commerce links. The aim was to sever Britain's supply routes through a cunning use of Germany's U-boat fleet, thus ending Britain's ability to trade and even to feed itself. Peace would then surely follow.

That was the theory, and the threat to Britain was profoundly serious. In 1939 two-thirds of Britain's food was brought in by ship. Many of these merchant vessels were destined for the bottom of the ocean. The British Isles had fertile land but also had a large population and lacked sufficient produce to fill its inhabitants' stomachs. That was why the agricultural revolution, innovation, and industrialisation had been essential to Britain's national development. Necessity had driven Britain's global quest for, and reliance on, overseas resources. This enabled Britain to become even more densely populated, and just exacerbated the problem. (The UK remains overcrowded and comparatively under-resourced to this day). Imperial produce fed mouths, but, in 1940 this supply was at risk. Attacking Britain's sea-lanes was surely a winning strategy for Hitler; even though, when it was tried a generation before in World War I, it was Germany that was starving as the war drew to a close. The fourth prong was diplomacy. Hitler sought to isolate Britain internationally. Hitler had a diplomatic campaign against Britain first seeking to get Spain into the conflict against Britain by promising Franco territory, but the Spanish Head of State, or Caudillo, priced his service to highly. Hitler then tried to get the Vichy regime of Pétain more embroiled in the dispute in exchange for captured British territory, the Old Marshal, however, refused. It was a fraudulent strategy akin to the multiple selling of shares in real estate interests that were not even owned or controlled by Hitler. Spain and what remained of France were being asked to go into debt and invest in an outcome that was far from certain in the hope that the market, the military conflict, would swing in their favour. The dictatorial leaders of those nations were wise to be sceptical.

Generally, Hitler's approach to winning Britain as an ally was the very toughest of tough love, a strange way to court the British political establishment. To Hitler, a man who was always overbearing in his desires and personal relationships, such an approach was logical. Yet, like many spurned lovers his wrath would in time be unleashed in multiple acts of vengeance on the object of his desire. Hitler thought himself a military genius, but he was at most, if one is charitable, a gifted amateur when dabbling in military affairs. His main skills were in ruthless political manoeuvring and above all else his greatest ability was in the craft of communications, and not the art of war.

Project fear

Blitzkrieg was as much political as it was military; its beauty was that it convinced its victims to cease their resistance without too much of Germany's limited resources being expended. Germany's next step was to take this approach to a whole new level. As Prime Minister Winston Churchill said, "Hitler knows that he will have to break us in this Island or lose the war." Everything was to play for.

On 16th July 1940 Führer Directive No. 16 was issued. Operation Sea Lion had come into being. This was ostensibly the plan to invade England by force. It was, however, nothing of the sort. Operation Sea Lion was little more than a hoax, part of Hitler's great bluff to bring Britain to heel. Hitler was a reckless degenerate gambler, when he did not hold a hand sufficiently strong enough to guarantee the win, he feigned threats and used guile and bluff to secure victory. However, this ruse was seen, and his bluff called.

In 'plane' sight aerial reconnaissance would have shown a German invasion fleet primarily made of converted river barges to be towed by tugs being constructed to land the Wehrmacht on the southern coast of England. Could they have safely delivered the jackboot to Britain's green and pleasant land? The reality was that this armada, with its flat-bottomed craft, was totally unsuited to the channel crossing. They would have been unable to cope with the English Channel's choppy waters when out on the open sea, presuming they would have even made it that far. The Royal Navy, when they castoff from their berths on the Orkney Islands' Scapa Flow naval base, would have obliterated Hitler's ramshackle 'invasion' fleet. The British fleet could steam south from its natural harbour sheltered from both the high seas and from attack by the Luftwaffe whose bases were far away, the ships would have easily covered the putative landing sites and cut-off any German forces that made it ashore, preventing resupply, and reinforcement.

The moat

British leadership knew that invasion was impossible. Renowned military theorist Basil Liddell Hart wrote in his 1939 book *The Defence of Britain*, that "The risk of sea-borne invasion by a foreign enemy has become so slight under modern conditions as to be almost negligible". Unable to destroy the mighty Royal Navy, the German's response was to mine Britain's waters to destroy both shipping and choke-off the sea lanes thus strangling the UK. This was a technological conflict as much as it was one of resources. British countermeasures against the German sonic and electro-magnetic activated mines beat the immediate danger of the nation being forced into a state of famine because the Nazi strategy had been anticipated. As early as 1938, as the war clouds rose on the horizon, and before the blood red sky of the following year, plans were underway to develop food security. Appeasement had bought time for a country that was slow out of its peaceful slumber.

Detailed plans were developed to ensure that the British people would not go hungry. The Dig for Victory campaign was propagated to the whole nation, but especially to the industrial working class. It encouraged people to develop green fingers so that even those in cities and urban areas could help produce the food that would keep Britain in the fight. Royal Horticultural Society publications such as *The Vegetable Garden Displayed* detailed how all could turn their gardens as well as urban parkland into farmland. Because of universal compulsory education British people had the ability to follow these comprehensive guides to growing their own sustenance.

The dirty industrialisation of the UK during the Victorian era, a far from ecologically friendly time, had led to early and highly successful efforts to green the urban environment. The industrial working class, who lived cheek by jowl with each other and in the shadow of belching factory chimneys, were, even in crowded London provided with great parks through which the air would be freshened and made not only benign but life giving. These "lungs of London" would be turned into the original urban farms that would help feed Britain's manufacturing centres, and substantially reduce food miles allowing for a better allocation of resources.

By 1945 there were 1.4 million allotments that produced 1 million tons of food. The little battalions of amateur farmers had helped thwart Hitler's plans just as the little ships had saved the Army from capture at Dunkirk. By the close of the war Britain had halved its reliance on food imports. More shipping was thus reserved for the ferrying of armaments. The temperate climate, though at times inclement, benefitted Britain. The UK is mild for a land at a high latitude. Its surrounding seas and the Atlantic conveyor belt, part of which includes the Gulf Stream and its North Atlantic Drift, bring relatively warm waters, and weather, from the Caribbean to the British Isles. This along with the once extensive farming, flora, and historical tree cover throughout Albion gave the UK rich soils that could, with care, be turned back to wholesome food production even in the cities. Underdeveloped, and in some cases, non-existent sewage systems throughout large parts of the UK provided easily accessible fertiliser for the kitchen garden. The nation of shopkeepers had become a nation of farmers. Hitler's dream of an agrarian economy had been surpassed.

These measures augmented the UK's farming industry. By the end of the war Britain was producing 91% of its food within the UK. Tractors, the vehicle that helped Britain win the First World War when they had been the inspiration for the tank, helped the UK in this the Second part of the great enduring conflict with Germany. The production of tractors was prioritised and were provided to farmers to ensure that agriculture was efficient. As in World War One, women were deployed to the farming front as part of the Women's Land Army. Originally the Land Girls, as they were known, were volunteers, but as the war continued women were conscripted into the Women's Land Army. Britain was not going to go hungry and could not be starved into submission.

Even though Britain was safe from conquest, at least for the time being, the defence of the UK from sea, air, and land remained an urgent priority. Churchill's administration requested 50 destroyers from the United States. The aim was to sure-up the UK's naval defences in exchange for providing the Americans with bases on the many island possessions which the UK held close to the eastern seaboard of the United States. This was amongst the worst deals in British history; most of the donated ships were not serviceable, with only 30 operational nearly a year later. This was the beginning of both the 'special relationship' between the cousins and *Pax Americana* with the United States taking up, as Rudyard Kipling saw it, the white man's burden over much of the globe. President Roosevelt, however, did little to support non-white communities in his Democrat Party's southern homeland. The putative partnership between the two English-speaking colossi, the British Empire and the United States of America created a new order where the sun would never set on America's extensive network of bases. The goal of embroiling the might of President Roosevelt's USA in the war had however been served and British fears of an immediate German threat were somewhat assuaged.

Churchill, whose mother was American, had US soldiers firmly in his sights and wanted their active involvement. The British Prime Minister tried to use charm as well as guile and dire warnings. He sought to win over Roosevelt, by often referring to himself as a former naval person in his letters to the American President. Roosevelt enjoyed sailing, and Churchill hoped to use this connection to build rapport with his US counterpart. Churchill wrote to Roosevelt on 14th June 1940 warning that a German dominated United States of Europe would threaten the New World, that is the Americas. That was certainly the aim of Hitler, who wanted to challenge the racially mixed capitalist and mostly democratic US behemoth. Yet, in Churchill's quest for more support, he was not entirely open and honest with his American counterpart. Churchill withheld from Roosevelt the fact that he knew there would be no German invasion of Britain in 1940. Later he would use his oratory to try to coax America into being ever more deeply embroiled in this European conflict. Despite Churchill saying in early 1941 to the US Congress, "Give us the tools and we will finish the job". He knew that this was not possible, and that Britain could only fight a holding action until the Americans came into the war. Nevertheless, Britain was still independent, its sovereignty endured.

The defence of the skies was well underway before the war began. Military production focused on aircraft and farsighted British authorities had invested in an early warning radar system. This network of radar stations reporting back to a central command was known as 'Chain Home'. British ingenuity and inventiveness had provided the technology that gave the Royal Air Force the information it needed to defend Britain's skies, and by extension the homeland, from the Luftwaffe.

The British nation's defence was not confined to the RAF in the skies and the Royal Navy at sea. The Army still had a role, and preparations were also made on land. Concentric stop lines were created to defend the Empire's capital city from advancing German forces. This antiquated defensive planning was later replaced by more modern tactics but for the time being multiple mini-Maginot lines were conceived. Indeed, the original inspiration for such fixed defences against a theoretical invasion came from France. The alarm caused by a French naval build-up towards the end of the nineteenth century generated fears that Britain's great rival across the English Channel would cross this short waterway and advance on London. To defend its capital Britain established a defensive line known as the London Defence Positions with supporting strong points, or redoubts, called London Mobilisation Centres. These, however, quickly became antiquated as were earlier iterations of fixed defences such as the Palmerston Forts, and the earlier constructed Martello Towers which were built in response to the Napoleonic threat. During the Second World War, attack by sea was also defended by bastions erected in the Thames estuary. Since the decommissioning of these Maunsell Forts the sovereignty of some of these armed towers in the sea have been disputed between the United Kingdom and the internationally unrecognised Principality of Sealand.

In the unlikely event of a German invasion the shore was defended by pillboxes, and the beaches where a German landing was deemed to be most probable had petroleum mines planted. These flame fougasse, as they were known, would incinerate both men and materiel that were in proximity to these weapons. They were also installed inland as part of the stop lines that stretched across southern-England and circled London, the epicentre of opposition to Nazi hegemony over Europe. Numerous European governments in exile, from Poland to Norway, were based in the UK's capital.

Britain was at this point still fighting the last war, employing outmoded tactics based on static defence. This was to be shaken up by an innovative commander who was to achieve fame and take a pivotal role in the fighting that was to follow, General Bernard Law Montgomery. His defensive plans focused on mobile defence rather than fixed positions. In 1941 he was made Commander-in-Chief, South-East Command. After assuming command of XII Corps, he was placed in charge in the most probable place where any German invasion could take place, the southeast of England. Montgomery improved the British Army's ability to defend the south coast by emphasising the need for a mobile aggressive defence should any attack come. But what would have happened if the Nazis had attempted to cross the channel?

What if?

Operation Sea Lion would have entailed German forces crossing the English Channel from embarkation points in northern France and Belgium. They would have had assistance from coastal guns, the Kriegsmarine, Luftwaffe, and even from Mussolini's Italian fighter aircraft and bombers. The result of this hypothetical invasion has been tested and the outcome as good as proved without the need for any weapons to be discharged in anger. In 1974 a wargame was conducted at the Royal Military Academy, Sandhurst, the elite British training college, as to how Operation Sea Lion would have progressed. Senior British and German military personnel were the wargamers playing the key roles of each of the senior protagonists including the main commanders. The real-life control structures were also mirrored. This veritable anthropoid computer produced a probable invasion date of 22nd September 1940. This allowed for the supposed grinding down of the RAF's capabilities, time for the Axis to prepare, assemble the invasion force and its shipping. It also considered when fair weather would be likely, tides, and real-life meteorological reports before the window for clement conditions would close.

It surmised that the invasion force, to be delivered over several beaches in several waves, with the *Fallschirmjäger*, parachutists, delivered by air, would consist of 330,000 men. Ten divisions would make it to England but did not manage to cross in their entirety and they lacked supplies from the beginning. Capturing and holding major ports, especially those that were undamaged and still suitably usable, beyond the unloading of token amounts of troops, proved beyond the invaders. Arguably that was a moot point, the Kriegsmarine were not in complete control of the channel, and many transports were lost. That was even before the Royal Navy's capital ships were committed to the fray, which would only have happened if Germany had committed the Kriegsmarine's big ships. In this wargame they did not venture into the English Channel. The Luftwaffe, despite being considered stronger than the Royal Air Force in the invasion, was not able to eliminate its British counterpart. The RAF's fighters, interceptors, and bombers continued to harry those Germans who made it ashore and harass and sink Hitler's ramshackle invasion barges, 65% of those in the second wave were sunk.

The result of this exercise, and the application of thirty of the best military minds available, was that any putative invasion would have seen a British victory after as little as six days of fighting. Despite a predicted rescue attempt the wargame estimated that only 15,400 German soldiers would make it back across the channel to occupied Europe. The rest would have been killed or captured with many wounded. For them, the war would have been over. As the disaster unfurled Hitler was compelled to move German reserves to Poland. This would have been to protect his seemingly vulnerable eastern flank. The losses experienced in Germany's vain attempt to conquer Britain, could have had geopolitical consequences emboldening Hitler's great rival, the Georgian dictator of the Soviet Union, Joseph Stalin, and his Red Army. To put it simply, Operation Sea Lion was not a credible plan It may also be theorised that an invasion force could never have succeeded in even crossing the channel in significant numbers to extend the fighting to as much as the six days which the wargamers generously ascribed to the German occupation of small parts of southern England.

The five years of warfare that lay ahead were to become almost as much a war in the sea, and the air, as it was on land. The evolving and expanding conflict tested the requirements for a successful operation across water be that the English Channel, the Pacific Ocean, or even the Rhine River. Demanding criteria had to be fulfilled for such an operation to be anything but an abject failure. The conditions for success included control of the sea as well as superiority in the air. It also required the delivery and the means to deliver and then reinforce and continually resupply the men who made the crossing with arms and fuel. How the German army, which still used horse-drawn transport, could have met this enormous logistical challenge was never satisfactorily answered. The German High Command was relieved when the real Operation Sea Lion was indefinitely postponed. Enlightened armies, even the Wehrmacht in the 1940s, unofficially relied upon a covenant with their soldiers to keep their consent for the operation and to protect morale, especially when facing an enemy that would abide by the rules of war. In order to maintain their enthusiasm, it would also have been necessary to provide a means to evacuate and treat sick and wounded personnel, yet another challenge that could not have been met.

Such an assault required extensive planning and preparation. Fair weather and favourable terrain on the opposing bank, or shore was needed. Then a secure beachhead would have to be made. Following that, the holding and aggressive expansion of a lodgement was needed and then an invasion would have to force a breakout into the surrounding land. This was as much of a requirement as getting ashore. Indeed, there were at times hard lessons to learn along the way especially by Canadian forces during the Dieppe Raid, or by the US Army at Anzio, and by the US Marines on the numerous D-days in the Pacific. It is inconceivable to think that Hitlerian forces could have scrambled across the English Channel in autumn and not only hold their positions but also exploit them to conquer the small but densely populated island of Great Britain which was still able to manufacture weapons in her defence.

Answering 'what ifs' produces other possible scenarios that would have cascaded through the war. The immediate aftermath beyond the obvious destruction of the invasion forces would have echoed across the globe. It is likely that the inevitable British victory would have garnered more support from Britain's American cousins. It would have not only generated sympathy but also admiration, it would have been an overwhelming triumph. Americans like a winner. This would have given President Roosevelt even more latitude to support Britain's war effort. It would have been a great advertisement for British resolve. Such a success would have proved that the UK had the stomach and means for the fight. And would send a much bigger message than even that which the Royal Navy had sent when on Churchill's orders they attacked the French fleet in North Africa on 3rd July 1940. Incidentally, the fact that Churchill dispatched naval forces to the Mediterranean prior to the Battle of Britain showed that the British Prime Minister was merely scaremongering and sabre-rattling when he had told the House of Commons that "we will fight them on the beaches". It was hyperbole.

Defeating a Nazi invasion of the UK mainland would have proved to the Americans beyond all reasonable doubt that supporting the British war effort was an endeavour worth investing in. The extensive backing that would have surely followed may perhaps have been delivered without US leaders thinking they had the *carte blanche* right to request that the British Empire be relinquished as the price of Uncle Sam's support.

As will be explained in later chapters, Japan, who was concerned about missing the boat, would have seen that aggression had its limits and that Nazi Germany's militarism was not infallible. Demonstrating that an attack across even as short a distance as the English Channel was unviable may well have led Japan to question the efficacy of attacks across the vast expanse of the Pacific Ocean.

Japan may well have thought twice before launching their military adventures against the numerous islands dotted across the south seas. The Battle of Britain never became the Fall of Britain. It remained a conflict that, apart from naval skirmishes, manifested itself primarily in aerial combat. What this signified for warfare, a whole battle fought in its own right in the skies and not merely to assist ground forces but to decide who controls the seemingly all-important airspace, was of equal magnitude to the outcome of the aerial battle. Was the Battle of Britain as crucial as the propagandists enunciated?

The myth of the few

"Never in the field of human conflict was so much owed by so many to so few."—**British Prime Minister Winston Churchill, 20th August 1940.**

The mythology of the Battle of Britain is epitomised by the imagery of the Supermarine Spitfire, a slick single-seat fighter. It is believed to have both saved the UK, and to have defeated the Luftwaffe. In fact, the slower but more manoeuvrable, and numerous, Hawker Hurricane shot down more German planes during the battle. The rugged airframe of the Hurricane, though quickly outdated as an interceptor, found a second purpose as a ground attack aircraft, a veritable flying gun mount which delivered its deadly payload in theatres far afield from the British mainland. In this role its 40mm cannons would open up and destroy German tanks in North Africa and at the least pinned down the Germans and denied Rommel's forces the opportunity to concentrate and manoeuvre en masse. At the same time its tubular framed steel skeleton wrapped in canvas gave it the advantage that even cannon shells fired directly at it could pass straight through without seriously damaging this warbird. This later usefulness was an instance of serendipity and came from the need to defend the skies, which it did admirably, but it also helped deliver a victory on land during one of the first turning points of World War II. This was in the fighting in North Africa as well as when it defended the skies over Malta, the Hurricane's other service was to prove crucial to the outcome of the war.

However, the Spitfire, a fighter plane that was state of the art even when compared to the Hurricane, was to capture the public's imagination; indeed, it was a PR man's dream. The Spitfire became a vehicle to sell the war to the British people and to make them invest in the outcome. This iconic plane, a Jaguar

E-Type of the skies, was the poster child for a fundraising effort to help finance the war. The public, including local authorities, and businesses, were encouraged to give towards 'Spitfire Funds' the monies raised would seemingly be used to pay for the plane's production. The English County of Kent was the only shire that purchased their own squadron for the RAF through the Kent County Spitfire Fund. However, these fighters were more often based in neighbouring counties. Generally, the government did not entirely allocate the funds as advertised. A serious case of mis selling. Nevertheless, the home front now had a tangible stake in the war and felt that they at least in part owned the outcome. It had become their war; the British would do whatever it took to win.

The wartime economy was also to benefit from voluntary taxation. Funding the war effort partly through such contributions, rather than relying solely on borrowing to fill the deficit between what was taken in taxation and what was spent, helped prevent the spectre of inflation from developing. The contributions helped give the government the financial firepower it needed to fund the war. It not only helped keep down ruinous levels of debt and allowed the government to avoid flooding the economy with borrowed cash. Thus, an oversupply in the quantity of money in circulation was averted. Otherwise, there may have been devaluation and runaway inflation, perhaps it even kept hyperinflation out of the system. Although the beautiful lines of the Spitfire and the shape of its elliptical wing were not the most efficient to produce, they were arguably the most elegant solution to the lift-to-drag conundrum. Only this stylish design could seduce the nation into supporting the war effort to the extent that they were willing to give without resorting to coercion. The Spitfire Fund contrived to make people feel involved. The public were even asked to donate their old saucepans, being told they would be made into a Spitfire, but were however completely useless in that regard. The scrap metal collected did not build the aircraft. Yet, the British public's romance with the Spitfire lives on.

The RAF's heroic knights of the sky were also assisted in their battle by the signals provided by Chain Home (codename for a chain of early warning radar stations) and the RAF took full advantage of airbases in close proximity to the battle above. Damaged planes could easily be repaired and reintroduced to combat. Pilots would rest, refuel and be back in service the same day. This gave the Royal Air Force, which was fighting over its home territory, a relative local superiority in numbers over their German adversaries. The Luftwaffe in having to cross the channel would expend most of their fuel making the journey to Britain and back to their bases in France. Some were fated to never make the return journey. When a German plane was damaged in combat the likelihood would be that both man and machine would be lost to Hitler's war effort. They would either be downed over enemy held territory or would ditch in the seas that guarded the British Isles; and these waters were policed by the Royal Navy. Some German pilots were shredded by machine gun fire or killed when they crashed.

The pilots of the Royal Air Force were aided by superior British aircraft production that outstripped that of Germany. Nazi aircraft production could not replace the losses it was experiencing in its reckless attacks over skies defended by barrage balloons, 'Ack-Ack' also known as anti-aircraft artillery (triple A and AAA) as well as the RAF's Spitfires and Hurricanes. This made it a battle that Hermann Göring, the head of the Luftwaffe, could not win. If the German attacks had continued, the Fatherland would have had few planes and pilots left. Their overconfidence, understandably spawned after early victories on the continent, along with the fog of war, led them to believe that they were ahead in the numbers game. The Germans overestimated their successes over the skies of England and Wales. In the confusing scenario of a dogfight the Luftwaffe had, on occasion, mistakenly double counted their victories. The Nazis were to receive a shock. The British in possession of the land and exercising control of the seas below knew the real military situation. The RAF was winning and in time this became clear. Britain's aircraft industry during the war produced 131,500 planes and by 1944 employed more people than were serving in the British Army.

Churchill's famous quote about the debt owed to the pilots was rhetoric from the original master of spin and was not a succinct and precise military analysis. Britain could defend itself and was secure in its island fortress – what Shakespeare had described as a moat. The untarnished strength of the Royal Navy was of prime importance in denying the Germans the opportunity to test Britain's superiority on home soil. Furthermore, it was a myth that the United Kingdom was standing alone. It had the might of the British Empire and Commonwealth of nations behind it. Countries such as Australia, who had close ethnic and political links with the mother country enthusiastically joined the war effort. As did New Zealanders, and not just those whose families originated from the British Isles. The Māoris, a group of native Polynesian inhabitants of New Zealand, also took part and fought against Germany; this is despite their ancestors several generations before being involved in uprisings against British colonial authorities. The resistance against the Victorian era New Zealand government was, however, far from uniform. Some Māoris fought for the colonial forces against those tribes that were in revolt. Today some renegade Māori motorcycle gangs use Nazi symbolism and salutes to signify their rebellious nature. However, these strange rituals do not represent an endorsement of Hitler's ideology which they would despise.

The Union of South Africa also joined with the UK, despite many of its citizens having been fighting, often with great success, and with some support from Germany, against the British Empire in two Boer Wars. The second of which had only ended as recently as 1902. Yet, South Africa was loyal to the Allied war effort. Indeed, so much so that the South African Prime Minister and polymath, Field Marshal Jan Smuts, was named by Churchill as his successor as British Prime Minister, should Churchill have been killed or otherwise incapacitated. No less remarkable a feat for this remarkable man as he had once led commando operations against the British in the Second Boer War. Incidentally, after World War Two Smuts opposed the introduction of apartheid in South Africa but was defeated in the 1948 election in his homeland. The new government then introduced the policy of separateness, i.e., segregation of the races. Smuts also helped draft the United Nations Charter and was a potential candidate for the Nobel Peace Prize.

Canada also voluntarily fought alongside the British. Whilst the *Québécois* were generally less willing to become involved in Britain's war, Canada remained loyal to the UK, sending many troops. Indeed, this was first proposed by General Andrew G.L. McNaughton as early as December 1932 in 'Defence Scheme No. 3'. This plan was devised to send an expeditionary force to aid Britain in time of war. He wrote to his British counterpart, the Chief of the Imperial General Staff, "the most serious or important issue for which we ... require to be organized concerns itself with the mobilization and dispatch of a Canadian Expeditionary Force to take part in an Empire War of first magnitude." McNaughton was to lead this force, the 1st Canadian Infantry Division, into action in 1940. As the number of Canadian soldiers grew, this division became an army; and McNaughton subsequently took command of the First Canadian Army. However, McNaughton was not a supporter of conscription instead he favoured a volunteer army. This perhaps only emphasizes still further the level of commitment from Canadians to the war effort. Newfoundland was then not a province of Canada; it was fully part of the Empire and automatically joined the war effort when Britain declared war.

Innate strength

Nine governments-in-exile were based in Britain and put their limited resources at Britain's disposal. These conquered continental European states provided men for the war effort, this especially strengthened the RAF which benefited from

Czech and Polish pilots who had fled their German occupied home countries. During the Battle of Britain, the most successful squadron was the Polish 303 Squadron, one of 16 Polish fighter groups serving with the RAF. They exhibited a blood lust driven by a thirst for revenge over what had been done to their native land. They were angels of vengeance on behalf of their defeated land and enslaved compatriots.

The Germans were likewise not unaided during the Battle of Britain. A division of the Italian air force, the *Regia Aeronautica*, also did their worst. The *Corpo Aereo Italiano* was dispatched by Mussolini to northern France during the later stages of the aerial conflict. Their contribution was far from decisive and in no way equalled, let alone countered the international elements working in Britain's defence. The Essex port of Harwich was bombed as was its counterpart across the Stour and Orwell estuaries, the port of Felixstowe, in the county of Suffolk. Deal and Ramsgate in Kent were also targeted after the Battle of Britain had already been decided in favour of the Royal Air Force. The arms race in quantity was being won by the British as was the technological battle. Developments in fuel gave the RAF a boost, literally. During the Battle of Britain aviation spirit was upgraded from 87 to 100 octane fuel. This allowed the engine to deliver more power and it increased efficiency; it also reduced emissions; it is unlikely that the environmental benefits were considered at the time. The Germans could not understand how the performance of British planes increased until a Spitfire, downed over occupied Europe, was analysed.

These events, taken together, meant that militarily Britain was secure. Over-stretched German airpower was fighting at the limits of its range in a misplaced offensive. The geography with the need to expend time and energy crossing the Channel was the key factor. The Germans attempted to counter the fatigue and cope with the demands of combat by drugging their pilots with methamphetamine, later dubbed 'crystal meth'. This perfect imitation of their Führer provided a short-term stimulant and energised their attacks, but the long-term implications of this drug abuse was a loss of performance. The chemical became a catalyst for German defeat. The British countered this move by providing amphetamine, a less damaging stimulant, to its pilots.

The moat served to not only protect Britain but also inhibited its offensive capability and in the first half of the Second World War it especially hampered the RAF's ability to take the fight back to the Germans. Following the Battle of Britain Churchill ordered the RAF to take the offensive across the English Channel against the Luftwaffe based in France. Here the RAF suffered a setback like the one experienced by the German air force when it fought over the skies of Britain.

The assembly lines would keep Britain free. There was a simple equation at work. If the rate of shooting down the opponent remains greater than losses and aircraft production stays higher than the enemy, then victory is assured. The businessman Lord Beaverbrook was made Minister of Aircraft Production in May 1940. Under his leadership the weapons the RAF needed were provided in plentiful numbers. Britain was producing the most planes in the world. By 1942 Britain had produced 23,672 aircraft, Germany just 15,409. The seemingly desperate need to produce more aircraft included bombers. By the wars end Bomber Command had the tools to drop 100 times more bombs than the Luftwaffe. The firestorm was coming. They destroyed more of the enemy's machines and men than were lost. The equation extended to more than just aircraft.

Nazi economic humanity vs Anglo-Saxon free market efficiency

German philosopher Professor Martin Heidegger, author of *Being and Time*, put into words what the Nazis were thinking. He sought to influence, even use, the Nazis to bring about a more natural and people centric system of economic organisation, a new era where lives were not ruled by the clock where people are serving a machine. It was a rejection of Anglo-American automatonism and was thus a denial of modern economic reality.

The Nazis intellectually rejected the mechanized labour system where the worker was an extension of a machine, serving a process he did not understand and where he never saw the fruits of his labour. They objected to men being just some part of an almost abstract process, that somehow and somewhere away from his workstation, miraculously produced a finished product out of his sight. They also intellectually rejected the hours of the working day as well as the working processes that were born out of the industrial revolution. In advanced economies workers would be abruptly woken from their slumber by the knocker-upper unfeelingly tapping at their bedroom window with a long pole or through a peashooter until they were awake. They were being summoned to obey and worship the whims of a machine in a dark satanic mill. The employees were paid according to the time that they spent toiling as an extension of that device carrying out just one process. Paid in Lsd, pounds, shillings and pence, the worker was remunerated at an hourly rate determined by an abstract formula applied by a managerial class; this was dehumanising. It contrasts with piece work where the individual worker is paid according to each unit of what they actually produced.

The hours of work undertaken in almost all developed economies are an unnatural invention stemming from the industrial revolution. It is a system that is still in existence today, though the abuse is now self-inflicted and coming from the electric tones of an alarm clock or a mobile phone. The introduction of home and flexible working hours and a more scientific understanding of how different people are more productive at different points in the day, or night, as the case maybe, may change this callous order. The benefit of being in communication with other time zones is also beginning to gnaw away at the edges of this modern concept and organisation of time. Yet, during the Second World War the battle of economic visions was won by the capitalist nations, the consequences of which still upset many people's circadian rhythms. Even in the post-industrial economy workers are seated in large office blocks, serving information systems in employment that deprives them of exercise and daylight. That is unless one has been lucky enough to remain working from home.

The British however celebrated the stupidification of its workers and celebrated the system that the Nazis despised. Indeed, wartime propaganda extolled its virtues in "The Thing-Ummy Bob (That's Gonna Win The War)" song, performed by English actress, singer, and comedienne Gracie Fields. She sung,

"I can't pretend to be a great celebrity.
But still I'm quite important in my way
The job I have to do may not sound much to you.
But all the same I'm very proud to say.
I'm the girl that makes the thing that drills the hole that holds the
Ring that drives the rod that turns
The knob that works the thingy a me-bob.
I'm the girl that makes the thing that holds the oil that oils the
Ring that takes the shank that moves
The crank that works the thingy a me bob.
It's a ticklish sort of job making a thing for the
Thingy a me bob especially when you don't know what it's for.
But it's the girl that makes the thing the drills the hole that
Holds the ring that makes the thingy
A me bob that makes the engine roar.
And it's the girl that makes the thing that holds the oil that
Oils the ring that makes the thingy a me bob that's going to win the war.
I'm not what you'd would call a heroin at all
I don't suppose you'd even know me name

But though I never boast of my important post
I'll strike a blow for freedom just the same.

That works the thingy a me bob.
That works the thingy a me bob.

Its a ticklish sort of job making the thing for the
Thingy a me bob especially when you don't know what it's for
But it's the girl that makes the thing that drills the hole that holds
The ring that makes the thingy a me bob that makes the engines roar and
It's the girl that makes the thing that holds the oil that oils
The ring that makes the thingy a me bob that's going to win the war.
It is 'n' all."

This explained how the war was to be won. It is this industrial process in Britain and America, both of which aided the Soviets, when the USSR stopped aiding the Germans, that won the war. The ruthlessly efficient and unnatural work pattern developed by industrialists to serve their profit margins rather than respect the circadian rhythms and creative needs of their workers was to win the war for the Allies. Conversely, the Germans were romanticising about the eternal forest and everyman controlling his destiny on a small holding.

There serves no better example of the German failure to embrace the Allied economic system and throw away what industrial advantage they had than the case of the German aviation industry. Prior to the war Germany possessed an advanced aircraft production capability. This was not surprising as civil aviation companies were secretly working with the German military as early as the 1920s, long before the Nazis came anywhere close to power. The aim of this, the original military-industrial complex conspiracy, was to bypass the terms of the Versailles Treaty which forbade Germany from having an air force. The clandestine cooperation sought to have an oven ready functioning Luftwaffe primed to be deployed when the time was right for Germany to retake its place as a leading European power.

German industry produced military planes but pretended they were civilian. These covert weapons were tested at secret bases in the Soviet Union where pilots and tactics were honed. These two pariah nations, both of which were given a belated entry into the League of Nations, had a Faustian Pact. The Germans provided military knowledge to the USSR in exchange for the use of secret military training bases in Russia.

Notwithstanding, the early problems, the foundations of the German aviation industry were flawed. Whilst the end product was superb, the production process was not. The Nazis did not like modern production methods. They idealised handicraft and small-scale production where the worker could use their skill as an artisan employing their trade. The work of these craftsmen was slower and not as efficient as modern mass production methods. Instead, it relied on men working by hand, shaping metal using an English wheel. Germany was dominated by industries whose antiquated working methods could not easily be scaled up. Even at the time this was an outmoded system compared to how factories worked in the USA, the UK, and those provided by America to the USSR. The Germans did not employ efficient production lines, conversely, they relied on labour intensive work practices that were both costly and slow. Too many spare parts had to be manufactured by hand and were not uniformly produced and interchangeable across different types of weapons. They were therefore not readily available close to the front. This prevented the German military from establishing a system for replacing damaged parts on planes close to where they were needed. Both the Luftwaffe, Germany's air weapon, and the *Deutsches Heer*, the German Army, thus lacked an efficient forward repair system, requiring the time consuming and logistically difficult process of removing the damaged vehicle and transporting it far from the frontline. This meant taking weapons out of the fighting for too long, adding to Germany's local inferiority in the number of machines in combat at a given place.

Furthermore, to train up a skilled sheet metal worker would take as much as four years, sometimes more. As the war progressed there was a shortfall of skilled labour, so Germany turned to cheap slave labour to fill the gap. These workers were even less efficient. Nazi racial theory led them to despise certain peoples as subhuman; many slaves emanated from ethnically diverse Russia and the rest of the USSR. This general contempt for their fellow man, combined with the belief that conquered people existed to serve the state, led the Germans to demand work without providing any incentives or positive inducements beyond not being hung or shot. Instead, in time they chose to work their minions to death. Failing to not only keep the workforce healthy but even neglecting to keep them alive was to further damage productivity. It also bred resentment. The slaves, ultimately totalling 12 million in number, vandalised much of their production. Through employing an alienated work force using processes that relied on handmade assembly, skill, and the attentiveness of the worker there were ample opportunities for sabotage. A missing ball bearing here, a cracked shaft there, would ultimately render the product unusable.

The German socialised system further undermined itself by taking industry out of the private hands of those who had built it and could innovate. The Nazis placed companies under the management of bureaucrats in the Reichswerke Hermann Göring, the German industrial state conglomerate that dominated industry in conquered Europe. The middle-manager pen-pushers centralised control was not a recipe for efficiency. And ultimately, they would be at the whim of the Führer and gave this paper hanger turned politician ample opportunity to intervene in matters he did not fully understand. Hitler would change production priorities with little consideration for the implications this would have on bringing out a finished product that could be delivered en masse. The Allies avoided this affliction and outproduced the Germans in all areas.

By 1942, even in tank production, Germany lagged behind the United Kingdom with as few as 2,159 tanks produced in the war so far, compared to 8,622 made in Britain. At the time Britain had the second biggest car industry in the world, its creative industrialists quickly adapted its factories to produce tanks for the war effort. As the war progressed Britain had enough spare capacity to send 3,000 tanks to Russia to help them in their desperate fight for survival. The United Kingdom was more than able to defend itself from attack. An attack that could not succeed because by 1942 Germany had built just five capital ships compared to the great ship building island nation that was the UK which had put 78 comparable vessels to sea in the same time frame.

Germany, despite being one of the largest economies in the world, would not develop in a way that could compete with its rivals. The German war economy was inefficient and lacked the ability to apply hyper-efficient and sophisticated production techniques that could put workable war machines into the battlespace in enough numbers to make the difference between victory and defeat. They could not donate enough resources to sufficiently develop their manufacturing to cope with the war of attrition which the Nazis had blundered into. History and geology had not fated Germany with a strong enough industrial economy to prosecute a drawn-out war against its more economically advanced rivals. The capitalist, free market economy that was developed in Britain, which incidentally Hitler despised, was too strong to be cowed. In time another Anglosphere country the United States, once an enemy of Great Britain and her Empire, would unleash upon the Nazis the full force of its free market might.

Like that of the UK, the American economy originally grew and developed in the absence of state control, and expanded because of the rarity of government interference. The business of America was business. Its enormous manufacturing base and economic potential was honed by the demands of consumerism and the profit motive. German minds were closed to learning from this system; the Nazis regarded it as Jewish and bourgeois and hence such economics would not be imitated. The individualism underpinning the industrialisation of both Britain and America deployed the most effective tools for prosperity and the war economy, namely incentive and initiative. Statist systems with collectivist cultures, where people expected and perhaps even desired to be told what to do, created and reinforced obedience; that comes at the expense of creativity. Systems built on personal responsibility encourage and reward innovative and ingenious solutions throughout all ranks and sectors of the economy. Germany could not compete and was ill-prepared. The aerial conflict of 1940 was the first German setback and demonstrated the absurdity of their deluded claim to dominion over Europe. They had conquered as far as the English Channel but would not and could not get further.

A damn close-run thing?

Whilst the fighting above was intense and British airspace was defended bravely, the land below was never in immediate danger of German occupation. The threat had become asymmetric, submarine versus ship. Instead of an invasion Hitler settled on trying to bring Britain to defeat via a war of attrition. He had the overriding aim to strangle the United Kingdom and isolate the British Isles from its overseas empire and loyal allies. German U-boats were the trident that would be used against Britannia.

The realisation that the Führer's invasion plan was bogus allowed Churchill to release more ships to defend the Atlantic convoys whose merchant mariners kept the United Kingdom afloat. However, even though a German crossing of the channel was anything but imminent, it still did not stop plans for the defence of southern-England from continuing to be enhanced and refined. The Fall of France, not to mention serious setbacks in Norway, Greece, and North Africa, had clearly left as deep a psychological scar on Britain as it had left physical damage on so many young men. The decline of Britain where the UK retreated from being a global power to just another European state was almost as much a loss of belief in herself as it was driven by economic materialism. In relative terms, especially when compared with the Soviet and American behemoths, the UK's post-war economy had been stagnating. Global growth was happening elsewhere. To compound this, in the decades that followed the Battle of Britain, many lacked the confidence that Britain could stand on its own. This was further compounded by events like the Suez Crisis, where both the USA and the USSR strenuously objected to Britain, France, and Israel acting in the middle east without superpower consent. Yet for some the rot had already set in. This in part stemmed from the belief that our freedom was close to being lost.

The belief persists that Britain was there for the taking if Germany had fought the Battle of Britain differently, such as by recognising the importance of the Chain Home radar early warning system. Or continuing to attack airfields rather than switching to a campaign of terror bombing. This led to a British inferiority complex relating to Germany which has, on occasions, shown itself; particularly when England plays Germany at football. It was represented in the tabloid press with the infamous 'Achtung! Surrender' headline in the *Daily Mirror* which appeared during the Euro 96 football tournament. After England lost to Germany, on penalties, some English football fans even took to the extreme lengths of vandalising Mercedes-Benz cars. The existence of these German cars on British streets stems from the middle-class belief that German marques and their engineering are somehow superior and to be coveted. Their alcohol fuelled desecration by working-class Londoners was the mirror image of bourgeois reverence. Whilst expressed differently these two quite contrasting phenomena were essentially expressing the same attitude, they both thought Germany was better.

The fact that Operation Sea Lion was never activated, there was no Nazi invasion of the United Kingdom, deprived Britain of the opportunity to achieve a decisive victory. Such a triumph that early in the war would have been a major fillip to the UK's national psyche. Any invasion would have not only surely failed but it would have led to the annihilation of German forces if they had been so bold as to attempt a channel crossing. Destroying numerous divisions and their arms, permanently removing them from the order of battle, would deprive Germany of much of the strength that was to still wreak havoc across Europe and North Africa. The Wehrmacht was, for the time being, free to do just that and would have to be destroyed later under circumstances and terrain that was less favourable to Britain. If there had been an invasion attempt the lack of self-confidence, may never have come into being. Such a folly on the part of Hitler would have given the British the opportunity to show to themselves that they can stand on their own two feet and win. The inevitable British victory would have been amongst the most celebrated of the war and seen as the decisive turning point. A victory that would have been secured without massive American support and without the Soviet's sapping German strength. It never happened because there was no truth to the myth of the few. Yet, romantic fables based on the reality of the RAFs very real gallantry, saving Britain's sovereignty, and preventing the UK from becoming a vassal state of the German suzerain was to have real implications.

The thinking which ultimately lead to the formation of the European Union was the belief amongst continental countries, particularly France, that Germany could not be constrained militarily. And therefore, France had to hold Germany closely in a political union to dissuade them from becoming belligerent. This view was shared by many in British politics and accordingly the UK first admired and then decided to enter this embrace believing the pooling of sovereignty was a necessary evil to protect some measure of peace and self-government. When the generation that fought in the war achieved political power it was seen by many in their cohort that Britain's vital interests could only be safeguarded by joining a European federation. The failed 1962 application to join the European Economic Community began the near six decades of British attempts to ingratiate itself with continental Europe. This long experiment was to ultimately fail and merely led Britain down a *cul-de-sac*.

If the UK had shown that England's defences were not overly vulnerable, then perhaps Britain would not have become part of the European Union. Instead, it would have followed both Winston Churchill's and Charles de Gaulle's advice that Britain should look to its overseas interests instead of Europe. It may have been better for the UK if it had instead collectively remembered the humorous paraphrasing of Churchill's famous oration on the role of the RAF made by his loyal lieutenant and future successor Anthony Eden. This came when Britain achieved its first major victory over Germany's Axis partner, the Kingdom of Italy, in North Africa during the Western Desert campaign. Following the destruction of the Italian 10th Army, which included the large-scale capitulation of its Italian and Libyan troops, Eden quipped that, "never in the field of human conflict has so much been surrendered by so many to so few". Fundamental flaws in military organisation and economic efficiency were not the sole preserve of the Italians.

The myth of the Nazi war machine
Hitler was a gambler; he had a grand vision of where he wanted to be, but he sought to get there one throw of a dice at a time. What strategy there was barely looked over the hill. Everything was short termism, for immediate gain, with little thought to long-term needs. When Hitler spoke of future successes, he was merely telling tall tales, yet Hitler believed his own fantastic ravings and Germany proceeded according to those whims. Like its Führer, the German economy was consumed with short term needs and could only cope with a

short war. Certainly, it started well, but there were two distinct phases to the war which itself was in two halves. Hitler was by nature indolent and shirked difficult decisions that did not fulfil his immediate desires. As the war took its toll on the German economy, instead of investing in developing better and easier to produce machines and munitions to meet the strain of military production, Hitler's first response was the opposite. In 1940, Hitler forbade the development of any new weapons which took more than a year to develop.

The Germans lacked everything. They had just five million tonnes of merchant shipping compared to the Allies 46 million. As there was a very small consumer car market in Germany there was also a paucity of motorised transport. In fact, the *Deutsches Heer*, the German army, relied upon horse drawn artillery. Indeed, the German soldier, if he did not walk, often had to rely on a horse for transportation. Beyond the use of submarines and a few outlying capital ships, the Nazis could not project their limited might much beyond the territory they controlled. Germany never even managed to produce a functioning four engine long-range bomber that could truly devastate opposing forces and Allied infrastructure. Nor did Germany possess a single battle-ready aircraft carrier. Germany lacked oil, and key metals such as aluminium that were needed for both engine and aircraft production. Tungsten and chromium, that were also needed for the war effort, were likewise not readily available.

Whilst the autobahns had been a triumphal improvement in German infrastructure, the opposite was true when it came to the Reich's train network. In the debt-fuelled rush to throw together the *Heer, Kriegsmarine,* and *Luftwaffe,* the train network had been neglected. Germany, a country rich in coal, and had seized many more coal fields from its neighbours, could not transport enough from its disparate mines and pits to its industrial centres. To alleviate these problems the Germans put soldiers in charge of running the railways, displacing professional managers that were experts at timetabling. The new management did little for improvements in punctuality. Indeed, it made the railways even more inefficient. This was especially the case in occupied lands; the effect of removing local expertise from positions of control engendered dissatisfaction. Where once there was loyalty to managers there developed a desire to disobey the new military masters.

This meddling created a serious backlog in the supply of coal. Veritable mountains of this combustible carbon emerged. This important fossil fuel had been dug out of the earth but could not be transported to where it was needed in a timely fashion. This held up the production of steel at a crucial time and prevented the Germans from producing enough materiel. The heart of the problem remained a chronic lack of investment which created the difficulties in the first instance, and this was exacerbated by amateur controllers. Germany's rush to rearm had meant they had ignored their railway network. German infrastructure was not able to support a war economy. They had the resources, and especially more than enough coal but not the means to get it to the industrial centres in sufficient quantities when needed. Britain was much better organised.

Fighting for freedom, not practising it

On 12th July 1940 Winston Churchill told generals Paget and Auchinleck that "the great invasion scare", as the war leader called it, was "providing us with the finest offensive army we have ever possessed, and it is keeping every man and woman tuned to a high pitch of readiness". The British increased their will to win, and fulfilled an important part of modern combat, namely the desire to take their opponents life. Soldiers were more willing to shoot to kill in this global conflict than their fathers were during the First World War a generation before. The phenomenon of an increased desire to aggressively engage with the enemy was also aided by the military identifying that in previous conflicts there was a problem with soldiers actively seeking to kill Germans as previously, some servicemen chose not to directly target the enemy. Accordingly, the British Army developed training techniques to resolve this problem and make sure that the target, as the other soul was known, would be marked, firmly fixed in the weapons sights, aimed at, and the soldiers would pull the trigger.

It was not just an offensive army that was being built. Civilians were mobilised for defence in the Home Guard and a separate guerrilla underground army was established that would terrorise the Germans and instigate an insurgency. This was markedly different to the Dad's Army Home Guard. The populace was also encouraged to sacrifice themselves in near suicide operations under the slogan of "You can always take one with you". Even as late as 1942, powerful yet quintessentially British films such as *Went the Day Well?* kept the nation primed for war. This film glorified civilians, young and old, taking the fight to the Germans with whatever tools came to hand to kill collaborators and Nazi troops. In the movie, men of the Wehrmacht had, by some means that was never explained, found themselves in the Home Counties occupying an English village. The film glorified the plum and clipped accented matriarchs that fought back against the Germans. Amongst other fictional brave acts carried out by civilians against the invader included, one lady taking a hatchet to the head of a German radio operator, taking his life, but receiving a bayonet in return from the dead man's comrade. When the Germans were attempting to storm a home housing the local resistance a Nazi throws a hand grenade through a window and into the nursery of children sheltering from the fighting. The film extolled the saving of their young lives by the children's governess and grandmother who took the deadly object out from the room and away from the little ones. The grenade then explodes off camera, but the sound of the blast leaves no doubt as to her fate and sacrifice on behalf of the innocents. When a wife realises that her husband is a collaborator, he had taken down a barricade at a window, she willingly shoots him dead with extreme prejudice, the malice on her face was all to see. She now held her traitorous late husband in contempt. Ultimately, with civilians and soldiers working in unison the area was cleansed of Germans.

Later, and with the fortunes of war swinging in favour of the Allies, films such as *The Life and Death of Colonel Blimp* used subtle and sophisticated propaganda to extol the need to deliver unto the enemy the destruction which the German's had practised so ruthlessly elsewhere. In glorious Technicolor the British cinema goer was nudged towards accepting total war. They must do whatever it took to annihilate Nazism and turn their evil against them. Notions of gentlemanly conflict were a luxury that could no longer be countenanced. Churchill, along with the British film industry and the creativity of war propagandists such as the poster designer Abram Games, had built a highly motivated nation dedicated to war and fighting for freedom.

Yet, Britain was not practising the freedom for which it took up arms to defend. The scare of Nazi invasion had allowed the British state to amass more power. Restrictions on the press were established, censorship was widespread, and restrictions on civil liberties were imposed. The war effort came before all else, even at the expense of democracy and traditional freedoms and rights. Duty, country, and killing came first. Nevertheless, the populace had inherited the virtues which made the small island of Britain great. That which was bequeathed from the past had not yet been extinguished.

Look east

With Hitler's forces held at England's veritable moat, the British Empire remained at large and a thorn in the side of the Nazis. On the continent of Europe, the only country that was both a potential ally for the UK, and at the same time a threat to German ambitions, was Soviet Russia. It was the Slavic peoples of eastern Europe who were to have Hitler's venom unleashed upon them in a full-scale invasion of Soviet held territory and not the peoples of the British Isles.

The new war in the east at first seemed to empower Hitler's empire. The land and the resources which the German's captured, including the Slavic slave class, would surely add to German might, not bleed it white. Indeed, Churchill was worried that with the collapse of the Soviet Union in the early days of Operation Barbarossa the Germans would soon turn their focus back towards Britain with renewed gusto and strength. Churchill ordered that the UK be on 'concert pitch for invasion from 1st September 1941.' The future as to whether Britain would remain free rested on how the war would fare on the blood-stained steppes and the sacrifice of the Russian men and women who paid the highest price to win. War in the east was coming one way or another. Historical forces were pushing towards that great clash.

Stalin had a desire for war against the capitalist powers. To serve the interests of global communism the Chairman of the Council of Ministers of the Soviet Union, Joseph Stalin, devised a scheme which he hoped would see the USSR triumph against the weakened west. He hoped that the war would see Germany, France, Great Britain, and the United States engaged in a permanent and debilitating conflict. When critical mass was achieved, the Red Army would attack and 'liberate' the workers. Whilst Britain held out and remained at war with Germany, Stalin's grand strategy seemed to be the correct path but, when Germany invaded the USSR before the Soviet dictator could launch his attack it initially appeared that Stalin had made a major miscalculation.

For the time being, the political battle to bring Britain to the negotiating table was an abject failure. The scheme to subdue the British Isles was little more than a propaganda exercise to steal by cunning what could not be achieved through force of arms. Hitler's focus once more became fixated on eastward expansion and plans for Operation Sea Lion continued in an effort to trick Stalin into believing Germany still aimed to attack Britain and not the USSR. The Führer thought he had little alternative but to invade Russia. Napoléon Bonaparte in 1812 went to war with Russia for similar misplaced reasons, his obsession with Perfidious Albion led to the French usurper forming the continental system, a trade block, designed to exclude the United Kingdom from doing business with Europe. French economic warfare against the UK could not succeed unless the entirety of the continent was closed to the British. Tsarist Russia, who could not afford to lose trade with England, came to reject the French system and opened their ports to Britain's merchant navy. In response Napoléon Bonaparte raised the largest military force in the history of the world to that date and sent them eastwards. On 24th June 1812, to bring the Russian bear to heel, 685,000 Frenchmen and their European subordinates crossed into Russia, most of whom would never return. Napoléon's empire ultimately shrunk to a wind-swept rock in the southern Atlantic Ocean called Saint Helana. Hitler would repeat this history.

Field Marshal Bernard Law Montgomery's first rule of warfare was 'Don't march on Moscow.' Bonaparte's decision, in 1812, to do just that proved to be as fateful for him as it was fatal for his followers. In the following century Hitler's ambitions led Germany into also breaking Montgomery's first rule of warfare. The Nazis would be broken by the intractable Russian army and, like France, trapped in the vast frozen Russian steppes attempting retreat. Yet, before that Hitler would have other European adventures.

Churchill's Odyssey

"One day the great European War will come out of some damned foolish thing in the Balkans."— **Reputedly said by Otto von Bismarck in 1888.**

Pax Britannica

With Britannia secure in her island fortress, Hitler's gaze turned east, where his substantive ambitions truly rested. But before he could direct his full attention, and not insubstantial military, to the drive east. The Führer faced distractions that complicated his plans, most notably he was compelled to drive South, making him miss his schedule and drain his resources, military, and otherwise.

Britain may have been isolated but the British Empire was still uncowed. Since the age of Nelson, who had fought and decisively won the Battle of the Nile against an earlier pretender to the role of European hegemon, Napoleon Bonaparte, the United Kingdom had known the importance of the Mediterranean Sea. The word 'mediterranean' means in the middle of land. Several of its chokepoints connect to other seas and oceans that were also under British control and many Mediterranean islands were incorporated into the British Empire. The British lock on the Mediterranean Sea only increased when the French constructed the Suez Canal, giving the United Kingdom's shipping a more direct route to the jewel in the British Empire, namely India. British influence had grown further with the decline of the Sublime Ottoman State. After the final defeat and elimination of the Ottoman Empire at the end of World War One, large parts of the oil rich Middle East were mandated by the League of Nations to the UK making them effectively a part of the British Empire. Incidentally, the League of Nations would not approve of Italian ambitions in Abyssinia, nor those of the Japanese in Manchukuo.

Despite a challenge from Italy, Britain now dominated the Mediterranean trade routes. Ancient sea lanes had seen the emergence of some of the world's most fascinating and influential civilisations. A number of these, Lykia, Sparta, and Rome had even provided templates for the Founding Fathers in their development of the American Constitution. In a different way, Fascist Italy and Nazi Germany also drew inspiration from Ancient Mediterranean civilisations. Britain, as the naval superpower, with her control of the waters in which the boot of Italy was such a prominent projection, had become a particularly galling situation for Italy and specifically Mussolini. *Pax Britannica* had turned *Mare Nostrum*, our sea, into just *mar Mediterraneo*, Mediterranean Sea. With Italy now in alliance with Germany, the Italian Royal Navy, known in Italian as the *Regia Marina*, began a long struggle with the British Royal Navy to turn the Mediterranean Sea into an Italian lake. Yet it was not the British Empire on Germany's southern flank that was the immediate threat to Hitler's dreams of conquering the Slavic peoples to his east. It was Italy that proved to be Hitler's undoing and gave Churchill the success he needed to keep confidence in his administration alive.

In economic terms, Italy's assistance to Germany's war effort was a negative marginal product contribution. Italy was a liability for the Allies in World War One and subsequently became a burden for the Germans in the Second World War. Italy had frustrated Hitler's plans and made limited German resources in both men and materiel even more unproductive in battle. In assisting Hitler, Mussolini's original overriding goal had been to undermine German power but unfortunately for Mussolini and Italy his 'assistance' had unintended and disastrous consequences.

In 1940, Mussolini had concluded that the war would end in a British defeat. He thought that he had to defeat the British before the United Kingdom sued Hitler for peace, and in such a scenario the spoils of war would then go to Germany, not his new Roman empire. At the very least Mussolini, not wanting to be overshadowed by Germany, wanted a place at the conference table. As soon as Italy entered the war, the growing hostilities in the Mediterranean between Italy and the United Kingdom erupted into naval warfare. This conflict had been simmering since Britain had failed to prevent Mussolini's earlier invasion of Abyssinia and was compounded by the Arab Revolt in Palestine, both of which occurred just several years before World War Two.

These crises made Britain appear weak. Perhaps Mussolini's time had come. The consequent Battle of the Mediterranean was amongst the most creative theatres of conflict in the earlier part of the Second World War. In November 1940, at the Battle of Taranto, the Royal Navy conducted one of the first ship-to-ship attack exclusively using airpower, it sank Italian vessels whilst at rest in harbour. This strategy was extensively studied by the Japanese. They saw its potential and were soon to employ this bold approach against America just one year and a month later.

Italy fought back at sea as well as on land. On the water Italy showed panache. On 19th December 1941, the *Regia Marina* deployed elite frogmen from their *Decima Flottiglia MAS*, known in English as the 10th Assault Vehicle Flotilla, to attack the British fleet docked in the Egyptian port of Alexandria. Italian midget submarines, effectively manned torpedoes, destroyed two battleships and a tanker. For the time being the Royal Navy ceased to be an effective offensive force in the Eastern Mediterranean and Britain had to fortify its Egyptian harbour. Incidentally, after Italy changed sides in the war, the 10th Assault Vehicle Flotilla joined with the Royal Navy to attack German controlled Italian shipping. Whilst Italy had some success at sea, the story on land was another matter.

Britain's *blitzkriegs*

In August 1940, to gain more territory for Italy and to also bolster his hand against Herr Hitler, Mussolini set out to take part of North Africa from British control. Despite Churchill recognising the importance of North Africa, Indian troops were sent south from that theatre to protect East Africa and eliminate the Italian colonies around the Horn of Africa. Indian soldiers were then replaced by Australian troops. This would not be the only instance of Churchill weakening his forces in the deserts of Egypt. In East Africa, the Italian Invasion of British Somaliland was initially a success. However, the situation was soon reversed, and Italy's empire in that region was dissolved. Abyssinia, now known as Ethiopia, was restored to independence by Britain, and its returning Emperor, Haile Selassie, continued the Italian and British introduced policy of stamping out the practice of slavery. After the war Britain returned Italian Somaliland to Italy. Upon decolonisation the British encouraged the two portions of Somali to unite. Most of the former British colony has since separated from the failed state of Somalia yet Somaliland has only received limited international recognition. The Republic of Somaliland, the successor to the British Somaliland protectorate, is one of the few success stories in modern African politics.

After months of border skirmishes, and a British incursion into Libya the Italians responded in September 1940 with their full-scale invasion of Egypt. Mussolini sent forces to drive the British out of Egypt, aiming to take the great port city of Alexandria and the Suez Canal. However, this mission was not to fare well. The invasion did not progress far and soon came to a halt with Italian soldiers seeking to reinforce their position after having achieved little. In December 1940, the British struck back, unleashing armoured units against the Italians in a bold flanking movement known as Operation Compass. The Italian losses were staggering in men, materiel, and territory. By early 1941 not only were the Italians thrown out of Egypt but also from much of the coast of Cyrenaica, the eastern part of Libya, including Tobruk which was now in British hands. The Western Desert Force had reached as far as El Agheila. The Italians feared that even Tripoli, the principal city in Italian-occupied Libya, would be threatened. Mussolini's African empire was unravelling.

The commander of the British forces, General Wavell, had consistently out-manoeuvred the Italians, cutting them off and capturing whole swathes of disheartened soldiers; it was an attack worthy of the most audacious blitzkrieg. The decisive British victory was, however, undone by Churchill's decision to focus on another theatre. When Hitler deployed units to assist the Italians the British Prime Minister reacted. Overall, Mussolini's going to war with the British was a blunder that was descending into ignominy, but not content with the growing crisis that had been created across the Mediterranean Sea, Mussolini also involved the Kingdom of Italy in affairs across the Adriatic and Ionian seas in the Balkan Peninsula. A region whose politics were highly combustible, war was just policy by other means.

The Balkans

The Balkan Peninsula, with the Adriatic Sea in the west, the Ionian Sea in the southwest, the Aegean in the southeast, the sea of Marmara and the Bosporus in the east, and the Black Sea to its northeast, had a mix of rival peoples. It was a political minefield. Its many mountain ranges were a gift for partisans, and its rugged terrain a trap for conventional forces. Yet, the lure of creating a new Roman Empire in this region was too much for Mussolini to resist. Italy had long held territorial ambitions in what was then Yugoslavia, the land of the Southern Slavs, a country that was created following the end of World War One. Throughout much of its modern history it had been the fault line between great transnational imperia namely, the Austo-Hungarian, Ottoman, and even the Venetian empires. Italy also had a traditional interest in the region and had its own border disputes, Italy occupied Albania in 1939, ousting King Zog, and possessed parts of what is now Greece.

The catalyst for the latest cataclysm coming out of the Balkans was the USSR. At the end of June 1940, the Red Army occupied Bessarabia and Northern Bukovina, much of which is now known as Moldova, forcing the Romanians to withdraw. The Russians then annexed this region to the Soviet Union. This aggressive act was not endorsed by the Molotov–Ribbentrop Pact. Indeed, Hitler took this as a serious provocation, and as always saw an opportunity to take advantage of this crisis. Partisans from Bukovina would reject both Romanian and Russian control and take up arms against the Red Army towards the end of the war. The region is still split and not sure whether to face Russia or to Romania and the European Union, whose largest contributor is Germany.

Romania, which had been an Allied nation in the First World War and had taken Transylvania from the disintegrating Austro-Hungarian Empire, dramatically took an about turn in its international relations. Romania installed a pro-German government, joined the Axis, repudiated its leanings towards Britain and France, adopted Nazi racial laws, and left the moribund League of Nations. German troops then entered Romania. Not all members of the Axis were happy with this new acquisition. Mussolini, already smarting from German *détente* with France, was both angered and alarmed by Germany moving troops into the Balkan Kingdom. *Il Duce* considered Romania to be in his sphere of influence.

Not only did Mussolini want his own empire to his east but as the German behemoth was beginning to encircle Italy at a geopolitical level, he now felt vulnerable. It was an indirect threat to Italian sovereignty. Mussolini felt that he had to redress the balance of power in Europe and get even with Hitler. Resources had also become a serious issue and Germany could cut-off supplies of both Romanian and Russian oil. To protect supplies of this most important energy source, Mussolini would have to expand his power in that region. His answer to this strategic conundrum was to invade Greece.

The Kingdom of Greece had long feared invasion, and not just from Italy which occupied neighbouring Albania. The Kingdom of Bulgaria, a German associated state in World War One, again aligned with the Axis in World War Two. Irredentists wanted to unite Bulgarian speakers in Greek Thrace, and Yugoslav North Macedonia. Alarmed at Bulgarian rearmament, Greece planned for war. Similar to the Maginot Line, the Greeks constructed its own defensive shield known as the Metaxas Line, a series of forts and defences along its border with Bulgaria. Should Italy attack, the Greeks planned to contain them in the mountains which made up the border between Greece and Italian controlled Albania.

On 28th October 1940, Italy invaded Greece. Mussolini had decided to present Hitler with a *fait accompli* by invading without first consulting his unwitting partner in crime who would read about it in the newspapers. This was extraordinary considering Hitler and Mussolini had met earlier that month at the Bremer Pass on 4th October 1940. Despite Mussolini's manoeuvring, Hitler remained loyal to his Italian counterpart. He had originally modelled himself on Mussolini and sought to replicate his successful seizure of power. Hitler's adoration of Mussolini was perhaps a case of Hitler, who had an abusive Father, seeking out a less than positive male role model by which he would live his life.

Yet ultimately Mussolini became dependent upon the German leader. Mussolini eventually adopted Nazism and tried to convince Hitler that the Italian people were Aryan. Mussolini also began to persecute the Jews, a dramatic turn from the time when there had been Jewish members of his Fascist Party. The imitation game also included Hermann Göring modelling the Luftwaffe on the Italian Flying Corps. As the war progressed the balance of power had clearly swung in Germany's favour. Mussolini wanted war, just not yet as and although he knew that Italy was unprepared still entered because he did not want to be upstaged by Hitler. Ironically, the Italian leader's fear of German domination of Europe led to his unholy marriage with the Nazis and German hegemony over Italy.

Italy's lack of preparedness became apparent with Italy's invasion of Greece. There was a stalemate between the two armies and Italy's prestige was irreparably damaged. By March 1941, the invasion had in effect been defeated by Greece. Although Greece was initially wary of angering Hitler, its armies had received some supplies and support from the British including assistance from both the Royal Navy and the Royal Air Force. The Greek victory over the invading Italians can be considered the first Allied victory of World War II but was, however, to be short lived. The Greeks were desperately short of materiel, they especially lacked ammunition for their artillery. British intervention was not enough to guarantee their security, so the Greek Prime Minister requested much more than that which was supplied by Churchill, it was not the full measure. Hitler had wanted Mussolini to stand firm to tie-up the British and stop them interfering in Greece from where the all-important Romanian oil fields could be threatened. The Führer, increasingly alarmed at the presence of the Royal Air Force in Greece, just a short flight from Romania, had a *casus belli* for another invasion which was quickly becoming just a matter of time.

Anticipating a German invasion of Greece, in March 1941 Churchill ordered General Wavell to move four divisions, largely consisting of 60,000 Anzac and Polish troops, from North Africa to the Balkans. The effects of Operation Lustre, as it was known, were to cascade through the war. The British Prime Minister feared that if Greece fell to the Germans, Hitler would then be able to pressurise neighbouring Turkey, the successor state of the collapsed Ottoman Empire, to join the war on the side of the Axis. Indeed, Hitler had made overtures to the Turks. A renewed alliance between the two still to this day intricately linked nations of Germany and Turkey, could have led to the British being driven out of the Middle East, and to Germany taking control of Turkey's neighbour, Iran; thus, depriving the UK of that country's oil. Though Turkey was not to officially enter the war on the Nazi side, they did supply the German war economy with important raw materials such as chrome, which was an important component in Germany's jet fighter programme. During the First World War, the Turks were on the side of the Germans. Though the war was a defeat for the once powerful transnational Sultanate and Caliphate, it did manage to hold of the British and French for a time, most notably during Churchill's Dardanelles Campaign. This attempt to supply Russia via the Bosporus failed, costing Churchill, the architect of the plan, his position in government as the First Lord of the Admiralty. Churchill then departed to fight on the Western Front. Though Churchill's latest escapade across the Mediterranean had fewer casualties it was far from successful. The Germans were soon to intervene in Greece but not before another actor entered the equation.

Again, the actions of the Soviet Union proved to be a catalyst for German expansion. Each Russian move was checked by the Germans. Russia recognised the new anti-German Yugoslav government, which had taken power after British intelligence had encouraged a popular uprising. Stalin quickly concluded a pact with the new government and within a week Hitler and his satellites Hungary, Romania, Bulgaria, and Italy invaded Yugoslavia. German forces also attacked Greece to both keep Germany's grip on Romania and to save the blushes of his friend, Benito Mussolini. Hitler had to bailout Italy in Greece, and elsewhere, when Mussolini's ambitions did not live up to his ability. Italy however was too big to fail and took too much from Germany, sucking the Third Reich into new conflicts that cost much blood and treasure.

A large part of Yugoslavia's, now Croatia's, Dalmatian coast, once known as the Republic of Ragusa, was incorporated into the Napoleonic Kingdom of Italy in 1808. This had resulted from the upheavals in Europe caused by the Little Corporal (*le petit caporal*) – Napolean Bonaparte. Less than a century and a half later, a jumped-up corporal, Hitler, would unleash yet more chaos, dissolving the Kingdom of Yugoslavia. The main part of the land that was part of the Austrian Empire, namely Roman Catholic Croatia, became a German puppet state known as the Independent State of Croatia. This region remains the fault line between the Roman Catholic and Eastern Orthodox faiths which have been officially in schism since 1054 AD; the area is also split between Christians and Muslims. In the late fifteenth century, following conquest, the Ottoman Turks had a policy of converting the local population to Islam.

With Hellenic forces tied up on the Albanian front, other sectors of the Greek border with Yugoslavia and Bulgaria were undermanned. Germany was to attack across those frontiers, and even directly assaulted the Metaxas Line. Despite also lacking personnel this formidable network, like the French Maginot

Line, performed well against German attacks. However, the German blitzkrieg bypassed it and come through Yugoslavia outflanking the Greek wall.

The British were driven back and retreated to the island of Crete. The Germans did not let up and unleashed Operation Mercury. In the second half of May, in one of the boldest operations of the Second World War, a German force of mainly paratroopers, the *Fallschirmjäger*, led by Kurt Student, were sent to capture the island. In Greek mythology Crete hosts the cave which was the birthplace of Zeus and is the reputed home to the labyrinth, the Minotaur and King Minos, the monarch after which a British archaeologist named Crete's bronze age Minoan civilisation. It has been mooted as a possible, but improbable, inspiration for the perhaps allegorical story of Atlantis. For Britain, the island may well have sunk into the sea. Crete, even with help from Britain, fell with great loss of life. For Germany the cost had also been high and the operation, though a success, very nearly ended in Nazi failure. Though it remained a German victory, it was one that devoured many German servicemen in both the initial operation and the bloody occupation that followed. The Wehrmacht were continually harried by Greek partisans. On a psychological level, Hitler perceived it to be a pyrrhic victory. Yet, despite what was on the face of it a failed venture, Churchill never gave up his fascination with Greece and the eastern Mediterranean.

The depletion of British Empire forces in North Africa, when Britain was on the verge of victory, was a major setback. It could not have come at a worse time. The weakening, rather than the concentration, of the army in the desert diverted resources from where they were most ably being applied and seriously hampered the fight to claim Africa for the Allies. It came just as Germany was sending its own expeditionary force under Erwin Rommel, the Afrika Korps, to secure Italy's overseas empire. Nevertheless, migrating British personnel across the Mediterranean to a whole new theatre of war had other consequences that inadvertently helped turn the tide against Germany on its southern flank. The dire situation in North Africa, caused by weakening a winning army, encouraged President Roosevelt to become more committed to backing Britain. He was moved to give more help after the fall of Tobruk. Of greater importance was Hitler's became timid when it came to using his airborne forces. No longer would men be dispatched from the air as they had been in decisive fashion such as when they seized Belgian forts the year before, and the important island of Crete. This newly found reluctance to drop men into battle from the skies was to have a decisive effect on the outcome of the battle for control of the Mediterranean and thus World War Two. The same was not true for Churchill. After seeing how parachutists could dramatically change the military situation, Churchill, as the leader of Britain's war effort, demanded the creation of airborne forces that could be dropped into battle from parachutes and flown behind enemy lines in gliders. These would be used extensively as the war progressed especially in support of the decisive waterborne landings in Normandy, the much bigger operation that crossed the Rhine in 1945, and in seizing a different Mediterranean island, Sicily, from the Axis. In all these operations Allied forces were commanded by Bernard Law Montgomery. Yet, the Germans would not use the same tactics again.

For the time being, with Crete conquered, all modern Greece then came under German, Italian, and Bulgarian occupation. A collaborationist government was also set up. This had the ignominious duty to pay their occupiers for the costs of their occupation. If that was not bad enough, the Germans took Greek resources and food to support their own war effort. The Royal Navy then blockaded Greece in order to starve the Axis forces out, which resulted in a great famine. There was much resistance to foreign control and German reprisals were brutal. The resentment from this bloody time lasts to this day. Despite Greek forgiveness of German debt owed to Greece as reparations after the Second World War, the terms of the so-called bailout of the Greek economy from 2010 onwards saw harsh terms and austerity measures imposed on Greece. As members of the Eurozone, Greece is reliant on funds from the European Central Bank in Frankfurt. With little political will to issue a parallel currency, and despite a referendum rejecting the cuts, the Greek government felt it had no realistic choice other than to accept Chancellor Merkel's terms. This reignited resentment from World War Two.

The German victories over both Yugoslavia and Greece were both stunning and brave but were also pyrrhic victories. The easy wins had inflated the German army's collective ego. Believing their tactics, systems, soldiers, and equipment were superior, the Nazis were drunk on victory. The biggest cost, however, was time. The escapade into the Balkans, not part of Hitler's immediate plans, pushed back the scheduled invasion of Russia from 15th May by five weeks to June 1941. This delay gave the Red Army more time to reorganise and prepare. It also put back the German march on Moscow to a period when the invaders were more likely to run into Russia's difficult winter climate. This was not the only problem. The tightening of Germany's grip on Bulgaria and Romania, meant the acquisition of more partners that, like Italy, were not always helpful to German ambitions.

Giant pincers

Hitler recognised the vulnerability of Italy, and his southern flank, if the British beat the Italians in North Africa. On 3rd February 1941 Hitler told his commanders that if the British defeated the Italians in North Africa, they would hold a pistol to the head of Italy. Within days he ordered Rommel to lead the newly formed Africa Korps in aid of the Italians. Big things were expected of the Afrika Korps, Hitler, who was an admirer of Erwin Rommel (the feeling was mutual) said on the dispatching of this German expeditionary force to North Africa, *The world shall hold its breath.* Its exploits did indeed become famous. And its commander, despite being committed to the Nazi cause, even managed to win the respect of his foes.

Hitler's directive number 32 on 11th June 1941 further expanded on the importance of the middle east. Whilst he could not directly take Britain in its island fortress, the Führer devised a plan to weaken the United Kingdom. This would be accomplished via a series of massive pincer movements aiming to converge on the centre of power that enabled Britain to stay in the fight, the region from which Britain obtained much of its oil, namely Arabia and Iran. One thrust, envisaged in Hitler's plans, would come via Russia and cross the Caucasus mountains near Iran's northern border, and would then descend on British interests in that country. This thrust was soon to begin with Operation Barbarossa.

Another arm would appear from the Western Desert of Libya. Hitler envisaged Germany taking Egypt and the Suez Canal thus jeopardising the sea lanes on which British merchant shipping relied. He intended to defeat the British in the desert where the Italians had earlier failed and from where Transjordan and Iraq would lay before the Wehrmacht. This force would then link up with its counterpart coming via Russia. Hitler also hoped to send his armies via Bulgaria to Turkey. The Nazis could then unilaterally drive Britain out of Iran. The troops would then take over the middle east and link up with Rommel advancing from North Africa. It was a strategy on a megalomaniac scale. The plan for a concentration on the middle east fitted together in theory, yet each of the thrusts whilst on paper appeared to be complementary, they were in fact competing for resources against each other. During 1941 Hitler had a Russia-first strategy and this deprived Rommel of resources. The big build-up of forces was in the east, not to Hitler's south in Africa. However, to assist his planned aggressive takeover of the middle east, he hoped to deploy a fifth column.

These thrusts would be assisted by the local population, many of whom were not well inclined to their current masters, be that the British in North Africa and the near east or the Russians in the southern Soviet Union. Hitler intended to initiate rebellion in Iraq against British rule and use Vichy French bases in Syria to help him achieve that end. It was a holistic solution to the problem of British dominance of the near east. Whilst the Allies were fighting a crusade against Nazism, Hitler was attempting to lead the Muslim world in a quasi-Jihad against Britain. Hitler would not only make friends wherever he found them, regardless of their race or religion, but in fact found common cause and identified with many in the middle east.

Hitler's holy war

During World War One Germany, in effect, inflicted Communism on the world by returning Lenin to Russia to stir up revolution. Germany was successful and Russia left the war, and in the process handed over much of eastern Europe to the Germans. Communism has now vanished from the earth, and States that claim to adhere to the dogma have at least some degree of private enterprise, even North Korea has some non-state shops which follow the profit motive. Imposing Communism on a part of the world was not Germany's only instance of meddling in extreme ideologies which they hoped to exploit and export for their own ends. The Germans in the First World War had attempted to incite Jihad and thus bring the Islamic world over to the anti-French and anti-British, German side. The Germans sought to radicalise Muslims and recruit them for Jihadi operations. The same attempt was made in World War Two. Unlike communism, the legacy of external Jihad is still with us.

As German war aims continued to grow, Hitler planned to use Crete as a steppingstone to reach Cyprus and from there take Palestine from the British and the Zionists who were in the process of colonising the Mandate. Palestine had, on the eve of the Second World War, been pacified by Bernard Law Montgomery who defeated the Arab revolt in that region. This conflict ran from 1936 until 1939 and was brutally quelled by the British commander within six months of his arrival in late 1938. The Arab Revolt was led by the Grand Mufti of Jerusalem, in Arabic Jerusalem is known as al-Quds. The Mufti was the head of the metropolis' Islamic places of worship, as a leader of Islamic jurisprudence he was prominent in the Muslim religious hierarchy. He was appointed Mufti by Herbert Samuel, the British High Commissioner, in 1921. Initially, he was considered an important ally by the British authorities, but later, due to growing nationalist sentiment, and popular Arab opposition to mass Jewish immigration, he called for a nationalist uprising and jihad, a Muslim Holy war, against the British Mandatory authorities. By seeking help from Nazi Germany to expel the

British from Palestine, he received weapons as well as public shows of support from Hitler, who spoke out against human rights abuses carried out by British forces against the Arabs

The Zionist paramilitary militant organization, Lehi, also known as the Stern Gang, sought to establish ties with the Third Reich for the same reason — to liberate Palestine from British control. However, their overtures were not fruitful. Fearing alienating potential allies across the wider Muslim world, Germany favoured the Mufti. Despite this, and the fact German anti-Semitism associated itself with the resentment across the Arab world against the unjust Zionist policies being pursued by the British, 12,000 Palestinians volunteered to serve in the British Army during the Second World War.

The Nazis admired Islam because its adherents were prepared to sacrifice their lives for their cause. Furthermore, as the Nazis were opponents of Judeo-Christian heritage, they thought that Islam could be a useful tool in undermining the traditions which the National Socialists despised. Nazi ideology and Islamic dogma also shared an interest in social justice for insider groups and to varying degrees had punitive policies against proscribed practices. The Nazis sought to incorporate Muslim soldiers into the *Waffen-SS* wherever they could be found, for instance in the parts of Russia where mainly Muslim Turkic peoples reside, such as the Crimean Tatars. Some Turkmen that had been conscripted into the Soviet Red Army, but were later captured by the Germans, volunteered for the Nazi Turkestan Legion. The Caucasus, large parts of which are Muslim also provided recruits for the Germans. *Waffen-SS* units were also formed from Islamic volunteers from what is now Bosnia and Herzegovina, once part of Yugoslavia. Bosnia and Herzegovina's capital city is Sarajevo; incidentally, this was the location where the Archduke of Austria-Hungary was assassinated, the act which sparked the First World War. In the Second, the conquest of Yugoslavia, and the areas populated by Bosniaks, as Bosnian Muslims were known, brought these followers of Islam under German control.

The Grand Mufti helped the Germans recruit troops for the Nazi cause, specifically the 13th SS Mountain Division, from amongst the Muslim population of Bosnia. They had been banned from collaborating by their local religious leaders but the Mufti's prestige in the Islamic world was so great that his call to arms motivated many to fight for the Nazis. Also, at the instigation of the Grand Mufti of Jerusalem, aid and saboteurs were sent to the middle east, in particular Iraq, to ferment rebellion against the British. This region had been taken from the Ottoman Turks during the First World War. Britain later installed members of the originally Meccan based Hashemite rulers of the Hejaz as the monarchs of Arab territory mandated to the British by the League of Nations.

The Axis also sought to undermine the British in Palestine and saw the oil pipeline which ran from Kirkuk in Iraq through the Mandate to the Mediterranean Sea as especially important. The Italian air force targeted oil refineries in Palestine as well as Bahrain. Despite this being part of a wider German strategy to undermine Britain in the Middle East, the head of the Luftwaffe Hermann Göring could not spare the planes to bomb British positions in Palestine. With the Afrika Korps far away in North Africa, the main German battle against Britain in the Levant, Mesopotamia, and beyond had to be mainly conducted by proxy with only limited German and Italian support being made available.

To this end Germany inspired a coup in Iraq that aimed to make the country fully independent of British control, although prior to the coup attempt, Iraq did have some autonomy. In April 1941 Iraqi nationalists, with the connivance of German intelligence, attempted to take over the country. Bombers from the German Luftwaffe, and aeroplanes from the Italian Royal Air Force, the *Regia Aeronautica*, attacked British forces from above. The Axis powers were assisted from bases in neighbouring Vichy French Syria where the aircraft refuelled on their way to assist the Iraqi rebels. This revolt was resisted by the British who fought back. Despite the initial success of the coup, the German associated government was quickly overthrown and by the end of May 1941 Iraq was again in British hands. As a result of German interference in what is known as the Anglo-Iraqi War, and due to France allowing Germany to use its bases in Syria, the British were compelled to start a new campaign. In June 1941, the British invaded Vichy France controlled Syria and Lebanon. By July of that same year these areas had been placed under British control. The UK did not hand these countries to the Free French but administered Syria themselves. Just as the First World War led to Britain seizing much of the German Empire in Africa and a significant proportion of the Ottoman controlled territory in the middle east, the Second World War was producing a similar outcome. Britain had now captured Arab lands that were once dominated by the Turkish Sultan and Caliph of Islam. Britain had also succeeded in taking part of Italy's holdings in Africa and was still to take yet more of Vichy France's African possessions from Madagascar to Tunisia. The war was progressing well for the British Empire.

The Nazi entanglement with the Muslim world even stretched to Iran. This land was known in Europe at the time as Persia. Its ruler had already requested that the international community use the area's correct name which remains Iran, meaning 'Land of the Aryans'. Hitler and the dictator of Iran, who styled himself as Shar, had become politically close and established strong trade links. Reza Khan, as he was called, wanted to avoid a close association with countries that had imperial ambitions in the region. Hitler was especially interested in Iran because of its connections with the Aryans, the name also attached to the Nazis' fantasised master race. Though the Farsi language spoken in Iran is part of the Indo-European language family, of which Germanic is a significant part, there is no clear direct connection between the two uses of the word Aryan. However, it is a matter of not only conjecture but also scholarly linguistic study that the Indo-European language group may have possibly originated from what is also known as the near east and Anatolia. Intriguingly, this area developed agriculture and it has been proposed that due to a deficiency of vitamin-D in the diet of these farmers, a process began where melanin was reduced. The lighter skin enabled the production of the vitamin D micronutrient through synthesis of cholesterol in skin cells and ultraviolet B light rays emanating from the sun. Despite the at times poor nutrition the farmers economic, social, and techno-logical system was superior to that of hunter gatherers. The farmers' reliable food source allowed for greater numbers. They spread to Europe replacing possibly dark-skinned Europeans with Indo-European speaking agriculturalists that had a fairer complexion. The Germans and Iranians were at best only very, very, very distant cousins. At the time, however, there was little evidence, apart from lin-guistics, upon which any link could be construed. The middle east appealed to Hitler for very practical reasons and not just his ethnographic fantasies. These practical aims were however to be thwarted.

In August 1941, in a coordinated but largely unopposed attack, the British invaded southern Iran and the Red Army occupied the north of that country. This both secured the middle east, eliminating Axis leaning rivals, and created the so-called Persian corridor through which war winning weapons would be supplied to the Soviets. These were desperately needed but the Red Army already had some impressive weapons. When the forces occupying Iran linked up, the British soldiers were in awe of Russian armour. The Soviets were impressed by British short trousers. The UK had much experience of operating in the heat of the near east and India. Hitler's fanciful strategy was not achieving the results he desired yet he would divide his focus and forces across much of the atlas.

The Pillars of Hercules
The Mediterranean had other chokepoints, at the other end of this sea lay the Strait of Gibraltar. Control of this narrow waterway was crucial. To the south

of the straight lies two candidates for one of the pillars that featured in Greek mythology. The location of this has been attributed to either the mountain of Jebel Musa (then in the Spanish protectorate in Morocco) or a less prominent mountain known as Monte Hacho in Ceuta, a Spanish enclave in North Africa. It is thought that the northern pillar was, what is known in English, as the Rock of Gibraltar.

Spain had long been of interest to Hitler. The Spanish Civil War ran from 1936 to 1939, and German aid had helped ensure Spain fell to the Nationalist side, the *Nacionales*. The Nationalists and their Falangist allies came to be led by the Spanish general Francisco Franco. Indeed, the coup against the Republican government, and subsequent civil war, was aided by the Nazis as well as Fascist Italy. German planes helped bring Franco's Army of Africa from Spanish Morocco to mainland Spain. These troops would quickly push back forces loyal to the Republican government and those of its Soviet ally and the international volunteer units. In time *Generalísimo* Franco, the youngest general in Europe since Napoléon, would become the *Caudillo*, dictator, of Spain.

A key German aim was to prevent a Republican Spain from allying with the French Republic. Furthermore, helping to install a regime sympathetic to the Germans would isolate France. Yet it was not just a matter of an aggressive geopolitical foreign policy. There was also a defensive consideration. Supporting the nationalist takeover of Spain would prevent Soviet backed communists, to whom many in Spanish politics were sympathetic, from gaining a foothold on both the Mediterranean Sea and the Atlantic Ocean. Joseph Stalin was supplying aid to the Republicans, but the military equipment was below par. In the 1930s Soviet tank development had yet to produce the decisive weapons that would later become associated with the Red Army. Indeed, the suboptimal performance of their equipment in other conflicts in the late 1930s, including against the Japanese, led to a much-needed reassessment of their armaments. The Soviets were not alone in testing their weapons and tactics in the crucible of the Spanish civil war.

Hermann Göring, head of the German Luftwaffe, was a hawk pressing for German intervention in the growing tensions which erupted as the Spanish Civil War. He had ignoble reasons for being involved on the Iberian Peninsula and Spain's North African possessions. He desired a testing ground in which the Germans could deploy and prove the Luftwaffe's latest technology and tactics. The full weight of these would soon fall upon the civilians of the Basque town of Guernica. They would experience first-hand the German experiment of terror bombing. It was just a foretaste of what could be expected, as much more was to come. Although Germany and its friends were successful in Spain, this victory led to the false presumption that their weapons would be sufficient for a future conflict.

The Pillars of Hercules feature heavily in the Spanish coat of arms and other symbolism. The northern pillar, however, like many strategic points in the Mediterranean Sea was under British control, along with its harbour, dockyard including a dry dock, airport, and military base. It was a veritable fortress. Gibraltar was of vital importance, if Britain lost control of the rock to Hitler, Germany would have been able to isolate the British in North Africa and beyond. It would have been a theatre changing strategic blow to the British Empire, closing-off the western Mediterranean Sea to British shipping, and severing Britannia's preferred route to the east. This would have helped the Nazis defend their soft underbelly and it is why Hitler wanted Spain in the war. Whilst Spanish volunteers were later sent to fight against the Soviet Union they were ultimately withdrawn when the tide of war turned against Germany. Franco was unwilling to give Hitler much more without a significant *quid pro quo*.

Germany proposed to take Gibraltar numerous times. As early as June 1940, General Heinz Guderian advised Hitler that Germany must enter Spain and take the British Overseas Territory. This was even planned and given the code name of Operation Felix. Franco was unwilling to formally put Spain into the war on the side of Germany and placed onerous demands on his benefactor. Hitler repeatedly requested that Franco allow Germany access through Spain to attack Gibraltar, but Franco remained reluctant to offend Britain and found excuses to stay neutral yet was still twice tempted to take the same path as Mussolini. This was firstly, after the Fall of France, and secondly during the invasion of Russia. Without Germany meeting Franco's demands, which Hitler found excessive, including supplying arms, aid, and energy, along with the promise of land, there would have been little reward beyond seeing Gibraltar taken from the British and put into German hands. Germany could not and would not spare the resources to bail out an impoverished Spain let alone build Franco's proposed Iberian empire. Yet without this aid Franco would not acquiesce to Hitler's demand.

Hitler baulked at supplying the Spanish Dictator with resources that Germany could not spare and territory in Africa which he could not deliver. Franco wanted land that belonged to Hitler's other putative potential Axis member, namely Vichy France. Furthermore, the Germans were content with the flow of resources going the other way to what Franco envisaged. Hitler was reluctant to supply Spain with resources, he was content with Spain supplying tungsten to the Nazis, that element is a key component in the production of steel. Information was also the other important resource that was passed from Spain to Nazi Germany, but it was not always reliable...

Germany was also being heavily compensated for its support for Franco in the earlier Spanish Civil War in other ways. German merchant shipping and U-boats of the Kriegsmarine were given access to bases in Spain's Atlantic possessions. These submarines posed a significant threat to British shipping during the Battle of the Atlantic. Spain's assistance to Nazi Germany was eventually countered by a neighbouring country – Portugal.

That other Iberian nation allowed British sub-hunting planes to use the Azores, an archipelago in the Atlantic. Portugal's Prime Minister and dictator, Dr Salazar, was opposed to Nazism, and wary of Spain's ambitions to dominate the whole peninsula. Portugal's assistance was also a continuation of the Anglo-Portuguese friendship, which is the oldest alliance in the world and has continued from the late-fourteenth century to the present day. Both nations have worked to support each other and have never been at war, nor on opposing sides in global conflicts. Following the Second World War Portugal joined with Britain as a founder member of the European Free Trade Association, an organisation which sought to be an alternative to the European Economic Community which later evolved into the European Union. Under the terms of the Treaty of Windsor of 1386 between the two states, British aircraft used the Azores to refuel during the 1982 Falklands War with Argentina. However, Britain has not always reciprocated and failed to come to Portugal's assistance when India invaded Goa in 1961, the UK however deplored the Indian action but recognised the anachronistic legacy of Portugal's former colonial possession on the Indian sub-continent. Still, the ties were strong, especially as Britain had defended Portugal against Napoleonic Spain and France during the Peninsula War of 1807 to 1814. The invasion was ordered by Emperor Napoléon Bonaparte, who then went on to take over his Spanish ally resulting in an especially gruesome war. The historical parallels for Franco, allowing an 'ally' to attack a neighbouring power, did not bode well.

The once great power of Spain had declined to such an extent that, had Hitler pressed the matter, Franco would have been unable to resist a German invasion. It was a missed opportunity, yet there was another factor at work. Admiral Wilhelm Canaris, the chief of the *Abwehr*, one of Germany's military intelligence services, knew Franco and dissuaded him from agreeing to allow the Germans in. At the same time the spy master sought to persuade Hitler that the operation was infeasible. He cited the problems of incompatible railway gauges between France and Spain, and that Gibraltar itself was invulnerable. Canaris could see the strategic opportunity in taking the Rock and was willing to use his subterfuge to make sure that his own side did not win the war. The key installation that is Gibraltar would remain secure in British hands as it does to this day. An opportunity to seriously undermine Britain was lost.

Franco's alliance of sorts and flirtations with Hitler led to Spain being isolated after the war and became little more than a pariah state. To resolve that, the myth was spread by Franco that it was he who had faced down Hitler in order to keep Spain out of the war. The Allies, in his false narrative, owed him a debt of gratitude. Amongst the propaganda was the myth that before he met Hitler to discuss the terms on which Spain would join with the Axis powers at Hendaia in the French Basque country, Franco deliberately made himself late to the meeting to unnerve Hitler. The fact is that despite Franco's best efforts he was both late and anxious. Not all Fascists could make the trains run on time. One that could at least provide punctual public transport was Benito Mussolini of Italy. He had his own troublesome British fortress to the south of his country.

Malta story

Initially, the struggle in the Mediterranean can be seen as largely a battle to, politically or otherwise, isolate the United Kingdom by seizing key points and arteries of the British Empire, namely the Suez Canal, Gibraltar, and, last, but not least Malta. That country, part of a small group of islands south of Sicily that pricked out into the sea between Italy and Libya, like Gibraltar has a significant natural harbour Accompanying the Port of Valletta or Grand Harbour, as it is known, was a British military base and airfields and formed another choke point near the centre of the Mediterranean. Hitler had come to realise that the Mediterranean was a decisive theatre in the war and recognised the need to drive the British out of Malta.

Vessels travelling across the sea between east and west, and from Europe to Tunisia and Libya, would have to pass close to this bastion. It had the potential to litter the seabed with planes, submarines, and ships that ventured within range of forces operating out of this stronghold. Malta was the reconnaissance base for the attack on Taranto on 11th November 1940 which sank much of the Italian navy. However, unlike Gibraltar, which was never seriously challenged, Malta's fate hung in the balance.

All the dominant powers in the Mediterranean had craved this small but strategically important island. The Ottoman Empire, which had aimed to conquer much of Europe, tried to seize Malta in 1565 from what was a crusading order, namely the Knights Hospitaller. They are also known as the Knights of Malta, and officially called the Order of Knights of the Hospital of Saint John of Jerusalem who are still in existence and have official permanent observer status at the United Nations. Although the Knights managed to repel the Ottoman Empire, they later lost the islands to Napoléon, whose French forces took Malta in 1798 whilst he was on his way to Egypt from where he would seek to imitate Alexander the Great. Just two years later, after a siege the United Kingdom won them for the British Crown. From then on Malta remained in British hands. Mussolini coveted the small nation of Malta including its neighbouring island of Gozo. It may have taken the islands in exchange for neutrality, but it could not be transferred without approval from the Maltese, and, at the time, they were determined to stay British.

In June 1940 Italy attacked Malta. The Italian state had a dubious claim to the islands that went beyond their close proximity to Italy. Malta had once been part of the Kingdom of Sicily, of which the modern state of Italy is arguably a successor state. However, since then Malta had declared its independence before eventually becoming a British Crown Colony. Furthermore, the Maltese language is not part of the Romance language group of which Standard Italian (the Florentine dialect of Tuscan) and Sicilian belong. Malta has two official languages; Maltese, which descends from Sicilian Arabic, and English. Although, Italian had been an official language and was widely understood. Regardless of Malta's legal status, the presence of a British base near the coast of Italy could not be tolerated. The Italians identified the threat posed by the British air and naval bases and acted accordingly.

The Royal Navy and Royal Air Force was to prove a major threat to the Axis. In January 1941, the Luftwaffe began its operations from Southern Italy and Sicily in support of *Regia Aeronautica* attacks on Malta. Hitler hoped that Malta would be bombed into submission forcing the islanders to surrender and throw out the British and Commonwealth forces based there. Churchill recognised Malta's importance as a military base as did the American President Franklin Delano Roosevelt, whose son, Elliott Roosevelt had been based there. Yet, Churchill did not give Malta all the defensive armaments they needed, holding Spitfires back to defend mainland Britain. However, lack of armaments did not prevent both the Royal Navy and the Royal Air Force from fighting back hard against the Axis.

British T-Class submarines sank ships, submarines, and harried Axis shipping, sending much of the supplies to the German and Italian war effort in North Africa to the bottom of the Mediterranean Sea. Consequently, depriving Rommel of the resources he needed. Even in the defence of the islands, the Royal Air Force was tenacious and aggressive. Despite the RAF being outnumbered, British Air

Chief Marshal Keith Park adopted the strategy of an aggressive defence. German and Italian attacks on Malta, and the base's British supporting convoys, were deprived of adequate Luftwaffe firepower because many of the Reich's planes were withdrawn to support Operation Barbarossa. The bombing of Malta then eased but it was only a brief and limited respite. In March and April 1942 more bombs were dropped in Malta than fell on London during the entirety of the Blitz. Plans for a Cretan style invasion by both sea and air were then adopted by Hitler and Mussolini. This was known as Operation *Herkules*. A Ptolemaic temple to the Greek hero Heracles existed in a part of Malta called Marsaxlokk. In the Roman era a cult to the Roman equivalent of the demi-god, Hercules, existed on the island.

Detailed and extensive plans for invasion were developed. Kurt Student, who had been the successful commander of the *Fallschirmjäger's* attack on Crete, was appointed to lead the airborne forces in the invasion of Malta. He was, however, unable to persuade Hitler of the efficacy of the plans and prove that they had solved the problems experienced in the earlier Cretan operation. Both Hitler and Göring, the head of the Luftwaffe, lost faith in Operation *Herkules* and especially doubted the airborne element's chances of success. Both Germany and Italy were already overstretched and were finding it difficult to supply enough manpower for the invasion of Malta, too many soldiers were embroiled in the campaign in North Africa, so opening another front would be too great a risk. Operation *Herkules* was quietly dropped. As the situation in North Africa turned against the Axis, the problem of Malta had been superseded by a far greater series of crises, and German attention had to face elsewhere. British Malta had survived. It was an epic struggle for survival, seemingly without end. The fight was to continue for nearly 2 ½ years and during this time Malta had a pivotal role to play in the war. The island was subsequently awarded the George Cross by King George VI and its flag still proudly displays this emblem.

Into Africa

Churchill's gamble in Greece failed and his bluff had been called, Hitler then raised the stakes in February 1941 with a move reminiscent of Scipio Africanus. The *Deutsches Afrikakorps*, initially sent to Libya as a defensive force to steady the Italian lines, and was officially placed under Italian control, quickly became a force to be reckoned with. This coincided with Archibald Wavell being ordered to halt his advance and then send his best forces to Greece as part of Operation Lustre. Not only had the momentum in North Africa been thrown away but the British Empire's Western Desert Force in Libya and Egypt were now in danger. The Afrika Korps under the command of Erwin Rommel had several advantages, namely the 88mm anti-aircraft artillery whose elevation could be depressed enough to make it an excellent tank killer and its shells destroyed many British vehicles. The German Mark IV tank was also a formidable machine. Although a minor advantage, the Germans also benefited from American lose lips. The Italians supplied information about the plans and dispositions of British forces in the Western Desert of Egypt to the Germans obtained from Americans based in Cairo.

There was another factor that aided the Germans in the Desert Campaign – geography. Apart from at the periphery with the mountains that rose in Tunisia and the Qattara Depression in Egypt, there were few natural obstacles to halt an attack and with the Sahara Desert to the south there was only a small strip of fertile land in which major human habitations were viable. Therefore, there were few man-made barriers, such as cities, through which attacking tank armies would have to pass. Where they did exist, the tank could easily bypass any fixed defences by sweeping through the arid land to their south. In contrast Rommel, in France the year before, was forced to stop when he reached the English Channel. In Europe, throughout the war, to capture a bridge over a river or bypass a mountain range or swamp meant the attacker would eventually need to take what were easily defendable conurbations, slowing the advance. To fail to do so would endanger the flanks and rear. When navigating his way across North Africa a bold commander, with enough transports and the fuel to power them, could make the most astounding advances; yet therein lay the issue. In so doing would create a problem – that of supply lines. Despite the Germans being able to feed and fuel their army in Africa from both Italy and later Greece, the sea, which had been the highway of the ancient world, was now a significant hurdle to overcome. Some supplies did succeed in crossing the Mediterranean, but it was far from guaranteed that they would reach their intended destination. The fast-paced advance covering hundreds, and in some cases thousands, of miles meant that supplies and reinforcements had to travel to the front along a coastal road that provided little tree cover. Interdiction from above by airpower that knew where to find the convoys on the long road meant that even basic aid would take time to arrive, if at all.

As both the British Empire and Nazi Germany were fighting on the same terrain, these unique circumstances and conditions applied to both sides. The open terrain afforded the attacker ample opportunities to outmanoeuvre an over-stretched opponent and a series of battles would ebb and flow across a giant sea of sand. Conversely, the concept of the blitzkrieg broke down in North Africa and breaking through only gave an illusion of victory. An inattentive general would be hit back by fast counterattacks and forced to retreat from whence they came. Only the most conscientious commander could handle these logistical issues and not leave their soldiers exposed to a shimmering counterstrike appearing out of the desert.

Much has been made of the Axis forces in North Africa not being cohesive as they consisted of both Germans and their less well trained, motivated, and equipped Italian Axis partners. However, during the more than 2 ½ years of fighting in North Africa these very same Axis forces were facing an even more multinational force. The Allies consisted of British, South African, Australian, New Zealand, Greek, Free French, Polish, Czechoslovak, and Indian Army soldiers. Also in the theatre were a significant number of Jews from Palestine. In time, American G.I.s would also enter the mix.

From March 1941 the Germans, now in *de facto* leadership of the Axis effort in Africa, struck back against the British Empire's depleted multinational force. The Afrika Korps quickly pushed the British out of Libya, bar one important port, Tobruk, which remained in Allied hands and was being supplied by the Royal Navy. The success of Rommel's army was not derived from his imagined superhuman abilities as a commander; he was to suffer reverses and make some poor decisions. According to the British commander in the theatre, Archibald Wavell, the British failed to initially meet the challenge posed by the Afrika Korps because Allied forces were ill-equipped and not battle hardened. Wavell, himself was not entirely confident of success and had plans to evacuate Egypt if the need arose, as did his successor Claude Auchinleck.

Seizing Tobruk would both shorten the supply lines of the *Panzergruppe Afrika*, as German and Italian forces became known. It would also be a real blow to Britain. Yet, victory for Rommel must include seizing the Suez Canal, anything less would keep Britain in the fight, so it was vital that he take this waterway and advance to the east. Churchill knew that Britain had to defend the Suez Canal and hold Britain's naval base in Alexandria. Yet, strategic issues were not the only considerations. Public relations were also an issue. Churchill needed a win in North Africa to show the Americans that the British were not wasting their support. Later Churchill wanted to show that his strategy in the Mediterranean theatre of operations was worth pursuing. Churchill desired to hold onto the port of Tobruk at all costs. Indeed, it became of totemic importance in his battle for the heart and mind of the American President. Tobruk was to change hands numerous times, and in 1941 it endured an epic 242-day siege.

It was relieved after a breakout which linked up with the advancing forces of Operation Crusader which ran for approximately the last six weeks of that year. The Australian troops at Tobruk had already been relieved by British soldiers who came by sea before the siege ended. A British contingent remained during the entirety of the siege.

The British forces in North Africa became known as the Eighth Army and were amongst the most famous formations of the Second World War and would launch the career of one of its later commanders into public consciousness. For the time being, Operation Crusader was commanded by an Ulsterman, General and later Field Marshall, Auchinleck. He had been Commander-in-Chief of the Indian Army. Operation Crusader was not without its problems, but it did drive the Germans back, securing Egypt and the Suez Canal, at least for the time being. Rommel was pushed back to El Agheila. However, in January 1942 Rommel's forces, now renamed *Panzerarmee Afrika*, benefitting from regrouping and shorter supply lines, struck back. Auchinleck was forced to withdraw his Eighth Army to Gazala, still in Libya but close to the Egyptian border. There was to follow the Battle of Gazala from May 1942, but this would be overshadowed by the fighting on the Eastern Front. The struggle for the southern shore of the Mediterranean Sea was to swing from triumph to disaster and back again until February 1943. Much more was to come.

Churchill's obsession

Churchill's strategy in the Mediterranean and the Balkans did not appear to be paying dividends. His judgement was not entirely dependent upon military affairs. Politically, Churchill was looking for another conflict so that he could demonstrate to President Roosevelt his desire to fight. There were also other motives at play. Churchill, looking beyond the war, wanted to not only preserve Britain's Mediterranean empire but also there was a deeper and creative logic at work in his approach to warfare in the Mediterranean and the Balkan Peninsula which projected into those waters. He was searching for a new route into the enemy's homeland. This would occupy Churchill's thinking throughout the war and was not too dissimilar from his approach in World War One where he was looking for an alternative to break the deadlock on the Western Front. The commitment to the Balkans was not outlandish. In World War One British soldiers fought alongside Greek forces in a desperate struggle against the German supporting Kingdom of Bulgaria, one of the Central Powers in the Great War and a follower of the Axis in World War Two.

Although Churchill had given Hitler a pretext to invade Greece and achieve more conquest, the British Prime Minister's strategy was inadvertently working. Italy had helped Churchill draw the Germans deeper into the Balkans, not only delaying Operation Barbarossa but also tying up the German army which found itself fighting partisans in both Yugoslavia and Greece. These partisans were armed by Britain and assisted by Churchill's Special Operations Executive (SOE). As well as British commando raids against Hitler's occupied coast, the SOE in the Balkans was setting Europe ablaze, just as Churchill had intended, and even supported communist forces. Just as Spanish guerrillas, aided by Britain, had been a bloody ulcer for Napoleon, the latest would-be conqueror of Europe found that he too was losing valuable resources to prevent another British expedition to Greece, which in time would come.

Yugoslavia was especially difficult terrain for the Germans. Britain later switched its support from the Serbian nationalist Chetniks to the National Liberation Army and Partisan Detachments of Yugoslavia – a communist resistance movement. After the war, Josip Broz, also known as Marshal Tito, the leader of the Yugoslav communist partisans was to strike up a rapport with British Field Marshal Bernard Law Montgomery. British support for communists in Yugoslavia was not the only instance of Churchill aiding the armies of an ideology he despised. In Greece, the UK supported both the Communist and Nationalist Greek resistance movements and tried to encourage these belligerent groups to work together. It remained a difficult and confusing conflict. German backed Greek collaboration forces were created to fight the communists and prevent a Red takeover of Greece in the event of Germany's inevitable defeat. Later, after Germany left Greece, British forces were to eliminate the communists. However, in the meantime Churchill's maxim became, my enemy's enemy... and British support for communist forces was soon to increase exponentially.

The Superman versus the Superpowers

"Behold, I bring you the Superman! The Superman is the meaning
of the earth. Let your will say: The Superman shall be the meaning
of the earth!" — **Friedrich Nietzsche**, *Thus Spoke Zarathustra.*

The man of steel

The concept of the *Übermensch*, or Superman, was twisted beyond all recognition by racialists, chief amongst them Adolf Hitler. The German philosopher
Nietzsche intended his Overman to be neither master not slave, but the Nazi
interpretation brought to the fore the notion of the *Untermensch* or sub-humans,
thus completely distorting Nietzsche's idea. The German Führer thought his
supermen, misidentified as Aryan, would rule over the sub-humans, who would
have to make way for the Germanic master race. However, the Nazi Superman
needed time to grow and develop, and unfortunately for Hitler was about to
come up against two emerging superpowers.

Hitler thought that Russia must be eliminated, though colluding with each
other, the peace was not expected to last; both the USSR and the Third Reich
were playing for time, both trying to avoid opening another front. Soviet Russia
remained the last significant power left in Europe which could become an ally
of Britain. Furthermore, with Russia's resources and its peoples enslaved and
put at Germany's disposal, Hitler would have the power to facedown Britain.
With the USSR liquidated, and Japanese advancing from the east, Axis power
would increase to such a level that the United States would not risk conflict
with Germany. Besides, the Germans coveted Russia's land. Germans would be
restored to the prominent positions they recently held from Estonia to Ukraine.
Furthermore, the Aryan would be able to live free of industrial capitalist exploitation, using the local serf population to tender the settler's land. Hitler believed
that only invasion would deliver that, he was preparing to turn on his associate,
Joseph Stalin, and expand the Reich eastwards, destroying the Soviet empire in
the process.

The Soviet leader was originally Ioseb Besarionis dze Jughashvili, but before
the First World War he took the pseudonym Stalin, meaning 'man of steel'. Stalin

had become accustomed to recklessly sending men into battle throughout the Bolshevik's consolidation of power during the Russian Civil War using this brutal strategy in the defence of Tsaritsyn on the Volga River, a city that would later bear his name. He did not mind accruing large casualties, nor was he averse to carrying out purges with summary executions and would burn villages to the ground. On the eve of Operation Barbarossa, however, the now leader of the USSR was a much less decisive character.

Despite his natural tendency to seek violent solutions to political problems, Stalin was desperate to avoid war with Germany. And beyond establishing a series of buffer states against the Reich, he had left Russia unprepared for war in 1941. Stalin had expected that Germany would be engaged in a long conflict with a British backed France but with the French and Belgian collapse the ground war in western Europe came to a premature conclusion and allowed Hitler to look east. Stalin rejected the invasion warnings from the Soviet General Staff, particularly the calls from Georgy Zhukov, Aleksandr Vasilevsky, and Semyon Timoshenko who urged the mobilisation of the Red Army. Stalin rejected these pleas for fear that they would spark a war, which is what had happened when The Tsar mobilised Russian forces in 1914. Stalin shouted at Timoshenko "What do you want... A war?" Stalin had replicated the same mistake that the Poles made nearly two years previously.

Stalin did have some cause for hope. German invasion was repeatedly predicted but did not initially materialise. The expected date was regularly put back, the intelligence services became like the boy who called wolf. However, Hitler's plans were delayed by the war in the Balkans and the desire of the Germans to avoid the Russian spring floods, known as the *rasputitsa*, when unpaved roads would become impassable. The delay into the summer, however, just increased the likelihood that the Wehrmacht would run into this meteorological occurrence later in the year. The autumn rains would create a sea of mud, slowing transport across Russia's underdeveloped road network.

The clouds of war now augured the spilling of blood on Russian soil. Yet, Stalin hoped, even on 14th June 1941 that the German build-up of troops on the borders of Soviet occupied Poland, and along the USSR's other western frontiers, was a negotiating position. Indeed, with Germany at war with Britain in the skies, the sea, and North Africa, it would have been nonsensical to open yet another front. Stalin had made the mistake of considering Hitler, a man he admired, to be rational. The Soviet leader had said of his German counterpart that he is not "an idiot". It was beyond Stalin's comprehension that Hitler would embark on a war on two fronts. He had not considered that Hitler was in fact a fantasist, whose deluded gambles had so far only succeeded because of political crises amongst his opponents causing them to effectively fold before the battle had begun.

German arrogance

The Fall of France created a false air of German invincibility. Reinforced by the lightning conquests of Yugoslavia and Greece, the Germans drew the wrong lessons from their early victories. They mistakenly believed they had superior armoured fighting vehicles, but they were about to get a nasty surprise, this bombshell came from Russian heavy KV tanks whose armour was all but impervious to anything bar the most powerful German anti-tank guns. In addition, the colossal KV's armament could rip-open all German tanks used in Operation Barbarossa. German arrogance had blinded them to the possibility that the Soviet Union could produce such effective weapons, there were many more to come. It was only superior German tactics and training that allowed the panzers to manoeuvre themselves into a position where they could overwhelm these mighty but slow vehicles.

France was undone by their own social, strategic, and tactical failings. Contrary to the thinking of the German High Command, Germany did not have better equipment than their enemies, the fortunes of war had turned on the fact that Germany had developed better tactics and strategy than the French and her allies. And not least of all, France, after its many political divisions and demographic problems essentially made the collective choice to fail. The science of collapsology did not apply to the Russians, they were determined to succeed whatever the cost.

Hitler was confident. He boasted that, "We have only to kick in the front door and the whole rotten Russian edifice will come tumbling down." This overconfidence was based on his view of the superiority of the Germanic race over the Slavic peoples and the superiority of Nazi ideology over communism. Hitler did have history on his side. Applying lessons from the First World War, where Germany was successful on the Eastern Front, and observing the abysmal performance of the Red Army in the Winter War, contributed to the logical conclusion that a German invasion would be straightforward. The Axis and its subject peoples also had greater economic potential. However, they underestimated the enormous British and American aid that would be supplied to Russia, nor did Hitler fully appreciate Russia's will to resist. The short termism of blitzkrieg was not going to succeed.

The failure of Germany to recognise their own lack of strength, both in terms of equipment and economic muscle, meant that new weapons were slow in coming to mass production. And when suitable arms were developed that could meet the challenges of a mechanised world war, these new designs could only be produced in numbers that were too few to change the course of the conflict. For instance, German Tiger and Panther tanks were over engineered and per unit they were too much, too late, and therefore could not appear on the battlespace in large enough numbers to be decisive. Whilst the Germans had learnt some lessons from their earlier invasion of Poland and had applied those lessons to the battle in the west against France, such as the need to keep fuel and maintenance available to the tanks, that innovation was not enough when the fighting was extended over the large Russian front. The Russians, on the other hand, had learnt from their battle against Finland in the Winter War. They had realised that they were weak and indeed they were, but the Soviets did something about it-they rearmed and retrained the Red Army whilst the Germans just rested on their laurels.

Totalitarianism and total war

The USSR, with its cult of personality for both Lenin and Stalin, had made the state, and its leaders, all important. They were attempting to create Soviet man; everyone was expected to conform to communism, and the science of socialism pointed the way forward. Individualism was not only discouraged but even considered suspect. The self was nothing, the state was everything; questioning and dissent would not be tolerated.

The mindset that created such disdain for personal freedom led to a complete disregard for human life. Soviet leaders saw the lives of their citizens as expendable; the modern war in Ukraine suggests that such a callous attitude endures. The Russian slave character gave the population the ability to not only endure hardship but to also accept harsh conformity. The Germans did not possess these same dark qualities, and indeed, Hitler fanaticised that his Germany was the modern incarnation of the Spartan state, whose warrior class were beaten and bullied into being amongst the finest warriors of classical Greece. He thought Sparta was an early embodiment of a national socialist state akin to his own Reich. They were, in fact, very different. Sparta was a constitutional diarchy whose laws, customs, and constitution created checks and balances, whereas Nazi Germany had leaders that knew no such restraints. The societies were also different, and the truth is that molly-coddled Germans bore few similarities to the Laconian peoples of old. Germany, today, has a welfare state and health service that originated under Chancellor Otto von Bismarck as long ago as the 1880s and so its citizens were protected from the baptisms of hunger and other privations which the Russians, and Spartans for that matter, experienced in their youths.

In the 1940's the forebears of many Russians had only recently been freed from bondage; this came in the same decade that America ceased practising chattel slavery. Indeed, the cultural similarities between the two downtrodden groups in Russia and America were manifold. Both expressed life's sorrows singing to music using stringed instruments yet kept and expressed a lust for life, an unreserved and exuberant warmth, passionate in love in hate, and an ostentatious desire to express what little wealth they had, coupled with a fatalistic and strong religious devotion. The only difference is that the oppressed were the majority in Russia, whereas in the United States the subjugated were a visible minority. Hitler had provoked an enemy that would tolerate and withstand much barbarism and Germany's repeated poking of the Russian bear would come back to haunt him. Carl von Clausewitz had long ago observed that the socio-economic conditions of the population was a factor in war, he declared that 'poor men, used to hard, strenuous work and privation, are generally more warlike.' The Russian, including the Turkic and Mongolian populations from which the Red Army also gained conscripts, were well suited to war. Russia, like the United States, had a frontier to the east where pioneers expanded and overcame opposition from natives who in some cases were not too dissimilar to America's Red Indians. This struggle on their Eastern frontier had forged a spirit in the Russian character that was to find its greatest expression in the fighting to come. The eastern frontier was made up of successor states to the once great Eurasian power – the Mongol Empire – and in the process of defeating them, the Russians learnt an important military strategy. The Mongols were known for annihilating their enemies and to this day the goal of annihilation remains a central tenet of Russia's battle doctrine.

The people of Russia survived, rather than thrived, in the harsh climate of summer heat and winter cold and endured severe Spring and Autumn floods. Local Russian populations also had experience of the cruel conditions that steppe land, forests, and swamps presented, all suitable in one way or another to disrupt the German advance. The Soviets also had the home advantage of defending cities in which the Wehrmacht could get bogged down and once embroiled in built-up areas were unable to exploit their greatest skill, the ability to manoeuvre. The Soviet population were the perfect fodder for a war of attrition. Their tolerance of hardship suited the gritty, and hard-fought war. The German advance was swift, but this would not be allowed to become a lightning war.

Russia performed dismally in the First World War, its many failings came from a lack of development, coupled with the difficulty supplying its troops on the Eastern Front. Despite their overall performance, the Russian soldier still showed remarkable endurance and ruggedness. This was remarked upon by British military observers who saw how they could withstand hardship and manage on meagre rations. This was a national trait that had long been in existence and had been added to by the miseries of the Great War, followed by suffering caused during the Russian civil war, and compounded by the introduction by Lenin of War Communism. This policy amounted to state theft, or acquisition, of food. The outcome of this redistribution was famine as was Stalin's policy of collectivisation of agriculture. Both caused mass starvation, killing millions. After enduring those tough conditions Soviets were even more able to suffer and yet still survive. This they did with a mix of both their traditional melancholy, fervent hate towards the enemy, and a passionate love of home. The population had been beaten, bullied, and starved into obeying the powers that be.

Despite the hardships, or perhaps because of them and the need for stability, most Russian's identified with their masters and were loyal to leaders that spoke the same language as them. This attitude was, however, only a recent phenomenon. Up until 1812 the Russian aristocracy spoke French. This practice, designed to separate the rulers from the uncouth lower orders, ceased after Napoleone di Buonaparte's invasion. This created common cause between the higher and lower castes. Russian nationalism had been born, but not all spoke the same language.

German speaking aristocracy were also tolerated in the Baltic parts of the Tsarist Russias. Indeed, the foundation of Russia occurred when the local population invited back Swedish Vikings, the Rus', to govern the unruly Slavic people. Since then, however, a distinct European culture had developed that chose to reject imposed foreign influences. Religion was another important factor in the development of this otherness. The Russian Orthodox Church was officially under the Archbishop of Constantinople, the New (Second) Rome based Patriarch – he was the first amongst equals. However, Russia saw itself as the temporal leader of the Orthodox world and the Slavic nations. When Moscow was the capital of Tsarist Russia, before Peter the Great's move to St Petersburg, it had claimed to be the successor city to Constantinople, also known as *Nova Roma*. After the second Rome fell to the Ottomans in 1453 Moscow was in the Russian mindset the political leader of Orthodox Christendom. Indeed, the founder of the Russian Empire in the early modern period, Ivan IV, took the title Tsar of All-Russia. This designation in the Slavic languages is derived from the Latin title assumed by Roman Emperors, Caesar. Ivan IV's Grandmother,

Sophia, was the niece of the last Byzantine Roman Emperor. She had married Ivan III, the Grand Prince of Moscow. Through supposed prophecy, the presence of theologians that had fled the Muslim Ottomans, and her imperial lineage, Moscow inherited the mantle of being the Third Rome and successor to the Roman Empire. This was not a nation that intended to be a suppliant of other powers, truly they wanted to dominate the Russian speaking peoples and the wider Slavic and Orthodox world.

After the Bolshevik takeover of Russia and the later establishment of the USSR, Soviet rulers saw themselves as the leaders of worldwide communism. Despite some Tsars earlier aping of the Germans and mimicking the French, Russia had become a country that sought to lead rather than follow other nations and influences. It rejected foreign interventions, even those of more benign intent such as during the Russian Civil War were eschewed. Soviet dictators of the early twentieth century were statistically at least as vicious as those from Germany, but few would tolerate a malignant German invasion. Russia was and remains a patriotic country.

The politics of the truly totalitarian Soviet regime pervaded all aspects of life in the USSR, especially those matters that concerned the military. In the communist mindset, the political battle was all important. Control came from the top. Conversely Russia's rivals, especially Germany and Japan, practised mission command. In this doctrine commanders were given the right to act *carte blanche*. The British Defence Staff could and did stand up to Churchill and respectfully revoke by persuasion his unsound military suggestions, as Alan Brooke regularly did. Yet, the paranoid Soviet empire practised a quite different system. Even experienced Red Army generals were subordinated to bureaucrats controlling their unit's ideology and often military decisions. These officials, known as political commissars, were an innovation introduced into the armed forces of revolutionary France in the late eighteenth century. They were an important part of the Red Army from 1918 until 1942. Their place in the command structure during Operation Barbarossa proved to be disastrous. Commanders were afraid to act, they would not and could not use their individual initiative, nor properly apply their talent for warfare. Generals were more fearful of making decisions without approval from higher authority than they were of what the Germans would do to Mother Russia. Indeed, at first Stalin forbade the army from being properly prepared to defend the Soviet Union. The many disasters which befell the Red Army led to this system being reformed with a reduction in the political commissars' power. Soviet commanders were then given more freedom and officers were to be addressed by their rank rather than as 'Comrade.'

Hitler, conversely, increased political control over the German army. He had given orders that captured Red Army political commissars should be summarily executed but in 1943 Hitler then adopted a similar system to that which had been rejected in Russia. This sought to indoctrinate the Wehrmacht and make its commanders subordinate to the Nazi Party and its ideology.

Hitler and Stalin did not lead parallel lives, they were two ships passing in the night, however there are some eery similarities. Stalin's wife killed herself and most of the women in Hitler's life either attempted suicide or succeeded in taking their own lives. Nevertheless, they were polar opposites. The differing control and command of mobile units illustrated how these great dictators approached war. At the start of the fighting on the Eastern Front, German mission command was set against Soviet order tactics. Hitler and Stalin reversed their approaches through the course of the war. Stalin was prepared to let go for the sake of the victory but Hitler's ego led to him to meddle ever more greatly. Despite the proven success of mission tactics, and the failures when they were not followed, most notably Hitler agreeing to pause his Panzers before Dunkirk, operational freedom was later abandoned. In time Hitler sought to control units down to the level of the division. The result was disaster in the field.

Hitler's many interferences were flawed military decisions. However, the rationale behind these orders, which often went against the advice of his senior officers, was political. Hitler, despite his artistic ambitions and even his own military service, was first and foremost a wily political operator. He felt that he could not allow the German army to operate independently of his will. It was an organisation that had been dominated by a class of men, the Prussian military aristocracy, that had a natural aversion towards the uncouth Nazi upstarts that were now their masters. Hitler, himself, spoke with a lower-class German accent. The German Führer had to show them who was the boss even at the expense of making decisions which cost him his dream of building a lasting empire. The alternative to this strategy of humbling the German military establishment was to risk a coup against his own rule.

Conversely, the Soviets at first followed directions being imposed from on-high, resulting in many of their early defeats. In 1941, Soviet forces were refused permission by their high command to escape from the Kiev pocket. After the defence of Moscow, a general advance pushed the Red Army on too far after the initial success. That was all to change. The spirit of reckless abandon passed onto Hitler who would make similar blunders at a time when Soviet commanders on the ground were given more operational freedom. Soviet success ensued and Germany's later top-down model led the Third Reich into utter ruin.

Whilst Stalin and the Russian's were willing to do whatever it takes to at first survive and ultimately win; Germany and the Nazis were not. Hitler had blundered into a war of attrition, yet, to justify Nazi rule, still sought the adulation of his people by placating their whims. Hitler and his henchmen must have questioned their own legitimacy and doubted their righteousness. The attempt to hide their most serious crimes was a sign of guilt. The Third Reich never had the same level of self-assurance about the rectitude of their cause than that possessed by the Soviet leadership. The Russians were sure that their historic mission was justified, they had a religious zeal for their holy books, the works of Marx and Lenin. Sacrificing the individual for this cause was not only right but the victory was inevitable, there is no better motivation. Soviet leaders did not crave the love of their people, they demanded it. Their moral superiority gave them all the justification they needed to drive their soldiers forward in mass waves. Or force their workers to relocate behind the Ural Mountains where before they even had homes, they would reconstruct factories far away from the fighting and out of range of German bombers. Choice was not a commodity available in the Soviet Union, one had to accept what one was given, especially if it was an order.

What Russian soldiers and tank crews lacked in training they made up for in motivation derived from their nation and ideology. They possessed a willingness to be used in remorseless massed attacks. Lenin has said quantity has a quality all its own. Red Army commanders were also a new breed of officer that had risen-up from the ranks during the bitter fighting of the First World War and the Russian Civil War. They too did not shrink from murderous and suicidal offensives. They were accustomed to disturbing losses. Mercy, pity, and remorse were not a part of their lexicon. These ruthless men also thought the individual was irrelevant. Indeed, they had few choices but to deploy soldiers in a way which made massive casualties inevitable. In the absence of enough equipment something, or, more precisely, someone had to make the initial breakthrough in the enemy's line. The most available resource to achieve that tactic was manpower deployed as massed infantry. Only when British and particularly American equipment, such as trucks, were provided could more sophisticated methods be employed by Red Army commanders. Yet, at the start of the war they had to bludgeon their way to victory.

Soviet battlefield tactics were retarded by the purges of the 1930s which took out many of the most able commanders who were replaced with lower ranking and less experienced men. This coupled with poor technology and a general lack of sophistication made the situation worse. To meet the German onslaught and make up for the enormous losses that the Russians had to endure, they had little time to adequately train their servicemen, this further exacerbated the numbers that would be killed in action. Ultimately, those who conducted themselves poorly or were found to be incompetent would be weeded out. The refusal to let the invader pass would prove enough to blunt, wear down, and ultimately stop the German advance but a terrific, and unnecessary, cost would be paid.

At the start of the fighting Russian authoritarianism combined with communist totalitarianism, which required complete subservience to the state, was to hinder the Red Army's defence. The USSR had a constitution which claimed to defend human rights and even limit arrest without a warrant, however, the political culture was everything, and Soviet society did not honour the concept of civil liberties. All power centred on a small clique, a citizen's life and death was in the hands of men who had struggled for power and were determined to hang onto it. No one was safe, not even the highest politician, their wives, and senior generals; all could be laid low through a stroke of Stalin's pen if their name was unfortunate enough to appear on a list. The NKVD, the Soviet secret police, would be willing to oblige the communist leadership. This culture spread and was all-encompassing in Soviet life. Stalin's mental breakdown in the mid-1930s led him to demand ever more egregious amounts of executions. To advance in the state apparatus, random targets for routing out dissidents had to be met. The state existed to repress.

To gain social credit in the system and advance economically, or just to prove that one was a good and loyal communist, a culture of denouncing your neighbours and colleagues developed. An accusation of a thought crime could condemn someone to death or deportation to a Siberian gulag, often they were one and the same. Eventually, this culture reached the Red Army. Stalin was concerned that he would lose power in a military coup. Germany had a part to play in this. Hitler's 1934 Night of the Long Knives where, he efficiently eliminated his rivals and cemented his power, appealed to Stalin's ruthless streak, The Soviet leader and officially General Secretary of the Communist Party, and later its Chairman, had seen the way forward. This not only inspired Stalin, but also led him to overestimate the German Führer's abilities and he especially feared a confrontation with Germany. Stalin did not realise that Hitler was indolent and ineffectual and far from wanting to rule, planned to retire after the war to the town of Linz in Austria and indulge his desire of becoming an architect. Stalin drew the wrong lessons and received information from Germany that destabilised his army.

In a plot inspired by Reinhard Heydrich, the Director of the Gestapo, Germany's secret police, false evidence was provided to Stalin that led him to believe that Red Army commanders were plotting to overthrow him. The result was that a third of the senior officer corps were liquidated by the Soviet leader. The development of innovative and practical tactics and technology stopped when the bullet entered the brains of these men. Even aircraft designers, for instance, found themselves in a gulag.

The Soviet military was still suffering from the purges at the time of Operation Barbarossa. This decapitation of the Soviet military helped encourage Hitler's optimism. The recklessness of this policy was only possible in a state that demanded obedience and had no checks and balances to restrain the rulers. It was as if serfdom and absolutism had been reintroduced into Russia by the Bolsheviks. Private property had been outlawed and all production was, in theory, under the control of an elite who used compulsion to control the economy. With agriculture collectivised, farmers were once again tied to the land which would be under the control of a state official. Internal passports were introduced to control the movement of Soviet subjects within the USSR and workers would be compelled to work however the edinonachalie manager so decreed. These 'little Stalins' were akin to a baron or count. Russia's ancient socio-economic mediaeval traditions with peasants tied to the land had been reasserted by the Bolsheviks with workers tied to the factory or collective farm. They laboured at the whim of a master that owed their power to their political abilities and not their proficiency. After the fall of communism, a different set of oligarchs took power and used force to assert economic control. A country cannot escape its history.

The Stalinist neo-feudal system was a double-edged sword, creating both misery and, for that part of the world, an unprecedented level of economic output as workers had no alternative but to accept employment in the cities. However, the mass famine of 1932-1933, particularly affecting western Ukraine is known as the *Holodomor*, meaning 'hunger plague'. It caused mass death and was one of the great atrocities of the twentieth century. It resulted from the rejection of biology, replacing established science with Lysenkoism developed by the Ukrainian Trofim Lysenko. His agricultural theories disregarded genetics and science and instead reinterpreted the natural world and applied communist revolutionary principles to nature and farming. Scientific opponents that would not divert from science-based biology were purged. The disaster was accelerated through the failed policy of agricultural collectivisation and the liquidation of the Kulaks, the most productive farmers. As part of these hellacious policies, those who owned a cow, or refused to cooperate, had their property stolen or were shot or both. The collectivisation policy of the Georgian born Stalin was enacted by Lysenko and enforced by fellow communist Ukrainian Lazar Kaganovich, the catastrophe that followed added to the bitterness toward Soviet rule in some parts of Ukraine. This did not dissipate even after the Germans sought to impose their own hunger plan to kill 20-30 million Soviets by starvation. Like the communists, the Nazis would requisition (steal) food.

The statist, socialist, and totalitarian Germans, Japanese, and Russians had a hugely different mindset to the capitalist democracies of America, Britain, and the old Commonwealth. The population of the latter group of nations were in their formative years predominantly of Anglo-Celtic and Dutch descent. They established a national ethos that later waves of immigrants assimilated into. Peoples in those countries knew not to throw money at something that is not working. The same mindset applied to the class of decision makers from which Britain, America, Canada, Australia, New Zealand, and South Africa drew their general staff and military commanders. To put it simply they learnt not to reinforce failure. The socialist and its sister statist mindset, which could call on resources at will, with no incentive to be efficient and strive for economy, took their wasteful worldview into their war plans.

Representative democracies with constitutional checks and balances and diffused power and decision making within their nations preserved the lives of their citizens. The countries that possessed totalitarian systems repeatedly made the military mistake of throwing away the valuable lives of its soldiers in fruitless human wave tactics. Dictatorships also attempted to hold territory at all costs despite there being no strategic rationale. These tactics were a major misallocation of resources. Soldiers could best be of service through staying alive so they can kill, not die, for their country on another occasion or fight at a different point in the battlespace where they could get a better return. The Nazi, Japanese, and Soviet leadership never saw value in that concept. Preservation of lives as a concept only emerged and really took hold in property owning democracies who fought to win without paying an exorbitant butcher's bill.

Newly created states, namely the Soviet Union, Italy, Germany, and Japan had no dissolution of power outside of a small clique. Indeed, the power of the inner circle would ultimately reside in the hands of the most prominent member of the gang who became accountable to no one, this made all politics personal. The rivalry between these undemocratic dictatorships became personified in the leaders who owned the lives of their subjects. Competing interests became personal slights. War was an expression of the dictator's will. Victory and vengeance were the same, overcoming one's personal rival became the overarching grand strategy in such states. This mindset, when combined with the power to impose it, led to reckless demands being made of their subjects whose lives would be thrown away to redress personal grievances.

The unstoppable force versus the immovable object

The invasion of the Soviet Union, and Russian occupied Poland, was a battle between two men which could deploy two different strengths. It was German speed versus Russian manpower. The Germans had to win quickly within the first few months before the USSR could grind them down. Although the invasion was on an epic scale, with three million men assembled for the conquest of Russia, the invasion itself was often delayed; the date was repeatedly pushed back. These were just temporary reprieves, but the rescheduling gave Stalin hope that the calamity could be avoided. Finally, the invasion was set for 22nd June 1941 and named after a Twelfth Century German Crusader and Holy Roman Emperor of an earlier Reich, Frederick Barbarossa, meaning 'red beard'. This giant of his age had also conquered parts of Italy. The General staff in the German High Command, responsible for their armed forces, believed the Soviet Union to be a threat and supported the principle of the invasion. This body was later to lose much of its power and was bullied into submission by their Führer. Yet, in 1941 they did not need to be intimidated into carrying out aggressive war. However, they were to have reservations about the final plan.

The initial invasion strategy was developed by General Marcks, and named Operation Draft East, and so was also known as the Marcks Plan, he proposed a two-pronged attack on Russia with diversionary attacks to hide the true objectives. There would have been two main army groups. Group North to attack towards Vitebsk in modern day Belarus, with an arm aiming to stride out for Leningrad where it would link up with the Finns, eliminate Soviet forces in the Baltic region then swing south-east to attack Moscow. Separated by the Pripyat marshes, in the southern sector Group South would take Kiev and other cities along the Dnieper River. It would also seize the Black Sea city of Odessa in the south. The two pincers would then begin to converge, first on Smolensk and then on the Soviet capital itself, Moscow. They would form a simultaneous conquest of this key transportation hub and home to the Kremlin, the seat of Russian power. From there the remainder of much of Russia west of the Urals would be taken under German control. Marcks thought the Red Army would at first retreat in the face of these ultimately converging thrusts and later try to form and hold a defensive line.

This plan was later revised by General Halder. Hitler's meddling was to prove to be the invasion's undoing. The Führer could not decide on the objectives and settled for three main thrusts that not only diverged but left German forces overstretched. The final plan for Operation Barbarossa had three army groups on different trajectories. Army Group North was tasked with taking Leningrad. Army Group Centre were meant to seize Moscow. Army Group South would conquer Kiev.

Germany's generals opposed Hitler's ideas, especially General Halder and Gerd von Rundstedt. The Field Marshal thought the diverging operation to be a nonsensical plan. He even spoke up against Hitler's favoured ideas. von Rundstedt recognised that the attack on Russia would be a long war, not a short one. Rather than Hitler's dramatic headlong rush into a climatic clash of civilisations, von Rundstedt advocated that Germany should go for objectives step-by-step. He wanted the advance into Russia to go only so far as a line running from Leningrad in the north to Odessa in the south passing through Orsha in the centre, in what is now Belarus. Only in 1942, if resources and the situation allowed, should German forces then push onto Moscow, with Army Group North moving first to Leningrad and from there go on to attack Moscow. Army Group Centre would strike directly at the Russian capital. Hitler, however, buoyed by earlier victories wanted to push ever deeper into the giant landmass that is Russia and was not willing to apply the precautionary principle.

Heinz Guderian was appalled that the thrusts in the scheme finally approved by Hitler were not being focused on an ultimate objective. Blitzkrieg depended upon the concentration of force against a single point. The dissenter's vision of how things should have proceeded was not to win out and the invasion went ahead as Hitler and one of Operations Barbarossa's planners, General, later Field Marshal, Paulus envisaged.

Götterdämmerung

Whilst the USSR did have ambitions to expand its borders and spread communism to less enlightened nations, it was not immediately preparing to attack Germany. If the Red Army had been about to attack it would have been in a higher state of readiness and better prepared to deal with the Nazi onslaught. The Soviet strategy still rested on defence, and initially it was a woeful resistance. By noon on the first day of the invasion, 22nd June 1941, one quarter of the Soviet air force had been destroyed; much of it on the ground where planes were parked next to the runways. Not only had the Soviets lost 2,500 planes; but one week after the beginning of the invasion the Germans were a third of the way to Moscow. The Red Army had lost over 1,300 tanks.

Fearful of provoking Hitler and a major cataclysm, the Soviet leader had stalled plans to reinforce Russia's defences and prepare a response to the imminent German invasion. When it did eventually start, Stalin, a man with his own mental health problems, who suffered from both paranoia and a tendency to have nervous breakdowns, retreated in a state of despair to his dacha, his grace and favour home in woodland. The Soviet one-party state was for four days rudderless, its government was built around one man, and after years of purges, other members of the politburo, the Communist Party's policy making committee, were dependent upon Stalin. After a few days of desolation with Stalin secluding himself away, his underlings arrived, not to arrest him and have him shot, as he had arranged for so many, but to ask him to give direction to his minions. Stalin had not been completely incapacitated and had been issuing some orders, but from now on the Soviet Union was dedicated to the war it had expected since the mid-1920s. The game was now on. Where there was ineffectual resistance to the Germans and the other Axis invaders the commanders were, as per Stalin's *modus operandi*, shot.

In the face of this devastating offensive, the Red Army did not melt away and lure the Germans into a trap. There was no land for time strategy. The Russians fought back with all their might and were determined not to cede any territory. Poland was conquered in 28 days; France fell in 38, yet the Germans were slowly but surely beginning to get worn down by the Red Army's constant pressure. German commanders reported back the unprecedented damage they were taking. The toll on German lives and equipment was like nothing they had experienced so far. The Red Army's dogged opposition was deeply unsettling and unnerving. It was not going to be a short war. Despite the rapid advance, Operation Barbarossa did not follow the pattern of the Wehrmacht's earlier battles. Troops cannot consistently fight and would need to be withdrawn from combat after 70 days. During the First World War, to avoid exhausting the soldiers and prevent combat fatigue, soldiers would have to be regularly rotated out of their relatively static position in the trenches. In the Second World War, the demands would be even more sapping. There was little cover to be had from Red Army artillery and rockets. Germany's resources were split between too many fronts. The overstretched campaign against Russia had men travelling on foot and often suffering the inconvenience of using horses to move artillery across the vastness of the USSR. This had a debilitating effect on the Germans. They were not alone in their suffering.

The Red Army also suffered cases of disillusionment and desertion. Stalin and his chief henchman, Lavrentiy Beria, re-established blocking units, also known as barrier troops, to encourage discipline and in some cases prevent any retreats. These were mainly drawn from the NKVD. Blocking units were first used in Russia during World War One and were known as Death Battalions. These troops executed fleeing soldiers; and when first deployed against Russians facing the Kaiser's army, had stopped retreats turning into routs. However, in time this strategy only increased disillusion with the Provisional Government and with Alexander Kerensky, the temporary leader of Russia after the Tsar's overthrow. He had decided to continue with the war and this paved the way for the Russian army and navy to switch their loyalties to the Bolsheviks. In the resulting civil war, blocking units were then deployed by the Red Army against the Red Army to prevent their comrades from retreating from combat with the White forces and their foreign allies. Stalin's barrier-troops were successful.

Lavrentiy Beria came from the Republic of Abkhazia, a region that is recognised by the UN as being part of Georgia but has since decided to incorporate itself into the Russian Federation. Stalin's Order 270, and Beria's ruthlessness, terrorised the Red Army into fighting back against the Germans. This decree demanded the execution of soldiers who did not resist and the imprisonment of their families. This even applied to Stalin's daughter-in-law who was imprisoned when his son was captured. Stalin said, "It takes a very brave man to be a coward in the Russian army". In the Red Army any lack of discipline or cowardness led to soldiers being put into penal battalions known as *Shtrafbats*. Those sentenced to serve in these brigades were given the most arduous, dangerous, and deadly tasks right on the front line. Through heroism or injury, the condemned men could win their rehabilitation. Lessons learned they would be returned to their regular units. Here they would no longer be considered completely expendable and would be used in combat in a more effective way that did not entirely waste lives.

The Red Army did not just rely on tenacity for its defence. The Soviet Union also sought to depend upon fixed defences and a series of fortifications. This was known as the Stalin Line, and consisted of a series of zones secured by a network of interlocking bunkers. These were not designed to stop the enemy, their aim was to provide strong points which would be hard to take and would need to be avoided. The intention was to channel an invader into certain chosen areas where mobile units could engage the enemy, halt their advance, and defeat them allowing for a counterattack which would see the enemy driven out of Mother Russia. Construction of the Stalin Line began in 1928 but following the USSR's advance westwards, conquering the Baltic States, the Bukovina region, and reclaiming land from Poland, work was abandoned in favour of defences closer to the new frontier. However, the Molotov Line, as the newer defences were known, was not completed in time for Operation Barbarossa. The older Stalin Line, having been neglected, was ill-prepared and could not provide adequate defence against the German *blitzkrieg*. Stalin did not overly help these defence lines; he prevented their improvement in case the work provoked the Germans.

Whilst these lines did not perform as originally hoped, there were instances of forts delaying the Wehrmacht. The Brest Fortress, in modern day Belarus, stood guard over the designated *Panzerrollbahn 1*, the road that led to Moscow. Brest was also a railway hub and held bridges over the Bug River. Part of the German advance was held up at this fortress for seven days. Some Soviet elements in the fortress were even prepared to fight to the death, holding out for more than a month. Notwithstanding their heroism Brest still fell to the enemy. Russia's only option was to let slip the dogs of war. In some cases, this was literal. Dogs, trained to find food under tanks, had explosives strapped to them and were unleashed in the face of the Panzers.

The Nazi advance into Russia was devastating for the Soviets. As in 1812, in Russia's first patriotic war, the Russians sought to deny the enemy access to their resources and the bounty of the land. They enforced a scorched earth policy although in many instances there was not much to destroy. Large parts were sparsely populated and with this came a paucity of settlements and therefore a lack of shelter. On the Eastern Front, this made even a village of great importance. The Soviets destroying many of these hamlets as they retreated denied refuge to the Germans. Those towns that the Russians did not wish to destroy were made inhospitable. In advance of the Wehrmacht, as the Red Army withdrew, the Russians would often bobby trap settlements, and even parts of cities, to kill their future occupiers and give the German no respite from the war which they had initiated.

Food and shelter from the elements were not the only thing they denied to the enemy. Soviet industry was also evacuated. The speed of the German advance and the unlikelihood of stemming this headlong dash into Russia meant there was a serious risk of the Germans overrunning Soviet industrial centres. To avoid this, the Russian authorities had to order the disassembling, packing, and transportation east of whole factories. These would then be reassembled, beyond the Ural Mountains, out of range of not only the Wehrmacht but even the Luftwaffe's bombers. This caused a temporary, but acute, loss of production until these plants could be re-established. Yet it kept many factories out of German hands and in the service of the Russian war effort. This was a feat of Soviet organisation and included the movement of millions of workers to the east. It was the most rapid industrial relocation in human history. This was a massive logistical success conducted under the most extreme duress. The United States was also to have a major industrial relocation, including large workforce movements, which was achieved through a different mode. The Russian war effort was not just aided by their ability of its industry to run away but also by their capacity to get the fruits of this industry to the front.

The Red Army also possessed superb armour. Alarming reports to the German High Command came back from the front about the fearful beast that was the KV tank which the Wehrmacht was facing. These would soon be complemented by the less heavy medium sized T-34 tanks. The reports of these large insurmountable vehicles on the Eastern Front caused incredulity. It was unimaginable that Bolshevik Slavs could produce such behemoths. The German racial prejudices towards their eastern neighbours had failed to realise that the Soviet Union's industrial strength and superb military equipment were not homemade but borrowed from the United States of America and Britain. Soviet socialists were more open minded than their German national socialist counterparts who despised all things American. The Nazis thought Americana was tainted by other ethnicities, namely Jews, and Anglo-Saxon capitalism, which again was seen to be Jewish in origin and influence.

Blood and treasure
The Soviet Union was resisting the creation of a Eurasian Reich. In this noble cause, much Russian blood would be shed but the treasure came from her new allies, the British Empire and America. The USSR was not alone in its struggle. President Roosevelt was determined that his country would be kept safe by preventing the Germans and Japanese from controlling the oceans. He was not only angered by the Axis' Anti-Americanism, but also by German, Italian, and Japanese expansionism, and their lack of respect for national sovereignty. Roosevelt turned the United States into the great arsenal of democracy and purposing its mighty industrial potential to aid Britain, China, and in time it would assist the Soviets as well.

It was not yet clear that Russian survival was guaranteed but the possibility of victory for the Red Army was becoming more likely as German losses mounted. Nevertheless, Russia's eventual triumph in the Great Patriotic War, as the struggle is known in Russia, was made in the west and achieved through Western aid given to the Soviet Union which kept them in the fight and prevented an economic collapse. Soviet industrial strength was merely a mirage. During the conflict, Britain produced more fighter planes, bombers, vehicles, and warships than the much larger USSR. America produced more tanks than the Soviet Union. British and US combined tank production exceeded that of Russian by 25,000 vehicles.

Indeed, the homegrown Soviet tank that was unleashed on the Germans to drive the invader back to Berlin, owed its parentage to the marriage between British and American technology. The UK's Vickers 6-Ton tank was licensed to Russia who renamed it the T-26, it was then mated with the American Christie suspension system, and markedly improved to create the legendary vehicle that was the T-34. Later in the war this again evolved into the T-34 85 which carried an even more deadly main gun and was the perfect partner to the heavy KV tanks and its successor the IS tank. Soviet tank production owed the United States a great debt.

The industrial giant which the Soviet Union became borrowed heavily from the United States of America. Lenin, the Marxist theorist and revolutionary, was originally opposed to capitalist developed scientific theories of management. However, upon taking control of Russia and founding the USSR, he realised its worth and became particularly enamoured with Taylorism. This was a system of production named after its founder, Frederick Taylor. The goal was to increase output. To increase industrial production in the interwar years, Russia also adopted Fordism, using the assembly line techniques pioneered by motorcar magnate Henry Ford.

The Russian factories that produced such war winning weapons were designed on the drawing boards of Detroit. Albert Kahn, formerly of Ford, and the architect of Motor City, known as Mo Town, was the designer of Soviet factories and his bureau trained the next generation of Russian industrial architects. The tooling for Soviet plants also came from the United States and in some cases whole workshops were purchased from America, transported to the USSR, reassembled, and put to work. To build the workers' paradise and defeat its enemies, the communists acquired these American latter-day temples to mammon by selling grain for US Dollars which was then used to pay for American factories. This practice continued even during famines and exacerbated the problems caused by requisitioning the food and property of the most efficient and productive peasants.

The Union of Soviet Socialist Republics communist leadership also employed American energy firms and their experts to develop and manage its oil production. The borrowing of expertise and technology was not a new phenomenon. Britain had been the role model in the nineteenth century when a Welsh industrialist John Hughes, manager of the London based Millwall Iron Works, founded a mill which quickly grew into the then Russian city of Donetsk, making this area a centre of mining and industry which well into the 21st century still provided products for the Russian market. In 1918 Donetsk and the surrounding regions declared their independence from Ukraine after the Ukrainians entered into an alliance with Germany. The Bolsheviks would put Donetsk back into the Ukrainian Soviet Socialist Republic when they took back control. Yet, it again seceded from Ukraine in 2014 when a pro-European Union government took power after an uprising in Kiev. The city is now a part of the Donetsk People's Republic, a little recognised statelet bordering the Russian Federation.

Taylor, Ford, Kahn, and to a degree Hughes, were the midwives of Soviet labour and delivered the fruits of Russian industry. However, other lessons from the capitalist states were not learned by the Soviets. The lack of consumer power in the USSR led to an inability to have effective quality control mechanisms for checking a factory's produce. This in turn led to unreliable vehicles being sent to the front line. Soviet tank crews and airmen, just like Soviet citizens, had to accept what they were given. Indeed, unless they were politically correct, the civilian would not have the right to receive anything. The lives of the workers were almost as expendable as those of its soldiers. Little concern was given to their welfare and few incentives were applied. Unlike the Nazis, the Soviets did not prioritise consumer goods, in fact the interests of its citizens were ignored as the war economy took over all aspects of production. Even agriculture was deprioritised, resulting in people becoming hungry thus making them less efficient workers. It was a vastly different story in the United States which had a quite different economic model. In America living standards were growing and there was a massive industrial migration of men and machines to new centres of work. This was achieved through providing better pay and opportunities for staff in the private sector. Companies even provided schools, cinemas, and services to the people of the new towns that sprung up to serve America's war effort. Workers willingly flocked to these sites.

Whilst the Germans still produced consumables for their people, the Americans took highly efficient tools and techniques used in consumer industrial production and turned its factories from peaceful purposes towards the making of weapons. Privately owned companies, freed from the harmful restrictions of Roosevelt's New Deal, would compete to win contracts from the US Government, which had taken on the role of the consumer previously occupied by individuals. However, free market principles still ruled. America's automotive industry, the largest and most efficient in the world, served the globe's biggest and most advanced consumer car market. In the task of bringing weapons to the Allies it would lead the way. Logistics wins wars, but the application of logistical science depends upon both vehicles and values. The ability to produce weapons and their transports in such abundance could not have happened if people were not free to sell their services, goods, and labour at a price agreed with the consumer.

The Red Army was kept moving by the Americans and the British. The USA supplied the Russians with more than 400,000 jeeps and trucks, double the Soviet production. The trucks were produced by Studebaker, and so common were they that Studebaker became a loan word in the Russian language as another term for truck. Other forms of transport came from America, including trains and motorcycles. Indeed, ⅔ of Soviet vehicles were built in the USA. Britain also supplied boots. Men and machines were fuelled by supplies of food, oil, and petroleum by way of the UK and America. The Red Army was however willing to use one resource that it grew and held in abundance, namely the lives of its citizens.

Whilst the USSR appeared to be on course to collapse, the character of the many peoples that made up Russia coupled with the support of both Britain and America would dictate a different outcome. The Soviet war effort also had assistance from an unlikely source. Under pressure from the United Kingdom, the Soviets and the London based Polish Government-in-exile signed the Sikorski–Mayski agreement, where Polish prisoners of war were released from their Siberian detention. These were the lucky ones; many officers had earlier been liquidated in the Katyn massacre. Despite Soviet outrages against Poland, the Russians could in time rely on Polish armies to supplement and serve alongside the Red Army's struggle against Germany.

The Soviets would also export some Poles to Britain via Iran. These former prisoners of war formed a corps that would fight alongside the British in the middle east, Italy, and France. A generation before, their forefathers in World War One had also fought against the Germans in France. Following that war, they were sent by the French to fight against the Bolsheviks in Ukraine where the Poles committed anti-Semitic pogroms. After the Second World War, many Polish soldiers of the so-called Anders Army would not get the opportunity to emigrate back to eastern Europe. Poland, the USSR, and Germany were not the only participants on the Eastern Front, supplies from Britain, Canada, and the USA gave the Soviets important assistance, but the Germans also had support; indeed, Russia had pushed others into the German camp. Politics and propaganda would decide how the fighting developed.

Partners in crime

The gradual expansion of the Grand Duchy of Moscow, evolving into Tsarist Russia, and its absorption of lands formerly held by Tartar Khanates, and the Swedish, Polish, and Ottoman empires had irked its European neighbours. This process began with Ivan IV's quest to control over warm water harbours on the Baltic Sea. These ports would remain open in winter, through which Russia could trade with the rest of the world all year round.

To that end Ivan IV, known in English as Ivan the Terrible, the epithet being a mistranslation of Грóзный (Groznyy) meaning strict, formidable, fearsome, went to war with the German speaking Teutonic Knights. This Roman Catholic Crusading Order held lands on the Baltic coveted by the founder of the Russian Empire. To mobilise support for their war with the Russians the Teutonic Order produced anti-Russian German language pamphlets. The propaganda depicted their Russian Orthodox opponents as cruel savages, a barbarous child devouring people. The production of these anti-Russian tropes proved to be successful propaganda. Poland and Sweden were to wage war with Russia and denied Moscow access to the ice-free ports. Sweden took the Baltic region for themselves. Just as the quest for a warm water port remains Russia's historic and enduring mission governing its statecraft to this day, so the Russiaphobic propaganda continues in an attempt to thwart their overriding aim of securing a window to the west.

When the USSR inherited the mantle of *de facto* successor state to the Russian Empire, the Soviets began to re-establish hegemony over its traditional spheres of influence. From 1939 onwards, the ethnically Georgian Soviet leader, Joseph Stalin, no longer practised Socialism in One Country and began to export communism to his neighbours. These adjoining countries saw Nazi Germany as the lesser of two evils. Eastern European nations in alliance with the Axis joined Operation Barbarossa. Amongst those accompanying the German invasion were volunteers from Spain and other western European states. Many were soldiers from Romania and most importantly Finland. The Finns saw this as a continuation of the war from the previous year.

The Continuation War lasted from 1941 until 1944. Finnish statesman, Mannerheim, aimed to reconquer land ceded to Russia the year before. However, Finnish forces lacked artillery and could not press deep into the USSR. Accordingly, Mannerheim could not complete the encirclement of Leningrad from the north and make up for the Wehrmacht failing to meet their objectives. Consequently, the Red Army kept a route into the city open, this passed over a lake that was frozen so hard in winter that its ice road could support trucks. The supplies brought in enabled Leningrad to be defended. Finland's war did not stop at the former Russian capital. Finland was still trying to defeat Russia, indeed, their resumption of war had aggressive intentions. They aimed to not only recapture their lost territory but also sought to create a greater Finland. Finnish nationalists wanted a greater Finland and sought to ethnically cleanse Russians from Karelia. These expansionists were also trying to ensure that other vital Russian cities were cut-off and conquered. They also allowed German forces to use Finnish territory.

Finnish forces, along with their German partners, working from both Finland and Nazi occupied and aligned Norway, tried to take the vital Russian port of Murmansk on the Barents Sea. In Operation Silver Fox Hitler wanted to attack northern Russia, cutting the Soviet's supply. Hitler sent the Finnish army and a German mountain division to seize the port of Murmansk. Often ice free due to the gulf stream, this proved to be a vital route by which essential war materials were delivered by British Arctic convoys coming via the North Cape. The thinking was sound but despite devastation wreaked upon the city the Axis forces failed to capture Murmansk. This failure was to have a decisive effect on the course of the war. The port of Murmansk and the manufacturing centre of Manchester would be linked by the Arctic convoys. The British merchant navy supplied the Red Army through Murmansk with the Manchester made materiel they needed to help defeat the Axis powers. Finland was being overambitious, the Finnish economy could not stand the strain placed upon it by the war, its massive mobilisation of men meant economic collapse; Finns were going hungry. It was a situation that could not be sustained.

Germany had other less than always completely helpful collaborators. The Romanians sided with the Allies in World War One and reaped the rewards of new territory. They took Transylvania from Austria-Hungry and were awarded parts of Maramureş, Crişana, and Banat. However, Romania aligned with the Axis powers in the Second World War and supplied troops to the invasion of Russia. To all intents and purposes Romania was a German satellite, with a small German speaking population. Like Finland, Romania had lost territory to the Soviet Union; however, unlike the Finns, Romania's soldiers were not an effective fighting force; this was to have dramatic effects in the years to come. Later in the war they shared a similar policy of taking dramatic U-turns as did others. The foreign policies of those two nations would resemble each other.

The Kingdom of Hungary, a landlocked country run by an Admiral, but with no ruling monarch, nor even a royal family, also joined the Nazis on the Eastern Front. As did soldiers from the Kingdom of Italy as well as those from the Slovak Republic and the not very Independent State of Croatia. The Kingdom of

Bulgaria initially refused to fight against the Russians as their Slavic co-linguists had helped them against the Ottoman Turks. The Bulgarians did, however, take anti-communist measures at home and supplied logistical help to the Wehrmacht, such as driving vehicles and helping in a non-combat capacity. They were still to pay a heavy price in the war for their alignment with Hitler. Bulgaria did declare war on the other Allies, namely Britain and America.

Some Soviet citizens from the Baltic States also fought with the German army. Both sides conscripted people to fight for them when they were in control of Baltic State countries. Resources were also taken from these littoral peoples. The Germans would attempt to pay for them, the Russians would just requisition whatever they wanted. There were some Russians, and various Muslim tribes, who also collaborated with the Germans. The Nazis were also joined by a potpourri of collaborators from western Europe, particularly Belgium and Norway, where some citizens joined the *Waffen-SS* in what they thought was a crusade against Russian Bolshevism. Some Spaniards also joined; Spain sent volunteers to the Eastern Front known as the Blue Division which served with the German Army. The Ukraine was particularly fertile territory for finding recruits to collude with Germany. The leader of Nazi collaboration forces, Stepan Bandera, is honoured to this day in Ukraine as a patriot. After the war, in 1959, Bandera was assassinated at his new home in Munich, then part of West Germany. This was carried out by the KGB on the orders of Russian leader Nikita Khrushchev. The weapon of choice to kill this dissident, and in Soviet eyes traitor, was an exotic one. A KGB assassin, who had feigned defection to the west, used cyanide gas, to take revenge on Bandera.

In parts of Ukraine nationalism had been stirring for some time and was accelerated by the dreadful famine caused through communist agricultural terror. To this day many in the west of Ukraine would prefer to be in the German orbit rather than being a satellite of Russia. They are not alone; other nations have sought to integrate Ukraine into central Europe. As part of the appeasement campaign in the late 1930s it was even muted that Germany be given back the Ukraine, a land it had ruled briefly in 1918 after the Bolshevik capitulation to Germany during the First World War. Germany would not be so successful the second time. Yet, there were some Ukrainian nationalists that supported these aims and fiercely objected to Russian domination; the most notorious of these was Bandera. However, the Nazis treated most Ukrainians with utter contempt. And despite the crimes committed by the communists most residents of Ukraine did not support Germany's occupation even though it came under the innocuous slogan of liberation from the Bolsheviks. The hostility to German control was not surprising as the area was the original crucible of Russian civilisation, Kiev being the principal Russian city until the Grand Duchy of Moscow took pre-eminence. The later fighting in Ukraine during the Second World War was especially vicious. In addition to the Soviet Red Army fighting against the *Deutsches Heer* (army) and *Waffen-SS* there were also pro-Russian partisans and pro-German militias. In the middle were other irregulars who opposed both the communists and the Nazis, desiring neither German nor Russian overlordship but instead favouring neutrality and real independence. In the First World War, Russia, politically divided and set against itself, folded to demands to cede its empire, even the Ukraine, to the Germans. In World War Two, communist Russia had a common purpose and would not accept defeat.

Ministry of Truth
The Nazi and Soviet states would in time use every tool at their disposal, including propaganda, to motivate their people, and was integrated into the military conflict. Totalitarian regimes already used their control of information to mobilise and manipulate their populations to serve the whims of the state. The German fear of Bolshevism was used before the war to justify the Nazi dictatorship and during the conflict to keep the population frightened and fighting. Germany spun the line that Russia was a threat to them and was planning an invasion, only Operation Barbarossa had forestalled it, so the story went. This was another big lie but based on a partial truth. The Soviet Union certainly had been seeking to expand its power westwards and improve their security. The Russiaphobic fear of their steamroller enslaving the rest of Europe was just a myth at the time, Stalin had wanted to avoid war, almost at all costs. However, socialism in one country was a temporary solution, a practical answer to the problems created by the Trotskyite failure to successfully export revolution to other countries whose peoples were still wedded to faith, family, and flag. The intervention of foreign nations in other country's affairs was rarely welcomed by workers in the invaded state.

Stalin had made his name in Bolshevik circles after writing a pamphlet titled *Marxism and the National Question*. This work, which won Lenin's praise, concluded that national identity and independence should be replaced by a superior culture under a vanguard elite. Diversity amongst different peoples would not be tolerated. The endgame was therefore always world revolution. However, society was not yet amenable to such notions, and would need to come after the conflict, or follow the culture war. Yet, such radical cultural policies were not implemented at home.

Stalin, a Georgian by birth, and a theorist who criticised the value of national identity, encouraged the people to resist the Nazis by unleashing patriotism, and love of *Mother Russia*. The Soviet Union was officially an atheist state but was willing to use religion to serve its cause, the communists even reopened Russian Orthodox churches. The theology of Russia, and the protection of orthodox Christian religious rites and sites was a fundamental part of their heritage. Nearly 90 years earlier, the Crimean war was sparked by French Emperor Napoleon III's desire to promote the rights of Roman Catholics to control religious sites above those of Eastern Orthodox Christians in the Ottoman controlled Holy Land. Religion was key to Russian nationalism and whilst faith was anathema to communists, those concepts were crucial components of the Russian anti-Nazi cause. A powerful reference was made to the resistance against Napoleon Bonaparte's invasion, known in Russia as the Patriotic War. The modern battle against the latest invaders to come from the west was known as the Great Patriotic War. Heroes of past conflicts from the war of 1812, where the French invasion of Russia was joined by Napoleon's German and Polish allies, were celebrated. The Russian fight against the Teutonic Knights was also remembered and used to fuel the fight.

The promotion of patriotism stopped after the war and the communists would return to their aim of suppressing national identity. Stalin's Russia had merely taken a brief and practical political detour that helped them all face in the right direction and concentrate on the foreign enemy. The German army, under the interfering and vacillating leadership of the Commander-in-Chief, Adolf Hitler, also switched between different strategies and objectives.

Diversions and detours
In July 1941, the Red Army Air Forces bombed the Romanian oilfields on which the Nazi war machine depended. The attack came from bases in Crimea, then a part of the Russian Soviet Federative Socialist Republic. This attack so alarmed Hitler that the Führer decided to use resources to seize this peninsula. Adolf Hitler was also influenced by General von Manstein, who warned Hitler that they should not leave a Russian bridgehead behind German lines. This ran contrary to the principles of blitzkrieg and contrasted with the devil may care attitude shown by von Manstein when he confused the French. The epic conquest of the Crimea began. This was not only a major misallocation of resources, but

it also began to take both Hitler's and the German army's focus away from the fight for Leningrad and the all-important drive towards Moscow. Instead, it deflected attention southward towards the Ukraine and its capital Kiev. The Führer's Crimea fixation turned into a major distraction as it had in the previous century. Another battle for the Crimea, a disputed region to this day, began. Hitler ordered three objectives: the capture of Moscow, the Ukraine, and the Crimea. These goals were mutually exclusive. Other instances of schizophrenic war making would emerge.

Hitler was to develop an obsession with capturing famous cities such as Stalingrad, once known as Tsaritsyn and now called Volgograd. At the time he coveted Sevastopol, the largest city on the Crimean Peninsula and a major warm water port on the Black Sea, something which is of enormous value to the Russians. The German and Romanian forces in the Crimean Campaign took eight months to secure the peninsula. Hitler could have left Sevastopol with a small screening force and use the bulk of 11th Army to cross the Kerch Peninsula and assist Army Group South's drive to the Caucasus. Instead, they had bogged themselves down, it was a major blunder.

Heavy German cannons were prioritised for the siege of Sevastopol and therefore not in use at Leningrad when they could have made a difference. Army Group North, besieging that city, was always the poor neighbour of its counterparts to the south. Army Group Centre and Army Group South generally received priority. In the summer of 1941, and again in 1942, the honour and the accompanying materiel went to the most southern of these three deadly sisters. Despite the lack of provisions, the objectives were not reduced. German forces, and those of their Axis partners, were overstretched. Hitler still wanted Leningrad, another port city to the north at the head of the Gulf of Finland, part of the Baltic Sea. Hitler decided Leningrad should be reduced by attrition and not by being stormed. German forces pinned themselves down besieging the city. One in five German troops on the Eastern front were involved in the siege and its surrounding campaign but to no avail. Either the Wehrmacht should have received all the artillery they needed to take Leningrad, or the soldiers and equipment should have been used elsewhere.

Germany's strength was in manoeuvre warfare, using better tactics and technology such as radios, to make up for their lack of manpower and shortage of equipment but in the sieges of both Sevastopol and Leningrad this strength could not be utilised. The investment of a city can be nearly as damaging for the morale of the besiegers as it can be for those encircled inside. The Russian composer, Dmitri Shostakovich, composed Symphony No. 7, titled *Leningrad*, in honour of the city. This was played for the besieged inhabitants every night to raise morale. The Russian nation likewise listened in on the broadcasts. They were with the people of Leningrad; they too would stand firm and resist the invasion. The situation was very different for the Axis besiegers and the Finns. Conversely, knowing that the city was enduring, *Leningrad's* performance lessened Nazi determination. The Russian authorities refused to mass evacuate civilians from Leningrad as this would have been considered defeatist.

Many in the Baltic States welcomed the Germans as liberators. It appeared that the Nazis would restore Germanic hegemony over the Estonian Baltic islands of Saaremaa, Hiiumaa, and Muhu, which the Germans captured in Operation Albion in 1917 during the First World War. In the late summer of 1941, the Germans launched a similar attack. This was codenamed Operation Beowulf, the name deriving from the hero of Old English literature who, among many other great legendary deeds, swam the Baltic Sea. However, despite Finland's best efforts the war beside the Baltic was not unfolding as Hitler wanted. Events further south were to scare-off the Führer from ordering a frontal assault on the Russian contender for the title of Venice of the North. Hitler was unnerved by the Soviet use of mines during costly German assaults. Hitler became very risk averse. When placed under pressure, he turned out to be unwilling and unable to make bold decisions. This was reminiscent of his reticence to take Malta even after the successful capture of Crete. Leningrad had been missed. With German forces tied up by the Black Sea, Hitler became alarmed at Army Group South's slow progress. In the centre, Moscow was still in play.

Moscow was not only the political and symbolic heart of Russia it was also a major transport hub from where the railways branched out to supply the front with both men and materiel. Capturing it would have limited the Soviet ability to wage war. The railway network which fanned out from Moscow was the logistical key that allowed the Bolsheviks to win the Russian Civil War. It allowed them to move troops around to key positions, even to use the Kronstadt sailors, based on an island in the Baltic, to be moved from Petrograd, later to be renamed Leningrad, to the east near Yekaterinburg. There they halted the Czechoslovak Legion which was advancing westwards from Siberia. These soldiers were originally intended to attack the prison house of nations that was the Austro-Hungarian Empire but with Russia's premature exit from World War One these volunteers and former prisoners of war found themselves assisting the White cause in the Russian Civil War. In March 1921 the socialist sailors would later be largely killed-off by the Red Army when the Baltic Fleet rebelled against

Lenin's dictatorial policies. Pro-Moscow forces crossed the ice to take the island base. Some Kronstadt sailors did manage to escape to Finland.

The loss of Moscow would have been a devastating psychological blow to the Soviets and would have precipitated political discombobulation. German generals wanted the symbolic victory of capturing that city. This glittering prize was alluring to the proud Prussian army commanders that still dominated much of the German High Command. However, Hitler had other ideas. He accused his army commanders of not understanding the economic foundations of war. Hitler's strategy sought the economic extinction of the USSR. The German leader wanted to capture Ukraine's resources, including its grain, the fertile farmland, and agribusiness potential. And at the same time take its population into the servitude of his Reich and eliminate large swathes of the Red Army. To achieve this, he again split his resources leaving him unable to fulfil most of his goals. Hitler, alarmed with Army Group South's slow pace of advance, redirected troops and tanks from Army Group Centre and sent them south away from Moscow. They were now tasked with completing the capture of the Ukraine.

The defences of Kiev were reconstructed just two days after Operation Barbarossa began. The citizens of the Ukrainian capital were conscripted to dig ditches and sure-up fixed positions. Despite this late work Army Group South still needed assistance to take Kiev. This would come by diverting troops south away from the march on Moscow. Hitler ordered Guderian's Panzers to take a more than 90° right turn away from Moscow. Guderian disagreed with this strategy. He thought the focus of the German advance should be Moscow before the Russian winter set in but obey he did.

Russian bombers attacked the advancing German troops. The Soviet southwest was also defended by the Stalin Line. The Germans had to use heavy artillery to destroy its bunkers. Assault guns were used as infantry support to attack and destroy Russia's fortified strongholds. The Red Army had often retreated intact from the many German onslaughts that made up Operation Barbarossa; but at Kiev the Soviet High Command insisted that the Ukrainian capital should be held. Losing Russian speaking Kiev, where most people were in communion with the Moscow Patriarchate of the Orthodox Church, would be a devastating blow to the Soviets. Stalin rushed hundreds of thousands of troops into Kiev to defend the city, but to no avail.

Prior to taking Kiev Hitler sought to capture more Soviet soldiers in a large encirclement, but the Wehrmacht had lost the element of surprise as it sought to draw the nose tighter. Hitler sent German forces away from the Ukrainian capital to the southwest of Kiev to encircle Russian forces in the Battle of Uman.

The Germans also captured ports on the Black Sea coast. They chose not to take Kiev directly, but surround it, cutting-off the Red Army which had been part of a salient that extended Soviet lines. This was then eliminated and the Russian's whole southwest front had been destroyed.

Hitler may have thought his Kievan detour to have been a stroke of genius. Out of the 532,000 troops that were surrounded by the Germans only 20,000 avoided capture by escaping. It succeeded in hauling over half a million Red Army prisoners of war and hundreds of thousands of civilians who were attempting to flee. At the time it was the largest encirclement in history but, NKVD agents had planted bombs in key locations in the city and burnt down buildings, a strategy similar to the Russian immolation of Moscow in 1812. The Germans paid a high price for their advance. The defence of Kiev cost the Germans two months and thus ruined Hitler's battle plan for a quick blitzkrieg victory. Guderian, who had the motto; "Don't tickle, smash!" thought the detour was a great tactical success but questioned its strategic significance. Indeed, the Red Army had been smashed in the south, but the gleaming towers of the Kremlin were now even further away.

Wilderness

The German transportation problems in Russia necessitated some creative logistical solutions. From 1942, the Luftwaffe employed the Messerschmitt Me 323 *Gigant* (Giant) transport plane to carry men and materiel closer to the front line. This six-engine pterosaur, though used in the north African theatre, was an evolutionary dead end. It was almost too big and was difficult to get airborne, a special plane was created to help it get into the air. This was the Heinkel He 111Z *Zwilling*, meaning twin as it was two planes joined together. Otherwise, three separate planes were needed to tow the *Gigant*.

In Russia, distance over time equals disaster. The German advance lacked the velocity it needed to be successful. This was not just because of stern resistance. Russia's separate development from Germany had hindered and slowed the Wehrmacht. The Soviet train tracks that were not broken up by the retreating Red Army, nor destroyed by partisans, used a different railway gauge from German locomotives. The Nazis did not develop trains that could take advantage of the wider Russian railway gauge.

Germany did not have a strong enough railway industry to exploit the full potential of this important logistical mode of transport on the Eastern Front. Hitler's obsession with the Autobahn meant that there was not enough investment in the railway network. Again, the German military was put in charge of this mode of transportation, whereas it should have been under the control of railway professionals who knew how the network operated. With much inconvenience and lost time, the railway gauges could be adapted but even so, many German trains were not robust enough to aid the war effort as they could not operate in the harsh winter which followed Operation Barbarossa; others were to be used for an even more nefarious purpose.

With Leningrad still holding out and the Crimean Campaign still not completed, attention switched back to Moscow. The advance resumed but became impeded by the autumn rains turning the roads into rivers of mud, bringing the Germans and their partners to a standstill. To this day the Russian road network, though more developed, is infamous and is only exceeded in notoriety by the quality of the drivers which use it. The Red Army was better prepared for this inclement eventuality than their German rivals who had developed Panzers with thin tracks that would enable them to be fast and efficient on the well-built highways and autobahns of central and western Europe. Red Army tanks had wider tracks, giving them better weight distribution than their German counterparts, thus enabling them to traverse rough ground and sodden conditions. Russian vehicles could also cope with the cold much better and were less liable to freeze than German armour. Even though the Wehrmacht's tanks were petrol driven, that fuel has a lower freezing point than the Russian diesel-powered engines, the Red Army vehicles could better withstand the severe conditions which would soon be unleashed on these hapless invaders of Mother Russia by Mother Nature. The same was true for the soldiers. With shorter supply lines and not suffering the same logistical challenges which the Germans faced, the Red Army could better maintain and fuel their vehicles than the Nazis who had advanced too deeply into enemy country. The lightning war was but a distant memory. Obstructed first by a sea of mud and then the cold; the Wehrmacht was as thoroughly unprepared and ill-equipped for a long-drawn-out war. The march on Moscow was delayed again. The balance of power was moving in Russia's favour.

Pyrrhic victories
Operation Barbarossa was succeeding in taking territory, but came at an excessive cost. The German gains did not capture enough resources to compensate for the losses expended in taking them nor did they offset the demands placed on the army by the occupation. Hitler's belief that he understood the economic needs of

warfare had been disproved by this self-defeating invasion. The drive into Russia was not only a strategic failure but even on a tactical level it had fundamental problems. Units would often advance beyond artillery support which could not keep up with the tanks. Russian permanent resistance was exhausting German men and materiel. German command tanks, with their radio antennae, were especially vulnerable as the Russians had learnt to target them. A well-aimed Molotov Cocktail could disable a panzer.

It was a myth that Stalin lured the Germans into the interior of Russia, the Germans were made to pay for every inch they took. Stalin attempted to resist the Nazi advance as much as possible and even hoped that a series of counterattacks would see the Red Army advance into Germany. Whilst Stalin was himself delusional the incessant fight back wore down the Nazis. Stalin by accident and through a stubborn dictatorial refusal to accept the loss of land had stumbled upon a strategy which would lead the German army into a deadly battle of attrition. The price of victory was costly, but the Soviets were forcing Hitler to fight in a way that played to Russia's strengths.

In Nazi occupied USSR there were too few Axis units on too large a front. The *blitzkrieg* began to break down. The German mad dash into the Soviet Union was their undoing. The concept that Germany could achieve a quick victory over Russia was flawed; this was known, but through Hitler's political manoeuvrings the military had been thoroughly subordinated and would follow his many foolish whims. German generals feared that Operation Barbarossa was spreading the Axis forces too thinly, but they could not voice their concern and instead continued to indulged Hitler's fantasies. For a short lightning war to be successful it required the different arms of the thrusts to converge on one point, cutting-off and destroying the enemy and inspiring a political collapse. However, in the vastness of Russia the three main thrusts of Operation Barbarossa were diverging. The Prussian theorist, Carl von Clausewitz, which every Wehrmacht officer would have been expected to study, had long ago warned about the danger of overextended lines. The vast steppes of Russia and the Ukraine, a seemingly endless expanse of grassland, provided little opportunity to trap the enemy that was always there on the horizon. The lack of features was unnerving for German soldiers who came from a land of cities, towns, farms, and forests. The nothingness of Russia's big country was delirium inducing.

German weakness, especially its lack of industrial output, and general unpreparedness for war meant that the would-be conquerors had little alternative but to throw caution aside. They were not equipped for a war of attrition and would time and time again gamble, but this would merely allow themselves to become over extended. In other theatres, commanders were similarly forced to try and steal a victory. The same mistakes would be repeated at the First Battle of El-Alamein, the Battle of Alam el Halfa, the Battle of the Bulge, and Operation Nordwind, to name but a few.

The war in the east was not just a battle of attrition where the accountants would tally up the scores and losses on each side to determine to whom the victory should be awarded. The need to seize and hold territory was important. Transport hubs needed to be both controlled and denied to the enemy. There was also a practical need for control of the battlefield; to recover armour, especially tanks, which may have belonged to either side but became abandoned or disabled. They could then be repaired and brought back into use. Nevertheless, property came with an expensive ground rent.

Defiance

The speed of the initial stages of the advance created other problems. Blitzkrieg, particularly Operation Barbarossa, left many Soviet troops behind enemy lines. They formed partisan groups which encouraged further local resistance, and generally harried and tied up German forces. These insurgents especially damaged the Wehrmacht's logistics. When German pilfering of their own resources was coupled with the attacks on the overstretched supply routes it meant that adequate amounts of food and clothing rarely reached those on the front line. Resources disappeared into the ether of the long logistical train. The German soldier hated the Russians, but they despised their own logistical corps who stole the food and clothing that should have otherwise been for those in combat.

The deliberate omission to mop up those left behind Red Army formations created a malignant cancer eating away at the German occupation from within. This problem was left to fester until it became near impossible to root out. It necessitated large sweeps of the wilderness through forests and swamps, they were failing attempts to locate and eliminate these irregular combatants. In just one severe case a whole Russian army was trapped in the Oranienbaum Pocket west of Leningrad. This held out for three years until relieved. The Soviet forces in this pocket were a constant menace and hampered German attempts to capture Leningrad, it also played a major role in lifting the siege. Pinned against the Gulf of Finland, the soldiers in the Oranienbaum Pocket were assisted by troops supplied by the Soviet Baltic Fleet. The Soviet Navy's large guns protected the Red Army and their important naval base which connected them to the main

Russian fortified island city base of Kronstadt. The breakout from the pocket finally destroyed the remaining forces besieging Leningrad.

In time, the Stavka, the Main Command of the Armed Forces of the USSR, would orchestrate the delivery of aid to the partisans and Red Army units operating behind German lines. This went some way to hollowing out the German army on the Eastern Front from the rear. Ultimately, too much occupied territory was defended by too few Germans. The enormous gaps would be filled by Germany's partners who were less than capable. On too large a front, blitzkrieg forces can themselves become isolated and surrounded and suffering from exactly the same problems that they were trying to inflict upon the enemy. A grizzly fate was awaiting the German army in the east. German victories would soon turn to defeats. In the south the Germans had reached Rostov-on-Don but in the first Battle of Rostov the Germans found themselves defeated and forced back. There would be two more battles for this city over the course of the war. The Red Army had learnt how to stop and push back the Germans, this did not bode well for the Battle of Moscow.

Defence of Moscow

Stalin ordered the creation of a defence line west of Moscow which ran through the site of the Battle of Borodino when Russian forces had been defeated and left the path clear for Napoleon's entry into Moscow. French losses at Borodino had been heavy and much of the Tsarist army had managed to escape to later take the fight back to the invaders, so it was a Russian success of sorts. In this, the latest and greatest patriotic war, although Stalin's defence line would be swept aside, this time Moscow would not be delivered up to the enemy. Beria (head of the NKVD) had wanted to abandon Moscow but Stalin, supported by General Zhukov, at the last-minute overruled Beria and cancelled the defeatist evacuation order. Zhukov had been confident that Moscow could be held and would later have Beria arrested. Beria was tried and shot.

Fresh divisions equipped with T-34 medium tanks and aircraft were available for Moscow's defence and a counterattack. These had been kept in the east guarding against another potential Japanese invasion. Yet through eavesdropping on coded Japanese transmissions, which had been deciphered by the Soviets, it was clear that the Japanese empire had turned its attention away from Siberia and were not preparing another attack on Russia. This was confirmed by Richard Sorge, a Tokyo based Soviet agent of German nationality. The Soviet high command, safe in the knowledge that a new front would not be opened in the east, at least for the time being, used its fresh eastern reserves to defend their capital. The Germans, not realising that the Red Army had ample men and machines, were checked, and driven back. Moscow had a temporary reprieve but could still be threatened if another Axis force could be assembled.

After the failure of Operation Typhoon, the German codename for the Battle of Moscow, the Germans were suffering a manpower shortage that prevented them from adequately defending themselves against Red Army. Germany's failures buoyed Stalin who now believed he could push the Germans westwards. In his desperation, and excessive optimism that aggression will work, he ordered a series of major counterattacks on German lines. This ground-away Soviet lives as well as those of their Axis enemies. This was not the end of Nazi travails on the Eastern Front as the winter of 1941/42 was to prove devastating. The elements were passing their judgement, but German logistics, and a failure to prepare for anything but the most optimistic outcome, were the deadliest factors.

German winter coats did not offer enough insulation against biting temperatures. The German jackboot, so feared in England by some appeasers, was well suited to the parade ground but was not suitable for combat in such harsh conditions. These boots, rising towards the knee, had iron nails in their sole which allowed the cold to be conducted through the footwear into freezing feet – frostbite and immobility were the result. The Nazi leadership appealed to its citizens to donate their furs and winter clothing for the soldiers fighting in the depths of the Russian winter, but this was far too little too late and did not reach them in time. In Germany itself, people were beginning to realise the war was going badly. However, *blitzkrieg* did not just end thanks to the actions of Marshal Mud and General Frost, German strategy had broken down on the altar of Hitler's ambitions.

Events had now spun out of Hitler's control. To regain the initiative; his instinct was to go on the attack and seek to confront new enemies. With resistance against the Axis being underwritten by American capital, machines, and labour, World War Two had evolved into a proxy war with Britain, China, and Russia carrying out the hostilities against Uncle Sam's Axis enemies. This situation was now rapidly evolving to the chagrin of Hitler, as the United States was becoming an active participant in the Battle of the Atlantic. There would also be a conflict on the other ocean that abutted America's western seaboard. Hitler was now eager for war to break out between the United States of America and his Axis. This would soon be delivered courtesy of events in the Asia-Pacific region – the attack on Pearl Harbor. The German Führer, the would-be saviour of Germany, had been compared to the mythical Norse/German hero Siegfried.

This legendary man slew a dragon, taking the beast's treasure, and covering most of his body with its protective blood. However, Hitler's strategy had awoken three sleeping superpowers, the British Empire, the USSR, and the USA.

Chasing the Dragon

"Now at this very moment I knew that the United States was in the war, up to the neck and in to the death. So we had won after all! … Hitler's fate was sealed. Mussolini's fate was sealed. As for the Japanese, they would be ground to a powder. All the rest was merely the proper application of overwhelming force."
— **Winston Churchill on Japan's entry into World War Two**

Paradise lost

The Second World War in the Pacific did not begin with the Japanese attack on Pearl Harbor. US imperial outposts were not the first bases to be violated. Japan's immediate neighbours were the first to fall victim. Korea was put under Japanese control after their invasion of 1910. Early Japanese attempts at conquest in the late sixteenth century had only limited and transitory success, the Japanese were soon forced to withdraw. China had fallen prey towards the end of the nineteenth century and suffered repeated incursions in the 1930s in what is known as the Second Sino-Japanese War which concluded as late as 1945. The word Sino is convolutedly derived from the Arabic name for China loaned to Latin via Greek. Next to fall were European imperial outposts. Even German possessions in China had been taken by the Japanese during World War One.

In 1904, after a series of territorial disputes, Russia was targeted and decisively defeated by Japan. This would not be the end of the hostilities. By the late 1930s Japanese grand strategy was dominated by the need to subdue China, this was their overriding aim. Despite Japan expanding their empire to control significant parts of China's seaboard much of the interior of this great landmass remained free from foreign interference. China's huge population continued to provide men that resisted the Japanese invasion. Throughout the fighting in China, both before and during the Second World War, Japan could achieve victories over the Chinese but could never deliver the knockout blow. Nevertheless, the Chinese suffered some of the twentieth century's worst atrocities at the hands of the Japanese. In some cases, Japanese bombing of cities helped eliminate pockets of resistance. Yet, still China's ancient civilisation endured, as it does to this day despite suffering even more agony at the hands of their own communist leaders during Mao's Great Leap Forward and the Cultural Revolution.

Japan sought to control China's ports, and areas rich in natural resources. Conquering China was impossible as there were simply too many people, and the country was too vast. The Chinese forces could simply retreat westwards and regroup. Even with their steady march across the orient, the seemingly endless landmass was never overpowered by Japan. Any advance just left the Japanese vulnerable to guerrilla attacks from the Nationalists who were also involved in large scale pitched battles with the Japanese. China, however, was divided. Chiang Kai-shek, the Chinese President, had a great rival, the Communist leader, Mao Zedong, author of *On Protracted War,* this text was the insurgent's handbook. At times Mao colluded with the Japanese, yet, for the most part the communists fought their own guerrilla war against the Japanese presence in northern China. There was communist resistance in the interior of China before they were expelled by the nationalists. Mao was ever careful not to expend too much strength on the war, he would save his soldiers for his revolution. The communist forces, largely keeping out of harm's way, subsequently increased and were to benefit from captured Japanese weapons after the war, then the Chinese Civil War resumed.

China was to Japan what Russia was to Germany. Both leading Axis powers chose to take one foot out of the quagmire they found themselves in and declare war on the United States of America; a task for which they were wholly unsuited, Japan especially so. Like Germany, Japan took on too many opponents. China had been at the mercy of Europe's industrial powers for much of the nineteenth century. As the twentieth century dawned these countries, in an alliance with the United States and Japan, defeated Chinese attempts to restore their cultural and political sovereignty. In the 1920s this changed, and the situation had completely reversed by the 1930s. The international community were appalled with Japan's aggression and China's resources became an international asset to be traded. Both Britain and Germany supported Chiang Kai-shek's Kuomintang. The Wehrmacht even helped train elements of China's army. However, Hitler chose to ally with Japan in 1938 and renounced Germany's support for China.

Despite his opposition to communism, the nationalist and Russian trained Chiang Kai-shek received backing from the USSR, this came in exchange for natural resources. The Soviets hoped that aid to the Chinese would tie-up the Japanese and deter aggression against Russia's eastern frontier. Throughout the 1930s the Soviet Union and Japan clashed over the poorly defined and disputed borders. The Japanese had recently occupied land adjacent to that which had been already colonised and incorporated into Russia as long ago as the seventeenth century. The Japanese were the newcomers in that part of Asia. Disagreements over the boundaries of Russia's Mongolian satellite also led to border disputes.

As well as Manchukuo imperial Japan created a further dependency named Mengjiang, the Mongol United Autonomous Government. In 1939, on the eve of war in Europe, the Red Army led by Georgy Zhukov, decisively defeated the Japanese and the forces of its dependent state in the Battles of Khalkhin Gol. Japan was forced to abandon its desire to make Mongolia and Siberia a part of its growing empire. Two years after the conclusion of the Soviet-Japanese border war the belligerents agreed to the Soviet–Japanese Neutrality Pact. This peace deal, coupled with America positioning itself in opposition to Japan, made the Yamato people look out over the Pacific Ocean in the direction of the rising sun for the focus of their aggression.

The Japanese preoccupation with China set Tokyo on the road to war with America and hastened Japan's ultimate defeat. Indeed, China became an American proxy. The US gave aid to China to prevent a Japanese victory that would have freed up masses of troops and resources that could be used against the US in the Philippines and directed at Australia. The USA even supplied men to the war in China long before America officially entered the conflict. The American Volunteer Group (AVG) also known as the Flying Tigers were recruited to fight against the Japanese.

One of Mao Zedong's senior commanders, General Tao Hanzhang, unsur-prisingly acknowledged China's key role in aiding America's victory over Japan. Indeed, the Japanese had since 1937 been steadily provoking American and British interests in China by targeting their vessels on the Yangtze River; this aggression led to Britain supplying more financial support to the Chinese. Both nations had long been interfering in Chinese affairs. The situation was exacer-bated when Britain's imperial outposts in China, the so-called treaty port trading concessions such as Hong Kong, Tientsin, and Shanghai, gradually came under Japan's influence. With Britain sheltering Chinese soldiers and Japan demanding customs duties, war was just a matter of time. This was part of a wider problem. Japan was doing little to adhere itself to the United Kingdom and the United States of America. Indeed, Japan was taking over their long-established role as peacekeeper, and exploiter, of China's troubled land. Both the UK and the USA took part in the occupation of Peking in 1900, Britain even had a presence in Manchuria at the turn of the twentieth century; the UK sought to defend it from the Russians. Britain then feared that Russia would take Manchuria, to stop that eventuality the UK even entered into an alliance with Japan. Japan's militarists were, however, damaging all the good will that had earlier been built with Britain. The United States would further make sure that Britain would be set on the path to war with Japan.

Following Britain's alliance with Japan in the First World War, the UK helped the Japanese develop naval airpower tactics and even taught them how to construct aircraft carriers. These cordial relations were tested by the terms of the Washington Conference, concluded in early 1922. The resulting Washington Naval Treaty limited Japan's sea power, restricting its ability to exploit China, and keeping Japan, a nation in a hurry, behind both Britain and America.

The aim had been to reduce costs and the chances of conflict by preventing a naval arms race. However, in the long run the legal attempts to maintain Japan's subordinate position only increased tensions. By 1936 the Japanese repudiated the treaty and strove to equip their military for war. The following year its militarists reignited the war with China, and began to look elsewhere for friends. Fellow outcasts Germany, and Italy appeared to be suitable candidates. These were belligerent and aggressive emerging powers; and were set against the predominately European imperial nations that dominated much of the Pacific rim at the time. Japan's new partners would not inhibit the empire's desire to expand beyond the crowded home islands.

By agreeing in 1936 the Anti-Comintern Pact Nazi Germany and the Empire of Japan also found common cause in their opposition to the Soviet Union. This was later joined by Italy, and other Axis occupied puppet governments. By 1940, with Germany at peace with the Soviet Union, the Tripartite Pact between Japan, Germany, and Italy, later joined by much of Eastern Europe, identified the United States of America as their main enemy. The Tripartite Pact was not only a mutual defence alliance, it also sought to build a new world order with the three Axis powers dominating much of the globe. Japan wanted to remake what they thought of as their part of the world, breaking the traditional power structures in the Pacific and Indian Oceans. Just as Germany supported Arab and Indian independence movements, so too did Japan in the Pacific and beyond. Without any sense of irony, Japan actively encouraged anti-western and anti-imperialist sentiment in Asia.

Ancient Athens, an earlier naval power in the Aegean Sea, exploited opposition to the Persian Empire to create what was known as the Delian League. This quickly became an Athenian protection racket with delusional Greek city states bound into the Athenian Empire. This hegemon had ambitions to dominate and control the Greek world stretching across the Mediterranean Sea. After much success in the Peloponnese war, Athens was stopped by its great rival Sparta. This came after the Athenian system of direct democracy led it to make absurd and extreme decisions such as being seduced into an ill-prepared and reckless overseas attack against Syracuse. The result was the destruction of much of Athens' fleet. Towards the end of the Athenian empire, its democracy even decided to execute six victorious commanders. The Spartans and their constitutional system of checks and balances, which provided much inspiration for the Founding Fathers of the American Constitution more than two millennia later, triumphed over Athens' crypto empire. Sparta became the leading power in mainland Greece. Japanese statecraft followed a similar pattern to Athens with comparable disastrous results. In a vain attempt to justify reducing their neighbours to servitude, Japan drew on the idealised notions of pan-Asianism, anti-European, and anti-Americanism. To that end Japan created the Greater East Asia Co-Prosperity Sphere. This was the Japanese empire by another name. Its members were merely Japanese puppet states. The world was descending into an Orwellian block war. The Axis powers attempted to create their own spheres of influence. Germany was seeking *Lebensraum*, Italy wanted its own living space, *Spazio vitale*, in the Balkan Peninsula, Arabia, and north, east, and central Africa.

Hell to eternity

Japan had the wrong strategy for war. Throughout the conflict they were looking for the definitive victory that would overturn gravity. Like their art, they were not dealing with the world as it was. They were attempting to impose their will and create a mode of warfare that reflected their desires. Eventually Japan's enemies would forcefully reject such designs. Japanese experience in China should have shown that when fighting a well-resourced and resilient foe winning was a fanciful concept. Still, they persisted in their delusional approach to war, but it had successful precedents and was remarkably triumphant in the war against Russia which culminated in a shock Japanese victory in 1905. Japan's British influenced imperial navy had observed the British in action against the Italians at Taranto and how this dramatically shifted the balance of power in the Mediterranean further in favour of the Royal Navy. Could such a tactic have a similar effect in the Pacific Theatre? The British would show Japan the way.

Naval cooperation between Britain and Japan was deeply ingrained and one of the reasons the Japanese had such a strong navy. A succession of naval delegations from the UK helped the Japanese amass their skills. The Royal Navy introduced Japan's sailors to curry powder, naval discipline, and strategy. And amongst other things brought them Association Football. One mission in particular was led by Admiral Sir Archibald Douglas GCB GCVO. In 1873 he was chosen to command the second British naval mission; and until 1875 he even served as an advisor to the Japanese navy. He trained Japan's fledgling officer class at the

Japanese Naval Academy in Tokyo. Douglas also provided the Japanese with advice in aid of their 1874 invasion and occupation of Taiwan. His was not the only foreign input, the Americans were also involved, namely Lieutenant Commander Douglas R. Cassel and Colonel James Wasson.

British industry also enabled Japan to embark on its fateful imperial voyage to war. Armstrong Whitworth in Newcastle-upon-Tyne constructed many of the ships in the Japanese fleet which decisively defeated the Russians in 1905. Other shipbuilders in the northeast of England supplied the Russians. And fatefully, in the 1920s Britain also gave Japan naval aviation. It started as goodwill to encourage trade, but this temporarily ceased with the attacks in 1941. Military cooperation has now resumed and continues to this day. There is burgeoning defence collaboration between the two island nations. The UK is also again increasing its involvement in the Pacific region. Britain applied to join the huge oriental free trade area called the Comprehensive and Progressive Trans-Pacific Partnership (CPTPP) of which Japan is a member. Britain is also actively involved in trying to keep international waters free from Chinese control. China inherited the mantle of expansionist Asiatic power from both Japan and America. Japan also learned from the USA.

The concept of the 'decisive naval victory' was adopted by the Japanese from an American theorist, Alfred Thayer Mahan. However, they had only learnt half of his lessons and failed to appreciate the importance of the blockade and the devastating effects this wrought even against land-based empires of yesteryear such as Napoleonic France, and Wilhelmine Germany. The Japanese adoption of the decisive-battle doctrine, making use of a blitzkrieg at sea, polluted their thinking throughout the Pacific war. It was a seductive but outmoded dogma. Like the Samurai, who tried to perfect the art of killing with one effective and efficient strike with their Katana, the concept of the decisive victory sought a quick end to any fighting. The Second World War, however, was an industrial war of production and attrition. The Japanese pinned their hopes on a quick victory delivered through the decisive naval engagement because they knew they could not compete with America's industrial power. Therefore, they did not plan for a long war and failed to develop more advanced weapons such as state-of-the-art aircraft.

The size obsessed Japanese also skewed their war production in the wrong direction. To win their putative decisive battle they spent valuable resources building large battleships such as the *Yamato* and its sister ship the *Musashi*. These were the two most powerful capital ships ever to be constructed. The

Japanese were fascinated by this class of warship and the prestige they thought it gave them. Pride however is not a valid military strategy.

To make up for Japan's lack of industrial capacity, as compared to that of America, they had to find an alternate strategy to a war of attrition. The seductive concept of the decisive battle sought to resolve these inherent weaknesses and lead the Japanese to conclude that they should build large battleships that can defeat the more numerous warships in rival fleets. Like their battles, the Japanese placed quality above quantity, ranking firepower, and displacement to be superior to numbers.

The *Yamato* class battleships, who's moniker comes from the ancient and poetic name for Japan, were designed to be able to take on several US capital ships at the same time. Through their unbridled strength they hoped to address the dilemma of their numerical disadvantage. The problem was that the battleship was no longer the decisive tool in naval warfare that it once was. The banner had passed to the aircraft carrier, making those supersized battleships expensive white elephants. Instead of being powerful floating weapons platforms they were slow moving targets in which their men would soon be entombed. Japan should have been investing its limited time and resources on constructing more aircraft carriers and submarines; they should have also sought to develop a suitable strategy against their American adversaries.

Master and commander

Franklin Delano Roosevelt's strategy in 1940 was to win an unprecedented and now constitutionally barred third term in office. He promised the American electorate that he would not send "your boys to fight in foreign wars". He then sought to extricate himself from this aspiration. The American President was steadily nudging America to war. America defended British shipping west of Iceland. Roosevelt first established, and then extended, the Pan-American Neutrality Zone which gave British shipping a degree of security. Churchill wanted America in the war against Germany, Roosevelt wanted in too. Merely being the arsenal of democracy, providing arms and ammunition to Britain, was no longer enough. The Japanese would serve as the useful idiots that would enable America to join the fight. Hitler's alliance with Japan would harm the German Führer. Churchill and Roosevelt both wanted a Japanese attack as a means of getting America into the war against Germany. Whilst Roosevelt was wary of being seen to be manipulated by Winston Churchill, the US President would have attempted to declare war against Japan if British imperial possessions in Asia, such as Malaya, were attacked. Roosevelt was looking for a pretext for war and even encouraged events to proceed as he wished. The catalyst was China.

Japanese planners deduced that they needed to expand operations to isolate their great Asiatic rival from outside assistance. One Japanese war, the war in China, led to the need for other wars to close-off supply routes, and gain resources to feed the carnage. It was the same rationale that led to the invasion of British Malaya, and the Japanese occupation of Tonkin in northern Vietnam, which so angered the Americans. Likewise, this attack was to cut-off supplies to the forces of the Kuomintang, the Chinese Nationalist Party, who actively opposed Japan's brutalisation of China. They were led by Chinese Premier Generalissimo Chiang Kai-shek. The Japanese invasion of Burma, now known as Myanmar, was also part of the mission creep to end the Kuomintang's resistance. The Japanese were assisted by forces from Thailand and later those of the Burmese puppet state, as well as a small army of Indian rebels. This convoluted conflict was again spurred by the need to try and close what was the only supply route available from the western hemisphere to the Chinese resistance led by Chiang Kai-shek.

Roosevelt sought to provoke an incident that would make the American public demand war and from there allow the US to enter the fight against Germany. American planners and policy makers had been preparing for such an eventually for a considerable period. To that end they devised War Plan Orange. This was developed after the First World War. The plan was to defend the Philippines with a blockade against the Japanese Imperial Navy. American forces on the islands were intended to hold out against a Japanese attack. US forces would then turn north to engage the Japanese in a decisive naval battle. This was one of many colour coded war plans against every possible and even improbable adversary, encompassing every colour in the rainbow and much more. There was a sheer multitude of colours preparing America against multiple opponents, including Britain and the Dominion of Canada.

1940 Admiral James Richardson the Commander-in-Chief of the United States Fleet recognised that America lacked men and materiel to prosecute War Plan Orange as it involved amphibious assaults on well-defended Japanese held islands. General Douglas MacArthur concurred, he also thought that the war plan was unworkable but believed the US could make a stand in the Philippines. However, the initial focal points of the attacks occurred elsewhere. In Spring 1941, the Japanese began planning for an attack on the western powers.

Pearl Harbor

The attack on Pearl Harbor did not come out of a clear blue sky. The Japanese felt they were encircled by four enemies: the Americans, British, Chinese, and Dutch. Bar the fighting in China, the Second World War in the Pacific officially erupted on 7th December 1941, yet not with the Japanese attack on Pearl Harbor, but with Japanese landings against the British colony of Malaya. The invasion of Malaya, and ultimately Singapore, came from Thailand which was in league with the Japanese. The Pacific War had begun in earnest several hours before Japanese planes bombed much of the US Pacific Fleet at anchor in Pearl Harbor, a US base at Honolulu in American occupied Hawai'i. Due to Malaya being on the other side of the international date line, it appeared that the attacks occurred on following days.

These events were the long-running culmination of Japan coveting the pacific rim. Japan had been preparing for an attack against the British base in Singapore since the early 1930s and may even have reconnoitred mineral-rich Australia as early as the 1920s. However, the Japanese were not the initial aggressors in the events that led up to this totemic and infamous strike on a lazy Sunday morning. The antagonists were the United States. America had become all too eager for war with Japan.

This was a dramatic U-turn from when the United States had literally fuelled the rise of fascism and militarists. During Italy's invasion of Abyssinia in 1935 the United States imposed an arms embargo against the Italians, yet still allowed American companies to continue selling oil to Italy. In 1936 American neutrality prevented the lawful Spanish government from receiving aid, giving the advantage to the forces of Hitler, Mussolini, and Franco. Throughout the 1930s the anti-Semitism of Nazi Germany was not an issue for Roosevelt's America, a nation in which large parts pursued policies which discriminated against specific ethnicities. Germany, Italy, and Axis leaning Spain, were not the only regimes which the USA appeased. Recognising that Japan had special interests in China, the United States also had a long history of assuaging Japanese imperialism, particularly against the Chinese.

The United States saw events in south-east Asia through an economic lens. Japanese expansionism and its desire to cut-off aid to Chinese nationalist forces led its military to demand access to part of Vichy France's territory, then known as French Indochina. This is now divided between three states, Laos, Cambodia, and Vietnam. The weakness of Vichy France vis-à-vis the Germans encouraged the Japanese to take over French Indochina, a move which the US greatly objected to. Japan now dominated those areas in the South China Sea which produced oil, rubber, and tin, much of which was destined for the US market. Consequently, America began the policy of provoking Japan into war.

In July 1941, America froze Japan's assets and imposed an embargo of oil, petrol, and scrap iron. This left the Japanese with few options other than war. The American sanctions threatened not only Japan's chances of success in the Second Sino-Japanese War but also negated its whole purpose, namely, to secure the resources and living room that Japan's exploding population needed. Sanctions are often justified as a tool to stop conflict, deterring aggression, and making supposedly belligerent nations comply with international norms, what is now called the rules based international order. There are, however, few examples of sanctions having the explicitly stated effect. In fact, far from resolving international disputes such measures exacerbate tensions. They further ingrain divisions and cut-off the commercial and financial links which foster mutual dependency and prevent war.

By November 1941, it had become clear to the US State Department that war was coming between these two less than peaceful Pacific empires. It was just a matter for the political spin doctors to sell to the American public. The Japanese were soon to give Roosevelt a great political gift. The US had earlier moved its fleet to Pearl Harbor ostensibly to deter Japanese aggression, it would however tantalisingly invite hostility upon itself. Indeed, the US knew its ships were vulnerable, Admiral James Richardson who was alive to Japan's intentions had repeatedly warned Roosevelt, but the Commander-in-Chief of the United States Fleet was dismissed for his labours. US ships at anchor in Hawai'i were duly attacked by Japan, as Roosevelt intended.

This was not the decisive battle that the Japanese had hoped for. Pearl Harbor was a flop. The problem was that the Axis commander, Admiral Yamamoto, was too cautious to deliver repeated blows against the American facilities in Honolulu. The nation that was economically underdeveloped in comparison to its ambitions failed to understand the economic necessities of war. Japan did not fight to disable America's ability to wage war. It only set out to deliver a short, sharp shock which they presumed the Americans would blithely accept. The raid's planners failed to consider objectives that were as important, perhaps more so, than the battleships in the harbour. The ship repair facilities were not targeted, nor was the submarine base. No attempt was made to strike at the vulnerable oil facilities. This omission allowed the United States Navy to keep ten months' worth of fuel. The bombing would have been more successful if the oil facilities at the port were destroyed, the US Pacific Fleet would have been confined to the docks. American Admiral Chester Nimitz said striking at Pearl

Harbor's fuel would have set back the American war effort by two years. That would have bought Japan enough time to build its defensive ring and isolate Australia from the United States.

Nothing was more critical to Japanese thinking than the need to obtain oil. One of the militarists' overriding aims was to seize control of hydrocarbon energy production in the Dutch East Indies. After the Japanese attack on Pearl Harbor the in-exile Queen Wilhelmina of the Netherlands declared war on Japan. This gave the Japanese the pretext to invade the Dutch East Indies as intended. The Japanese had been easily manipulated and just assumed that they would be victorious without ever carefully considering let alone planning for a response that did not suit their strategic goals. They believed they could easily remake the world as they wished.

Those obvious objectives were excluded because hitting them did not correspond with the Japanese marshal code. The planners did not think it honourable to strike at soft targets, instead they were solely focused on bombing the battleships as they posed the most direct threat. Yet 18 of 21 vessels hit were back in operation within months. What is more, the Pacific Fleet's four aircraft carriers were missed by the Japanese strike force as they were already at sea. They would have a crucial role to play in the coming months. Soon a further seven would be produced to take on the Japanese Imperial Navy. However, there was one notable success.

The damage wreaked on the Pacific Fleet's capital ships did fleetingly weaken America's naval presence and made it impossible for the ships based at Pearl Harbor to support their allies' ports, namely the British naval base at Singapore. This lay between the South China Sea and the Indian Ocean; it was now vulnerable. Winston Churchill had hoped that the naval bases of Singapore and Pearl Harbor would be mutually supporting each other but with the US presence in the Pacific initially weakened, Singapore was imperilled. The British position was further enervated through the dual sinking of the battleship HMS *Prince of Wales* and the battlecruiser HMS *Repulse* in December 1941, just days after America's losses at Pearl Harbor. They were lost in the South China Sea on their way to intercept the Japanese landings on the Malay peninsula. These vessels, now war graves, still lie where they sank.

Despite the avoidable carnage on the President's watch, the attack was a political triumph for both Franklin Delano Roosevelt and Winston Churchill, the British Prime Minister could not conceal his glee. Winston Churchill had pledged that Britain would join in a fight against anyone who attacked the USA within an hour. The British Prime Minister even went to the House of Commons seeking a declaration of war against Japan before Roosevelt addressed Congress on the attack on Pearl Harbor. Roosevelt, who wanted to announce it first, tried to stop his British counterpart, the message, however, did not get through. Churchill was not the only foreign leader keen to participate in America's conflict with Japan. As 1941 began to draw to a close, Hitler thought international Jewry was driving the world to war and expected a declaration of war from the United States. When this did not materialise, he became somewhat confused. Hitler then thought that Germany had to take the initiative. The Führer was already bitter, he was vexed by the US's unofficial participation in the Battle of the Atlantic where Americans defended shipping from German U-boat attacks.

Hitler unilaterally took the decision to declare war on the USA, announcing it on 11th December. Whilst Hitler remained loyal to his Axis partners, the Japanese did not consult with the Germans about the attack on Pearl Harbor, nor did they inform them of the other impending strikes. Hitler perceived that he had little choice but to declare war on America at that time. Mussolini too declared war and soon after the eastern European signatories to the Tripartite Pact followed suit.

In response to the German declaration of war, Congress, with no dissent, declared war on Germany and were from then on committed to a war on multiple fronts on opposite sides of the globe. The actions of Hitler and Mussolini *et alia* were enormous blunders. The Japanese strike had given Roosevelt everything he wanted. Hitler, however, thought that the Americans would be tied up by Japan and would not have the will to fight, he also thought that the ethnically diverse Americans were racially inferior to the German. America, however, adopted a Germany first policy where they used the bulk of its power to win the war in Europe. Furthermore, Japan, despite its early successes and martial spirit, would not be able to tie-up the Americans as Hitler was hoping. Indeed, Japan at no point wanted a protracted war with the USA. Japan's military code and poor planning, coupled with its lack of development, would prove to be its undoing.

Clash of the empires

Japan's flawed logic led it to believe that to normalise relations with America it must first attack its great Pacific rival, the USA. Japanese unquestioning obedience and rigid hierarchy produced one of history's most devastating cases of groupthink. They had failed to understand their enemy and appreciate its strengths. The Japanese martial spirit only saw weaknesses and opportunities to win honour. Two quite different philosophies rammed into each other in the Pacific Ocean. The sea and land battles between the Empire of Japan and the United States of America were the theatres where these ideologies and worldviews were fought out. Two vastly differing nations, who were poles apart, expressed their differences with raw energy and aggression. This conflict turned what were island paradises and the seemingly serene seas in the east into an area of torment. The Japanese fought against not only America but also Britain, China, Australia, and the Soviet Union.

An example of the strategic thinking at work, and its fateful consequences is best illustrated by the employment of the Japanese concept of *Bushido* and their *Senjinkun* military code. Both a hangover from a society that had only recently emerged from feudalism, itself a consequence of Japan's physical and intellectual isolation. The concept of *Senjinkun* means 'never become a prisoner of war'. This also meant that enemy soldiers were not held in high regard. Whereas 2% of Americans that surrendered to the Germans died, a staggering 37% of US service personnel that were taken prisoner perished at the hands of the Japanese; this meant the Allies learnt to fight with more ferocity. Few Japanese were ever to surrender. When they did, they were often acts of perfidy, surrendering in bad faith to lure the enemy into an ambush. Japanese false surrenders would even involve the defeated soldier apparently capitulating only to set off a grenade killing himself and his would-be capturer. These tactics became recognised as war crimes and led to a reluctance amongst US servicemen to take prisoners.

Japan's warlike ethos led to the arrogant belief that they were destined to become a great world power. This led to over confidence and a lack of security which hampered their preparations in the run-up to many of the battles which they hoped would be decisive. There was a massive under estimation of their enemy's resolve and ability to fight back. The Japanese thought that as the Americans were individualistic and would lack the common purpose to keep fighting when the casualties would inevitably begin to mount. The Japanese thought that US teamwork would break down, America appeared to be the land of the gangster, a country set against itself. Whilst this had an element of truth it was the Japanese taking literally American art as expressed through the medium of film. The attraction of screen portrayals of violent Thompson submachine gun toting Americans should have rung alarm bells. Of even greater significance, the genre's depictions of America's criminal element were popular because the protagonists represent rugged individualists who are free to follow their id. Individualism was the key component at the heart of American society that would be one of the defining differences between these two empires.

American art also had other cultural expressions which the Japanese misunderstood. Music and dance in the United States during the Jazz Age became synonymous with excesses and immorality. This contrasted with Japan's militarists who sought to tie their subjects into traditional cultural practices that fostered obedience. America nurtured individuality and this resulted in its citizens increasing their initiative, imagination, industriousness, innovation, ingenuity, and inventiveness; all of which are improved by incentives. Japan, however, like the Nazis and the Soviets favoured intimidation to compel its people to follow and not lead. Thus, those raised in statist societies did not learn personal responsibility, thinking for oneself was discouraged, the hive was everything. Japan, still one of the most homogenous countries in the world, disparaged America for being a melting pot of different peoples. The Japanese divined that the United States would remain divided, and this lack of unity would lead to their defeat against a cohesive foe. That, however, was a misunderstanding of American society. The lack of homogeneity ensured that policy makers in the USA forged a common national loyalty and identity to unite its many peoples, most of which had come to America because of the economic opportunities its freedom, resources, and open space allowed. America was united. Indeed, its Latin motto is *E pluribus unum*, meaning "out of many, one". It was a motto that was born in war when the original thirteen colonies violently revolted against rule from Britain. America was unified against its external enemies; its population was rightly angered by the attack on their military which came before Japan officially declared war. These many different peoples were employed to build the weapons by which its citizens would wage war against its identity politics practising Axis enemies. This shared purpose and celebration of all things 'Merican still endures despite the introduction of divisive identity politics into modern American public discourse.

The war in the Pacific was prolonged in the face of terrible Japanese suffering by enforced militaristic totalitarianism. Those that did not support Japanese expansionism were persecuted by the Kenpeitai, these secret police terrorised their own people in the home islands. When the tide of the Pacific War turned against Japan the aim of the Kenpeitai evolved into ensuring continued support for the war by routing out 'defeatists' and those who wanted peace. The pursuit of these realists was dubbed the "Thought War." Persecution at the hands of a secret police were not the only tools at the aid of the militarists. Poetry was also employed with deadly effect. *'Duty is heavy like a mountain, but a soldier's death is light like a feather.'* Japan's rich artistic tradition and high-brow society sought to mould perfection out of nature be that the ancient practice of enhancing natural phenomena such as boulders or pruning even large trees to improve their aesthetics. Artistic representations were idealised impressions rather than literal interpretations of natural beauty. Rather than working with the environment and the reality of existence, the Japanese elite wanted to reorder the world and human nature to make it comply with their whims.

The expendables

Japan had gone from being mediaeval to modern in just a number of decades. They had taken forward their ancient Bushido martial code and utilised it alongside the horror of modern mass-produced weaponry in an age of total war. They now had the means as well as the motive to brutalise their surrendered opponents and civilians alike. Yet, it also led to their own brutalisation. Following the suicide of a Japanese officer taken during the fighting with the Chinese in Shanghai in 1937, Japanese officers who were captured were openly pressured to take their own lives. Surrender ceased to be an option. Only fanatical resistance was tolerated. Dying in a suicidal charge was considered virtuous. The counterattack took on cult like proportions with its Japanese servicemen exclaiming *banzai!* as they charged, or flew, at the enemy. This exclamation, their battle cry, was the shortened form of *Tennōheika Banzai* meaning "Long Live His Imperial Majesty the Emperor". Massed suicidal frontal charges, were little more than an act of *Seppuku*, by proxy. *Seppuku*, also known as *hara-kiri*, is the celebrated Japanese ritual death by where the dishonoured would disembowel themselves with a short-bladed weapon called a *tantō*.

The pointless gesture would also be celebrated and immortalised in poetry. The suicide mission would be justified through verse comparing sacrificing one's own ephemeral life to the falling of the cherry blossom, a beautiful natural event revered in Japanese literature. It perverted this cultural expression into a sacrament that celebrated the moment of death as the fulfilment of life's purpose, just as the perfection of the cherry blossom is achieved when it falls. The romance of *Bushido* with its attacking spirit was not the only self-inflicted wound. Perverse tactics accounted for the wasting of men and resources. Whilst the Japanese gave great latitude to commanders to apply the principles of mission command, Japanese society produced different results. Their traditional hierarchical structure demanded compliance. Unquestioning obedience, masquerading as loyalty, created a situation where soldiers engaged in combat would repeatedly reinforce failure by slavishly following orders. In crucial battles to come the Japanese followed commands to continually attack against secure American positions rather than probing for weak points. The result was an enormous loss of life that hampered the war effort in the long run.

The United States' more liberal inheritance allowed them to delegate tactical decisions to soldiers, sailors, and marines. It encouraged individual initiative. Americans were creative enough to use and apply their resourcefulness and make enterprising decisions. Ultimately, the biggest difference was that whilst the Japanese soldier was willing to die for their Emperor, Allied servicemen were willing to kill for their country. One US commander, Admiral 'Bull' Halsey, adopted the mantra "Kill Japs, kill Japs, kill more Japs". The Japanese made this easy.

American support for the war also relied on propaganda and persuasion drawing on the art form for which their creative culture is best known, film. They could deftly deploy the common touch in the service of the war. The Hollywood film industry inspired Americans and their allies to fight. Many of its leading men implored the public to buy war bonds, as did decorated soldiers. Film stars volunteered for the war; the traffic went both ways. Heroes such as Audie Murphy, the most decorated US soldier in World War Two, later became a major Hollywood star. American movie makers adapted to the war's changing circumstances; they knew what their public needed to see. When US soldiers and marines were being driven back before the Japanese advance, the hero GI, often played by John Wayne, was portrayed as the near invincible superman that could and would beat the rampant Japanese. As the war progressed and American soldiers, sailors, marines, and airmen were securing victory after victory a more human and sympathetic character emerged to which the American public could relate. America had what amounted to vast factories producing the art at which they excelled, the motion picture or movie. Despite the Great Depression lasting throughout most of the 1930s, the United States also had some very real factories producing automobiles, aeroplanes, and aircraft carriers. American firepower would soon be sent back to the location where the story began less than ninety years previously, Tokyo.

The Japanese, with their poor economic foundations, did not appreciate the law of marginal gains when applied on a strategic scale. They could refine a product, such as their renowned fighter the Mitsubishi A6M Zero, they continually made improvements to upgrade its offensive capabilities, yet its development could only go so far. After Japan's rapid industrialisation and technological progress, it was well within their capabilities to produce what were for the time advanced weapons, the Zero fighter being a case in point. At the outbreak of war this was more than a match for American interceptors. However, the war with China negatively affected Japan's development of tanks. Throughout the 1930s Japanese tank design was superior to those put into combat by the underdeveloped Chinese. This led the Japanese to believe that their weapons were adequate for a modern war. However, against the Russians in 1939 and then again in 1945, Japanese machines were found wanting. In Burma and the Pacific War Japan came up against tanks produced by at the time America's far superior automotive industry. Light-weight Japanese models fared badly, even against the American made twin turreted M3 Lee tank which was considered outmoded in the European theatre. The only cannon which could fully traverse on the Medium M3 tank was the 37-millimetre, this proved to be inadequate at dealing with dug in Japanese fortifications. Its main 75-millimetre sponson mounting only had limited movement. Later, the M4 Sherman tank, which carried the more powerful turret mounted 75 mm gun, proved to be successful where its less well armed predecessors were not.

Japan's tactics negated what few effective tanks they had. The tank's great utility as a weapon comes when it is used on the offensive, but it has few defensive capabilities, especially when they are poorly armoured. The Japanese strategy was, after their lightning advance, to establish a defensive perimeter; a role not suited to the tank. Where they were used offensively, the Japanese, like the French, employed them as infantry support vehicles. They did, however, innovatively use tanks to support amphibious landings. Yet were not used in massed attacks to break an enemy's line, nor did they consider that there would be tank-on-tank battles. Japan's poor application of armoured warfare resulted in their tanks and accompanying crews suffering badly at the hands of the Allies.

Japan's obsession with offence was coupled with a self-defeating disregard for the lives of their servicemen. Their marshal code had always considered the lives of subordinates to be expendable. Their purpose was to fight and die if needs be. The Anglo-Saxon world which had more regard for the individual coupled with its Judeo-Christian inheritance, which held life in higher regard, lessened the impulse to make a virtue of losing men. The generation of commanders now in charge of the Allied war effort had seen first-hand on the First World War's Western Front how a failure to protect the lives of their men was both bad for morale and a waste of manpower. The Japanese historical experience had shown that aggression worked but this was on a more limited scale than what they now unleashed. Overall, little consideration had been given to preserving lives.

The absence of adequate defensive armour was found not only on Japan's tanks. Its aircraft were also designed for one purpose. Japanese attacking principles drove their technological development. The planes used in anger by the Japanese and the Americans represented their opposing martial philosophies. The Zero, and its shore-based counterpart the Oscar, were superb offensive planes which carried quite a punch; it was designed to down an enemy in as few blows as possible.

Axis fighter planes generally used 20-millimetre cannons as their main armament. Japanese fighters were no different and possessed a couple of such weapons as well as a further two 7.7-millimetre machine guns which would do considerably less damage compared to the bigger munitions. These large weapons fired heavy shells but at a slow rate. American aircraft followed a different ethos. US planes primarily shot .50 calibre (more than half an inch in diameter) rounds; these were approaching half the width of their oriental enemy's guns. However, more of these weapons could be fitted to the aeroplane and they had a much faster rate of fire saturating and overwhelming the opponent in a volley of bullets from multiple weapons. Less is more.

The Zero and the Oscar were also greatly manoeuvrable, with an exceptionally long-range enabling them to attack from a far, yet they had no defensive armour and did not possess self-sealing fuel tanks. These planes easily caught fire and broke-up when hit by either American fighters or anti-aircraft artillery. Conversely, American designers took extensive measures to increase the survivability of their warbirds. US planes, and their pilots, lived to fly and fight again. This was the superior strategy. Keeping pilots alive allowed them to knock their opponents out of the skies, or bomb their ships, on other occasions. Statistics show that once a pilot achieves a certain level of experience, they are much less likely to be shot down and they become more effective aerial warriors. Due to protective measures, US flyers managed to make it back to the aircraft carrier whereas the Japanese were less likely to survive combat and thus went onto the next form of existence.

The belief that the divine took precedence over the material world and the spirit will overcome the reality of human frailty caused the Japanese to have little regard for the needs of their flyers. American pilots were rested and the most experienced were taken out of theatre to train new recruits and pass on what they had learned. This gave the US a ready supply of skilled pilots, the Japanese kept theirs in combat; many of which would eventually perish. This meant that they had fewer competent and experienced pilots as the war progressed. Japan, a country with a long history was in a desperate hurry, trying to steal a quick victory in the name of their sacred ruler who had to be safeguarded.

Thirty seconds over Tokyo

The Japanese were an angry enemy and easily irritated. Roosevelt responded to Japan attacking his ships at Pearl Harbor in the most direct and provocative way. The United States would combine its naval strength and air power to strike at the

215

head of imperial Japan. On 18th April 1942, named after its leader, Lieutenant Colonel James Doolittle, the Doolittle Raid, as it was known struck Tokyo with 16 B-25 Mitchell medium bombers launched from the aircraft carrier the USS *Hornet*. The Mitchell bomber was named after the US military aviation pioneer, Billy Mitchell. He had been court-martialled and convicted in 1925 for accusing both the US army and navy of neglecting America's air power and defence. The year before he had also predicted the war with Japan and its attack on an inadequately defended Pearl Harbor. Douglas MacArthur had the distasteful duty of being one of Mitchell's judges yet dissented from his peers and cast the only not-guilty ballot when the court made its judgement.

Seventeen years later, this brief attack against Japan on the face of it achieved little and was in tactical terms not much more than an American public relations exercise from an embarrassed president needing to strike back against a foe that had wrought such humiliation. Whilst the damage caused by the counterstrike was small, it was a foretaste of the peril that Japan had found itself in. The strategic effect was enormous. The Japanese were drawn into one of their greatest mistakes in the war. It was the intersection of Japan's political and military culture that again led its military planners to be so easily provoked into yet more foolish and unproductive aggression.

A strong ethos of submission derived from their feudal culture, Japanese military officers were pledged to defend the Emperor above all else. They had to respond to an attack that had put the life of the *Tennō* at risk. He was much more than a mere ruler. Yet a gaping hole in Japan's defence ring allowed this outrage to be committed. Superstitious and fanatical devotion was to prove to be Japan's undoing at the hands of the Americans. Indeed, the Meiji restoration and the elevation of what is known in English as 'the Emperor' to political as well as spiritual importance came about through the shockwaves that engulfed Japan when the US fleet arrived in Tokyo bay in 1853. In time the US forced the Japanese to enter a trade treaty with the modern industrial power that was the United States. The Japanese, realising they were behind the industrial nations, then embarked on a period of rapid growth. The word *Meiji* translates as enlightened rule. The aim was to combine modern industrial development with traditional values. This was not enlightenment as someone from the European inheritance would understand it. It was economic power without a corresponding development in the power of the *demos,* a very Asian solution. This was to be a deadly development for both Japan's neighbours and its own people.

The Doolittle Raid on Tokyo led the Japanese to realise that they could be attacked. From this however the Japanese came to the wrong conclusions. The

Japanese decided to further expand their naval strength when resources should have been put towards increasing their airpower. The Japanese, like their German Axis partners, did not have a significant heavy bomber force that could destroy strategic targets in the same way that US bombing raids were to inflict devastation on Japan in the latter stages of the war.

The Japanese responded by expanding further into China to wipe out airfields that could be used to attack the home of their Living God. At the same time, Japan kept back some forces for home defence. The other response was to seek to extend the defensive line further towards the United States so that no carrier borne bombers would ever be in range of the home islands again. This meant using its even more stretched, divided, and limited resources and military capabilities on a fool's errand far away from what was the decisive theatre of the time, the battle in the Solomon Islands in distant Oceania. It would be Japan's undoing. The Japanese again allowed themselves to be provoked into making another attempt at winning a decisive victory over US forces, this culminated in the Battle of Midway. This was a decisive naval engagement but not as the Japanese had planned.

The thin red line

The Japanese had planned to seize the land that could provide the resources their empire needed and turn the many islands that dotted the Pacific into an impenetrable defensive ring. From there it was hoped that the home islands would be secure, and from behind this shield they would await the offer of negotiations. Despite Japan's early triumphs, talks to find an honourable settlement with the Americans never materialised.

Japan, a nation that for much of its history had barely been able to impose its power beyond its home islands, had massively overreached. The result was that soldiers stranded themselves on desert islands. It was far from romantic. The American held Wake Island quickly fell to Japanese marines at the beginning of hostilities. Following their victory, the occupiers became essentially irrelevant, playing no other part in the war bar the inhuman treatment of their prisoners. Cut-off, and all but forgotten, the commander felt that he had no other alternative but to commit the atrocity of killing his captives to preserve supplies for his own men. This was not an isolated incident. There were other instances of starving Japanese servicemen imprisoning themselves in paradise, cannibalism was not unknown.

Initially, Japan's conquests were amazingly successful. They quickly built upon the Japanese conquests in Korea, China, and its Pacific islands north of the equator, namely the Mariana, Caroline, and Marshall Islands. These specks in the ocean were taken from Germany by Japan during World War One and were then mandated to the Empire of the Sun by the League of Nations. The co-prosperity sphere, after their rapid victories at the close of 1941, into early 1942, became for a fleeting moment among the largest empires in history in both size and population, approaching half a billion souls. It stretched from Burma across to Borneo, and from the edges of Siberia in the north, down through Guam in the Pacific, to the Solomon Islands in the south. It included Hong Kong, Singapore, Malaya, the Philippines, central Java, Sumatra, much of New Guinea, the Dutch East Indies and extended along to Guadalcanal, which was to play host to some crucial battles. It also stretched out to the Gilbert Islands. This empire encompassed the resource rich lands the Japanese needed to continue waging war against China and to put them to the forefront of the leading nations in the world. Yet it was not enough to give Japan the security they needed. To defend their Emperor, they surmised that they had to extend their conquests still further.

Japanese strategy erred between cutting-off Australia from US support along with denying the Americans the islands off the northeast of that country to again seek the glory of a decisive battle. Naval staff wanted to extend the defensive perimeter by landing in southern New Guinea, finishing the job there and extending their control to conqueror New Caledonia, Fiji, and Samoa. However, the combined fleet staff led by Admiral Yamamoto wanted a full-scale engagement against the US Navy south of the Marshall Islands. From there it was hoped that he could destroy the US fleet which had survived his Pearl Harbor attack. Finishing the job started on 7th December 1941 became an unhealthy obsession.

The Japanese, appeasing the pride of its senior commanders, adopted both strategies. In Operation *Mo*, a naval force coming from Rabaul attacked Port Moresby in New Guinea. This engagement became the Battle of the Coral Sea, the US carriers had to withdraw but the Japanese achieved a pyrrhic victory and abandoned the naval invasion of southern New Guinea. Little did they know that they would only have faced just a brigade of Australian soldiers. Most of the Australian armed forces were away fighting for the mother country in North Africa and Greece. Only after the Australian Prime Minister, John Curtin, had a fiery confrontation with Churchill would they be brought back to defend their homeland.

The Battle of the Coral Sea, the first fought between opposing aircraft carriers, ruled out two of Japan's leviathans, the *Zuikaku* and *Shōkaku*, from the impending attack on Midway. This fatally weakened Yamamoto's chances of success in this risky venture. Japan did score some successes, such as inflicting considerable damage on the USS *Yorktown*, this however was to be part of their undoing. The Japanese thought they had sunk that aircraft carrier. However, it managed to make it back to Pearl Harbor, where it was repaired and readied for battle. It was to have a pivotal part to play in the forthcoming Battle of Midway. The Japanese did not have the advantage that they thought they had. Admiral Yamamoto's calculations were flawed.

The Japanese should have focused on fighting for control of Guadalcanal in the Solomon Islands. Japanese victory there would have isolated Australia, severed vital sea lanes, and, as land bases would be lost, it would prevent the American army from striking back at the Japanese for some time. The US navy was still not logistically ready for a direct assault into the Japanese defensive ring.

The decision to attack Midway Island used the Imperial Navy for a battle that need not have been fought. The Battle of Guadalcanal should have taken precedence. An even greater naval presence coming down from the north in support of the so-called Tokyo express, the Japanese nightly naval attacks on American units in the Solomon Islands, would have done more than harry US forces, Japan could have won. However, at no point did the Japanese make it easy for themselves. Uncompromising Japanese discipline meant that dive bombers in the Battle of Guadalcanal kept formation and did not take evasive action when under attack from American Wildcats, this made the Japanese easy targets for the US fighters. Directly to the north of Australia in New Guinea the Japanese campaign had likewise stalled. When Major General Horii complained that 'You can't fight with supplies like this' in the Battle of Kokoda in Papua New Guinea, the Japanese high command treated this and other similar complaints as instances of cowardice. The Japanese militarists did not fully appreciate the material aspect of the Second World War; their superstitions elevated the metaphysical above the material world.

Ultimately, after a desperate struggle in which the Japanese were repeatedly mowed down by machine gun fire, the Japanese lost in both New Guinea and Guadalcanal. The Empire of Japan's chance to cut-off Australia and deprive the Americans of an important base of operations in the south Pacific was gone. The US victory at Guadalcanal was a tremendous propaganda success, forever smashing the myth of the Japanese superman. The British in Burma, however, were still behind the curve and believed that the Japanese had an inbuilt and genetic advantage enabling them to fight in the harsh conditions that Myanmar's mountains and rainforest presented. In time the British would believe that the jungle was neutral; however, it wasn't, it was an enemy to all.

On a tactical level, the division of Japanese forces to secure a strategic objective was not unknown. Indeed, it was their *modus operandi*. Their army would often split into two, one portion would fix the enemy the other would outflank their befuddled foe, and attack from the side or rear. Often as found in Malaya their opponents would retreat in the face of the Japanese scorpion allowing Japan to achieve lightning advances, a veritable *blitzkrieg*. However, splitting their strategies caused a dangerous over extension and division of an already divided force. It amounted to another distraction undermining their own ever diverging and dwindling power.

The attack on the island of Midway was born out of a desperation to secure the defensive ring, create a barrier, and sink the aircraft carriers which could again threaten the Emperor. The capture of Midway Atoll would have enabled the Japanese to sail further up the Hawaiian island chain onto Honolulu, a target they could have devastated six months previously. Moving fantasy fleets about in a stupendous game of battleships, the Japanese also planned a foray far to the south to capture Fiji, and Samoa.

Half a year after the destruction of Pearl Harbor, Admiral Yamamoto aboard the *Yamato* lost all four aircraft carriers used in the Battle of Midway, they were ultimately sunk by being scuttled. They also lost hundreds of aircraft along with skilled, and as it would transpire, almost irreplaceable pilots. In total they lost more than 3,000 men, ten times the number of Americans killed in the Battle of Midway. The US Fleet finally saw *Yorktown* sink beneath the waves but only after it had done its duty. Yamamoto had failed to consider the impact of this ship and found himself surprised by the other American aircraft carriers and supporting vessels including cruisers and submarines. Midway Atoll itself was a fourth American aircraft carrier involved in the battle and had planes operating from an island base. Its preparedness was also a factor. The American navy had cracked Japan's codes and managed to surmise that Midway Atoll was the likely target. Yamamoto had fallen into a trap of his own making.

The Japanese strategy was flawed and even during the battle they relied upon faulty overly positive assumptions as to their likely chances of victory. Wishful thinking as to the damage they thought they were inflicting clouded their judgement. After suffering severe losses, instead of responding to the peril they were in and acknowledging the catastrophic situation, they ignored the evidence and broke the dictum not to reinforce failure. Only optimism was tolerated until it was too late. The Japanese at every level robotically followed their pre-programmed procedures and routinely and recklessly changed weapons and refuelled, making themselves especially vulnerable to an American strike. Their only thought was to make their offence more deadly, they thus left themselves vulnerable. The problems ran throughout the Japanese task force. Not only did the operation's commanders fail but under fire and in the heat of combat the Japanese sailors did not perform well in fighting back against the destruction of their ships. A decapitated leadership left men rudderless. They were less able to act without direction. The Japanese obedience to orders remained all important, conversely the American sailor's initiative was crucial in keeping the *Yorktown* afloat long enough to keep it operational and to fool the Japanese into thinking this repeatedly hit aircraft carrier was two different ships. The Americans proved to be more creative and resourceful under pressure than their Japanese counterparts. The bold initiative of the American pilots in locating their enemy first was of supreme importance.

The operation against Midway was itself divided, yet another front was opened in the north Pacific with the invasion of the Aleutian Islands of Kiska and Attu, which are a part of Alaska. The Japanese wanted to control the sea-routes in the north of the Pacific Ocean and prevent an alliance between the USA and Russia, which once held these islands along with Alaska and even part of California. The Japanese feared those nations would descend upon them from the north. The Axis aim would be both to deprive these islands to the enemy and to build more bases to aid further expansion. The cold and windswept Aleutian Islands were a world away from the key battles in the more southerly parts of the Pacific. Their temporary loss to the Japanese did mean that the Empire of the Sun had captured yet more American controlled territory, but these islands were a part of Alaska which was not yet a state in the Union. Still, it was a propaganda success and an important part of Japan's strategy to dominate the north Pacific. The Americans were able, however, to capture a Zero. Analysis of this intact plane helped the United States to refine tactics that would give America control of the air. That reckless loss harmed the Japanese militarists cause and the diversion north further hampered their other escapades.

The Japanese, from a small nation compared to America, spread themselves too thinly, with too few men, ships, and aeroplanes guarding their predominately nautical frontier. What strength Japan had was dissipated not just on too many fronts but on defending too large an area and a multitude of islands and atolls with too few resources. The defensive plan was little more than an act of self-mastication. The United States was free to concentrate its army and navy at points of its choosing. The Japanese in America's way would be destroyed, the rest would wither on the vine. The whole concept of the defensive line, especially when it encompassed many seas, was a fallacy as big as the vast wide ocean they were trying to control.

When the Japanese failed to take the islands at Midway and destroy the US Pacific Fleet's aircraft carriers, the chances of even delaying the American advance across the Pacific was lost. These decisive attacks were disasters for the Japanese. Nevertheless, the Japanese planners would continue to seek other decisive naval engagements. They endeavoured to overcome their industrial and military weaknesses by devising more overcomplicated battle plans and other blitzkriegs at sea. Japan should have focused resources on the Battle of Guadalcanal, the American victory in that confrontation was the real turning point of the war in the Pacific. A Japanese victory there could have been achieved if they did not send their other ships and aircraft on a fool's errand into the big blue expanse of the Pacific.

Yamamoto's naval forces were weakened and unable to deliver a decisive result. This split strategy was failing. When one defends everywhere, one defends nowhere. Correspondingly, simultaneously attacking on multiple fronts with differing objectives just created an indefensible divergence that led to Japan's imperial forces suffering a gaseous dissipation. Their big bang could not resist the external pressure placed on it, at its heart was a vacuum of economic impotence, weak leadership, and poor planning. The muddled strategic thinking had characterised Japanese expansion since 1937 when the ambitions of its militarists were allowed free range to embroil Japan in a war that was never properly thought through let alone adequately prepared for. Japanese planners were hoping for a quick war and did not even think they had the capability to resist their multitude of self-made enemies for long.

The defeatist realisation at the top of Japan's military even meant that beyond epoch changing fanciful super weapons based on pseudo-science, they actively decided not to develop new conventional weapons until it was late. They thought these could not be deployed in time and in enough numbers to turn the tide. Before their last desperate gamble with the lives of Japan's vulnerable indoctrinated young men, its industry merely tried to upgrade existing models to enhance their capabilities. This worked for a time. There was capacity to make incremental improvements in machines such as the Zero. Adjustments to its radial engine's exhaust pipes created a jet effect where the direction of the gases eked out a little more power, making a small increase in its top speed. This limited research and development was no substitute for the technological developments in fighter aircraft underway in Britain, the United States, and later the USSR. As the war progressed the Zero, one of the most able carrier-borne planes in 1941, was hopelessly outdated by 1945. Yet, given Japan's limited industrial base, the decision not to invest in new tooling and technology had its logic. Yet it only brought forward the date of Japan's inevitable defeat along with the destruction of its cities, laid low from the undefended skies above.

Whilst Japan followed Germany in many regards, its technological investment differed greatly to its Axis partner's approach to developing weapons. These two extreme nations could find no middle way, both were at different ends of the spectrum. Germany, in marked contrast to Japan, tried to address its industrial weakness by inefficiently looking to rush wonder weapons into production. Germany was searching for quality to address its quantitative gap, and in this hurried gamble failed to deliver either. The difference was that Germany fought the war to win and remained fighting to deliver victory even after that had become impossible. In their delusional state they hoped, like Wilkins Micawber, that something would turn up. Japan, despite its insistence that its common soldiers must be prepared to die and never to surrender, had a different hope. Its hierarchy only ever wanted a favourable peace with America and then a face-saving surrender. Management of decline is to invite and ordain one's own destruction.

Japan's experience with the modern world led them to enter a delusional Freudian overcompensation on a devastating scale, driving them to a state of excess. They even believed they were superior to much more substantial and sizeable nations and peoples. Occasionally the reality of their insecurities would break through, and they knew that their triumphs were transitory. Japan's unsustainable megalomania, and conversely, it's unrealistic hopes to force an exit from the war, made the coming defeat as much of an implosion as it was the result of the triumphal Americans. Japan had neither the men nor materiel to make any of their contrasting strategies work. Further diminutions of the limited firepower that could be directed against the Allies was the height of recklessness, Japan's strength had already dwindled from being split between fighting China, Britain in Burma, and against the Australians to name but a few. It was a world war in the Pacific involving representatives from all corners of the globe.

East meets west

Japan's expansion had been checked, though the militarists devoted to the Chrysanthemum Throne controlled a vast empire on both land and water. Its size, including large swathes of the Pacific Ocean, was many times greater than Hitler's Reich. It was a remarkable achievement. Japanese racialists could exploit their subject peoples through their co-prosperity sphere. With the British driven out of their Burmese colony, Japan was on the edge of India. The Japanese even had at their disposal Indian dissidents who were willing, in perhaps a not well thought out plan, to work with even Hitler to remove the British from the sub-continent. Some Indian soldiers captured by Rommel's Afrika Korps formed the Free Indian Legion. This came under the leadership of Subhas Chandra Bose who had fled from India to Germany where he was to meet with Hitler. The Indian Legion was only a small force that would provide some assistance and political cover to German attempts to end the British Raj, however, it only ever operated as a military force in Europe. With the Japanese capture of yet more Indian soldiers after the fateful surrender of Singapore more recruits for the anti-British Indian National Army (INA) were obtained by the Japanese. Subhas Chandra Bose after being smuggled out of Germany by Hitler would come to lead this small army. Despite the INA's collaboration with the Axis powers, and even though its numbers were dwarfed by the British Indian Army, to this day they are lionised in some sections of India and commemorated in public monuments in New Delhi. The much more substantial numbers that remained loyal to Britain and fought against Nazi Germany, Fascist Italy, and militaristic Japan have been whitewashed from India's historical memory.

For a brief period of time, it must have seemed to the ambitious Axis leaders that the dream of linking up on the border of India and Iran with the Germans coming from the west and the Japanese from the east could be achieved. From there the plan to partition Eurasia along the 70th meridian east all the way north through Russia could be achieved. Despite these fanciful aims being quickly abandoned, the Japanese plans for an empire, masquerading as a political union, found parallels on the other side of the world where the Germans were to create their own fraudulent institutions. Karl Haushofer's vision was for a time a reality, the Japanese had created its co-prosperity Sphere and its European counterpart was established in 1942 when Nazi Germany formalised its plan for a *Europaische Wirtschaftgesellschaft* (European Economic Community).

A new world order was coming, but it was not the one in which the Axis powers would have a leading role. They would become subservient to the Allies and incorporated into the United Nations, which was born out of the 1942 "Declaration of United Nations" drafted by President Roosevelt and British Prime Minister Winston Churchill. This would enforce the principles of the Atlantic Charter developed by these two leaders in August 1941. These men built the UN's intergovernmental system that guides the affairs of independent nations to this day. It is very separate to the German and Japanese vision of supranational regional power blocks ruling over subordinated states that were independent in name only. Before Roosevelt could realise the vision his administration had been working on since 1939, German and Japanese hegemony would have to be driven back. This fight would be fiercely resisted, to overcome Axis stubbornness the Allies were the first to unleash total war.

Operation Pacific

Initially, the Japanese were looking for a victory built upon success in a decisive battle. Later their defence also sought to use pivotal engagements in order to preserve their ill-gotten gains. The Japanese were as unadaptable as their history suggests. America had a hugely different approach and recognised that this was a war of attrition and like its fighter planes the Americans practised death by a thousand cuts.

Whereas Japanese submariners primarily took on warships, the Americans had no reservations about targeting Japanese merchant shipping. Cutting off an invader's supplies by sinking its merchant ships was unromantic and less 'honourable', in Japanese eyes, than attacking hard targets. The Americans understood the economic necessities of both business and war, they are the one and the same. America's liberal and capitalist society installed an ethos that placed the celebration of results and the outcome above other concepts such as glory in battle. The Japanese were fixated on counting coup. However, from General Sherman ordering the shooting of buffalo on America's Great Plains to the sinking of merchant vessels, the United States had no compulsion against deliberately starving an enemy into submission.

Japanese cargo ships were attacked from the skies and the sea, many were destroyed by speedy small craft such as PT Boats. These patrol torpedo boats destroyed Japanese supply ships heading to their many occupied islands. One was commanded by John F Kennedy, a future President of the United States. Indeed, he had an outstanding war record and was severely injured for his service. Other Japanese merchant ships were sent to the bottom of the ocean through the stealth of the submarine. US submarines sank over 1,700,000 tons of Japanese shipping, accounting for more than half the losses of Japan's merchant fleet. The United States Navy adopted the German Wolf Pack tactics in the Pacific and groups of up to 20 American Cato Class submarines attacked Japanese merchant ships and deprived the Japanese soldiers and marines of the resources they needed. This proved decisive in the Battle of Guadalcanal and many other battles in the Pacific. Ultimately, they succeeded in cutting Japan's jugular.

The Japanese made this easy for the Americans. Japan's aversion to anything that can be considered cowardly, meant that they did not develop defensive measures for their merchant fleet such as initiating a convoy system. In this arrangement a group of ships would sail together for protection under the watchful eye of warships who would be equipped for the defence of these supply and troop-carrying vessels. The omission of a convoy strategy was a major factor in America winning the one-sided war of attrition. For Japan, a naval power from a nation of islands with an oceanic empire, this was a major dereliction of duty; it was not their only failing. At the start of the war Japanese anti-submarine depth charges used by their warships exploded at a depth that was too shallow. American submarines could out dive these underwater explosive devices. The Japanese did not have the same luxury.

Japan's use of submarines to attack military shipping meant that they suffered massive losses and missed the opportunity to target supply ships and fight an effective war of attrition. Another factor was Japan's desperation to bring the war to a conclusion on favourable terms. Merchant vessels were deemed to not offer the opportunity for a decisive victory. And in their aggressive Bushido marshal code such ships were not an honourable target. More kudos came from attacking warships. Consequently, as many as ¾ of Japan's submarines were lost. Bar those that volunteered for martyrdom operations, Japanese submariners were more likely to die than those from any other service branch. This was in stark contrast to American submariners who had an exceptional chance of seeing the conclusion of the war.

Abroad with two Yanks

At the heart of the US strategy was the aim to seize Japan's occupied territories and thus deprive the empire of its resources, strangling Japan's arms production industry to death, starving it into surrender. America had its own resource issues that influenced how it chose to fight the war. The strategic decision to defeat Germany first meant that there were only limited supplies of men to use against Japan. More was spent killing Germans than was put towards liquidating the Japanese. These limitations fell heavily upon the US navy and prevented them from going straight to the centre of the Japanese empire.

Roosevelt decided the strategy in conference with his two main commanders in the Pacific Theatre. These were, sailor and submariner, Admiral Chester Nimitz, Commander-in-Chief of the United States Pacific Fleet. And the soldier, General Douglas MacArthur, who held the title of Commander of U.S. Army Forces in the Far East and when the war was underway, he was appointed Supreme Commander of Allied Forces in the Southwest Pacific Area.

These two rivals from different services had contrasting visions of how the war should be prosecuted. Reversing Japan's conquests and driving closer to the home islands was the goal but getting to Japan was quite an undertaking and a serious matter to contend with. MacArthur, based in Australia, favoured a southern route. Having been ordered to depart from the Philippines he wanted to return and regain those islands. MacArthur also aimed to capture important resources in Borneo and Indonesia, these were all land masses in which his infantry could operate. The navy had an alternative strategy.

The US Navy wanted to bypass these large islands and their deep impenetrable forests. Nimitz desired a direct route to Taiwan sailing east from Pearl Harbor snaking across the Pacific's small islands of the Marshalls, Marianas, Iwo Jima, and Okinawa along the way. They would then turn these into strategic barriers to attack Japan's supply lines, the all-important shipping lanes. The navy argued that this approach would be swifter and much more economical. Both the navy and the army were authorised to go ahead with their two different approaches. Like the Japanese, Roosevelt was not immune to splitting his forces, the difference was that these two thrusts using different services, and utilising distinct operational methods, would cover each other and converge on their enemy.

Resources were the deciding factor through much of the war. Whereas US soldiers were pouring into Australia, there was a relative lack of fighting men in the marines, so the navy did not have the resources to adequately prosecute an offensive via the more direct northerly route.

The way back
To capture the atolls of Tarawa and Makin, in the Gilbert and Marshall Islands campaign, the navy conducted a massive bombardment before the amphibious landings were underway. Tarawa was a particularly deadly battle because the marines had to wade ashore; it was also well defended. During the initial stages of the Battle of Tarawa the issue was nearly in doubt. A night-time Banzai attack may have worked during the early stages of the fighting at Tarawa, but this was never ordered; the Japanese commander, an Admiral, and his senior staff had been killed when they were caught in the open. The American forces had a reprieve and eventually conquered the island in a matter of days.

A massed charge at the Americans whilst proclaiming *Banzai* may have been temporarily rewarding for the ego of those that took part, but it was a worse than ineffectual military tactic. The suicidal charge on Saipan saw the death of 3,000 Japanese soldiers, including their commander who killed himself by ritual suicide; this mass folly saw the final defeat of Japanese resistance on that island. Similarly, Banzai attacks against US forces on Guam in 1944 led to 80% casualties and likewise hastened the defeat of Japanese forces on that island.

The US did not have the resources to immediately overwhelm the Japanese nor the time to deal with every Japanese outpost. A new kind of mobile warfare was needed, this was one of amphibious vehicles taking the US Marine Corps to far flung islands. At the start of the conflict there was also a lack of landing craft making landing operations difficult. It would take a herculean effort and American innovation to invent and produce the Higgins boats as the landing craft became known. Without these, taking America's young men ashore the task of engaging the Japanese in battle, and defeating them, would have been much more problematic. The marines were backed-up by airpower from aircraft carriers which could cover great distances across the Pacific Ocean. Where the navy was used, its ships, marines and aircraft had to follow a strategy of bypassing some islands, whilst devastating others. Those with significant bases, and were strategically important, would be devastated under a naval barrage or through aerial bombardment or both. Often, the Japanese would endure this before US Marines invaded and captured these outcrops. This strategy was known as island hopping. It was an enormous feat of arms; there were seventy-five major amphibious landings, 75 veritable D-Days, carried out in the Pacific by the Americans. The US Pacific Fleet was an enormous armada of warships of all classes, aircraft carriers, submarines, amphibious tanks, and the all-important landing craft. And these all tied back to the American mainland via a network of tankers and other logistical and support ships. It was the greatest fleet ever to have been assembled. It was crewed by the greatest generation.

The twin thrusts of the US advance split the Japanese defences, what is more, the naval attacks had the advantage of being able to determine when and where they could strike. They could pick their battles. Still the main thrust was to send MacArthur's army up the Solomon Islands, New Guinea, and beyond rather than the more direct approach of Admiral Nimitz using the Navy and the Marines. Even as late as 1943 the naval resources for a direct attack straight onto Taiwan, then known as Formosa, were not available, therefore the Japanese defences had to be rolled back using the army along MacArthur's line of approach. Operation Cartwheel, General Douglas MacArthur's two-pronged attack in the Solomon Islands and New Guinea to isolate the Japanese base at Rabaul still took nine months to succeed. The few quick victories in the Pacific theatre were attained at sea, and in the air. They came in response to Japanese attempts to finally achieve a decisive result. The next stop would be the Philippines.

Originally, America's strategic focus was on Taiwan. MacArthur, however, had other plans. And lobbied for a major invasion of the Philippine Islands from whence he came. This was not controversial. Chester Nimitz, in their meeting with Roosevelt, supported the logic behind the attacks on the Philippines. The sea lanes around these islands were all important. Japan had seized territory in south-east Asia to give it the resources it needed to survive. Taking the Solomon Islands, New Guinea, and then the Philippines would isolate much of Japan from Borneo, Burma, Malaya, and the entirety of the Dutch East Indies.

MacArthur's thrust into the Philippines would disrupt Japan's ability to wage war. The thought process was flawless. Depriving them of the Dutch East Indies and the resulting loss of oil would be particularly damaging to the Japanese war effort. This rationale behind taking back the Philippines was romanticised by General MacArthur; his superb spin caricatured the operation as him personally returning to avenge the defeat he had suffered earlier in the war. The twin US thrusts over an enormous battlespace ultimately trapped the Japanese in a giant pincer movement. From the Philippines, the Japanese home islands lay directly in the American sights. Before wreaking devastation on the Japanese, the Americans would learn the art of war against the Germans in North Africa, Italy, and in the skies above Europe. The lessons learnt there would be refined, perfected, and unleashed against Japan causing their utter ruin.

In the Red

"Ah, Stalingrad! All the same, they are a great people, a very great people." — **Charles de Gaulle, future President of France, praising the Germans after touring the devastated Russian city of Stalingrad.**

Block war

As the German army stormed eastwards, and despite encountering setbacks and privations on the way, it would have appeared to Hitler in his deluded state that the war was his to lose. With the false appearance that the military struggle was reaching a positive outcome, the political battle to remake Europe was about to get underway. It was a plan that had long been in the making and left a powerful legacy.

On 9ᵗʰ May 1950 the French Foreign Minister, Robert Schuman, made what became known as the Schuman Declaration. This called for a supranational higher authority above the governments of European states. The 9ᵗʰ May has since been adopted as 'Europe Day.' The plans he espoused led to the European Economic Community, later renamed the European Union. This was not the first time that such an idea had been proposed. In 1942 the *Europäische Wirtshaftsgemeinschaft* (European Economic Community) was implemented by the Nazis, this association did not last long, it was dissolved by British-led intervention. The vision outlined by Schuman was to endure. It was the latest iteration of other visions for a German-led Europe.

In 1942 the Reichsbank, the central bank of Germany, organised a conference in Berlin to create a new Zollverein. This convention was titled *Europäische Wirtschaftsgemeinschaft*. It set out how, once the war was over, a supranational German dominated bureaucracy would sit above the conquered nations and manage the economy of Europe. It involved restoring the idea of a customs union and even introducing a single currency; Britain would have the opportunity to opt-out of monetary union. Both the Germans and Japanese offered a regional top-down order, with separate institutions exercising authority over once sovereign states. In both the EEC and the Greater East Asia Co-Prosperity Sphere, single currencies were envisaged, and political and economic decision making would be linked.

Both these visions had their idealistic supporters who were perhaps somewhat naïve. The nature of power meant that the interests of the mightiest nation in each respective bloc would come to dominate lesser members. And economically, the central area within a currency union benefits more than the periphery. Instead of creating égalité between the nations, the Eurocentric vision subordinated France to Germany. The Nazis were using the Gallic nation to fulfil the Teutonic aim of *Drang nach Osten*. However, German political plans were meeting tough resistance; theirs was not the only vision at work.

The same year that Germany relaunched its supranational scheme, the United States offered an internationalist alternative. The Allied vision was a world structured around a system where governments agreed between themselves, hence the term 'international', meaning between nations. The idea of the United Nations was born. The UN as it is otherwise known, originates from 'The Declaration by United Nations' of January 1942; it was initially signed by 26 national governments with a further 21 adding their names soon after. The United Nations was considered the formal name of the Allies in the conflict. The Axis powers were losing the political war; their military struggle was also beginning to falter.

Year zero

In 1942 in North Africa there were four German and eight Italian Divisions, in Western Europe and France there were 26 German Divisions, 12 German Divisions defended Norway. Five German and twelve Italian Divisions were operating in the Balkans. There were, however, 197 German Divisions tied up on the Eastern Front. Hitler had broken Bernard Law Montgomery's first rule of war, the dictum warning against marching on the Russian capital. The Nazis came close, but success was proving to be a mirage, especially as the Red Army was learning how to win.

The Soviet's had found the antidote to blitzkrieg; no longer did the desperate Russians use massed infantry attacks that resulted in the wholesale slaughter of its men. The Red Army had relearnt the tactics that they had carefully developed in the interregnum between the two world wars but were forgotten in some quarters following Stalin's great purge of the military. The Soviets also adapted villages to establish heavily defended strong points which slowed and ground down the German advance. Such an approach had already halted the march on Leningrad. They stopped blitzkrieg with gradual but deadly attrition. The invasion had also floundered on the railway network and the mismatch of train track gauges. The logistical nightmare of advancing in Russia was made worse when the Germans decided to expand its war by targeting civilians. Mismatching railway widths were not the only problems regarding Germany's transport infrastructure.

The Nazis commandeered train wagons and their supporting network for nefarious purposes. Germany's strained and congested railway system would be used, not to aid the real war effort, but to conduct a racial war against civilians, not soldiers. 1942, the year that long term goals were put into motion, was also the date when the Wannsee Conference was held. This meeting between German government bureaucrats and the Nazi SS coordinated what they called the Final Solution to the Jewish Question what we now know as the Holocaust. Mass murder with millions of people losing their lives did not begin in 1942. It had started earlier when the Second World War got underway and accelerated after Germany invaded the USSR. The armed forces deployed Nazi viciousness. They hunted civilians in missions that were often far from the frontline. These murderers would have been better used against actual, rather than perceived, enemies. However, it did take advantage of latent anti-Semitic attitudes in many of the occupied territories and enabled the Nazis to recruit more support from those inclined to collaborate. The Ukraine and Baltic States provided much assistance to the Nazis. Volunteers joined the German fight against Judaism and Bolshevism, which were often misconstrued as being part of the same phenomenon.

Before 1942 the killing of proscribed peoples was carried out by special squads called *Einsatzgruppen* and *SS-Sonderkommando*; these units would personally shoot those they were tasked with hunting down. The slow pace of killing as well as the psychological damage wrought on the perpetrators made the Nazis and the collaborationist authorities that assisted them realise that another method was needed. The Germans were also using mobile vans that killed victims with carbon monoxide. These were, however, inefficient forms of murder and were replaced with a network of concentration camps to which millions of victims were transported by rail. Here the Germans showed their potential for efficient industrial organisation. Some camps were for slave labour where the inmates were expected to produce weapons or other manufactures to aid or fund the war effort. At these locations they would be worked to death if they were not executed soon after arrival. Other camps were dedicated to robbing and then killing with a chemical named Zyklon B though some did not receive an immediate death sentence; instead they were starved and worked until they died. Neither outcome could be considered one that spared the imprisoned.

The Nazi's anti-Semitism had an almost spiritual zeal; it was a part of many religions but for Hitler it was his religion. Purging Europe of Jewry was the Nazi faith's most holy sacrament. To the Nazis this *Ragnarök* was the cleansing fire that would bring about the millenarian rule of just Aryans. Hitler's faith was a perverted belief system that turned the Judeo-Christian inheritance on its head and sought to literally eradicate every vestige of both the Jewish ethnicity and their belief system. It was a quest for a cultural year zero. From the ashes produced by the ovens of the slave labour and extermination camps a new Europe would emerge where oppressed workers would no longer be strangled by the interests of capital. Hitler, like the proto-Nazis before him, hoovered up ideas that were already in existence and formulated them into his national socialist ideology. Collectivists which believed in the near unlimited right of the state to dominate the totality of people's lives were often opposed to Jews. Anti-capitalists frequently believe the trope that the Jew was obsessed with money and mammon. Cash was something the Nazis did not want to be king; they desired a more fulfilling purpose.

The ideology of Nazism presumed that different groups had different character traits; from this they ascribed a moral worth according to the ethnic definition applied to individuals by the state which categorised people into groups. The Nazis defined who was oppressed and who was an oppressor according to Nazi notions of identity. The Jews were considered the oppressor and the 'German' was their victim. One's place in the Nazi eutopia, if they were to have one at all, was defined by race. This was an early expression of what is known as identity politics. The road of identity politics ends in Auschwitz.

Such Nazi social attitudes retarded the development of Germany's war economy. People were not judged on the content of their character but by the state's definition of their ethnic group. Similarly, scientific works were judged not by their merits in a process of peer review but by the ethnicity of the author. Jewish scientists had no place in German academe. This problem was compounded by the racial Nuremberg Laws introduced in 1935. These had the effect of driving out many of Germany's top technologists. Discriminating against them on the grounds that they were Jewish meant that the physicists that Germany would have needed to develop nuclear weapons, and win the war, were not only lost; their skills and influence were gained by the United States. Two Jewish physicists that prudently eschewed Germany upon Hitler gaining power were Leo Szilard and Albert Einstein. They went west and both became instrumental in warning President Roosevelt about the dangers of the Nazis acquiring an atomic bomb. This led to America making a massive investment in developing their own war winning nuclear weapons. Other Nazi attitudes also hindered German chances of winning World War Two.

Socialist dogma

Germany believed that the role of women was to produce the next generation; demographics is destiny. A society cannot survive let alone thrive without at least replacement levels of fertility being reached, in times of peace that means at least one woman having 2.1 children or more. Yet these were different times, servicemen were losing their lives at the front and were away from their wives for long periods of time. And when they were on leave, they and their civilian families and children were dying at home from Allied bombing raids and the many privations brought by war. Such an environment was not conducive to child rearing. Baby booms in Britain and France followed peace, they did not come with war. Pronatalist policies introduced by the French following their liberation proved successful in increasing the population. In Germany there was only a weak baby boom following the outbreak of peace. The Nazis maintained their pro-birth policies when it was not a productive time. A pragmatic short-term sacrifice that would have aided the war economy would have been more likely to achieve a victory and allow its women to get back in labour as nature intended at the earliest practical opportunity. Flexibility would have lessened the chances of the Nazi regime and its ideology dying out. However, the Nazi refusal to use women in the labour force until it was too late meant that Germany could never fulfil its industrial potential. The Soviets, not only publicly professed notions of gender equality but even went some way to enacting them. Like Britain and America, the Russians included women in the labour force. This freed up more men for combat.

Manpower

The Red Army soldier had the option to fight or face arrest. Civilians in the workers' paradise had a similar extreme Hobson's choice, work or die. It had long been a principle in the Union of Soviet Socialist Republics that he who does not work, neither shall he eat. Soviet social innovations freed up massive amounts of people to fight the Germans. Whereas the Nazis intended women to serve the state by going into labour and childrearing, the communists were less accepting of traditional gender roles. In the dash to build a socialist state and then protect it from its enemies, the Soviets made sure that women laboured to improve the material wealth of their nation. The Soviet's also used under-age labour; teenagers were put to work in the factories as well as women. This was something that the Nazi would not and could not do. German industry relied upon highly skilled craftsmen employing labour intensive techniques, Soviet industry had imported the latest production methods from the United States, even literally importing the factories and their equipment. The production process was simple and straightforward. Machines did the heavy lifting. Even women and youths could do this work with little training.

The Soviet's, however, went one step further and even used women on the frontline. This tradition still exists to this day, pro-Russian females volunteered to fight alongside their men in the conflict which engulfed eastern Ukraine in 2014. During the Second World War the use of women helped address the manpower shortages the Red Army faced and were made even more egregious by its heavy losses of both men and materiel. Women's inherent physical weakness when compared to most men of fighting age could also prove to be a useful attribute which the Red Army could use to their advantage. Soviet industry produced vehicles to meet targets and paid little consideration to the end user, the consumer. With next to no concern for those driving a tank even the excellent T-34/76 was not user friendly. Chief amongst its poor ergonomics were its cramped conditions. However, women who on average are smaller than men, excelled as T-34 tank drivers as they could operate more freely in their tight surroundings. A major contrast between the Soviet and Nazi forces was that the Red Army had 1.5 million women serving in it, even on the front line. This was a resource that the Germans were reluctant to draw upon. The Russian women were mostly treated like their male comrades, though things were not quite equal. The difference was that the women received an extra ration of soap. The use of women in the army was anathema to the Germans. This was especially so when they were employed at the front be that driving tanks or in the Red Army Air Force where all-female bomber regiments would harry the enemy by night. These aviators took the fight to the enemy with a vengeance and spitefulness, consequently they received the epithet of "Night Witches" from their unfortunate adversaries.

In some cases, the communist indoctrination of its soldiers was made more furious through the use of women volunteering to fight to avenge the death of their husband. They were prepared to unleash hell on the enemy. Ideological fervour played a part in motivating soldiers on both sides, the strongly held regressive social attitudes of the Nazis would have therefore played a part in motivating those who fought alongside the German army, or *Heer*. The Nazi Party's fighting units were determined warriors and as a part of the SS had been indoctrinated with the necessary requirement of seeing their enemy as less than human. It makes the task of killing them that much easier. The *Waffen-SS* were often used in emergencies and as firemen or shock troops in the hardest battles;

they gave no quarter and expected none. They were often notable by the absence; there were no *Waffen-SS* at the debacle that was Stalingrad.

Hitler's racial attitudes often proved to be a hindrance. The Führer believed that the 'superior' Germanics would overcome the 'inferior' eastern Slavic race. He therefore could not focus on the real problems in hand, nor could he understand why Germany was beginning to lose the war. The Germans did, however, quickly adapt, and even abandon the practical application of some of their racialist notions.

The Germans were already willing to work with the Japanese, Arabs, and even use Indian soldiers. As the war progressed the Nazis even showed flexibility to those of Slavic background. The Germans sought foreign recruits and formed many divisions of the *Waffen-SS* from volunteers from eastern Europe and even conscripted some into the German Army. The Nazis were also willing to have Russian soldiers fighting alongside them and used them to conduct atrocities against the Poles which even some Germans were reluctant to carry out. Numerical expediency trumped the Nazi belief in racial purity. Ultimately, Hitler's racial theories were to take a bizarre twist. Once Hitler believed that the Slavs, from where the term slave originates as they were widely used as forced labour by Muslims, were a mongrel race with too much of an Asiatic influence. Yet, at the very end, this embittered man concluded that the German people had failed him and that his own nationality was inferior to the stronger Slavic race to the east. Nevertheless, for the time being the Nazi hatred towards the Slavs had a dramatic affect.

Behind enemy lines

Whilst the Nazis were desperate for their own people's affections, Soviet psychology was vastly different. In contrast, the Soviets, like many communists, were convinced of not just the 'scientific' inevitability of their cause but they also believed that they were morally superior. They knew that their cause was liberation, whether the people wanted their form of freedom from capitalism or not. As such they forced their worker and soldier ants, their *Stakhanovites*, to dig deeper and harder in the service of their idealistic masters who themselves were convinced they were on the right side of history and morality. They did not need to prove their legitimacy, they demanded obedience without question. Nor would many of those Russians living under German occupation be cowed by Nazi brutality.

The Russian character accepted the melancholy of their existence. For the Russian, the privations of war were merely a way of life. Another hardship to endure. Russia along with its 'partner' republics in the Soviet Union, had little experience of liberty and limited government. The freedom that briefly emerged after the overthrow of the Tsar had merely led to a vacuum that was quickly filled by the ruthlessly efficient Bolsheviks. In Russia, the stick of the state had always been the favoured motivational tool rather than the carrot. The population were mercilessly forced to resist the invader. On 3rd July 1941 Stalin encouraged the Partisan War and called on those living behind German lines to resist the occupiers. They responded as demanded. Matriotism for Mother Russia remained strong.

Those unwilling to surrender and unable to return to their own lines had their chances of survival increased by German tactics. The speed of the initial German advance and the use of blitzkrieg to wander far into the Soviet interior deliberately bypassed enemy units leaving many Red Army soldiers free to continue the fight as best they could. Indeed, they had little choice but to resist the Axis forces. After learning of the maltreatment of their surrendered comrades who were kept in exposed conditions and deprived of sustenance, the Red Army was no longer willing to surrender en masse as they had in the early stages of Operation Barbarossa. Enduring the appalling conditions of a German prisoner of war camp ruled out capitulation as an option; it added to their motivation to resist. Similarly, if surrounded it made the option of escaping to fight on as a partisan far more attractive. However, like conventional fighting, the Soviets were not ready for the partisan war.

For reasons of internal security and to prevent a challenge to the ruling Soviet authorities, the Russian leadership had not prepared for a guerrilla war on their home soil. Before the purges, the Red Army had planned to protect the Soviet Union by taking the offensive and fighting on an enemy's territory rather than their own. They were therefore unprepared for resisting the German occupation. Following the wiping out of much of the Red Army's senior officer corps, plans for defence were lost, many of its top military theorists were silenced by a bullet in the head from their comrades in the NKVD. The Russians also planned to defend themselves with fortified lines with strong points that would funnel the enemy; these defences, however, had been neglected. The Axis swept through leaving many bewildered Soviet soldiers behind them.

These once conventional soldiers turned to irregular warfare and mounted small scale hit and run attacks and carried out acts of sabotage against German logistics. The Heer's advance was already hampered by the poor state of the road network. Insurgents would take advantage of fighting on home soil which they knew better than the invader. The few highways meant that the locations of German advances could be predicted and checked, cutting access on just one road could be key; if that were blocked then there were not many realistic alternative supply routes, and the invader could be cut-off and destroyed. The Russian partisans could often both choose when and where they could use guerrilla tactics and even dictate German movements. The irregulars' bases were safely hidden in the vast forests and swamps that made up much of the Eastern Front. Or they could be hidden in plain sight in the Soviet Union's settlements be they cities or remote hamlets. These partisans had a ready supply of recruits from the local population who could feed and clothe them as required. Conversely, the Axis forces could expect to find little shelter. The infrastructure and resources had either been evacuated to the east or was destroyed by the retreating Russians as part of their scorched earth policy.

There were occasions in Estonia when German occupiers would attempt to make some form of payment for food and supplies requisitioned from the local population. These people were however not considered to be ethnic enemies of the Ayran race. However, the war on the Eastern Front had become a cultural and racial *Ragnarök* with the Slavs, who would have their food stolen in a fashion that was not dissimilar to Lenin's war communism. German exploitation exacerbated the partisan problem and encouraged more peasants to aid the insurgents. In response to partisan activity the Germans carried out reprisals against the civilian population. On the Eastern Front, as it did when tried again in Italy later in the war, this drove people to join the rebellion. German atrocities were a recruiting sergeant for Russian irregulars. At the very least the local population was willing to supply them with the food and information upon which they relied. The renegade in the forest or hills resisting the invader or even just an oppressive lord is a popular motif, indeed human psychology leads to many becoming attracted to such rebels. Despite the dreadful and fearful conditions in which they resided they are often romantic figures. As long as they are surviving and scoring successes against authority, they will receive popular support. Their state also came to their aid.

Sabotage groups infiltrated German occupied territory to conduct a guerrilla war. Resistance behind enemy lines grew to such an extent that whole German divisions were used chasing their tail far away from the front. Repressive anti-partisan measures further alienated the local population. The guerrilla war was stoked by the Soviet High Command which both actively coordinated and aided these irregular soldiers. Airdrops provided arms, ammunition, and explosives. Radios were also supplied so that the Soviet command could coordinate their activities and issue instructions. Offensives that were organised ranged from Operation Rail War which began on 3rd August 1943 and Operation Concert which began in September 1943, this aimed to assassinate leading Nazis.

The British also added to the popular insurgency against Nazism by aiding resistance groups in the west from occupied France to Norway and in the east where Churchill's Special Operations Executive aided partisans in Yugoslavia. It also sent assassins into Czechoslovakia and provided support to the Polish Home Army which was still fighting an underground war against the German occupiers and had fought Soviet forces in the east of the country before June 1941. After Operation Barbarossa the Russians favoured their own Polish resistance group and provided support for communist forces. Despite the political divisions these Polish partisans also played an important role tying up German forces and creating logistical problems for the Wehrmacht on the Eastern Front. The climatic conditions also aided resistance. Great forests, the last home to the aurochs, the extinct giant cattle admired by the Nazis, stretched from Poland to Belarus and beyond. These woods and their neighbouring swamps made the area inhospitable. Nature ruled this wilderness, not man. German conquests had stretched too far, and this opened up new opportunities for the enemies of the Third Reich which was forced to hold back men from the front line. The ever-present fear of attack, even when not on an operation, eroded morale. The guerrillas also slowed the supply of materiel to where it was needed. Ultimately, the partisans helped bleed the German army white.

The Nazi strategy of exploitation of the east and its people also further alienated the population. The General Plan Ost made life unbearable for many; people flocked to the partisans to avoid being conscripted as slave labourers who would be deported to Germany. Nazi brutality against civilians did however have its advantages. German anti-Polish attitudes, like its anti-Semitism, drew support from people that were willing to fight with the Nazis. The Ukrainian Insurgent Army keenly carried out ethnic cleansing of Polish people. The Polish–Lithuanian Commonwealth had once ruled over land that is now considered to be a part of Ukraine. Certainly, not all guerrillas were fighting with the Allies and German excesses against civilians could win over some people as easily as it alienated others. There were other benefits that came with the Nazi terror; it aided their economic plans.

The German war on their conquered subjects gave them the opportunity to plunder food; it also provided a ready supply of forced labour for the Reich's economic planners. The many partisan uprisings gave the Nazis the moral justification, as they saw it, to deport rebellious populations and use them as a much-needed source of slave labour and even as conscripts. The German economy, like that of the Soviet Union, relied upon central controls and workers having little choice but to work, and often toil in atrocious conditions. The difference was that Russian serfs spoke the same language as their masters. Increasingly those serving the German war economy spoke a different tongue to their Nazi overlords.

The madhouse

The Nazis took industry and put it under the control of the state incorporating once private businesses into the Reichswerke Hermann Göring conglomerate. This was under the dead hand of Hitler's deputy and President of the Reichstag, Hermann Göring. As Germany expanded the borders of the Third Reich from 1938 the Nazis seized the industry, factories, and many other businesses of subject nations and took them from their previous and lawful owners. The Nazis did not put these assets into the private ownership of Germans, nor their collaborators; instead, they were placed under the control of the German state and administered by the Reichswerke. After Germany's lightning military success, this behemoth controlled much of European industry. Germany, along with the resources that they had seized from the Atlantic Ocean in the west to the Black Sea in the east, was now on paper a great economic power. The Germans were getting closer to rivalling the United States of America and the British Empire.

In quick succession they had taken control of Austrian steel works, acquired after *Anschluss* in 1938; the same year they seized the Czechoslovak Škoda Works based in the Sudetenland. This plant was amongst the greatest factories in Europe, it produced arms for the Third Reich. The rest of Czech industry fell to the Nazis the following year as did Poland's coal mines, steel works, and oil refineries. The Germans also had Romanian oil at their disposal and that Kingdom's refineries. In 1940, Belgium, the second country in the world to industrialise, had its plants taken over by the Germans who now ran their coal and steel production. French industries that could efficiently produce cars, trains, and aeroplanes also now existed to serve the Nazi state's whims. As did the resources of Ukraine, including the industrial city of Donetsk, which fell to the Nazis in 1941. This former Soviet Socialist Republic was transferred into the German and Italian occupied *Reichskommissariat Ukraine*. The bulk of continental European production was now under Axis control; it was a great achievement, but it quickly turned to dust. The now centrally planned European economy could not maximise the enormous potential that lay under German dominion. The Nazis' answer was even more state intervention.

Many factories belonging to the Reichswerke were taken from this corporation and put under the direct control of Germany's Reich Ministry of Armaments and War Production. The Nazis had achieved the nationalisation of industry to create a socialised economy. In Hitler's book, *Mein Kampf*, he called for the collectivisation of agriculture and the nationalisation of industry. The ministry was under the direction of Albert Speer, he was an architect, but as a favourite of Hitler had become Europe's economic dictator. However, the German state completely mismanaged the resources and people at their disposal. National socialist price controls hurt producers who were not incentivised to make things. A short-term measure to please people seized up the system leading to shortages. This dire situation was exacerbated by the problems caused through Nazi plundering. The Germans took the gold reserves, food, and even the artwork of conquered countries, it solved immediate economic issues at home but contributed to their undoing in the long term. The now impoverished nations under German control had been prevented from effectively aiding the German war effort. Nazi desperation for success and rapacious desire to enrich their *volk* was hampering the war economy.

A pure motorised instinct drove the Nazis. The conquered were given little positive incentive to use their labour producing goods for the Germans. Militaristic managers used coercion, rather than encouragement, to force obedience from workers; this did not deliver. Across occupied Europe, employees, with little hope of reward, became deliberately unproductive. There were en masse informal individual and unofficial strikes. When workers did their jobs, they performed inefficiently and the output was of an insufficient standard, making a range of produce from munitions to vehicles unusable. Where work required precision, disgruntled staff delivered shoddy equipment. This was particularly prevalent in France; it was known as passive resistance. This was similar to the civil disobedience shown to the French and Belgian armies when they occupied the Ruhr between 1923 and 1925. Building an economic model based on duress only succeeded in lowering productivity. The Nazi response was to add even more oppression into their economic system. This virtually non-functioning economy was then further infected by the introduction of slaves abducted from other countries. Starved, bullied, and beaten, this forced labour was both unable and unwilling to help their captors.

The dismal economic system was made yet worse still through incessant bombing and even precision acts of sabotage. Churchill's Special Operations

Executive enabled the French resistance to conduct their own economic war against the Germans. Factories in France ground to a halt. However, some foreign arms factories were obedient to the Nazis. The Škoda Works in Czechoslovakia continued to produce its renowned tanks for the Germans throughout the war. The killing in Prague of Reinhard Heydrich, the Acting Reich Protector of Bohemia and Moravia, in June 1942 by SOE trained assassins did not stop Czech collaboration. Indeed, many fearful Czechoslovakians attended his first public funeral.

By 1942 it had become apparent that the war was not going to end quickly. The hope remained however that the fighting would soon be over; to that end senior Nazis lobbied Hitler to put the Germany economy onto a full war footing. Joseph Goebbels, Hitler's Minister for Propaganda, was chief amongst the agitators for making all industry and civilians of working age serve the war effort. However, the Führer delayed mobilising women into the workforce and continued the production of consumer goods for too long. Eventually, Hitler acted, and the following year approved the call for total war. Nevertheless, the policy goal was not to win a long-drawn-out war of attrition, instead the hope was that these measures would shorten the conflict in Germany's favour. Men like Goebbels and Speer were given the power they needed to increase output, nevertheless, it was still too late to save the one-thousand-year Reich.

With this new economic policy came a new message. The aim of Goebbels propaganda was to arouse outbursts of fury, organise hatred, and suspicion. An accompanying arm of this strategy involved positioning the Nazi Party as the answer to the problems posed by invented enemies. Now with his trademark ice-cold calculation he adapted the Nazi message away from selling the public fanciful dreams of a wonderful future, he now spun a darker message. The dream of conquest and success had changed to hoping for survival. Total War used fear and the threat of what would happen to ordinary Germans if they lost the war, they were now presented with a *fait accompli*; they were told that they had no choice but to toil in support of the war which must be won. Output did increase but the German economic miracle was a mirage. Speer used statistics to prove that the production of weapons was massively increasing, nevertheless, like other bureaucracies, figures were massaged to please political masters.

German technological developments were also being hampered by institutional failings inherent to Nazi Germany. The secretive and plural Nazi state did not have a unified weapons technological development structure, this meant there was not a cross fertilisation of ideas. Nor were enough resources allocated to German weapons programmes. There were too many competing ideas, each not adequately resourced, and managed by people who had little information about what they were meant to be investing in. German science became like a series of cottage industries. There were attempts to make German industry and innovation more efficient, but these were not always helpful. Hitler did understand the issue of overburdening the German armaments industry and forbade the production of different calibre firearms. However, this prevented the production of the Sturmgewehr 44 which was a successful and popular assault rifle. It was introduced by changing its official designation to hide its new calibre. Hitler learnt of its capability and ultimately relented and allowed it to be produced in greater numbers. If introduced earlier and in higher quantities, it may have delayed the demise of the Third Reich.

The German were looking for shortcuts to countermand Germany's inherent weakness, this went as far as hunting for magical and mythical items that Nazis hoped to weaponise. The leader of the SS, Heinrich Himmler, sent his *Ahnenerbe* pseudo-science research group to hunt for the spear of destiny also known as the Lance of Longinus. The legendary lance was purported to have pierced the side of Christ when he was on the cross. Its convenient discovery in 1098 during the Siege of Antioch had reportedly inspired the crusaders to sally forth from the city, win the Battle of Antioch, and defeat the besieging Muslim forces. The crusaders were now able to resume their march towards Jerusalem. Other obsessions of Hitler were the Holy Grail of Arthurian legend. Richard Wagner composed an opera titled Parsifal that romanticised Sir Percival's quest for the object. Similarly, the Führer fixated about Tacitus' book of spells. He believed both of these legendary items contained properties that could deliver a miracle. None was to come. If that were not deluded enough, Himmler diverted resources and the SS from the battlefront. He sent men to search for 'evidence' of Atlantis, the origins of the Aryan race, and used them to convert Wewelsburg Castle in Germany into the Vatican of the SS. Neither Himmler's other worldly fantasies, nor Speer's fanciful figures, could compete with real economics. German dreams were competing with countries that had at their disposal the real-world effectiveness and efficiency of the American economy. This arsenal equipped Germany's enemies with the resources they needed to resist the Axis powers. For some this came at a price.

The foundations of exponential American economic growth, both during and after World War Two, and the emerging special relationship between the United Kingdom and the United States would benefit the USA. In the hope of exchanging information for American manufacturing capacity, the Tizard Mission transferred British technology to the US. This included information on jet engines, proximity fuses, nuclear fission, gyroscope gun sights, engine superchargers, rockets, devices for submarine detection, self-sealing fuel tanks useful on aircraft, plastic explosives, and radar. Ultimately this technology was just surrendered, the Americans did not even handover in exchange the Norden bomb sight. Britain therefore lost technology that was of enormous commercial value after the war.

Britain was in debt to America financially and politically. This obligation to Uncle Sam would help shape the post-war world. Britannia, once the motherland of the former thirteen American colonies that formed the USA in 1789, would in time become the junior partner and chief cheerleader for *Pax Americana*. Franklin Delano Roosevelt lectured British Prime Minister Winston Spencer Churchill on the inequities of the British Empire. Churchill resisted the temptation to castigate the American leader over the treatment of black people in Democrat controlled southern states, FDR and the segregationists were part of the same political party. Roosevelt appeased their unjust rule in the south. Yet he attacked the long-term viability of British colonialism by forcing his British ally to reform its Empire preference trade policy thus weakening Britain's links with what would become Commonwealth countries. Roosevelt was against British tariffs that favoured trade with the Commonwealth and the UK's imperial possessions. Thus, he ended the economic rationale for empire and opened these markets to American producers, rather than keeping then the preserve of British manufactures. Trade is politics by other means.

President Roosevelt had a world vision for a post-war America that expanded its power, prestige, and prosperity. He had been preparing America for war with Germany from 1940, he introduced conscription and rearmament was already underway. Despite that the US military was not combat ready and a year before the conflict the army was the same size as Sweden's. Whilst it was true that the US armed forces were still thoroughly unprepared for war; in 1942 G.I.s started arriving in Britain. The balance of power was shifting further against the Axis. American soldiers, sailors, and airmen were now in the European theatre. America had become much more than just the arsenal of the democracies. Roosevelt saw the United States' role as protector of the world from aggression and to protect America's four freedoms: freedom of religion, freedom of speech, freedom from want and fear. Despite America's economic difficulties, its industry was still more advanced than that of Germany. The great wealth of the United States helped grow its greatest generation into formidable soldiers.

The fat of the land

Rich American diets that consisted of plenty of meat helped not only produce robust G.I.s, but also gave them the tools to obliterate their Axis enemies. US housewives were encouraged to donate the left-over fat from their family meal to the war effort. This was then used to produce highly explosive nitro-glycerine. This chemical was a key component used in producing other explosives and the smokeless propellant used in firearms called cordite, which was also the substance used to detonate the Little Boy atomic bomb over the Japanese city of Hiroshima. Before that auspicious occasion in the American war effort, the adipose tissue was used to even greater effect in conventional weapons. These were produced on a gargantuan scale.

Unlike Germany, which became a command economy, the United States relaxed government controls. Roosevelt ended his statist economic experiment, known as the New Deal, to get business on side and give them the freedom to produce the armaments the war economy needed. In this global contest for survival American businesses competed to win government contracts and the War Production Board was essentially the consumer that bought goods and services from the private sector. Not only were American industrialists given the policy concessions and payments they wanted to produce the machinery for the war, in some instances experts in production were brought into the army to make its procurement as productive as possible. William Knudsen, a former employee of Ford, General Motors, and President of Chevrolet, was commissioned by Roosevelt as Director of Production. Knudsen used the knowledge and skills which he had utilised in America's car industry to help make America the leading producer of war materiel in the world.

Again, the car industry, a sign of a healthy economy, came to the rescue of the democratic world. Much of America's industry was built upon a consumer society that had the greatest level of car ownership then seen in the world. The USA's ability to bring to market mass produced cars brought with it many mechanics who could then be employed maintaining vehicles on the front or producing them at home. And, unlike in Germany, it did not take skilled labour to manufacture weapons. Consumer society produced productive, economic, innovative, and yet simple production techniques; these were then adapted to make weapons. Like in Britain, the efficiency was so great that America's mass production methods became streamlined enough to allow unskilled labour and women to join the workforce. The same simplicity and ease of use also existed in the Soviet Union which had largely imported its plants and know-how from capitalist America. Similarly, these factories were powered by generators and power station engineers paid and purchased from Britain's Metropolitan-Vickers which manufactured electrical engineering equipment. The communist leadership of the USSR were also knowledgeable in the finances of a war of attrition. The Russians knew this was an economic war, and the currency that they traded for victory was the lives of its warriors.

The meat grinder

After the Russian victory outside Moscow the Red Army became overstretched. Zhukov wanted a limited offensive after the successful defence of the sacred capital, he only had limited resources, but Stalin wanted a general advance; this ran into trouble. However, the Soviet command refused to give up ground, this led to a confused front where it was difficult to get supplies to isolated Russian units. Soviet logistics were so stretched, and some Red Army units so isolated, that the Russians had to use airpower to supply their forces. The front lines would swing back and forth for several more years yet. Indeed, the Germans were still capable of striking back themselves.

An overly aggressive Soviet approach was the bane of Russia's war effort for much of the first two years following Operation Barbarossa. In the north, attempts to liberate Leningrad were rushed and failed. In the centre the Nazis and their Soviet foes fought over the strategic railway hub based in Rzhev, west of Moscow. The German occupation of this town prevented the Red Army from adequately supplying their units on the front west of Moscow. The ground around Rzhev was to absorb much Russian blood over a series of to and fro battles for the town that lasted more than a year from when it was first liberated until it was finally freed for good in the Spring of 1943. In the south, the Russians counterattacked in the Crimea before they were ready. The Soviet army's chief political commissar, Lev Mekhlis, who enforced Stalin's earlier military purges, insisted that the attack go ahead. Stalin's enforcer was not to be refused and the Crimea was eventually lost to the Germans. After the capture of Sevastopol, Hitler transferred von Manstein and a large part of his 11th Army all the way from the Black Sea to the north with the task of capturing Leningrad. Hitler had once sought strategically important economic sites, now he was beginning to become obsessed with trophy cities that would tie down his once superbly effective mobile army. There were more diversions to come and further opportunities for Hitler to fracture his own army in the pursuit of diverging and unobtainable objectives.

Hitler said of Soviet resistance to invasion that, "The Russians fight with a truly stupid fanaticism". That was not the only problem which the Third Reich faced. Whilst the Russians were losing both their men and materiel in reckless and desperate attempts to push back the invader. They were, however, able to tap deeper levels of commitment. The difference between the two sides was that the Soviets managed to harness communist ideology to expand their totalitarian writ into all areas of life. The USSR's leaders could marshal enough human cannon fodder to be able to bear enormous losses. What is more, the Russians also had enough fuel to get their soldiers, sailors, and aircrews into combat. Conversely, the Germans lacked the resources to give their men the mobility they needed.

Life blood

Prior to its entry into World War Two, companies in the United States were willing to do business with anyone, including Nazi Germany; indeed, American supplies of oil were vital to fuelling Germany's war on Russia. Much of this trade ceased following the declarations of war that came after the attack on Pearl Harbor. Though some trade continued through third countries, the Germans desperately needed oil. They had to replace the Danegeld supplies that came from the Soviets under the terms of the German–Soviet Commercial Agreement of 1940. Hitler would have to seize control of this vital fossil fuel for himself.

A renewed German attack was expected by the Russians, they just could not be sure where the hammer would fall, nor could they determine the objective. The goal, however, for the Axis in 1942 was to finally achieve what they were aiming for when they launched Operation Barbarossa the year before, namely defeating the Soviet Union. Stalin thought the main attack would come from Army Group Centre and aim for Moscow. When the main offensive was launched, however, the job fell to Army Group South, there were multiple targets, but the ultimate prize was the source of Soviet oil.

The German plan was not entirely novel. During World War One German General Erich Ludendorff, later a political associate of Hitler, devised a plan to seize the Caspian Sea region. Germany sought to dominate this region and secure access to the oil fields around the city of Baku. They planned to take control by attacking through German controlled Ukraine and the pro-German Democratic Republic of Georgia. This expedition ultimately failed and on the point of collapse the German Empire withdrew from the region. The Ottoman-led Islamic Army of the Caucasus also tried to conquer Baku but was checked by British empire and local forces.

A generation later, in 1942 the Soviet Republics in the Caucasus region, along with the oilfields that lay beside the Caspian Sea, were the main strategic objective.

Hitler also aimed to seize southern Russia's industrial region, including the city of Stalingrad which contained a sizeable tractor factory that had been retooled and was now turning out T-34 tanks. The Nazis believed that the Caucasus region was the centre of power in the world from where they could eventually dominate the globe. Even American newsreels referred to the 'world island' and the fear that Germany would dominate the supposed Eurasian navel of the world. Believing in that theoretical geographical entity encouraged the Germans to overextend and create a self-fulfilling prophecy; the struggle for the Caucasus would join the pantheon of the greatest battles in world history.

When the Axis launched its 1942 summer offensive, codenamed Case Blue, Stalin thought it was a trick, and kept the Soviet's focused on defending Moscow, as such they remained unprepared for what was to follow and consequently suffered grievous losses. Victory for the Germans would have awarded them the oil their economy urgently needed. The Nazi war machine was running out of fuel, and it was predicted that they would be suffering severe shortages by mid-September 1942, the Germans needed to capture Baku, the Soviets main source of this most fundamental resource. Defeat would have been catastrophic for the Russians. The capture of the Caucasus would deprive the Red Army of much of their fuel. Furthermore, losing Stalingrad would have allowed the Germans to control traffic on the mighty Volga River and allow the Axis to close navigation on this vital waterway. Soviet tankers transporting oil up the Volga would not be able to pass, nor would supplies coming from the USSR's western allies, namely Britain and the United States. Russia relied on the supply of trucks, tanks, and aircraft coming through Iran. This southern supply route was vitally important. It was free from the incessant U-boat attacks and was not threatened by the Kriegsmarine's big ships, both of which plagued the Arctic convoys in the frozen north. Losing the Caucasus and the Volga would have isolated the Soviet Union and denied it the weapons and the means to wage war. To achieve such a pivotal outcome Army Group South was divided in two. There was now Army Group A, which would head for the Caucasus, and covering its northern shoulder was Army Group B, which included the Sixth Army, it aimed to take Stalingrad.

The Stavka, the main Command of the Armed Forces of the USSR sought to prevent further losses of territory. On 28th July 1942, Stalin's issued order number 227, which mandated "Not a step back!". Blocking detachments were created to prevent any retreat, the idea being that soldiers fleeing from the Germans would be shot by their own side. Their use, however, was limited and they were of little significance. The Red Army fought hard enough on its own volition to stop the German advance, and even drive back the Axis and annihilate the invader.

Communist Russia sought to use all the tools at their disposal to motivate its men to keep persevering, propaganda poetry being an effective weapon.

Russia has a great literary tradition and its communist authorities believed in the value of education and intervened to improve literacy; even peasants were more than willing to learn to read and write. This gave the authorities the opportunity to deploy the written word in aid of the war effort. Soviet propaganda was explicit in what the regime expected of its people. Articles were published that urged the people to 'Kill the Germans'. Poems were also penned that extolled the same message, one example is the poem 'Kill Him', it reads,

If you don't want to give away
To a German, with his black gun,
Your house, your wife, your mother
And everything we call our native land.
Then know your homeland won't be saved
If you yourself do not save it.
And know the enemy won't be killed,
If you yourself do not kill him.

Accompanying the poem was a poster visualising the threat, it also dehumanised their inhumane enemy. It showed the German soldier as a beastly ape, submachine gun in hand standing over the corpse of a slain woman, her lifeless children lay beside her. This was a recurring theme. Another poster was produced showing the Nazi soldier as a spectre that would abuse Russian women. Mother Russia was a patriarchal society, its men would be willing to fight for their women, indeed defending one's opportunity to reproduce is a biological instinct as is sacrificing oneself for one's family. The propaganda posters were not too dissimilar to British works of art that showed the Germans in a similar light during World War One. There were other parallels with the previous great war, German ambitions in the Caucasus and Caspian area would again ultimately meet with defeat. Yet, as would become a pattern for Germany, the initial stages of the offensive went well only to flounder later.

In terms of progress being made, and the number of casualties, it did appear that the Wehrmacht was again winning in 1942, yet that was under extremely costly circumstances. Russia was making the Germans pay a high price for the ground they captured. For the time being, after a number of Russian defeats the Axis powers had the numerical advantage at the start of the Battle of the Caucasus.

Storm the heavens

The Soviets were pushed back by German, Romanian, and Slovak troops. They also had to contend with a German backed Chechen uprising against Russian rule. The Muslim insurgents from the Checheno-Ingush Autonomous Soviet Socialist Republic were eager to reject Russian rule and sided with the Nazis. Chechnya was only incorporated into Russia as late as the nineteenth century and managed to briefly revive their independence after the Russian Revolution before their reconquest by the Soviets. World War Two presented another opportunity for self-rule and through assisting the German war effort they became independent once again until Stalin retook the region and deported many of its people. Following the collapse of the USSR they again revolted against Russia and were only brought back into the Russian Federation in the early twenty-first century. Chechnya has since been reconstructed and enjoys autonomy within Russia and is allowed to enforce the Sharia as long as its once rebellious leaders retain an outward loyalty to Moscow and respect the Russian Federation's territorial integrity. For the peoples of Chechnya and their neighbours war is a way of life. To this day Chechens, like their fathers before them, will navigate themselves towards any number of conflicts around the world serving as soldiers of fortune on either side of civil wars or insurgencies around the world. They are formidable warriors. Some of those from the Caucasus, who choose not to engage in war, will gravitate towards combat sports. Combining their martial spirit with a thorough grounding in Sambo, people from northern Caucasus republics have become notable pugilists and accomplished mixed martial artists. The outcome of the Battle of the Caucasus means they compete as Russians rather than as their local ethnicity.

The drive to dominate the land between the Black and Caspian Seas, like other German campaigns in Russia, suffered from a further dissipation of forces. Hitler had already divided his forces in the attack. In the original plan there would be a thrust directly for the Georgian capital of Tbilisi and then Germany would proceed on to the Baku oilfields in Azerbaijan. He compounded the subdivision of Army Group South by even splitting the objectives of the new Army Group A. Desperate to end the Soviet Navy's operations on the Black Sea which could threaten Romania, Hitler diverted forces to capture naval bases. To that end he diverted the elite Bavarian and Austrian mountain divisions to the western Caucasus to capture the coastline.

The divided objectives were starting to take their toll on Hitler's ambitions. Valuable Luftwaffe squadrons were sent to support the Sixth Army in its battle in and around Stalingrad. This meant that the German Army in the Caucasus had little defence against Russian airpower which attacked the German forces on the ground. Hitler was becoming obsessed and not a little distracted by the still Soviet held city of Stalingrad. The Führer had high hopes and even greater expectations for his Sixth Army; he had said that the Sixth Army would "Storm the Heavens". On the contrary it was the forces of Army Group A that came closest to that lofty ambition. On 21st August 1942, German mountain troops managed to capture the summit of the strategically insignificant Mount Elbrus, the highest mountain in the Soviet Union and Europe; and after this highpoint also captured many other peaks. Nevertheless, the coastal oil producing areas on the Caspian were at sea level and safe.

The Russians retreated to a defensive line which used the Caucasus mountains and a river as a defence, here they dug in. Even Beria's NKVD internal security forces were deployed to fight the Germans rather than kill their own comrades. The Soviets also moved some of their Baku based oil production facilities to the north of the Caspian Sea. Whilst this cut their oil output, they were free from being overrun by the Wehrmacht. Neither the attack on the oilfields, nor the second thrust to control the entirety of Russia's Black Sea coast succeeded. The Germans could not break through. Case Blue was failing, the offensive was using up limited resources and the stubborn Soviet resistance wore-out the German army. Similarly, Army Group B's drive to Stalingrad was also subdivided.

Turning point USSR

The Case Blue offensive, which initially appeared to be a potentially decisive German move, was in reality a series of pyrrhic victories the sum of which constituted the real turning point on the eastern front even before the Axis defeat at Stalingrad. To protect the Sixth Army's thrust towards the great city that stretched along the Volga River, General Paulus sent his armoured units to the area north of Stalingrad to hold back the Red Army. Paulus now had little reserves nor tanks for his attempt to capture the city which bore the Soviet leader's name.

Stalin's chief henchman, Lavrentiy Beria, described the confrontation between Hitler and his Soviet opposite number, Stalin, as like "a confrontation between two rams". Stalingrad had been levelled by the Luftwaffe; its streets were strewn with rubble. This made the advance even more difficult. A German officer wrote of the fighting 'The streets are no longer measured in metres, but in corpses' It was costly for the Russians. The Red Army forced troops to fight and did in some instances kill them if they retreated; indeed 13,000 Red Army soldiers were shot for withdrawing. The Soviets also killed their own men through recklessness, the

Red Army was willing to take massive casualties. In one charge, 10,000 newly arrived troops coming from the opposite bank of the river were ferried across the Volga to Stalingrad, only 300 survived. A greater sacrifice than other acts of heroism with a similar numerology.

The Germans managed to capture nine tenths of the city that lay along the west bank of the Volga. Both Hitler and Paulus believed they had been victorious; this ignored developments far away from the ruined husk which they were still fighting over. Zhukov, the Red Army commander, who at the time had the distinction of never losing a battle, was soon to unleash two decisive blows. The planets would soon align to foretell a great victory.

In November 1942, the Russians launched twin attacks on different fronts against the Axis occupiers. The first, would come in southern Russia and was called Operation Uranus. It was designed to encircle and trap the Sixth Army in Stalingrad. This was to be followed shortly after by another great offensive further north, and to the west of Moscow, where another series of battles were still underway; this was codenamed Operation Mars. It aimed to tie-up German forces at Rzhev and ultimately take this important transport hub. An added benefit of this operation was that it would stop Germany's strategic reserve being transferred south to the sector around Stalingrad. Both Operation Mars and Operation Uranus were overseen by Zhukov.

The Germans believed their defensive lines to the north and south of Stalingrad were secure, but they crumbled in the face of the Red Army. The Axis forces were overstretched, and Germany's allies could not cope when attacked. The Italians facing Operation Uranus' southern thrust were overrun, the Hungarians and Romanians in the north were swept aside. The Hungarians were short of ammunition and the Romanians lacked anti-tank weapons; they were no match for the Russians. The city was now invested, the Sixth Army in Stalingrad were in a cauldron.

Field Marshal von Manstein did attempt to relieve the besieged men. He launched Operation Winter Storm, however it failed to break through to Paulus, there was now no possibility that a link-up with relieving forces could be achieved. Hermann Göring thought the Sixth Army could be supplied by his Junkers Ju 52 transport planes. The Luftwaffe had managed to supply trapped German armies before; this time however was different. There were too many demands that could not be met, and it was all together much too difficult a task for the Luftwaffe. Soviet airpower by this time posed a greater threat to enemy aircraft. The dreadful winter conditions conspired to make reaching the besieged forces in Stalingrad much more difficult. Furthermore, the encircled Sixth Army was drifting away. German air bases close to Stalingrad fell to the Russians, pushing back the Luftwaffe, lengthening the range they had to fly and thus shortened the numbers of journeys the relief planes could make; supplies dwindled.

Further north also saw reverses for the Germans. The Axis could not commit enough of their strategic reserve to defend Rzhev, they were needed elsewhere and could not be deployed to hold back Operation Mars. Army Group Centre was however faring better than their counterparts to the south. The Russian attempts to directly retake Rzhev tactically failed but did succeed in tying up the Germans, so it became a strategic success of sorts and therefore helped the Red Army elsewhere along the line. Despite the Wehrmacht's stubborn defence, ultimately the Germans had to withdraw from Rzhev to avoid their troops being surrounded like they were at Stalingrad; they would carry out their own scorched earth policy. The levelling of bridges and ripping up of railways did hold-up the Red Army advance, it damaged the Soviet's logistics; they could not get enough material to the front line in a timely fashion. Nevertheless, Soviet deep battle overcome German defence lines just like the Nazi *blitzkrieg* had overcome the French in the west. When retreating from Rzhev, German general, later Field Marshal, Walter Model not only organised the destruction of towns and transport infrastructure but also oversaw the killing of civilians and deportation of others to Germany for use as slave labour. At Stalingrad, the Germans would become the slaves.

Russian success against the Sixth Army was not due to Soviet soldiers fearing more brutality from their own side than that which they could expect from the Nazis. Compassion was shown by the Red Army to their wounded comrades. The Russians at Stalingrad had excellent medical care. They had the best recovery record of any Russian army. Conversely, as the fighting dragged on the Axis forces inside the city could expect little help, some wounded could be evacuated but those that remained quickly became emaciated. So bad was their starvation that when they were finally given high-calorie fatty food their bodies went into a hyperglycaemic crisis; this caused more fatalities.

Despite the harrowing conditions, the trapped Axis forces were prevented by Hitler from breaking out. Their strangulation became so severe that they soon lacked fuel and ammunition, and escape became impossible. However, they had to keep fighting to tie-up the besieging Red Army, failure to do so would have freed up the Russians, allowing them to push west even harder and faster; this would have ensnared the Germans in the Caucasus. This was a very real fear. As the debacle was still unfolding in Stalingrad, the Red Army launched Operation Little Saturn which aimed to capture Rostov-on-Don. The Germans, realising that the Russians could breakthrough all the way to the Sea of Azov to the north of Crimea, had to begin a hasty retreat from the Caucasus. Consequently, the Germans and their allies escaped back towards Ukraine. The failure to win the Battle of Stalingrad had implications along the front. The whole theatre of operations had collapsed, Case Blue had failed and what was meant to have been the blow that would have knocked Russia out of the war had conversely weakened the Axis.

The final destruction of the Sixth Army at Stalingrad came after it had been dissected multiple times and only held out in isolated pockets of resistance. Paulus was raised to the rank of Field Marshal, the next day the fighting reached his headquarters, he was captured alive, he denied that he surrendered. The fighting in Stalingrad officially ceased on 2nd February 1943, however, not all Axis soldiers immediately surrendered to the Russians. Some hid out in the sewer system and continued what the Germans called the 'rat war'.

Of those that were taken into captivity, few would ever see the Fatherland again. However, before they were transported to Soviet slave labour camps the defeated soldiers were forced to partake in a triumph where they were paraded through the streets of Moscow. This was a mistake, it showed the Germans for what they really were, bedraggled, emaciated human beings. This shattered the illusion in the Russian mind that their German adversaries were the beastly savages of the crude posters that propagated the message that the German must be hated, resisted, and annihilated in equal measure. After their ignominious march through Moscow, the streets were washed to remove any vestige of the 'unclean' German prisoners of war. The few German survivors of their captivity were only allowed to return to their dismembered Fatherland in 1955, a dozen years after their surrender.

The defeat was not just a major setback for the Germans, the Romanians, and Italians also paid a high price. Consequently, the debacle that was Stalingrad strained relations between two European Axis leaders, Mussolini, and Hitler. The Italian leader was a man that was naturally against German adventurism but had fallen under its spell, however, he began to turn against Hitler's maniacal war. Mussolini urged Hitler to make peace with Stalin. *Il Duce* thought that Russia was too well defended, too big to be quelled, and could not be held. Stalin, a practical man, had considered making a separate peace with the Nazis. There was latitude for an accord on the Eastern Front, however Hitler's Manichean world-view could only perceive two possible outcomes, glorious victory or shameful defeat. Hitler rejected the plea from his junior partner. Mussolini was not the only world leader that was moved by events in Stalingrad.

In December 1944, General Charles de Gaulle, on his way to Moscow, passed through the ruins of Stalingrad and observed the uncovering of dead bodies that were unearthed by the rebuilding works that were already underway. The leader of the Free French stated *"Ah, Stalingrad! C'est tout de même un peuple formidable, un très grand peuple."* ("Ah, Stalingrad! All the same, they are a redoubtable people, a very great people.") In response Alexander Werth, a BBC correspondent in Russia responded *"Ah, oui, les Russes..."*. ("Ah, yes, the Russians...."). Charles de Gaulle replied, *"Mais non. Je ne parle pas des Russes, je parle des Allemands. Tout de même, avoir poussé jusque là!"* ("No, I'm not talking about the Russians; I mean the Germans. In spite of everything, to have pushed so far!")

Germany may have won the respect of de Gaulle, but they had lost an entire army and a Field Marshal, the first time in their history a man of such rank had been taken alive by an enemy. Friedrich Paulus, who had been the commander of the Sixth Army inside Stalingrad, eventually began to cooperate with his Soviet captors and made anti-Nazi broadcasts. Hitler wanted him returned to Germany and even offered to return Stalin's first-born son in exchange for the defeated commander. Stalin refused this offer and Yakov Dzhugashvili, son of the Soviet leader, remained languishing in a prisoner of war camp until his suicide by electrocution in April 1943. He had mental health difficulties throughout his life. Hitler had also offered Stalin his progeny back in exchange for the Führer's nephew who like Paulus had also been captured by the Soviets at Stalingrad. Likewise, this second offer was also refused.

Many Romanian and Italian soldiers in this Caucasian adventure had also been lost. This made Axis numbers even more stretched. Attempts to increase the size of the German armed forces by cajoling Russian captives into joining the German cause provided little benefit. Despite the appalling treatment inflicted on them by the Nazis in prisoner of war camps, few joined with the Germans, and many of those that did collaborate ultimately chose to rejoin the Soviet side. Germany needed another way to deal with its manpower shortage and restore momentum to its campaign in the east. The question was whether or not the German high command could devise a winning strategy.

The racket

Hitler imposed himself as the overall operational commander of all German forces. The Führer frequently made decisions on the movements of his army even down to the divisional level. The withdrawal of forces, even for sound tactical reasons, was something which Hitler forbade without his express approval. It was not just a matter that he coveted his stolen empire so greatly that he could not countenance a retreat; Hitler suffered from false hope syndrome. His excessive resilience made him seek out more aggressive confrontations. The trauma of repeated setbacks made Hitler even more stubborn in trying to hold on to his ill-gotten gains. Neither Hitler's denial of the worsening military situation nor his obstinate refusal to abandon indefensible positions could reverse the worsening military situation. There were, however, other ideas as to how the war should be handled.

Those with competing opinions would be isolated, if a commander made a military decision of which Hitler disapproved, they took their life into their own hands. German generals had a choice, their life, or the lives of their men. The way the Nazi state was set up was one where the army had to compete amongst itself to receive the favours of the ultimate commander Adolf Hitler. To advance their careers, receive preferment, the material benefits of plunder, and often to stay in a position of authority, or even just keep themselves alive, many commanders chose to play the game. Hitler was using his generals to live out his war fantasy, they in turn were using his largesse to enrich themselves financially and receive large estates. Their fate was intertwined with Hitler's. They had to appease his many reckless whims. That did not make for a sound military strategy. Hitler should have allowed a professional soldier, an experienced general, to take charge in the east. However, Hitler's lack of trust of the Prussian officer class, and his own ego, prevented this.

Despite the atmosphere of oppression and manipulation amongst the German general staff there were some alternate ideas that would have provided at least a semblance of a coherent strategy. Hitler's refusal to allow retreats did however lead to a clash with one of his favourites. Heinz Guderian proposed the use of strategic withdrawals that would draw the Russians in and use Germany's superior mobile tactics and tank communications to obliterate the enemy. This was not new; the Mongol hordes had used similar tactics to conquer early Russian principalities in the thirteenth century. Seven hundred and twenty years later, in 1943, it was proposed that this so-called 'backhand method' should be deployed. The Germans would retreat, wait for the Red Army's attack to become overextended and then hit them hard with forces that had local superiority and greater tactical skill. Such a strategy had worked before most notably twice in both the Second and Third Battle of Kharkov, each nearly a year apart. In May 1942, around Kharkov, the Red Army drove into a trap and were surrounded and annihilated, losing more than a quarter of a million soldiers and more than 1,200 tanks.

In February 1943, the penultimate and Third Battle of Kharkov took place and lasted for more than three weeks. This followed von Manstein's managed retreat away from the defeated Sixth Army and his failed attempt to rescue them. The Soviets were advancing on this widely fought over city. Knowing that it could not be held, the *Waffen-SS* withdrew despite Hitler's orders not to. Yet, they counterattacked the overstretched Russian forces that briefly occupied Kharkov, the Red Army was driven out. The bold backhand method was a proven strategy, yet it required a well-balanced temperament, panache, and a willingness to accept granting the enemy a temporary triumph in order to achieve a greater victory. It contrasted with the so-called 'forehand method' which envisaged German forces taking the strategic lead and attacking. The latter approach, one which took fate into one's own hands, was the one chosen by Hitler. In time this led to another climatic and disastrous battle.

The Axis needed an opportunity to reset their war on the Eastern Front. Yet, Hitler was reluctant to give up any territory. After all, the war was started for lebensraum, it meant that any concept that involved giving up hard won land, as recommended by Guderian and Manstein, even to achieve a later military victory, was anathema to the Führer. Nevertheless, Axis losses had been great, after two years of exhaustive fighting, the Germans needed the opportunity to build-up their strength, regain the initiative, and then deliver the knockout blow the following year. Field Marshal von Manstein developed the elastic defence theory. Here he envisaged a series of localised offensives to drain Soviet resources, especially manpower, whilst the German army rearmed and reequipped, and restored its manpower. Similarly, Heinz Guderian proposed a strategic defence whilst the under-strength Wehrmacht could re-build itself. Both were rejected by Hitler in 1943. Despite his dabbling in military affairs, the Führer was above all a politician and self-publicist. Hitler felt taking the offensive would better serve his wider political campaign. He wanted to fight a decisive battle; the supposed victory that would follow would provide him with the propaganda triumph he felt he needed. Hitler would use this to both reassure his Axis partners and win over new ones to the Nazi cause. Similarly, Hitler hoped that by delivering a powerful blow against the Red Army, he could force the Soviets into granting him a favourable peace and thus allow Germany to then turn and face the western Allies. The obvious place for this titanic battle was a bulge into the German lines, at the centre of this salient was a city that was once a garrison town centred on a fort. A citadel was originally founded there to prevent raids into Russia. The city is called Kursk, the plan to capture it was Operation Citadel.

Every battle is won or lost before it is ever fought

Intelligence agencies have on occasions throughout modern history provided reports that tell their political masters what they want to hear. Or in a similar vein they can produce findings that just reflect already established presumptions. Like archaeologists they have a habit of finding what they are looking for and the phenomenon of groupthink takes hold. The German intelligence services were no different, indeed in the Nazi state the very real need to please their master made this situation arguably worse. Indeed, they had hampered German preparations from the beginning of the war.

In the forthcoming Operation Citadel, German secret services underestimated Soviet strength and the Abwehr failed to predict the full size of the Red Army's reserves. The Wehrmacht was heading for a trap of its own making. The situation was not the same for the Allies, mathematicians, and computer scientists were able to exploit the Führers centralised command and control strategy over his Wehrmacht. The sheer size of the theatre of operations and the demands of mobile war meant that fixed lines of communication could not possibly reach a fluid front line. Only insecure radio transmitters could be used to exercise authority over forces in the field. The British intercepted and deciphered German transmissions to and from the front line. Britain was a leader in radio technology and could detect and decode German messages that flowed to and from Hitler's headquarters. This vulnerability was exploited by British codebreakers at Bletchley Park which provided information for the Soviets to use. This was not the only source of information that the Red Army could rely on to further their revolution.

The romantic attraction to communism, an ideology that had a universal vision of a morally superior system, also proved to be a highly lucrative source of information. For some ideology trumped national loyalty. The USSR claimed leadership of all communist movements, it did this through its control of Comintern, the international organisation that strove for world revolution. Many with communist sympathies thought they had a higher loyalty that rose above oaths made to the country. As such they were willing to provide secrets to the Soviet Union in the belief that they were serving the cause of socialism; indeed, they were. These phenomena were even apparent in Nazi Germany, a country that faced ruin should Russia be triumphant in the war. This ideological zealotry was one of the motivations behind some in the so-called Red Orchestra which supplied information on Operation Barbarossa to the USSR. This lose network was later broken up by German counter-espionage agents. Incidentally, not all communist sympathisers were listened to. On the eve of the German invasion, Alfred Liskow, a would-be defector, escaped from the Heer to warn the Soviets about the impending invasion. His message was not welcome and later he may have been executed for his troubles. Other people and their networks proved to be instrumental in helping the Red Army defeat the Nazis.

Many involved in supplying information on German intentions were conservative in outlook. These officers were opposed to Hitler and his dictatorial and revolutionary creed. And were appalled by his extreme and inhumane racialist policies. The 'Lucy' spy ring, which operated out of Switzerland, was part of a network that included high ranking anti-Nazis in the German military. Before it was largely dismembered following a near successful plot to kill Hitler, its members succeeded in supplying the Russians with the plans for Operation Citadel. This gave the Red Army the opportunity to prepare for the Battle of Kursk that was to come.

Nazi bickering

Erich von Manstein envisaged that the aim of the attack on Kursk was to free up tens of thousands of German soldiers that could help resist the Allied invasion that was expected in southern Europe. To that end he would use hundreds of thousands of soldiers to eliminate a bulge, shorten the overall front line that stretched from the Baltic to the Black Sea and capture Kursk. It was a bold investment. Whereas the Germans had little in reserve, the Russians had ample men and materiel. The Wehrmacht had lost too much in the previous two years of fighting on the Eastern Front. At this point the Germans had lost over two million men, killed, wounded, captured, and missing in action, since the start of the conflict. Germany would struggle to replace them.

Field Marshal von Manstein thought an early attack in 1943 could have taken Kursk and thus the front line would be straightened, shortened, and simplified, saving manpower. However, Hitler, afraid of the risk of launching the operation, delayed to build-up more men and materiel, he then postponed the attack yet again to wait for the introduction of new tank designs. Hitler turned what was meant to be a limited operation that originally merely aimed to pinch out the Red Army's positions jutting into German lines into a major offensive. It would become a pivotal attack and proved to be decisive, just not in the way the Germans expected.

The planning for this took on a life of its own, the operation had morphed out of all proportion. The gold-plating of Operation Citadel filled Hitler with dread. Despite this the momentum was too great. When Hitler was warned by Guderian that the attack on the Kursk salient would be a mistake he replied that the thought of it "turns my stomach" but in his mind it was too late to cancel. Time was not a luxury the Germans had. The offensive was first scheduled to begin in May, but it was not until July that it finally got underway. However, the new weapons for which Hitler delayed the conflict, the medium Panther tank and the heavy Tiger panzer, proved to be inadequate and needed more development. They were also unreliable. Whilst still individually better than their Red Army counterparts their introduction was not enough to break the Russian defence.

Not only was the Kursk salient an obvious location for a German attack, but the Russians also knew from their spy network what was being planned and prepared accordingly. Marshal Zhukov convinced Stalin to fight a defensive battle. The Russian plan was one of strategic defence. The Red Army would absorb the German attacks and then hit back hard, this plan was developed to negate and then eliminate the mobility of the German army, wear them down, and achieve a victory through the counterstrike. This defensive approach was favoured by Zhukov and Russian general Nikolai Vatutin.

The Soviets used the extra time that Hitler had awarded them to build multiple, six in total, robust defence lines throughout the bulge. Zhukov and his planners also planned to strike back. To that end the Red Army amassed a massive force of reserves, poised to take the offensive as soon as the Wehrmacht lost energy. In the battle the Russians made use of what are known as fire pockets where Soviet tanks were dug in, they would let the panzers come into range, luring them into the pre-prepared kill zones. Soviet artillery would also take their deadly toll. It required patience and a commander that would not be overly aggressive. Vatutin wanted to attack before the German offensive was sufficiently degraded but he was told to wait. Stalin intervened and allowed Red Army general Mikhail Katukov, commander of the 1st Tank Army, to resist premature calls to launch what would have been a suicidal counterattack on the southern shoulder. Katukov, a renowned tank commander, received the honour of being featured in the film about another general that was also a notable leader of armoured units, General George S Patton. In the multiple Oscar winning movie titled *Patton* the two commanders, when they met in Germany at the end of the war, exchanged insults calling each other respectively a "son of a b**ch". They begrudgingly won each other's respect. In the Battle of Kursk, the Germans were again being forced to appreciate the deadliness of the Red Army. The German pincers, one attacking from the land to the north of Kursk and the other driving up from the south faced dogged resistance. The advance was slower than had been planned. The Germans were, however, not without their successes.

In the Battle of Prokhorovka, part of the wider Battle of Kursk, the Germans achieved a great victory, destroying a much larger force of Soviet tanks with minimal losses. However, they could not exploit this success. A tactical defeat for the Soviets had become a strategic success. The United Kingdom made a limited contribution to the Russian victory. British tanks were used by the Soviets. Indeed, the only heavy tanks available to the Red Army at Prokhorovka were little more than thirty Churchill tanks. Away from that battle, the Germans that managed to break through one defensive line around Kursk were forced to pay a high price, only to find yet another ring of defences blocking their advance. Ultimately, the outcome of Operation Citadel was decided far away from the Eastern Front by another Churchill, who was rigorously pursuing his Mediterranean strategy. The final blow which halted the German advance fell on the island of Sicily.

Erich von Manstein believed that Germany appeared to be winning the Battle of Kursk but during the fighting Hitler visited Operation Citadel's commander. The Field Marshal explained to his Führer, "We have suffered losses, but so have they (the Russians)."von Manstein wanted Operation Citadel to continue. Hitler, however, ordered a halt to the offensive; he had become concerned with the Allied invasion of Sicily and consequently moved divisions from the Battle of Kursk to Italy. The Germans now went over to the defensive on the Eastern Front, indeed they had little choice. However, German losses of armour, particularly assault guns, made it difficult for the Wehrmacht to establish new defensive lines. When the Red Army counter attacked the Germans were unable to prevent the Russian forces from breaking through.

Massive Soviet reserves, that dwarfed even those defending Kursk, struck back; this counterattack had a devastating effect, it outflanked and drove back the Axis forces from whence they came. Notwithstanding that, Zhukov had learned from earlier mistakes where the Red Army had advanced too far and too fast. Danger lies at the point of victory. The Soviet strike did eventually become vulnerable with elements of the German army successfully reversing some Russian gains. Yet generally the Red Army counterattack did not become too overstretched, as such it was successful.

The result of Kursk was that the frontline was both shortened and straightened but in the wrong direction to what the Germans had anticipated. It was now 100 miles closer to Berlin. Kharkov changed hands for the fourth time in World War Two. Churchill tanks also played a role in this battle. After a political dispute within Ukraine, known as the Euromaidan, its status was again disputed in 2014. A revolt over the future orientation of that country had taken place and led to a successful attempt to overthrow the elected President who had delayed implementing a trade and association agreement with the European Union. There was an alternative proposal to remain closely allied to the Russian Federation. With pro-EU forces in control of Ukraine's capital, Kiev, separatists who favoured retaining links with Russia took control of Kharkov. However, these were quickly expelled by the Ukrainian security services. Nevertheless, other parts of the country were still disputed, and Russia recently resumed the war for this territory.

Up Periscope

"England in effect is insular, she is maritime, she is linked through her interactions, her markets and her supply lines to the most diverse and often the most distant countries; she pursues essentially industrial and commercial activities, and only slight agricultural ones. She has, in all her doings, very marked and very original habits and traditions." — **Charles de Gaulle, as President of the French Fifth Republic, 1963**

Blue-water navy

Britannia had ruled the waves, and just a generation before the Second World War the United Kingdom held the undisputed mastery of the seas. The envy that this created, as well as the political and economic benefits that Britain's grand fleet accrued, drove leaders with a point to prove to seek to emulate and even try to surpass Britain's success. The Kaiser, and King of Prussia, Wilhelm II, though himself part British and the favourite grandson of Queen Victoria, whom he lovingly cared for in her final days, coveted naval superiority. At the turn of the century, his delusions of grandeur even extended to using his High Seas Fleet to reduce New York and Boston on America's eastern seaboard. Shortly after the dreaming up of those fantasies, however, President Theodore Roosevelt sent the so-called Great White Fleet on its mission to project America's newly established maritime power around the globe which it duly circumnavigated. When Germany, with a new autocrat, returned to menace world peace, there was a new Roosevelt in the White House. Franklin Delano Roosevelt was now President of the USA, incidentally his wife Eleanor was the niece of Teddy Roosevelt. At the start of World War Two, the United States' Navy was on paper the equal of the United Kingdom's. Germany had two superior naval rivals to overcome, this further stoked Hitler's inferiority complex who like the head of state of an earlier Reich sought a world class naval presence. The possession of such a fleet became a prime objective in Hitler's preparations for war. He was not alone; the Kriegsmarine craved an expansion of their nautical prowess.

Admiral Raeder advised Hitler on naval matters; the militarist head of the Kriegsmarine thought the big guns of large capital ships were the route to naval domination. He planned to produce super-sized battleships that would outgun the British. Plan Z was commissioned, this scheme was a blueprint setting out the production of ever more massive battleships, the largest of which would be ready by 1944 in time for when Hitler planned to move beyond pinching out Germany's borders and into launching his all-out-war. They aimed to construct an aircraft carrier but lacked capacity to complete such a kraken. Other competing priorities intervened.

World war came earlier than Hitler and his planners had envisaged, Germany had to go to war with an ill-prepared navy. Without the ability to project German might at sea, the Third Reich would go the same way as the earlier German Empire, namely that the Royal Navy, and Britain's allies, would cut off from the rest of the world. In 1918, starved of resources the German war economy failed, its war machine faltered and then faced defeat on the battlefield. Ultimately, riven by privations, soldiers, civilians, and sailors alike no longer served their military masters; its politicians were forced to sue for peace. Hitler knew he needed a world beating blue-water navy. This was, however, merely fantasy. If Hitler's belligerence had not provoked war in 1939 and if Germany unencumbered by war was allowed to accumulate the resources to build its mega battleships would this have allowed the Nazis to rule the waves? The reality was that this was beyond Germany. Battleships were then, and remain, an expense few could afford. Super-sized ships were something which the indebted German economy could ill-afford in peacetime let alone during a conflict. Despite appeasement British political objections to rearmament had already been neutralised. If Germany had provoked a new big gun naval arms race other nations would not have stood idly by. An even more powerful Kriegsmarine would have been met by an even greater opposition. Germany's rivals would have developed more numerous vessels in more powerful blue-water navies, furthermore these fleets would not be built around outmoded ships. They would be based on aircraft carriers, control of the skies was the prerequisite to victory at sea. Unlike foresighted nations such as Britain and America, Germany did not invest in aircraft carriers early enough and was wedded to the concept of the battleship. The Allies capital ship was the aircraft carrier, and they had many.

Despite some ships already being in construction, Plan Z was ultimately cancelled. The would-be battleships were scrapped and broken-up, their steel used to strengthen the Atlantic Wall, not sailing upon the ocean. Instead of trying to rule the waves Hitler had settled on trying to hold back the incoming tide of superior Allied forces. Just as the 11th century King Canute proved he could not turn back the incoming sea in the apocryphal story of the tide, the less pious Hitler could not stop the inevitable seaborne invasion.

Germany had managed to produce some powerful battleships, namely the *Bismarck* and its sister ship the *Tirpitz*. These leviathans for a brief period of time allowed Germany to follow a "fleet in being" strategy where it retained a surface fleet purely to act as a deterrent and to make the far more powerful Royal Navy cautious. Indeed, the British kept back many of their ships to guard against potential German maritime attacks which as the war progressed became ever less likely. As the fighting came to its inevitable conclusion the threat posed by Germany's surface fleet never really materialised. Over the course of the war the Kriegsmarine was gradually whittled down by the Royal Navy. Even the German navy's successful operations, such as aiding the Nazi victory over Britain and France during the Norwegian campaign, came at an excessive cost with the loss of cruisers and destroyers that were irreplaceable.

Despite lacking numbers, the Germans made up for their paucity of ships with inventive solutions to win the war at sea. One of the overriding aims was to keep the sea lanes open to merchant ships. These brought supplies from their business partners in Sweden across the Baltic Sea and their Turkish commercial partners which shipped raw materials across the Black Sea from where they reached German industry. One solution to keep Allied warships out of these waters, thus keeping the Nazi's nefarious trade routes open, was to deploy magnetic mines. The Germans also used this technology in an attempt to keep British ships trapped in their home ports. The magnetic mine was designed to detonate should a metal hulled vessel pass above the explosive device. They would be activated when the mine detected the disruption caused to the earth's magnetic field by the ship or submarine as it drew near. British vessels were uncowed by this form of warfare.

A new Hanseatic League

The Germans were not just concerned about the great naval power that was the British Empire, but also that of nations that were perceived to be predominantly land based powers, namely Russia. To this end Germany, using its occupied and client states, sought to control the Baltic Sea and use this vast expanse of water in the middle of northern Europe to defeat the Soviet behemoth. Likewise, in order for Hitler to keep control of his empire to the northeast of the Fatherland, the Baltic Sea had to be a German lake.

The Military Maritime Fleet of the USSR had been built-up by Joseph Stalin but like every arm of the Soviet military it had suffered as a result of the purges and did not receive priority when the Germans invaded in 1941. The lion's share of Soviet arms production went to the Red Army. The Russian lack of vessels was partially addressed by both Britain and the United States of America which under the Lend-Lease program supplied the Soviet Navy with ships. Yet even before that the Russian navy was a potential menace which the Germans attempted to neutralise. Unlike the Japanese who attempted to destroy the American Pacific Fleet anchored at Pearl Harbor, the Nazis planned to blockade the Soviet Baltic Fleet and did not intend to annihilate it. Similar to the use of mines deployed in vain against Britain's Royal Navy, Germany tried to imprison the Soviet Baltic Fleet at Leningrad and keep it in its traditional naval base on the island of Kronstadt. When the Nazis began their drive to the east and encountered Russian vessels resisting their invasion. These Soviet ships were often subjected to successful attacks from the Luftwaffe. Initially, the Germans did not consider Russian submarines as a threat, these were however both numerous and active in the Baltic and wreaked havoc against German merchant vessels. In response to this unseen threat Germany, along with their Finnish associates, strung a net across the Gulf of Finland to lock up the Soviet submarines, keeping them in the vicinity of their bases.

This was reminiscent of the Eastern Roman Empire in its earlier fight with the proto-Russians known as the Kievan Rus'. The Byzantines of Constantinople had stretched a great chain across the Golden Horn, the waterway to the north of the great city, to the original Galata tower. This boom could be raised to act as a barrier to navigation or lowered to permit access. In the early 10th century, the Rus' managed to negate this chain by dragging their ships overland and into the Golden Horn. Despite the danger Constantinople won a reprieve for the time being, Nazi Germany, however, was not to survive the Russian response to Hitler's aggression. The German-Finnish net was at first successful, yet it only remained in place whilst Finland was fighting alongside the Nazis. When the Finns switched sides and joined the Russian war effort the net came down. This allowed Soviet submarines to once again navigate their way through the Gulf of Finland and enter the Baltic. The result was a renewed submarine offensive and the terrorising of the Baltic Sea which included the sinking of a German refugee ship as the war drew to a close.

Soviet naval strategy

In 1919, after the cataclysm of the First World War, there were numerous foreign interventions along Russia's coast, some penetrated deep into the interior. Their mission was to quell Lenin's Bolshevik revolution. Whilst these were seen as a failure, British action in the Baltic by the Royal Navy, which included providing arms and ammunition to the natives of the nascent Estonia, proved successful and aided the creation of a new country. Its Finno-Ugric speaking population managed to oust German, Russian, and communist influence which came from other Baltic states and nations as far afield as China. The remains of two Chinese communists were commemorated by the Soviet authorities who erected a small memorial where they died near the Estonian town of Tõravere. Estonian independence was short lived, and it was returned to Russian rule in little over two decades and was put into the USSR.

The Soviet's initially conceptualised their navy as one that would help them resist a seaborne invasion from the more advanced capitalist powers. It was intended that the Soviet navy's submarines, light ships, and even aeroplanes were a key part of this strategy to repel a seaborne attack. The submersible was especially favoured; indeed, the Russians had more submarines than the Germans. The Soviet Baltic Fleet was on paper stronger than the German forces sailing on and under this contested sea. Russian's not only had a powerful fleet, their navy was also alive to the danger it was in. Soviet admirals expected the German attack and was on high alert 3 days before Operation Barbarossa began on 22nd June 1941, this readiness was not reflected by its political leadership. Consequently, it fell prey to the Luftwaffe when war broke out between the Nazi Reich and the USSR.

Despite its losses at the start of the war, the Soviet Baltic Fleet had its own Dunkirk moment. In August 1941, the Russians managed to evacuate their forces from the port city of Tallinn, the capital of the Estonian Soviet Socialist Republic. There the Old Town, and seaport, were surrounded by German forces which eventually took Tallinn but only after important vessels had managed to escape. This was not before many fleeing ships were attacked by the Germans. The Russian authorities were more concerned with securing the safety of its warships and consequently neglected to protect the transports which duly suffered badly. However, whilst the Baltic Fleet left the cargo ships to their fate the big-gunned vessels managed to escape and were able to fight again. Indeed, they were helpful in the defence of Leningrad and would prove their worth throughout the war. The ruthless Russian and communist mindset had taken the tough decisions that they deemed necessary.

Not only was the Soviet Baltic Fleet's bombardment of the German army a boon to the Red Army, these seagoing big guns delayed the German army's advance on Leningrad, they also helped win this key battle in the northern theatre. The Russian navy supported Red Army attacks which finally broke the siege of Leningrad. Their opponents also used this tactic. The German Baltic Fleet similarly helped its army. In 1944, Kriegsmarine ships bombarded the Red Army which helped the Germans breakout from Estonia. The Germans would have otherwise been enveloped and trapped against the Baltic Sea.

When the fight against Germany dragged on the Soviet Navy sought to win the economic war against their German foes and Hitler's subordinate satellite states. Soviet submarines went over to the offensive and conducted a war of attrition disrupting supplies of iron ore and ball bearings from Sweden to Germany, both vital to the Nazi war effort. Towards the end of the conflict the Soviet Baltic Fleet successfully severed the supply lines to the isolated and cut-off German pockets holding out in Courland, Latvia, and Pomerania, much of which is now in modern day Poland.

During the later stages of the conflict, the land war alongside the Baltic was also assisted by Soviet submarines which dropped reconnaissance units behind German lines. Likewise, the submarine became crucial to German strategy in this region. Grand Admiral Dönitz, as the Supreme Commander of the German navy, used the Baltic Sea as a training ground for his U-boat crews. He desired that the Gulf of Danzig on the Baltic be held as long as possible so that his submariners could be trained in the new Type 21 U-boat. This gave further justification for Hitler to keep his army in the east when it would have better served the Third Reich by defending the approaches to the capital of the Fatherland. In the face of the Red Army's overwhelming firepower, this area was soon lost to the Soviets; thus, rendering this strategy useless. The Führer had hoped that the now cut-off Hitlerite forces on the Baltic would help him in his fanciful fight back against the Russians from where he could reclaim territory in the east. This was not to be won back by force. What remained of more than 26 divisions, amounting to nearly two-hundred-thousand men, became trapped and isolated in the Courland Pocket. These soldiers of what was called Army Group Courland became their own gaolers. They finally surrendered to their fate soon after the war had officially ended in Europe.

The Soviet navy did not just play a crucial role in the Baltic. Russia has a massive coastline that touches different seas and even oceans, consequently their vessels influenced the fighting in many regions and time zones. The Russian navy had a powerful presence in the Arctic where its Northern Flotilla defended the allied convoys that were supplying the USSR with vital materials from the west. In warmer waters the Black Sea Fleet also affected how the war developed.

Black seas

Russia's historic quest to control the sea to the south of its historic fulcrum, Kievan Rus', and secure a warm water port led it to dominate the Black Sea. Russia's progress towards this expanse of water followed the Swedish Vikings route to the sea down the mighty Dnieper River. These men, the Varangians, used this river and others including the Don to traverse the landmass from the Baltic to the Black Sea. After generations of struggle against the Ottoman Turks, and other Turkic and Tartar forces in the region, Russia secured access to the Black Sea, its associated limans, and the Sea of Azov, as well as the warm water port of Sevastopol. The Soviet successors to Tsarist Russia inherited a formidable navy. Its Black Sea Fleet, which during World War Two was initially headquartered in the Crimea, then part of the Russian Soviet Federative Socialist Republic, also had bases around the Black Sea, indeed, it dominated this waterway. This force included a battleship, many cruisers, and submarines.

The attack on Russia by Germany and their Romanian junior partners in turn begot attacks on Romania's oil installations across the Black Sea by Soviet ships. These economic targets were crucial to the German war effort and defending this supply of oil was an important consideration for Hitler. This stretch of water had to be closed to Russian shipping. Throughout the war, the Soviet fleet's naval guns attacked German positions. Its ships and submarines supplied the Red Army and even carried out amphibious attacks against the Heer to hamper the German advance in the south during Operation Barbarossa. Landings behind enemy lines disrupted the German push towards the important naval base at Odessa in the Ukraine. Ultimately it fell to the Germans when the Red Army evacuated their forces to reinforce the key naval position at Sevastopol in the Crimea. This port was also supplied from Russian bases on the eastern Black Sea and defended by veritable floating artillery platforms. German attacks were delayed when the Soviet navy's marines and the Red Army launched attacks against the eastern coast of the Crimea forcing von Manstein to divert resources away from the attack on Sevastopol. Ultimately, the attacks on the Germans occupying the Crimea were stopped as they proved too costly for the Russian fleet, but they slowed the Wehrmacht's advance. Lost time was amongst Germany's biggest enemies.

When the Germans sought to take the land to the north and east of the Black Sea along with the oil rich Caspian Sea region the Soviet Navy continued to harass the Nazis every step of the way. Army Group South's drive to Baku on the Caspian had divisions split from the main objective, not just to capture Stalingrad and close the Volga to river borne transport, but also to seize naval bases on the east coast of the Black Sea. Hitler's diversion of resources in the Battle of the Caucasus towards the Russian naval bases was equally disastrous. The Nazi war machine's divisions were further dissipated, checked, driven back, and finally destroyed. Ultimately, the German navy lacked reach to win the war.

A new hope
Originally it was conceived that the role of aircraft carriers was to support the main ship of the line, the battleship. The aeroplanes carried across the great distances of the oceans would spot enemies and guide the artillery fire emanating from the capital ships' mighty cannons. However, as the war developed the aircraft carrier became king, and indispensable to the fleet without which victory could not be achieved. Fleets were reconfigured around the aircraft carrier with the battleship reduced to fulfilling a supporting role to the seagoing airbase. Though it operated under the cover of the now even bigger vessels accompanying the battleship, this older concept remained the main arm of action. Furthermore, in the Pacific theatre, battleships, less sizable cruisers, and destroyers sank a greater tonnage of Japanese shipping than the planes carried on floating leviathans. Whilst dominion over the sea depended upon achieving air superiority, the battleship was far from obsolete. These mighty floating gun platforms found a new role in supporting landings of troops on enemy held shores. This was not always successful.

The navy's guns did not help in the Pacific theatre as much as was hoped. At the Battle of Tarawa in November 1943, the low trajectory of the American 15" naval guns meant that the mighty shells did not penetrate deep underground. Their explosive force bounced off and was deflected away from the Japanese who were secure in their underground fortresses. Nearly one and a half years hence, a barrage from the plethora of US Navy during the preliminary bombardment before the Battle of Iwo Jima likewise had little practical effect. The Japanese were again too well dug in around this volcanic island. Ultimately, there was no alternative to putting boots on the ground. Nevertheless, another great power that abutted the Pacific did make good use of sea going vessels to expand its empire.

Russian naval power, first established by Peter the Great in the late 17th century, provided, just as he intended, another dimension to his empire. He had stated that, "a ruler that has but an army has one hand, but he who has a navy has both." The Soviet's used their naval power to not only defend and consolidate a land empire but also spread its dominion to neighbouring islands, seizing overseas territory from the once powerful Empire of Japan. The United States and the UK requested support from Joseph Stalin. They wanted him to join the war in the Pacific. As the war drew to a close, as per its agreement with the Allies, the Soviet's repudiated their non-aggression pact with Japan and then declared war on the Empire of the Sun. The result was the occupation and annexation of South Sakhalin, part of an island that had long been fought over between Japan and Tsarist Russia. It had been ceded to Russia as part of The Treaty of Saint Petersburg in 1875. However, aggressive and expansionist Japan later took part of the island. Sovereignty over Sakhalin remained a source of dispute into the Soviet-Communist era. The Russians also took the opportunity that war presented them to capture the Kuril Islands, some of which did have a Russian presence before they were ceded to Japan as part of the agreement of 1875. The islands annexation in 1945 would not have been possible without a significant Soviet Pacific Fleet supporting the Russian ground forces advancing in these islands by bombarding the positions of a capitulating Japanese army whose soldiers were forced to down arms. British and American ground forces would also benefit from naval power in other battles.

The Pacific theatre was not the only conflict that required the use of naval big guns. Having been driven out of continental Europe, the route to victory in Europe for the British Empire and her American ally was from bases in Britain and North Africa. To defeat their Nazi and Fascist enemies they had to cross seas, then seize and hold the coastline from where they would advance inland. Naval guns developed in an earlier arms race which was spawned by the British introduction of HMS *Dreadnought* in 1906 which rendered all previous designs obsolete. These ships evolved to have ever larger guns capable of hurling increasingly powerful explosive shells at enemy vessels over great distances. They found their heyday in clashes at sea during the First World War, this was also to be their zenith, yet only the most foresighted military planners understood their limitations in the age of airpower. These dreadnoughts, however, proved to be of use to the two great naval powers of Britain and America in a vastly different way. They successfully supported the landings of soldiers and marines and kept them safe until the beachhead was secure. The big ships supported the 1943 Allied invasion of Sicily and saved General Patton's forces when they were attacked by German Tiger tanks at the Battle of Gela. That same year, on the peninsula of Italy, the American landings at Salerno were again saved by the power of the naval guns forcing the German commander Albert Kesselring to order a retreat away from the coast. The situation had been exacerbated by the decision of the American commander, Mark Clark, to dispense with the idea of a preliminary naval bombardment. This left the Wehrmacht intact and able to oppose the spread too thinly US forces. The surrender of Italy, brought on by the loss of Sicily, coincided with the Eight Army landings at the toe of Italy leading many to believe that there would be little resistance to the Salerno landings; this proved to be a false assumption. The following year in France, during the campaign in Normandy, Erwin Rommel was similarly forced to move German forces out of range of withering fire from massive naval guns. This mode of warfare, big ships attacking shore-based targets, was not a new innovation.

Monitor ships were used in the War for Southern Independence, also known as the War Between the States, and the American Civil War. This class of ship was used to bombard fortifications, and through sailing up the Confederacy's river system the Union navy attacked anything inland from civilian to economic targets. Arguably this was not new, Peter the Great had captured the now Russian town of Azov from the Ottomans in 1696 after a bombardment from both land and sea. Monitors also found use in the Great War. HMS *M33* was such a ship whose specific role was to provide a supporting bombardment against targets on the coast. This was used to aid the ultimately unsuccessful Allied landings during the First World War's Gallipoli campaign which aimed to knock Ottoman Turkey from the war and force open a supply route to Russia. Monitor ships, though powerful for their size, lacked the punch of a battleship. The failure in the Dardanelles showed that bombarding the shore was a task for bigger vessels. Hence, a generation later, capital ships were deployed to perform this duty.

The battleship was not just restricted to aiding offensive operations, it could also be deployed in a defensive function. Hitler used the last of his capital ships, the *Tirpitz*, along with its four platforms of twin near 15-inch guns, as a floating battery defending the coast of Norway from the perceived threat of a British invasion. The insistence of British Prime Minister Winston Churchill and the inventiveness of British scientist and engineer Barnes Wallis forced the ship to capsize when his Tallboy bombs were dropped on the vessel by RAF Lancaster bombers. The incessant targeting of this vessel, the sister ship of the *Bismarck*, by Churchill increased Hitler's paranoia that an invasion of Norway was a likelihood. This misreading of Allied strategy forced the Führer to keep back troops in Norway that could have been much better deployed elsewhere.

The battleship gained a new lease of life even as far into the future as the latter part of the twentieth century when the World War Two era USS *Missouri*, recommissioned by the American Reagan administration, was deployed to the Persian Gulf by the first President Bush. The aim was to first deter and then defeat the forces of the dictator of Iraq Saddam Hussein. The *Missouri* used its powerful guns to bombard Iraqi positions in the 1991 Gulf War. During Desert

Storm this large and adaptable weapons platform also launched Tomahawk cruise missiles at its foe. Its sheer presence in the vicinity of the battlespace helped convince the Iraqi forces, then unlawfully occupying Kuwait, that the coalition forces would attempt a seaborne landing on the Kuwaiti shore. The real attack was, however, delivered elsewhere in a vast outflanking movement.

The other often overlooked heroine of the war at sea was the destroyer. Despite its awe-inspiring name, it was a relatively small, but fast and manoeuvrable, long-distance warship. Its nomenclature derives from its original purpose and designation as a torpedo boat destroyer. This vessel entered its own in World War II. It proved to be highly useful as an escort to the larger ships of the fleet, convoys and, armed with a phalanx of anti-aircraft guns, it was the last line of defence guarding the vulnerable and too big to fail aircraft carriers. In the Pacific its Bofors guns were the perfect foil to Japanese aircraft. Anti-submarine action also became an important part of the destroyer's duties. Such was the destroyer's utility that Churchill asked for 40 or 50 destroyers, and only those that were surplus to US requirements, from his American counterpart, to help defend the UK during the Battle of Britain. This was not a too onerous demand and President Roosevelt supplied vessels but at a cost. To this day the Destroyer class of ship remains the mainstay of most nation's navies and the weapon of choice to commission when building surface combat vessels. Its economic viability is such that it has helped cause the global extinction of the battleship and the battlecruiser. The latter being a heavily armed but, in comparison to the battle-ship, lightly armoured warship. The smaller destroyer is also compatible with modern stealth technology. Weapons systems from guided missiles to electronic warfare, and developmental railguns no longer give pre-eminence to big guns which are now firmly anachronistic and can only be carried on ships with the largest displacement.

Pole star

Whilst Germany did not have a serviceable aircraft carrier, the Nazis still followed a combined arms approach, employing airpower, alongside its battleships, and submarines to disrupt the passage of merchantmen carrying their vital cargo to Britain. The UK's naval capabilities were, despite the many perils posed to both its merchant ships and its complementary Royal Navy, so numerous and ambitious in their scope that Britain's fleet could be used to export materials and fuel from Britain to her allies. The UK used its industrial capability to deliver supplies to continental resistance networks fighting against the European hegemon, Britain was setting Europe ablaze. Its merchant navy also supplied the Soviet Union; this aid was a vital contribution to Russia's Great Patriotic War against the German invader. Indeed, the Red Army's war effort depended upon the many convoys of ships sent from Liverpool to Russian ports such as Arkhangelsk and Murmansk via the Arctic Ocean north of Norway.

These Arctic convoys became a major target for Germany submarines, ships, and aircraft operating out of Nazi occupied Norway. Such was the importance of these convoys and so great was the threat posed by German forces in Norway, Hitler thought it logical that the Allies would reinvade Germany's most northern possession. This would have deprived the Nazis of some of its Swedish iron-ore and its bases to attack the convoys. Ultimately, Hitler's fears were well founded but the invasion came not from the west. Later Norway was invaded from the east.

Despite having to run the gauntlet of German forces operating from occupied Norway, Britain still managed to deliver 400 million tons of supplies to the Russians via the Arctic convoys. These fleets had to traverse treacherous seas, overcome gales, all whilst having to evade or destroy their spiteful German enemy who were just as intent on destroying merchant ships as they were military vessels. Controversially, the sailors serving on the convoys were not initially issued with a commemorative award. This however was rectified in 2012 when veterans of this campaign were belatedly awarded the Arctic Star medal. This was not the only time when their sacrifice went unappreciated. Convoy PQ 17 is a notable example. In July 1942, a naval commander, fearful of a phantom impending attack from the German battleship *Tirpitz* ordered his ships to scatter. Merchant vessels in tight formation with mutually supporting watchful eyes and closely defended by supporting warships were well defended against German U-boats. However, they would present a vulnerable target if engaged by the might of a battleship. It would be bait to be devoured by the leviathan in one bite. The threat posed to the convoys by the *Turpitz* was a possibility should it have sighted the merchant vessels. However, the mighty battleship was sailing away from convoy PQ 17 and thus the danger was illusory. When German U-boats attacked the ships, which were no longer mutually supporting each other, the effect was devastating. Out of 35 merchant ships only 11 reached Murmansk to deliver their important cargo to the Russians. So great was the wreckage that the Soviet authorities at first refused to believe that so many ships had been sunk and instead accused the British of not supplying as much help as the UK had claimed. They were not the only ships to have been ravaged by German submarines.

Das Boot

Like a generation before, the greatest threat to Allied shipping and Britain's war effort came from Germany's U-boats. Yet, they could not defeat the UK. German submarine construction, mindful of the need to improve their efficiency, attempted to copy multiple assembly line mass production techniques combining the different sections at the final stage into a complete unit. This contrasted with the previous mode of mass production that developed one-unit station by station until the manufacturing was complete. Whilst their ambitions were correct, and this innovative multiple line system was on paper the most productive technique, German industrialists did not possess the knowledge to deliver it in practice. In many instances, when the different sections of *U*-boats were combined, they were found to leak and thus for any seagoing vessel, let alone a submarine, were completely unseaworthy. Fixing the flaws in the manufacturing process took too long. The weapons that they hoped would throttle Britain surfaced too late and were too few to beat the British Royal and merchant navies. German industrial know-how was not quite advanced enough to enable streamlined and seamless processes. Hitler's dreams were retarded by a comparative lack of development in his adoptive country. Thus, Germany was not properly equipped to fight a modern war. If Germany had entered the war with a more sophisticated economy and the most up-to-date production methods, then these manufacturing issues would have been teased out before the fighting began.

Not only was Germany incapable of flooding the seas with the quantity of submersibles that they needed if they were to have any hope of victory, but their pre-war preparations invested resources elsewhere. They produced costly and complex battleships. This was a major misallocation of finite resources. Hitler was keen to undo the unfavourable terms of the Treaty of Versailles which limited the size and quantity of German naval vessels. Banned from possessing the largest and most modern battleships, the Führer craved those symbols of past prestige. He became fixated on investing in building-up Germany's surface fleet. However, due to the Weimar Republic obeying the Treaty of Versailles, Germany started from a position of naval weakness that could not easily and quickly be turned around.

Ultimately, Plan Z was to the detriment of the Kriegsmarine's *unterseeboot* capabilities. German U-boats were still numerous and effectively deployed in wolfpacks, and certainly capable of alarming British Prime Minister Winston Churchill, yet they were too few to force the United Kingdom to surrender. However, the British Isles were not acting in unison against the peril of the U-boat and the threat these vessels posed in the Battle of the Atlantic.

Malin, Rockall, Shannon, Fastnet

Great Britain is an island, but the United Kingdom has a presence on another land mass, Ireland, with which it shares a land border. The British Isles were united in 1801 with Ireland becoming an integral part of the UK. However, in the time immediately before World War One Irish politics again began a descent into violence as militias formed to either fight against or fight for the British Government's policy of Home Rule for Ireland. The German Empire supplied arms and ammunition, first to the loyalist anti-Home Rule Ulster Volunteers and then to the nationalist Irish Volunteers that formed in response. This enabled Irish politics to enter periods of recurring militancy. Nevertheless, putting aside their differences most Unionists and Nationalists backed Britain's war effort in the fight against the German Empire.

The tumults of the First World War gave new life to the put-on hold crisis. Germany deployed its *modus operandi* of seeking to ferment internal revolution in its opponent's territory and aided militant Republicans who in 1916 enacted the so-called Easter Rising which was mainly limited to Dublin. One of the leaders was the Scottish born socialist James Connolly. They represented few but themselves and their little supported revolt in the city collapsed within days. Nevertheless, the execution of its leaders created sympathy for their cause. Amongst the most radicalising factor at the time was the British government's attempts to enact conscription in Ireland to aid the war effort against Germany. This measure alienated much of a mostly loyal population, and war in Ireland soon followed.

The result of the fighting was that in 1922 Ireland became a divided island with two parliaments one in the north in Belfast governing six of the nine counties that made up the province of Ulster. This area remained in the United Kingdom. Another assembly in the south, based in Dublin, controlled a self-governing Dominion within the British Commonwealth of Nations. This was not radically different to an earlier iteration of the British Government's home rule plans, contained in the Government of Ireland Act 1920. The bitterness created by Republican ethnic cleansing of protestants pushed back the process of reconciliation between the two sides and kept the conflict between Ireland's civil authorities and the British government simmering. This was to have consequences when Germany was again to endanger the peace of Europe a generation later.

Ireland both achieved *de facto* and *de jure* independence from the United Kingdom in 1937, though it was not yet declared a Republic until nearly a further dozen years later. It was officially neutral during World War Two. Its position as the most westerly part of the British Isles, jutting further out into the Atlantic Ocean, made its 26 mostly southern counties of crucial importance during the Battle of the Atlantic. The threat from German U-boats during the First World War led the British to retain three naval bases, one in the north and two in the south, in the newly independent Irish Free State which came into being in 1922. This was agreed in the Anglo-Irish Treaty signed on 6th December 1921. To resolve a trade and financial dispute with the Irish government, which ceased to be a dominion in 1937, the British vacated these so-called Treaty Ports in 1938 and handed them over to the control of the now independent Ireland, known in Irish as Éire. This attempt at winning goodwill was essentially an act of appeasement. The Irish government maintained its claim over Ulster and militant Republicans were still active in that province. Indeed, as war clouds again loomed over Europe, the surrender of these ports was a reckless decision.

Ireland was a source of concern for Britain throughout the war for numerous reasons. One such worry was the Irish Republican Army. These terrorists neither recognised Northern Ireland's right to self-determination nor the government of Ireland. Nevertheless, the IRA was willing to take Ireland's financial support. The IRA also collaborated with Nazi Germany passing secrets to the *Abwehr*, the German Military Intelligence organisation. Furthermore, from 1939 – 1940 the IRA conducted the S-Plan campaign against the UK. This was a series of sabotage operations against military, economic, and civil infrastructure in Britain. Another problem was Ireland's passive obstruction of Britain's war effort. Yet at times they were helpful. The Irish government was not unwilling to work with Britain. During the Irish Civil War which followed the creation of the inde-pendent Irish Free State, the lawful authorities used British arms, artillery, and even British gunners to defeat the anti-Treaty rebels who did not accept a peace deal with the United Kingdom. The G-2, the Irish Secret Service, also at times co-operated with the UK's MI5; helping to round up IRA spies.

The government of Ireland was also willing to allow Britain to reoccupy the remainder of Ireland should the Germans invade. Nazi plans to invade Ireland were even less credible than Operation Sea Lion. It was merely a feint aimed at distracting and unnerving the British authorities. However, Ireland's acquiescence to British wishes at least demonstrated a small degree of willingness to at least not impair the Allies' war effort. There was even an occasion when a British naval reconnaissance plane was permitted to use Irish airspace. This helped locate the German battleship *Bismarck*, which was later sent to the bottom of the Atlantic. The sinking of the *Bismarck* showed that airpower was decisive at sea; it came after Swordfish torpedo planes from HMS *Ark Royal* damaged its rudders, thus preventing its escape back to occupied France. This allowed the Royal Navy to engage the German battleship. The *Bismarck* sustained a multitude of severe hits from British vessels that would have sent it beneath the waves had it not been scuttled.

Notwithstanding that assistance, the loss of the three Treaty Ports and the failure of the Irish government to join the war effort proved to be a serious impediment to the Royal Navy and the Royal Air Force. It hampered their efforts to protect the shipping that kept Britain's mouths and factories fed. Britain's occupation of Iceland in the north Atlantic helped mitigate the problem of the UK no longer possessing the Treaty Ports. It provided a base for convoys traversing the Atlantic, shortening the sea route to North America, and shrinking the gap in which German U-boats could operate unimpeded by Allied air power. Yet, the absence of the Treaty Ports and Ireland's omission to enter the war impeded Britain's desperate struggle to win the Battle of the Atlantic.

Britain's retaining possession of Northern Ireland, as per the Anglo-Irish Treaty of 1921 and Ulster's opting out from being part of the Irish Free State, saved the British Government from having to invade southern Ireland. This however remained an option. The British had planned to invade Ireland to drive out Nazi influence from there and open its ports and airfields to help with the Battle of the Atlantic. This, however, never came to pass.

British Prime Minister Winston Churchill had offered Éamon de Valera the Irish Taoiseach, otherwise known as Prime Minister, a degree of Irish unity if the south entered the war against Hitler on the Allied side. However, this was turned down by de Valera who feared that it would create political difficulties in Ireland. Despite this the Allies still managed to win the war at sea and win the Second World War. Churchill said in his victory radio broadcast of 13th May 1945 that,

"Owing to the action of Mr de Valera . . . the approaches which the Southern Irish ports and airfields could so easily have guarded were closed by the hostile aircraft and U-boats. This was indeed a deadly moment in our life, and it if had not been for the loyalty and friendship of Northern Ireland we should have been forced to come to close quarters with Mr. de Valera or perish for ever from the earth. However, with a restraint and a poise to which, I say, history will find few parallels, His Majesty's Government never laid a violent hand upon them . . . and we left the de Valera government to frolic with the Germans and later with the Japanese representatives to their heart's content."

Upon learning of the death of Adolf Hitler in 1945, Éamon de Valera sent his condolences to the German Ambassador in Dublin; he did not pay such respect to the American Ambassador on the passing of President Roosevelt. Despite de Valera being Ireland's leading politician, he did not represent all of his countrymen. During the Second World War, more than 10% of soldiers in the Irish Army, a number more than 4,000 men, deserted to join the British Army's fight against Hitler. Upon their return to Ireland, they suffered terrible treatment. de Valera had them placed on a blacklist where they were denied public employment and pensions. Their children were often taken into care where they were singled out for abuse. Furthermore, following the Second World War, Ireland became a home for German Nazis exiled from their Fatherland.

Notwithstanding the anti-British and pro-Nazi leanings of Ireland's leadership, the innate characteristics, and economic interests that had made Britain great were able to keep the United Kingdom open. The strength of the Royal Navy was not the only factor, the merchant navy, and its commercial ability to dominate the oceans also proved pivotal. Indeed, the Royal Navy was made into a mighty force to defend these business interests. These commercial concerns also created a powerful ship building industry that could not only replace losses caused by German U-boats but also provide shipping which safely transported Allied servicemen to the UK from where they could take the fight to Hitler.

Conspicuous consumption

Cruise liners such as the *Queen Mary* safely transported soldiers around the world in the global war fought by Britain and America. The conspicuous consumption that was the cruise liner industry was fed by the increasingly consumer-led economies of Britain and France. They produced large and luxurious cruise liners. These crossed the Atlantic and took advantage of this burgeoning trans-Atlantic trade with the United States. They served the travel tastes of upper-middle class consumers. The competition for this market between the French Compagnie Générale Transatlantique and the British Cunard-White Star Line produced large and fast ships, most notably the *Queen Mary*. This famed vessel transported in total 800,000 troops during the war at such a pace, over 32 knots per hour, that it could evade Germany's U-boats. Perhaps just as importantly for the course of the conflict it also transported British Prime Minister and Secretary of State for War, Winston Churchill, across the pond to meet the US President, Franklin Delano Roosevelt. The bond between them produced an alliance that was to aid Britain's war effort, though not always as Churchill had hoped and with consequences for the British Empire and eastern Europe that the British Prime Minister did not approve.

The sterling service of the requisitioned for the war effort *Queen Mary*, which had been repainted and became known as the 'grey ghost', was supplemented by the *Queen Elizabeth* and the French liner the *Normandie* which was interred by the Americans and renamed the USS *Lafayette*. This liner also served as a troop transport ship. They could likewise evade the German wolf packs.

Sea wolves

Hitler knew that if his U-boats could isolate Britain this island fortress would be unable to feed herself, nor have the materials to wage war against his Reich. The United Kingdom would have been at his mercy, and unable to lead in the liberation of the continent. In terms of manpower, for most of the war more servicemen and women engaged in the fight against the Third Reich came from Britain and her Empire than from the United States of America. That was until late-1944 when US troop numbers began to outnumber British and Commonwealth forces. Yet neither of these substantial build-ups of men and their accompanying materiel would have been possible without the Allies winning the Battle of the Atlantic. Nevertheless, total victory in this part of the conflict, which lasted from the beginning of the war in 1939, only came when Nazi Germany surrendered, and hostilities ceased. The main weapons used in this long battle were the submarine targeting what were civilian merchant vessels defended by warships which operated above the surface of the water.

Unrestricted submarine warfare against Britain came to be the norm in the Atlantic and beyond. Though the wanton sinking of nonmilitary ships was outlawed by the Second London Naval Treaty, this agreement had a clause that came to be known as the London Submarine Protocol. This permitted the sinking of merchantmen if they were armed vessels or assisting the navy in hunting submarines. Arguably therefore German U-boats in many cases may have been operating within the laws of war. The Nazis nefarious intention were however clearly expressed in Führer Directive 23, 'Directions for Operations against the English War Economy.' Hitler intended to deny the seas to the British and her Allies regardless of the circumstances and legalities.

The Germans planned a U-boat campaign prior to war being declared. The Kriegsmarine had war-gamed the best tactics to use and realised that attacking in groups was indeed the most effective approach. This concept had initially been trialled during Germany's *Handelskrieg*, the war on trade, during World War One. It was now renewed and reinstated for the rematch; the wolf pack came back with vengeance. Instead of hunting alone and stalking its prey, the U-boats under the command of their alpha, Karl Dönitz, who micro-managed the attacks, would lie in wait across the likely advance of their quarry and once located converge on the target. From there they would attack any lone straggler or if they encountered a convoy, the U-boats in the pack would seek to split the convoy from its defending escort ships who would be provoked into attempting to engage the submarines. The warships would be drawn away from the defenceless merchantmen which would now be vulnerable to the U-boats, at first many such ships were sunk. On the British side, the convoys' fight was managed from the Western Approaches Headquarters based in Liverpool. The convoy, if watchful and prepared, would have a much better chance of survival than ships sailing alone without defence.

The British, despite having a technological advantage as well as a much stronger navy, were ill-prepared for the wolf packs which from the onset of unrestricted submarine warfare were scoring success after success. The long-running Battle of the Atlantic became one of convoys versus wolf packs of German U-boats and in some instance's Italian submarines. British shipping was also bombed by German Condor planes. These aircraft were described by Winston Churchill as the 'scourge of the oceans.' Yet the greatest threat remained the U-boat, their weapon of choice was the torpedo. This self-propelled underwater missile was an Anglo-Italian invention that came into being during the Victorian era.

The U-boats concentrated their efforts in the part of the north Atlantic Ocean which could not be covered by Allied anti-submarine aircraft. Submarines throughout much of the Second World War were mainly restricted to operating for most of their days at sea above the waves, not beneath them. They needed to be on the surface to function properly and could only spend relatively short periods underwater. Indeed, the U-boats were designed to operate on the surface where they could achieve greater speed and efficiency than when diving. The German term *U-boot* was therefore something of a misnomer, they were more submersible than submarines. Once they had broken the surface the U-boats could be detected from the air, engaged, and sunk. In the Black Pit beyond the range of Allied aircraft the U-boats could operate with little fear of attack from above. However, they could not attack with impunity. The Royal Navy could detect submarines through sonar, which in an earlier incarnation was originally known as ASDIC. The Sonar technician would listen for the presence of enemy submarines. Upon their being located these vulnerable craft could be struck by devastating hydraulic shockwaves emanating from detonated depth charges or hit directly by hedgehog anti-submarine mortars, rupturing the hull and causing a catastrophic breach.

The Royal Navy was not alone in its struggle for rule of the waves. The Royal Canadian Navy also fought in the Battle of the Atlantic, this young nation came to the aid of its mother country by providing men and equipment for the fight. At the start of the war the RCN, also known as the *Marine royale canadienne*, was a small force but by the end of the war it had 400 ships which linked up with the British and helped close the gap in the Atlantic. Britain in her hour of need was also assisted by the United States Atlantic Fleet which had recently been reformed and had become belligerent in all but name even before Hitler declared war on America. Upon war being declared on the United States, the U-boats immediately went into action attacking American shipping on its eastern seaboard. At first the United States Navy did not institute a convoy system and its merchant fleet suffered heavy losses at the hands of the Kriegsmarine. The Americans quickly adapted to this danger and instituted convoys. The United States Navy also fought back, forming hunter killer groups. The wolf pack hunters had become the hunted. There would be no more happy times for the U-boat crews.

The Battle of the Atlantic was a fight where each measure was met with a countermeasure. The British had already learned to fight back. As wolf pack tactics evolved, so did those of the convoys. Among the innovators of new naval tactics was Captain Johnnie Walker. Aggressive use of escort carriers to defend the commercial ships proved to be superior tactics and many convoys were able to cross the seas without being engaged. What losses there were, despite the loss of life, could be sustained, especially by American ship production. US shipyards, some created especially for the war, adapted a British design to mass produce cargo ships on a gargantuan scale; the easy and quick to manufacture Liberty Ship was born. New American construction techniques produced vessels that helped keep Britain supplied and more than replaced losses. Their production produced a latter-day industrial revolution in America. Workers flocked to purpose-built metropolises by the sea, with new schools and cinemas to work in these private shipyards where they would receive better pay and conditions than before the war. The Allies were winning the industrial battle as well as the tactical and technological struggle.

The Royal Navy also established rapid response units which were rushed to engage the wolf packs whenever and wherever the German U-boats were spotted. Not only did strategy and tactics develop, so did technology. The Royal Navy embarked on an arms race against the U-boats. Radar was used to detect the submarines when they were on the surface. Even when they had dived, they could be detected and destroyed by warships. The U-boats were particularly imperilled by the fact that the German naval codes and their enigma machine had been captured and cracked. This allowed the Allies to decipher their orders.

They knew where to find them and destroyed them accordingly. The U-boat's centralised command and control system proved to be somewhat of a disadvantage that could certainly not stop the appalling losses which the Allied navies inflicted on German submariners. The dire situation was exacerbated when the U-boats found that the area in which they could hide was shrinking. By the end of the Battle of the Atlantic more than 28,000 Germans lay dead on the bottom of the ocean floor, entombed in a watery grave. The *U*-boat was their coffin.

With aircraft range increased and with planes operating from the British Dominion of Newfoundland, now a part of Canada, as well as from Iceland and the United Kingdom, the Black Pit triangle shrank until it disappeared entirely. Furthermore, with the introduction of escort carriers accompanying the convoys, the U-boats were even more likely to be caught by Allied planes hunting them from above. These small carriers were vulnerable, nevertheless as they were low cost and quick to produce the escort carriers were, to a degree, expendable. Their service to the convoys was nonetheless vital. The elimination of the mid-Atlantic gap effectively defeated the U-boat campaign by mid-1943, though the threat never fully subsided. They could still strike at Britain.

U-boat attacks on the Allied fleet on the D-Day landings sank some 56,000 tons of shipping, yet it came at a high price. The Germans had sacrificed much of what remained of their depleted fleet in the vain hope of disrupting the invasion of Normandy. Defeating the U-boats at sea was not the only option. British airpower was also brought to bear on them at their base. The Germans had constructed massive concrete armoured *U*-boat pens to keep the submarines safe in their French ports. These were bombed by the British but without success. The Nazis, like all socialists, had an affection for concrete, here their use of cement proved its worth. The Germans not only hid their submarines in near impregnable bases but also developed more stealthy craft to operate under the water. They produced a class of midget submarines, but these met with no success, indeed their intoxicated crews who were given a cocktail of drugs, often did not survive training. The submarine was not the only platform to deliver a torpedo.

Under the terms of the Versailles Treaty, Germany was restricted from producing larger ships. Accordingly, it developed a speciality in smaller faster boats. German *Snell* (fast) boats, known in Germany as S boats, and in Britain as E boats were designed for raiding by firing torpedoes at enemy vessels. This was not a new concept, but they were used to deadly effect by the Kriegsmarine in World War Two, especially when the seas should have been under the command of Allied navies. In April 1944 German E boats penetrated Exercise Tiger, a rehearsal for the impending invasion of Normandy. They devastated the American ships taking part in this operation and the soldiers and sailors they were transporting. This became known as the Battle of Lyme Bay, named after an area on the south coast of England.

The British countered the German E boats with corvettes and their own motor torpedo boats, MTBs, and motor gun boats, MGBs. These Royal Navy D boats as they were also known, were fast and manoeuvrable but not entirely stable in heavy seas. Britain later produced larger more effective D boats to take on the Kriegsmarine's fast craft. The United Kingdom's ingenuity in small vessel design came from the British desire to enjoy sailing on the UK's many waterways. They were developed from light and fast pleasure cruisers built on the Thames in Chiswick by Thornycroft. This boat builder, which specialised in steam powered yachts, was first commissioned by the Norwegian Navy to make torpedo boats in the Victorian era. The Royal Navy quickly followed suit as did other navies. During the Second World War Britain's versatile torpedo boats were used across the Atlantic Ocean as well as in the North Sea and in the Mediterranean. They even supported partisans on the continent and raided Hitler's Fortress Europe. The Americans also deployed torpedo boats, and in the Pacific theatre John F Kennedy, a future President of the United States of America, served with distinction on one such vessel.

German and Italian torpedoes, be they delivered from E boats or submarines, could not strangle Britain. However, a more effective seaborne battle of attrition would have been possible if the Germans had concentrated on U-boat warfare much earlier. The crucial Battle of the Atlantic could have been even more alarming for the British Prime Minister had Germany been able to develop and deploy its more advanced *U*-boat, the Type XXI class, much sooner. These superior submarines were exactly what Germany needed to knock Britain out of the war, however they arrived too late and in too few numbers to contribute to German efforts to win the Battle of the Atlantic. Whilst the right technology did eventually exist, it could not have been developed earlier, not by Germany. The Fatherland's naval and industrial capabilities had been retarded by the Treaty of Versailles and the French and Belgian occupation of the Ruhr in the 1920s. Technical innovation and production had been stymied particularly by the Versailles *Diktat* and what was under development would take too long to come to fruition to save the Third Reich. In these circumstances defeat for the Kriegsmarine was just a matter of time. And besides any naval developments, pre-war, or during the conflict would have been countered by the Allies who were starting from a much more advanced position.

The success of the Allies in the Battle of the Atlantic enabled more shipping to cross the Atlantic Ocean. As Allied ship building more than compensated for the losses, the convoys were able to increase the number of vessels in each group. This expansion aided their defence and thus success bred more success. This not only kept hope alive but also helped hand victory to the Allies not just in the Battle of the Atlantic but also in the war. The fight was, however, long, and hard and though the Germans were defeated Nazi submariners equipped themselves well. The braveness, loyalty, and self-sacrifice of the U-boat crews was reflected in Hitler choosing their commander, Grand Admiral Dönitz, to become his successor upon the death of the Führer. The Admiral's surprising appointment made him the head of the Nazi state with the title of *Reichspräsident*. He and his government managed what remained of Nazi Germany from the town of Flensburg near the border with Denmark. His overriding aim was to make sure that as much of Germany's armed forces surrendered to the western Allies as possible and thus stay out of the clutches of the vengeful Soviets advancing over land from the east and from the north in Norway.

Hitler's Crocodile

"We came, we listened and we were conquered."— **US military planner, General Albert Coady Wedemeyer, on the United States being manoeuvred into adopting Churchill's Mediterranean strategy.**

Churchill's soft underbelly

In 1942 the Red Army was being put under enormous pressure by the Wehrmacht, many times the Soviet Union appeared to be close to the point of collapse. To alleviate the situation its leader, Joseph Stalin, implored his British and American counterparts to relieve the pressure bearing down upon his country by opening a second front in France. British Prime Minister Winston Churchill, and US President Franklin Roosevelt were minded to positively respond to his appeal but with varying degrees of enthusiasm.

The Americans were gung-ho for opening another front against Germany on mainland Europe. There were tentative plans for an invasion of France scheduled to take place as early as 1942. This aimed to come across the English Channel, capture the Cotentin Peninsula and French ports on the Atlantic coast. The following year would see the breakout from these substantial bridgeheads into the rest of the country. This invasion was codenamed Operation Sledgehammer. With America only recently in the war an invasion so early was not realistic. The postponement was not intended to last long. Alternative plans were produced under the supervision of General Dwight D. Eisenhower, a man that would become the Supreme Allied Commander in Europe and the 34th President of the United States. This envisaged a cross-channel invasion in 1943 and was codenamed Operation Roundup. Similarly, this was not feasible, the landing craft were not ready, and neither was the American soldier, their opportunity to get their blooding would have to come elsewhere. Neither were the Allies fully united. General Eisenhower was sceptical about Churchill's commitment to an invasion of France across the English Channel; indeed, Churchill had his own ideas as to where the G.I.s should be deployed.

The British Prime Minister's ancestor, John Churchill, 1st Duke of Marlborough, fought against the French Sun King, Louis XIV. At the time England, and then Great Britain, followed a grand strategy that included exhausting the economic resources of the enemy. Marlborough's descendant, Winston, supported a similar strategy. Prime Minister Churchill also favoured using American personnel, as well as their glut of weapons, and combining them with the British to win the war in North Africa and from there attack Germany via Italy and the Balkans. It was not the shortest way to Berlin, but the British Prime Minister saw his circuitous path as the surest and safest route. There were also strong historical precedents for attacking Britain's continental enemy via southern Europe. Churchill, a student of history, later the man that wrote it, knew that it took nearly two decades to defeat revolutionary France. He was in no rush to stop Hitler.

In the Napoleonic wars a British naval blockade helped achieve victory over Bonaparte. The threat which Britain posed to the French continental system provoked a series of errors that allowed Napoleon's enemies to whittle down the French army. In cataclysms such as the 1812 invasion of Russia, the might of France, and that of their collaborators, was destroyed. This was not the only folly embarked upon by the French emperor. Britain had earlier defeated Napoleon in the middle east. And on the other side of the Mediterranean Sea in the Iberian Peninsula; the British, rebel Spaniards, and Portuguese patriots would time and again defeat the French. Bonaparte's armies paid a high price for his desire to spread the continental system throughout mainland Europe. In the Iberian Peninsula, France haemorrhaged men fighting in the so-called Spanish ulcer. The original soft underbelly had reaped rewards and when the Duke of Wellington crossed the Pyrenees Britain was firmly at the top table of European affairs. In the next century, Winston Churchill thought that attacking the Axis powers at their weakest point was the key to victory. It also provided important political benefits.

Meandering towards Germany was not too dissimilar to the Gallipoli campaign in 1915, where he hoped that attacking the Ottoman Turks in the Dardanelles was the key to victory in World War One. That invasion attempt was intended to help the Russian empire, by securing the epeiric seas that connected it to the Mediterranean, it failed. In the Second World War, Churchill hoped that using the sea would afford him the opportunity to outflank the Red Army. And help him keep Soviet Russia in check by depriving the communists of the opportunity to conquer eastern Europe. Conversely, Stalin wanted Britain and America to invade from the west to keep them far away from his territorial ambitions.

Even though US Commanders opposed Churchill's Mediterranean strategy, in June 1942 the British Prime Minister met with Roosevelt in America and convinced him of his logic. The American's conceded and committed to fighting in North Africa. It was not unreasonable that the USA should follow Britain's lead, at that point in time there were more British soldiers holding arms in Europe than there were Americans in the theatre. Churchill's attitude to the Soviets was not entirely malevolent. Russia had not been abandoned and aid continued to flow to the USSR. Furthermore, the British Prime Minister did want to appease Stalin by demonstrating that the United Kingdom was standing beside the USSR and willing to engage the Germans in France. What followed demonstrated the folly of invading France until such time as Allied firepower could sweep the Germans from the French coast.

Whilst Churchill was unable to reopen the Western Front, he was willing to provide support for the Soviets by tying up the Wehrmacht in France. To that end a raid in force on the French port of Dieppe was proposed. It was hoped that this would show the British Empire's commitment to the conflict with the Germans. The UK's consistent North American allies, the Canadians, formed the largest contingent in this assault codenamed Operation Jubilee. The Dieppe debacle was meant to be the biggest in a series of raids. The port of Dieppe, across the English Channel, was to be held for just six hours in August 1942. In this combined operation there would be five main points of attack from the sea.

It was a poorly planned operation and launching an assault against a well defended port was always likely to result in horrendous casualties. British general Bernard Law Montgomery had advised that the operation should be postponed, permanently. Despite that, it still went ahead and indeed it did face difficulties from the start. The Germans guarding Dieppe may have suspected that the assault was imminent from intercepted BBC radio broadcasts. Whatever the reason, the British and Canadians as well as their tanks struggled to make it off the beaches without being killed or taken into captivity. It has been alleged by historian David O'Keefe that Commander Ian Fleming, later of Bond novel fame, devised the raid to seize an Enigma machine along with its code books and rotor setting sheets. This may have been one of many secondary motivations; a fourth rotor had been added by the Germans to those encryption devices, consequently British intelligence based at Bletchley Park were unable to crack the new code system leaving them blind. Whilst, capturing the Enigma was an aim it was not the mission's chief concern; it came as an afterthought after the decision had already been made.

The great discovery of the failed raid was that the operation clearly demonstrated what not to do and where not to attack. The conclusions were that for an Allied invasion of France to be successful there were several requirements. The element of surprise was demanded, sufficient supporting bombardment had to be delivered, and shingle beaches in which tanks would sink would need to be avoided. The cross-channel invasion would have to come ashore on sandy beaches; however, it would have to wait and first a victory would need to be secured in the mountains and deserts of North Africa. The failure of Operation Jubilee also proved *ex post facto* that attacking the weaker underbelly of Europe, far from the armoured north, was the prudent course of action. Britain would persistently push this southern strategy to its American partners.

Soft power

To advance British interests in the Americas Winston Churchill approved the establishment of British Security Co-ordination (BSC). This was part of the UK's Secret Intelligence Service (SIS), also known as MI6. Its agents sought to counter Axis influence, protect British interests, and influence American public and political opinion to support the United Kingdom. Amongst the most creative and expressive artists of modern English were enlisted to persuade the Americans to stand foursquare behind Britain's war aims. These ranged from authors such as war heros Roald Dahl and Ian Fleming, to philosopher Isaiah Berlin, classicist Gilbert Highet, and advertising expert David Ogilvy to name but a few. Also involved was the playwright, singer, and film director, Noël Coward. As well as his covert work for SIS he also openly produced propaganda for consumption on the home front. This ranged from the 1943 song *"Don't Let's Be Beastly to the Germans,"* mocking the notion of being merciful to Britain's enemies. Coward also directed the 1942 film *In Which We Serve* which was based upon Lord Louis Mountbatten's naval exploits. Mountbatten was also involved in supporting the work of the BSC.

These artists led a cultural campaign that was in terms of influence greater than the so-called British Invasion two decades later where England's popular rock 'n' roll beat musicians conquered America in the mid-1960s. The BSC influencers often used fake news. So successful was this campaign that most of the information passed to President Roosevelt by the Office of Strategic Services (OSS), a predecessor of the Central Intelligence Agency (CIA), originated from Britain's secret services. They even managed to convince Roosevelt that Hitler had a plan to invade South America. The President was incensed and publicly attacked this 'plan' on 24th October 1941. Hitler too was so outraged that he had been misrepresented that it may have contributed to the Führer's decision to declare war on America.

This was not the first time that Britain had manipulated the United States. Britain had established its empire, not through solely using the force of arms of its own citizens, but by co-opting foreign peoples to subjugate their neighbours and even fellow natives. The United Kingdom rarely won wars on its own. Both the First and Second World Wars saw British political leaders coax and cajole its one-time US opponent into supporting the British Empire. The UK's global dominance, propensity for innovation, and commercial ability to monetise the flow of information enabled Britain to establish as early as the Victorian era the so-called All Red Line telecommunication network that transported messages through cables laid on the ocean floor. One such wire linked the British Isles with North America. Britain was prepared for the information war. At the outbreak of war in 1914 the UK managed to sever German communications.

Germany was forced to communicate with the outside world via radio, which could easily be eavesdropped on from Britain's extensive radiotelegraphy network. Alternatively, they could use third countries cable networks that stretched to North America. Yet even those had to pass through Lands' End in the English County of Cornwall where the signal would be boosted before diving down under the Atlantic Ocean. Here Britain could and did intercept telegraph messages. One message that was intercepted and decoded by the British Admiralty's Room 40 cryptanalysis department was the infamous Zimmerman Telegram. This was a message promising support for Mexico to reclaim some territory annexed by American settlers and later incorporated into the United States. After a plausible cover story was invented that disguised the surreptitious source of the information, the message from the German Secretary of State for Foreign Affairs, Minister Arthur Zimmerman, was leaked to the United States. This enraged American public opinion and the US Congress voted to declare war on Germany in 1917.

There was also a wider strategy where Britain made sure that the information reaching the United States was what the United Kingdom wanted them to receive. With British and English language points of view being the most accessible to the American media and other opinion formers it was inevitable that Britain's political and wartime agenda would come to be a powerful influence on American foreign policy. Undersea cables remain important to this day, though they use more advanced fibreoptic technology. A British computer scientist, Sir Tim Berners-Lee, later invented the world wide web. In the modern age data is largely transferred between computers and servers via a network equivalent to the All Red Line. The level of security and privacy of this modern network is a matter of debate.

The British efforts and escapades during the two world wars would not be the last time that the United Kingdom used its soft power to sway American presidents to get involved in foreign adventures. Having established the wartime alliance and the post-war special relationship the UK more recently moved from black propaganda to open political influence and persuasion. When American Ambassador, April Glaspie, gave her seemingly near tacit prior approval of Saddam Hussein's plan to invade Kuwait, the Iraqi dictator, however, had the misfortune of occupying that country when Margaret Thatcher was in the US. The Iron lady told the American president, George H W Bush, "this is no time to go wobbly". The Prime Minister strengthened his backbone and America became committed to war in the middle east. A later UK Prime Minister, Tony Blair, manipulated Bush Snr's successor, Bill Clinton, to become more deeply involved in the Kosovo dispute. In that conflict ethnic Albanians Muslims in the Serbian region of Kosovo were fighting to secede from the Federal Republic of Yugoslavia, also then known as Serbia and Montenegro.

British Security Co-ordination, and Roald Dahl in particular, also helped Churchill understand the mind of Roosevelt and thus ensured that the two leaders would remain on good terms. Specifically, the British wanted to keep America focused on its Germany first policy. In US war planning this was given the code Rainbow 5. This originally proposed a large assault on Europe in 1943. General of the Army George Marshall, who was Chief of Staff of the United States Army, did not always support victory in Europe first, but Roosevelt, manipulated by Britain, kept him true to the original American goals, keeping his eyes on the prize but with a British twist.

Churchill desperately wanted American support to defeat Germany, yet stead-fastly held to his position of striking at Hitler through the soft under belly of the Nazi crocodile what was devouring freedom. Churchill's proposed strategy for 1942 to 1943 had three main facets. Firstly, supply the Soviets with arms and ammunition, secondly, launch a bombing campaign against Germany, and thirdly, attack the Axis powers via the Mediterranean and thus shift resources from western Europe so that the Allies would face less resistance when they attacked France. In 1943, the Prime Minister set out his strategic objectives; a cross-channel invasion was the bottom of his list. Churchill's grand vision for the future conduct of the war was not a Germany first policy but more specifically it put victory in North Africa as the prime mission.

Shifting desert sands

The first Allied victories of sorts over the Germans came in November 1941 from the newly formed British Eighth Army under Claude Auchinleck, Commander-in-Chief Middle East Command. This soon to be famous army was commanded by General Alan Cunningham, and later General Neil Ritchie. During Operation Crusader they drove the Axis forces back, relieved Tobruk, and even forced Rommel to flee as far back as El Aghelia close to the border between Tripolitania and Cyrenaica. This was essentially the point in Libya where Rommel's forces, then called the Africa Korps, had stated their assault against Britain the year before. The situation was to turn again. The British-led army had overreached itself, as had its commanders; Rommel struck back forcing the British to retreat.

At the Battle of Gazala in late May to June 1942 Rommel's Panzer Army attacked the multinational British Eighth Army commanded by General Ritchie, a man who had been promoted beyond his capabilities by Claude Auchinleck. To counter Rommel's lightning tactics Ritchie grouped his army together within a series of strung-out rigid boxes, each may have been defensively strong, but they were outmanoeuvred and could be eliminated one-by-one by Rommel's free flowing units. The overwhelming force triumphed against Ritchie's very moveable army which galloped from Gazala all the way back to Egypt; leaving the important port of Tobruk, along with its supplies and tens of thousands of men, to fall into Axis hands. The loss of Tobruk, a vital port, was a great blow to Churchill and British military prestige. Despite this, President Roosevelt responded by increasing supply to the Eighth Army in North Africa. Included in the provision of weapons were, the most up-to-date American tanks, M4 Shermans, and heavy bombers from the United States Army Air Forces. Spitfires came from the RAF. This build-up of interdiction aircraft would be to the detriment of German and Italian supplies.

The speed of Rommel's success also played a part in his undoing. Not only did he reach beyond his supply lines, but he also created the mirage of an impending Axis victory against Britain in Egypt. The appearance that the middle east would fall, along with the important port of Alexandria and the Suez Canal, and all the oil that lay beyond it, encouraged the cancellation of Operation *Herkules*, the plan to capture Malta. Albert Kesselring, a Field Marshal in the Luftwaffe, and Commander-in-Chief South wanted to take Malta but Hitler and Göring instead gave Rommel the resources for another push in North Africa. Rommel ignored his previous advice that Malta must be secured, or North Africa would be lost, and drove into Egypt. Many of the Luftwaffe planes that were harrying the Maltese archipelago and preparing to support the purported invasion, were transferred to the fighting in Egypt's western desert. That switch of airpower, along with the continued strength of the Royal Navy, made an assault on Malta unfeasible. The British from those islands were now free to continue disrupting Axis supplies to North Africa and to use their Maltese base to defend their own logistics.

Auchinleck ordered a retreat that went as far as a defensive position in Egypt, west of Alexandria, to an area centred around a small town on the coastal railway that ran across northern Egypt. The town is called El-Alamein. Auchinleck made a number of important changes; Ritchie was sacked, and The Auk, as he was nicknamed, took direct control of the Eighth Army. Ritchie's failed concepts were also abandoned, and Auchinleck with the assistance and advice of one of his staff officers, Major General Eric Dorman-Smith, devised brigade groups. These were smaller mobile units containing armour, infantry, and artillery that could react in unison against Rommel's Axis forces. The Eighth Army was now more flexible. Independent artillery was also added and put under a unified command, this allowed for the concentration of barrages on enemy weak points. The Eighth Army was now in a better position to fight and they could do so from a much more secure location.

The geography of the area where Auchinleck sat his army offered the enemy few options for attack other than a direct assault, there could be no sweeping movements around his flank. The potential battlefield consisted of just a 40-mile front line with the sea to the north and the Qattara Depression to the south. The southern flank abutted a 200-mile expanse of below sea level salt marsh that was described in the 1958 British war film *Ice Cold in Alex* as being, "Liquid, with a dried crust on top rather like a mouldy rice pudding." The topography also included sand dunes. Whilst an Austin K2/Y ambulance, known affectionately as a Katy, could in theory navigate the Qattara Depression, it was however, almost impassable to a large army. And where the front line's terrain could support armoured vehicles there were several ridges that aided the defender.

Throughout most of July 1942 Rommel tried to break through in the hope that he could then capture Cairo, capital of the nominally independent Kingdom of Egypt. The Eighth Army struck back, often scoring victories against the hapless Italians, but were unable to force the German army from an equally defensible position between the sea and the great marsh to the south. The narrowness of the front and mutual exhaustion meant that the First Battle of El Alamein became a stalemate. August 1942 saw the high watermark of the Third Reich. German troops sat on the Volga and atop the Caucasus mountains and were on the face of it bearing down on the Suez Canal. The situation on all fronts was, however, about to change dramatically. Winston Churchill removed Claude Auchinleck and replaced him as the C-in-C of Middle East Command with General Sir Harold Alexander. Churchill also appointed the tired, and admittedly out of ideas, Lieutenant-General William Gott to become the new General Officer Commanding Eighth Army, likewise replacing Auchinleck who had been acting in that role. Fate however intervened. Gott was killed soon after his plane was shot down. Upon making a crash landing the aircraft was then strafed by Luftwaffe fighters on the runway in Cairo. Lieutenant-General Bernard Law Montgomery was then put in charge of the Eighth Army. His destiny and that of Rommel would be intertwined for much of the next two years. Rommel was effective at making bold attacks but did not pay enough attention to administration and logistics. He could often read the enemies movements but could not see the bigger picture. Montgomery could marshal the home front, he would visit munitions factories to motivate the workers, and deploy all the talents and strength that his substantial and growing army had to offer.

Magic and *Materialschlacht*

The Second World War produced many great commanders, two stand out as masters of *materialschlacht*, or the material battle. In such a confrontation victory would be achieved by overwhelming the enemy through the successful application of a superior quantity or quality of weapons. One notable commander that excelled at the war of attrition was Georgy Zhukov, another, Britain's Bernard Law Montgomery. Monty, as he was known to his men, called his approach to attritional warfare 'crumbling'. This involved a series of limited attacks that were designed to wear down and destroy the enemy whilst preserving enough forces in reserve to defend from counterattacks. These kept back forces would also allow a commander to retain balance, or flexibility, so that he can respond to changing circumstances as the battle unfolds. Unlike Zhukov, who sacrificed soldiers and tanks at Rzhev, the British general carried out his materiel war whilst trying not to waste the lives of his men. Monty considered his soldiers to be an important asset that should be physically fit, skilled at fighting, motivated, and knowledgeable as to the task that was expected of them. Montgomery excelled at enthusing his army with those attributes, as a trainer and communicator he was second to none.

Bernard Law Montgomery transformed the dejected Eighth Army. The situation with the British and Axis armies sitting on either side of substantial minefields could not endure for long; another battle was coming. Monty scrapped Claude Auchinleck's plans to retreat up the Nile should that battle be lost. Monty's spoke to his troops, and said,

"Here we will stand and fight; there will be no further withdrawal. I have ordered that all plans and instructions dealing with further withdrawal are to be burnt, and at once. We will stand and fight here. If we can't stay here alive, then let us stay here dead."

Monty trained and motivated his men to fight. He told them that the "bad times are over". He also provided the fresh approach, new ideas, and the confidence in those ideas that Winston Churchill and General Sir Alan Brooke, the Chief of the Imperial General Staff (CIGS), were looking for. Montgomery observed that the desire to achieve a breakthrough was leading to only a temporary respite and would be followed by a counterstrike forcing a retreat back to the original starting point. The new British commander envisioned that a novel approach was needed that would end, permanently, the to and fro fighting in North Africa, which was categorised with rapidly shifting back and forth frontlines. Montgomery's solution was to use his crumbling tactics, not just in one battle but over the course of two. Rommel elected to attack first before Montgomery's supply of soldiers and tanks reached a critical mass that would all but guarantee him victory over the Axis forces in the autumn.

Attrition at El Alamein

The ridge at Alam el Halfa, to the south of El Alamein, was transformed into a strong bastion. Atop this hill were placed anti-tank weapons, even armour was to be used in the role of providing anti-panzer artillery. When the attack came in late August 1942, Montgomery's soldiers wore down Rommel's armour. The German general was forced to retreat back behind his own network of mines, machine guns, and anti-tank weapons. These would in time be used in an attempt to try and destroy Montgomery's attacking tanks, but the advantage in the western desert of Egypt was now forever with the British. Montgomery was free to launch his attack when the build-up of men and machines was complete, this would be October 1944, the Battle of Alam el Haifa had only briefly delayed the assembling of his strike force. The only question was where Montgomery would attack.

The German position, between the Qattara Depression and the sea, could not be outflanked. The only option was to crack and then break through a short stretch of land heavily defended by minefields and interlocking fields of fire from the dreaded 8.8-centimetre anti-aircraft and anti-tank guns. A battle of attrition was required, with Rommel now on the defensive, where would Montgomery direct his initial assault? Conventional wisdom dictated an attack in the south, pinning the Axis forces against the British controlled sea. Montgomery, however, chose to strike first in the north. That was not what Rommel was expecting, the German commander had been outthought before his army was outfought.

Dudley Clarke, a South African officer in the British Army, and Archibald Wavell, during his time in charge in the middle east, established 'A' Force to devise deception operations. Their maxim was 'that every real operation should have a complementary deception.' They had already devised Operation Cascade which successfully exaggerated the size of the British forces facing the Germans and unbalanced Rommel's' plans. There was even a contribution from a magician, Jasper Maskelyne, who devised a plan to hide the Suez Canal. In the prelude to the Second Battle of El Alamein, Operation Bertram fooled the Germans into thinking that the attack was not imminent and that it would be in the south. It was a complete success.

On 23rd October Montgomery launched his offensive against the Axis forces in the north, close to the Mediterranean Sea. Monty predicted that his battle of El Alamein would last 12 days, it lasted twelve days. He predicted that there would be three stages to his battle: the break-in, the dogfight, and then the breakout. Montgomery's armour, artillery, and airpower were decisive. The effect of his Spitfires in support of the ground offensive had a debilitating effect on Axis morale. The German and Italian forces were routed. Montgomery and the Eighth Army pursued the German-Italian Panzer Army across North Africa fighting several other battles and engagements on the way. Rommel was chased as far as Tunisia in what was one of the longest and swiftest advances of World War Two. The retreat did not stop at North Africa, the Nazi German empire was now past its zenith, from then on bar a few isolated successes the Wehrmacht would be forced to retreat all the way back to Berlin.

Croque monsieur

Whilst Montgomery was pursuing Rommel from the east, the Allies did launch a substantial new front in the west coming in a region known as Tamazgha. This was technically an invasion of France. Italy, Britain, and Spain were not alone in ruling parts of the coast of north Africa. France, another colonial power, had also taken control of large parts of Africa from the Sahara Desert to the Mediterranean Sea. In those lands Arabic and Berber languages were predominant. It was the perfect soft launch for American soldiers to enter the war.

In November 1942, the Allies executed Operation Torch, as the Anglo-American invasion of French North Africa was known. In three taskforces, under the overall command of Eisenhower, British and American soldiers landed on soil controlled by the regime of Vichy France. On the Atlantic coast of the French protectorate of Morocco, US soldiers in the western taskforce, under then Major General George S Patton, landed and quickly took Casablanca. Further east, coming ashore via the Mediterranean Sea, the centre taskforce took Oran, scene of the British naval attack more than two years before. A further predominantly British contingent in the eastern taskforce assaulted Algiers. Both those two cities were in French Algeria which since 1848 was an integral part of France and administered as if it were the same as any other part of the metropolitan French state. Following the Second World War many Muslims in Algeria fought a bloody war to achieve independence causing a political crisis in mainland France. Following the collapse of the Fourth Republic, a referendum was held to determine the future of Algeria, most voted for independence. In 1962 Algeria left both France and the European Economic Community to which it also belonged.

To make the Allied occupation of this territory more palatable to the French it was presented as an American operation, Churchill feared that there would be strong resistance to a British invasion. There was resistance from forces still loyal to the Vichy regime, though this quickly ceased when French admiral, and politician, François Darlan, ordered their surrender in exchange for his receiving political power in North Africa. His switching sides, from the Vichy government to the Allies, so enraged Hitler that he responded to Darlan's betrayal by occupying the remainder of mainland southern France, the *zone libre*, which according to the armistice was meant to be free of German forces. Hitler also tried to seize the French fleet at anchor in Toulon, a port city on the French Riviera. However, to keep these vessels out of German hands the fleet was scuttled, though some submarines escaped to join the Free French in Algiers. The Axis did, however, succeed in occupying the French protectorate of Tunisia.

The destination of Operation Torch would be the capture of Tunis, the capital city of Tunisia. With Montgomery and his Eighth Army advancing from the east a link up with Operation Torch coming from the west, would give the allies control over the entirety of the southern Mediterranean coastline. This would not be achieved without substantial resistance, yet that was to the advantage of the Allies; Hitler was pouring in troops into what was to become yet another self-guarding prison camp.

Between a rock and a hard place

Erwin Rommel was again at odds with his colleagues. Rommel had earlier thought that Kesselring was not supplying enough airpower to support the doomed campaign to drive Britain out of Egypt. Their views contrasted again over strategy in Tunisia. Kesselring advocated a defensive strategy using the advantage the mountains gave them, whereas Rommel wanted to be bold and attack. On the occasions when they agreed the *Comando Supremo* of the *Regio Esercito*, Royal Italian Army, based in Rome, meddled in Rommel's plans.

Neither of the contradictory strategies could square the equation. The choice was between expand and die or hold the line and be killed. If the Axis remained static it would be corralled and then crushed. Driving forward would push their supply train to breaking point, superior Allied naval and air airpower would complete the shattering of Axis logistics. The enormity of the British empire was too great; Germany could not advance far enough to defeat it. Beyond the Mediterranean Sea, with the rock of Gibraltar and the Suez Canal under British control, lay the Anglosphere. America, Canada, Australia, New Zealand, the United Kingdom, India, and South Africa to name but a few of the colonially produced network of anti-Nazi states dominated the seas and could suffocate the Third Reich. In North Africa there were no obstacles that could prevent a withdrawal, it was always possible to take the British Army out of harm's way. With the League of Nations mandating UK control over much of the middle east and with the British occupying southern Iran, the UK still had an empire that stretched from Egypt to India. The subcontinent itself provided soldiers for the fighting in North Africa. They were supported by a mighty fleet of ships and aircrafts that could resupply Allied servicemen. Germany lacked resources and, due to its historic focus on central Europe, did not have the global links to win a world war.

History is littered with examples of imperial overreach that should have been apparent to all but those who were obsessed with the 'will' as the determining factor in military affairs. Germany's own tactics should have demonstrated the folly of recklessly overreaching their limited logistics.

Parthian shot

One tactic that did give the Germans success was the sword and shield. It was a modern iteration of the ploys used by the Greco-Persian influenced Parthian Empire which came to dominate much of Iran and fought to both defend themselves and establish Parthia as Rome's nemesis. They used a stratagem known as the Parthian shot. This was an ancient and tried and tested tactic where horsemen would draw in the enemy and shoot arrows from their technically advanced and deadly composite bows. The Parthian light cavalry ploy involved horsemen feigning retreat only to turn on their stead and fire their arrows at a bewildered and exhausted enemy. The job was complemented by Parthian armoured knights known as Cataphracts, these heavy cavalrymen would then charge and obliterate their foe. The Parthians repeatedly used such combined assaults to defeat and Roman *triumvir* Marcus Licinius Crassus at the Battle of Carrhae in 53 BC.

Rommel's panzers would perform the role of the cavalry, they would draw an enemy's tanks into range of the glorious 88 mm anti-aircraft gun. These cannons which served as both flak and artillery weapons had superb range and power, they fired a high-velocity shell at its intended target with reassuring precision coming from the accuracy of its analogue computer aiding the gunner. The use of *Flugabwehrkanone*, flight-defence cannons, to kill tanks was not novel. The Germans used similar weapons in such a role in the First World War during the 1917 Battle of Cambrai to counter a British armoured blitzkrieg. In that engagement the British used massed tank attacks, supported by airpower. A generation later, Rommel's forces combined the use of armour and anti-tank weapons to devastating effect.

In February 1943 Rommel set a trap for the Americans into which they were all too willing to advance. His chosen battlefield was the Kasserine Pass, here he had the dual aim of inflicting a psychological defeat on the Americans that would give the G.I.s what Rommel described as an 'inferiority complex.' The second more tangible objective was that the German general hoped to seize the American supply base at Tébessa in Algeria. Heavy losses were first inflicted on the Free French at Faïd in Tunisia and then on the Americans at Sidi Bou Zid and the Battle of Kasserine Pass. US tanks, charging like cavalry, were easily ambushed. After US failures in Tunisia, the Allies adapted to these cunning and effective German tactics.

The old one-two

During the interwar years, the United Kingdom had been developing modern warfare and devised how for instance armour and airpower could be integrated. Conversely, the United States, without a substantial overseas empire had reverted to its original isolationist ideology, and thus neglected to invest adequate resources into its military. Least prepared were its commanders who were at that early stage devoid of the knowledge needed to fight a war.

General Sir Harold Alexander, who was overseeing the Allied fight in the Mediterranean basin, with perhaps some old-world arrogance, was politely disparaging of the unfulfilled potential of the American army in Tunisia. This was not entirely unfounded. The British had been actively fighting the Germans since 1940, and sometimes with success. They had learned valuable lessons and proved the quality of its battle tested commanders. Those that were incompetent or could not command the trust of their companions were removed from their positions. Operation Torch was the first opportunity in the European theatre to carry out this Darwinian process. A notable sacking was that of Lloyd Fredendall. The fighting exposed the fact that he had been promoted beyond his abilities, the US general was held responsible for the debacle at Kasserine Pass and was duly sent back to America by Eisenhower.

In the Tunisia campaign British generals shared their experience with their American comrades and instilled in them the knowledge of how to win. General Omar Bradley of the US Army commended Harold Alexander for nurturing the American field command into effective leaders. Bradley explained that during this time the Americans had "learned to crawl, to walk — then run." Clearly in 1943 it was still too early for them to attempt a cross-channel invasion of mainland France. However, after gaining experience of their own in Tunisia, Sicily, and then mainland Italy, the G.I.'s grew to become a mighty band of brothers. Yet, some snobbery was still directed towards the Americans whose soldiers were as inexperienced as their generals.

For the time being America's raw recruits could not be relied upon to perform the crumbling operations at which the UK's soldiers were beginning to excel. The British Army was known for its resilient martial qualities. The British Isles with few natural resources demonstrated that a country's biggest asset is its people. The traditionally small size of the British Army had necessitated its professionalisation. A well-schooled officer corps produced highly drilled soldiers and sailors whose rate of fire, be that from a line of ships at battles such as at Trafalgar or the line of men at Waterloo, could outpace that of continental conscripts. Whereas Soviet commanders, for example, achieved victory through the blood of their own men pressed into service, British commanders had learned to triumph by making the enemy lay down his life for his country and creed.

A division of labour subsequently emerged between the two English speaking peoples. The British soldier took the responsibility for battles of attrition, fixing the enemy, and directly taking on the *Heer* and *Waffen-SS* at their points of strength, tying them up and then grinding them down. In the same offensive operation, the Americans would use manoeuvre, aided by their superior trucks, to get into the enemy's rear at weak points and from there the enemy was surrounded and defeated. This was described by Harold Alexander as 'the old one two'. This approach to warfare was replicated in Sicily, northern Italy, Normandy, the Ruhr, and even into the modern era where the differing roles were undertaken in the 1991 Gulf War. Its success was self-evident, and reminiscent of an earlier Alexander whose phalanx formation held the enemy whilst the Companion cavalry was the arm of decision breaking through and falling upon his foe's flanks and rear. In World War Two, the Anglo-American alliance had perfected these hammer and anvil tactics, but the different tasks led to the mistaken belief that the British were slow.

Montgomery's Eighth Army was advancing from Tripoli into Tunisia. In early March he repelled Rommel's attack at the Battle of Medenine. Rommel was defeated and conducted a rapid withdrawal with himself finally leaving Africa. Upon calling on Hitler to abandon the north African littoral he must have also appeared to be dejected. General von Armin, who in March 1943 succeeded Rommel as commander of the recently formed German and Italian Army Group Africa, favoured a more cautious and defensive approach. It was logical, yet the approach of his enemies was remorseless. The next obstacle in Monty's way was the Mareth Line, a series of fortifications built by the French in the 1930s close to their protectorate's border with Italian occupied Libya. Montgomery, attacking through a mountain pass to the east, circumvented these defences and by the end of March had won the Battle of the Mareth Line. The Tunisian campaign had decisively turned against the Italian German occupiers which were now being pressed back from the west and south. Tunis, and its wealthy suburb of Carthage, fell to the 7th Armoured Division, who are known colloquially by their appellation "the Desert Rats." They had been transferred from Monty's Eighth Army.

Casablanca

With the British Empire still the biggest contributor in men to the fight and with His Majesty's forces victorious, triumphs on the battlefield were matched by successes at the negotiating table. At the Casablanca conference in January 1943 the British delegation adopted General Sir Alan Brooke's proposal for an invasion of Sicily and then Italy proper. The Americans were manipulated into agreeing this as the next target, there was little British compromise; the US failed to secure a firm commitment as to when the cross-channel invasion of France would take place. General Marshall's principal adviser at Casablanca, Brigadier General Albert Coady Wedemeyer wrote, ' …we lost our shirts and… are now committed to a subterranean umbilicus operation in mid-summer…. We came, we listened and we were conquered.' However, it did not all go Churchill's way.

Churchill had given little thought to war aims and what the goal of victory was; the vacuum was filled by his American counterpart. President Roosevelt unexpectedly announced to the media that the Allies were demanding the unconditional surrender of Germany, Italy, and Japan. This, perhaps as much as the totalitarian nature of the Nazi Reich, made sure the war endured longer than it may otherwise have. It left influential Germans little room for manoeuvre other than fight onto the bitter end. Roosevelt may not have understood the full implications of this announcement. Political theatre played a role. A former US President Ulysses S Grant was, prior to entering politics, known as Unconditional Surrender Grant. He earned this name from the successes he had against the armies of the Confederacy at a time when he was one of the few successful Union commanders. Despite Grant being a pro-emancipation Republican, and FDR being a member of the segregationist Democrat Party, the current President found the demand of unconditional surrender to be politically important to his domestic audience. Field Marshal Montgomery, in his seminal work *A History of Warfare*, critiqued the demand for an uncompromising victory as it gave Germany no way-out bar total defeat and the enormous loss of life that this entailed. It did however reassure the Soviet Union. Joseph Stalin feared that the western Allies would make a separate peace with the Germans, leaving the Soviet Union to face the full onslaught of the German army. The communist leader could now be assured of his Allies commitment and he, still embattled around Stalingrad, need not come to terms with Hitler.

Whilst Churchill may have negotiated with a non-Hitlerite Germany in 1940, Britain was no longer looking into the abyss. The Soviet dictator need not have worried, the bird of peace had already flown. German overtures to the British had already been rejected. In 1941, Rudolf Hess, Deputy Führer of the Nazi Party, flew to Britain with Hitler's approval to offer a possible peace treaty and leave western Europe in exchange for a free hand in the east. Making Britain neutral in a war between Germany and Russia. Hess was hoping to contact the Duke of Hamilton, a Scottish nobleman, and ask him to contact Churchill. However, it was too much of a mountain to overcome and Hess found himself captured by a pitchfork wielding ploughman called David Maclean. There were Nazi sympathisers in Scotland, but the duke was not one of them. Support for the Germans came from a former SNP leader Arthur Donaldson who wanted to establish Scotland as a Vichy style state in Germany's wider European empire. He was not alone and boasted a network that was willing to act to undermine Churchill's war effort. Other notable Nazi-lite Scottish Nationalists were William Power, and Andrew Dewar Gibb an SNP Chairman. Scots entreating with continental demagogic regimes was a regular occurrence. Generations before Scottish leaders had aligned with Roman Catholic France to undermine their old enemy, England. Nevertheless, this mission failed and according to Hess' suggestion Hitler then encouraged the myth that his Deputy was acting on his own. Hess would not be the last Nazi to try and entreat with the Allies. Head of the SS, Heinrich Himmler, later tried to negotiate with the Allies but to no avail. Himmler, in April 1944, believing in the power of international Jewry, sought to rectify Germany's shortage of transport vehicles, and reduce the German reliance on oxen by trading Jews for trucks and other wares. The Allies did not entertain these overtures.

Churchill's Mediterranean strategy was seen to be vindicated when in May 1943 the Axis forces surrendered in Tunisia. In that theatre alone Germany and Italy had lost more than a quarter of a million soldiers, killed, or captured. It was a defeat comparable to the Red Army's victory at Stalingrad, yet Britain and America achieved it at a substantially lower cost. What is more, the Third Reich forfeited much materiel. German attempts to resupply their forces in North Africa led to the destruction of Axis weapons that instead of being on their way to the Eastern Front, found themselves sent to the bottom of the Mediterranean Sea. The final capture of Tunis was one of many British inspired victories. Churchill's strategy in North Africa also complemented America's preference for the precision bombing of crucial Axis controlled installations. Benghazi in Libya was the base from which USAAF B-24 Liberator bombers set out to try and destroy Romanian oil refineries in Ploieşti. The jaws were closing on Germany. With the severe setbacks on the Eastern Front and with North Africa cleansed of Axis forces, Germany was now losing the conventional war, the clandestine conflict was also faring little better.

The secret war

Britain was the proverbial spanner in the works of Hitler's plans for dominion over Europe, sometimes literally. Agents from the United Kingdom, working with national resistance movements, disrupted industry across the continent from Norway to Greece. Closer to the UK, agents from Churchill's Special

Operations Executive carried out Operation Josephine and worked with the French resistance to destroy electrical substations serving Axis submarine bases on the French Atlantic coast near Bordeaux. Churchill's Ministry of Ungentlemanly Warfare achieved great success, many more were to follow. The SOE were not the only threat to German logistics and infrastructure. Other commando raids also targeted shipping in Bordeaux. Operation Frankton carried out by the Royal Marine Boom Patrol Detachment (RMBPD), applicable to the Special Boat Service, attacked vessels carrying German imports of rubber via the French port. This was one of the great raids of the war and the sacrifice of the British commandos was immortalised in the film *The Cockleshell Heroes*. The multitude of UK linked attacks on the continent raised British morale and forced the Germans to divert forces from the frontline and redeploy them to work in internal security. The response of the Nazis to such sabotage operations often involved reprisals against the civilian population in the locale of the attack, such a response further alienated already embittered people. This just created more passive resistance which further undermined the economic battle to produce enough war materiel. Similarly, it encouraged civilians to switch sides and join British assisted resistance organisations, Nazi Germany was entering a death spiral. The only question was how much damage their eventual collapse would leave behind.

Germany was destined to lose the secret war. Nazi ideology and German control over nations that had experienced freedom ran contrary to peoples' hopes and desires for life. This state of affairs would be resisted. The excesses of Nazism were repulsive to even many Germans. Admiral Canaris, the chief of the German military intelligence organisation known as the *Abwehr* was decidedly working on a covert basis to undermine Hitler, Nazi Germany, and even his own country's war effort. Not only had he hid from his Führer the date of the Torch landings, but Canaris even actively worked with British intelligence.

Deception, *doppelgängers*, and delusion

British creativity and high cunning were put to good use in the Mediterranean theatre. After the surrender of Axis forces in North Africa the next logical steppingstone was the island of Sicily. It had been fought over for millennia by Greek city states, Epirus, which partly equated southern Albania, Carthage, Rome, Vandals, Ostrogoths, Byzantium, Arabs, Vikings, and Normans. From the late twelfth century Sicily was even briefly ruled by Germanic kings. With other owners having come and gone, namely Spain and France, Britain and America then wanted to control this strategic island. To ease their conquest the Germans would need to be convinced that the Allies would come ashore elsewhere. Fascist associated Falangist Spain, and its intimate relationship with Nazi Germany would be the mark, or patsy, in this British game of trickery.

Generalissimo Franco, dictator of Spain, turned a blind eye to German spies, in particular those monitoring British shipping through the Straits of Gibraltar. This led to the loss of many Allied ships, but Britain was about to equalise the score. One *Abwehr* agent, Adolf Clauss, was identified as a target who would be duped into providing false information as to the impending Allied landings. This plan, that may have originated from author Ian Fleming, was called Operation Mincemeat. It involved a false letter planted on a corpse purporting to be a British Acting Major in the Royal Marines. The cadaver was brought ashore in Spain where it came to the attention of Clauss. Fictional correspondence planted on the deceased person suggested that the Allies will land in Greece and Sardinia instead of Sicily, and that any suggestion that Sicily was the target was just a clever ruse. The German spy passed on this false information regarding the location of Allied attacks in the Mediterranean in 1943. It was then taken to Germany by an agent known as the Shadow, Major Karl-Erich Kühlenthal, he was a half-Jewish spy for Nazi Germany. Hitler was convinced and accordingly the Peloponnese and Sardinia were reinforced to the detriment of Sicily. As Kühlenthal was a protégé of Canaris one cannot be sure as to the Shadow's real motivations.

Later in the war the British were to unleash other plans to dupe Hitler. Actor, and British Army Lieutenant-Colonel, David Niven, had a role in sending a Bernard Law Montgomery lookalike to Gibraltar and North Africa to dupe the Germans into thinking that the main invasion of mainland Europe would be mounted against southern France rather than against the northern French coast. Actor M. E. Clifton James, the man who impersonated the British general played himself in a 1958 film about the deception titled *I Was Monty's Double*. This operation was known as Operation Copperhead. There were also other schemes that helped fix German attention away from the Normandy beaches.

Decision time

There were other dashing missions carried out in the Mediterranean. Britain's Special Operation Executive kidnapped German Major-General Heinrich Kreipein from Crete. However, this provoked severe reprisals on the local population from the man that was the original intended target. Hitler was obsessed with the threat of an Allied invasion of Greece and saw possible sites for the opening of a new front in all places other than the location for the main landings that were to come in France. It was a reasonable belief, actions in the Mediterranean theatre were substantial in size. Indeed, the invasion of Sicily, codenamed Operation Husky, was, in the number of men involved, larger than the quantity that landed on the Normandy beaches on D-Day.

The Trident Washington Conference held between Roosevelt and Churchill took place in May 1943, it confirmed the details for the attack on Sicily and put the invasion of France back a year to May 1944. Churchill insisted on Italy being the next target and even made suggestions about further operations in the Balkans. There was further dissension between American and British strategists, whilst negotiations did reach an accord, George Marshall had only wanted to commit to an invasion of Sardinia. Eventually Alan Brooke persuaded Eisenhower to support the invasion of Italy, but the Americans would only do so if the invasion of Sicily was successful.

In July, the Anglo-American Operation Husky was underway. It gradually took over Sicily and opened more of the Mediterranean to Allied naval and air traffic. The next steppingstone was mainland Italy. Montgomery and his Eighty Army, preparing for the invasion, left Patton's Seventh Army to take Messina. The German army had retreated from Sicily to Calabria, the toe of Italy, which was less than two miles away across the narrow Strait of Messina. With Sicily secured in August, the Italian peninsula would soon be assaulted by sea and from the air. Allied bombers were to contribute to what could have been a theatre changing event. US planes targeted Rome's railway marshalling yards and industrial areas. Yet, they also destroyed civilian parts of the city, including the San Lorenzo district, causing much loss of life. The high death toll encouraged the Italian population to protest the war. The bombing proved to be a catalyst for Italy's departure from the Axis.

The boot

After these shocking aerial attacks and a string of military defeats the Italian people, rarely united behind their many governments, were now largely unified in opposition to the war. No longer would they tolerate the hardships caused by this conflict that had found its way to Italian soil. They were also firmly against their country's disastrous alliance with Germany. This feeling ran even as far as Benito Mussolini himself; he was minded to seek an exit from the war and cancel his agreements with Hitler. The Italian dictator, however, dithered but members of his own government acted.

Plots to remove the leader of the Italian government were now underway. In July, Mussolini's Fascist Council told him at a meeting called by *Il Duce* that they had no confidence in him, the next day King Victor Emmanuelle III formally dismissed Mussolini, kicking him from office and having him placed under arrest. After the overthrow of Mussolini, the King appointed Marshal Pietro Badoglio as Prime Minister. He announced that Italy would remain fighting on the Axis side yet began covert negotiations with the Allies. His plan was to find an accommodation with Britain and America; however, little was done in Italy to establish what they themselves would find acceptable. Regardless of that, Badoglio was hesitant not to provoke an aggressive German reaction. This was to have grave consequences.

With the Sicilian steppingstone secured, mainland Axis Italy was next in line. The Eighth Army amphibious assault on the toe of Italy, called Operation Baytown, came ashore on 3rd September. The initial landings were a success; Italian resistance was quickly overcome; they had been bamboozled by the supporting barrage. Montgomery, despite commanding the operation, objected to the plans for this landing. Monty rightly felt that the location of the invasion was too far south and correctly surmised that the Germans would retreat and not give battle making the whole endeavour a waste of time and misallocation of resources. Kesselring ordered that his forces withdraw north and disrupt the Eighty Army's advance by destroying bridges. The commitment of resources to Baytown was one of many missed opportunities in Italy. Six days later the British, in Operation Slapstick, also made a successful amphibious assault on the heel of Italy capturing the port of Taranto on the Ionian Sea.

The landings on Italy's Calabrian coast were intended as a diversion to tie-up German forces and thus make them less able to resist Operation Avalanche, the Anglo-American landings at Salerno, south of Naples. This was scheduled for 9th September. The Italian government under Marshal Badoglio wanted the landings to be nearer Rome to prevent the Germans from seizing the capital, which the Nazis duly did. Rome's Jewish population paid a particularly high price, in October 1943 many were deported to Auschwitz. The following March, in response to an attack by the Italian resistance, the SS massacred 335 Italians in the Ardeatine caves in Rome and concealed their bodies which were discovered after the war.

Italy sought an armistice with the Allies and signed the surrender on 3rd September 1943, yet it was announced on the 8th day of the month. Italy had admitted defeat in a war they were never capable of properly prosecuting. Italian industry produced some effective piston driven aircraft, fighter planes with flare. The *Regia Marina* possessed at the start of the war a not insignificant navy. This was logical for a nation that was primarily surrounded by water, with colonies across the sea in Libya, Somalia on the horn of Africa, and briefly Ethiopia. In time those colonies became independent countries but are now amongst the most troubled nations in Africa.

Salerno was chosen as the location of the main American landings in Italy as it was within range of Allied fighter cover based on Sicily and near to the important port of Naples, which was indeed captured after the landings. This strike at the shin of Italy was a close run. The Americans at Salerno were still inexperienced, and this showed in the desperate fighting that followed. Superior numbers, along with Allied airpower, and naval fire, did save the troops at Salerno who were under threat of being pushed back into the sea. The US commander, Lieutenant General Mark Clark, actually considered a withdrawal, where they would re-embark on the ships from whence they came. Despite the armistice there was still some Italian resistance to the Anglo-American landings. The political loyalties of many Italian soldiers would remain divided.

The new Italian government not only left the German-led Axis but also eventually joined the side of the United Nations and from October fought against Nazi Germany. Though not all Italian soldiers came over, some stayed loyal to the Nazis. Despite Admiral Canaris seeking to hide the fact that Italy was due to switch sides, Hitler still surmised that his Axis partners would defect. His suspicions were correct. The Kingdom of Italy, prior to World War One, had been aligned with the so-called Central Powers of Germany and Austria-Hungary and was expected to enter the war on their side. Yet, they received a better deal from the Triple Entente. In return for joining with the Allies, they were promised the opportunity to annex part of Austria. This inversion of grand strategy was effectively repeated in the Second World War. Germany had anticipated this and acted decisively.

It had become clear that with the fall of *Il Duce*, and without the Italian forces supporting the Axis war effort, the German position was further weakened. The Führer was forced to move German troops from western Europe to keep the Balkans secure, and protect their all-important oil supplies from eastern Europe. There were two schools of thought as to how Germany should respond to the war in mainland Italy. Field Marshal Erwin Rommel favoured falling back to the Alps; he hoped this would give the Germans more time to form an impregnable defensive barrier, or so he thought. Albert Kesselring, however, favoured a different strategy. He observed that Italy's mountainous terrain, a spine running down the country, dissected by rivers, formed natural barriers to the Allies. These could be reinforced with fixed defences. Despite his earlier retreat from southern Italy, Kesselring favoured occupying the parts of Italy that did not already have an Allied presence. The Nazis, and what remained of their Italian collaborators, could tie up the Allies and force them to expend resources in both men and materiel in a slow gruelling slog up the peninsula.

Maintaining German control over Italy was important to both Kesselring and the Führer. They wanted to keep the war as far away from Germany as possible, Hitler also saw the need to keep the Allies engaged to prevent them from entering the Balkans. The near German success against the Americans at Salerno encouraged Hitler to make the German stand south of Rome instead of in the north of Italy as his favourite Rommel had suggested. Hitler consequently followed Kesselring's plan. It was a bold decision as elsewhere fixed defences were seen to be wanting. Germany put their plan into action and decisively occupied much of mainland Italy, disarming bewildered Italian soldiers. What followed was that Italy was divided between a series of near parallel defensive lines crossing the Apennine peninsula from the Tyrrhenian Sea on the west coast to the Adriatic Sea on its eastern shoreline. The mountainous terrain in the middle did not lend itself to mobile warfare. Indeed, the Germans most able medium tank the Mark V Panther and its high-velocity main armament found a use in these static defences. Panther turrets were buried in concrete emplacements known as the Pantherturm. Italy was also dismembered politically.

In the northeast of what was then considered part of the Kingdom of Italy, Germany directly administered some provinces, this area was known as the Operational Zone of the Adriatic Littoral. Much of it now forms part of Slovenia and Croatia. Germany also took control of the German speaking South Tyrol. What remained of German occupied Italy was turned into a puppet state known as the Italian Social Republic. Benito Mussolini was the nominal head after his rescue from captivity in a bold combined *Waffen-SS* and *Fallschirmjäger* operation requested by Hitler. Famous Nazis such as Otto Skorzeny were involved in this propaganda success as was Kurt Student, this pioneer of paratroopers approved Mussolini's rescue mission. When the operation was underway, the Carabinieri police guards, who should have fought back, were ordered not to resist the German forces by Italian police general, Fernando Soleti; he had been press ganged into helping the raid. Previously Soleti had assisted the coup against Mussolini, he was now forced to aid and abet his release. Mussolini was, in time, flown to meet with Hitler. After being paraded in front of the media, he was restored to some semblance of power as the puppet head of an alternative Italian state. The man that had done much to oppose Hitler in the 1930s and limit his power was now the lacky of the Nazi leader. Mussolini was always a concern for Hitler, first as an opponent, and then as a dependent providing political cover for German control of northern Italy.

Mussolini had entered World War Two with the intention of negating Hitler's dominance of Europe. He had spent much of his life opposing the ambitions and the attitudes of both Wilhelmine Germany and the Third Reich only to find himself collaborating with a predator. History has shown that there can be no accommodation with a powerful aggressor. Hoping that through siding with one's enemy you will be devoured last does not change the final destination of one's fate. Indeed, through cooperation comes contagion and ultimately assimilation. The malevolent power will taint the weak and naïve. The man that had mocked the racial identity notions of the Nazis found himself trying to persuade Hitler that the Roman was an Aryan and even went so far as to adopt Germany's genocidal anti-Semitism. All to curry favour with a maniacal dictator that genuinely filled Mussolini with dread. Mussolini, a man that believed in the nation-state, had turned his back on Italy and became an agent of German control, subservient to their National Socialist ideology. For a moment in time in late 1944 to early 1945 the political map of central Europe was not too dissimilar to what it had been a millennia before. Then northern Italy was a part of the Holy Roman Empire which was led by the Kingdom of the Germans.

Backbone and spine
Montgomery's Eighth Army, after linking up with the US Fifth Army who had fought their way off the beaches at Salerno, advanced up the eastern coast of Italy along the Adriatic coast. Mark Clark's forces took the western side which abutted against the Tyrrhenian Sea. Both Allied armies aimed for Rome, they intended to capture it in a pincer movement. The Germans at first retreated but then fought against their foes from a series of interlinked defences and forts known as the Winter Line. The most formidable section of Kesselring's defences was called the Gustav Line. It stood firm across central Italy. The line stretched from north of where the Rapido and Liri rivers converge and flow into the Tyrrhenian Sea, to the mountainous terrain around the town of Cassino which sat beside the Route 6 road to Rome. The line then ran through land on the northern side of the Sangro River which flows into the Adriatic Sea. The Gustav Line terminated south of the port town of Ortona. Montgomery wanted to take the town then

pivot west and descend on Rome. Ortona's port was vital part of the strategy to supply his army. Failure to take it would have meant supplies would have to continue to be brought up from Taranto and Bari further to the south. The town of Ortona was defended by the elite German 1st Parachute Division. The Battle of Ortona ensued on 20th December 1943 when infantrymen of the 1st Canadian Division were sent in to secure the town.

The Battle of Ortona saw house-to-house and even room-to-room fighting with the soldiers using mouse-holing tactics. Here soldiers would move through buildings and engage the enemy not through doors but by using explosives to make breaches in walls. This caused much devastation and loss of life but was safer than being caught enfilade in the streets where snipers could shoot them in the open. The battle was known as the Italian Stalingrad. Soviet military observers, who were present at the battle, should have been suitably impressed that the Allies were not shirking their responsibility to have their own blood shed in the service of victory. The battle resulted in a Canadian victory that spanned Christmas, after just over a week of costly fighting the Germans, contrary to Hitler's orders, withdrew.

The day following the victory and with the task of penetrating the eastern flank of the Gustav Line complete, Montgomery ceased to command the Eighth Army. He returned to Britain to lead the 21st Army Group and develop and plan the invasion of mainland France. He would also motivate factory workers and inspire Allied soldiers amassing in the United Kingdom. General Eisenhower had wanted Sir Harold Alexander to lead the ground forces on D-Day and the subsequent Normandy Campaign, General Sir Alan Brooke, however, intervened, thinking Alexander unsuited to the role. As history does not look upon Alexander's overall command in Italy with great admiration, and as Montgomery was successful in France, Alan Brooke was perhaps right to show such faith in Monty. The fighting in Italy continued. The western arm of the Gustav line had not entirely been overcome. Nevertheless, the campaign in Italy had drawn German forces south, away from the Eastern Front and northern France.

By 1944 there were 45 German Divisions in the Mediterranean Theatre leaving just 60 Divisions in western Europe to defend against an attack that may come in France, the Low Countries, or even against Norway. Italy was the underside of a larger campaign, but it was not a side show. Germany poured hundreds of thousands of troops into Italy and even made use of its most modern materiel. The Italian theatre not only saw the use of old school fortified lines but also the latest Axis technology was put to work to slow Allied progress. Germany utilised fast reconnaissance planes, adapted from the jet engine powered Arado Ar 234

Blitz, a high-speed turbojet bomber. Thus, the Luftwaffe could also observe Allied troop movements and be safe from most British and American airpower which German jets could simply outrun. The USAAF reacted towards the end of the war by deploying then still experimental P-80 Shooting Star fighter jets to hunt down the German intruders, however, they were not successful. It mattered not, the war was already being won in Italy and what is more, the Italian peninsula, provided a valuable base for Allied bombers to attack deeper into Nazi occupied Europe and its satellites. The fighting on the ground remained challenging but stern German resistance was not the only obstacle faced by the Allies.

The United Nations fight against the Germans and Mussolini's National Republican Army was slow and laborious, not least because of the muddled command and failed generalship exhibited by some American commanders. A determined and well led German defence was hampering the poorly coordinated advance. Italy's geography and geology made Kesselring's strategy possible and the logical choice. The Allies, having to look up at an enemy at a high elevation made the task harder still. Harsh climatic conditions and a stout defence made the Apennine mountains near impenetrable. As the altitude increased the density of air decreased, forcing it to expand, thin, and cool. In winter, the snowy cold mountains were even less conducive to swift mobile warfare; Italy's other seasons also produced problems. The spring and autumn wind and sea around Italy brought rain clouds which shed their deluge upon the mountains which collected in the gorges between the mountains and would descend downstream in a torrent that made rivers impassable. The Apennine mountains also provided lush cover. Land that was not dissected by rivers could be dominated by dense shrubland known as *macchia*. All of which hampered those who sought to advance.

General Alexander, the overall commander in Italy, focused the direction of the advance on Rome though the western side of the peninsula. The Eighth Army in January 1944 attempted to reach the eternal city via Route 6, yet this was under the watchful gaze of Germans holding the imposing rocky hill of Monte Cassino which loomed above the Allies. Their attacks broke time and time again against the limestone peaks of the mountains of Lazio. There was a way to circumvent this near impassable terrain and Winston Churchill surmised a solution. In Italy, the only way to outflank the Germans was to make an amphibious landing. There was another road that led to Rome. Route 7 traversed western Italy close to the Tyrrhenian Sea. A new American-led amphibious landing was planned for 22nd January 1944 which would come ashore at Anzio to the south of Rome.

Kesselring had envisaged such an outflanking attack and kept back reserves for this eventuality. The Anzio landings were met by *Generaloberst* Eberhard von

Mackensen's Fourteenth Army. German soldiers were rushed in to surround the Anglo-American force that were now surrounded and unable to break out from their beachhead. The Allies also had to contend with Anzio Annie, the nickname for the giant railway gun, the Krupp K5, that sent its enormous shells down on the soldiers kettled on the beach. Part of the problem was caused by the American commander, Major General John Porter Lucas, consolidating his position rather than striking out and expanding his lodgement. Lucas was relieved of his position, but he was only guilty of following his commander's orders. Mark Clark had rewritten his instructions to Lucas at Anzio urging caution. It awarded Kesselring the opportunity to form another defensive line around Lucas' stranded whale below. A stalemate ensued that lasted for a third of a year, it was almost another Gallipoli. It was a similar situation around Monte Cassino.

The mission of pushing the Germans out of the Italic Peninsula was made even more arduous by the fact that there was near parity in troop numbers between the Axis and the Allies. Military doctrine surrounding force concentration usually mandated that for an attacker to be successful the aggressor needed three times the manpower of the defender or possess superior firepower which would provide a comparable qualitative advantage. The Allies did possess superior airpower, but this was not always helpful. In February 1943, New Zealander, Lieutenant General Freyberg, ordered that the abbey atop Monte Cassino be destroyed. He only requested a few bombers at knock out the monastery, General Alexander sent 250 to try out a new tactic of precision bombing from high altitude in support of ground troops that were due to make another push up the slopes. The bombing attack was pointless, it was brought forward by a day, yet the ground troops were still scheduled to attack the day after. Only one in five bombs hit the target, nevertheless, the destruction wrought on the Abbey of Monte Cassino by American bombers merely allowed the Germans to occupy this ruined monastery, the rubble now provided superb cover and accordingly its defiled precinct was occupied by the Fallschirmjäger.

The Gustav Line remained intact for the time being but in May 1944 General Alexander, later Field Marshal, launched Operation Diadem. He had the strategy of grinding down and destroying the German defences in the Liri valley and on the route to Rome. This push threatened to isolate Monte Cassino and cut-off the German defenders perched upon the mountain from their supply lines. The 1st Parachute Division, that was holding Monte Cassino, withdrew as they had done from Ortona five months previously. The multinational force had seen off the Nazis and Polish soldiers scaled the hills craggy heights and proudly flew their national flag above Monte Cassino. The Poles had excelled at that battle and throughout Italy. Alexander hoped that his big push in May would link up with Mark Clark's Fifth Army breaking out from Anzio which would simultaneously strike south and fall upon the Winter Line from the north. Between them they would capture the German 10th Army. However, the American General Mark Clark had different intentions. He sought fame and sent his forces to Rome; he wanted to be the first to capture an Axis capital. Rome was taken on 4th June 1944; however, he had allowed the Germans to escape the trap Alexander had set for them. The Germans fled and formed new defensive positions to the north; namely the Trasimene, Arno, and Gothic Lines. Hitler feared more amphibious landings, but politics intervened. The Allies' war in Italy was hampered by the acquisition of landing craft that were earmarked for the invasion of France. It was a much wider conflict.

Migration era

One and half millennia before the Second World War all roads led to Rome, disparate tribes, often making up confederations of different peoples descended on the eternal city. Their origins were in northern and eastern Europe. The Ostrogoths once occupying the area of what is now Ukraine. Another group known as the Vandals, even came to Rome by way of North Africa via Carthage. They may have originated in what is now Poland. The mysterious Huns, whose origins are a matter of conjecture, may have amalgamated into what became the Soviet Union or one its satellites. They also assimilated many Germanic peoples, and at one point marched on Rome. Incidentally, the Hun was a pejorative term for German used by the British in World War One. History was now repeating itself again but on an even grander scale. Italy in the 1940s again saw many different peoples descend on it.

The German and Soviet invasion of Poland at the start of World War Two helped the Allies in the Mediterranean Theatre. Many Poles escaped through Romania and made their way to Britain and France. Those who could not immediately escape were not entirely lost to the war effort. When the Red Army invaded Poland in September 1939, reclaiming territory lost to the Poles in the 1920s, the Soviets captured more than a third of a million men. Later the NKVD secret police deported perhaps a million more to Siberia, where they were forced to reside in appalling conditions and slave in labour camps. Following Operation Barbarossa, the Polish prisoners of war that had not been executed by the Soviets became pawns. Stalin was lobbied to release the Polish prisoners. The Soviet leader was initially paranoid about the role of Polish soldiers on the eastern front; many ethnic Poles had little love for Russia. Nevertheless, Stalin was willing to use their lives for his cause, with Soviet occupied Poland annexed to the Lithuanian, Byelorussian, and Ukrainian Soviet Socialist Republics many Poles could be considered citizens of the USSR.

General Władysław Anders, freed from Soviet captivity, wanted the Poles to fight alongside the Red Army on the Eastern Front so as to be nearer to liberating their homeland. Stalin, desperate for manpower, did absorb some Polish divisions that fought beside the Red Army. Political friction and poor supplies dictated that some would go west. General Władysław Sikorski, the Prime Minister of the London based Polish Government in Exile, wanted the Poles to fight alongside the western Allies. There were already Polish pilots serving with the RAF. The number of combatants working with the British would increase exponentially when the Soviets allowed a mass evacuation of Polish military personnel and civilians to leave. The Anders' Army, as it was known, first came to the middle east, from there they would fight alongside the British Empire forces in the Mediterranean theatre. Some Poles had already been serving the French in the middle east but left Syria when France capitulated, they then joined the British Army. They were now joined by many more determined soldiers who formed a Polish parachute brigade and the Polish armoured division. Together they would help the Allies win in Italy and later in France. However, diversity was not their strength.

The Allies in Italy were hampered by the lack of homogeneity amongst their forces. Different equipment was used by the British and American armies which exacerbated supply problems. What is more there were Indian soldiers and Free French north African troops amongst other nationalities, many of which spoke different languages. There were also a multitude of religions, some of which mandated strict dietary requirements on their followers. The need to provide different foods was also problematic for Allied logistics. The Germans, however, were homogeneous; the same could not be said for Italy.

Social war

The war in Italy descended into a civil war between two equally sized forces. On one side was the Kingdom of Italy (the Kingdom of the South) and its Italian Co-belligerent Army, Navy, and Air Force, operating alongside revolutionary partisans. On the other were the Fascist National Republican Army fighting for Mussolini's Italian Social Republic. The *Duce* of now just northern Italy had chosen to remain in office but not in power. However, his military alliance with Hitler had inadvertently fulfilled his original and once overriding aim, it helped prevent Nazi domination of Europe; but not by adding a counterweight. Instead, Italian involvement was a millstone around Hitler's neck, dragging down German soldiers, airmen, and sailors away from the frontlines where they were truly needed. And when the Italian soldiers did fight on the critical Eastern Front their contribution was of limited value. Mussolini, however, paid a high price for his inadvertent gift to the Allied war effort.

Political divisions meant they were not a united force, the man beside an Italian soldier may have a completely different agenda and worldview. This was exacerbated by the fact that the Kingdom of Italy was a modern invention. Military force had unified disparate polities with differing dialects and, according to some linguists, differing languages. Southern Italy was not the organised powerhouse that small areas of the north became after the war. Indeed, there is no word in Italian for 'busy'. To this day much of Italy has a reputation for disorganisation, corruption, and unreliable political leadership; this was not entirely abolished by Mussolini. The aim of his Fascist state was to unify the country and bring together its competing factions under Mussolini's statist rule. Yet even the revolutionary sentiment of northern Italy was not eradicated by his tyranny. He was to pay for his inability to resolve Italy's inherent contradictions.

The poverty that Italy endured after the First World War had sparked a new Italian social war of sorts, the *Biennio Rosso*, reminiscent of the conflicts that plagued the dying days of the late Roman Republic. Then civil strife led to civil war that saw the emergence of the dictator Sulla. And then the First Triumvirate, with Rome governed between; the general Gnaeus Pompeius Magnus, property plutocrat Marcus Licinius Crassus, and politician turned military commander Gaius Julius Caesar. In time he was the last man standing, his eventual successor enacted the social reforms of the *Populares* and ushered in rule by emperors. Forward two millennia to the end of the Great War, over a period of two years communists and anarcho-syndicalists occupied factories, went on strike, and agitated for revolution. This had so frightened Italy's oligarchs that in the early 1920s they were encouraged to turn to the Fascist Black Shirts to restore order. Having split from the Italian Socialist Party over the latter's opposition to the Great War Mussolini also resented his former party because they failed to address the national question and for their insistence on following a narrow class-based politics. Mussolini remained against capitalism, but he was willing to fight against those revolutionaries that did not follow his correct path. The industrialists' support for Mussolini may appear to be counter-intuitive, but his corporatist anti-capitalist vision served their interests. Fascism enabled businessmen to become monopolists. Its corporatism ended free markets; state management of the economy created barriers to new entrants thus stopping competitors from emerging that would have challenged those that already had privileged positions. Mussolini's socialist origins and collectivist goals did not trouble Italy's industrial leaders. To this day multinational corporations, especially Silicon Valley's tech giants, seek to align themselves with political movements that originate from forms of socialism that conveniently do not challenge property rights. American President Ronald Reagan defined Fascism as "private ownership, private enterprise but total government control and regulation"; a state of affairs he vehemently opposed. The 40th President of the USA also predicted that, "If fascism ever comes to America, it will come in the name of liberalism."

Whilst Mussolini did defeat those who would nationalise industry, communist political agitation was only temporarily suppressed. The interregnum of Fascist corporatism came to an end in 1943 and communist and anarchist partisans renewed their war against Mussolini. Northern Italy had gone full circle and produced a mirror image of the events two decades before. The Agnelli family, the owners of Fiat automobile company, had helped Mussolini in the 1920s but were aiding the partisans in 1945. The revolutionary activity which led to the birth of his political power in 1922 now caused his death. In April 1945 Mussolini was captured by partisans, and, along with his mistress, eventually shot and then strung up in Milan. Hitler's Axis partner and friend had been humiliated along with *Il Duce's* loved one. Hitler was determined to delay and, if possible, avoid the same fate.

It has been argued that Mussolini was executed on Churchill's orders to disguise the British Prime Minister's wartime negotiations with the Italian leader. There are faked letters from Churchill to Mussolini offering peace negotiations. This would have been controversial as the Allies, at the instigation of Roosevelt, were demanding that the Axis surrender unconditionally, but it may not have been surprising nor too outlandish. Mussolini had been offered Malta by the British to stay out of the war. What is more, America had acquiesced to Mussolini assuming power in 1922.

The entry of Italy into the war had been nothing but a drain and a distraction for the Germans, it drew German troops further south away from the main battle for the heart of Europe. The dissatisfaction, disillusionment, and ultimately the defection of Italy compounded this diversion of resources. It also affected how Hitler planned to fight the war. Kesselring's superb defence in Italy gave Hitler hope that he could hold the Allies on other fronts. However, the lessons were not transferable to different theatres. The western and eastern fronts proved to be less static and consisted of terrain that allowed for much greater mobility than that which was permitted on the southern front. Movement was difficult across the many mountain ranges that stretched across the northern Mediterranean. The near impassable terrain was created by tectonic forces unleashed in long distant epochs prior to World War Two. Geological forces likewise separated the body of water that became the Mediterranean Sea from the Atlantic Ocean. This became a conduit for the spread of Phoenician and Greek civilisation; it was now a highway for Anglo-Saxon armies to re-enter continental Europe. There would soon be another front opened.

The Tehran Conference, held in the capital of Iran, took place in late November and early December 1943. It mapped out and decided the future of the war. It involved the big three world leaders, Joseph Stalin, Franklin Delano Roosevelt, and Winston Churchill. The British Prime Minister, after having bounced the Americans into supporting his Mediterranean strategy, was himself manoeuvred into the invasion of France by Stalin and Roosevelt who were often in agreement. Stalin wanted Britain and America to be concentrating their efforts on the opposite side of Europe to where his struggle for control was taking place. There was military as well as political logic behind his request, it would draw German soldiers further away from Stalin's embattled Red Army. Nevertheless, the agreement mandated that there would be a corresponding Soviet offensive in the east that would complement the western Allies invasion. The interests of communism were also furthered at the conference by the parties agreeing to remove support from Yugoslavia's Royalist Chetniks and instead redirect it to Josip Tito's National Liberation Army. His communist partisans were to grow into a substantial army.

Stalin was even asked for his suggestions on where the next Allied blows should fall. It was agreed that the cross-channel invasion, now renamed Operation Overload, would take place in June 1944, shortly after there was also to be a second complimentary invasion that would land on southern France, this other amphibious assault was named Operation Anvil. Planning began for the big push on France in earnest from late 1943 after this conference. With a pathway being laid down to give the Allies a military victory over the Axis powers, the big three leaders would next be attempting to use their influence to determine and design the post-war world.

From sea to sea

Whilst the British and Americans were affirming their domination of the Mediterranean Sea region, to the northeast the Soviets were reclaiming dominion over the Black Sea. Germany was determined to keep control of the strategically significant Crimean Peninsula. To that end the Nazis tried to retain the land to the east of the Crimea in the north Caucasus. This area was separated from Crimea by a small stretch of water known as the Kerch Strait. The pocket of German occupied land across that waterway was known as the Kuban bridgehead; it had become isolated after the debacle following Stalingrad. The pocket was eliminated by late 1943 with great German loss, including the destruction of much Axis airpower. By the end of the year the Crimea could be attacked from the north and the east.

Crimea was occupied by the Germans far beyond the point at which it ceased to be militarily sensible to do so. However, even after the peninsula was cut-off in 1943 it was feasible to keep troops there. The German and Romanian soldiers on Crimea were kept supplied by sea, therein lay the attractiveness of possessing that peninsula. Its projection into the water made it a fundamental part of the naval Black Sea campaign. If reconquered by the Red Army, it could again serve as a base from which Soviet air and sea power could threaten Romania. It would allow air attacks on Balkan oil and gas production; and the port of Sevastopol would provide a harbour from which the Soviets could increase amphibious operations against Axis partners along the Black Sea coast. Russia could even apply political pressure on its old enemy Turkey. Militarily the Soviet air forces could threaten German supplies of chromium from Anatolia. Chrome was an important part of the engines of the Luftwaffe's Messerschmitt Me 262. Turkey had an agreement to sell all its Chromium ore to Britain but was illegally supplying it to Germany, its ally in World War One.

Spring 1944 saw Russia retake the Crimea and decisively defeat the outnumbered German and Romanian forces still stationed there. Evacuating those troops earlier would have kept more alive to be able to fight another day. The battle to control the sea to the south of Crimea was now turning in the USSR's favour. From the beginning of Operation Barbarossa through much of the war the Russian navy had fared badly against an assortment of Axis flotillas and the fleets belonging to Germany's satellites. The penultimate year of the war saw the Soviet's victorious over enemy vessels operating in the Black Sea. Not for the first time in World War Two, the change of fortunes came through airpower with the Russians knocking out German U-boat bases and attacking Axis shipping. The Black Sea also saw Soviet submarines ply their dark trade from the depths.

Control of the Crimea was pivotal to Russian security, it helped deliver a Soviet victory in the Black Sea theatre of operations. With the Soviet economy now firing on all cylinders they were more than able to match German output, and, with supplies from Britain and America, the Russian steamroller was driving back the Axis on the Eastern Front.

Diversity

Nazi industry had foreign slaves that were forced to work for the war effort. Similarly, those in occupied territory were likewise compelled on pain of death in some cases to work for the Germans. This did not enamour the subjugated to their rulers. The lack of positive incentives encouraged workers to sabotage the production process providing substandard materiel and in woefully low quantities. There were massive resources and industrial potential under the control of the German state. This was organised into the Reichswerke Hermann Göring industrial conglomerate and its three main subdivisions, despite this the Nazis were never able to realise Europe's economic potential. Compulsion did not work. With Nazi planners lacking the ability, and even the inclination, to offer positive incentives to foreign workers the conscripted staff would have little desire to produce weapons for the Third Reich. The Allies, however, were able to utilise both patriotism and a perceived or real stake in the endeavour of defeating their enemies. This motivated the home front to deliver a level of industrial production the Nazis, and their economic model based on coercion and plunder, could never match.

The British and Soviet economies had deficiencies, but these were alleviated by American muscle. The industrialisation and mechanisation of the Soviet Union and its armed forces was still not complete. Nevertheless, the USSR's lack of development was not always a hindrance. The Tsarist Russian empire had expanded east and north into desolate lands dominated by the taiga, the largest boreal forest on earth existed in a world which is dominated for large parts of the dark winter by ice and snow. Beyond that to the north lay the tundra where even less grows. Both these inhospitable environments could not enable economic developments nor support large scale populations. Man was forced to exist in a state of nature that was little more developed beyond the stone age and yet people still lived there in the era of the aeroplane.

The Turkic tribal peoples that resided in Russia's far north lived within communal societies and made a subsistence living; these indigenous inhabitants of Russia could, however, still contribute to their overlords war effort. Soviet communists thought their ideology was the last word in modernity. However, the native's unique society and economy, built on the reindeer, gifted the Red Army useful and unique talents. The Russians used these reindeer herders, and their beasts, to pull artillery and ammunition in the war against Nazi absorbed Norway and the German forces based there. The vastness of Moscow's empire led it to have dominion over other vastly different environments.

To the south of Moscow, the steppe stretched east from the Black Sea in the west, almost towards the Pacific Ocean in the east. This vast land, that includes what is now Ukraine and Kazakhstan, first saw the domestication of the horse. Men from the Eurasian steppe developed the stirrup and took this technology to produce fine cavalry. Amongst the most able were the Cossacks, the word has the same root as Kazakh; both derive from a Turkic word describing a people free to wander, adventurers. The Cossacks were primarily a Slavic Russian Orthodox people and owed their military allegiance to the House of Romanov; the Tsars of all the Russias. These Cossacks were renowned for their martial skills.

Despite the Bolsheviks undertaking a program of decossackisation, a process akin to genocide few of these horsemen chose to collaborate with the Nazis, instead they joined the Soviet war effort with gusto. They complimented the Red Army's plans. It was originally envisaged that mounted troops would be used in a role like that traditionally undertaken by a dragoon. Horse and rider would move quickly to affect a rapid breakthrough, the troops would then dismount, and the horses sent to the rear. Later cavalry was used in its traditional role in conjunction with mechanised attacks as part of their deep battle doctrine and operations. Indeed, the Russians kept cavalry units in the Red Army until 1956. In this modern day and age, the US military still trains soldiers to use horses to transport men and supplies to where vehicles are unable to reach. In the Second World War the use of mounted troops was even less outlandish and the Cossacks at times had a decisive effect.

In early 1944 the Red Army was trying to eliminate the Korsun-Cherkassy Pocket. The Germans were fighting to defend an airfield which was being used to evacuate wounded troops. The Nazis were also trying to breakout from their encircled positions in central Ukraine along the Dnieper River. Cossack cavalry played an important part in the Russian victory, they overran the *Waffen-SS* Units in the pocket and massacred fleeing German soldiers. With this victory the Red Army now had a springboard from where they could threaten Romania and German controlled oil production.

Following the war, the limited number of Cossacks that did collaborate with the Germans surrendered to the British Army. These were however handed over to SMERSH, an organisation set up by Stalin to stop counter revolutionary infiltration. Its name derives from the Russian term 'death to spies'. Upon their repatriation to the Soviet Union many were executed. The Nazis did make use of German speaking mounted troops and had their own cavalry regiments in the *Heer* and *Waffen-SS*. They were not greatly used and were often tasked with hunting Jews and other civilian non-combatants despised by Hitler. Mounted patrols were especially useful in the swamps of Belarus. For the most part the Germans used horses to complement their oxen to pull equipment into combat. The equines were making up for the lack of mechanisation in the German army rather than making a direct contribution to the fighting.

The Germans did not have access to such an eclectic mix of peoples whose unique skills could be brought to bear on an enemy in sufficient numbers. The Russians could use horse soldiers to a much greater degree, deploying the tried and tested military techniques that a large and accomplished cavalry force could deliver. Instead, Hitler chose to follow a different path.

Wunderbar and vengeance

Just as blitzkrieg was looking for a breakthrough, Nazi-led scientific innovation was striving for a technical quantum leap that would deliver super weapons that would snatch victory; time constraints were a problem and they turned out to be military dead ends.

Blitzkrieg scientific thinking failed in Europe but was successfully used by the Americans in their development of nuclear weapons which were deployed against Japan and helped bring the war to an end. This development succeeded in the United States, but only with collaboration from the United Kingdom and Canada, which had their own joint nuclear weapons programme code-named Tube Alloys. The United States could invest more resources than other nations, especially Germany. These three Anglosphere nations, where freedom of thought was cherished, combined their knowledge and expertise with American capital to make the Manhattan Project a success. The USA could also marshal human capital that was unavailable to the Nazis, namely Jewish scientists. The director of the Los Alamos Laboratory, which designed the weapons, was Robert Oppenheimer, a man of Jewish descent; he is known to some as the father of the atomic bomb. Despite Allied fears of German wonder weapons, the Nazis were not able to develop such theatre changing devices. Nor were they willing to cooperate with other nations and their scientists; they therefore lacked the necessary requirements for anything but a rudimentary nuclear weapons programme. The Germans did, however, have some advanced conventional weapons.

German research did produce some highly technical arms. However, the great achievements of Germany's scientific strategy in creating wonder weapons were wasted on a futile quest for vengeance. This was mainly directed against the United Kingdom. Like a scorned lover, Hitler's admiration of the British Empire had morphed into hatred. He wanted to retaliate against the capital of his intractable foe, London was the target of his reprisals. Germany invested its limited capacity in developing the V weapons, or *Vergeltungswaffen*. Not all were state of the art high tech solutions. The first vengeance weapon, or V-1s, were flying bombs using pulsejets, a basic form of jet propulsion. These were simple devices that ran on low octane petrol. The operating life of a pulsejet was short, this did not matter as the whole cruise missile was to be sacrificed in return for inflicting terror on Britain's civilian population. In time, British-led forces overran the launch sites of the doodlebugs, as the V-1s were also known. The Germans then only had the option of launching them from aircraft. However, the parasitic doodlebugs made the host planes slow and cumbersome and they were both easily destroyed by Allied fighters. This did not spare the south-east of England for long.

Next came the V-2, a ballistic missile, they were guided onto a target, first by gyroscopes, and then by radar beams. They were ground-breaking long-range rockets, each with a powerful warhead close to its tip. Similar in design to a 7.62mm bullet these sleek supersonic missiles were almost impossible to stop, but they did have an Achilles heel. V-2s were effectively targeted by Allied aircraft when the rockets were in transit along the ground. Britain's elite Special Air Service Regiment, the SAS, were used to hunt and locate the stealthy carriers. The pursuit of the V-2 weapons programme was itself a serious foible that distracted from the development of arguably more important anti-aircraft rockets. Hitler coveted the V-2s and won over his armaments minister, Albert Speer, into investing in their production. Yet they remained resource hungry, unreliable, and inaccurate vengeance weapons that unlike other technologies did not defend Germany's skies from Allied bombers.

Development of these weapons pre-dated their application and were a drag on Germany's faltering war economy. Their entire concept was flawed, the consequence of a polluted mind that wanted to watch the world burn. The vengeance weapons were not intended to win the war on the ground. Some V-2s were however used for more practical purposes. When the Belgian port of Antwerp fell into British hands, Hitler hoped to use them to knock out its facilities, denying its use to the Allies. They were even used tactically. Some missiles were aimed at the Ludendorff railway bridge at Remagen which spanned the Rhine River and had fallen to Americans. The V-3, a supergun, whose giant cannon was intended to shell London from as far as the French channel coast, was a failure. Its base was destroyed by British earthquake bombs dropped by the RAF. The entire V programme, and investing in the very human desire for revenge, took away resources from the production of weapons that would have had a more tangible efficacy. Yet not all of Hitler's weapons programs were about vengeance, even in the dying stages of Nazi Germany there was still development into conventional weapons.

Armour race

German tanks had quickly become outdated. Indeed, many underperformed as early as the Fall of France. Yet, there was not just a quality gap, there was an even greater disparity in numbers which only grew worse as the war progressed. Germany tried to make do and mend, finding quick, easy, and cheap solutions to address the imbalance of tank numbers between the Axis and the Allies. The easy answer was to continue upgrading and producing more of the already effective Panzer Mark IV. German panzer crews started with an advantage; they had a saying, "Don't worry about the Russians, they always miss their first shot". Superior training and better communication with more use of radios in German panzers were not the only solutions to the tank gap.

The Germans tried to achieve parity in numbers, not through producing more tanks, but instead they would try to manufacture the tank destroyer. These hunter-killers main armament could depress and elevate but lacked a rotating turret, so the entire vehicle would have to move to aim at its target. The chassis from Panzer II and Panzer III and light Czech tanks were used as a platform on which a powerful high velocity cannon could be placed. These German tank hunters, often generally known as *Jagdpanzers*, killed 20,000 Russian tanks. The Germans also produced self-propelled guns such as the Hummel and Wespe; the mobile howitzers could deliver a powerful blow. Yet even though this part of Hitler's war-machine was cost effective the devastation caused by Allied bombing meant that the Nazis were still not able to produce even those simple designs in sufficient numbers. They were manufactured in no more than the hundreds rather than the many thousands that were needed. And the German concentration on developing unexacting armoured vehicles, such as assault guns, meant that their tanks remained inferior to those under development in the Soviet Union. What is more, the Russians also had both self-propelled artillery, such as the SU-76, and dedicated tank hunters, the SU-85 and its successor the SU-100. The numerical designation of those vehicles reflected the width of its gun barrel in millimetres. The British Army also had a dedicated tank hunter, called an Achilles. This was essentially an American vehicle but with an upgraded main gun, it had the British quick firing 17-pounder gun. Its weighty shell could rip through any Axis tank. It was adapted from the M10, a tank killer produced by the United States. The Americans also put into battle the M-18 Hellcat, also a tank hunter. The American models differed from their German and Soviet counterparts in that they did not use the fixed casemate structure; the US vehicles, with their moving turret, had more of a semblance to a conventional tank. However, the M10 and M-18 were both lightly armoured and even had open topped turrets. Their main defence was speed. The great numbers of Allied vehicles were by far the greatest offensive weapon. The Nazi leadership had compounded its inherent weakness by striving for extravagance when efficiency was needed.

Traditional German tactics compensated for the penury of vehicles. Instead of spreading the German heavy tanks out along the front where their power could be diluted, the Germans used the limited number of Tiger tanks on the Eastern Front in mobile units concentrating this modest but powerful force in small areas where they could achieve local superiority. This non flying circus of panzers were rushed to trouble spots, where elite German tank commanders would unleash their deadly beasts on their enemies. These German counterattacks on the Eastern Front were led bravely by men such as General Hyacinth Graf Strachwitz and Lieutenant Otto Carius. The Russians also reorganised their armoured units. Massed armoured brigades were reordered to form smaller, but more numerous, and more flexible brigades. Yet where appropriate powerful Soviet shock armies with extra components of artillery and armour would tear apart German defences.

National strategy affected production of weapons and even helped determine the design and utility of tanks. The Allies were waging a war of attrition, one that aimed to wear down and destroy the Axis in its entirety. This shaped what they used in the field of combat. The M4 Sherman, the most produced tank of World War Two, and the Russian T-34, both medium sized tanks, had their problems. Indeed, the T-34 was overrated and its American counterpart somewhat underrated. However, they did however lend themselves well to the needs of mass production. Ease of manufacture was a key component in their design. It was almost as if the consumer could have any colour of tank they wanted as long as it was green.

The Germans, however, lacking economic efficiency were unable to compete in the long-term, therefore the Nazis favoured what is known as blitzkrieg. And accordingly produced weapons that they hoped could deliver a quick knockout blow. These ranged from; jets, rockets, superguns, and unworkable vortex machines to target Allied bombers. They diverted resources and the rockets burnt through Germany's already depleted cash reserves. German tank design also followed this misguided thinking. The blitzkrieg sought to achieve a breakthrough on a focused point. To this end the German's produced highly effective, but over-engineered tanks that could offer a localised superiority. However, because of their complexity not enough could be produced in numerous and sufficient quantities and were thus subsequently overwhelmed. German attacks also relied upon shock and awe to be successful, encouraging their enemy to fold. This strategy took on an even greater impetus as the war progressed and was reflected in the often-impractical weapons that the Germans tried to produce. German tanks sought to take advantage of the blitzkrieg fear factor to psychologically intimidate as well as destroy an enemy, this led to weapons which even dwarfed the complex and often unworkable Mark V Tiger and Mark VI Panther panzers.

As the war was no longer under German control, Hitler's desperation increased and this had a corresponding increase in extreme tank designs, they grew and became ever more complex. The Führer envisaged the super tank. The Royal Tiger upgraded the Panzer Mark V to a mass where mobility and reliability had been seriously compromised. This was not only over engineered, but its considerable size made it an easier target from the air. Allied fighter-bombers such as the Hawker Typhoon would try and rain down rockets upon this lumbering vehicle. It did not stop there. The Mark VII Lion was conceived but not developed. Tank evolution skipped a stage, the next great beast that Hitler coveted was the Panzer Mark VIII, the Mouse, known in German as the *Maus*. This supersized behemoth was more land cruiser than tank. Here the concept came not from the desire to have an irresistible force that could crush those who would stand in Germany's way, but it was more of a defensive weapon. The Mouse was intended to be a mobile replacement for a lost bunker. This gargantuan tank would be defensive, and function as part of Hitler's hold the line strategy. Usually, the tank can only be used for offensive action, however, just two were built. Each used a gallon of fuel to travel as little as 500 feet. Hitler's mobile fortress was a waste of resources and an entertaining distraction for the Führer from the very real need to have more men and materiel. It had also been proposed to develop an even greater weapon, the *Ratte*, or Rat. It would have had a mass of approximately one thousand tons but was never constructed. Nevertheless, Hitler's strategy had changed. Blitzkrieg was no longer the strategy of choice, defence at all costs was Hitler's latest whim.

Fortress Europe

This new approach was congruent with Hitler's common refusal to allow retreats, even under almost any circumstances. In time this came to be known as *Fester Platz*, which translates as 'fixed place; it meant turning cities into fortresses. Commanders had the liberty to select what cities would be selected as a *festung*, or fortress, yet they were not free to abandon or surrender without the agreement of the army group's senior commander and then only with the Führer's approval.

Hitler must have thought that his general refusal to allow any retreats would keep Germany in the war, instead it shortened the conflict and condemned the Nazis to an early defeat. When the fortresses held strategic locations they did briefly slow up the Russian advance, however, generally the *Fester Platz* strategy concept actually aided the Red Army's alternative notion of deep battle which sought to bypass Wehrmacht strong points. It meant that much needed German troops became isolated behind Russian lines and could be annihilated at leisure. Indeed, the result was that the Nazis were quickly surrounded and destroyed losing both men and materiel.

Holding onto prestigious cities became a source of pride, however, the fall of Germany soon followed. Military strategy and political propaganda began to intermingle until they became one and the same. In the dying days of the Third Reich the Nazis even used valuable resources producing a film named Kolberg, the title of the movie came from a town that stubbornly resisted a French and Polish siege during the Napoleonic wars. Troops were even withdrawn from the Eastern Front to take part in the motion picture that extolled the virtues of fighting on to either death or victory in what is known in Germany as the War of Liberation. This film cost 8 million Reichsmarks and used railway wagons which could have been supplying the army. 187,000 soldiers and 12,000 sailors were used in its production; they would otherwise have helped the war effort in a more tangible way. Salt was even used for snow. It was intended to be a part of an effort to motivate the people to keep fighting. In the film Kolberg remained free, and its people were ultimately victorious. Hitler designated the real Kolberg as another *fester platz* as well as many other cities. The success of these German redoubts is shown by today's map of Europe and the names of many cities. Kolberg, once a predominately German speaking town in Pomerania, is now a part of Poland and is known as Kołobrzeg. The Germanisation which began in the late medieval period with the cultural and linguistic obliteration of Slavic influences would be reversed by Russia. Other *fester platz* fortresses were to share the same fate. Further along the Baltic coast was Königsberg. Germany's most eastern city, in what was then East Prussia, was overwhelmed and is now part of the Russian Federation. The city has been renamed Kaliningrad and acts as a bulwark against German-led expansion eastwards. This political relic of Stalin's Soviet meddling with Europe's borders is now holding out behind enemy lines. The border between the Russian enclave of the Kaliningrad Oblast region, and neighbouring Poland and Lithuania is heavily fortified. In Silesia the once Austrian, Prussian, then German city of Breslau was also used as an outpost that was intended to fight until the bitter end. Like the other former fortresses, it was soon crushed and given the Polish name of Wrocław.

The *Fester Platz* should have been located using sound tactical judgements, yet resources were even wasted on building giant fortresses in the west on the insignificant Channel Islands. The Nazi obsession with propaganda led Hitler to waste German resources on the occupation of these islands, part of the original Duchy of Normandy. They were of little strategic value, but Hitler became obsessed with occupying Britain's Crown Territories. Instead of sending troops to the Eastern Front, where they were desperately needed, he stationed them on relatively small islands. At one point in 1943 there was one soldier to every two islanders on Guernsey. Nazi propaganda also confused strategy and propaganda by creating the myth of *Festung Europa*, fortress Europe. To guard against a seaborne invasion from Britain the Nazis established the Atlantic Wall which stretched from Norway in the north to the Pyrenees in the south bordering Spain. To defend Europe's skies from intrusion by British and American bombers the fortress concept deployed an air defence line. However, *Festung Europa* was about to meet two irresistible forces coming from the east and the west.

Blue Sky Thinking

"Now I am become death, the destroyer of worlds." — **The incarnation of Vishnu, manifested as Lord Krishna, in the Bhagavad Gita, a sacred scripture in the Hindu epic *Mahābhārata*.**

The bomber dream

Destruction from sky borne weapons had long been a part of the human psyche expressed through sacred myths that some still pass on to their children as fact. This has been depicted as lightning or fire or iron arrows or bombs of stone raining-down from above on a foe that cannot escape the coming righteous judgement. The demise of evil from such arms appears in many religions. This theme is told in the Hindu epic the Mahābhārata where weapons known as *Astras* are used by Arjuna in the Kurukshetra War. It emerges again in the *Quran's* chapter of *The Elephant*. The Islamic story recounts a tale where birds dropped stones on an army and its mighty war elephants that were advancing on what was to become the Muslim holy city. This bombing raid destroyed the elephants, leaving nothing but ashes and saved the site of pilgrimage known as the Ka'bah. It was in the mid-nineteenth century that bombing moved from the realm of myths and magic; in 1849 the Austrians attacked Venice with bomb laded hot air balloons. The effect was negligible, but the age of the bomber was coming.

The development of aviation and the ever-expanding capabilities of the aeroplane put into motion for the time being the theoretical development of airpower as a war winning weapon. The Italians were to lead the way. Their bombing of Turkish troops in the 1911 war over Libya was judged to have demoralised the Ottoman soldiers, helping the Italians in their campaign to seize that part of North Africa. The experience of this led to Italian officer, Giulio Douhet, theorising that airpower's main use would come in the form of strategic bombing. Rather than tactical bombing aimed at individual military targets, strategic bombing could deliver a decisive victory in the war through the levelling of transport infrastructure and industry. It was thought this would destroy both an enemy's desire and ability to wage war. Giulio Douhet, like his American counter-part Billy Mitchell, was court-martialed and convicted for his overly zealous advocation of airpower and criticism of his country's military leaders over their short-sighted attitude regarding the use of planes. Douhet, however, was exonerated and promoted to General. His theories, expressed in the seminal work, *The Command of the Air,* which he released in 1921 was to become very influential in many nations from Italy to the USA.

The Italians were not the only country that even before the First World War had seen the potential of strategic bombing. Tsarist Russia was an early pioneer of aviation. As early as 1913, they produced an airliner and, for the time, a heavy bomber named after a Slavic mythical figure called *Ilya Muromets.* This had four British engines and its military version had state of the art defensive machine guns capable of shooting down enemy fighter aircraft that attempted to intercept this vision of the future. Both the passenger aircraft and the *Ilya Muromets* bomber was designed and built by Igor Sikorsky. His company would later develop fixed wing aircraft and helicopters in the United States of America. The Russian heavier than air vehicle was quickly put to good use in World War One targeting German troops on the front line and attacking train depots and other transport infrastructure. Despite losing Sikorsky, who emigrated to the USA in 1919, Russia's new Bolshevik masters remained men that were willing to innovate. In the 1930s the Soviet Union had the biggest strategic bomber force of the time. The Soviet air force possessed the Tupolev ANT-20 Maksim Gorki, then the biggest plane in the world, it sported a staggering eight engines.

Other nations were not so advanced, during the First World War planes were initially used for spotting and guiding artillery fire but were soon deployed in both strategic and tactical bombing raids. As the war developed, the British even used airpower to eliminate ground targets in combined operations with tanks and infantry in an early iteration of blitzkrieg. War begot bigger and bigger bombers, and more outlandish ways in which airpower could influence the battlespace. In 1918 Billy Mitchell advocated for the deployment of men with parachutes from planes to attack the German held city of Metz in north-eastern France. His plan called for 12,000 men of the American 1st Infantry Division to become parachutists. This was ahead of its time and was not considered feasible; it did not proceed. However, the horizons of military commanders were expanding.

Germany had begun the development of airships known as Zeppelin's in the late nineteenth century. These rigid hydrogen inflated dirigible balloons were lighter than air and used by the Germans to bomb London during World War One. They did succeed in creating panic in the British capital and destroyed some military production. They were however a technological dead end and were superseded by the aeroplane. German Gotha G. V. bombers attacked London in the First World War. Those attacks were not without response.

The British belief in bombing began in earnest when in October 1914 Sopwith Tabloids of the Royal Naval Air Service undertook strategic bombing raids against German Zeppelin bases in Düsseldorf. These raids were successful. The following month Avro 504s carried out similar attacks against German infrastructure and airships at one of their bases. By 1918 General Jan Smuts, who fought against the British in the Boer war, but became loyal to the Crown, and commanded South African forces fighting for Britain during the First World War commended the use of bombers. He predicted that the outcome of a war could be decided by them in the future. General Smuts also prophesied during WWI that airpower could evolve into an independent arm of decision which would target industrial centres and troop formations. During the First World War British airpower was split between the Army's Royal Flying Corps and the Royal Navy's Royal Naval Air Service. The need for an independent air arm had become clear. The Royal Air Force was formed in 1918. Due to the Armistice of 11th November, British plans to bomb Berlin in the last year of the war were shelved. Whilst British bombers could reach and did attack German cities in World War One, one man, Winston Churchill, was not yet convinced that bombing could destroy a modern industrial city, this was despite theoretical physics showing that a resulting firestorm could in theory do just that. A generation later that theory would be put to the test by Britain and other nations.

Following the First World War men such as Walther Wever of Germany, Billy Mitchell in the USA, and Marshal of the Royal Air Force, Viscount (Hugh) Trenchard, along with Douhet, became amongst the most influential people in the theatre of airpower. They not only saw the future of conflict, but their ideas, not always completely accurate, actually shaped strategy and coming events. Supporters of strategic bombing thought that airpower would alone be war winning.

1931 US War Games strengthened the view that the bomber will always get through. In this exercise pursuit planes failed to catch the bombers in time before their theoretical payload was dropped on imaginary civilians below. When it was tried for real and in anger the results were promising. They appeared to justify the proponents of strategic bombing's beliefs in this new form of an old theme in warfare, namely harrying an enemy population into defeat. Winston Churchill supported the Air Policing policy to control Britain's newly won lands which it had seized in the middle east from the ashes of the Ottoman Empire. These airpin tactics, as they were known, were successfully used in Iraq in the 1920s against Kurdish rebels. And, in Palestine in the 1930s, it helped Bernard Law Montgomery quash the Arab Revolt.

The implications on the morale of guerrillas were as great, as the physical damage caused through the bombing. It broke the insurgents' will to fight on. Local villagers were also taught the hard way the need to disassociate themselves from partisans who relied upon a civilian base of support to be effective. Britain was not alone in testing these pioneering tactics. The Condor Legion's bombing of Guernica during the Spanish Civil War was judged a complete success by the German High Command. Basque resistance to Franco collapsed. These preliminary uses of aerial bombardment proved promising and outweighed any legal hurdles. It was conveniently ignored that the Geneva Convention, as developed by the Hague Jurists in the 1920s, outlawed the targeting of civilians via a bombing campaign.

Yet, airpower still had limitations, chief amongst them were gravity and an aeroplane's drag coefficient. The technological inefficiencies of piston driven aero engines using propellers restricted the payload and range of machines that were pushing what were then the edges of science. Until the Boeing B-29 Superfortress was deployed in 1944, bombers were vulnerable to anti-aircraft artillery and enemy fighters and not yet capable of delivering a strategic victory on their own using conventional weapons. Only in the form of the B-29 was there a bomber able to fulfil the dreams of early aviation theorists. Its development and production costs exceeded that of the Manhattan Project, the fruits of which the Superfortress would soon drop in anger. It could reach an altitude and speed that could allow it to evade all but the most powerful ack-ack and interceptor aircraft whilst also carrying a devastating payload of bombs. For those fighters that came close, its fire control system operated through an analogue computer was able to provide defence and shoot out of the skies aircraft that would otherwise down the bomber. Human nature, however, and the psychology of aviation pioneers and early adopters of such technology overestimated airpower's effectiveness. The influence of these men could not be overestimated.

The pre-war theory that bombers could be used to win wars and the thinking that the bomber will always get through was both a seductive and fearful theory. Politicians and military planners believed strategic bombing would allow for a war to be fought over someone else's soil and airspace with the minimum of casualties. This was a requirement in democratic countries where leaders were accountable to its citizens. The reality was that bomber crews were far from safe. In the inter-war period, whilst it was believed that all nations were vulnerable to bombing that would devastate civilian areas, there was little option but to be prepared to deliver corresponding levels of terror on one's enemies. Stanley Baldwin, the Prime Minister of the United Kingdom in the mid-1930s was one of those politicians who believed that the bomber will always get through and the only defence was offence. Under his leadership Britain began building its soon to be mighty bomber force. Others, however, experienced another phantasmagoria, Germany had other priorities.

Strategic versus tactical

Continental European nations had a long history of favouring the development of ground forces above the needs of their navies, naturally so as the threat and opportunities came from soldiers storming over a national land border. Germany's immediate need was for landships rather than those that took to the air. There were also other reasons that held down German aviation. It was retarded by the terms of the Treaty of Versailles which forbade them from having an air force.

When the Nazis rejected the repugnant treaty the primary aim of the newly created Luftwaffe was to support ground operations to aid their blitzkrieg, not to unleash a destructive strategic bombing campaign. Despite their history of targeting Basque civilians, and their general disregard for the lives of those upon which the Nazis waged war, Germany's immediate aim was not to flatten foreign cities as part of a protracted war of attrition. Indeed, upon Britain's declaration of war against Germany, the feared burning of Britain's cities did not at first materialise, nor did it happen to some other countries that found themselves at war with Germany. At first, where German strategic bombing did occur it was a means to an end, and not an end in itself. The Germans used it as part of their shock and awe strategy to encourage, if not force, a political collapse. It is an irony of the war that Germany won infamy for its area attacks on civilians in Guernica, Rotterdam, and London but had not built a bomber force that could crush whole conurbations. And occasionally Germany had little desire to even attempt it unless it proved necessary. France famously capitulated and made peace with the Germans after the Nazis threatened to bomb Paris. Germany overestimated the strength of their air power.

The German bombing of Rotterdam in 1940 was unnecessary as negotiations for the cities surrender was already underway. It is probable that the Dutch surrender coming shortly after the aerial bombardment gave Hitler and Göring the impression that the Luftwaffe's bombers were capable of achieving a decisive result, forcing a quick surrender. And they surmised that attacking civilian targets would lead to a quick capitulation. The reality was that the German planes were just medium bombers and were not well suited to such missions. Indeed, the bomber had been instrumental in the fighting for the Netherlands, but the

Nazi bombers were not the dominant arm of decision. Part of the rational for the German invasion of the Netherlands was to deprive the RAF of a base for their bombers. Hermann Göring insisted that the Dutch nation be added to the German campaign in the west. If it were not for this, and the fact that the German invasion of France would in part be via a small part of Dutch territory, the Netherlands may well have been bypassed as it was when Germany attacked France in 1914. However, that was not to be and Dutch cities were indeed vulnerable to German aircraft. British bombers tried to defend Rotterdam by bombing the bridges that led to the city but as the Allies did not have air superiority they were mauled by the Luftwaffe's fighters.

German aircraft production concentrated on building medium sized bombers to assist the Heer's thrusts by breaking open gaps in enemy's lines. Large lumbering heavy bombers were not ideally suited to such a task. It was the path of least resistance, the most convenient strategy but it was divorced from the full reality of industrial warfare and failed to address its demands. The Nazis envisaged a short lightning war, as such the Germans did not concentrate on developing effective long-range heavy craft for strategic bombing. The failure to produce such a valkyrie bedevilled the Third Reich throughout much of the war. As the conflict's demands grew and spread both geographically and in scope, becoming a true war of attrition, the Germans found themselves unable to devastate Allied and especially Soviet arms production. Russian factories, along with workers, were relocated from Europe to the east of the Ural Mountains and lay outside of German reach in Asia.

The seeds of the German failure to wipe-out the Red Army at the start of Operation Barbarossa had already been sown by Hermann Göring, head of the Luftwaffe. He had not been able to unleash heavy bombers. These remained almost entirely absent throughout the war. Powerful bombs delivered from aircraft that could lift them into the air would have been able to eliminate the Red Army's stubborn defence of the Brest fortress much sooner. This was a pattern repeated throughout the Eastern Front. The German lack of strategic airpower meant that they could not knock Leningrad out of the war, nor could they fatally destroy the Soviet Baltic fleet which helped defend Russia's window on the west.

Without suitably sized heavy bombers there was little chance that Hitler's Reich would rise like a phoenix from the ashes of the conflagration which he had unwittingly unleashed too early. Germany's limited abilities meant the Luftwaffe could not prevent Russia from bringing reinforcements of both men and materiel up to the front. The way was clear for the Soviets to deliver fresh divisions that went west from Siberia to defend the Russian capital during the

Battle of Moscow. The Germans did use their medium bombers to attack civilian targets, but as they were not ideally suited to the ambitious task given to them, the Luftwaffe could not finish the job. The 1940 Blitz on Britain's capital and her other industrial cities was bad, but London could take it. In 1941 the Russian capital was identified for similar treatment. The seat of Soviet power was pulverised, but it was also costly for the Germans who lost aircraft in their savage assault and more importantly it used resources that could have been better used tactically rather than strategically. The Luftwaffe flight crews were on a fool's errand. The Germans could not destroy Moscow because they simply did not have strategic bombers. Nor would German bombing break the political will of nations that due to Nazi belligerence and their numerous atrocities had settled on becoming intractable enemies of Germany and would not take the knee for Hitler. These Allied nations had settled on victory or death, and often both. They would not be cowed by the German bullying that succeeded against the French.

Germany had little choice but to focus on medium sized aircraft. They did not have the industrial capacity and expertise in aviation to overturn the bomber gap. The costs of heavy bomber production exceeded Germany's overstretched and indebted economy. However, the will did emerge. The Germans initiated the Ural bomber program that aimed to reach and destroy Stalin's asian industry. However, Allied bombing of Germany deprived the Nazis of the resources they needed to complete the program. German industry did manage to deliver one workable heavy bomber, the Heinkel He 177. The concept was sound, and the final product was eventually made to work and proved to be more than adequate; but too few were produced to make a real difference. There were even ideas to deliver Hitler's vengeance across the Atlantic Ocean and strike the USA.

An attack on New York was a fantasy of Kaiser Wilhelm II who had envisioned invading the USA at the end of the Nineteenth Century. Hitler's aims were more measured. He just had the idea to bomb New York. The delivery mechanisms varied from submarine launched V-2 rockets to 'Viking' sea planes launched off the coast of America supported by U-boats, dropping a dirty nuclear bomb. Other ideas included suicide piloted pulsejet powered V-1 flying bombs piggybacking underneath a large transport plane. Another suggestion was to use Condor planes to cross the Atlantic and reach New York. The pilot would then bailout after delivering its weapon. It was even hoped that the planned development and introduction of the A-10 rocket, which would have a second stage V-2 combined with it, would be able to reach New York and begin the process of turning that city into a moonscape. The aims for this ballistic missile were ambitious and terrifying, especially if it carried a chemical or nuclear warhead.

It was, however, merely a fantasy. The Allies conventional weapons not only existed in reality but were also so numerous that the very heart of the Axis power was being hammered from above. There was one plan that was more realistic.

The *Amerikabomber* program had many candidates for planes that could be developed into heavy long-range bombers that could cross oceans and continents to reach the United States. The Junkers Ju 390 was amongst many of the contenders but was not put into full production. These projects were suitable distractions to divert the German Führer's attention away from the hordes of Soviet and Allied soldiers that were step-by-step coming ever-closer to Germany. Yet the delusion was not his alone, the culpability stretched across the Third Reich. However, Göring was willing to transfer the blame upwards. He said of his Führer that "Hitler would never ask how big our bombers are, but how many?"

The search for a suitable heavy bomber ended when thousands appeared in the skies above Germany, but these belonged to the Allies. Some of the planes that hit the German capital even belonged to the Red Army Air Forces, but this was a rare occurrence. The German response to the multitude of British and American bombers was to realise that their limited resources had to be diverted in 1944 into an emergency fighter program to try and clear the skies of those devastating machines. The efficacy of the heavy bomber was clear. Again, the German response was too little and far too late.

Not all German thinking on the use of airpower was misguided, their combined arms operations did at first deliver some stunning victories. Opposing armies found their armour was harried to the point of distraction and destruction by well-coordinated tactical bombing. The Stuka JU-87 dive bomber and ground attack aircraft initially provided superb close air support. It was used against enemy tanks and even shipping, their wailing sirens made a terrifying noise before delivering their deathly blow. However, they were ultimately too slow and lacked manoeuvrability making them vulnerable to Allied and Red Army Air Forces fighters which proved to have more than sufficient platforms to carry out interdiction and close air support.

For an advanced economy with enough resources, strategic and tactical bombing were not mutually exclusive approaches to warfare, indeed, they could be complimentary. In the run-up to D-Day, originally planned for 5th June 1944, the heavy bombers that were being used to attack civilian and industrial targets in the Reich were largely taken from national control and placed under the command of the Supreme Allied Commander, General Eisenhower, whose Deputy was Arthur Tedder of Britain's Royal Air Force. They were used to disrupt and cut road and rail links, especially the bridges over the River Seine. Aerial attacks to stop enemy supplies reaching the front were known as Operational Bombing. The intention was too severe the connection between German industry and the Normandy beaches on the English Channel where a new front against Germany would be opened. This disruption would also isolate and immobilise *Heer* and *Waffen-SS* troops based in France. This was managed in such a way that they achieved that task without laying clues as to the intended location of the landings. The bombing was close enough to Normandy to cause disruption but far enough from the beaches that they would not give away where the Allies impending invasion would come ashore. It was not completely total war; the British Prime Minister was concerned that the operational bombing of transportation links in France in the build-up to D-Day would cause too many French civilian casualties. Churchill sought to place a ceiling on these raids.

Following the invasion of France, heavy bombers were used to hinder the German defence and support the British, American, Canadian, and Polish advance. In September 1944, after the successful conclusion of the Battle of Normandy, the bombers that had been used to support Operation Overlord were taken back under their respective national control. The tactical use of heavy bombers was in complete contradiction to what the initial advocates of strategic bombing had intended for these aircraft. Yet unintentionally their advocacy of an approach to warfare that led to the massive investment in such planes had greatly aided the tactical necessities of warfare. Bombers would be made available to aid the ground effort throughout the remainder of the war. Nevertheless, operational bombing was a significant departure for the Allies in general and Arthur Tedder in particular. Tedder, had helped develop saturation bombing, also known as carpet bombing, which sought to subject a large area around a target to a sustained bombardment to obliterate the entire mark and its surrounding vicinity. So instrumental was he in developing this concept that it also received the epitaph of 'Tedder's carpet'.

The problems created by being too fixated on the immediate needs of the *Heer* extended beyond the size of bombers to other types of aircraft. The Messerschmitt BF 109, though an outstanding fighter plane at the start of the war, had poor range and was therefore at a major disadvantage during the Battle of Britain. It had not been created to fill a strategic role, but as a tactical support plane that would be operating in conjunction with blitzkrieg forces operating on the ground and would take-off from airfields close behind the advancing army. Adding sufficient range was never a consideration, a major drawback during the Battle of Britain.

This situation was compounded by the German High Command initially favouring the medium bomber above even fighter aircraft. They committed the strategic mistake of not prioritising the production of fighter planes early enough. When the Germans did provide planes to their Luftwaffe, they would be near world beaters. The Focke-Wulf Fw 190, first introduced in 1941, was an outstanding contribution to their fighter force. This excellent Luftwaffe fighter, which even became an effective ground attack aircraft, was initially beset by production difficulties and was not present in sufficient numbers until too late in the war. Likewise, the Messerschmitt Me 262 jet and an assortment of rocket powered planes were deadly attempts to answer the problem posed by Allied heavy bombers that were unleashing firestorms throughout Germany. Despite the ME 262 being amongst the most advanced fighters of its day its production was hampered by the enemy it was intended by its designers to destroy. Its production was reduced to nearly zero as the supply routes to the factories were cut by Allied bombers.

The British were amongst the pioneers of jet technology, but this was largely provided to the Americans, surrendering the UK's advantage in the Anglo-Saxon world. This was not before the important development work was completed that ultimately led to the Gloucester Meteor. This twin turbojet engine fighter plane entered service in 1944 and was used in the spring of 1945 in a ground attack role. However, it was not allowed to fly too far in case it was shot down and its technology, in particular the advanced metals that were used in its construction, could be stolen by the Axis. Later German technology was appropriated by the British who took the Luftwaffe's swept wing design and used it in the ill-fated Comet commercial airliner after the war. The British and the Germans were not the only countries to be developing jet power. The Italians were also amongst the first jets, but their experimental aircraft was not a great success, and it did not enter full production.

Italy did manage to produce effective fighter planes using the conventional configuration of a tractor propeller powered by front mounted engines. The Italians showed their creativity and willingness to experiment by producing different types of aircraft using either an inline or radial engine. Just as the Italian's showed panache in the air and in naval attacks, they also showed élan in their aircraft design. However, these aircraft did not give Italy's Royal Air Force, *Regia Aeronautica*, anywhere near the same dominance in the skies that their car marques enjoyed both before and after the war on the racetrack. Italian fighter planes in North Africa were too elegant and not sturdy enough for the tough demands of this desert environment. Britain's rugged Hawker Hurricane was better suited to the ground attack role.

At the heart of the problem was the Fascism of Benito Mussolini. The corporatist state he established sought to limit competition between the classes and unify all sections of society from industrialists to trade unions under a central bureaucracy. It ran counter to the entrepreneurial spirit at which Italy excelled. Government control from Rome of businesses and Italy's diverse regions was not effective, those entities managing their own affairs would have been more productive. The mountainous nature of Italy encouraged its people to have different customs, languages, and their own separate administrations based on the city state. During the Middle Ages competition between these polities made the cities on the foothills of the Alps, in the Po Valley, and down into the northern Apennine Peninsula amongst the most prosperous and scientifically advanced areas in Europe. Free from central control they led the way in physics, metallurgy, finance, and art. The dissemination of power to the local level enabled the laying of the foundations for the renaissance and moved Europe from the medieval era into the modern age.

Excessive state control was a rational response to the anarchic and divided nature of Italian life and a practical form of socialism that was intended to eliminate the class conflict that Karl Marx had critiqued but not solved. Yet corporatism was stultifying and suppressed the competitive spirit and drive for excellence which would have otherwise been a hallmark of the Italian economy and its society. Fascist corporatism did not work effectively, neither did the corporatism of social democratic states of western Europe in the 1970s and the European Union in this age, which also failed to spark growth. As such, in the interwar years the Italian automotive industry was nowhere near as productive as it could have been. This meant that unlike countries such as Britain and America, which transferred their automobile production skills to making planes, the Italians were unable to utilise quality control and efficient assembly techniques. Alternatively, a freer Italy with the productive northern regions of Italy left to their own devices would have given their wartime aircraft industry a stronger footing to produce world beating designs which could be made en masse.

The air race

Belief in the knockout blow from bombers theory led to the development of their antidote, fast interceptor planes to shoot them down. Here again Britain and Germany followed different courses. Whereas the British concentrated their efforts in the run up to the Battle of Britain on the production of a few models of fighter plane the Germans handicapped their production capabilities by producing too many different types of planes and in too many variants, The Messerschmitt Bf 110, a twin-engine heavy fighter, is an example of this; it was designed to escort the bombers into combat but ultimately required an escort of its own. This division of resources helped British fighter production outnumber that of Germany, even though the Germans entered the conflict with a much stronger air force.

Fighter Command in the summer of 1940, when the Battle of Britain began, was outnumbered by the Luftwaffe. Nevertheless, Britain's Ministry of Aircraft Production was phenomenally successful. This body, and the equipping of the UK's car industry that switched from making automobiles to aircraft, enabled more than 131,500 aeroplanes to be produced in the war, this was a great achievement. It was a massive build-up of airpower. This great transformation was an accomplishment that had long been planned and prepared for. From as early as 1935, the UK established shadow factories next to car plants, these enabled the industrial sites to churn out war planes. The American automobile industry also helped in the air war.

Ford Motor Company turned to producing bombers and constructed the famed Willow Run plant. This was a child of consent not compulsion. A key component of Henry Ford's strategy to build his company was though improving the terms of his employees, paying a proper wage and attracting the best workers who were therefore motivated and conscientious. His enlightened employment policies were profitable for him and made his company successful; Henry Ford also employed black, female, and disabled workers. He believed that prosperity would bring peace, which was to the betterment of humanity. Ultimately, he was correct but not before his productive factories and workers had helped annihilate the enemies of peaceful industrial progress.

Britain and America took different approaches as to how best to build up their air power. President Roosevelt in the United States rolled back his New Deal policies that had constricted and constrained American industry. Henry Ford, who was originally against US intervention overseas, came to back the war effort and allowed his company's considerable skills and potential to produce weapons. Roosevelt won him and other industrialists over to his cause by limiting state interference and freeing up the economy. Through cancelling his failed New Deal initiatives, the American war economy was built on allowing manufacturers to be free of state control. They would also compete with one another for US government contracts. In the UK, the British government took a different approach. They amassed emergency powers to conduct the war, and limited individual freedom and property rights. They also abolished the right to strike but did not stop some miners from downing tools during the war. Performance related pay, and the sending of the Bevin Boys down the pits rather than to the front, increased coal output. Britain's relative decline began when it took a socialist mindset into the post-war era. However, these policies have now been reversed and the UK is again a motor car manufacturing success story.

The ability of both Britain and America to rule the skies, enabling them to win the war came from their advanced automobile industries. That was itself driven by their competitive consumer car markets. They allowed a creative and efficient industry to prosper. Britain and America had overtaken that of Germany which in 1885 produced the Benz Patent-Motorwagen, considered to be the first automobile. Since the Second World War the defeated Germans and Japanese have built their industrial strategy around the production of the automobile. Germany in particular had learned the lesson that a free motor industry operating in a free market would benefit the state. It was those policies, known in German as *Ordoliberalismus*, that created their post-war *Wirtschaftswunder* economic miracle.

In the UK, the car industry was not the only contributor to Britain's aviation success. The de Havilland Aircraft Company was more than capable of producing modern designs using unconventional and traditional materials. They had long been experimenting with wood and plywood in their aircraft construction. Using such abundant materials in their aeroplanes had the advantage that they did not deprive other manufacturers of finite aluminium, steel, and other metal alloys. There were other practical reasons. The main benefit and rationale for using what appeared to be an antiquated material like wood in a plane's fuselage was that it had a higher strength-to-weight ratio than many metals. When such a wooden wonder was mated with two Rolls-Royce Merlin engines the Mosquito was born. This wonderous aircraft was amongst the fastest aeroplanes in the world when it was introduced and could outclimb its adversaries. The aircraft faithfully served the Royal Air Force in a multitude of roles. It was used as a night fighter to a pathfinder bomber dropping its incendiary bombs on a target and consequently pinpointing the drop zone in advance of the four-engine heavy Lancaster bombers who would obliterate all that was left. The Mosquito's production placed woodworking skills on a par with coachbuilding. Carpenters and cabinet makers amongst others could contribute to the war effort. This mightily impressive aircraft won plaudits from Hermann

Göring. When talking about the fast multirole plane he praised British geniuses for their inventiveness and described their German counterparts as nincompoops.

Anglo-American aeronautics

US military advisors had been helping the UK from mid-1941, particularly in matters to do with aviation and air war. The Allied cooperation was aided by the political and cultural closeness, and the common war aims shared between the western Allies. This made military co-operation much easier. This produced immediate successes ranging from the sharing of radar technology to producing possibly the most outstanding fighter plane of World War II, the P-51 Mustang. This model, produced by North American Aviation, vied with the Vought F4U Corsair, to be the war's most capable Allied fighter. The Mustang, however, with its low drag laminar flow wings gave it exceptionally long-range allowing it to reach the heart of Germany. This attribute, along with its superb speed, hastened the demise of the Third Reich. Yet, not only did it owe its existence to Britain, having been commissioned in response to a British order for more aircraft, but its functionality was only realised when the airframe was mounted with the Rolls-Royce Merlin engine. This unleashed the plane's full potential. Its utility was further advanced by the addition of the Malcolm Hood, a bubble canopy which gave the pilot excellent all-round visibility. This was invented by Robert Malcolm of R Malcolm & Co, both of whom were British. This concept had earlier been seen on the Westland Whirlwind, a British twin engine fighter. The hood was also inspired by the canopy of the Bell P-39 Airacobra, a plane which incidentally came to be rejected by the British Royal Air Force and the United States Army Air Forces in favour of the Supermarine Spitfire. However, the P-39 along with other British and American types performed useful active service with the Soviets on the Eastern Front.

The Americans did not only learn from the British but also borrowed from the Germans and adopted their finger-four fighter plane tactics which balanced defence and attack. The British RAF and the Soviet Red Army Air Forces also embraced that formation. The Luftwaffe's development of this four-plane tactic came from their experience during the Spanish Civil War, where older German aircraft were outperformed by Soviet fighter planes which had been supplied to the Republican forces. Whilst there was much cooperation between Britain and America, these two nations were divided by a common desire to defeat Germany. They had vastly different ideas as to how the air war against Germany should be conducted.

Divided allies

The contrasting approaches to the bombing campaign showed stark differences between the Allies. The British Army volunteered to fight in a style that pinned their enemy and wore them down in gritty attritional fighting. This enabled the Americans to sweep in and eliminate key strategic points, both making important contributions to completing the victory. Likewise, the two nations respective bomber forces undertook contrasting, but perhaps complimentary, strategies. However, the synergy was not fully realised nor appreciated at the time and not until now.

The British had no illusions as to the enemy they were dealing with and were willing to undertake the darkest measures to wipe Nazism from the face of the earth. Despite the size of the British Empire, its armed forces did not have an unlimited reserve of manpower at its disposal, the Royal Air Force especially so. It was hoped that attacking at night would preserve the lives of Britain's young men in the RAF and the airmen in the Royal Canadian Air Force that operated alongside the British. Manpower was always an issue for Britain and her empire forces. Area bombing under the cover of darkness had been forced on Britain. The heavy casualties from daylight raids could not be sustained. Yet, bombing by night made precision all but impossible. Not to use Britain's bomber force was inconceivable, therefore, the strategy of area bombing at night was a necessity. This RAF's decision was not an aberration, the Luftwaffe likewise abandoned costly daylight raids.

There were other less tangible factors that justified Britain's area bombing, namely important political considerations. There was the requirement to demonstrate to the domestic political audience that Britain, after being grievously bombed herself, was hitting back. The UK did pay Germany back and with substantial interest on top. International relations also had a part to play. Stalin was anxious that Britain expand operations against Germany. The air war against Germany was for a time the aerial equivalent of the second front against the Third Reich that Stalin had been calling for. Indeed, after being ejected from the continent it was at first the only way that Britain could be proactive in the war.

The Area Bombing policy was rigorously advocated by Britain's Charles Portal, the Chief of the Air Staff, during World War II. In 1942, Sir Arthur Harris, a veteran of both the First World War and the Arab Revolt in Palestine, became Air Officer Commanding-in-Chief of the RAF's Bomber Command. Bomber Harris as he became known was tasked with implementing Portal's strategy. A relentless and highly effective organiser, Harris made Bomber Command a force to be reckoned with; he followed a focused approach. Rather than attacking dispersed locations, he selected specific targets to be subjected to repeated attacks so that they would suffer absolute devastation. This even included bombing the city's transport links to hamper the emergency services reaching beleaguered denizens.

The bombing campaign was successful but not in the way they anticipated. It dislocated the Axis war economy, or at least prevented it from reaching its full potential, but it did not break the civilian population, nor did it win the war on its own as Harris expected. He had great ambitions for his approach to the air war, even repeatedly attacking the Third Reich's capital. However, Bomber Harris' 'Battle of Berlin', led to considerable losses amongst his aircrews in the sixteen raids which made up that campaign. It was considered a failure. Yet, the raids against Berlin never received the support of the USAAF that he would have liked. Perhaps with more American involvement the outcome may have been more advantageous, but the United States had a different philosophy.

The American strategic bombing campaign was devised in 1941 before the US entered the war. Its philosophy was to prevent the enemy from waging war and focused on trying to destroy factories and other industrial targets, in particular; plane, ball-bearing, and fuel production plants. Like the Russians, the United States bombed the Ploiești oil installation in Romania. Bombers even flew from North Africa.

Amongst the most influential US theorists of strategic airpower was Alexander P de Seversky. He had fought for Imperial Russia in the First World War as a bomber pilot. de Seversky was another émigré from Russia who decided to permanently settle in the United States following the tumult that came with the Bolshevik revolution. He founded the company that became Republic Aviation which produced the P-47 Thunderbolt. This excelled as a fighter and ground-attack plane. de Seversky became one of the most influential advocates of strategic bombing. He was a contemporary of Billy Mitchell.

Alexander de Seversky's book, *Victory Through Air Power*, was published in 1942. The following year Walt Disney adapted the book, turning into an animated movie of the same name. This extolled the value of long-range heavy bombing and showed heavy bombers clearing the skies of enemy planes. The reality for many American aircrews was different to the fantasy film. Despite bristling with defensive machines guns and flying in combat box air defence formations with each bomber providing an overlapping field of fire, the bombers could not entirely defend themselves from fast and manoeuvrable fighter planes. Despite shooting down some Luftwaffe fighters, the self-defence concept did not entirely work.

Attacking in the daylight made aircraft easy to locate and allowed fighters planes to engage the bombers. Their defences were also inadequate. The large and less manoeuvrable heavy planes were susceptible to the powerful cannons on Axis fighter aircraft. Despite having a slower rate of fire and less rounds available than the machine guns used on most American planes, large calibre guns were more than capable of knocking a bomber out of the sky.

Whilst the British developed direction-finding technology to aid their night-time navigation to the target, telling the bombardier where to drop his bombs, American aircrews also took advantage of technology. The USAAF had faith in their Norden bombsight. It was said that when using this a bomb could be dropped into a pickle barrel from 20,000 feet. The belief in this bombsight, that even took control of the flight, was a factor in pursuing their precision bombing strategy. The accuracy of American daylight bombing, even when using that device, was not in practice what the testing had led them to believe. The climate was also a hurdle to overcome. Northern Europe's cloudy overcast conditions negated the usefulness of even the advanced Norden bombsight.

Bombing campaigns were still in their infancy when the war began. As there was little practical evidence to rely on, commanders had little choice other than to apply untested theories devised in peacetime. After developing a position, humans often resist change and stubbornly refuse to depart from their *modus operandi*. Organisational inertia, groupthink, and commanders rigidly following their routine, all contributed to a lack of willingness to change course from their pre-war theorised national approach to aerial warfare. Both Britain and America were trying to make the tactics fit their individual theories. The stark contrast between British and American bombing was largely predetermined before the war began. When American losses began to mount up the British put pressure on the US to bomb at night to avoid the appalling loses incurred during their daylight raids. However, it was estimated that it would have taken too long to retrain the crews to operate at night, thus it was ruled out.

A great deal of disharmony existed between Britain's Sir Arthur Harris and his American counterpart, Curtis LeMay. The Allies, however, could agree on the policy of using strategic bombing to destroy German industry. As per the Casablanca Directive of 21st January 1943 – the RAF and USAAF would pay special attention to destroying transportation, oil plants, indeed any part of the German war economy was earmarked for destruction. Submarine construction yards, and the German aircraft industry received special attention. However, the inability to completely destroy the robust U-boat pens showed that the British belief in area bombing was the correct way forward. Nevertheless, the attacks on

German aircraft production reaped dividends. Operation Point Blank, beginning in mid-1943, lead to the round the clock bombing of Germany's aircraft industry, with the US bombing by day and the British coming at night. Ultimately, cooperation had won out and a compromise was reached, and differing objectives were divided up with all receiving some treatment. Despite the differences the competing strategies proved to be complimentary. All aspects of the German war economy were targeted without reprieve.

Harris wanted bombing to target cities, yet at times even Bomber Command successfully embraced precision bombing. Daylight precision strikes were not the sole preserve of the USAAF, such attacks were also carried out by Bomber Harris' Lancasters. French industry, most notably the armament factories at Le Creusot, the Schneider works, was repeatedly struck. The so-called Krupps of France served the German war machine by turning out guns, tanks, locomotives, and armoured vehicles. One attack, called Operation Robinson, even had a component that sought to disable this plant by destroying the substation which provided the factories with electricity; it was a success. To accomplish a similar end awe-inspiring bombs were designed by British inventor and aeronautical engineer Barnes Wallis. His Tallboy, Grand Slam and earthquake bombs destroyed specific targets. His research on seismic bombs showed that shockwaves could be a powerful destructive force. These weapons could destroy bridges, viaducts, coal mines, and dams. The devastation they wrought would make much of the German armaments industry impotent. He also famously invented the bouncing bomb. This device, first developed as an anti-shipping weapon, was successfully used in 1943 against German dams in the Ruhr Valley, damaging the region's industrial production. Operation Chastise, as it was known, forced the Germans to divert labourers and copious amounts of concrete from building the Atlantic Wall to repair the damage wrought on the dams. This hindered the construction of defences in Normandy, which were left incomplete, thus making it harder for the Germans to resist the D-Day landings which came the following year. The bold and daring operation was achieved at an excessively high cost, as did American precision bombing.

To avoid the alarming death toll the Americans had to increase the altitude of their bombers. Saving the lives of aircrews trumped the need for accuracy. Technically, this was an abandonment of the precision bombing strategy. American daylight precision strategy would take on a different purpose, inviting the Germans to allow themselves to be shot out of the sky. The introduction of the P-51 Mustang, a long-range fighter, changed the prospect of US daylight bombing. USAAF bombers, such as the B-17 Flying Fortress and the B-24

Liberator, now had escort fighter planes that could protect them over Germany. The Mustang's role, however, was not defensive. They flew in front of their charges and attacked German planes that sought to intercept the bombers. The single-seater P-51s pilots actively hunted their Luftwaffe counterparts. Jimmy Doolittle, now a USAAF general in the European theatre, allowed American escort fighters, especially the Mustangs, to fly in advance of the bombers eliminating the Luftwaffe from the skies. They were free to attack and destroy the enemy wherever they found them. The American bombers were in a sense bait. Doolittle's tactics drew-out the German fighters. Once the bombers had attacked their target, the fighter escort were then allowed to strafe German airfields and other infrastructure on their way back to base. In February 1944's Operation Argument, also known as Big Week, American and British bombers and fighter planes reaped further destruction on German aircraft and their production. The Nazis were losing the war on all fronts.

There is a mindset which makes a great fighter pilot and America's society produced such a mode of thinking in abundance. The United States of America, whilst having great industrial cities that could manufacture the planes also had more isolated rural communities that helped forge many of the USAAF's most successful pilots. Individualistic Americans from such a background could thrive in an environment where their decision making alone would be the deciding factor. Americans from a farming background would often hunt from childhood and learned from this the requirement of having to shoot ahead of a flying target, that would then fly into the bullet's path. Shooting warbirds was second nature to these men. The Mustang with its six .50 calibre browning machine guns, had replaced the shotgun as the weapon of choice for these self-starter farm boys.

The Mustang, described in popular culture as the "Cadillac of the skies", became a true American icon. When Göring saw the Mustang fighter planes escorting the bombers over Germany he knew that his Nazis had lost the war. Indeed, the introduction of the P-51 Mustang as an escort lead to a 75% reduction in bomber crew loses. When the Luftwaffe was devasted and ceased to be the deadly threat that it once was, Doolittle allowed American bombers to return to low altitude precision bombing. While the American fighters took on German interceptors, the USAAF bombers attacked industries vital to the Nazi war effort, especially what was left of German aircraft factories. However, bombing Germany created a sense of solidarity amongst its civilians and the feeling that they were all in it together, yet it did cause catastrophic disruption of Germany's infrastructure. An especially devastating attack came on 12th May

1944 when bombers targeted German controlled oil production. This was to become increasingly important.

General Carl Spaatz of the USAAF became a particularly strong and successful advocate for Allied air power to focus on destroying oil production as the number one target. Spaatz thought it was even higher in priority than Arthur Tedder's desire to support the ground troops by focussing on severing transport links. General Dwight D. Eisenhower, Supreme Commander of the Allied Expeditionary Force in Europe, considered Spaatz to have made one of the greatest contributions to the victory in Europe. Apart from the fire storms caused through Allied bombs and incendiary devices, the light was going out on the Third Reich.

The home front burning

The Americans had the luxury that threats to their industry were negligible. The only real danger to US factories came from ineffectual German saboteurs whose mission was betrayed and easily foiled. A negligible threat arrived from the opposite hemisphere to the east, Japanese balloon bombs carried on the jet stream across the Pacific to the United States of America aimed to inflict some damage. However, these bombs with timed fuses used a technological approach reminiscent of the equally impactless Austrian attack on Venice nearly a century before, US industry was unscathed. Japanese plane carrying submarines were also intended to be used to attack America's western seaboard with biological weapons. This mission was cancelled following Japan's surrender. US factories were free to maximise their output throughout the entirety of the war.

The air war and industrial production were intrinsically linked. The Soviets, with a long land border, were far more vulnerable to Axis airpower. The Russians survived the onslaught by moving their industry out of harm's way and relying on the fruits of American and British workers. Despite the Blitz in 1940, and the ongoing German bombing campaign against the UK, building up to a second, though less severe, aerial onslaught in 1944, Britain and her empire was able to continually expand production.

The United Kingdom relied on its centrally controlled and coordinated anti-aircraft defences. Britain's smart defences relied on analogue information gathered from its long-established early warning system, first built around a series of listening devices on the south-coast and then radar. This directed the RAF's planes, fighting in the big wing formation used in the Battle of Britain, on to the enemy. The en masse interception of German aircraft was partly a safety measure so that the British fighters could face the Luftwaffe on near equal terms rather than being picked off in small piece meal attacks. Aeroplanes were not the only means by which Britain's cities could be sparred. Where the bombers would get through, deception was used to divert them from their intended targets. Tactics ranged from vigorously enforced blackouts to deprive enemy pilots of visual clues, to fields of fire that mimicked the intended target and drew the German bombers away from real industrial centres. In a system that was planned and organised before the war, Firemen were used and Air Raid Precautions (ARP) wardens were recruited. When the conflagration came, they would put out fires, limit damage, enforce blackouts, and thus help to keep as many civilians as safe as possible. Workers were then free to focus the next day on building weapons which would soon be directed at the Third Reich.

The Germans could not escape their fate. In response to the destruction wrought on Germany by the Allied bombers the Nazis attempted to protect and enhance their industrial output by dispersing their often-bomb-damaged industry to underground sites. These were in the centre of mountains where slave labourers would tender machines that were intended to breath fire on Germany's enemies. The conditions of these factories, where the forced labourers would toil under pain of an almost inevitable death, was not conducive to supplying large amounts of vengeance weapons and aircraft for the war. The decision to construct these facilities was a major strategic error made out of desperation by people who did not understand the requirements of modern industrial production. The underground factories were simply inappropriate environments to produce complex and technologically demanding machines, particularly planes.

The desperate German need to produce aircraft led to the alternative strategy of further dispersing industry into new locations in the heart of Germany's vast woodlands. The Nazis romanticised the eternal forest and this fabled landscape did help their cause. It was hoped that allied pilots would be unable to see these wooden built factories under the trees. This approach worked, safely hidden from British and American reconnaissance flights, and aircraft production increased. Yet, there was a fundamental flaw that limited the success of this industrial reorganisation. These factories secreted away from the eyes of prying pilots, were themselves too thinly spread out to work at maximum efficiency. So all-encompassing was the Allied bombing, particularly British saturation bombing, as well as the more targeted attacks on transport links, that supplies could not readily be delivered and put into production. Regardless of that, Germany was just too far behind and outgunned. Most of the aircraft built at these factories were destroyed in the air war.

It was Allied air power that was winning the war in the west, and its successful co-ordination with infantry, armour, and artillery. Strategic bombing, either through carpet bombing or more precise strikes, destroyed arms production. Air superiority allowed the British and Americans to conduct operational and tactical bombing almost at will, destroying the enemy in the field and limiting their freedom of manoeuvre. 85% of Allied tanks that succumbed to the Germans were knocked out by panzers and anti-tank guns. Conversely, the reverse was true for German heavy tanks. Most Tiger tanks were destroyed by aeroplanes or were abandoned by their crews.

At times Allied air power was vital. Despite overwhelming American superiority, not all operations against the Germans were straightforward, indeed far from it. None more so than the issue in doubt US landings on Omaha beach as part of D-Day 6th June. Here tactical bombing helped save the Americans at Pointe Du Hoc above that blood-stained shore. It prevented German counterattacks on the US at Omaha and created craters and mounds of earth that provided cover from German machine gun emplacements, many of which were also destroyed. It helped negate the loss of British developed Duplex Drive amphibious tanks which did not fare well in the rough seas. Air power also assisted the Americans at Utah Beach and across the other Allied landing sites. Indeed, part of the rationale for choosing Normandy was that, as well as its long sandy beaches, it was easily in range of the most numerous Allied fighter plane, the Spitfire.

Tactical bombing not only helped Allied assaults but also hindered those of the Germans. As soon as the fog lifted above Belgium during the Battle of the Bulge the panzers below were exposed, the operation to seize Antwerp was doomed. The situation late in the war was markedly different from when the Germans had crossed the Ardennes in 1940, when they were at liberty to deploy their Stukas at will. The core problem was the Luftwaffe's lack of fighter aircraft. The Germans could not defend themselves from tactical airstrikes for which they had no answer. Any German counterattack, be that in Normandy, at the Battle of Bulge, or during the Allies advance to the Rhine were destined to fail. Such a move would be met by a flying taxi rank of Hawker Typhon fighter-bombers waiting for the next opportunity to fire their rockets and rip open a panzer as soon as German tanks broke cover. This plane was not well equipped for high altitude, so what would have been a design failure was turned into a successful tool for interdiction rather than interception. Tanks were not the Typhon's only target. They also destroyed anything from trains to German air defences.

In this day and age, aircraft have the technological edge over surface-to-air defences, which as soon as they become operational, unwittingly advertise their position allowing the plane to attack the missile site and seal its fate. The same was not true in the Second World War's Pacific theatre. The ship based Bofors anti-aircraft guns would fire proximity fuse shells in quick succession at Japanese aircraft. These munitions would explode when they came close to the lightly armed Japanese planes, the flak would tear them apart. So effective were they that these platforms have been labelled as war winning weapons. The Axis, however, did not have proximity fuse anti-aircraft artillery; resource limitations prevented them from investing in their development. The Germans and the Japanese had to rely on less accurate pre-set estimations of altitude when arming their anti-aircraft rounds. Anglo-American inventiveness and superior resources won the day. The defence of Axis skies was retarded.

German air defence

The Soviets on the Eastern Front not only indirectly benefited from the dev-astation of Germany, but Allied bombing also grievously weakened their Nazi foe. The Germans stripped planes and aircrew from the Eastern Front to defend their Home Front from the immediate threat of air attacks. The German armies fighting the Russians lost pilots and planes to the battle raging in the skies above the Reich. This movement of men and machines back to Germany was not just to stop the American daylight raids, but also the British who came during darkness and faced Luftwaffe night fighters and the dreaded 88-mm anti-aircraft guns. These were effective tank killers and could have been used to destroy Russian armour, instead they were stationed on Germany's western flank aimed at the sky. Along with them were 900,000 men. This host and the enormous firepower and resources at their disposal, were engaged in trying to knock the British and Americans out of the air. Despite these defences the Allies were gradually ruling the skies as well as the waves. Without those aerial assaults nearly one million men could have been used against the Red Army and the Red Army Air Forces. Instead, they were fighting a losing battle for the lives of their loved ones at home.

The German air defence system relied on what was known as the Kammhuber Line, this stretched across Germany's north-western frontier and had a massive array of radar stations feeding information to the lines of flack guns and sup-porting fighter squadrons. It was named after its founder Josef Kammhuber. When the British attacked, they would cross the Himmelbett defence system of radar. This network would detect the planes and direct search lights onto a bomber, other search lights were controlled by hand. Once the aeroplane had been illuminated, its position and path through the sky would be fixed and the flack guns would be unleashed. This system of night fighting using searchlights was known as the *Helle Nachtjagd*. It was introduced in 1940 and became the biggest threat to British bombers. The radar would also direct Luftwaffe night fighters onto their target. Some of these large *nachtjägers* were even equipped with radar and could fly at night, fulfilling a role that single-seat fighter planes could not perform as they would only operate at daytime and in good weather conditions.

One particularly effective German night fighter was the Heinkel He 219. This model was a twin-engine, radar equipped, and heavily armed night fighter. It was comparable to the British de Havilland Mosquito; it could and did destroy heavy bombers but was too few in number. German air defence would have been much more secure if they had been able to put this plane into full production. For the most part, however, the Luftwaffe had to rely on less able aircraft which could not stop the bulk of British bombers from getting through.

Evolving German air defence technology was matched by British technological developments that cracked Axis air defences. RAF Bomber Command also developed tactics known as the Bomber Stream. This overwhelmed and broke through the line of defences with as few losses as possible to reach the Ruhr Valley. Here they could attack industries vital to the German war effort from armaments production factories to synthetic oil refineries. Other important cities such as Hamburg were also subjected to bombing in large and sustained campaigns.

Fly 'til you die

German air defence policy was desperate to stop the Allied destruction of its industry, infrastructure, and spare the individual German citizens who were also targets. The Nazis, initially eager to please their own people, wanted to defend them from the war Hitler and his cronies had unleashed in their name. This positive attitude to their people would just bring more suffering upon them. German fighters flew continuous missions against the massed ranks of Allied bombers. This did enable them to shoot down many British and American air crews, indeed, the losses were appalling, but it also exhausted the Luftwaffe pilots and gradually killed-off their most skilled. Superior British and American aviation production, equipment, and technology were not simply going away. Despite German efforts they would return time and time again. Indeed, the desperation to stop this onslaught played into US hands. American military planners wanted the Luftwaffe to expose itself from where it would be destroyed. The German sacrifice of its own air power, death by the United States Army Air Forces, made a tangible difference on all fronts. The Führer's negligence with the lives of his flyers only led to the near murderous wasting of his pilot's existence. They were almost an oblation to the god of war. In desperation the Nazis organised their own near Kamikaze operations.

Hitler was a Laconophile, and drew inspiration from the Battle of Thermopylae, where, obedient to their laws, Spartans, Thespians, and Theban hoplites fought to the death against Iranians coming from the east. Similarly, the Luftwaffe's Leonidas Squadron, named after the heroic Spartan King Leonidas I, was expected to save the Reich. This German self-sacrifice squadron piloted a specially adapted version of the V-1 flying bomb. In the dying embers of the war the airmen were tasked with destroying bridges over the River Oder that flows to the east of Berlin. Unlike the Spartans, who bought time and created martyrs, the squadron's efforts were pointless. Nazi pilots that tried to crash themselves unto the bridges did not prevent the Russian advance for long, the Soviets spanned the river in one day. Theirs was not the only futile gesture. *Sonderkommando* Elbe were given the task of ramming Allied bombers with their fighters and thus rip the lumbering aeroplanes from the sky by severing a wing, or the fuselage, and sending it into a death spiral. The fanatical Luftwaffe pilot would hope to bail out and escape with his life. However, this was far from guaranteed. The extreme act of crashing a fighter plane into an Allied bomber made this a quasi-suicide squadron. It was hoped that this would fill the Allied aircrews with fear and stop the bombing raids long enough to restore Luftwaffe airpower by giving German industry an opportunity to produce enough jets. Nevertheless, for a nation with such economic problems and unable to supply enough men and machines this approach was indeed suicidal. The Allies could absorb their losses, the Axis could not.

Such acts of bravery were not the sole preserve of Germans. On 15th September 1940 Hawker Hurricane fighter pilot Ray Holmes, when out of ammunition, rammed a Dornier Do 17 as it approached Buckingham Palace on an attack run. He knocked the German light bomber out of the sky. Holmes survived and would go on to train Soviet fighter pilots. The Germans would plan other martyrdom operations. In 1945 a proposal to bomb power plants supplying electricity to Russian industry was revived. Aircrews involved in this putative operation were not expected to return to the Fatherland. This scheme was to be known as Operation *Eisenhammer*, it was cancelled due to the intended targets becoming nearly beyond range.

Red sky in the morning

On 22nd June 1941, the Luftwaffe found Soviet planes lying ready to be attacked beside their respective runways. The opening days of Operation Barbarossa saw the near complete destruction of the Red Army Air Forces, though they attempted to fight back many of Russia's obsolete designs were simply shot out of the sky. The situation had been worsened by Stalin, who did not trust flying nor even aircraft designers. The Soviet leader imprisoned aeronautical engineers in his gulag system, even men such as Andrei Tupolev experienced such treatment. Soon after the Axis invasion, he was quickly found and forced to work under pain of death for his design bureau. He and many others had effectively just moved from prison to better surroundings that were still tantamount to gaol.

Outmoded Soviet fighters and tactics at the start of Operation Barbarossa led to many losses. A lack of radios meant that there was poor communication between the pilots. The omission of this technology demanded that the Soviets fly in rigid inflexible formations that gave little freedom of manoeuvre and made them vulnerable to *Jagdwaffe* fighter wings. Pilots also received unsatisfactory training. The massive losses at the start of the war meant that new flyers had to be called up, the inexperienced are far more likely to be defeated in the air and die in combat. Notwithstanding that, better models and manoeuvres began to transform the dire situation.

The crisis at the start of invasion that befell the Red Army Air Forces gave the Soviets little option but to replace their defunct old aircraft with modern designs. They also took the opportunity to reorganise how air power, and their new models, were used. Fighter and bomber attacks would be integrated with the Red Army's ground forces. The Russians, in a desperate struggle for survival, had to hold back and repel the invader. They did not have the luxury of time and could not focus on hollowing out the Reich from within as Harris hoped to do. Conversely, it was the Soviet Union that was repeatedly being ravaged every day. As such the Russians had to focus on the immediate danger posed by an occupying force that threatened to wipe out Russian civilisation. The Red Army Air Forces' primary focus was against military targets rather than German cities, though their time would come. *Deutsches Heer* and *Waffen-SS* Divisions were harried by day and night.

Before the stagnation of state socialism set in, the Soviet authorities were creative and obsessed with modernity, they thought that science was on their side and they were willing to embrace new ideas. Yet, there are always practical limitations to how far this should go. The German invasion was a major crisis for Russia. The word crisis derives from the Greek κρίσις, meaning a turning point in a disease from which the afflicted could either make a recovery or die. Stalin, his scientists, and aeronautical engineers had a choice to make. They could either invest resources in state of the art, even futuristic, flying gun platforms such as rocket powered aeroplanes, that were indeed under consideration. Or conversely commit to conventional designs that were easy, cheap, and quick to manufacture. There was clearly a need to produce aircraft that in terms of speed could out compete German machines, which were initially superior to Russian fighters. The Soviet authorities desperately yearned for anything that could turn the tide of the war; however, it was soon realised that they did not have the resources for such an ambitious scientific program. Furthermore, the Russians needed weapons that were guaranteed to work and could be produced quickly. They settled for quantity and ease of production. History shows they made the right decision. Their German adversaries, however, came to make the opposite choice and were to invest in surface-to-air guided missiles and their own rocket fuelled planes in a vain attempt to find a solution that would stop the Allied bombing campaign. The Soviets made decisions that wisely used their resources, and those of Britain and America; the desperate Nazis squandered theirs.

The approach the Russians settled on was similar to that of their tanks. Whilst Russian armour was effective, it was by no means overengineered. The Soviets even produced what was dubbed "the flying tank" which was officially known as the Ilyushin Il-2 *Shturmovik*. This was a single engine but heavily armoured ground attack aircraft. It even had the defensive armament of a rear facing 12.7mm machine gun, congruous to the browning .50 calibre, operated by a rear gunner. This, and its successor, was the most produced aircraft in history. They were essential components of Russian victory on the eastern front, eliminating German tanks from above.

The Red Army Air Forces also used their medium bombers to decisive effect; indeed, they changed the course of German strategy, leading the Nazis into a cul-de-sac that diverted Axis resources. In 1941, when the Russians bombed the oil refinery at Ploiești in German aligned Romania, they succeeded in causing some damage. The whole German war economy was at risk. The bombing came from the Soviet Black Sea Fleet based in the Crimea. This made Hitler realise that the Russian air bases there had to be eliminated, consequently he designated the Crimea as a prime target, previously it had not been a major part of German military planning. This led to a massive concentration of forces in that peninsula which could have been used on other fronts such as Leningrad. These forces included the best tactical air force units, Germany's heaviest guns, and thousands of pieces of artillery.

The mission was not entirely in vain; Romania and its vital oil remained at German disposal for the time being. The peninsula, which Hitler considered to be a Soviet static aircraft carrier that threatened his oil, had been eliminated from the equation, at least for the time being. The Luftwaffe also made use of Crimea's air bases and launched attacks from there to support the attempted conquest of the Caucasus region across the Black Sea. The Crimea also allowed easier access for Hitler's eastward drive to proceed across the Strait of Kerch, bypassing the Sea of Azov.

Despite the Allied shipment of planes to aid the Russian war effort, aircraft were, like almost everything else in the Soviet Union, bar tanks and the Ilyushin Il-2s, still in short supply. Nevertheless, Russian tactical and operational bombing gradually wore away their Axis enemies. The Russians recognised that supplies and a lack of them would be a key factor. The aerial component of Germany's attempt to eliminate Russia, or at least its European element, became a conflict centred around the Red Army Air Forces' use of air power to interdict German supplies. This was set against German attempts to deliver the resources they so desperately needed. In the vastness of the Soviet Union's underdeveloped country, a land that still has appallingly bad transport links, this was an arduous task made worse by partisan attacks. Aircraft were at times the only practical German mode of conveying necessities; at first this worked.

Herman Göring, head of the Luftwaffe, successfully used transport aircraft to supply the German Sixteenth Army from January to May 1942. Following the failure to capture Moscow, this army was cut-off and trapped in the Kholm Pocket by the Red Army's winter counter-offensive against Army Group Centre. The same trick could not be repeated the following winter. Göring reassured Hitler that the Sixth Army encircled in Stalingrad by Operation Uranus could be kept in the fight by supplying them through the air. Success on the ground required victory in the air.

Russian airpower was used to cut-off supplies from reaching the beleaguered Sixth Army. Three aerial blockade rings were set up by Chief Marshal of Aviation of the Soviet Air Force, Alexander Alexandrovich Novikov. He also organised hit and run tactics to destroy German planes attempting to supply the trapped men. Such tactics also helped train Russian pilots. Luftwaffe supply bases were also captured by the Red Army, extending the distance the German Junkers Ju 52 had to fly until reaching Stalingrad became too risky and untenable. The Germans had too few aircraft for the task. The same aeroplane that brought Hitler to his Nuremberg Rally, in a brilliant propaganda exercise recorded by Nazi filmmaker Leni Riefenstahl, and had successfully delivered paratroopers into combat, could not save the besieged Sixth Army. Most of its men would never return to Germany.

Though Soviet fighter planes were not quite as effective as their German counterparts, the Red Army Air Forces kept up the fight. In time, the Russians helped gradually ware down and destroy the Luftwaffe and Axis ground forces. In 1945 during the Battle of Berlin, the last major clash of the war in the European theatre, Ilyushin's even attacked the beleaguered capital of Hitler's thousand-year Reich. German cities had been systematically devastated.

When the city of Dresden was bombed in mid-February 1945, the Nazi propaganda chief Joseph Goebbels spun the line that Dresden was an artistic city whose spires did not warrant the Anglo-American attack. Certainly, it was true that it was an architectural treasure, but that was not the whole story. Dresden was, by the standards of the time, a legitimate target. The Soviets requested that their western Allies bomb Dresden to aid their advance on that city. As Dresden was an important railway hub, it was of great importance. It needed to be controlled and it was vital that the enemy be deprived of that city. Furthermore, Dresden was also an important industrial centre. Prior to the bombing, a special British Joint Intelligence Subcommittee report to Churchill titled *German Strategy and Capacity to Resist* emphasised the need to end the war quickly by aiding the Soviet capture of important industrial bases such as Silesia, then a part of Germany. Hence the bombing, which aimed to assist the Russian advance, also helped make sure that another industrial area was eliminated and could not be reclaimed by the Third Reich. The bomber crews undertaking their strategic mission certainly fulfilled their objectives and at the time the war was by no means finished. The Russians, who were legally the innocent party, and had been attacked in what was deemed to be a war of aggression, a criminal act, still had much fighting to do. They would still suffer far more casualties in assaulting the German capital than the lives that were lost in Dresden when it was bombed. It was not a time to relax and give relief to the enemy.

Dresden was also a hotbed of Nazism, many of the residents had been fanatical supporters of Hitler. Whilst they may not have deserved the blame for what he did, those who aided and tolerated his crimes bear some responsibility for all that the Führer unleashed. In that sense, to wipe National Socialism off the face of the earth, there had to be consequences for those which enabled such an ideology to prosper in the first place. It was fitting that 'Bomber' Harris paraphrased the Old Testament prophet Hosea when he said... "They sowed the wind, and now they are going to reap the whirlwind."

The Third Reich was literally crumbling away. Both the British and the Americans were bombing German towns and cities reducing the buildings to rubble that would block roads, "putting the city in the street" as the American's called it. It was hoped that this would obstruct their defender's movements. This certainly did hinder mobility.

Bombing as a hindrance

Bombing was working, but sometimes too well. The use of air power could on occasions be a problem for ground forces. Levelling an area with an aerial bombardment had largely become standard military practice; they were often carried out at the behest of ground commanders. The 1942 German obliteration of Stalingrad, the heaviest aerial attack yet seen on the Eastern Front, turned this once great industrial city into a devastated moonscape of ruins and rubble strewn streets. This made it harder for both men and vehicles to advance through. Whilst it succeeded in destroying this onetime centre of tractor production, turned to producing the famous T-34 tank, the bombing created more opportunities for defence. Thus, the German 6th Army became worn down, which in turn allowed the Red Army to keep a bridgehead on the western shore of the mighty Volga River. And Hitler's eye was kept locked on his latest fixation.

The Germans were not alone in this experience. The bombing of the monastery of Monte Cassino just led to a defender's paradise of close quarter fighting in which the German paratroopers, the *Fallschirmjäger*, excelled. The ruins were not only easier to defend but prior to the bombing the abbey was not occupied in the first place. The Allies had inadvertently created a strong point which was only over come when the German defenders withdrew to avoid being cut-off.

Despite technological improvements to aid accuracy, be those advanced bombsights and even the development of electronic signals that could be used to direct the bombardier to drop his payload, precision was not guaranteed. There was still the tendency for the barrage to creep backwards as the following planes, seeing the explosion and fire of already dropped munitions, would release their bombs too early. This would cause the tragic consequences of missing the intended target, thus lengthening the war, and when used tactically the bombing could cause collateral damage and even blue-on-blue deaths, otherwise known as friendly fire. One such example of this came in the Battle of Normandy. The bombing at the beginning of Operation Cobra, part of the Allied breakout from the Normandy lodgement, impeded the initial advance. Smoke bombs were dropped too early killing 100 US soldiers, including Lieutenant General Lesley

McNair, the highest-ranking American Officer to die in the European theatre of operations, and injuring 500 more in the Saint-Lô area of France.

Even as the war drew to a close, and when the job was done efficiently and on target, bombing could create problems for the Allies in a similar bane to that experienced by the Germans in Stalingrad and in Italy at Monte Cassino in the Mountains of Lazio. As the allies pushed into Germany as part of Operation Veritable under Bernard Law Montgomery, Lieutenant General Brian Horrocks, accepted an offer to bomb the city of Cleves. The resulting rumble on the roads from the heavy bombing that preceded the ground forces again just hampered the advancing armour.

Airpower had become almost everything; it was vital to the ground forces and even decided where the army would fight its battles. This mode of warfare was a vital component that was used to take troops into combat and as in the Normandy campaign it was key to determining where the land operation would take place. From the landings on Sicily in the Mediterranean Sea, to Okinawa between the Pacific Ocean and the East China Sea, forces came ashore close to airfields so that these important pieces of infrastructure could be seized quickly. Depriving them to the enemy and turning their facilities to serve the Allied cause. The island of Iwo Jima was taken by the Marines and the US Navy to gain control of its airfields. Despite the controversy surrounding the operation and the islands' questionable efficacy as a staging post to attack Japan, Iwo Jima did provide airfields. These proved vital to saving many B-29s and their crews who would not have been able to return to their base in the Mariana Islands after encountering difficulties during their bombing of Japan. Ultimately, the air war, and particularly the bombing campaign, had paved the way for the liberation of Europe and the Orient.

The setting sun

It was thought that the Americans won the 'area' versus 'precision' bombing argument and that the United States had the superior mode of warfare amongst the Allies. However, the USAAF temporarily abandoned their drive for accuracy and adopted a more British style approach. And when the American advance in the Pacific put the Japanese home islands in range, Curtis Le May who had come from the European theatre of operations implemented a carpet-bombing strategy and used this against Japanese cities. This was highly reminiscent of Britain's RAF Bomber Command. LeMay had observed that Japanese daytime defences were inflicting heavy damage on low flying American planes. Flying in daylight at higher altitudes also gave little to no reward. Due to the atmospheric phenomenon of the jet stream, the belt of high-speed wind, that often manifested itself over Japan, bombs dropped from high altitude would often be blown of course, making precision bombing difficult at best. Furthermore, Japan had dispersed its production into micro factories in civilian areas making precision bombing impractical. This led LeMay to implement a new and devastating strategy.

Before night raids on Japan were started the US bombing crews could expect to be killed after as few as sixteen missions. Night-time attacks gave the Americans greater opportunity to inflict more damage, and as the American aircraft were relatively safer at night than in the day, they could fly low enough to inflict maximum destruction on their target and could expect little in return. Japanese night fighters were in even shorter supply than those available to the Germans and even less capable; they were too slow to sustain their attacks on the fast-moving American B-29s. Japan's Nakajima J1N1 *Gekkō* plane's radar was also of limited use. Generally, Japanese anti-aircraft defences were woefully inadequate. That was not their only deficiency. The sky at night even above Japan's home islands belonged to the Americans. These two belligerents were sharing the same time and physical space but lived and died in different eras.

It was a symptom of both Japanese under development and the ever-present risk of earthquakes that many Japanese cities, even as late as the 1940s, were still largely built of wood. These compressed conurbations were a veritable tinderbox at the mercy of American incendiary munitions. The firebombing of Japan from mid-1944 onwards shattered Japanese industry and its civilian workforce. Yet so ferocious were the flames that on occasions the heat would create a powerful vortex whose updraft could even make a B-29 Superfortress lose control and spin out of the sky where it would meet its own oblivion.

The US would try and warn Japanese civilians about which cities they were intending to bomb by dropping leaflets in advance. This policy was not followed in August 1945 when Hiroshima and Nagasaki were targeted with never before or since used in anger weapons to which Japan had no answer and no workable defence. Only at the final stages of Japan's war did they try a dramatic shift in strategy, unleashing creative airpower solutions to hold back their enemies. One attempt was to develop an interceptor capable of using its speed and firepower to shoot down the B-29. This plane, the Kyushu J7W, had a pusher configuration propeller engine, leaving the nose free to mount powerful cannons. With its swept back wings at the rear of the fuselage and its canard winglets emanating from its front the Kyushu J7W was reminiscent of a modern jet fighter. Yet, it was little more than a prototype. Japan had left it too late, besides, the bombing had ripped apart their already limited industrial capacity to produce this plane quickly enough and in sufficient numbers to defeat the exponentially growing in power United States. The perilous position that the Empire of Japan found itself in was becoming ever more acute. After the defeat of Germany, the US now had but one enemy in its bombsights.

The Japanese were not alone in being destroyed from the air. Even the stone, brick and mortar cities of Germany were engulfed by the all-consuming fire-storm. The Third Reich was burnt out from within. As the final embers of that great conflagration still glowed, in March 1945 Germany tried to send advanced weapons, ranging from jet engines to uranium, to the Japanese by submarine. This *U*-boat, however, was captured by the Americans. Even so, if it had arrived in Tokyo Bay, even the oriental talent of borrowing, adapting, and then producing en masse other people's technology would not have been enough to save the Empire of Japan so late in the war.

Liberation and Occupation

"Life is too short to learn German." — **Oscar Wilde**

Will power

Hitler believed that he only had to exert his will and victory would be achieved. The notion was not considered to be excessively outlandish at the time. Hitler's contemporary, the Indian nationalist, Mahatma Gandhi had said, "Strength does not come from physical capacity. It comes from an indomitable will." This belief in the superhuman and the triumph of the will, as if the mere desiring of victory were enough, gave latitude to ignore the reality of Germany's looming defeat. Hitler and his cabal stood firm and blamed the cowardice of the army for any reversals in the field. The Nazi revolutionary creed and belief in their scientific certainty allowed them to indoctrinate their soldiers and civilians, keeping them fighting beyond when it had ceased to be prudent. In that sense, Nazism was a boon to Germany's desire to dominate Europe and proved useful to those in Germany, particularly the military, who wanted to control neighbouring states. It was a German war, not a Nazi conflict. National Socialism was to a degree hijacked and internalised by those who sought to restore German leadership over Europe. Fanatics like Field Marshal Ferdinand Schörner, were all too happy to indulge Hitler's whims and wishful thinking by sanctioning a stubborn desire to stand firm.

Nazi notions were a useful supplement feeding German hunger for reordering Europe. Their ideals made defeat seem illogical and necessitated that the conflict continued as victory was always just one last push away. As such Germany remained at war; its peoples had little choice. The concept of Hitler as the saviour meant that the Nazis who governed the German state apparatus remained loyal to him and his flawed, feckless, and failing strategy. That, as well as an all-encompassing amount of propaganda, kept many Germans faithful to the belief in the *Endsieg,* the ultimate victory, when in reality all was as good as lost. Hitler could never achieve his nefarious goals. What the Nazis did not understand was that culture is everything; and their most consistent and enduring enemy had a quite different worldview.

The twentieth century would become a conflict between collectivism and individualism. Only one would achieve pre-eminence in the world, at least for a time. Anglo-Saxon societies in World War Two not only tried to preserve lives but also put this belief at the heart of their war planning. After witnessing the many debacles of World War One, Montgomery tried to win battles with as few casualties as possible. He also prioritised individual initiative, everyone had an important role to play. Those Anglo-Celtic notions that rejected the concept of an overbearing state made British individuals amongst the most inventive in the world. Indeed, the United Kingdom, and her Anglosphere progeny, led the world in the number of Nobel Laureates. Much of modernity was patented in Britain by its scientists and engineers. British eccentrics were at the forefront of this phenomenon and one such individual was Major General Sir Percy Hobart. He would give his name to 'Hobart's Funnies'. These were a plethora of specially adapted tanks that ranged from amphibious armoured vehicles to mine clearance machines, and to mobile bridging equipment. Hobart's armoured vehicles also included specialist anti-fortification tanks and the Churchill Crocodile, a flame-throwing tank. Incidentally, his sister, born Betty Hobart, was, before her passing, the wife of Bernard Law Montgomery and mother to Monty's son David, the 2nd Viscount of Alamein. Together, Monty and Hobart were to have an important role in a crucial battle to come, tearing down one of the barriers which guarded Hitler's domain. Hobart's adaptations of the US Sherman tank and the British Churchill helped the Allies win the Battle of Normandy. The Churchill was well armoured but at first it was believed to be an ineffectual design, it was slow, but its tracks were wide, this allowed it to navigate its way across difficult terrain. In other theatres, such as North Africa, it could even traverse mountainous ground. Its robust chassis was the perfect platform for Hobart's specialities. These adapted vehicles would break down the main barriers defending the Reich.

The wall

Germany tried to wall its empire in: the Ostwall, or East Wall, known as the Panther-Wotan Line, was anchored in the north on the Estonian city of Narva which lies near the Baltic Sea. The city is dominated by Hermann Castle and its imposing tower. It was once owned by German crusaders and still sits opposite the medieval Russian Ivangorod Fortress established to prevent the Teutons from restricting Moscow's access to the Baltic. Half a millennia later the same historical battle was again being played out. The two forts are separated by the short but mighty Narva river. The defensive line sat to the west of this waterway which flowed from the beautiful sandy shores of Lake Peipus. This wall ran along the western side of that great lake and the Wotan section snaked south as far as the Black Sea.

Where proper preparations were taken it was a strong defence and could slow the Soviet advance, however German construction work started too late. What is more, it was not adequately defended. The Axis had a shortage of trained soldiers and did not have the manpower available to defend such a monstrous undertaking. The east wall failed, but not before a substantial battle in the north around Narva which lasted from February to August 1944. That part of Germany's defensive network and its accompanying lines had endured longer than other parts, but this system ultimately collapsed; yet it was not the only such barrier. In the west lay the Atlantic Wall.

Hitler's Führer Directive 40 of March 1942 set out his vision for the building of substantial coastal defences in the west. It was a major misallocation of resources often using slave labour. Even some of its defenders were low motivated conscripts kidnapped from eastern Europe. The Atlantic Wall was not complete and flatlined because its defenders were stretched too thinly. Furthermore, there was no effective plan to integrate the series of forts into a wider defensive strategy. It took more than two years to build but was breached in just one day by forces under the command of Bernard Law Montgomery.

From the north

Normandy, in northern France, had been identified as the preferred location for the invasion. The land had taken its name after men had come from the north and colonised the region. More than nine hundred years later another invasion of historic importance would come directly from the north. Although the landings on the Normandy coastline were not against Germany's most daunting defences it would require a mighty host to breach the wall and an effective plan to continue rolling back the Hitlerite forces. The Allied codename for this great three-month long battle was Operation Overlord. It would be carried out by the 21st Army Group commanded by Monty. Montgomery's plan for D-Day was based on simplicity, he wrote it on one page. Of prime importance to Monty was the need to establish a firm beachhead that would link together the Allied forces and form a secure lodgement.

On 15th May 1944, Montgomery made the final presentation of his plans for D-Day and the Battle of Normandy. He knew that he was again facing the same Field Marshal who he famously defeated in the desert at El-Alamein, a victory that made the British general's name. Erwin Rommel would take the leading role in resisting the invasion and the following Battle of Normandy. Montgomery knew that Rommel intended to defeat the invasion on the beaches. Consequently, the invasion force would include enough armour to nullify German counterattacks. The date of when the invasion would take place was known as D-Day. As the British general first suggested to Eisenhower when Monty was first appointed to lead the ground forces, five divisions would land on Normandy's beaches. The day of the invasion would see one hundred and fifty-six thousand men fighting to establish an Allied bridgehead. Britain and her Empire, along with the Dominion of Canada, provided the biggest component. Of the 156,000 men, 73,000 would be American, and 83,115 were Britain's contribution. They would come by sea and air. A contingent of 7,900 airborne troops coming from the British Empire, and a further 15,500 Americans would also descend from the skies. Airborne troops would come at night in advance of the main force which would cross the English Channel, landing on the five beaches. Each of those strips of coastline are known to history by their codenames. From Britain, including Canada, 61,715 men would come by sea. Their landings, towards the east of Normandy, were closest to Germany. They aimed to land north of the City of Caen, a vital transport hub. 28,845 British troops would land on Sword Beach and on Gold Beach a further 24,970 men would stride ashore. Between those two stretches of shoreline was Juno Beach, where 21,400 Canadians would land. The Americans were to come ashore on the western flank, landing 34,250 men on Omaha Beach and 23,250 on Utah Beach. That was just the beginning, they would push forward creating room behind and beside them for millions more men to follow. This mighty invasion force would be supported by a shore bombardment from Britain's capital ships. The D-Day landings would not have been possible without the 195,700 sailors crewing the navy's 6,939 ships which would support the soldiers and carry them safely over the sea to fight again in France four years after Britain's departure from Dunkirk. Also, making a major contribution were the plethora of Allied bombers, they were pulverising German defences in advance of the landings. On D-Day, above the soldiers, the skies would be dominated by Allied fighter aircraft and ground attack aeroplanes that would seek to interdict any enemy that attempted to break cover and move.

As was characteristic throughout the war, and replicated on other fronts, the British and Canadian forces would fight around Caen and draw the bulk of German strength onto them. This would allow the Americans to break out from their lodgement. First the Americans would have to take the Cotentin Peninsula and Brittany before sweeping east. Montgomery envisaged that the British Empire and American forces would form two pincers that would meet to encircle the Germans west of the river Seine. Montgomery did not take battle for granted and developed his master plan for Operation Overlord. Whilst neither D-Day nor the extended Battle of Normandy would proceed without difficulties, indeed, it encountered many challenges, the ultimate result would be an Allied victory. The Germans would try and take the initiative, but the Nazis own internal contradictions and limited resources meant the Allies were imposing their will on the Axis forces.

Division and distraction

Despite being the undisputed leader of Germany, Hitler rightly observed that some of the Prussian military aristocracy, from which many of his senior commanders originated, held National Socialist ideology in contempt. Many even had disdain for their Führer. This revealed itself in numerous assassination attempts, all of which Hitler survived, and consequently added to his belief that the hand of history was on his shoulder. Nevertheless, Hitler enacted a divide and rule strategy to protect his dictatorship. This, however, contributed to division and defeat.

Even in the crucial sector of northern France, Hitler deliberately split the command between two Field Marshals and consequently hindered the development of an effective German defence in Normandy. Field Marshal von Rundstedt was the senior commander, but Rommel oversaw the defence of the coast. Furthermore, Erwin Rommel, as Hitler's favourite, had a direct line to the Führer, whereas von Rundstedt had to go through the military's bureaucratic channels. These imbalances would have been more manageable if the protagonists had been of one mind, however, they had competing visions. von Rundstedt favoured fighting the Allies inland where he could more freely manoeuvre the supposedly individually superior German armour. Rommel planned to meet the Allies head on with all resources as soon as possible to prevent them coming ashore. Rommel knew that the date of the invasion would be the "longest day". If the Allies managed to gain a beachhead the battle would be lost as their superior resources would lead to Germany being defeated. The question was what day would the Allies launch their great gambit?

The invasion could only go ahead when suitable tides and moon phases would coincide to enable landings from the air at night, and by sea in the morning. This had to be married with clement weather when the skies and English Channel would be calm. In June 1944, the first dates when invasion was possible were the 5th and 6th of the month. The next possible day was 19th June. The weather was unsuitable on the 5th and consequently the invasion was temporarily postponed.

Allied weather monitoring found that the skies would be clear on the following day. Eisenhower, after consulting with the members of his Supreme Headquarters Allied Expeditionary Force, ordered the invasion to take place, D-Day would be 6th June 1944. The date was set, and surprise would be achieved. The Germans did not consider the weather conditions suitable for an invasion and lowered their guard. The all-too-common poor weather in the English Channel also disadvantaged the Kriegsmarine ability to defend the French coast. Germany's E-boats could not be active during D-Day, these small vessels were kept at anchor and would not replicate the wreckage they caused when they struck the Operation Tiger rehearsal for invasion. The implications of that attack exceeded the loss of life and cast a shadow over Allied plans to liberate France. Many landing craft had been destroyed, consequently Operation Anvil, another invasion aimed at supporting Overlord, would face a delay.

Even if von Rundstedt and Rommel had been ready to face the Allies, neither of them could order the deployment of panzers that were kept in reserve awaiting the Allies to show their hand. Hitler would make the decision to release his armoured units. This confused command and control was systemic throughout the Third Reich. Under the Führer Principle, the functioning of the Nazi state was only brought together in the person of the Nazi leader, Adolf Hitler; he would make the final decisions. There was little delegation. This proved to be a major problem. There were social events that interfered with Germany's fight back. Rommel was away from the front attending his wife's birthday party. She was not the only distraction. Hitler's supposed paramour and companion, Eva Braun, had a sister that was getting married just days before the Allies were due to land. The drawn-out and continuing wedding celebrations of Eva's sister, Gretl, also hampered Germany's ability to resist the invasion. The gaiety concluded on the night of 5th June. Hitler retired to bed with strict orders not to be woken. Hitler was in the habit of sleeping until midday, despite the assault his aides dared not disturb his rest. Consequently, the Panzers could not be moved, and even if he were so minded the opportunity to prevent the formation of the Allied beachhead was lost. Once safely ashore the Anglo-Canadian and American armies overwhelming men and materiel would enable a lodgement to be formed in which there would be a substantial build-up of Allied firepower. Secure in Normandy the Allies would then be able to breakout and inflict a decisive defeat on the Germans.

A German rout was just a matter of time, however, upon hearing of the Allied invasion of Normandy Adolf Hitler welcomed the attack as he thought it would give him the opportunity to defeat the Allies. He did not comprehend the scale of the disaster that the invasion spelled for his Reich. Indeed, he persisted in the delusion that this was a diversionary attack, and the real invasion would be mounted elsewhere. The Nazis had been deceived and laboured under the false impression that it would come across the Pas-de-Calais, the shortest route across the English Channel. Operation Bodyguard, with its series of subsidiary schemes, fooled the Germans into thinking that there would be Allied landings in locations from Norway to Greece. When the Normandy invasion was underway, double agents persuaded the Germans that this was merely a deception aimed at hiding the location of the 'main' but completely fictional landings in the Pas-de-Calais. They allowed themselves to be fooled because they placed too much value on the opinion of their preferred sources of information. The problem for the Germans was that from the UK's point of view 'their' spies were 'our' agents. After being captured they were given a Hobson's choice of either working for the Allied cause or facing military justice. Consequently, they were turned to work for British intelligence. However, Nazified German intelligence placed too much emphasis on the status of the source of information rather than the quality of the evidence provided. The result was that facts would be changed to fit theories, evidence to the contrary would be discounted. This was a common occurrence, on other fronts the Nazis even held in high regard the duplicitous work of men such as the career criminal and spy Eddie Chapman, codename Zigzag.

The Allied deception succeeded and even survived the Free French leader, General De Gaulle, giving away the deception. In a radio address he described the Battle of Normandy as the supreme battle in the liberation of France. Despite this, the Germans still considered the Allied landings to be a mere ruse. The Nazi view of warfare was partly their undoing. The German blitzkrieg strategy dictates getting to the heart of the enemy as quickly as possible. It was thought that if the Wehrmacht were role playing Allied commanders in an invasion of France war game, the Germans would deduce that the logical area for the attack would be for it to take place along the Pas-de-Calais. Such a location offered the shortest Channel crossing and the most direct route to Germany. Lt General Sir Frederick Morgan, a British D-Day planner, decided that it was best to use this belief against them and deceive the Germans into thinking the Allies would land near Calais when in fact Normandy had been chosen as the location for D-Day. Consequently, Hitler and his commanders were caught by surprise. Despite this, the Führer remained convinced that there would be a series of diversionary attacks from Norway to the French Mediterranean coast that would mask the Allies true intentions. D-Day was no diversion. The reality, which absolutist tyrants often have trouble grasping, was that on 6th June 1944 more than one hundred and fifty-six thousand Allied troops invaded Normandy. By the close of the battle to wrest northern France from German control, this force would expand to more than two million men. None of that would be possible without first wading ashore and descending from the skies. The Normandy landings, just like the larger fight for northern France, were not without their difficulties, indeed the American landings on Omaha Beach were nearly considered to be in doubt. Yet by the close of the day an unshakeable bridgehead had been formed. Between 6,000 and 9,000 Germans were killed in action for the loss of 4,414 Allied lives from across all the many services involved in the operation. The fighting was not just on the ground. For the loss of 127 aircraft, Allied planes made 14,674 sorties against the enemy. The Germans were overwhelmed.

German problems on D-Day were not the sole preserve of Hitler. Rigid thinking had infected their armed forces. As invasion was not expected on 6th June, least of all in the Normandy sector, evidence that it was taking place was questioned. The presence of parachutists landing should have been a major red flag, however, for a time some did not act on this information as to do so would have diverged from accepted wisdom. The Allied situation benefitted from a markedly different ethos. Flatter Anglo-Saxon political culture gave those in Britain the opportunity to question failings and challenge leaders and failed assumptions. Such an ethos helped Britain in its quest to liberate France.

Pièce de résistance

In 1943, a British agent called Forest Frederick Edward Yeo-Thomas, known as Tommy, appalled at the state of the French resistance, was given the opportunity to personally lobby Winston Churchill for more resources. This contact proved decisive, and the British wartime leader dramatically increased British support for the French *Maquis*, as the resistance was known. This was transformative. The Germans were harassed throughout the country and became the victim of both active and passive resistance. The non-compliance of railway workers proved to be an especially frustrating hindrance to the Germans who found that moving tanks and troops across the country by train was a slow and laborious process. Though the various resistance groups were far from united they did have a common enemy but not always a shared strategy. In the event of the Allied invasion the communist resistance wanted an immediate revolt throughout France with a general strike and an armed uprising, other groups rejected this out of a fear of German reprisals. These came anyway. Ultimately, the resistance followed a policy of a gradual, phased insurrection, developing in accordance with the advance of Allied armies. However, less accessible parts of rural France, such as the highland Massif Central, to which many Frenchmen fled, became dominated by the *Maquis*. Throughout France, so great was the resistance's effect that General Eisenhower thought their military contribution was the equivalent of five Allied divisions in the field. They were not alone in their struggle.

Britain's Special Air Service, amongst the most elite forces produced by the war, were dropped behind enemy lines in France and the Low Countries to disrupt German supplies. They also attacked the V-2 sites from where rockets were being launched at London. British special forces operated alongside local resistance networks. In France they aided the *Maquis*, who were waging a guerrilla war against both the Vichy Regime and the German military. The SAS were a force multiplier. Such was their affect that they disrupted German military control of France aiding the Sixth Army Group's advance from the south. The SAS also operated close to the German border in advance of the American Third Army. However, despite the resistance network and the valiant efforts of the SAS, a lack of supplies to the Third Army meant that their progress was halted. This had dire consequences for some of the men fighting behind enemy lines. It was not possible to relieve the SAS troops and the Germans were able to release more men in sweeps to hunt them down. Nevertheless, they had an impact that greatly outweighed their minimal numbers. The Germans were also trying to make the most of their inherent lack of numbers.

Holding back the tide

Not all German troops facing the Allies on D-Day were inferior conscripts. Two months before D-Day, Hitler reinforced weak units that were to face the British landings at Gold Beach with the elite 352nd Infantry Division. When the time came this newly arrived division doggedly opposed the British Dorsetshire Regiment on 6th June. What is more, German defences were more than just the bunkers beside the seashore. Rommel put in defence lines up to ten miles long. Although Rommel was a master of manoeuvre warfare, he knew that his options were limited. To have any chance of success he had to fight the first waves of soldiers using a static defence close to the sea. Rommel believed that he did not have the luxury of being able to allow the Allies to secure a bridgehead, furthermore, Anglo-American air superiority would make it difficult for him to move his forces freely. However, if a breach in German lines was achieved a flood would surely soon follow; this eventuality came to pass, and Rommel had to conduct a more mobile fight back that aimed to prevent the Allies from building up their forces.

Rommel's counter invasion strategy on D-Day relied on fixed defences, not all of these were real. This was to have an impact as the Battle of Normandy unfolded. The Germans made the best of their modest means by using deception to fool the Allies, not all the Atlantic coast could be defended so Rommel faked it. False German artillery, gun emplacements, and large batteries of weapons distracted the Allies from real threats. Up to a point he was successful. The Allies developed plans and made extensive efforts to annihilate through bombing, naval barrage, and finally capture these pretend batteries from the Germans. Many of these were merely ruses to tie up Allied resources and distract them from very real threats that remained hidden. The fighting for control of Omaha Beach saw the Americans expend resources seizing Pointe du Hoc. This supposed gun emplacement had evaded complete destruction from the bombardment aimed at it and was finally taken by US Rangers. Yet it was not the greatest threat to the beleaguered troops arriving ashore. Indeed, the American forces were in a desperate fight to take the cliffs overlooking the beach, however, the G.I.s were coming under withering artillery fire; yet these attacks did not just originate from Pointe du Hoc. Embattled American soldiers on both their beaches faced deadly fire from an emplacement 1 ½ miles behind Omaha Beach, the so-called Maisy Battery. This extensive complex comprised a network of artillery pieces; however, orders to take it on D-Day were not passed on. For three days, until it was finally eliminated, its shells took US lives and disrupted the advance from both Omaha and Utah Beaches. This was not the only failure; more problems awaited the Allies inland.

Normandy was the logical place to get the troops ashore but beyond the beaches the temperate climate, suitable for farming, led to the development of a landscape dominated by small fields surrounded by thick tree lined hedgerows. This rustic countryside is known as the *Bocage*. Allied planners had failed to comprehend the enormous difficulties that it presented and how the shrubs and Normandy's sunken lanes between the fields were a gift to the German defenders. Although the longest day had been won, the fight turned into the drawn-out Battle of Normandy. Rommel, whose defences had been breached, now wanted a more flexible approach to the fighting. However, Hitler, as had become characteristic, insisted on holding every inch of French soil. Despite the alternative visions German forces were far from static. Allied attempts to expand the lodgement were met head on with German attacks aiming to dissect their enemy. The Bocage and fanatical German resistance delayed Allied attempts to expand their lodgement south. There was also a great struggle around the city of Caen. The Germans identified the area around this city as the crucial sector and the likely location for the Allied breakout. Its bombing on D-Day indicated to the Germans that this was a priority target, consequently German defenders fanned out to protect it against the forthcoming British attacks. Indeed, it was of great importance but not in the way the Germans expected. Like much of the Normandy sector it was the scene of great clashes of massed men, artillery, and armour abutting against those of their opponent. Any advance was slow with a cost that men like Montgomery thought it was unnecessary to pay. This desire to preserve Allied lives slowed the breakout but in the long term this guaranteed that British soldiers were alive to fight another day and take the lives of their enemies when battle offered more favourable conditions.

By July 1944 it was clear that the Germans were in a dire situation, they were losing the battle of attrition. Hitler made command changes on the western front; his reshuffle involved removing the defeatist von Rundstedt who was replaced by Field Marshal Günther von Kluge. Rommel, after being injured near the village of Sainte-Foy-de-Montgommery, was no longer able to lead the German defence, all the responsibility rested on von Kluge's shoulders. He recognised the need to withdraw but was fearful of being seen to be pessimistic. Few could disobey Hitler without suffering some form of retribution.

The Germans thought the main breakout would come from the forces on the eastern flank of the Battle of Normandy as this was the shortest way to strike into the heart of Germany. It was crucial for the Germans to doggedly resist what they thought would be the main Allied thrust east which would also lead to the capture of Hitler's pet projects. The Führer wanted to protect the launch sites of the V-1 flying bombs. And before British bombers put it out of action, Hitler had especially desired to prevent the British and Canadians from seizing the super-cannon known as the V-3 (Vergeltungswaffe 3) based in the Pas-de-Calais. This all demanded that German eyes were fixed on the Allies left flank. General Eisenhower was also expecting British and Canadian forces to make a breakout in that sector. He wanted the Allies to achieve such a feat of arms all along the line in all parts of Normandy, Montgomery stuck to his plan of drawing the Germans onto the British and Canadian forces in the east allowing for the Americans to launch an expected breakout in the west. At the time Sir Alan Brooke, Britain's Chief of the Imperial General Staff, observed that Montgomery's strategy was succeeding in drawing German armour away from the Americans.

The British build-up was wearing down the Germans and hid the Allies true intentions. Instead of coming in the east, the breakout came in the American sector. Whilst the British were distracting the Germans around Caen, Operation Cobra was launched in late July around the city of Saint-Lô. The US First Army punched a hole in the depleted German lines. With the British army protecting Operation Cobra's flanks, fresh soldiers from the US Third Army, fighting a relatively negligible enemy, poured through the gap that had been created. Both armies, after securing the northwest of France, would soon be able to rapidly drive eastwards towards Germany. Hitler's response was to order an attack at a narrow point in the American positions. The aim was to drive a wedge through American lines, cutting-off the Third Army in Brittany; von Kluge obliged his Führer. Operation Lüttich, aimed to capture and hold the town of Mortain, reach the coast and split the Americans. The Mortain counter offensive failed, leaving the Germans aggressors even more vulnerable. With the success of Operation Cobra, the Battle of Normandy had been transformed from a slog against a determined enemy across difficult terrain into a war of manoeuvre.

Not only had the counter offensive failed but it had also gifted the Allies a great opportunity to trap the Germans in a pocket around the town of Falaise. By rushing to capture Mortain the Germans had exposed their flanks and rear to an Allied attack. With the British Empire advancing south-east after winning the Battle of Caen and Americans having raced to Le Mans the Germans were caught between two powerful forces. Montgomery would have preferred to continue with his plan for a wider encirclement with the US Third Army blocking the Germans from crossing the Seine whilst the British advance would grind down the Nazis, catching them in a great cauldron. However, US General Omar Bradley requested the Germans be captured around the immediate vicinity of Falaise. Consequently, Monty ordered that the Germans should be trapped where they stood, the Battle of the Falaise Pocket ensued. Montgomery ordered the Canadians south from Caen and the Americans north. This would be the encirclement. It succeeded but was not immediately overwhelming. The Canadians were unwilling to take casualties and characteristically moved slowly, nevertheless, Canada's great commitment to the Allied cause was made evident by the great number of volunteers that came from the Dominion. Another problem was that US forces closing the pocket from the south were at risk of being overstretched and would have been swept aside if the US Army tried to complete the investment too soon. As such some Germans managed to escape. Nevertheless, August's battle to eliminate the pocket was a great Allied victory.

The Germans called the fighting in the Falaise pocket the "Stalingrad of Normandy". The German Seventh Army was devastated. They were now in full retreat, the fighting in northern France was all but over. Germany had put so much into the Battle of Normandy in a forlorn attempt to defeat the Allies that they were unable to defend the rest of France. They should have established a defensive line on the Seine; instead, they were rushing to get across the river. The defeat in Normandy was such an overwhelming rout that they had to flee towards the borders of Germany. The way was clear for both the British and Americans to make a lightning advance. Hitler's attack had hastened his defeat. However, Führer's stubbornness did present other opportunities to spite the Allies' cause.

Hitler recognised that the long supply lines from the Normandy beaches were the Allies' Achilles heel. He instructed special troops to hold onto the channel ports and thus in theory the Allies would be deprived of materiel. This was successful and many French ports remained in German hands for months after D-Day. However, it did not change the balance of power in Normandy. Hitler's hopes were dashed by British ingenuity and their ability to design, build, transport, and install their own harbours. These portable docks were known as Mulberry harbours. This concept was an important logistical aid in establishing the Allied lodgement. However, the Mulberry that was installed close to the American Omaha breach was not properly secured and was severely damaged in a severe storm which arrived on 19th June. This forced the Allies to rely on the Mulberry that remained in use at Britain's Gold beach. The Americans would also bring supplies directly to the Normandy coast using tank landing ships. Hitler's orders to hold the French ports did not stop the Americans from taking the city and harbour of Cherbourg. Despite extensive damage, the port was soon brought into use. Another inventive supply solution was the establishment of the pipeline under the ocean (PLUTO). This transported fuel from England to France. The capture of Port-en-Bessin-Huppain by the Royal Marines made the PLUTO operation possible. Although the task of getting supplies ashore was a continuing triumph throughout the Normandy campaign, as the Allies drove ever deeper into France, transporting fuel and munitions to the front became increasingly difficult. To solve this conundrum a fleet of trucks, the famed Red Ball Express, was established to expedite freight to the frontline. Despite this success, the Allies' supply system was put under great strain by the ever-increasing distances involved, and the sheer quantity of cargo being carried from the Normandy beaches. The Allies desperately needed to gain control and access to a major working port closer to the action. Those problems were becoming apparent but for the time being the Normandy Campaign was a decisive victory.

Operation Overlord had been 288 days in planning. Montgomery predicted that the Battle of Normandy would last ninety days, in fact victory was achieved in just 85. It ended with the Germans being driven across the River Seine and rushing back towards Belgium and the Third Reich. The Nazis had been overwhelmed in Northern France. The catastrophe facing Germany was being made even more dire by another operation that complimented the Allied advance coming from the west.

Under pressure

Along with the new front in northern France, the idea to invade the south of the country was reactivated. Plans for Operation Anvil were dusted off, renamed Operation Dragoon, and scheduled for mid-August 1944. The newly created Sixth Army Group, under General Devers, would take over the fighting in the south. It mainly consisted of American and Free French armies. To assemble the invasion force landing, craft, and resources were diverted from the fighting in Italy where they would have been gainfully employed. The loss of these contributed to the deadlock on the peninsula, preventing the Allies from driving the Germans out of Italy. Consequently, they lost the opportunity to link-up with the powerful Yugoslav partisans and make a beeline to eastern Europe from where they could deny the Soviets control over some parts of that territory. Furthermore, southern France was not a crucial sector, the theatre changing operations were taking place in north-western Europe. What is more, history had shown that to conquer France it was not necessary to overrun the entirety of the country; decisive victories in key sectors would suffice. Nevertheless, it was important to the French to see their country liberated as soon as possible and wipe away the stain of defeat suffered four years prior. Yet, victory in the war, and in the peace, would come from conquering Germany before the USSR. As such, the men involved in Operation Dragoon could have been better deployed elsewhere.

General Mark Clark, commander of US forces in Italy was critical of the taking of resources from the Italian campaign to use them in southern France. Montgomery also had deep misgivings about the efficacy of the attack as did Winston Churchill. Although there were good reasons why this superfluous operation should not proceed, Monty was obliged to support it and was required to employ his considerable power of persuasion to assuage Churchill's opposition to Dragoon. Monty dutifully obeyed and dragooned the British Prime Minister into dropping his opposition to the landings, they went ahead as planned.

The Operation Dragoon invasion was comparable in size to D-Day but was centred on Saint-Tropez on the Côte d'Azur. A major difference was that unlike in Normandy the overstretched Germans were both unable and unwilling to seriously oppose the landings. The German defenders, Army Group G, did not stay in Provence for long. They largely refused battle and retreated far from the French Riviera and formed a defensive line further up the Rhône valley. They were joined by troops who rapidly withdrew from south-west France and would now be able to join the fight defending Germany's borders. Nevertheless, Operation Dragoon did succeed in capturing the important ports of Marseille and Toulon and the Sixth Army Group did link up with the 12th Army Group approaching from the west. In 1945 they would also break into Germany and in the closing days of the war take control of the Nazis' Bavarian homeland. This, however, was not in the crucial northerly parts of the Western Front. Although its French and American armies could have been better used in other sectors, the Sixth Army Group did still contribute to the final victory. Notwithstanding that, Operation Dragoon was not the only operation timed to coincide with the Normandy campaign.

The squeeze

On 22nd June 1944, 3 years since the German invasion of the USSR, the Soviets launched Operation Bagration. It was named after a prince loyal to Tsarist Russia who sacrificed himself in the Patriotic War against Napoleon's invasion of Russia in 1812. Bagration was a suitable name for this decisive operation; like Stalin, and his henchman Beria, Prince Pyotr Bagration was Georgian. In just two months this major offensive reversed much of the German conquests of 1941. The strategic situation on the Eastern Front had forever changed. The focus of the Russian attack came against Army Group Centre, and quickly captured the capital of the Byelorussian Soviet Socialist Republic, Minsk. Into the twenty-first century Belarus, as it is now known, remains in Moscow's orbit. Yet, Operation Bagration did not stop there. The Red Army even reached the suburbs of Warsaw and forced the Germans to commit more resources to their doomed attempt to hold back this bulldozer of an offensive. The once mighty *Heeresgruppe Mitte* was all but annihilated. The calamity which befell them was not just a matter that they were being outgunned and outmanned, they had also been out thought. The Germans had been kept guessing as to the location of the Russian blow, when it came it was earth shattering. A massive artillery barrage shredded German defences into which Soviet and some Polish forces swept. It was the Red Army's deep battle doctrine *par excellence*. The Axis predicament had been made worse by coordinated partisan activity in the days preceding Operation Bagration, these guerrillas harassed the Nazis and their Allies behind their own lines. 1944 was a good year for the Red Army. The Soviet dictator, Joseph Stalin, was able to boast about the successful conclusion of ten blows delivering ten great victories against the invaders. As German troops were drawn into the centre in a desperate attempt to halt Bagration, other Soviet offensives swarmed over Axis positions. Fighting through the Ukraine in the south the Russian advance reached into Poland, as did troops coming through Belarus and Lithuania. On the Baltic, bar the isolated troops in the Courland pocket, much of Latvia, and all of Estonia had been reconquered by Russia. After murderous fighting, the Estonian Baltic islands of Saaremaa, and Hiiumaa were retaken by the Russians.

Along with British and American victories, the Third Reich was now being squeezed by giant pincers coming from the east as well as the west. And via the southern front in Italy and the aerial armadas of bombers in the sky, along with their faithful escorts, American fighters hunting the Luftwaffe, who were overwhelming Germany's increasingly limited capabilities. In the east the gains of Operation Barbarossa had been rolled back, in the west the Fall of France had been largely avenged. After France lay the conundrum of the Siegfried Line, also known as the Westwall, and the river Rhine, both of which ran north from Switzerland. These twin obstacles would give the Allies pause for thought and caused considerable delays.

The Westwall, and the Rhine, could have been taken out of the equation if Churchill's Mediterranean policy had been followed to its logical conclusion, an advance into central Europe from the south. Yet, US policy, partly driven by concerns regarding British designs for the Mediterranean, rejected these proposals and subsequently surrendered eastern Europe to communism. The confirmation of this abandonment of the very people for which the war was begun came at a time when these new European countries were ripe for tearing down Germany's imperial order.

Germany was struggling to keep hold of its eastern European Allies. Hungary sought an armistice with the Russians and the western Allies, Hitler, however, would not countenance this especially as the Wehrmacht needed Hungarian oil. The Germans occupied the country in March 1944. To this day the Visegrád Group of countries in eastern Europe, named after a town in Hungary, have been questioning Germany's unofficial leadership of the European Union and its policy of bringing in middle eastern migrants and dispersing them throughout the EU. The Visegrád Group have yet to transform continental Europe, however, in the Second World War other countries would change their national strategy and have a dramatic effect on the course of the war.

Geopolitik

The success of multiple Russian offensives changed the political map of Europe. German grand strategy, expressed through two world wars, sought to control eastern Europe. It was to fail spectacularly. The high summer of 1944 saw Germany begin to lose control over the east, friend and foe alike turned on the Führer. The Soviet offensives had brought them to the suburbs of the Polish capital Warsaw, taking the eastern outskirts of the city, the Red Army was encamped on the Vistula, the river which runs through that metropolis. Anticipating the Red Army's entrance, the Polish Home Army initiated an uprising on 1st August 1944. Initially it was successful and secured large parts of Warsaw, establishing control over the western bank of the Vistula. The Soviets, however, were seeking bridgeheads elsewhere. The Red Army beside the Polish capital was deprived of fuel by Stalin and ordered to halt; this left the citizens of Warsaw at the mercy of the Germans, though not entirely.

Some soldiers, serving in the Polish First Army, which fought alongside the Red Army, did eventually cross the river but they were too few. They had entered the conflict in the city too late to make a decisive difference and lacked support from their remaining Red Army comrades who sat on their hands. Involvement of the Russian National Liberation Army, a division of the *Waffen-SS*, meant there were more Russian, Belorussian, and Ukrainian Nazis fighting against the Poles than Soviet citizens assisting them on the ground. Some Russian help for the beleaguered Poles in Warsaw was forthcoming from the Soviets, they did bomb German positions and dropped aid to the Polish Home Army. It was not enough to change the outcome. The British Prime Minister, desperate to help the uprising, also directed the RAF to supply the Polish Home Army. Limited support also came from US planes dropping supplies. Nevertheless, the Home Army surrendered in early October. The Allies in the west, unsuccessful in Poland, would however assist with the successful liberation of another European capital.

Marshal Pétain, a hero of France turned collaborator, was cheered in Paris just months before D-Day when he visited the city in April 1944. The situation soon changed dramatically. On 19th August 1944, in advance of American troops, Parisians in the French resistance rose and fought to take control of the German occupied city. The liberation of Paris had begun. This battle for control of Paris was not just a matter of German versus Frenchmen; it can be viewed as a civil war between different factions vying for dominance in the *de jure* capital. Some Frenchmen were engaged in fighting against the resistance; these were members of *la Milice*, Vichy France's paramilitary organisation established to hunt down the French Resistance.

Eisenhower and Montgomery thought that getting involved in Paris, which was not strategically significant to them, would mean Allied soldiers would become bogged down fighting in a city. Indeed, Hitler hoped to turn Paris into an Allied Stalingrad which would draw in the British and Americans forces where they would be worn down and then destroyed. The Supreme Allied Commander and the man leading the ground forces in the Normandy campaign were unwilling to fall into such a trap. Paris did, however, have a great deal of symbolic importance. De Gaulle wanted to liberate the capital because he feared that if this task were left to the communist resistance, they would have a political powerbase. The city was also valuable to the German commander, General Dietrich von Choltitz. He was unwilling to execute Hitler's order to fight on and raise the city to the ground. Hitler asked his commander "Is Paris Burning?" But the general had already decided to surrender to the Free French army which he duly did on 25th August 1944. von Choltitz, has been called a saviour of Paris, after ignoring Hitler's demand to blow up the city which was liberated by its own citizens. General De Gaulle soon arrived to take over the leadership of a new French republic. Other European capitals and their countries would follow suit and leave their alliance with Nazi Germany. Russia's growing success on the battlefield was a catalyst for change.

The Red Army entered Romania at the start of August, the dire military situation which that country was now in prompted a dramatic course of events. King Michael I of Romania, at just 22 years old initiated a *coup d'état* against his nation's Axis overlords. On 23rd August 1944 he helped overthrow his pro-German government and thus changed the balance of power in eastern Europe decisively in favour of the Allies. The King dismissed his Axis supporting Prime Minister Marshal Ion Antonescu and had him arrested. Furthermore, effective action from the Romanian armed forces quickly outmanoeuvred the German ambassador. H.E. Manfred Freiherr von Killinger was the power behind *de facto* Nazi control. He shot himself soon after the coup. The young King declared war on Germany and Hungary, and drove them out of Romania which joined the Allies and importantly allowed the Red Army in. It is thought that this action shortened the war by as much as 200 days. Germany was deprived of Romanian oil, and the Red Army advance had been eased. Romanian armed forces also assisted the Soviets and fought alongside the Russians as they drove closer to the Reich. Indeed, immediately after the coup the Romanians took one-hundred-thousand German soldiers prisoner. There was a cost that Romania would have to pay. Soviet backed communists took power, and despite Stalin awarding King Michael I the Soviet Order of Victory in 1945, the King was forced to abdicate by the Russian backed communist Prime Minister Petru Groza in late 1947. The former King, and Prince of Hohenzollern, went into exile along with his mother in early 1948. There were also territorial changes.

Romania took back northern Transylvania from Hungary, but lost control of Bessarabia and Northern Bukovina to the USSR; they are now a part of Moldova and Transnistria. Some Romanians were also expelled from Bulgarian territory. The next domino to fall was the Tsardom of Bulgaria. In early September, Soviet troops crossed the Romanian border and entered Bulgaria which duly overthrew its pro-German government and joined the Allies. Bulgaria was required to withdraw from the parts of Greece it occupied in 1941 but fought to liberate eastern Europe from Nazism. Bulgarian armed forces drove west and linked up with Yugoslav partisans. Alongside other partisans, Tito's British backed communist forces helped drive out the German occupiers who nevertheless retreated to avoid being cut off as the Soviet's advanced on the Fatherland.

By the end of the war the Bulgarian army, supplied by the Soviets, became a powerful military force in the Balkans and even penetrated as far as Austria, linking with the British Eighth Army at the end of the war. The issue of Bulgarian expansionism, where irredentists wanted to absorb into a greater Bulgaria neighbouring North Macedonia, had been one of the destabilising factors in the Balkans. The future of Bulgaria remained a matter of international importance to the Allies.

In October 1944, Churchill and Stalin agreed in Moscow to divide eastern Europe and the Balkans into spheres of influence between Britain and the USSR. Control over Romania would be 90% Soviet, and 10% British. The numbers were reversed in Greece which was to be 90% British, with the USSR having 10%. Yugoslavia and Hungary were to be shared equally, and Bulgaria was 75% Russian and 25% belonged to the UK. This has been viewed as a betrayal of eastern Europe, the region that Britain had sought to defend in 1939. The reality was that Churchill had no choice. Duly, Bulgaria was forced to accept communism and the abolition of its monarchy in 1946. The former Tsar Simeon II, however, returned as Prime Minister of Bulgaria in 2001 as Simeon Saxe-Coburg-Gotha. In 2020 he regained ownership of one of his former royal palaces. Romania and

Bulgaria switching sides late in the conflict was not the only geopolitical event that helped bring the war to a close earlier than it otherwise would have.

Churchill had his own grand designs for eastern Europe, he had been in favour of finishing the job in Italy and then advancing through the Ljubljana Gap in modern day Slovenia onto Vienna, capital of Austria, and from there into Hungary. This would have both supported Red Army operations and interfere with Stalin's ambitions for eastern Europe. This idea had support at the highest levels of the Mediterranean theatre's military establishment. It was strongly advocated by General Wilson, Supreme Allied Commander Mediterranean. In 1944, Jumbo Wilson, later promoted Field Marshal and elevated to the House of Lords, lobbied unsuccessfully for such a strategy. The Americans by this point were winning the political struggle with Britain, and the USA was acquiescing to Soviet grand strategy. Nevertheless, there were other routes into Europe and despite the Allies being on Germany's western border the British Prime Minister did not abandon the eastern Mediterranean. Churchill still wanted operations against the Germans in Greece. Hitler, of all people, would soon give the British Prime Minister this opportunity.

With the loss of Romania and with the Russians taking Bulgaria there was a very real and imminent threat that German forces in Greece would be cut-off. The Balkans were now a much less attractive area to occupy, a retreat was warranted. Hitler agreed to a withdrawal from Greece, allowing for the consolidation of forces closer to the Fatherland. His Balkan adventure had failed and was at an end. In October 1944, the Germans withdrew; British and Greek forces rapidly moved back in. Conflict between royalists and communists soon broke out and Britain found itself involved in the Greek civil war. British forces set about attacking the communist guerrillas who had risen-up in an attempt to take power. In December, the British violently suppressed the communist partisans and their civilian supporters. Notwithstanding that the United Kingdom did try and broker a peace. At Christmas time Churchill went to Athens to establish a pro-British regency under Archbishop Damaskinos. The cleric installed a government that at least temporarily assuaged the violence. The fighting would however flare up again.

Southern Europe was lost to Germany, due north things were faring little better. Finland was to make an about turn, rejecting its recent leaning towards Germany; a policy which they had occasionally pursued with various degrees of enthusiasm since 1918. With the siege of Leningrad lifted in January 1944, the Red Army would attempt to retake Estonia. This Baltic nation is on the other side of the narrow Gulf of Finland from the Finnish capital Helsinki, if Estonia was back under Russian control this city would be vulnerable. This made Finland's continued participation in the war untenable. Finland was soon to reappraise renewing its links with Germany. The Finns kept ajar the possibility of extricating themselves from their alliance with Hitler. They sought a separate peace with the USSR but in April 1944 found their terms too harsh. Nevertheless, they were rapidly running out of options. Stalin, who had no desire to reincorporate Finland into the Russian empire, was however, minded to reach a separate peace with this now unwilling but hard to defeat belligerent. A further Soviet offensive in June 1944 retook territory that had been lost in the Continuation War, but they could take little else. Yet, although the Russian attacks had run out of steam by August, the offensive was a political success, Finland was willing to sue for peace. That was not before Mannerheim and Finnish President, Risto Ryti, essentially tricked Nazi Germany into giving them support against the Red Army's 1944 offensive which was conducted against Finland. Under the terms of the Ryti–Ribbentrop Agreement, Finland, in exchange for German arms and ammunition, promised to not conclude a separate peace with Stalin. The Finns, however, did not ratify this agreement in the Finnish Parliament and it was therefore not legally binding, however, Germany's military assistance had already been delivered. After the war, to appease the communists, the former President was put on trial and sentenced to prison for his collaboration with Nazi Germany. Risto Ryti and his advisors were the fall guys for Finland's geostrategic flirtations and dramatic changes in their choice of friends. Nonetheless, most of Finland had survived, the country prospered after the war and had a beneficial trade relationship with the USSR.

In September 1944 Finland signed a peace treaty with the USSR, ending the Finnish nationalist desire to conquer the eastern side of the Karelian isthmus. The Continuation War which had lasted for more than three years was now over. Soviet terms dictated that the Finns pay reparations and cede the territory which Stalin had been awarded at the conclusion of the Winter War in 1940. Russia was also given the nickel rich province of Petsamo in Finland's far north; Russia again had a land border with Norway. This frontier is beside the Barents Sea, but the Red Army still had to fight for it. The peace deal also obliged the Finns to use force to expel German forces from Finland. The Finns attacked the German 20th Mountain Army in the north of the country and the Lapland War ensued. Most Wehrmacht soldiers, however, managed to escape to German occupied Norway; they were pursued by the Red Army. With support from Britain and Norwegian forces, the Russians also conquered the most northerly part of mainland Norway called Finnmark. The Germans retreated and tried to establish *Festung Norwegen*, a putative base for a potential last stand of the Nazi Third Reich. This idea came too late in the war for it to be realistic. Nevertheless, the keeping of yet more German troops in Norway, away from the main battles on the western and eastern fronts, accelerated the demise of Hitler's one-thousand-year empire. The Soviets withdrew from northern Norway in September 1945, but according to East German files, they only did so after installing their placemen into key positions who themselves further appointed socialist leaning political figures. The National Socialists, however, were being burnt out from their lairs but a lack of a coherent strategy slowed the success of this latter-day European crusade. The western Allies were an alliance of theoretically equal democracies whose leaders were accustomed to diplomacy and deal making; political considerations crept into military decisions. Such sensitivities, combined with over confidence following the success of the Normandy campaign, retarded the development of a decisive focused strategy.

The fall

The breakout from Normandy and the subsequent dash across France had taken the Allied advance close to the borders of both the Netherlands and Germany. It was a magnificent victory, yet this Anglo-American blitzkrieg began to break down. Command changes that overburdened the limited in experience Supreme Commander allowed for a muddled compromise campaign to dominate the rest of 1944. On 1st September, Eisenhower, as was planned before D-Day, took command of the ground forces fighting in the western theatre of operations. Bernard Law Montgomery was promoted to the rank of Field Marshal and remained in command of the 21st Army Group, which became a predominantly British, Canadian, and Polish military organisation. Concomitantly the American Twelfth Army Group, with General Omar Bradley, at its head, took control of most American servicemen fighting on the western front. The other American army group, fighting in France, was General Jacob Devers' Franco-American Sixth Army Group which had landed on the French Riviera.

Eisenhower's stratagem was 'advance to the Rhine' and 'kill Germans'. Whilst there was merit in despatching the Boche it was not a particularly profound strategy nor was it even coherent. Eisenhower's lackadaisical management of the Allied direction of travel, the so-called Broad Front Strategy, was a diplomatic way of handling his generals. It was to all intents and purposes a political compromise, however, like most imposed from above solutions it pleased no one. It also prevented any Allied army from being strong enough to breach the Siegfried

Line, also known as the Westwall, the fortifications which guarded the internal borders of Germany between the Rhine and its neighbours to the west. Since the Fall of France in 1940 this network of multiple lines of ditches, tank traps, and bunkers had been neglected. The defences of the Siegfried Line had also been weakened to build the Atlantic Wall, which stripped resources from the defence of the Fatherland. However, following the disaster in Normandy Hitler had ordered that the western approaches to Germany be strengthened. The line's construction involved a third of Germany's industrial production and the labour of half a million men. It was a strong defence that could both slow and kill approaching enemies. What is more, the Siegfried Line was not difficult for the Germans to defend. Supply lines were short, and as it was inside Germany, troops were readily available. They could be brought up with less difficulty than the Wehrmacht experienced in the earlier battle of France where Allied airpower and French resistance hampered transportation. To help replace those units that were lost in France, to man the Westwall new divisions were created from the ranks of other shattered formations, these even included sailors and airmen. Montgomery, however, advocated a plan that would bypass the Siegfried Line and then attack the Ruhr, paralysing German industry.

After the many successes of summer came the gloom of the autumn. However, Eisenhower had not prioritised the opening of the approaches to Antwerp. Through this great Belgian port the Allies could bring in supplies close to where their war machine was devouring the food, fuel, weapons, spare parts, and munitions they needed to wage war. However, without Antwerp being accessible to Allied cargo ships, the many armies under Eisenhower's overall command would lack the resources to enable them to be ever victorious. Despite Antwerp being captured by the British Army on 4th September 1944, the banks of the waterway that connected the harbour to the sea were still occupied by the Germans who could threaten Allied traffic navigating the estuary. This vital conduit is known as the Scheldt. The task of controlling this watercourse fell to Montgomery. However, Eisenhower ordered Monty to defer clearing the littoral approaches to Antwerp; he wanted him to focus on reaching the river Rhine and seizing a bridgehead over this mighty river. Eisenhower saw that airborne forces would play a role in this. Such a bold move would get around the Siegfried Line's northern flank. The Supreme Commander also envisioned that opening a line going north from Allied controlled Belgium, reaching as far as Arnhem in the Netherlands, would cover the eastern approaches to Antwerp, defending it from any German counterattack. Eisenhower was opposed to stopping short of that Dutch city - he wanted to go all the way to Arnhem in a lightning thrust. Montgomery, as the Supreme Commander observed, energetically put this plan into motion. Building upon the concepts in Operation Comet, the much more substantial but hastily planned Operation Market Garden was born.

Market was the airborne element, involving several drops of paratroopers, and soldiers coming in on gliders, landing at numerous locations, to seize multiple bridges that they would hold for the ground element of the operation known as Garden. For this operation to be successful the Anglo-American airborne forces, with a following Polish force of paratroopers, would have to seize objectives culminating in the capture of the road bridge in Arnhem which spanned the Lower Rhine. If successful it would allow the 21st Army Group to trap the German 15th Army in the Netherlands, and from Arnhem, Britain's mechanised forces could pivot south-east and descend on vital German industry.

American military doctrine emphasises that operations should be simple. This was anything but, and as such some American commanders were sceptical as to Market Garden's chances of success. There were too many variables and if any of the objectives were not achieved the operation would fail. Furthermore, the flanks of the salient that would be created in the push towards Arnhem would be vulnerable to German counterattack, potentially threatening the movement of British tanks along the one highway that snaked to the far away bridge over a northerly branch of the Lower Rhine in the Netherlands known to the Dutch as the Nederrijn. Despite the many misgivings there was political pressure for the operation to proceed. The Netherlands was home to the V-2 launch sites. These rockets were terrorising London and it was imperative that this threat be eliminated.

Regardless of the risks, the many rewards of bypassing the Westwall and simultaneously crossing the Rhine, giving the Allies a path to the Ruhr and northern Germany, would have been theatre changing. Whilst Antwerp was still inaccessible by sea, and with supplies having to come via French beaches, there was not enough resources to supply all potential lines of attack; only one could receive priority. During the preparations for D-Day and the Normandy Campaign it had been agreed that resources would be allocated to Montgomery's army operating on the northern flank of the western front.

As the Allies drew closer to Germany, Eisenhower continued with the plan to give priority to Monty. Geography and topography were an important consideration. American forces under Devers and Bradley were largely in the wrong place, as was Patton's Third Army which was a component of Bradley's 12th Army Group. The Siegfried Line had been reached, but by no means had it been breached. Furthermore, the American dash east had not carefully considered early enough the terrain that lay beyond the Westwall.

In front of many US soldiers lay Germany's dark and near impenetrable forest growing on the country's low mountains. Conversely, Montgomery 21st Army Group was close to the industrial heart of Germany, the Ruhr, and the North German Plain, which was much easier to traverse. What is more, the low altitude plain stretched across the Reich to Berlin. Monty's proposed thrust afforded the Allies the opportunity to quickly navigate Germany. The Anglo-Canadian occupation of Antwerp also gave them easier access to the supplies which would flow through that port once its approaches were opened to Allied shipping. Backing Monty's Market Garden operation was the logical choice, but it did not receive full priority, Eisenhower considered it as just one component of his broad front strategy.

The operation was launched on 17th September 1944, even though SS Panzer divisions were in the Arnhem area it could have succeeded but for several unforced errors and climatic conditions. Plans were captured by the Germans; paratroopers were erroneously ordered to seize high ground instead of immediately taking the Nijmegen bridge; giving the Germans the opportunity to organise a fight back. The Polish airdrop was also delayed by fog, when it finally came the Germans were waiting for them. Furthermore, the threat of flak around Arnhem had been overestimated, consequently the airborne forces were dropped too far from the road bridge, only the northern end was taken and then only by a limited number of troops. So far were they from the forces that should have been relieving them that their radios could not transmit over such a long range. Despite those failures British tanks could have still broken through had it not been for their commander, a young Captain and peer of the realm, Lord Carrington. He chose not to advance into Arnhem when the road was clear. He later became Foreign Secretary but resigned for failing to foresee the 1982 Argentine invasion of the Falkland Islands, indeed he may have inadvertently encouraged it by suggesting that Britain would not defend this outcrop of empire.

The British withdrew from the north bank of the Nederrijn after 9 days. The Allies had paid a high price and had not been able to achieve their ultimate objective. Whilst the operation did liberate south-east Netherlands there was also a cost paid by Dutch civilians. To support the Allied advance towards Arnhem and beyond, the London based Dutch government in exile and its Head of State, Queen Wilhelmina, called for a railway strike. This brought severe retribution from the Germans who placed an embargo on supplies of food to the civilian population in the part of the Netherlands that remained under German occupation. This caused a famine. The Allies would make great efforts to feed the near starving Dutch by dropping food stuffs, rather than paratroopers, to the desperate people below. Despite the aid, their privations only ended in May 1945 with the surrender of German forces in the Netherlands to Montgomery but not before deaths through malnutrition occurred.

Market Garden's falling at the last hurdle also meant that the fighting in Europe would continue beyond 1944, and for the time being would remain as broad as it was long and drawn out. The operation has been much criticised; indeed, it failed, and forced the Allies to keep defending a corridor that had lost its initial purpose. At Arnhem, many airborne troops were lost, umpteen amounts being killed or captured, but with the onset of autumn the Market element was the last chance to use them in 1944. Indeed, the climatic conditions which delayed the Polish deployment proved that mid-September was perhaps already too late in the year for an airborne assault. However, it did succeed in killing some Germans, it moved the 21st Army Group closer to the Rhine and prevented a probable German attack aimed at immediately retaking Antwerp; that objective would have to wait. Hitler, recognising the importance of that port to the Allies, began hatching an ambitious plan to seize the city. In the meantime, to make the harbour facilities unusable he fired more than half his V-2 rockets at Antwerp. That failed but Eisenhower would soon gift Hitler the opportunity to recreate earlier glories and perhaps retake that vital port.

Despite its many controversies Monty's Market Garden gambit was still not the full northern thrust the British Field Marshal desired. Eisenhower in the autumn of 1944 had not given Monty the fuel, men, and machines that would have allowed him to sweep all before him. Similarly, the Third Army's advance to the south had run out of gas shy of the German border near the river Meuse. Indeed, for a time Patton's stationary forces were vulnerable to a German counterattack and were only saved through the ruse of blaring out the sound of tank engines through loudspeakers. This gave the Germans the impression that they were facing a mobile and deadly opponent that best be avoided. The splitting of strength and the diminution of resources that followed the decision to have diverging and disconnected thrusts prevented the Allies from either bypassing or breaching the Siegfried Line. It was making it harder to enter the dark heart of the German Fatherland.

With Arnhem over, but still with limited resources, Montgomery dispatched the Canadian 1st Army to clear the Germans from northern Belgium and Dutch Zeeland. However, Montgomery had overestimated the Canadians' ability to quickly secure the shore surrounding the Scheldt and thus make Antwerp accessible to Allied shipping. Eventually, with the support of the British Army and commandos landing from the sea, the Battle of the Scheldt was decided in the Allies' favour. However, the slow Canadian advance, the dogged German defence, and the need to clear mines meant that the Allies could not open Antwerp to shipping until late November. The armies in the west were still suffering from a paucity of resources and one group could not receive full priority without impoverishing and immobilising another. Yet, the pressure for Eisenhower to prioritise an unadulterated thrust continued.

Colossal cracks

Monty, a master motivator, was great to serve under. However, as a natural rebel who rejected the authority of others, be that his mother or even that of his Supreme Commander, he was a difficult man to control. He was also highly focused and by hook or by crook would try and make sure that the right military strategy was followed. As such he would not cease lobbying for his concentrated thrust. Montgomery's narrow front was the exemplar of the military logic he developed in the interwar years. He even devised his own vocabulary to define his tactical and strategic solutions to warfare. The term he used in the war to describe his overwhelming focused attacks on a narrow front was 'Colossal cracks'. Here he would use overwhelming firepower, materiel rather than men, to destroy a point in the German defence. Not only did this approach to fighting battles correspond with his philosophy of developing an overall master plan to which all other plans would be subordinated, there were very practical considerations necessitating Montgomery's methodology. It obliterated the enemy, guaranteeing success in the chosen battlespace. Importantly, it also maintained morale as it did not needlessly waste Allied lives. Artillery, the king of the battlefield, did much of the heavy lifting. The application of colossal cracks was the rational response to the manpower shortage that the British and Canadian armies were facing. The Supreme Commander disagreed, preferring his own Broad Front strategy.

Eisenhower did have some military logic behind his initial reticence to follow Monty's scheme. Ike, as the Supreme Commander, was affectionately known, believed that a single thrust, with vulnerable flanks would soon run into trouble. What that could be beyond a flank attack and the need to shed divisions to secure its flanks was not clearly defined by the Supreme Commander. Furthermore, those risks could have been mitigated by Allied intelligence, airpower, and artillery. If the 21st and 12th Army Groups were working in unison, they would have formed a force of more than two and a half million men. With the support of overwhelming allied airpower, they would hammer any German opposition into submission. They would be able to impose their will on the enemy. Alternatively, if they continued to operate in a piecemeal fashion the initiative on the front would be transferred back to Hitler. Indeed, that nightmare scenario would materialise, and it nearly cracked open the relationship between the leading Allied generals. Yet, Eisenhower remained wedded to his strategy even when it was clear that momentum was being lost.

In the Autumn of 1944, the Anglo-American forces were far from taking the objectives set by General Eisenhower on 28th October 1944, where he called for the capture of both the Ruhr and the Saar. Whilst Monty's 21st Army Group, which was predominantly composed of British and Canadian forces, was in a strong position and formed a cohesive and powerful front; to the south a vastly different situation was emerging. US forces, under General Omar Bradley, were stationed so thinly along the Ardennes that a chasm in their defences had opened up approximately one hundred miles. This area was guarded by a corps of only four weak divisions. This did not go unnoticed. Upon this weak spot in the Allied lines a ferocious German blow was to strike, cutting Bradley's 12th Army Group in two. History was about to repeat the tragic scenario of a German attack through the Ardennes, it was farcical that it was allowed to happen again. Eisenhower had been warned about this eventuality by Field Marshal Montgomery on 28th November 1944, Monty suggested to the Supreme Commander that the Third Army, commanded by General Patton, should move north to plug the gap and also seek out, engage, and annihilate the Sixth Panzer Army, which had disappeared from Allied observation. The failure to heed Monty's call would hand the initiative to that panzer army, the most formidable mobile force in that area, it was to have grave consequences. Despite the warnings Eisenhower did not put two and two together. Even though there were reports of a build-up of German forces opposite American lines, no action was taken to ameliorate American weakness in the Ardennes.

Eisenhower had his abilities; he was highly personable and possessed the skill to organise this crusade in Europe, but he himself had not seen combat. Yet he regularly received advice from a man who had, though this was not always welcome let alone heeded. British Field Marshal, Bernard Law Montgomery, had not only observed the positional weakness of the US 12th Army which was under the command of General Omar Bradley. Monty also saw that US forces were experiencing ammunition shortages and had continuing difficulties obtaining supplies. Similarly, Monty also knew that the Americans to his south were not operating at their full strength. Montgomery was alarmed by the growing number of casualties which they were sustaining, these losses were enough to cause a manpower shortage in the armies under Bradley's control. America could fill the gaps that German firepower inflicted on US units but that created problems of its own. The American system of replacing soldiers lost in combat involved throwing raw recruits into the front line to serve alongside battle hardened veterans. This did not add to the cohesiveness of units, the newcomers were yet to earn the status of brother-in-arms. It would be unreasonable to expect the comrades of fallen men to immediately accept their replacement especially as their life expectancy would be short. The result was an increased butcher's bill, the inexperienced soldiers rushed into the thick of battle were chewed up by the demands of combat. October's Battle of Aachen, though an American victory, disrupted their timescale and slowed their advance. Similar scenarios were being encountered along the front. The death toll was not the only issue. Throughout the autumn of 1944 the Americans fought the Battle of Hürtgen Forest. Over three months more than one-hundred-thousand US soldiers had been thrown into battle and failed to breakthrough Germany's western defences. The sapping fighting amongst the trees in this densely wooded area was America's first Vietnam. It was an appalling waste of time and lives, worse was still to come. On a macro-level, further unforced errors were to open a cavernous vulnerability in US lines.

General Eisenhower, the Supreme Allied Commander, along with General Bradley, the commander of the 12th Army Group, had split this formation in two, dissipating its power along contradictory axes, each thrust could not adequately mutually support the other. To the north the American First Army, which had captured the historic German city of Aachen in October, aimed to capture the Roer dams. However, the harsh weather of that winter delayed the main offensive capability of that thrust which was originally due to be launched on 13th December 1944. To the south the US Third Army was heading towards Germany's resource rich Saar region. The demands of these diverging prongs left the Ardennes poorly defended. The Germans were being presented with a real opportunity to shatter the dissipated Americans.

The Allied advance had lost focus and petered out; this not only gave Germany the opportunity to rebuild a secure west facing frontline but also create a strategic reserve that could take the fight back to the Allies. Hitler increased his divisions on the western front to seventy. There had been as little as twenty-three. A significant part of that mighty new host, supported by Germany's most advanced tanks, would be unleashed on the unsuspecting Americans. The offensive would begin as soon as the fog, for which the Ardennes was known, would ground

Allied aircraft. Caused by the high terrain and prevailing winds, that climatic condition is a frequent occurrence in the area. In mid-December 1944 water vapour condensed to form dense fog. Hitler's Ardennes Counteroffensive, named by Churchill as the Battle of the Bulge, could now get underway. Upon the skies inevitable clearing the Luftwaffe's fighter aircraft would harass the Allies in an aerial blitz. The quality of Allied military planning was to be critical in how this great battle would unfold.

Throwing in the hand

In military terms Hitler was a degenerate gambler, reckless in the extreme, but the German leader had a clear, just misguided, strategy which echoed that used by the previous Reich. The Führer was far from original and derived his actions from those of yesteryear. Historical events found an echo in Hitler's war and his plan to overturn destiny. The autumnal lull on the Western Front was, contrary to the opinions of Allied commanders, filled with plans for a major eleventh-hour offensive. The thinking was similar to another last desperate thrust made by Germany. In March 1918 the German Empire's Spring Offensive, or *Kaiser-schlacht*, meaning Kaiser's Battle, tried to steal a victory before the build-up of new troops would take their inevitable toll on a beleaguered Germany that was bereft of resources. This attack, also known as the Ludendorff Offensive, had initial success striking at the intersection of British and French forces. However, it was a largely directionless and confused offensive, it petered out. Hitler hoped that this new attempt would succeed, after all there were differences between those two schemes to save their respective reichs.

In 1944 Hitler had a clear military objective, and a desired political goal. He also had supporting follow-up offensives that contributed to a wider strategic plan. The location of the surprise attack drew inspiration from where the main thrust against France came in 1940, the Ardennes. Would another attack through these hills and forests be revenge for the Allies or a repeat of Hitler's earlier success? In 1940, the German attack was towards the south-west which followed the direction of the area's roads, this made the logistics less of a challenge. However, in 1944 the attack was aimed at Antwerp, this port-city was to the north-west of the Ardennes. The intended German direction of travel was not supported by adequate infrastructure nor was there enough logistical aid, like an army of days gone by they would have to forage for supplies. Germany would have to seize fuel to feed Hitler's unbridled offensive.

The Führer's generals, led by the Prussian Field Marshal von Rundstedt, favoured a more limited attack which would preserve the bulk of German resources that could then be made available for the Eastern Front. Hitler had grander plans that were intended to be theatre changing. He wanted to first defeat the Allies in the west, allowing for a full concentration against the Red Army later. That thinking was similar to the Schlieffen Plan. There was only going to be one winner, Hitler was the driving force behind these reckless plans, which were as much political as they were military. He wanted to drive a wedge, both literally and figuratively, between the UK and USA. Hitler hoped that splitting the western Allies militarily, the British to the north and Americans to the south, would result in a political schism and a potential end of their fight against the Nazis. Hitler also anticipated that he would win time which would give Germany the opportunity to develop its wonder weapons. The Ardennes Counteroffensive had three main prongs to its attacks. Two were towards Antwerp and had the task of denying the port to the Allies. If Hitler could seize the harbour, he would restrict the supplies reaching his enemies. To that end Germany's latest panzers would be unleashed and sent in the direction of the predominantly British and Canadian forces occupying that part of Belgium. They would attack via Liege and through Brussels. The third prong, an infantry attack to the west, had the aim of tying up American forces.

The blow fell on 16th December 1944. Early indications were that the attack was reaping rewards for the Hitlerite empire. The German offensive scythed through the American 12th Army Group led by US general Omar Bradley. As the growing bulge pushed into American lines two shoulders formed, one to the south, the other created a northern flank. Bradley's forces had been split in two. Eisenhower awarded two US armies, formerly under the American commander, Bradley, to the command of Bernard Law Montgomery; he would lead the fight back in the north. Most of the might of the German attack was headed towards his command. Monty calmly managed the fight back on the northern shoulder reorganising defensive lines, and he immediately began orchestrating his forces to mount a counterstrike, the timetable of which was agreed with Eisenhower and set for 3rd January 1945. It proceeded according to plan but has been airbrushed from history.

Hollywood has produced a filtered version of these events and glorified the role of General Patton, commander of the US Third Army, part of Bradley's army group that was to the south of the Ardennes. However, he was not in overall command. Eisenhower and Bradley postponed Patton's preferred offensive towards the coal rich Saar region, indeed the mercurial American general protested Bradley's order to attack the emerging German bulge. Patton had an alternative suggestion which he expressed to both his senior commanders, Bradley, and Eisenhower, at their meeting on 19th December, and it did not involve stopping the German offensive, conversely, he thought to let it continue. He said, "Hell, let's have the guts to let the bastards go all the way to Paris. Then we'll really cut'em off and chew 'em up." This proposal only succeeded in winning disdain from Eisenhower. Not only had Patton misunderstood the German's intended destination but also according to the Supreme Commander, Patton 'did not seem to comprehend' the level of threat posed by this powerful and unexpected attack. Nevertheless, reluctant to risk losing his command yet again he dutifully complied and swung his army north, to attack the southern shoulder, this move was not without consequences. Patton's pivot away from the Saar allowed the Germans to retake the approaches to this important sector. Nevertheless, the responsibility for this rested with Eisenhower and Bradley who decided both the direction and date of the Third Army's foray into the bulge.

Patton, when ordered to join the battle to his north, promised a speedy victory. Although the southern shoulder was not the main part of where the battle was raging, that was in the north, and even though the German divisions in the south were the weakest, Patton's progress was slower than he had pledged. Far from the rapid and all conquering attack of Hollywood legend, the Third Army attack was laboured and sluggish. Patton himself was disappointed and telephoned Eisenhower 'to express his disappointment' with the pace of progress. Patton had predicted that he would reach US forces defending the town of Bastogne, an important road junction, in his initial thrust into the Ardennes. The slow pace did not disturb Eisenhower who understood that Patton's original timetable was unrealistic. What is more, by the time Patton relieved American forces in Bastogne, the town had already been secured by the well supplied airborne troops occupying the municipality. The defenders were secure, and with artillery at their disposal, they had already defeated German attempts to take the town. Not one of the men of the besieged 101st Airborne Division stationed at Bastogne has stated that Patton saved them. Nevertheless, the all-American achievement on the southern shoulder did inflict heavy losses on the German Seventh Army. Notwithstanding that, the Germans did however manage to evade becoming encircled and escaped back to the Third Reich from where they could continue to wage war.

The fighting was desperate, and the number of American casualties started to mount, some of whom did not die in combat according to the laws of war. The *Waffen-SS* visited upon some G.I.s the brutality that had been shown to captured British and French servicemen in the Wormhoudt massacre of May 1940. Over four years later, as part of the Battle of Bulge, Germans executed American prisoners of war. On 17th December, close to the Belgium town of Malmedy, more than 80 Americans of Battery B of the 285th Field Artillery Observation Battalion were massacred by the men of *Kampfgruppe* Peiper who were under the command of infamous tank ace Colonel Joachim Peiper. It was premediated murder. Hitler had instructed his forces to fight stubbornly and to execute Allied prisoners of war. The Führer thought that massacring American prisoners would both allow the German forces to advance more quickly, he also believed that it would simultaneously demoralise the G.I.s, the reverse was true. In fact, it encouraged the US troops to fight back harder and begot a more stubborn resistance from Allied soldiers who learnt of the atrocities. The same contempt would be visited upon the Germans in the Battle of the Bulge. On 1st January 1945, eighty soldiers from the Wehrmacht were massacred in Chenogne, a Belgian village, by their American captors. Individuals slaughtering surrendered Germans was not unknown but was a rare feature of the fighting from Normandy onwards. There were even instances of British servicemen dispatching injured German soldiers and the isolated shooting of some concentration camp guards, they were executed under Rule 303. SAS legend, Blair 'Paddy' Mayne had also been known to kill grounded Axis airmen that his elite unit could not and would not transport to Allied lines. For those unfortunate souls the war was over and such callousness would have helped win the war. British commanders also perceived a need to remind West Indian servicemen based in Italy of the obligations which the Geneva Convention placed on them. Nevertheless, limited Anglo-American atrocities were outnumbered by those committed by the Nazis.

The Germans' experience of taking allied prisoners had not always been a happy one. In March 1944 airmen imprisoned in Stalag Luft III escaped en masse humiliating the Germans and triggering a massive manhunt that temporarily tied up many thousands of German personnel. Only three had managed to make good their escape, many of those who were recaptured were executed. It was a high cost to pay but Britain especially encouraged its captured airmen to try and break out from their confinement. Escapees could supply valuable information back to the Allies; furthermore, pilots and air crew were an asset whose training had been long and expensive. Consequently, the Germans used more troops guarding airmen than other types of prisoners. Some captives received special attention from the Nazis. German experiments on prisoners of war, notably techniques to safely aid the rescuing of downed pilots from the sea, did yield valuable information that saved lives though this came at the expense of violating the rights of others. Generally, the Germans used Russian POWs as slave labour. Both Britain and America put German prisoners to work and some in the United States continued in their servitude beyond the war's end. A rump of German prisoners that had managed to survive the Soviet gulag system were finally repatriated in 1955. On the long wagon train journey home unreconstructed Nazis took vengeance upon colleagues that collaborated with their Russian captors; they would never see the Fatherland again. Nor had the fight gone out of the Germans even as late in the war as 1945.

Eventually, both the metaphorical fog of war and the very real form cleared. Allied aircraft could now strafe German armour. The improved weather was, however, a double-edged sword. A massed Luftwaffe attack came on 1st January 1945, Operation *Bodenplatte* was underway. The intention was to use the German air force's fighter arm, the *Jagdwaffe*, to sweep away allied airpower and seize air superiority above the stagnating Nazi battle below. The chances of this attack achieving its lofty goals were always minimal. The attack hastened Germany's defeat by giving their many enemies the opportunity to weaken the Luftwaffe beyond a point from which both its men and machines could not be replaced. Attempting to force a breakthrough, be it on the ground or in the air, only managed to deplete limited German firepower. In early January on all fronts in the Battle of the Bulge the Germans would be pushed out from their stolen gains snatched briefly just weeks before.

Hitler's Battle of the Bulge was clearly failing but the attacks were just getting underway. To support the Ardennes Counteroffensive, the Germans tried to unbalance the Allies by launching an attack against US forces south of the bulging salient. This came in Alsace and Lorraine, a region that Germany and France had been fighting over for generations. This offensive was known as Operation *Nordwind*. It was hoped that this would force Eisenhower to shift troops away from the main front in Belgium and move them to the south. Whilst Hitler was having little success in the Battle of the Bulge, his southerly gambit forced more errors from the Allies. The leader of the Free French, General De Gaulle, was greatly concerned by this new offensive and became worried that the recently liberated French city of Strasbourg may be attacked. This city was the embodiment of the great power struggle and border disputes between France and Germany which had helped plunge the world into war. It was again under threat, and this caused dissention between France and the United States. Consequently, on 3rd January 1945, a worried de Gaulle threatened to remove his French army from Eisenhower's overall control and command it independent of the Supreme Commander and defend Strasbourg, a city which had repeatedly changed hands between the two European neighbours. However, such a drastic change in the command structure would have meant that the French would have removed themselves from being able to take part in future Allied operations. In response Eisenhower made it clear that he would cancel supplies earmarked for the French if de Gaulle attempted to unilaterally leave the alliance. The US general also made clear to de Gaulle that the threat to Strasbourg was exacerbated by the French failure to eliminate German forces who were holding out around the city of Colmar which lay to the south. Notwithstanding that, Eisenhower, ever the diplomat, did appease his French subordinate and accommodated his request by transferring soldiers from the north. This movement did secure Strasbourg's safety but further unbalanced the disposition of Allied soldiers. Eisenhower's undoubted diplomatic abilities would soon be tested again.

Hitler's attacks in the west had militarily failed, but there had been some political accomplishments. Not only had de Gaulle been at odds with Eisenhower but discord was also sowed between Britain and America. An existing rivalry was made much worse by the Battle of Bulge. That enmity became embodied between Monty and some of his American counterparts. The growing animosity was not helped by an ill-advised press conference held by the British Field Marshal on 7th January 1945. The German gamble had failed, and they returned to the retreat. Monty then took it upon himself to announce the impending total victory. In this briefing he extolled the principle of teamwork and praised Eisenhower, stating that he is "the captain of our team." Montgomery also complimented the superb fighting qualities of the American soldier. Yet, it was not politically correct to officially announce that the battle was won especially as crestfallen American generals were still smarting from the mauling their negligence had caused. The situation was worsened by Nazi fake news. A German propaganda broadcast falsified a news report of Monty's press conference by deliberately making it appear that the British Field Marshal had downplayed the role of American commanders in the battle. This disinformation was hastily accepted by the Americans as the authentic report, US generals were outraged, and their ire took on a life of its own. The Nazis had managed to dupe the Americans first on the battlefield and then in the black art of misinformation.

Nevertheless, Monty still won plaudits from some American commanders, even Bradley, who had lost two armies to Montgomery, acknowledged Monty's "notable contribution" in the Ardennes offensive. Furthermore, Major General Matt Ridgway, commander of the US XVIII Airborne Corps, also gave the British Field Marshal fulsome praise for his handling of the battle, writing in a letter to Montgomery which read,

'It has been an honoured privilege and a very great personal pleasure to have served, even so briefly, under your distinguished leadership. To the gifted professional guidance you at once gave me, was added your own consummate courtesy and consideration. I am deeply grateful for both. My warm and sincere good wishes will follow you and with them the hope of again serving you in pursuit of a common goal.'

Even though Monty was successful, or perhaps because of this, some American commanders would rewrite history. And sought to besmirch the reputation of Britain's military hero and most famous wartime opponent of German imperial ambitions.

Post-war prestige was important. America was a country that lauded success and saw the need for posterity to recognise the young country's emergence as the preeminent power and world policeman. In fewer than forty years from when President Theodore Roosevelt's Great White Fleet announced America's debut on the world stage, it had all but superseded the old-world powers and was in the process of putting the British Empire in the shade. That mission would not be served by allowing its mother country to outshine its war record. However, not all Americans were willing to bend history to serve industrial and military goals. Eisenhower admitted to the mistakes that gave the initiative back to the Germans, he wrote, 'The responsibility for maintaining only four divisions on the Ardennes front and for running the risk of a large German penetration in that area was mine... This plan gave the Germans opportunity to launch his attack against a weak portion of our lines.' Furthermore, he also acknowledged tactical failings that cost more American lives. In agreement with General Bradley, Eisenhower did not wait for reinforcements before counterattacking. Instead, they pushed back with understrength forces and fought 'to the extreme limit of our ability, and it was this decision that was responsible for the startling successes of the first week of the German December attacks.' This contributed to the high casualty rate. Conversely, Britain's cerebral commander, Bernard Law Montgomery, was to change this with his methodological approach to the battle; he lessened the danger in his sector. Monty did not rush too early to throw American soldiers into the meat grinder.

The German commander of the 5th Panzer Army, General Hasso von Manteuffel commented on Montgomery's role in the Battle of the Bulge. Stating that, "The operations of the American 1st Army had developed into a series of individual holding actions. Montgomery's contribution to restoring the situation was that he turned a series of isolated actions into a coherent battle fought according to a clear and definite plan. It was his refusal to engage in premature and piecemeal counter-attacks which enabled the Americans to gather their reserves and frustrate the German attempts to extend their breakthrough."

Hitler had thrown his hand in trying to capture Antwerp, the gamble had failed. His best divisions could not retake the city, nor could his latest technology render the port unusable. The Ardennes offensive cost the Germans six hundred tanks and assault guns, a staggering one thousand six hundred planes, and six thousand transport vehicles. They also lost as many as one-hundred-and-twenty-thousand casualties, yet the Nazi commanders only acknowledged losing ninety thousand men, still a hugely significant number. None of those could be adequately replaced. Yet, Hitler had taken the opportunity to give the Americans a bloody nose. Eisenhower estimated that he had lost over seven hundred and thirty tanks and tank destroyers. And suffered seventy-seven-thousand casualties of those 8,000 were killed in action, 21,000 were captured or missing, and a further 48,000 men were wounded. This severely affected the Allies.

Hitler had succeeded in delaying by a month and a half the western Allies' big push into Germany. Yet, the cost to Germany was high and the foregoing of so much materiel and the loss of so many men made the American and British Empire's fracturing of Germany's western defences much easier. However, with a new great power rivalry emerging the lost time would be critical. The Anglo-Americans were not the only armies that would benefit from the Führer's fanciful attack. To man Hitler's impulsive and reckless Battle of the Bulge offensive, the Vistula front, named after a river in Poland, had been deprived of troops. The idea to free up the forces in the west by shattering Allied unity allowing Hitler to refocus on the east had failed and further opened the door to the Russians. Therefore, the real winner of the Battle of the Bulge was Joseph Stalin. And as that major struggle in the Ardennes was drawing to a close the Red Army brought forward a major offensive of their own.

Hope springs eternal

Before being transferred west, Walter Model, the Führer's Fireman had proved himself capable of shoring up the front and could temporarily delay the Soviets in the east. It was only a brief respite. The all-too-common German refusal to make a tactical withdrawal, worsened the military situation. Wehrmacht forces became as cut-off in East Prussia as they were in Courland, and Hitler's futile forts did not stem the Soviet advance. German armies were either bypassed or annihilated and if they did finally manage to break out and stage a fighting withdrawal much of their equipment, notably tanks and armoured vehicles, would be lost and any new lines could not be properly defended.

In early January 1945, Soviet-led forces began their advance from the Vistula to the River Oder and soon completed their capture of Warsaw. The Red Army Vistula-Oder Offensive, as it was known, sent the overwhelmed German army reeling back. German civilians also fled west in its wake, they were not alone, concentration camp inmates were sent on forced death marches to the west by their German captors. On 27th January 1945, the Red Army liberated Auschwitz. By the end of the month the Russians were just over forty miles from Berlin. There was little beyond them bar ad hoc formations and an untried commander.

In late January 1945 Hitler made Himmler the Commander of Army Group Vistula, a new formation made from the remnants of other armies and cobbled together to hold back the Red Army. The Führer hoped that this leftfield appointment would motivate the soldiers to fight on; it did not work, and neither did Himmler. He was a man of no combat experience and added zero value to this crucial army group and left it rudderless. Himmler soon decamped to a sanatorium. And then resumed his attempts to broker a peace with the western Allies. The Third Reich's principal cities were now under direct threat from Soviet ground forces. The Germans tried to establish a new defensive line, the *Südostwall*, to guard Austria, this however, was unfinished and was quickly breached in March 1945. Vienna was now vulnerable to the Soviets. The fighting was not yet over. German assertiveness was enhanced by Russian brutality towards their civilian and military enemies. This made many Germans more willing to stubbornly fight on against the Red Army. To secure a faster victory the Soviet command tried to ameliorate its soldiers' rapacious attitude shown towards German female non-combatants. The Russians were looking to advance against the Third Reich on multiple fronts, one of which aimed to enter the Fatherland through western Hungary. The Germans were, however, desperate to keep control of the last patch of ground from which they could extract oil. To that end the Germans were even willing to mount an attack.

Operation Spring Awakening took place in March 1945, having failed to learn their lessons from the Battle of Bulge; this was the last significant German offensive of World War Two. It was mounted in western Hungary against Russian, Bulgarian, and Yugoslav forces. The rationale for the attack was like that which led the Führer to redirect forces from Moscow to secure resources in Ukraine. Hitler's understanding of the economic aspects of war again led him to divert troops from Germany to the Kingdom of Hungary to secure oil production in that country. Formations such as the Sixth SS Panzer Army, which could have been used to defend the approaches to Berlin, was instead put into combat around the shores of Lake Balaton. They aimed to advance to the Danube and from their spearhead north and retake Budapest. The operation lasted little more than a week and ended in abject failure. After the debacle, the Sixth SS Panzer Army Commander, Sepp Dietrich, said; "We call ourselves the Sixth Panzer Army because we only have six panzers left". The loss of both men and materiel in an offensive far away from the German capital simply made the Russian advance on Berlin easier. The Russians were not the only contenders for that prize.

Das Rheingold

Gradually the Allies broke down the Siegfried Line and by March 1945 had penetrated into Germany as far as the western bank of the Rhine. However, allowing the Allied generals to move in differing directions meant that they diverged. As they fanned out their strength dissipated when it should have converged on the seat of Nazi power, Berlin. Lost opportunities to rip open the Third Reich's borders were not the only cost to the Allies. Montgomery was not alone in his opposition to Eisenhower's drawn-out strategy. Churchill also opposed the broad front concept. The British Prime Minister wanted the troops to push further and faster into Nazi controlled territory and onto the important post-war political prizes of Berlin and Prague. This would have restricted Russia's ability to dominate central Europe after the war. The reverse happened. Eisenhower's failure to prioritise a major thrust in 1944 allowed the Russians to occupy much of eastern Europe. The USSR could also then claim much of the political credit for defeating Nazism. This contributed to the growth of sycophancy towards the USSR and its communist ideology. This tendency that emerged in post-war western Europe ignored the fact that much of the Red Army's firepower came from the UK and the USA or from industry that was either managed by Americans or utilised their manufacturing philosophy. And what was produced inside the USSR came from factories purchased from the United States and resembled in Russia. Pressure was mounting for a concentrated thrust to crack apart Germany. General Patton, a man that was even more anti-Russian than he was anti-British, also saw the need to back one main thrust, naturally he favoured his line of attack to the south. Eisenhower did not favour him.

Just as Hitler ignored the principle of 'he who defends everything, defends nothing.' So surely the reverse applied to Eisenhower's broad front strategy, he who tries to take everything, takes nothing. The advance to the Rhine was slowed by Eisenhower's failure to prioritise resources to a single thrust. It was not a mistake that the Supreme Commander would make again. Montgomery, and the more than a million men in his 21st Army Group, were chosen to make the big push across the Rhine and on into Germany. To all intents and purposes, the broad front strategy had been abandoned. Whilst the predominantly American forces continued their steady campaign to reach the Rhine and force a crossing into the remainder of Germany the main thrust was to be Monty's; it was known as Operation Plunder. It was the largest invasion across water in history, surpassing even Operation Husky and D-Day, which was also led by the British commander.

The assault across the Rhine began on 23rd March 1945. It had been meticulously planned and was well organised. It was another exemplary combined arms operation. It was supported by airborne operations and received substantial aircover from Allied bombing and ground attack aircraft which bombarded the Germans who were trying to defend the last major natural obstacle preventing the Allied conquest of Germany. Special army units and Royal Marine Commandos, along with regular forces made it across, again Hobart's funnies were deployed, and troops crossed in his amphibious vehicles. British engineers constructed pontoon bridges upon which armour could cross in great numbers. Operation Plunder was also covered by a smoke screen which for more than a week had concealed much of the Anglo-American build-up towards the river's western bank. The success of the crossing has since been obscured by the fog of war.

As had been agreed in February 1945, Bradley's army group would stage another crossing upstream of Operation Plunder to draw German forces away from Montgomery's attack. The Allies also made yet another crossing which came unexpectedly early. The earlier bridgehead over the Rhine was achieved through Operation Lumberjack which on 7th March 1945 reached the Ludendorff railway bridge at Remagen. The 9th Armoured Division, part of General Hodges First Army, had surprisingly captured the still intact bridge, which the Germans had failed to destroy. US forces soon crossed and were on the eastern bank of the mighty Rhine River. Incidentally, American soldiers crossed this bridge in December 1918 when assisting the occupation of Germany's Rhineland following World War One's armistice. This time the Americans would have to fight for the bridge. Montgomery welcomed the Americans making it across the river. Although the bridgehead was in the wrong location and surrounded by heavily forested and hilly southern Germany, the passage of G.I.s across the Rhine would draw German forces south away from Monty's major penetration into Germany to the north. The Remagen crossing was a useful diversion and distraction that hampered Germany's defence.

To complement Operation Plunder and join in the encirclement of the industrial heart of Germany, the Ruhr, Bradley's 12th Army Group was slated to cross before Monty's army group. In that supporting role General George Patton's Third Army bounced a crossing the day before the main attack to the north began. Still fighting a public relations battle against their British ally, Bradley's HQ press released this crossing to take some of the lustre from Montgomery. Militarily the manipulation of the news media made no difference to how the war progressed. Plunder was still the prime crossing.

Monty's earlier ill-fated attempt to slip across this great barrier had helped this much larger operation six months later. Market Garden and its supporting operations had gained ground from where the Allies moved closer to the German city of Wesel, which was a major focus of the Rhine crossing. The hard lessons from Arnhem had been learnt and successfully applied to Operation Varsity, the airborne component of Monty's March crossing. Drops of paratroopers and glider borne soldiers came on 24th March. Unlike in Market Garden, they were concentrated in a much tighter schedule, limiting the German's ability to regroup and engage piecemeal landings. Varsity was also better supported by ground forces who successfully used their artillery to help eliminate threats to their lightly armed compadres. The ground forces that had crossed the Rhine would also speedily reach those that came from the air. Their role was an important component but unlike at Arnhem, success of the crossing did not depend upon the airborne troops having to be relieved by units racing from the river. Operation Varsity suffered casualties and as with all actions involving dropping lightly armed men behind enemy lines, encountered difficulties. Yet, it was considered at the time by those present to be a major success. Varsity disrupted the Germans, destroyed their defences, and removed the Nazi's capacity to mount a punishing counterattack. Britain's elite Special Air Service was also involved in supporting Operation Varsity. The SAS would continue to support Britain's armoured units as they fought their way into the dark heart of the Nazi state.

The Third Army, which stole some headlines, went into the centre and southwest of what remained of the Third Reich. Other US armies also crossed the river, and as planned joined the fight to isolate and reduce the Ruhr. Beyond it lay the North German Plain which afforded the Allies a rapid route to Berlin. The question was would they be allowed to take it. Nevertheless, the many crossings of the Rhine shattered the Fatherland; the war would not last much longer and many senior Nazis could see that their Third Reich was all but over. However, a new hope was to emerge.

Wishful thinking

Even as Soviet forces were bearing down on the city that Hitler planned to remodel as Germania, the Third Reich's capital was largely in ashes, all that was left were the dying embers of Nazism; their eternal flame had all but burnt out. Nevertheless, hope came on 12th April 1945 when USSR-friendly American President Franklin Delano Roosevelt died. He was replaced by his Vice-President Harry S Truman. The Nazi leadership hoped this could create a dramatic change in grand strategy and end the alliance arrayed against Germany. There were historical precedents that had saved Berlin even as its people stared into the abyss. Two dramatic changes in fortune had twice saved Frederick the Great from the Russians. The First Miracle of the House of Brandenburg of 1759 saw the Russians and their Austrian allies fail to press home their advantage, Berlin was saved. Less than two years later Prussia was again facing defeat. The death of Frederick's enemy, Empress Elizabeth of Russia, led to the pro-Prussian Peter III becoming Tsar, he made peace with his idol Frederick the Great, saving this German King. Would the new US President save the Third Reich?

Truman was a cold warrior who gave his name to the concept of containing the Soviet Union and rebuilding post-war Europe, the Truman Doctrine. A man that had only briefly been a part of the US administration, and was not directly involved in foreign policy, quickly had the scales fall from his eyes and he learned to oppose communist expansionism. Yet, that was not before the Soviets had the opportunity to expand their grip on eastern Europe. A similar turn of events to the two 'miracles' that had saved Berlin was an unrealistic hope, fate did not intervene. Hitler was drawing the wrong lessons from history. Ironically, the Führer ignored the military principle of his hero Frederick the Great, "He who defends everything, defends nothing." Despite the Nazis exalting this quintessential Prussian militaristic King, his doctrine was abandoned and the empire he had toiled to establish was falling apart, the Germans were losing on all fronts. Any possibility that the Germans could defend their Fatherland and make it impregnable to the British and American assaults had evaporated. The Wehrmacht were unable to shatter the alliance between the UK and the USA. Nor could they make the western Allies pay a price that was so high it would dissuade them from conquering Germany and entering a separate peace with the Third Reich. Churchill and Truman would not entreat with the Nazis and abandon the Soviets. America and the British Empire, along with her fast Comet tanks, were racing along the Autobahn into the heart of the Third Reich. The western Allies had overcome the last great natural obstacle that could slow their advance. The threat from the east was also looming. To counter this the

Germans were still trying to hold or destroy the bridges that offered a route into the Nazis' sacred capital.

Horatius

The Nazis were obsessed with the cult of self-sacrifice, this ethos was inspired by the Teutonic Knights and other historical legends. Hitler believed that all that was needed for Germany to triumph was for his soldiers to refuse to retreat or surrender and be willing to fight to the death. This approach to war often had little military sense. History has a multitude of martyrs that laid down their life for their country. The Romans, whose symbols inspired Fascists and Nazis, drew inspiration from Horatius Cocles who, despite possibly being of Etruscan origin, is mythologised for his presumed role in holding back an Etruscan and Latin army at a bridge outside the eternal city. This was immortalised in a poem by Thomas Babington Macaulay who wrote,

'Then out spake brave Horatius,
The Captain of the gate:
"To every man upon this earth,
Death cometh soon or late.
And how can man die better
Than facing fearful odds,
For the ashes of his fathers,
And the temples of his Gods," '

There were many unrealistic plans that would not stop the red tide. In the final year of the war, and as the fighting came to Germany, the Allies would be met by civilians. In the autumn of 1944, even the old were enlisted in a militia set up by the Nazi Party. It was not a novel idea; various German states would often raise a Dad's Army at times of war. This new Nazi-led militia was called the *Volkssturm*. Men and boys from the ages of just 16½ to 60 who were not already in the Wehrmacht could be pressed into this militia and were expected to fight on the frontline. They would not hold back the Allies for long. Nevertheless, it was undermanned but not entirely ineffective. Older members were often veterans of the First World War, they brought with them their military experience. The resurrection of their frontline role was, however, a hopeless task, giving them the ignominious epitaph of twice failing to make Germany the hegemon of Europe. Youths in the *Volkssturm* could often be eager combatants. The young were amongst the most fanatical Nazis, and as seen in the Battle of Normandy, formations like the Hitler Youth were known on occasions to fight to the bitter end. Young people are attracted to the extremes of politics. This was not just a madness that befell young Germans during this conflict. Youths in the Soviet Union made up the Young Pioneers, in China, little red book carrying child communists were the Red Guards enforcing Mao Zedong's coup that enabled him to retake the helm of Chinese politics. From December 1944 even girls were recruited to serve the *Volkssturm* as auxiliaries and were even given weapons training. Hitler, however, would not fight to the death.

As early as May 1943, an American clinical psychologist produced a report for the Office of Strategic Services, which made several predictions as to the fate of the Führer. Considering Hitler's many mental health difficulties, one of the possible outcomes was that he would commit suicide. He would also try and take what was left of his nation with him. In March 1945 Hitler issued the so-called Nero Decree. He ordered that no German industry should be left to the now clearly victorious Allies. The Reich's infrastructure that had not already been destroyed by Allied bombs and artillery was to be demolished. Albert Speer, Hitler's architect, and armaments minister deliberately disobeyed this year-zero order. Nevertheless, the destruction of Germany, self-inflicted or otherwise, was not the end - it was merely the beginning of a new chapter.

German resistance behind enemy lines was to continue. An underground network known as *Werwolf* was established. These fanatical Nazis would continue the fight against the Allies in occupied Germany. These nefarious paramilitaries were involved in the assassination of the US appointed Mayor of Aachen, Franz Oppenhoff. Beyond that they had little impact. War weary and beaten, Germans were largely unwilling to resist the Allied occupation to the same degree shown by the Ruhr's striking workers who resisted the French and Belgian invasion of 1923. Whilst the *Werwolf*s were themselves insignificant, the mythology was however strong. Their lore was to have a completely out of proportion influence in how the final stages of the conflict played out.

Berliner or *Alpen*

Propaganda from Joseph Goebbels led Eisenhower to erroneously believe that the Nazis would mount a last stand in the *Alpenfestung*. This redoubt, high in the Alps, would, he thought, be a base for *Werwolf* fanatics. The Alpine region leant itself to being a natural fortress and was home to both the Berghof and the so-called Eagle's Nest, the Kehlsteinhaus, Hitler's mountain retreat in the

Obersalzberg above the town of Berchtesgaden. It was there that in 1939 the Führer hosted his parties and accepted the bloody future that fate handed to Germany. The Supreme Allied Commander instructed amongst his most able American troops to head south east to cut-off this fantasy last bastion of Nazism. It was far away from Berlin.

The alpine fortress was just a myth that gave Nazis time to escape justice. Hitler, however, remained in Berlin. Eisenhower made the mistake of considering the capital of the Third Reich to be strategically unimportant. Whilst the German war was as good as over, Berlin would be a key battleground in the cold war, which was to follow. In this great game former Allies would duel in a covert conflict across the divided city. It had already been decided to partition both Berlin and Germany into zones of Allied occupation. West Berlin, divided between the UK, France, and the USA, was to be surrounded by the Soviet zone, as such Eisenhower did not consider it worthwhile pushing on to capture a city only to hand much of it and its adjacent land away to the Russians. Eisenhower was also a man that believed in cooperation with Russia. He felt that if there had been closer collaboration between the western Allies and the USSR, with the UK, USA, and Russians forming a close-knit team, then the war may have come to a speedier conclusion. There would, in the general's opinion, also have been a better basis for post-war relations between the superpowers. This suggests a degree of naivety on Eisenhower's part as to the nature of Stalin and his communist regime.

The decision to split Germany and Berlin into zones and apportion them between the Allies had been confirmed in February 1945 at a conference between the co-called big three, Churchill, Roosevelt, and Stalin. It was held in Yalta, a seaside town in the Crimean Autonomous Soviet Socialist Republic. The imminent defeat of Germany was no longer in question, the battle for the post-war political map of Europe was underway. Both Roosevelt and Churchill effectively conceded Poland to Stalin. The promise to hold free and fair elections in Poland after the war was made mute by the Soviet's already establishing a communist backed Provisional Government that would control the Republic of Poland. Soviet hopes of spreading its form of state socialism were heavily incentivised by Roosevelt and Churchill, it was what Stalin wanted and rewarded the Russians for remaining in the war. Borders were also changed. Poland was to be pushed west, absorbing parts of East Prussia, Pomerania, and much of Silesia. The USSR would annex territory occupied by Poland in the 1920s. The new eastern border of Poland was not too dissimilar from the demarcation line suggested by British Foreign Secretary Lord Curzon in 1919. That part of the world had been turned upside down only to return to the starting point a generation before. Roosevelt was pleased that Stalin had agreed to join his new United Nations organisation. The American President would not live to see his international fora become a showcase for the proxy war between communism and capitalism that came soon after the defeat of Nazism and Japanese militarism. The ailing and increasingly infirm Roosevelt also naively thought it a success that he obtained a commitment from Stalin to enter the war against Japan.

Stalin's quest for his own hegemony over eastern Europe was being aided by other Americans who were naïve as to Stalin's real intentions. General of the Army Dwight D Eisenhower, Supreme Allied Commander in Europe, followed his commander-in-chief's useful idiotism. In mid-April 1945 Eisenhower unilaterally made his decision to not take Berlin and did not consult his superiors, nor inform his Deputy, Air Chief Marshal Tedder. Churchill was furious that Eisenhower had decided not to push for Berlin and accused him of surpassing his authority and straying into inter-governmental affairs. Eisenhower, like his President, had been politically outmanoeuvred by Stalin. The Soviet leader had sent him a message that Berlin had lost its military significance; the reality was that Stalin coveted the capital of the Third Reich. The communist leader would unleash his commander's competitive spirit, making them sprint towards Berlin in a deadly contest. Part of Stalin's plan to force his commanders to speedily drive to capture the great city involved telling Georgy Zhukov and Ivan Konev that Montgomery and Patton were about to seize Berlin and that his Red Army marshals had to act soon.

The Russians clearly won the political battle of Berlin with the western Allies, Stalin had broken the enemy's resistance without fighting. He wanted this prize for an array of reasons. Peppered around Berlin were Germany's atomic research facilities, Stalin wanted these laboratories, along with their scientists, and stockpiles of uranium. Gifting them to the Russians was a grave mistake that would hang a dark cloud over the world during the forthcoming cold war. Nevertheless, Soviet nuclear science was also aided by communist sympathisers who leaked details of the Manhattan Project to the USSR. Czechoslovakia also had significant stockpiles of uranium. Its capital Prague had partially been liberated in May by the Czech resistance which began a pogrom against ethnic Germans. The Czechoslovak government headed by President Edvard Beneš wanted to create an ethnically pure Slavic state by eradicating, expelling, or encouraging German speaking minorities to escape from the country. He hoped the violence unleashed would force German civilians to flee for their lives. Eisenhower also left Prague to the Russians; it was another betrayal of Czechoslovakia. American troops in southern Germany could have raced to the city before the Russians as could the British Eighth Army. This formation had advanced across North Africa, Sicily, Italy, into the Reich, and crossed the border from Austria into Moravia, a region in the southeast of what is now the Czech Republic. Nevertheless, the Red Army was to take the laurels of completing the liberation of the Czechoslovak capital. The Russian steamroller had been gifted Berlin, Prague, and the Austrian capital Vienna, giving the Russian motherland a great deal of leverage in post-war Europe. It need not have been so.

Montgomery's 21st Army Group was advancing at such a rate they could have made it to Berlin before the Russian and Polish armies, but Eisenhower sent Monty north. Once Berlin was deprioritised by Eisenhower Montgomery sent part of his 21st Army Group to the Netherlands to help the relief of the famine which the Dutch were suffering from after being vengefully denied foodstuffs by Hitler. Monty also raced towards the Baltic Sea; the aim was to prevent a Russian breakthrough.

Stalin's commanders were not just competing against the capitalist powers but also against each other. In communist theory, the two marshals were comrades, in reality the Soviet dictator nurtured a fierce rivalry between Georgy Zhukov, who commanded the 1st Belorussian Front, and Marshal Ivan Konev along with his 1st Ukrainian Front. The opportunity of reaping the rewards and glory of victory by taking Berlin as quickly as possible, meant that more Red Army soldiers died than was necessary. Indeed, the Germans were still able to maul the Russian and Polish soldiers that were descending upon the political heart of the Third Reich. Ironically, Konev was saved by Zhukov when Konev was being investigated after being defeated in 1941, previous investigations into other commanders had resulted in Red Army generals being executed. Ultimately the honour of taking Berlin was given to Zhukov and his 1st Belorussian Front. Zhukov had masterminded many Russian victories over both the Japanese and the Germans. His pushing the Axis back from Moscow, cutting them off at Stalingrad, and blunting and then repulsing the Germans at Kursk are to name but a few of his great victories, but he would have to wait for his ultimate triumph.

Russian restoration?
Stalin, as both a Marxist and an imperialist, saw war as being downstream from economics. Immediately following the Red Army victory over German forces at the gates of Moscow Stalin wanted to regain control over the eastern part of Poland and retake the Baltic States. Incidentally, Britain still recognised those

countries as being independent. The Soviet leader took this expansionist policy to great heights, even putting it at the forefront of his military strategy. In 1945, instead of driving straight to Berlin the Russians advanced into the northern Balkans to capture territory for communism and seize Romanian oilfields. Thus, most of eastern Europe and its resources would be tied into the Soviet economic system. Hitler inadvertently helped his Soviet socialist successor. When the Red Army entered the Balkans Hitler did not allow a retreat behind effective defensive lines anchored on Romania's Carpathian Mountains; this would have allowed the Germans to preserve control over at least some of the areas rich in hydrocarbons. All would quickly fall to Stalin.

The need to cover the flanks of Zhukov's advance on Berlin, provided a springboard for advances into Austria, and take the Reich's other resource rich areas. Stalin delayed the 1st Belorussian Front's strike at Berlin to prioritise Marshal Ivan Konev, and his 1st Ukrainian Front's attack into Silesia. During a meeting with his commander Stalin pointed at Breslau, the region's principal city, on a map and said to Konev "gold". The Soviets allowed the Germans to partly escape from Silesia so that they would capture this highly industrialised area and its coal fields intact. The loss in February and March 1945 of Silesia and its factories hastened the war to its inevitable conclusion. This along with the western Allies denying the Nazis access to the already damaged Ruhr industrial region meant that the war was as good as over. Even as the Red Army closed in on Berlin, Hitler had tied up his declining forces defending the indefensible, then raged that his generals could not hold back the enemy. Such a strategy was accelerating Germany's defeat. As the Third Reich limped on, the Soviet's sought to capture East Prussia. Germany could not hold onto this enclave, yet Hitler refused permission to withdraw from this province. With the Russian advance on Danzig, now known as Gdansk, East Prussia and the remnants of Army Group Centre would be cut-off. The capture of Danzig, a principal city in Pomerania, had a decisive effect on what was left of the war. Occasionally Hitler had moments of clarity and heeded sound military advice. The Führer eventually approved the withdrawal, yet this came nine days after it was requested, by which point it was too late and German troops were isolated. East Prussia is now no more, its capital Königsberg is now called Kaliningrad, and much of the territory of East Prussia is a region in the Russian Federation. The German speaking population was expelled and replaced by Russians. In what remains of Germany, Prussia, a by-word for German militarism and professionalism, was abolished as an entity by Allied decree.

With Zhukov's flank secured by Konev on the left and the Polish born Konstantin Rokossovsky and the 2nd Belorussian Front on his right, taking Pomerania, the assault on Berlin could get underway; but it was still not without its costs. The direct line to Berlin required Zhukov's army group to punch through a significant plateau known as the Seelow Heights that rose above the surrounding land to the east of Berlin. The Russian field marshal would deploy massive firepower though not always effectively. The German 9th Army partly withdrew from their first line of defence thus making Zhukov's initial barrage of massed Red Army artillery fire futile. In the Battle of the Seelow Heights the Russian and Polish advance was met by determined resistance and even counterattacks, the infantry faced withering fire from an enemy that had not yet been destroyed. The Red Army suffered dreadful casualties in the advance on Berlin. Clearly at times a German tactical retreat could reap dividends. Nevertheless, despite the mauling, the Red Army and its Polish subordinates broke through the gates to Berlin, encircled the city, and began reducing resistance in the capital of the Reich.

Meanwhile Hitler was in his bunker, and in a scene that had launched a thousand video memes was divorced from reality, issuing fanciful orders, and barking at the moon. The howling wolf was as good as stopped, and permanently so. In the Battle of Berlin, the planned counterattack by Germany's 9th Army was to no avail, it had been severely mangled and could not stop the communist force's investment of Hitler's capital. Hitler had grand plans to save the city. Army Detachment Steiner, under *Waffen-SS Obergruppenführer* Felix Steiner was tasked by Hitler with leading an attack against Zhukov's 1st Belorussian Front. Steiner, however, lacking the men and weapons to carry out his unrealistic mission he effectively countermanded the plan. On 22nd April, upon Hitler hearing of Steiner's reticence the Nazi leader flew into a rage and then finally acknowledged that the war was lost.

During the final death throes of the Third Reich, with the Russians closing in on the *Führerbunker*, Hitler, who recorded his occupation as author, concluded in his last testament that the German people had been unworthy of him and that the Slavs were the stronger race. Clearly Germany was lacking the inherent strength needed to win a world war and its rematch. On 30th April 1945, with the German defenders running out of ammunition, the Nazi leader and his newly married wife Eva Hitler took their own lives. The confirmed animal lover had earlier also killed his dog Blondi by testing cyanide on her. Following the death of Hitler, Flensburg in northern Germany, where Grand Admiral Karl Dönitz had decamped, become the seat of a rump Nazi government. Before its leaders were arrested the overriding aim of this pseudo-state was to drive a wedge between the western Allies and their Soviet comrades. The Germans still attempted to forge a separate peace with the UK and USA. Failing that the remaining Nazi President and his Ministers hoped to give an opportunity for Axis soldiers facing the Russians to flee west where they could surrender to the British and Americans, and thus avoided falling into Soviet captivity. Indeed, the Red Army was trying to metastasise over Europe.

On 2nd May Montgomery's forces reached the German port city of Lübeck on the Baltic just hours before the Russian's arrived, thus preventing the Red Army from entering Denmark. Germany had been dissected multiple times. On 4th May Nazi generals came to see Monty. Despite Germany's losses the British Field Marshal still had to force their unconditional submission in a one-sided negotiation. Montgomery told the German commanders facing him that they must surrender unconditionally, if they did not agree Monty said to them, "I shall go on with the war and will be delighted to do so, and all your soldiers may be killed." They quickly complied and unconditionally surrendered to Montgomery in front of a film crew at his Headquarters on Lüneburg Heath, near Hamburg. All German forces in northwest Germany, Denmark, Schleswig-Holstein, the Netherlands, all isles including the Frisian islands and Heligoland along with naval ships in those areas surrendered to Monty. It was a great success, but the military Battle of Berlin had concluded two days before in the Soviet's favour. The Germans did try to surrender to the British even those forces facing the Russians, Montgomery refused to accept that. Those fighting the Red Army would have to surrender to their eastern enemy, there would be no separate peace. Complete capitulation formally came when the Instrument of Surrender was signed on 8th May 1945. Notwithstanding that, some isolated units did not immediately lay down their arms, the Germans in the Courland Pocket finally surrendered two days later. It was over but the medium and long-term future of the defeated Germany was still largely an outstanding question.

Montgomery, Eisenhower, Zhukov, and French general Jean de Lattre de Tassigny on behalf of their countries formally took over Germany when they signed the Berlin Declaration in June 1945. The Allies in the west would impose a quite different vision to the Soviets. Whilst eastern Europe fell to communism not all state socialist countries were occupied by the Red Army. There were also non-aligned communist armies that took power in Yugoslavia and Albania. Another country in time became neutral but not socialist. The partition of Austria between the Allied powers, including the French, ended in 1955 in return for Austrian promises of perpetual neutrality. Accordingly, the occupation forces left that same year, and it became a fully independent and democratic state.

Communist revolution was also rolled back in parts of southern Europe. With the involvement of the United States, Italy, which became a Republic in 1946, remained in the democratic sphere of influence when the communist electoral challenge was defeated in 1948. Nevertheless, it remained a divided polity and subject to terrorism and corruption; as did Greece. Across the Ionian Sea in the Hellenic Kingdom the Americans along with the British assisted anti-communist forces and the Greek government in defeating a Marxist insurgency which lasted through much of the mid-to-late 1940s. Britain was exerting its influence in that part of the Mediterranean as was agreed between Stalin and Churchill in Moscow in October 1944. Controversially, former Greek collaborators, who had previously been fighting communist partisans, were later used to combat those very same Soviet backed insurgents after the Second World War had ended. *Plus ça change, plus c'est la même chose*. The competing forces were part of a new and wider great game between Britain and the Russians which is still being played today.

The United Kingdom reasserted control over part of Germany just as it had done following World War One. Both military phases of this intergenerational war had now ended for good. The wars were an interregnum bookended by political and trade agreements that sought to achieve the same ends. Notwithstanding that eastern Germany, bar west Berlin, was to be under Soviet occupation. Whereas Hitler had ordered the destruction of Berlin, in Russian occupied areas efforts were made to feed the population and restore the essential services that had been damaged by the war. Soviet commanders also imposed the death penalty on those Red Army soldiers that were caught looting or raping. It was a markedly different occupation to that which the Germans imposed on its subject peoples. With Soviet control came communist economics. As with all command economies eastern Europe, behind the emerging iron curtain, began a rapid reindustrialisation. West Germany was also transformed.

The new boss

Montgomery, after World War One, was part of the British Army of the Rhine, occupying a portion of Germany from 1919 until 1929. After the second great war his British Liberation Army converted into a reformed British Army of the Rhine. Field Marshal Montgomery was the BAOR's Commander-in-Chief administering and governing its area of the prostrate Germany. His rule was markedly positive. Monty stated, "Our present attitude towards the German people is negative, it must be replaced by one that is positive and holds out hope for the future."

Monty's merciful and forgiving attitude was reflected throughout the UK's political establishment. Indeed, Con O'Neill, a senior Foreign Office official and leading authority on Germany remarked that "in general, the impression that British Military Govt. has now embarked on a policy of Full Speed Ahead for German rehabilitation". Later Con O'Neil led the UK diplomatic team which negotiated Britain's entry into the European Economic Community. He achieved infamy by agreeing, under Prime Minister Edward Heath's direction, to surrender the UK's fishing waters to Brussels. This remains a point of conflict between the UK and the European Union even after Britain's EU exit. During the war O'Neil interrogated Hitler's former deputy Rudolf Hess upon his capture in Scotland.

Britain, along with the United States, made a positive contribution to rebuilding Germany and helped set it on the path to post-war success to become the hegemon at the heart of the contemporary European Union. America made a substantial contribution under then Secretary of State George Marshall called the European Recovery Program, known as the Marshall Plan. This replaced the previous scheme that would have seen the pastoralisation of Germany. The punitive Morgenthau Plan would not only have deindustrialised Germany but also dismembered it, transforming the former Third Reich into several separate states, create an international zone and award German territory to Poland, France, and Denmark. This approach was rejected as it would have made the German people a burden on the victorious powers. Similarly, it was viewed that it was better to give the Germans hope that a better future awaited them, and they could leave behind the privations caused by Nazism. Nevertheless, before the end of the war the existence of the plan was a propaganda coup for Goebbels who used those proposals to keep Germany at war, and himself in power, for as long as possible.

Britain had a forgiving attitude in the extreme. The War Damage Commission assessed that Germany had caused £1.45 billion in harm to British domestic and industrial property in 1945 prices. With the near geometric increase in property prices since then this figure would now run into trillions. Nothing like that amount was recovered in reparations by the Inter-Allied Reparations Agency. According to Alec Cairncross in *The Price of War* just $106 million's worth of assets was taken from Germany in restitution. The Soviet's approach to the defeated Germany was initially vastly different to that of Britain, America, and France. The Russians enacted reparations by seizing much German industry and deported manufacturing plants to the USSR and used captured soldiers as forced labour. These punitive policies were however soon reversed. Furthermore, Britain and America wanted to make Germany function again and make a positive contribution to the world by acting as a bulwark against communism. German financial reparations were often forgiven, and its debts were restructured so as not to hinder German recovery which the United States financed. Conversely, American post-war assistance to the United Kingdom came with conditions that diminished Britain's standing in the world.

The UK's World War Two financial debts to America remained in place, the final instalment of US war loan debt was repaid in 2006. Further US aid after the war required the Labour government that succeeded Churchill's administration to accept dollar convertibility, this led to Britain's longstanding balance of payments problems. America, in the driving seat of Allied affairs from the second half of 1944 onwards also established the Bretton Woods monetary system. British dominated markets were opened to competition from the United States which was now able to dominate the global economy. The General Agreement on Tariffs and Trade (GATT) signed in 1947 undermined the opportunity to expand upon the concept of imperial preference trade policies. Much of the rationale for empire was abandoned and Britain cut and ran from its historic links in Africa and Asia. Peoples in those countries achieved independence but did so before notions of representative democratic government, private property rights, and meritocracy could be properly established and engrained in society. Much of the new commonwealth remained dominated by tribal cliques and the corruption and nepotism that was inherent in such a system. The vacuum left by Britain was often filled by the Soviet Union and the United States. America had finally taken on what was known as the white man's burden, US foreign policy was however more concerned with preventing the spread of communism than good governance. They cared not that a leader was an SOB, so long as he was their son of a b***h. Across the pond, America politically pushed for a reversal of Britain's traditional foreign policy goals. Notably the United States encouraged political integration in Europe and in time cajoled Britain into applying to join this supranational experiment and unsuccessfully tried to encourage the UK to remain in the Europe Union. Nevertheless, much of mainland Europe at the time of writing is still subservient to Brussels, Frankfurt, and Berlin. Britain's continental interregnum, the ill-fated venture of trying to embark on a European future, undermined the close links with the old Commonwealth otherwise then known as Britain's white Dominions. The process of re-establishing those global links is now underway again after a brief European hiatus. The hand of history is a powerful guide and irresistible force. The overriding idea of looking to the sea lives on. Britain and its Empire had at one point stood alone against Germany and kept the flame of freedom alive and ultimately won the war, but it can be asked what did the United Kingdom actually win?

Along with a normalisation of relations between victor and vanquished, there was a process of de-Nazification in West Germany. Nazis were removed from positions of authority though not all. Some businessmen in the Third Reich metamorphosed into post-war industrialists. And in the case of Martin Heidegger, he was eventually allowed to remain in academia as a respected member of Germany's university system. Several leading figures in Germany's *Europäische Wirtshaftsgemeinschaft* also had successful careers after the conflagration. Dr Horst Jecht, Professor at the Berlin School of Economics, became chairman of the advisory board of the post-war German Federal Ministry of Finance. Dr Emil Woermann, Professor at Halle University, who was on the board of the Nazi *Mitteleuropäischen Wirtschaftstag*, also had an influential role following the war. He became a leading academic in agricultural economics and a prominent commentator on Germany's role within the EEC. Dr Anton Reithinger, Director of the Economics Department of I.G. Farbenindustrie A.G., became a post-war economist. Dr Bernhard Benning, Director of the Reich's Credit Company, joined the board of the Bank of German Länder and from 1957 was a board member of the German Federal Bank. Dr Carl Clodius, Ambassador of the Foreign Office, became German ambassador to Romania. Professor Dr Heinrich Hunke, Economic Committee Advisor to the National Socialist German Workers Party (NSDAP) became General Secretary, then Vice President of ARL. This was the influential German institute for civic, state, and economic planning. Increasingly, as the Cold War between the communist east and capitalist west developed, each bloc's part of Germany came to be seen by its occupier as a friend, ally, and tool in the emerging rivalry between the USA and the USSR.

The Allied zones of occupation were united. First the British and American parts were amalgamated in 1947 to form Bizonia. The following year the French occupied zone joined to form Trizonia. In 1949 it became the Federal Republic of Germany. The Soviet zone eventually became the German Democratic Republic (GDR) in 1949 and is often known as East Germany. Whereas the western Allies used their benevolence to legitimise their control, the Russians, like the Nazis, weaponised art to maintain order. To psychologically ease the Germans in the Soviet occupied zone into accepting the new communist regime and its agents of control the uniforms of the new state's police and military were like that of Nazi Germany. The hammer and sickle merely replaced the Swastika on cap badges. Posters were produced and put-on display showing fit young men in their new old uniforms. German military traditions were also preserved in the East. It was not altogether successful. In 1953, several months following the death of Stalin, and with the East German economy in a dire situation spontaneous strikes ensued in East Berlin and spread throughout the GDR. This quickly became an uprising against communist control and attracted elements of the German population who were still wedded to Nazi ideology. The unrest was quickly suppressed by the Soviet Army and East German police. A long period of stagnation set in.

The Nazi legacy continued in East Germany; Stalin kept open the Buchenwald concentration camp for opponents of his regime, the new bosses were the Soviet NKVD who took it over from the Nazi SS. To this day parts of the old East Germany exhibit amongst the worst aspects of racial politics seen in the new unified Federal Republic of Germany. To a small degree, communist rule just freezes identitarian and sectarian politics which re-emerge and break out again when changes of regime occur; this pattern has been seen over much of the former Soviet Union. Arguably the Second World War ended in Europe when Russian control over the last occupied countries in eastern Europe ceased in 1991. The USSR was initially an ally of Nazi Germany and occupied its neighbours as part of the agreement made between Molotov and von Ribbentrop. However, Poland, Finland, and Estonia have still not recovered all the territory that was lost to the USSR and its successor states following the end of World War Two.

Nevertheless, the age of total war had led to Germany being defeated in its totality. As Oscar Wilde may have written about German ambitions in Europe, 'To lose one war, Herr Hitler, may be regarded as a misfortune; to lose both looks like carelessness.' Or perhaps it was inevitable, was Germany unable to win great wars. Would a change of Axis strategy have delivered victory to Nazi Germany?

Twilight of the Living God

For the wind is in the palm-trees, and the temple-bells they say:
'Come you back, you British soldier; come you back to Mandalay!'
— **Rudyard Kipling, *Mandalay*, 1890**

A passage to India

The war in the Pacific Theatre had several clearly defined stages. At first Japan had a great deal of success, then Japan's advance was halted and checked. A period of stalemate then ensued whilst the Allies built up their resources. Then from June 1944 the Allies took the offensive and the Japanese empire began to be overwhelmed. Having expanded so far and so fast just meant that there was a vacuum of power towards the centre of the empire. Outside pressure made an implosion inevitable. In their quest to subdue China the war had spread like wildfire. Japan was the proverbial lady that swallowed a fly. Nevertheless, this did not stop them from further military folly. Indeed, the Japanese forces in Burma believed that the best defence was offence.

General William Slim, commander of the British Fourteenth Army, later a Field Marshal and Viscount, took the fight to the Japanese in Burma and supported aggressive patrolling. Long range penetration groups, known as the Chindits, were sent on foot behind enemy lines to harass the forces of the Empire of Japan. The Chindits were supplied by air drops and through runways constructed in the jungle, such as Broadway. The Chindits were the brainchild of Major General Orde Wingate. He was an accomplished counter insurgency commander, his operations utilised tactics akin to guerrilla warfare. Wingate, a British Protestant Zionist, was an Army Captain who helped crush the 1936-1939 Arab-Revolt in what was then Palestine. The rebels sought to stop Jewish immigration and expel the British. He devised the Special Night Squads that operated against Muslim radicals, particularly in the region known as Galilee. He also led other operations behind enemy lines. Earlier in the Second World War, Wingate conducted guerrilla style incursions into Ethiopia which played a key role in helping to liberate that country from Italian occupation. Wingate had become the master of unconventional and asymmetric warfare.

In Burma the jungle was the enemy. The Chindit operations had questionable levels of success, the rigours of rainforest life left many British soldiers unfit for combat, however, they did unnerve the Japanese. Wingate's mode of warfare, using soldiers as a guerrilla force, may not have been as effective as deploying them conventionally, nevertheless, the Chindits did have one major effect; they convinced the Japanese that defence would not work.

Japan attempted to disrupt the United States by aiming for the jewel in the British Empire's crown, India. Japan wanted to encourage the Indians to revolt against the Raj as this, they thought, would make the Americans divert resources from the war in the Pacific to reinforce a presumably beleaguered Britain. Hence Japan attacked the British Indian province of Assam, they launched Operation *U-Go* in 1944. It was as ambitious as it was deluded. Despite some Indians siding with the Axis, the attack did not have the effect that was intended. India remained loyal and provided millions of soldiers for the fight against Nazism, Fascism, and Militarism. The overall effect of *U-Go* was that the Japanese just broke themselves in a theatre far away from where the main battle for the future of their empire was being fought. At Kohima, a major British supply base, and Imphal, the Japanese lost a total of 65,000 men, and valuable resources. These major defeats hastened Japan's eventual loss of Burma to the British Empire and its Allied forces.

The fighting in and around Burma, had an area of operations that also included India and southern China, it became a veritable multinational melee. The Japanese were assisted by their Thai allies. Also fighting for Japan were anti-British Burmese forces, however, they would later switch sides and therefore assisted their former and future colonial masters. An equally international force was ranged against the Japanese-led armies. An ethnic group in Burma, now known as Myanmar, called the Karen people, were the victims of Japanese and Burmese atrocities, consequently they rose in rebellion and sought independence from Japanese occupied Burma. After the war their calls for autonomy were ignored and they fought an insurgency against the dictatorship that is Myanmar and continue to suffer persecution to this day.

Adding to the mix were American soldiers who were fighting in the China-India-Burma theatre. America also had long range deep penetration units. These were dubbed Merrill's Marauders, unofficially named after their commander, General Frank Merrill. They operated in a fashion similar to that of the Chindits upon which they were modelled. Another component of the Allied cause in south east Asia were the Nationalist Chinese. As mentioned, Indian forces were also heavily involved as were soldiers from Africa and mainland Britain. Other important contributors to the British Army came from the Kingdom of Nepal. At times the Gurkhas, as soldiers from Britain's Nepalese regiment are known, had a decisive impact. An example of the many acts of heroism in service of the Allied cause was that of Lachhiman Gurung who was awarded the Victoria Cross, Britain's highest award for valour in the presence of the enemy. His citation reads;

'On 12/13 May 1945 at Taungdaw, Burma, Rifleman Lachhiman Gurung was manning the most forward post of his platoon which bore the brunt of an attack by at least 200 of the enemy. Twice he hurled back grenades which had fallen on his trench, but the third exploded in his right hand, blowing off his fingers, shattering his arm and severely wounding him in the face, body and right leg. His two comrades were also badly wounded, but the rifleman, now alone and disregarding his wounds, loaded and fired his rifle with his left hand for four hours, calmly waiting for each attack which he met with fire at point-blank range.

'Additional information: He had only been with his battalion for two months when he was involved at Taungdaw as a member of the 9th Platoon of C company.

'87 of the enemy dead were killed by C company. 31 were dead in front of Lachhiman Gurung's position. He is reported as shouting "Come and fight. Come and fight. I will kill you." at the end of the battle, exhausted, he said, "I wanted to kill some Japanese before I Died on." '

He did not die that day; indeed, the author had the honour of officiating at his funeral in 2010. Beyond the bravery of individual soldiers like Lachhiman Gurung VC who prevented the Japanese from turning the British position; the Allies' key to victory in Burma was destroying the vulnerable train tracks that brought supplies to the Axis forces. Much of this railway was painstakingly built by prisoners of war in what was a marvel of engineering. The Allies knew that if these routes were destroyed the Japanese in the front line would lack resources. To that end the most able minds in a culture that encouraged and rewarded inventiveness were the difference. Technological innovation enabled America to develop the Azon bomb, one of the first smart bombs. This guided weapon was dropped onto the railway bridges thus cutting the Japanese off from resupply; this showed the future of warfare. The Japanese were behind the curve in the development of their guided munition, the *Ke-Go*. This could not be developed to a satisfactory and sufficient level in time to make a difference in the war. Therefore, the Japanese had no working comparable technology with which they could answer. Nor could they hold back the advancing forces of the British Indian Army.

Allied attempts to retake Burma began in earnest in late 1944 and by May 1945, after racing south down the Irrawaddy River, they had retaken Rangoon; the largest city and capital of Burma was back in British hands. The British advance was aided and assisted by Karen guerrillas who, along with the RAF, harassed the retreating Japanese. Defeat for the Axis in south-east Asia would follow and British rule would be restored, but not without the Allies having to overcome the most extreme resistance.

Suicide squad

Japanese soldiers, known as *Kirikomi tai*, would leave on a mission from which they were not allowed to return; for them it was goodbye and not *au revoir*. One of their tactics involved sacrificing themselves by diving under an Allied tank and blowing themselves up, taking the tank with them. In Burma, the Allies established special units of soldiers to defeat these Kamikaze attacks and defend the tanks. The Japanese were forced into massed attacks against armour, consequently it had the result of causing the Japanese to suffer mass casualties. The Japanese concept of self-sacrifice in the service of the emperor failed again. Nevertheless, this did not stop it being repeated time and time again. The Japanese fled towards the refuge of the Tenasserim hills which made up the panhandle at the far south of Burma which borders Thailand and reaches towards the Malay Peninsula. The Japanese clung to that part of Burma and finally surrendered on 13th September 1945, 11 days after Japan's official surrender. Other fanatics in the military also belatedly accepted the end of the war. On the same day in mid-September, the Japanese eventually surrendered to the Australians in New Guinea.

To a degree the Japanese empire, with the fig leaf that was the Greater East Asia Co-Prosperity Sphere, was a reaction against European and American colonialism. In this early iteration of identity politics, Japanese soldiers' purpose of living was to replace the old colonial order with a new one dominated by those who looked a little more similar in appearance to the governed underclass. However, they were soon enforcing the *status quo ante*.

In the period immediately following the Japanese surrender the problem of maintaining order in Japan's once occupied territories existed. The solution in nations such as Vietnam, then considered to be legally a part of the French protectorate of Indochina, was complex. Forces from the Republic of China had moved into the region of Vietnam to take the Japanese surrender. The Vietnamese had incidentally a long history of opposing Chinese imperialistic ambitions in their country. Upon the departure of Chiang Kai-shek's army back to China the American backed guerrilla leader Hồ Chí Minh asserted Vietnam's independence. British officers then moved in with some Free French forces and took command of the Japanese prisoners of war and remobilised them to reconquer the country and maintain European control. The Anglo-French-Japanese forces then handed

Vietnam back to France in 1946 who reasserted their colonial control over part of the country. Japan's conquest of Indochina, a move that had spurred President Roosevelt into pushing Japan into war, had been reversed, though it was not the end of history in that region. Nevertheless, for the time being the old European colonial powers were back in charge. Despite immediately reasserting themselves, in the long run the lustre for empire had gone; enforcing their claims in a protracted war would be difficult. What is more, European powers' reputations were now tarnished and would in some post-war cases be met with nationalist resistance that had co-opted the revolutionary zeal of communism.

Ultimately, victory in Europe was won on the ground with the assistance of properly deployed air power. In Asia War Plan Orange proposed that Japan could be defeated through a combination of blockade and bombing, this had been proved correct. Japan was reeling. Yet these were not the only elements that eroded the Empire of Japan. America also won great victories on the battlefield of far-flung islands as well as being triumphant on the sea and in the air. These victories resulted from the increasing disparity in firepower between these two nations whose homes were at either end of the Pacific Ocean. In the early stages of the war, Japan held sway over a vast empire that was large in both resources and manpower. Yet, like the Germans they could not convert this strength into an enduring war machine. The Americans, however, were able to turn their potential into an overwhelming force. The looming cataclysmic defeat of Japan resulted from its society and philosophy as much as it did from their equipment. War is downstream from culture.

Different strokes

Japan's military rulers sought to create a culture of conformity and obedience and built this upon existing social norms. The medieval concept of Bushido was resurrected by the military rulers of Japan who had taken over the government in the 1920s. Sacrifice and service to the Emperor led to a stubborn but foolishly uncreative and ultimately ineffectual defence that relied upon pre-war presumptions that were proven to be false. They depended upon a defensive ring that could not prevent the biggest invasion fleet seen in the Pacific since the time of the Mongols from drawing closer to the home islands.

The wishful thinking of Japan's leadership permeated down through the dutiful military; there was a devotion to groupthink. Considering alternative scenarios was disobedience. The thought that Japan's gambit against America may not work would not stop such a reckless policy from being pursued. To the militarists it was inconceivable that anything but a political agreement could be reached with the USA after all war is a continuation of policy by other means. 'Logic' dictated that a quick victory would be achieved, and a settlement would end the enmity. It was the same assumption used by Carthaginian general Hannibal more than two thousand years prior to the events of World War Two. The famed commander led his forces in a series of bold strikes against the Roman Republic which suffered grievous losses. Yet, the patricians of Rome did not accept their defeat, nor would they entertain peace. Eventually the superior resources at their disposal, particularly that of manpower, came to bear down heavily upon the invaders and the Italian states that had defected to Carthage's side. The burgeoning Roman Republic was evolving through force of arms into a formidable empire whose ability to manufacture weapons, most notably triremes, outstripped its rivals. A system that produced a thorough census of the population, a legacy from the time of Etruscan kings of Rome and inherited by the Republic, allowed the leader of the Latin tribes to locate and deploy its male citizens quickly and efficiently. The Roman manpower advantage was the product of effective bureaucracy. The forces of the Carthaginian anti-Roman alliance were worn down and then crushed by Rome and her steadfast and loyal Latin allies. Ultimately, Rome's great rival across the sea was annihilated. Japan was similarly being overwhelmed and would be fortunate if it were to avoid a Carthaginian peace.

The Japanese military reinforced failure with ever more extreme iterations of the costly Bushido code. The concepts of which were extended to the whole society. They were no longer waging war for conquest but to save Japan's political structure, the *status quo* that preserved the militarists grip on power. Unlimited discipline was the backbone of Japan's military structure, it was already a part of Japanese life and would grow to such an extent that there would be no separation of roles between civilian and soldier. All would be expected to die.

The militarist's psychology did not allow them to admit that they were defeated. The Japanese code of honour did not allow for them to surrender, they could not detach themselves from the war which they were clearly losing. The Japanese had little respect for those on their own side that did capitulate and even enemies could expect a dire fate should they make the misfortunate decision to lay down their arms. Japan had not signed the Geneva Convention because that would force the Japanese military to treat prisoners better than their own soldiers. The Americans knew what was in store for them should they be taken alive. This legitimised the brutalisation of the Japanese at the hands of the Americans who would be ruthless in response to Japanese atrocities. Japan's martial culture had produced a similar reaction in their opponents. Yet, towards the end of the war they were not equal in terms of firepower.

The lack of Japanese inventiveness and devotion to conformity was compounded by the belief that they were only fighting a short war. As such there was little need to spend resources on researching and developing weapons that could match American models. Japanese social norms at the time preceding World War Two prevented a society developing that could produce the materiel Japan's war economy needed. The militarists had at their disposal ample resources which they obtained from their empire, these included a more than an adequate amount of labour in its co-prosperity sphere. Japan would demand the servitude of conquered peoples who were pressed into work. Notwithstanding that they were unable to produce the weapons in the quantities that were needed, nor could they deploy them in a practical way. Their thinking was unsuited to the rigours of fighting a modern war of attrition in an industrial age, total war. As their excellent aircraft such as the Zero and Oscar showed, and as their complex and mighty battleships demonstrated, the Japanese had some suitable technology and fine weaponry which was highly honoured. The Japanese soldiers' rifles were considered the personal property of the emperor. They were stamped with the image of a chrysanthemum, the mark of the heavenly sovereign. Yet they were not used properly, theirs was to obey, not to think.

Japan was capable of so much more than its military industrial complex could provide. Its potential was shown after the war when the imposed American model gave Japan the economic and political tools to turn the home islands, now without any empire, into a manufacturing giant that rivalled the USA. The United States was built upon maximising the potential of its land and people through belief in the individual, weaponsing initiative and providing positive incentives. Americans displayed more inventiveness at more levels of their society than that exercised by the Japanese. Such a grounding allowed American troops to maximise their military's ability to improvise in the field. G.I. Joes and the Leathernecks in the US marines had a make do and mend mentality throughout the war; this gave American servicemen an innate advantage. This is demonstrated by the adaption of the B-25 Mitchell bomber which was added with extra armaments. The marines also took the Browning 1919 air-cooled machine gun from disused dive bombers and modified it to produce a powerful infantry support weapon. Americans were trained to kill, Japanese servicemen and even non-combatants were expected to die. The former is a much sounder method for winning a war, the latter a self-fulfilling prophecy. Another divination was soon to be achieved; General Douglas MacArthur was aiming to return to the

Philippines. Japanese soldiers, sailors, and airmen were ready to die to prevent this, America would assist them in their duty.

The gods weep

Sacrificing lives was not just the preserve of the Banzai charge, it was also a result of overly intricate battle plans designed on paper to win a victory that could reverse the course of the war. To this end the Japanese were willing to take great risks with their forces. To achieve the decisive battle, they were prepared to endanger entire battle groups of their fundamentally important navy. Everything and everyone were expendable.

Admiral Toyoda's Operation *A-Go* was planned to be another decisive battle. This became known as the Battle of the Philippine Sea which took place on 19th to 20th June 1944, it led to the disaster which became known as the Great Marianas Turkey Shoot. This saw the destruction of much of what was left of Japanese naval airpower in the Pacific. The Japanese had to defend the Marianas Islands because they knew that if these fell to the Americans then the Japanese home islands would be vulnerable to USAAF heavy bombers. However, the US bombers taking off from the far away Marianas Islands still lacked fighter protection and had a long way home which was a difficult journey if the bomber was damaged or suffered technical difficulties. Therefore, the decision was taken to capture an island nearer to Japan, the volcanic rock protruding out of the Pacific Ocean known as Iwo Jima was to be taken; but first other islands had to be subdued.

US Marines and American soldiers sought to capture the Palau Islands as well as the Marianas. This saw an evolution in Japanese strategy. Whilst still intending to destroy Allied servicemen; Japanese commanders also saw the need to kill time. Suicidal Banzai attacks were abandoned at Peleliu instead they adopted the policy of trying to hold out as long as they could and take as many American lives as possible, Colonel Nakagawa who requested a Banzai charge had this denied by Tokyo who demanded that he stick to the tactics of trying to kill US soldiers and marines. Nevertheless, compared to near total Japanese deaths, US losses were light. The American juggernaut was not thrown off schedule.

The United States had come within striking distance of the Philippines. They were on the cusp of retaking their archipelagic colony which sat across sealines crucial to Japan. The loss of these islands meant that Japan's factories, already limited in capacity, would be strangled. These workshops were the final destination of a huge set of now vulnerable logistics that snaked across Japan's diminishing empire. The loss of the Philippines would stretch them to breaking point. Without the service of a properly functioning supply chain factories, and their labour force, would become redundant.

To defend the Philippines, the Japanese response to the looming American plans to reconquer the islands was to devise an over-engineered battle plan. The success of Operation *Shō-Gō*, the attack on the US landing fleet, would depend upon the United States Navy performing according to the presumptions the Japanese planners made. Japan's hierarchies were accustomed to being obeyed, their deplorable subjects would conform to their whims; the Americans, however, had other ideas. The complicated plan was an exercise in groupthink and battle-ships. It had three main elements. Southern Force, Centre Force, and Northern Force were to attack the American fleet at the Battle of Leyte Gulf. The Japanese Imperial Navy hoped to use decoys to draw away American battleships and aircraft carriers so that the American ships involved in the landings could be sunk. The Japanese planners had not accounted for the possibility of seemingly irrational heroic actions and the serendipity that came with recklessness. These very American traits, coupled with individual bravery, created a naturally flexible and adaptable battle force. This was to show itself in the Battle of Samar; here the uncommon valour of the US ships of Taffy 3, a relatively small fleet faced down Japan's battleships, including the mighty *Yamato*, whose commander could not fathom an opponent that was not conforming to Japan's expectations. The human element had defeated Japan's robotic approach to war.

Other Japanese naval attacks on the US fleet defending the American landings on the island of Leyte in the Philippines were rushed. Admiral Kurita should have formed his ships up in a powerful line with their broadsides to the enemy allowing them to direct all the fleet's firepower at their American enemy. Instead, he ordered a general attack which was disorganised and as they were steaming towards the US vessels, they could not return fire with all their big guns. In the Philippines Campaign it was instead the Americans that managed to cross the T, as the naval manoeuvre is known, and use the full force of their cannons. The US fleet achieved what every good naval commander had sought to accomplish since Horatio Nelson, building on the tactics of Lord Howe, deployed a vari-ation of this method at the Battle of Trafalgar. The USA now ruled the waves. The American landing force was able to get its men ashore. Following the Battle of Leyte Gulf, a Japanese commander sent out a call for volunteers for a yet even darker chapter. The wounded tiger that was the Empire of Japan would exponentially increase their shocking approach to warfare, but only after the Americans drew near.

Territory that was officially a part of Japan was now coming into range. On 19th February 1945, a mighty US force landed on the island of Iwo Jima over which Japan exercised legal sovereignty. The landing parties were met with nothing. The Japanese did eventually strike back with an artillery bombardment and throughout the five weeks of raging battle the defenders conducted furious attacks at night from their extensive network of bunkers. The brutal opposition to the American invasion was effective but ultimately doomed, however, victory was never the aim. The goal of the Japanese was to use the carefully constructed caverns underneath the island to both buy time and deny the Americans the use of the airfields; in this they were not successful as the runways were quickly made operational and put into use. The Japanese, however, would not yield. The commander of Japanese forces on their island was General Tadamichi Kuribayashi, in the final stages of the Battle of Iwo Jima he wrote, 'Since the enemy's landing, the gallant fighting of the men under my command has been such that even the gods would weep.'

Sting in the tail

Next in line were the Ryukyu Islands, the main island of which was Okinawa. Though the native language of this chain was a member of the Japonic language family it was once its own self-governing kingdom. However, since the early seventeenth century Japan took suzerainty with the Tokugawa shogunate taking ultimate control and placing itself in charge of the Ryukyu's foreign relations. In the late nineteenth century Meiji authorities annexed the islands, incorporating them into Japan. The American pincers were now closing in on sovereign Japanese territory.

Okinawa was an important stepping stone towards the invasion of Japan's home islands. In March 1945 America would deploy its overwhelming firepower to take this springboard; the now outnumbered and outgunned Japanese would stubbornly resist from the island's interior. It was to no avail; the emperor's forces were hamstrung by a general lack of sophistication. Japan's military supplied inadequate medical support to their soldiers. As such not only would a wounded soldiers' chances of survival be greatly reduced, but also, they would be less likely to positively contribute to future fighting as they would not be treated adequately and thus become irredeemably injured. This was especially the case in the Battle of Okinawa. This contributed to the appalling death toll that was to follow. Suicide also accounted for much of the destruction of lives, yet it was not the only cause. Whilst the Japanese in the fight to control Okinawa proved adept at countering frontal assaults, they showed an inability to think laterally and were poor at dealing with flanking attacks. Their lack of tactical maturity was the product of a society built on hierarchy and only produced vertical thinking.

The Japanese were also no longer fighting to win, the logic of laying down arms once defeat was imminent no longer applied. Japanese soldiers and pressed into service civilians were expected to fight to the death. In the Pacific theatre they only had two main objectives. One aimed to delay the US so that Japan could improve the defence of the home islands. The other want was to make the Americans pay a high price for shrinking the empire. It was hoped that they could kill or maim enough American servicemen to make the USA believe that the price of total victory would be too high. Continuing the war would therefore be unacceptable. To achieve that end the Japanese deployed the tactics of terror and time. The Japanese would await American attacks and try and pin down their enemy on often carefully constructed fixed defences from where they could mount a bloody resistance. Defeat would inevitably come but not before they could inflict more carnage. Whilst the Americans were drudging through multiple lines made up of hidden forts on remote islands, the Japanese were striking back against near stationary targets unleashing the suicide bomber.

Japan used a version of the defence in depth strategy, holding back their enemy, delaying them, whilst deploying terror tactics. Many of these dreaded attacks would happen far out at sea, above, and even below the depths of the ocean. The *Tokkō*, or suicide weapons, were not just aerial strikes coming as a storm from a bright blue sky, often they were naval. These Kamikazes at sea included *Shin'yō* boats and *Kaiten* midget submarines. Even the mighty battleship *Yamato*, the vessel that bore an ancient name of Japan, was sent on a suicide mission in April 1945. The intention was that it would beach itself on Okinawa and become a fixed gun emplacement that would disrupt the American landings until the mighty vessel would have finally been overwhelmed. The Americans, however, having cracked Japanese codes, knew it had embarked for the Ryukyu Islands. US airpower remorselessly attacked the *Yamato* whilst it was still at sea. It was sent to the bottom of the ocean. The other Kamikaze raids were the cause of this suicide mission's failure. The *Yamato* was sunk because it received no defensive air cover. Japanese airpower was being used in the offensive Kamikaze attacks which dissipated the Imperial Japanese Navy Air Service's strength, it killed itself. That should not have been a surprise, self-destruction was after all the aim. The perfection of the cherry blossom is achieved when it falls.

By the closing months of the war desperate militarists had little choice. Axis suicide attacks were not unknown. The Nazis used similar tactics just on a limited scale. And even British wartime propaganda extolled the virtues of martyrdom with the phrase "You can always take one with you." The Japanese had once relied upon the Aichi D3A to attack Allied shipping, this dive bomber was known to the Allies as a Val, indeed they knew it well; this aircraft destroyed more vessels than any other Axis plane. Instead of focussing on proven tactics that required the crew to stay alive, if they could, these planes were pressed into service in suicide missions and even as night fighters to defend the home islands from Allied bombers. This plane, however, was hopelessly outdated, and towards the end of the war had become unsuited to the role for which it was designed. A faster and more up-to-date dive bomber, the Yokosuka D4Y or *Suisei*, called a Judy by the Allies, also failed to halt the American advance across the Pacific and was similarly used in martyrdom operations.

The Japanese even developed a single-seater rocket plane that was essentially a pilot-guided missile. This was developed for sole use in suicide missions. This aircraft was carried into combat under slung a bomber. When within range it was detached from its mother ship and with rockets ignited it would fly towards the intended victim. The concept was flawed. Its attack-obsessed designers, like those that developed Japan's vulnerable fighter aircraft which could not withstand an enemy attack, had given little thought to addressing a defect inherent in its design and application. Whilst in transit, many of these parasites, along with their host aircraft, were shot out of the sky by American planes en route to their target before they could even be released and transformed into predators to attack Allied shipping. These rocket planes were the epitome of the Kamikazes and were called Okha which means cherry blossom. The allies, however, gave them the reporting name *Baka*, this word in Japanese, 馬鹿, means idiot. The Americans had the measure of Japanese culture.

The reliance on the Kamikaze not only had a degree of logic, misguided as that may have been. The strategy to use martyrdom operations came from problems inherent in Japan's rush to war and their desire to keep feeding their war machine with new recruits. Japanese pilots by the end of the war were too inexperienced and so poorly trained that they could not effectively drop bombs or torpedoes onto US ships. This left the Japanese little choice but to turn the whole plane, including the pilot, into a flying bomb. The Japanese had faith in their strategy, believing in the natural logic of this mode of warfare. Bees die after they have stung. However, they could only inflict pain on their adversary once, and a determined foe could only be repelled by swarming their opponent. The problem was that, through exposing themselves to such danger, the life cycle of a Japanese pilot was short, there were simply never enough Kamikazes to make the strategy work. The white Anglo-Saxon protestant leadership of America had produced a mode of warfare that would devastate the Japanese.

The misguided concept behind the Kamikaze tactics and the loss of pilots meant that Japan no longer had any chance of developing experienced pilots, potential instructors had all been lost. The situation could not be salvaged. When they did seek to impart skills to their flyers the Japanese took too long to properly train pilots and were slower at this than the Americans. Ergo, with the pressing need to put men into combat effective training had to be circumvented. They were sent to their deaths as a result of the military providing young pilots with skills insufficient for battle, their predicament made worse by employing outmoded aeroplanes. As the Japanese empire regressed, the brainwashing of young men increased. They were encouraged to navigate the craft directly into the hull of a ship. These factors combined to deprive the militarists of trained pilots. This reinforced the belief that the only choice was to deploy the most extreme measures. It was a vicious circle.

Aerial Kamikaze strikes rose exponentially. As the Battle of Okinawa progressed the tactics of Japanese suicide missions evolved from individual strikes to massed planes flying in units known as floating chrysanthemums. In deploying such a strategy Japan's navy sunk to new depths. On balance it was not successful, the Kamikaze's only destroyed around fifty ships and no more than three escort carriers. They did, however, have one important impact.

The Americans found these Kamikaze attacks psychologically disturbing as their opponent's lack of regard for the lives of their own servicemen was a perversion of the norms of war. The converse US strategy, which sought to safeguard the lives of its soldiers, sailors, marines, and flyers, made prominent Americans further question the appalling cost in life that an invasion would have caused. In that respect Japan's strategy bore fruit. Notwithstanding that, the same could have been achieved by conventional tactics that did not needlessly sacrifice lives. Furthermore, the mental fallout from the Kamikazes would be limited to those serving in theatre. To prevent alarming the home front the Americans ordered a news blackout on Kamikaze attacks. Nevertheless, the families of the approximately seven thousand US servicemen killed by Japanese martyrdom operations would no doubt have suffered the distress of losing their loved ones to this spiritual mode of warfare as would the relatives of the doomed men.

Japanese Vice Admiral, Takijirō Ōnishi, was responsible for expanding Japan's Kamikaze program. Upon Japan's cessation of hostilities, he took his own life and apologised to the approximately four thousand Japanese dead kamikazes and their families. He died slowly from agonising internal injuries. Attempts to give the Americans a bloody nose on Okinawa just resulted in the destruction of the Japanese navy. There was now nothing in the way of the home islands. Island hopping was now approaching its inevitable final destination. The fall of Okinawa made Japan's home islands the next target.

Downfall

Invasion planners envisaged that the operation that would lead to the downfall of the Japanese empire would come in two main operations. Firstly, the conquest of Japan proper would begin with the invasion of Kyūshū, the most southerly of the main home islands. This would be the main part of Operation Olympic, as it was known. This was to be launched in November 1945. Taking the southern part of Kyūshū would allow the USAAF to turn it into an air base for bombing Japan's largest island, Honshū. It would also enable American airpower to eliminate the threat from Japan's kamikaze planes. Kyūshū would then become the staging post for the invasion of Honshū. This second invasion was outlined in Operation Coronet and was scheduled to begin in March 1946.

This was all contained within the overarching strategy of Operation Downfall, which included continuing to supply aid to China to either defeat the Japanese occupiers or tie up their troops on the mainland of Asia. Driving back the Japanese in China would also allow for more air bases to be captured from which the pummelling of Japan could continue apace. Britain and Commonwealth forces also offered troops towards the proposed final climactic campaign of World War Two, the offers were accepted. Ultimately, it would have become another Anglo-American invasion. The prize would be capturing Japan's capital, Tokyo, in a pincer movement. This would not be straightforward as the plain surrounding Tokyo was very well defended. Indeed, a captured Japanese colonel predicted that it would be impossible to conquer Japan. He explained that there are 100 million people in the Japanese empire, it will take 10 times that number to conquer them. It will then become a matter of generations. Indeed, they were preparing to fight; the Japanese were being prepped for destruction. The Japanese answer to invasion was Operation *Ketsugō*. An American estimate was that the conquest of Japan could lead to one million Allied casualties. Japan's militarists hoped to convey a message to the Americans. The Japanese dogged and determined desire to fight on to kill as many US servicemen as possible would let America know that the cost was too high a price to pay. They hoped that such a realisation would allow the Empire of Japan to snatch a peace deal out of the jaws of defeat.

Black hearts and minds

Japan was preparing to sternly resist an American-led invasion and that which the Soviet may have launched. If the home front were to become the front line, Japanese civilians were instructed in how to fight in the *People's Handbook of Resistance Combat*. Japanese propaganda and its rigid disciplined system of obedience had made this island chain a prison from which escape could only be achieved through an inglorious death or via the even more inconceivable act of surrendering. Fearful of the beastly American GI of Japanese propaganda, civilians, as well as soldiers, were willing to take their own lives and those of their children rather than be subject to the torments of captivity. The truth of American occupation proved to be vastly different. The myths spread by Japan's militarists of the US bogeyman, were intended to keep themselves relevant and in power by keeping the population fearful and serving their masters, it had a very real effect.

Armed in some cases with just agricultural equipment, pitchfork wielding Japanese civilians were expected to partake in a national Banzai charge in what would have been a desperate attempt to stop the advance of American progress. It would have been mass suicide by soldier. This would have more than decimated the Japanese population. The National Resistance Program required all over 15s, including women, to fight against the predicted US invasion. They would not be alone in their sacrifice.

In August 1945 there were 900,000 Japanese troops on Kyūshū. That number does not include the civilians that would be mobilised in the event of an invasion. Kyūshū would see the first allied troops landing ashore, they would be met by a fanatical resistance that would give no quarter, and none would be expected. The millions of Japanese personnel, including the militant civilians on Kyūshū, would be reinforced by trained battle-hardened soldiers brought in fresh from the fighting in China. To free up a further one million men, the Japanese resolved to negotiate a truce with the Chinese. The Pacific War was ignited to remove impediments against the militarists desire to conquer China. However, it had burned out of control to such an extent that they would have to forsake the endless fighting in Asia to defend their Emperor's home. Japan's cities were already inflamed.

On the other side of the Pacific Ocean patriotism was more efficiently channelled. US civilians were encouraged to invest in war bonds to finance the fighting and worked in gainful employment to produce the weapons their taxes and loans paid for. The home front in America was a world away from the expectations placed on Japanese civilians. The US social and economic system was noticeably more productive.

The Japanese men and women fighting on the ground would not be alone, they would receive assistance from above. This aid would not be in the form of the 'divine' descendant of the Sun goddess Amaterasu, and Susanoo, the storm god, but from more earthly tempests. There were 5,000 Kamikaze planes in reserve on Kyūshū and a further 5,500 based on Honshū. The desperation that was expressed through demanding the Yamato people martyr themselves was matched by a belated search for wonder weapons, some more practical than others. These ranged from physics defying death rays to more realistic advances in aeroplanes. However, the fruitless search for the microwave weapon of mass destruction took attention away from more practical solutions.

Japan had belatedly tried to develop new models of planes. However, the military situation was already too dire. The engine factory for the Kawasaki Ki-61 fighter was destroyed by US bombing retarding its production. Another interceptor, also manufactured by Kawasaki, the Ki-100, had the potential to strip US bombers from the skies. However, it was produced in too few numbers and was delivered far too late to save Japan from the fire storm. In the face of these setbacks the militarists reverted to the few viable weapons that existed in their armoury, namely the patriotism and obedience of their people. Death and glory charges were the military's default tactic when losing to the Americans. Japan's leaders hoped this would bludgeon the USA into a negotiated peace.

In America there began to be a realisation that compromises needed to be made, indeed, the demand for unconditional surrender had helped force Germany to remain in the conflict until total war turned into total defeat. On the other side of the earth the bitter fighting that was still underway, with the promise of even more to come, began to create a meeting of minds between the main belligerents. There were movements in both America and Japan that were trying to edge the warring sides towards a peaceful conclusion to the war.

George Marshall, Chief of Staff of the United States Army, wrote to Henry Stimson, the US Secretary of War, on 9th June 1945 that, 'We should cease talking about unconditional surrender of Japan. And begin to define our true objective in terms of defeat and disarmament.' Other leading political figures went further still. Fearful of mass casualties, former president Herbert Hoover even advised Truman to seek a negotiated peace allowing the Empire of Japan to keep Korea. Rewarding such a brutal and aggressive empire, by allowing it to keep control over one if its neighbours was unpalatable and contrary to the notions of de-colonisation which America was planning to install in the new international system. The United States of America was opposed to the concept of formal empires and supported the self-determination of peoples to have their own state. Truman rejected Hoover's advice and demanded unconditional surrender, yet compromises were to be made.

America's beleaguered but still belligerent enemy also began a gradual shift towards peace. Japanese Prime Minister Suzuki wanted to surrender but was powerless in the face of the military. The peace party in Japan needed a decisive event to swing power in their favour, they were to get two and still the matter was in the balance. The deadlock was only broken by the intervention of the Heavenly Sovereign. Yet, until that time came the Japanese stuck with the strategy of trying to wear down American resolve. However, the Americans regarded a negotiated settlement as anathema. The result was that this gave the US little option but to take a decision that has since never been made again.

Totalitarian regimes put their collectivist ideology above all other interests and saw their own citizens as expendable in the service of their state creed. Their peoples' sacrifice towards an end that its leaders approved would on balance be acceptable, it was even considered morally good. Conversely, leaders in societies that placed individual freedom at their centre, and had democratically accountable governments, did their utmost to avoid needlessly wasting the lives of their own citizens. Even the lives of those in uniform had to be preserved as best they could. And after years of fighting, they had learnt to win battles with minimum loss of their own blood. Science would take this concept to new heights.

One option that would have allowed the United States to conquer Japan without the extreme loss of American and British lives, was the use of weapons of mass destruction. In June 1945 President Truman's Chemical Warfare Service advocated to invasion planners the utilisation of gas attacks on Kyūshū in advance of Allied soldiers. Japanese cities were to be targeted. The USA, like Japan, had not signed restrictions on the use of a deadly miasma. And as Japan had already used chemicals in China it could be argued that America had a pretext for taking such drastic tactics. Nevertheless, this would have been an extreme course of action and was considered anathema. The former and deceased President Roosevelt had only wanted to use gas in retaliation and even Hitler was averse to using those weapons against combatants, preferring instead to use them exclusively on civilians. The Truman administration's flirtation with such a weapon was an extreme solution, moreover there was an alternative.

America had invested billions of US dollars in developing powerful bombs that would use uranium and plutonium to harness the power of the atom, the smallest part of an element that can exist. Truman kept the use of these nuclear weapons under his control. They could not be used by the military without his express approval. He was reluctant at first. President Truman hesitated about using the A-bomb. He was finally persuaded when he was asked what he would say at his impeachment hearing when they found out that he had a weapon to finish the war but did not use it. The United States resolved to unleash nuclear war; the only time such devices have been used in a conflict.

Atomic clock

The timing behind the use of radioactive weapons was to force Japan's surrender to the Americans before the Soviet Union entered the war. Whilst Truman's predecessor Roosevelt had missed the opportunity to negate Russian influence in post-war Europe, President Truman was in a race against time to make sure that communist influence over parts of Asia would be limited. The dropping of the bombs on Hiroshima and Nagasaki were the first American moves in the new great game of noughts and crosses known as the cold war. This conflict was to be fought by proxies whilst the forces of the main protagonists generally did not engage each other directly. In this simmering war between the two new superpowers, the USA and the USSR, would seek to check the other's strategic moves. However, contrary to Roosevelt's policy of provoking war with Germany and Japan, President Truman and his successors made sure not to make the Soviet's so seething with anger that tensions would become too hot causing them to boil over into an open conflict. That remained America's doctrine until President Reagan in the 1980s pushed back against the Soviet Union causing the completely rotten edifice to collapse from within. However, that was after communism had been allowed to run roughshod over both eastern Europe and the far east for more than four decades.

Whilst the two atomic strikes helped bring the Pacific war to an end, and led eventually to Japan's formal surrender, the cessation of hostilities also gave Stalin a free pass in the region. It was therefore the first self-defeating American move in the cold war and aided Soviet and communist expansion in Asia. This was inadvertent, what was deliberate was the Roosevelt administration's encouraging Russia to restore its power over the east. Indeed, it was even prepared to aid and abet this reconquest.

The Manchurian candidate

Former Vice-President Truman, who became the 33rd President of the United States of America, had inherited a difficult position from President Roosevelt. FDR, as the previous American Head of State was known, created problems that would plague future American administrations. Roosevelt wanted the USSR to join the war against Japan. Stalin, in exchange for entering the war three months after the defeat of Germany, required a high price. The infirm and fading President was not only willing to pay this but also enabled this communist power grab.

Stalin demanded the right to access Port Arthur in Manchuria, once a key Russian base. The Soviet leader also required recognition of Russian interests, a euphemism for control, over Mongolia and Manchuria. Both were once considered to be a part of China and were ruled by the Qing Dynasty who were themselves Manchu in origin and received Mongol support in their conquest of China in the 17th century. With the revolt against Qing rule in China and following the growth of Han nationalism, the Han being the largest ethnic group in China, Mongolians reacted and freed themselves from Chinese rule in 1911. Its independence was recognised during the era when China descended into warlordism. However, Mongolia soon fell under Russian influence.

Stalin also wanted possession of Japan's Kuril Islands. This archipelago stretched out northeast into the Sea of Okhotsk from Japan's most northerly main island Hokkaidō. The island chain reaches towards the Kamchatka Peninsula which extends down from the eastern edge of Siberia. Russia did have a claim over those northern islands. And besides, the Japanese had only recently incorporated the Kuril chain into their empire, in the process they deprived the native population, the Ainu, of their last area of autonomy. These peoples were the original inhabitants of Japan and descended from the Arctic region and were ethnically unlike most Orientals. The Ainu were comparatively fair skinned and hairy. Against the evidence of his top advisors Roosevelt agreed to Stalin's demands.

The long serving 32nd President of the United States was the mortal enemy of some dictatorial regimes. He weaponised America's economic might and deployed his young country into the great conflagration as the arsenal of democracy. Roosevelt then sent American servicemen into the conflict. These actions contributed more to sealing the fate of Nazi Germany, militarist Japan, and Fascist Italy more than any other Allied contribution to the war. Yet, Roosevelt consented to Stalin's Soviet regime spreading its writ along with communism into Russia's near abroad. Soviet socialism was every bit as wicked as collectivist

Germany and far more malevolent than Mussolini's Italy. Stalin was also as eager for conquest as Japan's out of control military.

There was, however, a difference between these totalitarian regimes. Apart from Stalin's presumed mental breakdowns, where his paranoid rage was directed at his own people, the Soviet autocrat was for the most part a rational actor in matters of international affairs. In contrast with Stalin's cold and calculating risk playing, Hitler and Mussolini were out of control fantasists. Japan's military knew not restraint. Roosevelt believed that Stalin was a man he could do business with. The Georgian communist despot knew that his American counterpart was a man that could be bent to his will, or at least neutralised. This was not a difficult task.

Roosevelt, wanting to hold the Soviet leader close to his bosom, offered Russia a place in his new world order and considered this a victory. This played into Stalin's hands as his involvement with the United Nations gave the Soviet Union a veto on the UN Security Council. Stalin was not tied into the liberal and democratic new world order as Roosevelt had hoped. Instead, Soviet Russia had thrown off the isolation that contained them before the Second World War and were now at the top table of global governance. Communism was emboldened.

Stalin kept his part of a near one sided bargain. Stalin had promised Roosevelt at the Yalta Conference that Russia would enter the war against Japan within three months of victory over Germany. The Soviets attacked on 9th August 1945. Roosevelt was not just appeasing Stalin's ambitions in the region by recognising Russia's historic ambitions but was even willing to offer practical assistance. As part of Project Hula, America equipped the Russian navy with the vessels the Soviets needed to seize Japan's northern territories. US navy personnel even trained Soviet sailors on how to operate these warships and transferred them to their new operators.

Roosevelt's Soviet sympathies and unfounded faith in the reasonableness of his communist counterpart, Joseph Stalin, was not the only factor in the American President's decision making. It was clear an invasion of Japan would have been costly for American servicemen. Roosevelt wanted the might of the Red Army to join this final climactic battle of World War Two. To that end, Roosevelt was eager for Russia to even invade Japan alongside America. Yet, a national strategy that could only see as far as defeating existing enemies to freedom and democracy, and failed to prepare for emerging threats, was extraordinarily myopic.

In line with his agreement to cooperate with America's war against the Empire of Japan, Stalin began preparing for conflict in the east. In April 1945 Stalin repudiated the Soviet-Japanese Neutrality Pact and began amassing a sizable force made up of Red Army divisions, bolstered by soldiers from the Russian client state of Mongolia. They would attack the Japanese, and the collaborationist forces of Japan's puppet states of Manchukuo (Manchuria) and Mengjiang (Inner Mongolia). The Japanese military in Manchuria, the Kwantung Army, once famed for its conquests in China was by 1945 greatly weakened. The army that had never before been humbled by the authorities in Tokyo had been a law unto itself. Its commanders took free rein to not only carve out an empire in a fit of hubris but also provoked Japan's entry into World War Two. However, they were finally weakened by the Imperial General Staff which took away its best units and equipment to fight against the Americans and also sent them south to deprive the United States of air bases in southern China. This was successful, a Japanese offensive in that region meant air bases had to be evacuated. Nevertheless, the proposed conquest of Manchuria by the Red Army was a bold undertaking, the Russian objective was to seize territory comparable in size to the area of Europe fought over between Germany and the western Allies.

During the war this vital industry and other Japanese controlled factories were conveniently out of range of American bombers. As World War II progressed in a fashion that was most certainly not to Japan's advantage, more manufacturing was moved to Manchuria to be beyond the range of American airpower. The Japanese military's biological weapons programme was tested on the people of Manchuria by the infamous scientists of Unit 731. Yet, after the Second World War the scientists avoided prosecution, receiving immunity in response for supplying the results of their experimentation to their American captors. The leadership of the Kwantung Army did however, face punishment by the Soviets, and from the Americans in the Tokyo trials for the crimes of human rights violations and waging aggressive war.

The Russian and Mongolian Red Armies used surprise to conquer Manchuria. Although the Kwantung Army had detected troop movements across Manchukuo's border, they thought it would be many more months before the Soviets launched an attack. It was another example of a spiritual people following wishful thinking rather than searching for and analysing hard evidence. The Japanese did not at first realise the scale of the assault. Previous performance served as a misleading guide to future events. Japanese troops had been kept in this theatre throughout the Second World War and prior to that great conflict there had been clashes between the Imperial Japanese Army and the Red Army, yet these were limited in scope and were often little more than skirmishes. The past proved to be a poor pointer as to the future. Millions of well-motivated and trained cadres, believing in their cause and an ultimate victory were soon to descend upon the Japanese occupiers. The situation had been made worse because the Japanese had been deceived. In December 1941 Japan was talking peace with America while planning for war. They were now to fall prey to similar tactics.

Stalin, who the Japanese had hoped would act as a mediator between their empire and America, had been misleading them as to the neutrality of the Soviet Union. He was just preparing his forces to attack Japan and seize the territory they held on continental Asia and in the Pacific. Stalin knew it would be crucial in the cold war which he was strategically preparing for. Indeed, it was already important. Manchuria was vital to Japan's war economy. It produced coal and synthetic fuel and its factories were outside the range of American bombers, its loss would be a devastating blow. Stalin also coveted these resources and wanted to take much of Manchurian industry to Russia. He would try and make it serve Soviet interests in the coming cold war. The Russian-led forces began their attacks without a preliminary artillery bombardment and achieved the element of surprise. Nevertheless, the Japanese and their subordinates, though weakened, had a strategy to resist a Soviet invasion. The Kwantung Army kept most troops in the interior of Manchuria. The plan was to react to any invasion and move defending forces to wherever in this vast province they were needed. It was a reactive rather than proactive defence.

The enormous scale of the potential battlespace and the technical and numerical inferiority of the Japanese left little choice. However, the Japanese military backwardness that was already prevalent in their earlier battles with the Russians in 1939 was even more marked six years later. The Japanese attempted to make up for their shortcomings in technology, materiel, and numbers with ferocity. Japanese planes made suicide attacks diving onto Russian tanks, these sorties were unsuccessful, and soldiers with explosives strapped to them ran at armoured vehicles. Neither of which was a good use of human potential, nor an effective way of deploying limited equipment. After years of desperate fighting, a nation that had become devoted to war, had highly disciplined soldiers who were reduced to penury. The once dreaded Japanese soldier had been enfeebled. The flower of Japanese manhood had largely been wasted in reckless and near suicidal human wave attacks. In contrast, Soviet man, thrown into combat and expected to fight or die had, through a process of natural selection, become a mighty warrior that thrived in the harshest of conditions. It had weeded out the incompetent, the coward had been liquidated. What remained in the Red Army and the Red Army Air Forces after six years of fighting first Japan, then Poland, Finland, and the Axis was a well-oiled killing machine. It was more than capable of annihilating the now poorly equipped Kwantung Army, whose tactics were even more antiquated than their outmoded weapons. Whilst the Russians also used massed wave attacks, these were for practical tactical reasons, not as a quasi-religious sacrifice to a 'god' as was the Japanese custom. Faced with the well-equipped Red Army the Japanese were rolled over and then even took the extraordinary step of cancelling what little resistance they could mount.

Softly killing

The Allies in the so-called Potsdam Declaration set out the terms of Japan's surrender as agreed at the conference held in the German city from where the pronouncement got its name. The choice for the last of the Axis powers to remain in the war was between justice for war criminals, with an end to their empire, or face prompt and utter destruction. The Allies' call for unconditional surrender and its opaqueness on the position of the emperor did not enamour the declaration to the Japanese leadership. Not only did it not mention his role in a post-war Japan, but there was also a problematic clause which demanded that,

'There must be eliminated for all time the authority and influence of those who have deceived and misled the people of Japan into embarking on world conquest, for we insist that a new order of peace, security and justice will be impossible until irresponsible militarism is driven from the world.'

The militarists' professed loyalty to their heavenly sovereign made this a difficult term to accept. Allied measures aimed at building their reign of peace were in danger of prolonging the conflict; this would lead to yet more soldiers and civilians losing their lives. Japan resolutely ignored this call to relinquish the fight. The strategy of treating the Allied ultimatum with a quiet contempt was known as *Mokusatsu*, silently killing the calls to surrender. The Japanese Supreme Council believed that they could reach a negotiated settlement that would guarantee that the position of the emperor would be maintained after the war. However, the nuclear attacks intervened.

Was the final victory delivered by the attacks on Hiroshima and Nagasaki? The emperor did indeed refer to the new and terrible weapon in his statement announcing the end of hostilities, which did not mention surrender, but declared "The war situation has developed not necessarily to Japan's advantage." However, few outside of Hiroshima and Nagasaki and Japan's supreme command new of what happened when the atomic and plutonium bombs were dropped. So their use did not create a groundswell of opinion to end the fighting. The nuclear devastation though great was matched by the great conflagrations that resulted from the American use of incendiary devices on Japan's wooden cities. Indeed, more died from those firestorms than in the dual atomic strikes. Civilian loss of life was never an overriding consideration for Japan's masters, their concept was that the people were there to serve and die if need be. Many political systems celebrate ideologies that enrich and empower the uber elite and still claim to be virtuous. Besides, the civilian death toll that would have resulted from a mass Banzai charge would have brought even greater loss of life than those lost at Hiroshima and Nagasaki.

Yet many historians still argue 'yes', the nuclear weapons brought peace. Nevertheless, Russia's entry into the war should also be considered as a major factor as the Soviet-led invasion not only thoroughly defeated Japan in Manchuria, but also could have led to a Russian invasion of Japan proper. It also ended the misguided notion that the USSR could be a possible mediator between America and Japan. This latter point was the most salient. Indeed, Prime Minister Kantarō Suzuki thought the Soviet attack on Manchuria made Japan's position hopeless.

All aspects combined to produce peace. The triple blows of learning what happened at Hiroshima, the further attack on Nagasaki, and learning of the Soviet attack on Manchuria merged to make an overwhelming case for surrender. Yet, the question was still not fully settled. Ultimately Japan capitulated after an 800 Super Fortress flypast over Tokyo on 13th August dropping leaflets, not bombs. The leaflets explained to the Japanese people the intransigence of their military leaders and detailed the enormous fire power which the United States possessed in the nuclear age. It was a bluff; for the time being America only had a limited supply of these new terrifying weapons. It is thought that this leaflet had a profound impact on Hirohito.

Japan finally gave in when President Truman sent a communique to the Japanese that the emperor's position would be safe and emphasising that a failure to capitulate would mean more destruction. Only then did Japan allude to surrender. The Emperor, after evading an attempted *coup d'état*, announced on 15th August 1945 via a pre-recorded message that his subjects must endure the unendurable. This was not universally welcomed at home, nor abroad. The Russians refused to recognise the Japanese surrender and ensured that the Red Army kept on pushing to capture more territory from their Asiatic rival. The bulletin of the Soviet General Staff of 16th August said that effectively Japan had not surrendered, they had only announced their intention to surrender. Technically the Soviets were correct, yet even when Japan had formally signed the Instrument of Surrender on 2nd September 1945 the Soviets continued their offensive operations for a further 3 days, completing their capture of the Kuril Islands on 5th September. The now hapless Japanese servicemen could only sit by and be taken prisoner and watch the Soviets consume Japan's hard-won conquests; they even lost some of their territorial integrity. The obedience that produced such ferocious fighters, which in just a matter of years carved out one of the largest empires in world history, both in terms of population and geographic size, could now no longer even try and defend themselves. Japan's earlier triumphs were just fleeting.

Red dawn

With the Soviet attack Japan had not only lost much of its empire on the landmass of Asia and the very *raison d'être* for launching the war in the first place but they had also lost a potential peace broker. The idea that the USSR would negotiate a face-saving exit from the war was a fanciful hope and a misreading of Russian ambitions in the far east. The Japanese misconstruing of the USSR's intentions was as big a mistake as Japan's vain belief that America would accept the Empire of Japan's hegemony over the USA's Asian possessions and tolerate an attack on its military. Wishful thinking does not make sound public policy. The reasons to accept peace with the Allies were now myriad. And what is more the threat of a Red Army invasion loomed over the home islands. This Russian threat was a key consideration in making sure Japan lay down its arms. Stalin was preparing to seize the Japanese home island of Hokkaidō. Japan was only saved by its one-time great adversary the USA led by the man that ordered the dropping of first a uranium bomb and then one using plutonium, President Harry S. Truman. More alert to the communist threat than his predecessor, he demanded that the Soviet's stop their attacks on Japan. Stalin dutifully complied, the Soviet leader's plan to invade Hokkaidō on 24th August was only stopped by US President Truman who ensured the USSR cease operations against the Japanese home islands. However, Truman and the Japanese had to accept the Russian acquisitions of disputed Japanese territory.

The Japanese abandonment of the war led to the Red Army taking Manchuria and Korea with next to no resistance. In Manchuria a Chinese leader, Mao Zedong, was installed as the ruler of a communist government. He would use this territory, its resources, and remaining industries to win the Chinese civil war. From there Mao took control over most of mainland China, declaring the People's Republic of China in 1949. To this day China and the Democratic People's Republic of Korea remain at loggerheads with the United States. Without the Japanese effectively downing tools before the official surrender on 2nd September 1945, there was no guarantee that the USSR would have occupied so much of China so easily, winning territory from where Asian communism was to be built. Japanese soldiers were to surrender to the Red Army with almost the same fanaticism that they showed when dutifully obeying orders to attack. It had the same defeating effect as the massed wave *Banzai* charge. This even entailed the surrender of islands in the Japanese archipelago. To this day Russia controls South Sakhalin and the Kuril Islands, which have been annexed to the Russian Federation.

Roosevelt's insistence that the Soviets enter the war against Japan ninety days after the end of the war in Europe was not the only problem. FDR's original and almost unilateral demand for unconditional surrender, bouncing Churchill into this uncompromising position, kept the world at war longer than it otherwise would have. He was not the only President at fault. Following FDR's passing, the administration of his successor, Harry Truman, also enabled the war to continue. Truman's delay in guaranteeing the survival, in name only, of the institution of the emperor also rightly bears some responsibility for the war's continuance. Nevertheless, ultimately the blame rests with Japan. The Japanese were culpable for the continuing loss of life for no substantive reward. Not only was Japan placed under American occupation, but the United States also imposed religious and constitutional innovations surrounding the position of the emperor. Hirohito became just a man, and it was for all to see that he was subordinate to General MacArthur. Neither side had gained anything substantive by prolonging the war beyond July when the Americans knew that the Japanese wanted out of the war, and that the demand for unconditional surrender was the only impediment to peace. Indeed, they had been considering surrender since as early as 1944. An early exit from the war would have preserved Japan's territorial integrity vis-à-vis Russia and may have stopped the domino run of Asian countries falling to communism before it began.

Fortress Japan
Whilst on the face of it Hirohito kept his position, the reality was somewhat different. Not only had he lost his temporal power, handing political control of the home islands to a military commander, General MacArthur. The US General was effectively a foreign Shōgun that co-opted the Japanese government, along with its head of state, into his administration; there was no illusion as to who the senior partner was. The emperor's political role became one of agent to the American occupation of Japan. A far more lenient and liberal regime than the Japanese imposed on their conquered subjects.

When the period of occupation ended the emperor's loss of political power was permanent. In a democratic Japan an elected Prime Minister was effectively supreme. The changes brought by the Meiji Restoration which put the emperor at the centre of Japan's executive was over. It had lasted less than a mere 80 years. When considering this country's long history this period was merely a brief interregnum. Indeed, in the 1930s the emperor's reign was at times little more than a smokescreen for rule by large corporations which in turn became totally subservient to the military, Japan' real rulers during World War Two. Whilst temporal power proved to me a mirage Hirohito's spiritual power was built upon many millennia of worship, this too was to end, though controversially the ritual would be maintained.

Hirohito was also forced by the US to renounce his divinity. The American occupation ended State Shintō. The religious ideology ruling Japan was over. In one sense therefore the position of Tennō or Heavenly Sovereign, a spiritual position, often wrongly translated into English as Emperor, was in effect abolished and merely exists in name only. However, upon Akihito's enthronement in 1990, a year after his accession to the Chrysanthemum Throne, following the death of his father, Hirohito, the old order reasserted some semblance of its divinity. The new Emperor controversially took part in the Daijōsai ceremony as part of his investiture. This ritual supposedly reunites the emperor with his divine ancestor, the sun-goddess Amaterasu.

Whilst, the nuclear attacks may not have immediately ended the war, they did permanently change Japan's historical and religious development similar to William Adams three centuries earlier. With the dropping of the second nuclear bomb on Nagasaki the penetration of Christianity into Japanese society was stunted. The port city of Nagasaki had been an important centre for Christianity and despite many martyrdoms had managed to cling on and survive the persecution under Japan's Shōguns. The dropping of "Fat Man", as the plutonium bomb was named, on Nagasaki did not discriminate in favour of Japan's Christians. The exceptionally brutal act not only killed many members of this struggling community but also created a barrier of embitterment against further conversions. Despite being the *coup de grâce* for a dying empire, the act of mercy did not prove to be a public relations success in the long-term. It damaged the moral authority that American society would have needed for Christianity to take a strong foothold and make inroads into Japanese society.

The lack of cultural awareness of foreign nations amongst American military planners prevented Japan moving even closer towards the United States. Oriental societies are not immune to Christianity taking hold. Nestorian Christians were once innumerable in the orient. Today, China has a growing Christian, and mainly Protestant community. This congregation produces many members of China's successful business class. Furthermore, most of the population of South Korea, a land that is under American protection with a large US military presence, is now predominantly Christian. Despite a benevolent American occupation, in Japan there was little post-war growth in adherence to Christianity.

The tumults and violence that were set in train when American gunboats sailed into what was then called Edo Bay and is now known as Tokyo Bay had reached their conclusion, the wheel had turned through 360°. The result was the USS *Missouri* sailing into Tokyo Bay to host the formal Japanese surrender ceremony which took place on 2nd September 1945. The Americans were again dictating terms to this now vulnerable state which lay prostrate before them. Japan had become a client state of the USA, history had gone full circle.

During the official signing of the Japanese surrender document the huge US Fleet, along with some British vessels, mirrored the situation in 1853 when US gunboats, the so-called Black Ships, forced Japan to end its isolation, and enter a trade agreement with America. This led to the emperor's position of power being restored and to the modernisation of Japan's economy and its industrialisation. Japan then embarked on the course that made it an aggressive regional power and thus created the Pacific war nearly nine decades later. The result, however, was that in 1945 the American empire was victorious and could again dictate the terms just as they had done in the middle of the nineteenth century.

The Japanese fight for imperial sovereignty over the home islands whilst becoming hegemon over neighbouring peoples had been a failure. Japan's aggression against European and American imperialism was the ultimate form of flattery. The Japanese national strategy was essentially one of imitation but with a Japanese cultural twist which mass produced and exported suppression on a monstrous scale. After their surrender, the Japanese were forced to become a pacific people. Once conquest had been celebrated, now the state constitution enshrines non-aggression. However, the past is not completely forgotten nor entirely anathema. The militaristic Shintō Yasukuni shrine, is still however, a centre for the reverence of fallen Japanese servicemen from the Second World War and other conflicts. This venue received a controversial visit from then-Japanese Prime Minister the late Shinzō Abe in 2013.

After the war, a people who had long been taught to conform quickly adapted to the new normal. Obeying orders, and their social superiors, came naturally even if the message contradicted earlier indoctrination by the militarists. Embracing peace therefore was not a radical departure, obedience was a continuation of this cultural phenomenon. Furthermore, isolationism in foreign affairs was also the norm, that is bar the infrequent forays into Korea and clashes with China, both of which failed. One occurred soon after the end of their medieval period, the other coming soon after Japan's modern stage began.

Nevertheless, after 1945 the Japanese embarked on a new nationwide voyage, one of replicating their master's success. At the behest of the occupiers, Japan separated spiritual matters from the state and established a stable democracy. It was very stable indeed, with the conservative Liberal Democratic Party winning most elections since its foundation in 1955. Japan has a bi-cameral parliamentary system with elected representatives in a body known as the Diet choosing a Prime Minister who in turn selects other members of the executive. The invariability of Japanese election results has as much to do with the gerrymandering of seats in the Diet as it has to do with the success story that was post-war Japan. Yet that success is now a distant memory.

Japan experienced phenomenal growth when after 1945 the power of large semi-autarchic industrial conglomerates was diluted and they themselves were broken-up. These mega corporations had dominated Japan's pre-war economy. That version of corporatism failed and initially under the stewardship of General of the Army Douglas MacArthur, Japan embraced the economic model that made America great. Soon the Japanese would, in some respects, again be competing with the behemoth on the other side of the great ocean. This time however it was in car production and technological consumer goods. More recently however, and since the 1990s, Japan's economy has stagnated. Its lost decades began when reckless lending caused an asset price bubble which duly burst and put the economy in the doldrums in which it remains. Japan is now burdened by an ageing population and has a falling birth rate. Despite Japan's many recent difficulties the Liberal Democratic Party has remained in government for much of this time.

The status quo remained because of the over-representation in the Diet of seats in less populated conservative rural areas, incidentally the parts of the country that were once home to feudalism. The overrepresentation of the countryside as opposed to the more populated cities, where voters would have a greater propensity to lean more towards social democratic parties, locks in the Liberal Democratic Party's majority. Clearly in terms of an aversion to change, aspects of the political culture remain intact. As do other facets of culture, namely that as expressed through fashion.

In both feudal and Meiji Restoration Japan, authorities attempted to impose modes of dress on their subjects and tried to discourage American fashions; in the pre-war period this was not always successful. The obsequious aping of American dress, occasionally with a Japanese twist, was seen before the war just as it is now. However, particularly in terms of business attire, American fashions are now the socially mandated norm. The trait of conforming to the most powerful can still be seen. Japan is no longer under US occupation but is now under American protection. Japan is occasionally harassed by North Korea and is in dispute with the communist controlled People's Republic of China which claims sovereignty over Japan's Senkaku Islands. Taiwan, officially called the Republic of China, also claims these specs in the ocean, yet the serious threat to Japanese sovereignty in this regard comes from Beijing. Despite Tokyo having its own military known as the Japan Self-Defence Forces, peace in this region is now maintained by the United States, and certainly not through the Greater East Asia Co-Prosperity Sphere. That model in Asia became defunct generations ago, Japan had little chance of success against its many enemies, chief amongst them the USA. Nevertheless, could a similar system, led by Germany, have triumphed in Europe?

How Hitler Won the War
The decisions that could have given the Nazis victory

'Victory is reserved for those who are willing to pay its price.'
— **Sun Tzu**

All glory is fleeting

Hitler, and Japan's militarists, established great empires that disappeared nearly as quickly as their violent birth. The intense flames burnt themselves out. Considering the forces ranged against them it is remarkable that Germany remained at war for so long. Against unprepared opponents they had the ability to deliver quick political knockout blows, indeed their entire strategy relied on intimidation to make their adversary surrender. However, they lacked longevity, and their warlike grand strategies were ultimately exposed as flawed when confronted by an enemy that would not be intimidated.

Japan and Germany had similar problems that were exposed by the industrial giants of the USSR, the USA, and the combined capacity of the British Empire. The leading Axis powers lacked the ability and know-how to manufacture the quantities of weapons needed to force a victory on their terms. Germany and Japan were gambling on a short war, snap military successes, forcing the 'inevitable' peace at the political level. Axis groupthink surmised that the American, British, and Russian empires would accept that history was on the side of the Aryan and Nippon peoples and those races would triumph and become the hegemons over their respective spheres of influence. This was not to be, their totalitarian cultures were not conducive to the economic dynamism that was needed to underpin their desires for conquest. Both however choose different strategies to redress their firepower production deficit.

Germany went for a technological solution, hoping that the quality of its highly functional but over-engineered weapons of war would augment the superior training of its soldiers. Thus, quantity was sacrificed. The Japanese realising from the start that their only chance of success was for a quick victory did not embark early enough on the fanciful production of highly technical materiel. They knew that this would limit their abilities to compete in the short-term and reduce even further the already improbable hope of winning a war of attrition. Following the German approach of heavily investing in new weapons would have hastened Japan's defeat. Japan's already limited capacity would have been further stretched by the need to retrain its workers and retool its factories. Trying earlier to make more complex weapons would have reduced even further the slim chances of a quick victory or honourable exit. In the end even the home islands had to accept occupation. Germany was, however, not as vulnerable as Japan.

Germany and their European Axis did have the potential for massive economic production to fight the war of attrition which World War II became. The population numbers were not against the Nazi's. The combined German and Axis aligned population outnumbered the Soviet population, indeed, 1.5 million Russians fought for the Germans. And the Nazis industrial potential was augmented by their use of slave labour in their workforce to keep arms production high. Many were prisoners of war, others were migrants, some were kidnapped from their homes in Germany and eastern Europe, others were given by collaborationist regimes. The Vichy Regime conscripted workers to serve the German war effort. Indeed, after Poland, France supplied the most foreign workers to the Reich to keep alive the Nazi's armaments industry. However, this policy began to be self-defeating. Those who wished to escape the conscription fled to rural areas where they joined the resistance.

Country lines

The near immutable characteristics that enabled an efficient and productive economy to emerge in Britain also gave it the ability to export its capital and capitalism to create a global business empire. In so doing the Anglosphere was born, the greatest scion of which is the United States. The shared inheritance of the English-speaking peoples defeated the most vicious tyrannies that arose in Europe. The largely protestant revolutions that were the English Civil Wars, and the Glorious Revolution of 1688 helped enshrine parliamentary democracy. This built upon already existing property rights, and through reasoned and rational debate, ensured that business and the financial reforms necessary for economic success would take place. With Protestantism in the ascendancy the religious conflict on the British Isles was settled. With peace and prosperity at home the United Kingdom could embark on establishing its epoch defining empire.

Britain, through its colonies, exported its open-source systems and the notion of economic freedom for all. In so doing, the UK waged war on the institution of slavery, a system that retarded economic development. Eventually Britain's former colonies used force of arms to spread the idea that people had natural rights, these free peoples would make the Anglosphere bigger and mightier yet. The religious zeal which fuelled England's civil wars, was reflected in America's northerly states who after a protestant religious revival, militantly opposed the expansion of the southern state's peculiar institution. This grew into a movement that sought the abolition of chattel slavery. The ultimate victory of the free soilers over the sleepy south made certain that the United States of America would grow to become a great powerhouse that could unleash its arsenal of weapons and financial might on the Germans. Collectivist and statist Nazis and communists built their systems on forms of coerced labour and inherited the wind.

Continental European and Japanese cultural traits allowed for the emergence of absolutist monarchies and less efficient economic systems. Such hierarchical societies with vertical lines of control put their militaries at a relative disadvantage in World War Two. Orders from Hitler could not be challenged, in the United Kingdom Churchill's less sober plans could be and were rejected, his general staff were free to persuade him as to the folly of his ideas. Military planning is underpinned by good information processing, this too is superior in a flat structure rather than in a top-down society where hierarchy is all important. The Anglosphere's meritocratic and more horizontal systems allowed for the assessment of intelligence on its merits rather than the rank or perceived status of the source. The wisdom of the crowd, with the greater number of inputs into decision making will always produce outcomes that trump the decision making of a single expert that owes his position to gaining the favour of a small clique to which they must remain obedient. The societies that enshrined the right of people to challenge perceived wisdom, were the ones which became democracies and further expanded the decision-making pool. In twentieth century Anglosphere society sovereignty rested with the individual and in families who were protected by, and were loyal to, their country. They had a stake in their nation's success and constructively contributed to the victory. More people had the right to be consulted, the right to encourage, and the right to warn. This allowed for unreasonable contrarians to be the light by which freedom lives. The Anglosphere did not demand that people meekly conform. Personal responsibility made people in those countries perform better than those who were broken by being compelled. Those Anglosphere countries that possessed the attribute of freedom prospered and had the strength to face down the Axis when war broke out between those incompatible models. The positivity of the Anglosphere created a real belief in the final victory, they were not wrong. However, in the United Kingdom this was far from universal.

Civil war

The centre of gravity in the war was the role of the British Empire. Nevertheless, not all in Britain were foursquare behind the national effort. Indeed, some sections which were near polar opposites had negative perceptions of the conflict. London's EastEnders who were heavily blitzed in 1940 found it difficult to see it in a positive light. Towards the other end of the spectrum were Britain's intelligentsia. Highbrow liberals in Britain had often been opposed to the growth of their own country's empire, and even sympathised with nationalist forces that threatened to break up the United Kingdom. George Orwell had observed this very unBritish phenomenon. In his essay, *The Lion and the Unicorn: Socialism and the English Genius*, he wrote of the intellectuals that:

'In intention, at any rate, the English intelligentsia are Europeanized. They take their cookery from Paris and their opinions from Moscow. In the general patriotism of the country they form a sort of island of dissident thought. England is perhaps the only great country whose intellectuals are ashamed of their own nationality. In left-wing circles it is always felt that there is something slightly disgraceful in being an Englishman and that it is a duty to snigger at every English institution, from horse racing to suet puddings. It is a strange fact, but it is unquestionably true that almost any English intellectual would feel more ashamed of standing to attention during 'God save the King' than of stealing from a poor box. All through the critical years many left-wingers were chipping away at English morale, trying to spread an outlook that was sometimes squashily pacifist, sometimes violently pro-Russian, but always anti-British.'

Orwell further observed that the working classes remained patriotic and that this culture would endure '...England will still be England, an everlasting animal stretching into the future and the past, and, like all living things, having the power to change out of recognition and yet remain the same.' British patriotism was not replaced by the narrow and divisive class-based politics that had led Germany and the Soviet Union down the political rabbit hole that led to Nazism and Communism. Hitler's bombs and empty threats were by no means enough to subjugate the British Isles and change its culture to one of subdued acquiescence under the knee of would-be European hegemons. Some however did not participate in the patriotic fervour. In May 1945 George Orwell wrote in his essay *Notes on Nationalism*:

'Within the intelligentsia, a derisive and mildly hostile attitude towards Britain is more or less compulsory…. Many people were undisguisedly pleased when Singapore fell or when the British were driven out of Greece, and there was a remarkable unwillingness to believe in good news, e.g. El Alamein, or the number of German planes shot down in the Battle of Britain. English left-wing intellectuals did not, of course, actually want the Germans or Japanese to win the war, but many of them could not help getting a certain kick out of seeing their own country humiliated.'

If their view had triumphed Hitler would have been given the free hand in the east that he and his henchmen so desired. Nevertheless, the Dunkirk spirit gave the optimists the advantage over the pessimists. The Germans were surprised by the high morale of British soldiers captured at Dunkirk, who despite being left on the continent retained their belief in their own nation. And were still confident of Britain's eventual success. The intelligentsia did not speak for England. The guilty men of appeasement were anathema and out of kilter with Britain's historic mission to oppose European unions in all their forms. The contradictions between the two traditions continues to this day in relation to the United Kingdom's evanescent membership of the European Union. Some would rather have seen Brexit fail and result in an economic crisis than see Britain's EU withdrawal become a success story. Nevertheless, the positive vision for an independent and defiant British nation proved to be the most popular alternative. Likewise, similar concepts existed in other countries fighting the Germans.

The national question
The Second World War rang the death knell of European states as colonial world powers. The roots of that war lay in the unresolved issues from just 20 years before the outbreak of war. The nation-state has been wrongfully blamed as the cause. This was not the case in the First World War, free countries do not attack other similar nations especially when goods are able to cross borders. However, empires do assault rivals, and multi-national prison houses of nations where peoples were given no right of self-determination were the cause of that great conflict. They were autocracies headed by largely unaccountable rulers. Democracies, however, do not go to war with other democracies because power is dispersed. Personal slights against a leader will not cause a conflict. However, placing the levers of state power under one man's control risks making all politics personal. Agitating an autocrat, humiliating a dictator, be they addressed by the

title of Comrade, Kaiser, Tsar, or even President can result in them committing their whole empire to war.

The concept of the nation-state followed the age of enlightenment and embodied the rational organisation of government. In time the state began to serve its citizens and not the whims of its sovereign. Those nation-states that had a longer and more developed political system were amongst the least bellicose nations in the 20th century. The Central Powers in pre-World War One Europe, largely became the Axis Powers European franchise of World War Two. They still had the inherent problems of a lack of democracy and the political need to build an identity where none had existed before. There was a phenomenon at work where newly created states turned to political extremism and war. Artificially forged political units were the major antagonists for war, countries that needed to develop a consciousness looked for conflict abroad to forge a unity at home. Their leadership professed too much their belief in their state's cause, they were overcompensating because they knew that their country was a construction less than a century in being. They also had a divided population whose loyalties often lay elsewhere.

Many of those polities were inherently unstable and susceptible to revolution. The upheavals brought on by World War One allowed totalitarian collectivists to seize control; from there they would merge state, party, ideology, and leadership. The stage was set for war. This conflict duly reignited after little more than a twenty-year armistice. Germany tried again to establish its hegemony with a new leadership at the helm. The National Socialists were, however, not nationalists, their politics was racialist, and they found willing support from other identarian ideologues across Europe. These quislings were all too willing to surrender their countries to gain personal preferment and align with the Nazis Social Darwinism which presented itself as a progressive, scientific, and modern belief system. Britain, however, with its notion of individual freedom was a parliamentary democracy; it was more stable and carried on its role as the foil of European demagogues. Today, Britain remains the largest military power in western Europe. The same can be said of Britain during World War Two when it was the last major free country standing against Nazi Germany. Britain has thus proved itself as Europe's constant insurance policy against insecurity and threats to its peace. If Britain had surrendered, surely, Hitler would have won the war. This, however, was not fated to be.

German attempts to replace national identity with a new higher culture based on racial awareness gathered few adherents in the occupied nations. Instead,

Europeans continued to identify with their country of origin, as such they would resist, passively or otherwise, German occupation. A nation can be defined as a large body of people united by common descent, history, culture, or language, inhabiting a particular country or territory. There are around two hundred separate states in the world, the number is still increasing, and is in part being driven by ideology unleashed in the English-speaking world, namely the right to self-determination. Churchill, and British aid for resistance movements across the continent, provided an answer to the national question. The desire to restore national self-determination meant that the German European empire was being hollowed out from within. A country's biggest asset is its people, and the over-riding loyalty of citizens to their nation-state prevented the Axis from being able to fully marshal the conquered resources at their disposal. Despite the dangers democratic nationalists never relinquished their hope of freedom.

Morale is exceptionally important as a facet of national character. A productive sense of nationhood is involving, embracing, and interacting, uniting the governed with their governors. The shared national interest increased *esprit de corps* and kept citizen soldiers and workers focused on their common endeavour. Democratic Britain and its former colonial Allies were able to foster those intangible factors. In Germany and Japan, the sense of commitment was, to a greater degree, imposed. Whilst fear is a powerful motivator it is still not as strong as the positive bonds that individually united the British, American, and Russian nations. If Nazi Germany were to have survived the war it would have had to find a way of overcoming its own inherent cultural traits. To change those characteristics would have meant they would have to cease being Nazis, the National Socialist ideology was not conducive to survival. The German Fatherland also suffered from its position sandwiched between its western and eastern enemies. To overcome that geographical and geological weakness would have meant they would have to cease to be German; Hitler knew this. The very concept of *Lebensraum* made it clear that Germany was not enough; land and resources elsewhere would need to be controlled. Hitler's plans even acknowledged that his people were inadequate, they would not only need a slave class to provide for them but also imagined ethnic rivals would need to be purged from the earth. Aggression can be the result of an inferiority complex, the pain of losing the Great War was enormous. The continuation of the same conflict which we now call World War Two would surely end with the same result. Nevertheless, some steps may have mitigated German cultural failings and negate the strength of the Anglosphere.

Stamping down the dirt

The jackboot on England's green and pleasant land… ? The possibility of this nightmare scenario was always remote. Yet, for Hitler's great gamble to payoff, it would not have required the Germans to successfully cross the moat that kept this island safe for what was then nearly nine centuries. Throughout this 'big history' several key decisions stand out as ones upon which the fate of the world turned.

If Grand Admiral Dönitz had sunk one million tonnes of British shipping per month it could have ended Britain's ability to wage war. German naval technology did eventually have the potential for that, yet it came too late by which point the US and the Royal Navy were more than equal to the task. Hitler's capital ship folly took the resources away from where they were truly needed. Giving the Nazis the ability to wage truly unrestricted and remorseless submarine warfare would have starved Britain of the life blood of war, men, materiel, and oil. Dönitz thought that 300 submarines would suffice. The problem was that Germany did not have the means to produce those U-boats. And any earlier build-up would have just initiated a greater Allied rearmament in response. Hitler, a man obsessed by the idea of competing races, could not win the arms race.

If Hitler had been able to invade Britain, keep his forces supplied in both men and materiel, and conquer these islands, then Germany would have won, but only in the short term. Resistance to the German continental system would have been snuffed out through extreme repression. Yet that would have left an empty husk that would have provided little benefit to the Nazis. Indeed, it would have been a burden on Germany making the Third Reich vulnerable to its enemies. Britain's example and efforts in supplying liberation movements on the continent and attacking the Reich itself and providing a base from which others could do so, enabled victory to be achieved by 1945. Yet, knocking Britain out would always have been difficult. Nevertheless, there were perhaps other paths to victory that would not have required the tall order of conquering the British Isles.

Britain's 'peace' party would have been emboldened if its army had not been able to escape from Dunkirk. Hitler's fateful decision to approve the halting of his panzers gave time for Britain's little ships, aided by the Royal Navy, to rescue the bulk of the British Expeditionary Force, along with 123,000 French soldiers. Although the continent was abandoned, it kept the bulk of the British Army away from Hitler's grasp. With its Royal Air Force and, most importantly, the navy still intact; a successful cross channel invasion even against a depleted army, would have been impossible. Yet, the will to win may have suffered a mortal blow. Certainly, after Dunkirk, even though there were still more British soldiers to be rescued from France's Atlantic ports, Britain was euphoric and flushed with a dogged determination. This was built upon by Churchill, not invented by this great orator.

It need not have been so. The return of French prisoners of war to the Vichy Regime was enough to secure further collaboration from Prime Minister Pierre Laval and the supply of workers to the German armaments industry. Returning over 200,000 of Britain's encircled 'boys' home to Britain may have had an even greater effect. Churchill had not yet fully triumphed over the guilty men, the appeasers, in his own Cabinet. Indeed, his victory only came on 28th May, when the evacuation, also known as Operation Dynamo, was underway, the panzers having halted four days earlier. Only then did Winston Churchill fully impose his will. He outmanoeuvred his rival Lord Halifax by winning over the full British government and secured the War Cabinet's support for the continuation of the war. Capturing the army may have swung the political pendulum towards the Holy Fox. Germany missed this great opportunity but there were still others. Events far afield were of great influence in the European theatre of operations. Japan, and its alliance with both Nazi Germany and Fascist Italy could have been a factor in Hitler's victory. Instead of providing a reason for Hitler and Roosevelt to lead their nations against each other Japan could alternatively have enabled the Nazis to win against the USSR.

If Japan opened a new front against the Soviet Union it would have tied up the Russian forces that saved Moscow. It is understandable why the Japanese were reticent about attacking the Red Army again. They had been soundly defeated in 1939, yet the Japanese achieved a victory against Russia in 1905. Further, in 1941, the Soviets this time around had to contend with Germany and the minor powers of Hungary, Romania, Italy, and Finland, to all of which the Russians were losing ground. Japan could have been the straw that broke the camel's back. Indeed, the 18 Divisions that Stalin kept in the east to deal with the probable Japanese attack proved decisive when transferred to the west to drive back the Wehrmacht from the gates of the sacred Russian capital.

Without the Soviet confidence that Japan was not going to attack, hundreds of thousands of men, 1,700 tanks and a further 1,500 aircraft would have remained in Siberia and the far east awaiting an illusory enemy. Without this transfer to the key theatre at a decisive time, Moscow, this key rail hub, and centre of Soviet resistance, may well have fallen to the Nazis. Another effect, which was perhaps just as pivotal, was that this major setback led Hitler to take personal command of the German army on 19th December 1941. His involvement in day-to-day military affairs was to prove disastrous. The contribution of Hitler's newly appointed staff officers who oversaw the fight was also detrimental. They were little more than 'yes' men, and dared not challenge his ludicrous directives, this also undermined the operational ability of a once all conquering force. The rot set in during the late winter of 1941.

The Japanese did not put the interests of the Rome–Berlin–Tokyo Axis first. Imperial Japan instead prioritised the preservation of their conquests by attacking the perceived American threat. They undertook to launch a pre-emptive attack on Pearl Harbor. Itself a serious provocation that not only brought America into the war but also raised Hitler's lust for the apocalyptic conflict about which the Führer had long fanaticised. Keeping the United States out of the war should have been a priority. Instead, Japan woke a sleeping giant. If the Empire of the Sun had not attacked Pearl Harbor on 7th December 1941, the USA would have no doubt remained the arsenal of democracy but, with little political will to enter another European war, it would itself have stayed out of the fighting for a longer period of time. Yet, the decision to attack America did not in itself seal Hitler's and Hirohito's fate. Not only could Japan have pressed the war in a far more productive fashion, but they also could have been a distraction for the United States taking America's attention away from Europe and thus aiding the German war effort.

Through observing British operations against the Italians, the Japanese knew that air power at sea was the decisive arm of any naval engagement. Yet the attack against Pearl Harbor missed the American aircraft carriers. Despite sinking powerful but increasingly outmoded capital ships they had missed the real prize. If, instead, Yamamoto's attack had at least disabled the aircraft carriers then the ability of the Pacific Fleet to resist Japan's conquests would have been all but eliminated for a time. At first the American forces did a bad job of defending their territory in the Pacific, and very nearly gave Japan the chance to establish their defensive ring. This would have made the reconquest, let alone forcing an almost unconditional surrender, an extremely difficult and time-consuming task.

Pearl Harbor was not Japan's first mistake nor was it their only near miss. Japan could have still prevailed over America's aircraft carriers at the Battle of Midway. A small amount of codebreaking and cunning aided the Americans there. Chance, however, was by far the biggest factor. The spotting of the vulnerable Imperial Navy carriers and being able to exploit it was by no means a forgone conclusion. A few stolen minutes allowed the US to overcome Japan's overly complex and overconfident drive into the central Pacific. It could have been vastly different.

If Japan had sunk the US fleet and seized the immovable aircraft carrier called Midway Atoll, then American strategy would have had to change. Whilst it was unlikely that this new world leviathan would sue for peace as the Japanese had hoped, failure in the Pacific Theatre, and the humiliation that would surely follow, would have made Roosevelt reappraise his Germany first policy. If the full might of the US war machine, both its military and industrial arms, had been sent against the Japanese instead of the Germans then Hitler's drive eastwards would not have been slowed by American men fighting in the west. Midway was not only a bad result for the Axis it was also the wrong battle.

The Japanese launched the Battle of Midway and its supporting diversionary attack on the cold Aleutian Islands of Alaska to keep their religious and constitutional head, the *Mikado*, safe. The pivotal battle however was far to the south in the Solomon Islands. If the resources used at Midway were deployed in the Battle of Guadalcanal, then America would have been deprived of a base from which they could hop and bomb their way through Japan's defensive shield.

7th December 1941 was when America was forced into a war with Japan, but not Germany as Churchill had hoped. War against Germany came a week later when Hitler declared war against the US. Invading the Soviet Union was a mistake but almost inevitable, picking a fight with America whilst still fighting the British and Soviet empires, was still his biggest folly. Despite Hitler's will, Germany's destiny was not fully under its own control. Japan was not the only country that influenced its fate. Italy also had a decisive effect. Mussolini entered the war on the side of his old foe, soon to be friend, Hitler. The loyalty that the Führer showed to him, would contribute to Germany's undoing.

To defend Italian expansionism, and Mussolini's 'power' games aimed at forging a new Roman Empire, Hitler lost one of the greatest commodities one can have in warfare, time. Operation Barbarossa, the invasion of the Soviet Empire, was partially delayed so that the Germans could support Mussolini's disastrous invasion of Greece. German involvement there and in Yugoslavia, both of which quickly fell under Nazi control, cost time and were to prove damaging drains on the German war machine. Ulcers, which bled away much needed resources.

The hailing of yet more victories led to Hitler being even more deluded, if that were possible, about the inevitable triumph of his will. The Führer was not alone in drawing the wrong lessons from their early triumphs. The German high command concluded that their tank designs were superior. Indeed, they were effective against foes in the Balkans, yet they did not have an advantage over the tanks used further east. The inventive Russian armaments industry was in the process of bringing out new designs ready for combat. Every delay gave the Red Army time to produce more war winning weapons and deploy them at a critical time. The German soldiers advancing on Moscow were to receive a shock when they first encountered the T-34 medium tank.

The greatest threat caused through the postponement of Operation Barbarossa, for which Mussolini was arguably culpable, enabled the Russians to benefit from a mighty foe, Marshall Mud. Hitler thought the conquest of the USSR would take just three months. The weather, not for the first time, had helped save Russia. Summer passed into autumn and the inevitable, but unplanned for, rains came. This unique circumstance is known in Russia as the *rasputitsa,* the time without roads. Russia become a mire making travel almost impossible. For this, the Germans were unprepared. The impassable Russian countryside also suffered from an immature road network, giving few options for easy transportation. Indeed, Russia's track ways would turn to a sea of mud, on which even Germany's caterpillar tracked tanks struggled. Their thin tracks were ideal for fast and efficient travel on the autobahn yet sunk in the sodden Soviet soil. Worse was to come. The German situation was relieved by General Frost. The mud froze and the armour could make way again. This, however, just heralded the onset of winter for which the Wehrmacht was woefully unprepared. The *rasputitsa* and the winter were to hinder Russia reinforcing the front, yet they were prepared for the extreme conditions and had shorter supply lines. All of which made Moscow, which was so close, seem a world away.

Not only were the German's logistics dangerously overstretched, but they also had other demands on their resources. Again, the Italians, despite supplying men for Operation Barbarossa, drew amongst Germany's best and boldest away from where the fighting really mattered. The difficulties caused through delay were just the beginning. The eventual elimination of *Heeresgruppe Afrika* in Tunisia with its accompanying losses, notwithstanding those sent to the bottom of the Mediterranean Sea, were equal in size to a major loss on the Russian front. Men and materiel that could not easily be replaced.

This was a misallocation of resources on a colossal scale. The involvement of Italy in the war on the side of the Axis had exacerbated the problem that was Hitler's underbelly. Hitler moved armoured units from the frontline during the Battle of Kursk to save the blushes of his co-conspirator during the fighting in Sicily in 1943, not a good use of ever decreasing manpower. The Germans had not been defeated at Kursk, indeed Field Marshal von Manstein wanted to complete what was emerging as at least a temporary military victory. This was thrown away to defend the Mediterranean theatre. Ultimately from Italy the Allies crossed into the Reich and took a million German soldiers into captivity.

Whilst Italy may not have been a reliable ally, the addition of one other may have made a significant difference. Spain was far from a force to be reckoned with, but if Franco acquiesced to Hitler's requests and allowed Operation Felix to go ahead then Germany would have had a new route to attack the British. The Germans could take Gibraltar and threaten Britain's access to much of the world. The credit for not proceeding with these plans does not rest entirely with the then head of Spain, Francisco Franco, but the fault rests with Hitler himself for not pressing the matter harder and demanding rather than merely asking. The Führer's boldness was absent here.

The African adventure need not have ended in failure. Rommel should have insisted on the capture of Malta. Hitler was reticent about using the vulnerable *Fallschirmjäger*, German paratroopers known as the Green Devils, in an airborne assault on the island. If they had been deployed to Malta the fighting in the Mediterranean could have swung in favour of the Nazis. Yet, Operation *Herkules*, as the German landing was to be known, was cancelled. If it had gone ahead Rommel would not have been starved of resources by this almost unsinkable aircraft carrier. Malta nearly fell, but its tenacious citizens of what was then a British imperial outpost stood firm.

If Rommel had been able to press home his advantage, the loss of the Suez Canal and the oil rich Arab and Iranian lands to his east would have dealt a body blow to Britain's war effort. It may also have facilitated the linkup with German forces ploughing through Russia and the Caucasus. In such circumstances, Stalin would have either been defeated or would come to the negotiating table and conclude a separate peace with his German counterpart. It was an option considered by Joseph Stalin. If this were to have happened at the earliest possibility, particularly in the dark days of 1941 before the USA entered the war, the USSR would have followed a similar path to Russia nearly a quarter of a century before. Then, Germany's eastern enemy's abdication from the war allowed for the army to re-concentrate efforts westward against Britain, her empire, and the French. If history had repeated itself the progress of World War II could have been very different.

The Italians were not the only peoples to undermine Hitler's chances of success. The brave Finns could have been of even greater assistance to Army Group North. Leningrad was never completely encircled. The depredations of its people were myriad, yet it remained out of German hands and tied up resources that were better suited to mobile warfare. It is not just a matter of assessing the mistakes Hitler made and how things could have been different if alternate decisions were made. The truth of what did happen in those tumultuous years between 1939 and 1945 is that the Soviet Union chewed up the Wehrmacht and bled the Third Reich white. This was not without great pain and sacrifice. The attention of the counterfactual can now focus on Russia. Could they have won on their own?

The bloodied army

Looking at alternative outcomes is not just a matter of how Germany lost, or could have won the war. The issue of whether or not the Red Army could have beaten the Germans on their own needs to be explored. Indeed, there was even the possibility that peace could have broken out between the two great dictators, Hitler and Stalin.

The seemingly diametrically opposed, yet eerily similar, Nazi Germany and Soviet Russia, were – along with their dependencies and subject peoples – two titanic empires that on the face of it could not mutually exist. Yet, prior to Operation Barbarossa they had been partners. The German Weimar Republic and the Soviet Union, two outcasts in the post-First World War international order, developed their war machines together. The Soviets allowed the Germans to develop tanks, and military doctrines, on their soil. It is a great irony that the military theories developed on Soviet territory would be used to such deadly effect by the Germans against their former hosts.

Some commentators have sought to present the victory over Nazi Germany as primarily belonging to the Soviets. A part of this has even included a rehabilitation of Stalin's memory. If it can be argued that as the bulk of the victory over Germany was achieved by Russia then the plaudits should go to the Red Army, indeed they paid the butcher's bill as did Soviet subjects. Yet, China also lost many lives in its war against Japan, but we do not credit the Chinese with subduing *Nippon*, the Land of the Rising Sun. And that is despite the fact that one of Japan's feet was firmly stuck in the quagmire that was China. Those forces could not be rapidly turned to face the Americans who are rightly credited with the victory. The difference is that 80% of German casualties were on the Eastern Front and the Red Army was allowed the prestigious honour of taking the Nazi capital, which despite the lateness of the war was still a costly endeavour. That in itself shows the fragility of the Russian war machine. The Red Army had more than 80,000 soldiers killed assaulting the city of Germania, as Hitler wanted to restyle Berlin. That is almost comparable to the 90,000 to 100,000 men killed defending the German capital in the Battle of Berlin.

The numerical superiority of not only the Red Army's materiel, but also its men, need not have occurred. Whilst the Soviet Union's population was greater than that of Germany, the number of people living in Germany and its European partners exceeded the population of Russia. The Red Army was allowed to focus its power, the German forces however dissipated their strength over too many theatres of operation.

The Red Army even began to have manpower shortages from 1944 onwards. Their response was to field under strength units but would avoid this as best they could by making up the numbers in the Red Army through conscripting men from countries outside of Russia that had been 'liberated' from the Germans. The maximum age for conscription was also increased in some areas to 45, those involved in war production were exempt. The young were also drafted to serve on the frontline as were some women.

Back in the U.S.A.

The industrial might of the USSR was also not what it appeared. By 1942 the Soviet economy was nearing collapse and was only kept functioning through aid received from Britain, the United States, and even Canada. Much was supplied under the American Lend-lease policy, it just did not include weapons but also aid and food for the home front.

Of particular importance was the provision of trucks, tanks, radios for armoured vehicles without which attacks could not be coordinated, and aircraft. Where equipment could not be supplied the raw materials were. The Soviets received for its own aeroplane production, aluminium and even the energy to power them. High octane aviation fuel for the Soviet Air Forces was supplied by Britain. It is remarkable to note that oil was supplied from the middle east, transported to Britain and America, there refined into aviation fuel, and then sent to Russia, all the time running the risk of attack from U-boats and having to be defended by the Royal Navy. This was more economical than that which could be produced in the USSR by the USSR. A state which was itself rich in oil.

Before the First World War and its resulting privations and destructive revolutions, Tsarist Russia was the fastest industrialising nation on the planet. It was starting from a low base and was still largely an agricultural economy. Serfdom, considered by some to be a form of slavery, had only finally been abolished in Russia in 1861, this had the effect of improving the economy in all sectors, but it was a late entry into the modern world. They were not alone in transforming their economic system, the USA several years later abolished chattel slavery, which like its Russian counterpart held back economic growth where it was practised. States and Commonwealths which had agricultural economies dependent upon slave labour were economically retarded by that peculiar institution. This gave them the epitaph 'the sleepy south' which describes their lack of economic dynamism. Russia would not have been able to resist Germany without the USA. America's help was much more than the aid provided under the terms of the Lend-Lease policy, whatever industrial might the Soviets possessed was largely imported from America and some café from Britain.

Stalin's policy of collectivisation, and its resulting destruction of much of the USSR's agriculture, forced people to work in the factories. In the 1930s, as his people starved, Stalin sold on the international market what little farm produce there was for hard currency to pay for much of the equipment that industrialised the Soviet Union. This was largely purchased from the United States of America, in some case whole prefabricated factories were bought from America, shipped to Russia, set-up, and put into production.

Operation Barbarossa failed but it was still delicately balanced. And without help from the capitalist west, whose industry was driven by the profit motive, there would have been no victory for the Red Army. The USSR most certainly did not win the war on their own and could not have won without the combined efforts of east and west bearing down on the Germans. It is true that Russia's capture of Berlin was a great achievement, but they did not have to go via Stalingrad. The victory was delivered by Russians, but it was made in places such as Detroit and Birmingham.

The sacrifice of those on the Arctic convoys was not a futile gesture. Despite the USSR being an industrial powerhouse, they still needed resources and even weapons from Britain, Canada, and the United States. This was of such importance that supplying the Russian war effort became a strategic consideration in its own right. Iran was secured as a route to supply the Soviets. Even British and Canadian built tanks found a valued home in the Red Army. British fighter aircraft were also supplied, as was information from the codebreakers of Bletchley Park. The Russian steamroller would not have rolled, and been so manoeuvrable, without the American trucks that transported its troops all the way to the German capital. Even the famed Red Army tank the T-34 was the product of American and British ingenuity.

The positive contribution was remarkable, the negative help of drawing away and ultimately destroying German forces that could have been better deployed on the Eastern Front was also a great help. The opening of the so-called 'second front' in France was itself a misnomer. Britain and her allies had been opening up new theatres over the continent aiding resistance movements from Norway to Greece, even supporting the communists in Yugoslavia who proved the equal of the Germans. In North Africa, Sicily, and Italy millions of Axis soldiers were tied up, the coast of Europe was filled with servicemen deprived from the Eastern Front, even in Norway 250,000 men of the Wehrmacht were held back to deal with an invasion which was always illusory. These were just some of the multiple fronts that were opened against the Third Reich and its partners. Indeed, the air war was a major campaign. Not only was the fate of the Luftwaffe destroyed in the skies above Germany and occupied Europe, the Nazis ability to wage war was also deeply retarded by the incessant and withering bombing. The 900,000 German soldiers, along with their 88-millimetre anti-aircraft / anti-tank guns, used to defend the Fatherland from British and American bombers would have been better used against the horde of Russian tanks.

Germany's tardy decision to fully engage the home front in total war and the development of a full war economy came too late. The Nazis, not wanting to alienate their own citizens relied on slave labour whilst many Germans remained idle, at least in relation to armaments production. For a regime that lacked democratic accountability it was surprisingly wary of angering public opinion.

The real wonder weapons

When Göring saw P-51 Mustangs above the skies of Germany he reportedly said that the war was lost. This Anglo-American warbird was not the only cause for much of the Reich Marshal's discomfort. Göring said of the mostly wooden, but all British, Mosquito that "It makes me furious when I see the Mosquito I turn green and yellow with envy".

The Dakota aeroplane, officially known as the Douglas C-47 Skytrain, was the workhorse of Allied transportation to the front and sometimes beyond it, dropping paratroopers behind enemy lines. This plane alongside the M1A1 rocket launcher, nicknamed the Bazooka were cited by the Supreme Allied Commander in Europe, General Eisenhower, as war winning weapons. Eisenhower's praise was not just for the tools of warfare. He also praised one particular inventor. The Supreme Commander, who had ultimate responsibility for D-Day said of Andrew Jackson Higgins, the owner and founder of Higgins Industries, that he "is the man who won the war for us." When it came to this remarkable industrialist both Eisenhower and Hitler were in agreement. The German Führer described him as the "new Noah". Higgins' achievement, and great contribution, was that he designed and built the Landing Craft Vehicle Personnel (LCVP) otherwise known as the Higgins Boat. He changed the face of warfare and made it possible for the Allies to effectively strike at the Axis from the sea, be that on the sandy beaches of Normandy or the atolls of the Pacific. Eisenhower further said 'If Higgins had not designed and built those LCVPs, we never could have landed on an open beach... The whole strategy of the war would have been different."

The Allies had many procurement problems. Much technology missed its mark, particularly in tank development, but when the Allies produced effective weapons, they were deployed mercilessly. The M1 Garand Rifle, the mainstay of the GI, was described by US General George C Patton as "the greatest battle implement ever devised". Yet, this had a competitor for such an epitaph. To strengthen a British platoon a soldier in that unit possessed the Bren gun. The author's grandfather wielded this to deadly effect in World War Two. This automatic machine gun fired the powerful .303 round. This highly accurate weapon is arguably one of the finest light machine guns ever produced and was in service with the British army from 1938 until as late as 1992. It saw action in all wars including the Falklands and the First Gulf War. This was a weapon developed from the Czechoslovak light machine gun. The British could make full use of their superb designs, yet the Germans could not.

British forces also possessed a submachine gun known as the Sten gun. This fired the 9x19mm parabellum round, itself a German invention, its magazine was also a copy from a similar German weapon. The Sten was not always reliable if handled incorrectly or poorly maintained, but, as it was very easy and cheap to produce, its use was an economic procurement decision. It gave good close-range firepower to British servicemen and was also supplied to resistance forces on the continent, helping to set Europe ablaze. For those not enjoying the Bren or the Sten, British soldiers would bring into combat the reliable Lee Enfield bolt-action rifle. Despite the drawback of the requirement to chamber each round using a small sliding handle operating the bolt, an experienced marksman could fire 30 aimed shots per minute. Slow by today's standards but it was the British Army's tradition that soldiers should not waste their ammunition.

Germany could produce state-of-the-art weapons such as the Sturmgewehr 44, meaning assault rifle 44. This formed the basis of the famed Soviet AK-47. This innovative German weapon, also known as the StG 44, could have helped make a difference, its firepower certainly helped the beleaguered troops on the Eastern Front. However, its entry into the war was still too little and too late to turn the tide back in Germany's favour. More than adequate weapons already existed when the Germans could have continued to use and adapt their already proven models. The Panzer IV was an effective tank. It was a design that allowed further development and improvement; it was also relatively easy to produce. In the Nazi desperation for quick success the German military produced ever more effective, yet complex and difficult to manufacture tanks. Focusing on the Panzer IV would have allowed German industry to supply their army with the numbers they so desperately needed. In this sense the Germans allowed themselves to be overwhelmed. Instead, Nazi-led German procurement sought over engineered new designs such as the Panther, Tiger, and King Tiger.

Allied procurement proved successful and delivered decisive firepower. Germany's mistakes were unforced errors. It need not have been so. Whilst German, and Japanese cities burned in the firestorm, the Axis could not answer back with a long-range strategic bomber. The Nazis answered with vengeance weapons and overly costly and slow to produce non-solutions. They would take too long to design and build, yet Nazi economic short-termists, who claimed to be building a 1,000-year Reich, could never fully level their enemy's cities. As the German war economy failed to deliver what was needed, Hitler was pursuing fantasy warfare based on wonder weapons yet ignored the one weapon that has ushered in a new epoch in Earth's history, the uranium and plutonium bombs. The Americans valued this approach to warfare and deployed the greatest of levellers. Hitler's *wunder* weapons were a dead end as was he and his empire. The Nazis could not easily scale up the production of low-tech weapons let alone deliver ahead of their time futuristic devices in significant numbers. The Nazis always did have an impractical concept of time and production.

Misallocation

The Nazi economic model relied on plunder, and the Reichsbank would eventually run out of other people's money. It was certainly unable to fund the war to the extent required for victory. Industrial capacity could have been sufficient to produce enough war materiel if the economy of Europe would have remained functioning, then states under German control would have provided what the Nazis needed. To do that Hitler's European Economic Community needed the consent of conquered peoples, however, Nazi compulsion could never win that. They could not make use of the pool of labour under German control, nor benefit from the resources of the Axis nations let alone those countries that were systematically being pillaged by extreme German asset stripping. If through a quirk of fate Operation Barbarossa had succeeded, and the British and Americans were at peace with Germany, that would only have been a temporary respite, just like Versailles was a mere postponement in hostilities. As resistance, both passive and aggressive, grew on the continent, external actors would have been there to face down Hitler's successors. Just like the Soviet Union was defeated and crumbled internally, the Third Reich would have inevitably declined as did the health of its leader. At which point its many global enemies would have been able to dismantle it should they so desire. The only question would be the size of the calamity the Third Reich would leave behind.

The hypnotic personality of Adolf Hitler held together the internal contradictions of the Nazi political structure. Without him its divisions would have erupted, a divided empire is one that will inevitably fail and fall. Hitler was unlikely to produce an heir to carry his nefarious work forward. Perhaps an intelligent and ruthless man such as Reinhard Heydrich could have inherited Hitler's crown. Reinhard's crimes had, however, led him to be assassinated. Ultimately, the one-thousand-year Reich lasted as long as it did because of severe oppression, Germans feared their own secret police more than they feared their external enemies. Those spreading defeatism would be executed at the hands of those who were clinging onto power and owed their position and prestige to the now failing structures of Nazi Germany. Without Hitler at the top holding the system together through cajoling and intimidating his immediate subordinates it would have collapsed. Many of the Führer's underlings held a quasi-messianic belief that somehow Hitler had the answers, he had been right before when remilitarising the Rhineland and in the Battle of France. The devotion in which they held their Führer kept German resistance going. Without him they would have had the opportunity to sue for peace, just as Himmler had attempted.

Germany was once the world leader in science, particularly physics. Nazi intolerance created an environment that was inconducive to many of these scientists, a great number of which hailed from a Jewish background. Germany was woefully behind in the nuclear arms race. Where the Nazis allocated resources to science it did not deliver tangible results in time to make a difference. The research and development they did invest in was to be realised, however, it reached fruition under American not Nazi leadership. Through Operation Paperclip German scientists were taken to the United States of America. Here these men served the interests of the USA, their former enemy, in the arms and prestige race in the cold war which soon followed the end of World War Two. Yet the object of their work remained the same. They continued the technological fight against Russian led communism, they were just serving a different master.

Phoenix rising

Hitler's dream went up in flames, as did his body, in the grounds of his bunker in Berlin. The Red Army was just a hundred yards away when he took his own life. Yet, the so-called Third Reich for what it was worth did not end with Hitler's suicide. Its remnants briefly lived on under the leadership of Grand Admiral

Dönitz, Hitler's appointed heir. This submariner, however, had the appearance of a low-grade bank clerk, to coin a phrase, so did not carry credibility to lead the other Nazis. And there were more senior Germans, namely Hermann Göring and Heinrich Himmler. Both men were technically traitors against their Führer, but after Himmler's suicide, Göring was left as the last outstanding Nazi, if that can be said, left alive. Weaned from his dependency on dihydrocodeine, a form of morphine itself a derivative of opium, his intellect and drive returned. It would not save his life, which he took before the hangman could exact justice on him. During the Nuremberg Tribunals Hermann Göring became the unofficial leader of the Nazis on trial and a powerful standard bearer for what was left of Nazism. Before his end, he was convinced that Germany would rise again. He thought Germany would be ungovernable without him. And in time, the Allies would turn to him allowing him to rule a kind of Nazi Germany 2.0. This was just a pipe dream. A hope against hope and the result of a giant ego as large as his once drug dependent girth.

Whilst Göring's vision differed from Hitler's belief that the German people through a later struggle would rise again and form a Fourth Reich, Göring, like Himmler thought he could do a deal with the Allies. Under such circumstances, perhaps there would be the snatching of some small victory out of the jaws of total defeat. It mattered not to the likes of former *Reichsmarschall* Göring, or SS head Himmler, that the 'victory' was merely survival and the opportunity for some power and prestige for their gang as the leaders of the shell of a once great nation. Yet it was not completely farfetched. He was not alone in thinking such thoughts. Many indeed thought that Nazi Germany would be squashed down and would contract under the weight of the Allied offensives, until Britain and America joined with Germany to fight the Russians. These overly optimistic Germans were perhaps far sighted enough to see that the post-war world order would be dominated by the cold conflict between the USA and her NATO satellites and those of the Soviet-led communist Warsaw Pact.

The unthinkable

It was not only the Germans that foresaw such a scenario. The British Prime Minister, a long-term critic of Bolshevism, also foretold this. Churchill was a student of history and sought to learn lessons from the past. He recalled that the greatest failing of Oliver Cromwell, a Bretwalda like the eminent man himself, was that the Lord Protector concentrated on fighting Spain and failed to check the rise of France. A decision that was, like the Second World War, to undermine

England's finances and economy. Cromwell's alliance with France to fight the Spanish in the Anglo-Spanish War of the 1650s only succeeded in catapulting the French into becoming the leading European power. France under the Sun King Louis XIV picked over the remnants of a weakened Spain and grew in stature and belief. The French were soon to prove a bigger threat to British interests than the Spanish had been for nearly a century. The situation was only saved by an earlier Churchill at the Battle of Blenheim in 1704. Winston Churchill vis-à-vis Germany and Russia did not want to make a similar mistake to Cromwell's foreign policy folly.

The British Prime Minister prepared for war with Russia. The aptly named Operation Unthinkable was Churchill's plan for war with the Soviet Union in 1945. Shamefully, this plan included the use of 100,000 German soldiers. With a four to one Red Army superiority in manpower over the western Allies, success was far from guaranteed. Indeed, despite the Red Army on occasions being every bit as beastly as the German forces, there was an enormous amount of sympathy for the plight of the Russians and their suffering at the hands of the Nazis. As the UK lurched towards socialism after the Second World War, Churchill's plan to attack the Soviet forces four days before the British General Election would have been viewed as a cynical attempt to hold on to power and prevent the creation of a land fit for heroes. There was no will for the fight. The American Trump card of long-range bombers and nuclear weapons may have been the deciding factors that would have reversed any quick Russian victories in the Third Great War. Yet as the evils of communist atrocities had not yet been publicly acknowledged the use of weapons of mass destruction against the Soviets, a people with which many were sympathetic, would have been unimaginable in the extreme.

The launching of World War III against Uncle Joe's Russia, known to many in Britain as Good Old Joe, could have been a bigger political disaster than it would have been in military terms. Churchill's well-meaning but reckless warmongery may not have been the only cause of war between the USSR and the USA along with her allies, indeed, some conflict had already begun. American planes flying over German airspace captured by the Russians found themselves engaged and shot down by the Red Army Air Forces. In various instances they were defending themselves from gung-ho Americans, in other altercations US planes had not properly identified themselves.

With now western Europe in peril, this time at the hands of their former allies, Britain, and America may well have turned to, if not Göring, other leading Nazis. Yet they thankfully did not have to. Britain, France, and America went instead on to the defensive and sought to contain the spread of communism. Winston

Churchill personally took on the fight and through his powerful oratory spoke about the fate that had befallen eastern Europe. Whilst still officially occupying Germany, in time, Britain, the USA, and later France did reunite the portion of Germany that was under their control. They reequipped its military and used their armed forces as a bulwark against the Soviet empire. Despite de-Nazification, soldiers in the German army were later to hold senior positions in NATO, the defence alliance set up to facedown Russia. The EU and NATO seek to expand into her space, a move that is resisted by Mother Russia, as it was generations before.

In the cold war that followed between the former Allies the ideological battle remained a conflict between two contrasting economic, social, and military systems, the pursuit of profit and professionalism versus plunder. Coercive systems, be they Soviet or Nazi, lost out to Anglo-sphere nations that had professional militaries financed and supplied by private industry following their own self-interest. It was this model that defeated the conscripted pillaging forces of Bonaparte, French forces that alienated the peoples they occupied. When industry and technology allowed brutal collectivist systems to emerge, the same requisitioning of supplies, industry, and wealth similarly disaffected whole populations, ruining the Nazi and Soviet occupation economies. Those ideologically driven dictatorships had come up against an alternative system and were found wanting. They could not compete with an approach that had competition at its core and did not practice looting, nor grind down those who could have been gainfully employed in the war effort. This model was pioneered in England, and perfected in the form of the American military-industrial complex which grew so mighty in its quest to defeat the USSR and Germany throughout the twentieth century.

Contrary to Hitler's belief Germany would not seek to reconquer Europe through military means. Instead, they would in time go on a different course. This once belligerent nation was to work with other European countries through organisations such as the Council of Europe and the European Union. The latter organisation, like the Nazi or Napoleonic continental systems before it, is seeking to expand eastwards and finds itself at loggerheads with a resurgent Russia. In the circumstances of the cold war between America and Russia becoming hot, it could have been the case that Germany, acting through the EU, would become the ultimate winner. They may have retaken their place at the helm of European affairs as the continent's hegemonic power; but that is a story for another day.

Index

Endorsements

"I thought I had a good knowledge of the origins and actions in both World One and Two, but I have been astonished that the detail and argument in this book has opened my eyes to much more than I expected.

The contents are all consuming and cover so much of the rationale and consequences of every part of these two extraordinary conflicts. From whichever standpoint you start, real reasons – politically, militarily, and culturally – emerge from every page. And what is clear is how the exceptional characteristics of the people of the United Kingdom and the leadership at every level, had a major impact on the success of the Allies.

There is so much in every section to absorb that I found that taking it in stages helped me understand the reality of every aspect and in every arena."

"This is the ultimate history of the World War and while it has taken a while to read it completely it was certainly worth it and you will become enriched in the stoic, determined nature of our predecessors and what they achieved and underlines the unique traits as well as our national independence, sovereignty, freedom, and culture which we must ensure the younger generations understand and follow."

Rear Admiral Roger Lane-Nott CB
Former Flag Officer Submarines and Submarine Commander

"With the subject of World War II, it is difficult to think of much new to say, but this book offers a unique and stimulating perspective, illuminating in particular the crucial role of ideas – moral and intellectual – in the outcome of the conflict."

Professor Michael Rainsborough
Academic Principal, Australian War College

"Astonishingly revelatory, this comprehensive reappraisal of the Second World War shatters many illusions of the prevailing narrative. A provocative cultural contextualisation links to the current problems of woke ideology, the European Union and global corporatism."

Dr Niall McCrae

"The UK fought alone for the values we hold dear in the opening months of the war. She was joined by the USA after the attack on Pearl Harbour. Together the English-speaking allies stood for the self determination of peoples, for the liberty of the individual, for freer trade and free enterprise and the rights of small countries to govern themselves. Ranged against us were the Axis powers proposing might is right, enforced union of countries under an autocracy, cultural uniformity and the mass murder of peoples they disliked or opposed.

"Liberty won. It won because people nurtured in liberty fight hard to defend this precious gift. It won because out of liberty comes innovation, initiative, and adaptation. They led to a surge of technology and war time production that outclassed the autocrats relying on hostile and sullen slave labour."

"Robert Oulds is right to centre his history on the English. When Churchill wrote his four-volume history he wrote of the English-speaking peoples, fashioning a global story out of the enterprise, ambition and venturing of the English around the world. It was that same spirit, that same love of freedom, which brought the USA into the second world war alongside the UK, fashioning what proved to be an invincible alliance against the tyrannies of Germany and Japan. The Anglo-Saxon freedom and free enterprise model out invented, out produced and out fought the autocracies of the Axis powers. The peace settlement they created allowed the self determination of peoples, urged more to adopt the democratic model, and pioneered the UN. Robert Oulds has shown an important light on the epoch-making events of the second world war and its aftermath."

Rt Hon. Sir John Redwood MP, D.Phil, FCSI